Fifth Edition

CRITICAL ISSUES IN POLICING

Fifth Edition

CRITICAL ISSUES
IN POLICING

Contemporary Readings

Roger G. Dunham
University of Miami

Geoffrey P. Alpert
University of South Carolina

WAVELAND
PRESS, INC.

Long Grove, Illinois

For information about this book, contact:
Waveland Press, Inc.
4180 IL Route 83, Suite 101
Long Grove, IL 60047-9580
(847) 634-0081
info@waveland.com
www.waveland.com

10-digit ISBN 1-57766-352-7
13-digit ISBN 978-1-57766-352-2

Printed in the United States of America

9   8   7   6   5   4   3

Contents

SECTION III
Management and Organization   129

SECTION IV
Police Deviance: Corruption and Controls   229

SECTION VIII
Hazards of Police Work   507

Preface

The fifth edition of *Critical Issues* includes many updated and new articles reflecting changes that have evolved in policing during the past several years. We are pleased that the authors we asked to update their material were willing to do so with dedicated attention, and we are proud to include the new articles that introduce fresh ideas on current topics.

It is instructive to view policing as an elastic profession. That is, it changes shape, often appears different than it has in the past, may have a shift in focus but seems to return to an original shape and function. The selected articles reflect that elasticity. Police work must be in concert with the community if it is to be successful. The agents of formal social control must rely upon citizens, or agents of informal social control, to perform successfully their duties, gain respect, and earn a sense of satisfaction.

In choosing our topics for *Critical Issues*, we selected those that have the broadest application. Rather than limiting the scope of our material to large, urban, suburban, rural, or small departments, we have selected issues that are applicable to all. As in *Policing Urban America*, a text designed to accompany *Critical Issues*, we are emphasizing the importance of involving community members in decisions concerning law enforcement—including tasks, objectives, and goals.

One of the major roles played by citizens is to help identify what is a proper measure of performance in law enforcement. In the past, the ultimate measure of police success was an evaluation of the crime rates. It seems that the comments made by Durkheim, as well as contemporary researchers, that a change in the rate of crime is influenced by factors beyond the control of police, has fallen on deaf ears. Politicians and police officials still take credit when the reported crime rate decreases and are blamed when the reported rate of crime increases. The use of reported crimes as a measure of success for police demonstrates an unsophisticated understanding of the role and scope of police services. While different styles of policing can affect many performance measures including response time and the nature and extent of community contacts, understanding changes in the rates of crime requires a far more sophisticated analysis.

Hopefully, we will soon see a switch from holding the police responsible for crime rates to holding them accountable for specific tasks and objectives and the general goal of law enforcement: promoting secure communities. In that spirit, we have revised *Critical Issues* to include information on the tasks, objectives, and the law enforcement goal of promoting community safety.

Acknowledgments

We are indebted to many people for their contributions to this collection. The collaboration and friendship of our colleagues who wrote the excellent articles in this book are sincerely appreciated. Our wives, Vicki Dunham and Margaret Alpert, offered patience, support, and understanding. Our collective nine children provided both incentive and distraction. Thanks to the many colleagues who used the fourth edition in the classroom and offered suggestions for the revision. This work was a cooperative effort and we thank everyone who generously shared their time, knowledge, and expertise.

The Foundation of the Police Role in Society

What is the basic role of the police in our society? What do we expect them to do, and not do? And how do these expectations correspond to the actual day-to-day behavior of the police? If the police get out of line or begin using their authority in ways deemed inappropriate by a majority of citizens, does society have the right or even the ability to control their behavior? In order to answer these questions we must recognize that the police are an integral part of government. In fact, they are located at the interface between government and the private lives of individual citizens (Pollock, 1994). The police represent and implement the government's right to use coercion and force to guarantee certain behaviors from its citizens.

Carl Klockers (1984) has described police control as having four major elements: authority, power, persuasion, and force. Authority is the incontestable entitlement to be obeyed. Power, which lies in the hands of the organization, is drawn upon by the individual officer and implies that if there is resistance, it will be defeated without compunction. Persuasion involves the use of symbols, words, and arguments to convince an individual that he or she ought to comply with the rules. Force involves something very different from the other elements of control: the element of physical control. Although the other three elements rely mostly on mental or psychological control, they function partially because of the underlying threat of force. All of these elements of control are used by the police, but the ultimate right to use force is what makes police unique and what allows the police to function successfully.

THE POLICE RIGHT TO USE FORCE

Where do the police get the right to use force to control citizens? Ideally, they get it from the citizenry through a governmental right invested in federal, state, and local governing bodies. Although we may wonder if we really need all the government we have, and may fear the tremendous power vested in it, most of us realize that governments are a necessary feature of modern societies.

Mancur Olsen (1965) made the argument that governments are unavoidable features of human societies. He argued that we need public goods (e.g., public safety) and that public goods can only be created by coercion. It is through the formation of a state or government that force is legitimized to coerce citizens into contributing to public goods. Fortunately, it is not necessary to apply force most of the time, as long as there always is a credible threat of force.

Richard Quinney (1970:9–10) said that "a society is held together by force and constraint . . . [that] values are ruling rather than common, enforced rather than accepted, at any given point in time." Although other institutional means exist to officially establish sets of values and rules (e.g., laws and fines), they mean little without some method of enforcement. To enforce the rules, we have created the social institution of police and authorized it to use physical force. In fact, the police are the only ones who have the legitimate right to use force in society. In a sense, the government must use organized coercion to prevent private coercion (Quinney, 1970).

In sum, we need the police in order to have a civilized society, to ensure safety from being harmed by insiders, and to make sure we contribute to other needed public goods. In his *Leviathan*, Thomas Hobbes tried to describe what life would be like in a condition of anarchy.

> Hereby it is manifest, that during the time men live without a common power to keep them all in awe, they are in that condition which is called war . . . where every man is enemy to every man. . . . In such condition, there is no place for industry: because the fruit thereof is uncertain: and consequently no agriculture . . . no society; and which is worst of all, continual fear, and danger or violent death; and the life of man, solitary, poor, nasty, brutish, and short.

While Olsen demonstrated that we need the state, historically, the state has often been an institution of repression. It seems to be in the disposition of most individuals that, when they are put in positions of authority and given the right to use force to maintain society, they succumb to the temptation to use that power and authority to exploit others. Most citizens will give in to the lure of power and force to benefit themselves individually. This has been called the great dilemma of the state: how to have the state and keep it benign, to avoid exploitation of its citizens (Stark, 2000). Given that the police are at the interface of citizens and government this is also becomes the central dilemma of policing. How can we authorize a police force to maintain our safety, ensure that our laws are obeyed, and keep officers from using that force illegitimately? Most of the important issues concerning the police emanate from this basic problem. The greatest issues surrounding the police are misuse of force, police corruption, and methods employed to control these problems.

Taming the police is a major aspect of the distinction between a police state and a democratic state. In a police state the citizens do not have adequate control over the police. The police are therefore able to use their monopoly on physical force to exploit citizens. In a democratic state, the people have maintained more control over the police, so that the police cannot exploit them.

THE SOCIAL CONTRACT

In discussing what has been termed the social contract, Jeffrey Reiman (1985) explains that democracy does not guarantee that the judgments of public officials, such as the police, will uniformly replicate those of the public. The power is delegated and must be exercised according to the judgment of the individuals to whom it is delegated. However, Reiman makes clear that "the public has a right to spell out the criteria by which the judgments should be made, and to insist on both competence and good faith in the application of those criteria" (1985:237). He defines the social contract as "embodying a general test of the legitimacy of the acts and rules of public agencies of law enforcement, namely, that such acts or rules must be such that the limits on citizens' freedom that they bring must result in a net increase of that freedom all told" (p. 246). His test gives us a way to exercise public control over the police's right to use force. To refuse to give the police the right to use force to enforce the law would undermine our laws and freedom and compel us to devote much of our time and effort to self-protection. Thus, according to Reiman, the public surrenders its right to use force and loans that right to the police to use it in the name of the group and to protect each member of the group against the use of force by other members. The sacrifice of this individual right results in a gain in real and secure freedom to live with minimal fear of victimization by others.

The real issue for citizens is whether they really decrease their personal likelihood of harm given the reduction of victimization by other members when they delegate the right to use force to the police, and thereby create the potential of being harmed by the police misusing that force. In a video series on the U.S. Constitution, entitled *Law and Order*, a victim of police misuse of authority, who later was able to obtain justice in the courts, said that he would still vote to give the police greater authority and risk the potential for misuse, rather than to have to fend off violent offenders in his community. He felt that with the police he at least had a chance for justice in the courts (*Law and Order*, 1987).

An argument against the social contract theory is that the police have always been instruments of the dominant class and seldom look out for the interests of all citizens equally. In fact, historically, the police have been extremely partisan toward those in power by looking out for their interests and by enforcing laws against opposing classes and groups. However, the idea of citizens actually delegating power and authority to the police has some historical support. Samuel Walker, a police scholar, attributes the rapid social change in the early to mid-1800s to the breakdown of the old system of law enforcement and the need to establish modern police forces (Walker, 1992). When many people thought the best solution to contemporary social disorder was to create modern police departments, modeled after the newly formed London police, Americans showed great uncertainty and hesitated to create them.

Despite the breakdown in law and order, Americans moved very slowly in creating new police forces. New York City did not create a new police force until 1845, eleven years after the first outbreak of riots. Philadelphia followed a more erratic course. Between 1833 and 1854, in the face of recurring riots, the city wrestled with the problem of police reform before finally creating a consolidated, citywide police force based on the London model. These delays reflected deep public uncertainty about modern police methods. For many Americans, police officers dispersed throughout the community brought to mind the hated British colonial army. Others were afraid that rival politicians would fight for control of the police department to their own partisan advantage—a fear that proved to be correct (Walker, 1992:7–8).

The dilemma created by the desire for police protection and the fear of losing control of the police was a factor in deciding whether or not to establish the modern police forces in American cities. The notion that the police received their authority and right to use force from the citizens of the young democracy was as much a part of policing in America as was the subsequent partisan policing and corruption.

This democratic model of police in society therefore retains a certain historical validity and also provides a valuable standard or ideal for modern policing. In the same way that much of our Constitution remains an unfulfilled ideal, so does our means of societal control: it seems evident that a democratic model of policing could provide a framework for improving the police and therefore society. It is encouraging to note that the history of the American police, especially since the 1960s, supports the idea that policing is progressively moving closer to this democratic ideal.

Following this model, Reiman (1985) outlines the implications of the social contract perspective for modern policing. He argues that "any coercive practice by legal agents that constricts and endangers the freedom of the citizenry, rather than expanding and securing it, reproduces the very condition of the state of nature that coercive legal agencies are meant to remedy" (p. 240). In other words, if the police use their authority and force in an exploitative fashion, it would literally undermine their own justification, because it would subject citizens to precisely the sort of risks they were given special powers to prevent. With regard to this tension, Reiman continues, "if law enforcement threatens rather than enhances our freedom, the distinction between crime and criminal justice is obliterated" (p. 241).

This view of the police is consistent with the idea of legitimate public power in which the power flows from the citizens to the police. To make this a reality, Reiman argues that the police must be accountable for their use of publicly assigned power, and accountable to the wider public, not just to other law enforcement agents. For the use of force to be legitimate, he maintains it must be viewed as owned by the public and loaned to police officers for specific reasons, and further, it must be exercised under specific conditions (Reiman, 1985). In fact, under the democratic model of policing, one major function of the police is to guarantee citizens their rights.

Throughout this book, many of the issues examined (especially the hotly debated ones) will tie into the dilemma of policing as above. Hopefully the following general analysis will help to set a valuable framework and foundation for thinking about the many topics covered in the book.

HOW AMERICANS VIEW THE POLICE

The social contract perspective discussed above demonstrates the the tie between the police and the public based on a moral or philosophical argument. Beyond this basis for authority, the police have learned that they need a cooperative public to be effective in controlling crime and maintaining order. This has been termed the "co-production of police services" (Reiss, 1971). Findings indicate that between 75 and 85 percent of police-citizen encounters are generated by citizens calling for police services, and this reflects the recent trends in policing strategy, which focus more and more on citizen involvement and cooperation with the police (e.g., community-based policing and problem-solving policing). This trend has sensitized the police to the importance of citizens' attitudes toward the police and how the police go about doing their job. Favorable attitudes toward the police are crucial to the success of this new wave of policing strategies.

A brief review of some recent studies on how Americans view the police can set the stage for understanding the critical link between the police and citizens. First, it is interesting to note that the general public is surprisingly satisfied with the quality of police work. On the average, between 70 and 75 percent of the public think that the police are doing a very good or fairly good job and rate police service as excellent or good (Huang and Vaughn, 1996). A slightly higher percentage of the public (around 80 percent) are satisfied with the police and have confidence in them (Weitzer and Tuch, forthcoming).

In a 2003 Gallup poll, citizens were asked how much confidence they have in various U.S. institutions. Sixty-one percent said "a great deal" or "quite a lot" when asked about the police. Only one institution had a higher percentage: the military (82 percent), which was inflated about 15 percentage points over its normal level probably because of the war on terrorism. Citizens had more confidence in the police than in the U.S. Supreme Court (47 percent), banks and banking (50 percent), public schools (40 percent), Congress (29 percent), newspapers (33 percent), big business (22 percent), and the television news (35 percent) among others (Maguire and Pastore, 2003). Further, confidence in the police has remained high (between 54 and 61 percent) since 1994. In another Gallup poll, respondents were asked to rate the honesty and ethical standards of people in different fields. More than half (59 percent) rated the police as "very high" or "high." Only five professions were rated higher than the police: nurses (79 percent), pharmacists (67 percent), military officers (65 percent), high school teachers (64 percent) and medical doctors (63 percent). Citizens rated the police higher on honesty and ethical standards than bankers (36 percent), journalists (26 percent), clergy (52 percent), business executives (17 percent), lawyers (18 percent), and Congress members (17 percent) among others (Maguire and Pastore, 2003).

While general support for the police has been consistently high, attitudes differ among diverse demographic groups, and according to the type of experiences people have had with the police. Race or ethnic group membership has been a strong predictor of attitudes toward the police. African Americans are usually less positive about the police and hold more antagonistic attitudes toward the police than do whites. African Americans generally score about 25 percentage points lower on favorable attitudes toward the police and on their ratings of police services (Weitzer and Tuch, forthcoming; Huang and Vaughn, 1996). Indeed, lower-income African Americans living in the inner city have the least favorable attitudes toward the police.

Hispanics, with the exception of Cubans in Miami, usually are more favorable toward the police than African Americans, but less favorable than whites (Weitzer and Tuch, forthcoming; Huang and Vaughn, 1996). The Cubans in Miami hold more favorable attitudes toward the police than all others, with the exception of recent immigrants (Alpert and Dunham, 1988).

Generally, people younger than 30 years of age have more negative attitudes toward the police than do other age groups (Maguire and Pastore, 2003; Sullivan et. al., 1987). This is especially true of adolescents, and has been attributed to this group having more negative encounters with the police than others and having a low level of identification with law enforcement officers.

One's political ideology even has an impact on how favorably people view the police. Conservatives and Republicans generally hold more favorable attitudes toward the police than Democrats and liberals (Maguire and Pastore, 2003).

Socioeconomic status is another variable that helps explain variations in attitudes toward the police. It is the lower-income people who hold least favorable attitudes toward the police. This relationship holds up even within ethnic groups. For example, whites generally hold more favorable attitudes toward the police than African Americans. However, middle-class whites are more favorable toward police than are lower-class whites, and the same is true for African Americans. Higher social class is associated with more positive attitudes (Maguire and Pastore, 2003; Huang and Vaughn, 1996).

In addition to demographic factors having an influence on attitudes toward the police, the types of contacts and experiences people have with the police seem to play a major role in how positively or negatively they view the police (Weitzer and Tuch, forthcoming; Huang and Vaughn, 1996). Generally, positive contacts and experiences with the police result in positive attitudes, and negative contacts lead to negative attitudes. Also, contacts initiated by the citizen, such as calls for police services, tend to be more positive than contacts where the police initiate the contact, such as giving a traffic ticket. The impact of contacts with the police are so strong in determining attitudes toward the police and police services that many believe that negative contacts explain why some groups have such negative attitudes about the police (such as African Americans and teenagers). These groups have many more negative contacts with the police than the general population. For example, African Americans and teenagers perceive the police as less friendly, less fair, and even less prompt, when compared with the evaluations of the police by other groups. The same is true for perceptions of the police use of force. African Americans are much more likely than others to think that the police are allowed to use too much force and to view police abuse of force as a problem. Huang and Vaughn (1996:41) report from their research that, "older, middle-income, rural, and conservative respondents tended to have more favorable perceptions about police use of force than did younger, urban, and liberal ones."

Huang and Vaughn (1996) conclude from their extensive research that direct police contacts were more important than demographic variables in explaining most attitudes toward the police. For example, most African Americans and youth who experienced positive contacts with the police were as likely as others to report the police to be friendly, prompt, and effective at crime control.

Current trends in policing have emphasized the relationship between the police and citizens, so that police administrators are becoming more and more sensitized to the value of a positive and supportive citizenry. Many police administrators have found that positive contacts and good policing can overcome negative attitudes of citizens and are making strong efforts to foster a conciliatory atmosphere and to develop programs and strategies, such as community-based policing, to cultivate positive police-citizen encounters as much as possible. Weitzer and Tuch (forthcoming) found that "the existence of community policing in one's neighborhood increases satisfaction with the police . . . for whites and blacks." While there is still much room for improvement, all of these measures lead to more police accountability to citizens. It is noteworthy, in spite of the fact that the role of the police officer has become increasingly complex and that citizens' expectations of the police continue to broaden, the attitudes citizens hold toward the police and toward how well they do their job are generally positive.

THE INCREASING COMPLEXITY OF THE POLICE ROLE

If we were asked to identify the most apparent changes in modern policing during the twentieth century, the raised level of expectations by citizens of the police would most certainly rank among the top. August Vollmer, police chief of Berkeley, California, from 1905–1932, and one of the first great reformers, once observed:

> The citizen expects police officers to have the wisdom of Solomon, the courage of David, the strength of Samson, the patience of Job, the leadership of Moses, the kindness of the Good Samaritan, the strategical training of Alexander, the faith of Daniel, the diplomacy of Lincoln, the tolerance of the Carpenter of Nazareth, and finally, an intimate knowledge of every branch of the natural, biological, and social sciences. If he had all these, he might be a good policeman! (cited in Bain, 1939)

As problems of social control have grown and become more complex, so have the actions and reactions required of the police. Unfortunately, the tendency has been to proliferate new agencies to meet specific needs, rather than to consolidate or to improve the effectiveness of existing organizations. The result has been an increasingly complex and uncoordinated development of law enforcement, mired in the multiplicity of agencies and the overlapping of jurisdiction and responsibility. Simultaneous with these developments has been the growing complexity of police functions and the growing public expectation of a more professional and competent police force. All of this has made the study of modern policing an exciting yet difficult topic.

There is a great deal of confusion over the terms, "policing" and "law enforcement." These terms are often seen as interchangeable. In common usage, a police officer is a law enforcement officer, but a law enforcement officer is not always a police officer. Another important distinction is that many law enforcement officers are not involved in traditional police work such as patrolling, traffic enforcement, service calls, and so on. For example, a private security guard or store detective may spend considerable time trying to detect crimes, but he or she is not a police officer. In the same light, a detective for a police department, or an agent of one of many state or federal law enforcement agencies, may have police power and authority but does not participate in traditional police work.

Law enforcement, whether practiced by a specialist sitting in front of a computer terminal or investigating a crime scene, or by the general practitioner cruising in his or her car or walking the beat, has an important role to play in American society. It is onerous to have to separate police work from that of law enforcement, as they overlap in many situations. However, it is the work of the local, uniformed officer that represents the major portion of police work and, consequently, is the major focus of this book.

Police agencies and departments come in all sizes and many shapes. The federal government supports more than fifty law enforcement agencies, including the Federal Bureau of Investigation (FBI), the Drug Enforcement Agency (DEA), the United States Marshals Service, the United States Secret Service, the Bureau of Alcohol, Tobacco, and Firearms (ATF), and the United States Customs Service, among others. There are close to 60,000 federal law enforcement personnel who work for these agencies. While it may be necessary to refer to the work of these and other agencies, we will focus our attention on the local police in urban America.

According to the most recent Bureau of Justice Statistics report that summarizes the findings of the 2000 census of state and local law enforcement agencies (see article 3), there are more than one million full-time employees, including 708,000 sworn police officers, in state and local police forces in America. The numbers range from approximately 40,435 sworn officers and a budget well over one billion dollars in New York to numerous rural areas that employ only one part-time officer. It is interesting to note that more than 93,000 sworn full-time officers work in the ten largest departments, but there are more than 10,000 police departments with ten or fewer employees. American police officers work for a large number of departments, but these are mostly small departments with approximately five sworn officers (Bureau of Justice Statistics, 2002). The focus of this book is on the larger urban departments and their problems (for information on crime and policing in rural and small-town America, see Weisheit et al., 1999).

OUTLINE OF THE BOOK

The purpose of this anthology is to provide a selection of readings that covers policing comprehensively yet focuses in on specific topics and issues. The readings are selected to provide greater insight and depth than is possible in a general text and to expose the reader to a variety of experts and specialists from several disciplines who study the police. For each section, we have provided a short introduction that summarizes the major themes and issues in the readings.

In Section I, Introduction and Historical Overview, we provide a socio-historical overview of policing, focusing on the social context in which the police function. A historical review is necessary to understand more completely both the present and the future of the police and to place police work in the larger context of the social control functions of our society. As only one form of social control, the police appear fairly recently in the history of society's attempts to control aberrant behavior. Specifically, policing represents the government's entry into the business of social control. Boston, in 1838, was the first major American city to sponsor a police department. New York followed closely behind Boston, establishing the first large police department in America. Our rapidly changing society led to many changes in policing. Changes that greatly impacted police work include the invention of the telegraph, the two-way radio, and the police car. These changes, among others, have led to the impersonalization of police work and the eroding of the bond between the police officer and the citizen. The disappearance of the officer on the "beat," who knew his neighborhoods and had earned the confidence of citizens, was followed by the appearance of an unknown officer behind the tinted glass of a patrol car, who often fears getting out on the street without backup and who often applies the letter of the law in an extremely bureaucratic fashion. The accumulation of these and other changes in American policing have led to the issues and dilemmas facing police officers and administrators today.

Section II, Selection, Training, and Socialization, contains articles that point out the significance and impact of these functions. Police work is a labor-intensive service industry in which approximately 80 percent of the budget is devoted to personnel costs. The most significant investment a police department can make is in recruiting, selecting, and training its personnel. Recent trends in policing present difficult challenges for law enforcement selection and training. For example, community-oriented policing strategies emphasize activities and skills that are very different from more traditional policing skills, which may require screening potential recruits for different skills and characteristics and altering training to prepare recruits for the new activities. Careful and knowledgeable selection and training can save a department many costly and embarrassing problems, as well as improve the quality of policing so that society is better served.

The first critical personnel decision is the selection of a recruit. Many may apply for police jobs, but not all applicants possess the personality and aptitude to make good police officers. There are several methods that are used to screen applicants. Psychological screening is the traditional method by which candidates are permitted to enter into the academy. If candidates demonstrate that they are unfit for police work they are prevented from attending the preservice academy. Progressive agencies employ a multi-hurdle approach to the selection of police recruits. That is, applicants must take a battery of tests, a physical examination, and a lie detector test. A background investigation is also completed, and only after a personal interview can a candidate be accepted into an assessment center. Here, candidates role-play a number of stressful scenarios and exercises under the watchful eyes of several observers to determine whether each candidate has the potential for handling the situations he or she will likely encounter as a police officer. These assessment centers can also be used for promotional purposes. Although the purpose of the assessment is to determine the applicant's aptitude for police work, it does not simply rely on formal education.

In the twenty-first century, an increasing emphasis is being placed on a college education as a prerequisite for police work. In fact, the state of Minnesota has developed a combined curriculum that leads to a bachelor's degree and police officer certification. The findings of some studies indicate that the college-trained officer is less cynical, less prejudiced, less authoritarian, less hostile, and less likely to use force than the non-college-educated officer. On the other side of the argument, college-educated officers are viewed by many as prone to dissatisfaction with the job, having a higher turnover rate, and possibly exhibiting hostility toward non-college-educated officers. In spite of the controversy, many departments are requiring some college education and are giving college-educated officers preferential assignments. Additionally they are frequently first in line for promotions.

The police academy provides the basic training for the new police recruit. More than a century ago, it was discovered that although very little training was required of police officers, good police work does require considerable knowledge and skills. To correct this inconsistency, efforts were made to formalize a model for police training around the country. The police academy was instituted to fill this void. Police academies throughout the country emphasize the technical aspects of police work but also cover topics such as human relations skills, intercultural communication, the structure and functions of the criminal justice system, and the organization of police departments. In addition to training received in the police academy, officers gain valuable training in the field from more senior officers. This type of on-the-job training is supplemented by in-service training, which continues throughout the officer's career.

This section also deals with one of the most interesting aspects of police work: socialization. As with other professions, the police go through a rigorous socialization process that results in the development of distinct attitudes and beliefs among officers. Many students of the police refer to this as the police subculture and the police personality. One aspect of the police personality that has received considerable attention is authoritarianism. This is a complex domain of personality traits that includes an exaggerated concern for authority, punitiveness, conservatism, and a rigid adherence to rules and societal values. Included in this personality constellation is a need for order and routine, inflexibility, and a proclivity to stereotype groups different from one's own. This personality type raises some concern when present among police officers because it is linked to toughness, aggressiveness, and cynicism among officers. An outgrowth of the authoritarian personality is its relationship to prejudice. Individuals with authoritarian personalities often have unfavorable attitudes about people belonging to groups other than their own and are likely to stereotype members of these groups. These traits, when present in police officers, have obvious implications for fair and equal treatment under the law.

The police subculture is a double-edged sword: it is extremely practical for the survival of officers and for the effectiveness of police work, yet it has been criticized for the tremendous pressure it exerts on officers to be loyal to the group. The pressure for loyalty and complete conformity among officers can create ethical dilemmas when it is used to cover up mistakes or to help officers in trouble with the system.

Also included in this section is a discussion of styles of policing and the ways police exercise discretion in fulfilling their police responsibilities. Police styles develop in response to the social environment in which the police operate, the individual officer's personality characteristics, and the political demands imposed on the department and on individual officers. Individual police officers develop personal styles of carrying out their tasks and responding to various problems. As these ways of approaching and dealing with demands and problems develop into patterns that dominate a particular department or unit, they are referred to as institutionalized characteristics and styles of policing. There is a great deal of variation among the institutionalized styles of police departments. It is difficult to determine which comes first: individual styles that begin to fall into distinct patterns and develop into institutional styles, or institutional patterns that socialize new recruits into particular styles. In reality, each has an influence on the other.

In recent years, there has been a call for changes in police style. An increasing emphasis on the professionalization of the police, on decreasing citizens' fears of being victimized, and on the safety and security of the community has focused attention both on styles of policing and on measuring the effectiveness of the police. Unfortunately, different types of communities desire different styles and levels of policing, adding another complexity to the issue of police-community relations. A recognition of this complexity has led to a call for community-oriented policing based upon the characteristics of the specific community and its citizens.

Section III, Management and Organization, includes selections that outline various managerial and organizational characteristics of police departments. Since police departments have such unique characteristics and functions when compared to other institutions in our society, we would expect the organization and management of these units to be quite different from other institutions. The single fact that police departments are charged with maintaining order and are authorized to use force when necessary does more to shape the organization and management of police departments than anything else.

Police departments are organized in much the same way as the military and use military ranks, such as captain, lieutenant, or sergeant, to designate authority. Most traditional departments are organized around a highly structured bureaucratic model, with specialized units and a well-developed division of labor. Police bureaucracy is characterized by a high degree of formalization and specification of rules and procedures. This is usually an attempt to control the discretion of officers in potentially controversial situations they may face, especially with regard to the use of force. Because of the detailed division of labor and the delegation of authority, a chain of command is set in place to delineate both authority and responsibility. Police responsibility and authority are generally very sensitive subjects, so most departments adhere to the "unity of command" principle, which maintains that each person in the organization is accountable to only one superior. Although agencies may differ in their emphasis, many characteristics of organization and management are common among most departments.

As a response to the movement for community-oriented policing and the need to decentralize authority, many agencies have changed their organizational structure drastically and quickly. One consequence of these rapid changes has been an emphasis on community expectations and a decrease in bureaucratic management. A solid bureaucracy and an emphasis upon community interaction are required for effective and efficient management (Reiss, 1992).

Another major change taking place within the police organization is the implementation of new technologies. Information systems and other computer-based technologies have led to a number of new organizational and management strategies, from processing and storing information to early intervention systems and Compstat, a computer assisted management process. Computerized management systems have increased the record-keeping responsibilities of officers and in turn have resulted in a greater degree of monitoring their activities by both supervisors and the public. Further, policing strategies and normal day-to-day decision making have become more information based and complex.

Section IV, Police Deviance: Corruption and Controls, addresses the potential for corruption and misuse or abuse of power, including the power to use force in the name of the state, given to the police and efforts to control police deviance. Over the years, police organizations have become more and more bureaucratic in an effort to control this high level of power, authority, and discretion. As a result, there has been progress in controlling all types of police deviance.

Unfortunately, there will always be two elements that result in corruption of our police: opportunity and greed. Police deviance is a type of occupational deviance, deviance that is made possible by an opportunity structure associated with a particular occupation. Police officers, by the very nature of their work, are constantly being exposed to opportunities for misconduct. Even in the most crime-free areas, there are opportunities to base arrest decisions on extra-legal criteria, or to accept money for not issuing a traffic ticket, or to use one's authority against someone or some group.

Additionally, a second form of deviance, that of organizational deviance, also presents itself as an issue of concern for the police. Organizational deviance is that which extends beyond acts of individuals to deviant acts sanctioned by the organization. For example, the Special Investigative Section of the Los Angeles Police Department has come under attack by a movie titled *S.I.S.*, which details police corruption in the California city. Similarly, a former detective with L.A.P.D.'s Organized Crime Intelligence Division (OCID) has written a book titled *L.A. Secret Police: Inside the LAPD Elite Spy Network* (Rothmiller, 1992), detailing the unethical and illegal acts of that division. The implied allegations, if true, paint a sordid picture of police activities in Los Angeles.

It is central to a police department's public image and survival to have a system for controlling police deviance and corruption that is both known and trusted by community members. Although much of the focus on controlling police deviance involves negative discipline, it is much more effective to focus on the positive. For example, it has been found that there are three main elements to an effective system of discipline. First, a department must have a well-formulated and consistent set of rules and procedures. Second, the rules and procedures must be communicated fully and effectively to the officers at all levels through proper training. Finally, proper supervision and leadership within the department can help to ensure conformity to the rules and to the maintenance of a good working environment. Focusing on positive aspects of discipline will serve as a preventative effort, which is more effective than focusing on the problems after they happen.

All types of police deviance and corruption, including simple acts of differential enforcement of the law, such as racial profiling, can weaken the legitimacy of the police in the eyes of the public. If such behaviors go unchecked, they can create a hostile environment for the police and have grave consequences for successfully carrying out everyday police functions.

In Section V, Minorities in Policing, the articles focus on the representation of African Americans and women in police work and the implications of any discrimination, both upon members of minority groups and upon the effectiveness of policing. The potential impact of minorities in policing has not yet been realized. The United States Civil Rights Commission stated in its report, *Who is Guarding the Guardians?* (1982), that police agencies were underutilizing minorities and women and that this underrepresentation was hampering the ability of police departments to function at their most effective levels. If police agencies do not represent the ethnic characteristics of those they police, they have a difficult time earning the respect of the citizens in the community and may actually increase the incidence of perceived or real prejudice or discrimination. This in turn increases the chances of racially based trouble and violence. Many students of the police, as well as civil rights groups, argue that minority representation in police departments is an important factor in improving relations between the police and members of minority communities. However, it has been found in many cities that if hiring, making assignments, and giving promotions are done for affirmative action purposes and not as rewards for competence and performance, a number of unintended and undesirable consequences will likely occur. Research indicates that, in such circumstances, there is an increase in confusion and a decrease in morale among officers in the department. This can lead to a decrease in loyalty and trust given to the department and to the public. Further, if such procedures result in a lowering of the quality and qualifications of officers generally, mistakes and poor judgment will often cost the department in the long run. As a result, social, political, and economic considerations must be balanced with the impact that hiring and promotion practices will have on the department and its ability to function effectively.

The selections in Section VI, Community-Based Policing, were chosen to provide the reader with the basics of the discussions concerning community-oriented policing philosophies and strategies. These arguments for community-based policing evolve from the idea that the community is a major source of social integration in our large-scale and often impersonal society. These "natural areas," as they were called by early students of the city, provide residents with a more intimate avenue for relating to a large, complex society. Communities influence individual behavior, which usually functions to maintain informal social control of members. Arguably, the formal system of social control operated by the police, which is based on written rules and laws and prescribed punishments, cannot be fully effective without being closely integrated with the informal control system in the community. The effectiveness of the formal control system (i.e., the police) depends on citizens to initiate and assist in the enforcement of norms and laws. The informal means of control, then, becomes a backup or support of local enforcement.

Community-based policing is a strategy that maximizes the integration of the formal control system of the police with the informal control system of the community. Emphasis is placed on building bonds of communication, interaction, and mutual support between the community members themselves and between them and the police, which will develop strong bonds of mutual trust.

Although there is an emphasis on community-oriented or community-driven programs, the crime-fighting function of police work must not be lost (Moore, 1992). Rather, innovative departments have linked their techniques of police work to their styles of fighting crime. Whether it is through the identification of high-crime locations, known as "hot-spots," or an innovative strategy to reduce the level of crime in these areas, e.g., problem-oriented policing, the police are demonstrating their involvement in, and respect for, the communities they serve.

In Section VII, Use of Force, the selections deal with an issue that has traditionally been one of the most controversial aspects of police work—the use of force by the police. Our society has given the police the right to use force to maintain order and to enforce the law. However, this is not a blanket authority, and police officers have many constraints on exactly when and under which conditions they may legitimately and lawfully use force. A mistake in job performance that merely creates an inconvenience in most occupations may result in an officer being suspended from the job, sued, or possibly even arrested for committing a crime. In the normal course of fulfilling his or her legitimate duties, an officer is often placed in legal jeopardy.

The beating of Rodney King in Los Angeles has become paradigmatic for the inappropriate use of force by the police. This event, as no other, has focused our attention on police violence and public responses to it. Although the events surrounding the beating death of Arthur McDuffie in Miami were hauntingly similar, they lacked one ingredient: a videotape. The technology and practice of capturing events on videotape has become a valuable tool for law enforcement, especially with respect to training and accountability (Alpert et. al., 1992).

It is little wonder, then, that the use of force is such a controversial aspect of police work. Since the beginning of policing, citizens have complained about excessive use of force by the police, and this has led to sporadic reform movements that have helped curtail abuse of what is undoubtedly an important tool for maintaining law and order. Reforms in this area have mostly consisted of minor adjustments to a system that needed an overhaul. It seems clear that we need to think differently about police use of force and not just tinker around with the timing and degree of force. Too much attention has been placed on specific beatings or shootings, while insufficient attention has been paid to the more general issue of the ways in which the police control citizens (Alpert and Dunham, 1988:158). Until the police change their training philosophy concerning the use of force and accept the goal of controlling situations without it, problems related to the use of force will continue to plague our society. A relatively recent concept in training is commonly called "violence reduction," "restraint" or "avoidance training." This relatively new philosophy of training puts an emphasis on the need to reduce violence and the excessive use of force and differs from earlier training by stressing communication and restraint rather than the traditional violent responses. Restraint training stresses tactical knowledge and the use of concealment strategies to avoid being placed in a situation that has a high probability of violence. Of course, force training is not the only solution to the problem of officers using excessive force, a problem that has plagued policing from its inception and seems to be of increasing concern to citizens.

The subject of Section VIII, The Hazards of Police Work, is perhaps the greatest concern of the police officer. Police work has several characteristics that present a unique set of personal hazards. Research has indicated that there is an unusual amount of stress generated by police work. This is due to the ever-present threat of danger to the officer and to others and the potential or actual use of force. This high level of stress has been associated with the relatively frequent occurrence among police officers of such personal problems as divorce, alcoholism, and suicide.

There are no simple solutions to the complex problems associated with police work. The most reasonable approach is to reduce stress as much as possible by changing stress-producing aspects of police bureaucracy, procedures, and operations. This said, it is clear that stress will always be an inherent part of police work. The alternative strategy is to help officers cope with the everyday stress they experience and to develop programs and services that help officers cope in specific stress-producing situations (e.g., when an officer is involved in a shooting or is traumatized by a domestic violence call).

A positive development is that police administrators are becoming more sensitive to the personal hazards of police work and their effect on the individual officer. This increased awareness is resulting in attempts to reduce stress whenever possible, and also in the provision of services to help officers cope with their highly charged role in society.

The articles that follow provide an exciting selection of readings that offer valuable insights into many of the important issues concerning the police role and police work. We will begin with a historical overview of policing.

References

Alpert, Geoffrey and Roger Dunham. 1988. *Policing Multi-Ethnic Neighborhoods*. New York: Greenwood Press.

Alpert, Geoffrey, P. William Smith, and Daniel Watters. 1992. "Implications of the Rodney King Beating," *Criminal Law Bulletin* 28:469–78.

Bain, Read. 1939. "The Policeman on the Beat," *Science Monthly* 48:5.

Bureau of Justice Statistics. 2002. *Census of State and Local Law Enforcement Agencies, 2000*. Washington, DC: U.S. Department of Justice, NCJ 194066.

Huang, W. S. Wilson and Michael Vaughn. 1996. "Support and Confidence: Public Attitudes Toward the Police." In *Americans View Crime and Justice: A National Public Opinion Survey*, edited by Timothy Flanagan and Dennis Longmire. Thousand Oaks, CA: Sage Publications.

Klockers, Carl. 1984. "Blue Lies and Police Placebos." *American Behavioral Scientist*. 4(27): 529–44.

Law and Order. 1987. Princeton, NJ: Films for the Humanities.

Maguire, Kathleen and Ann L. Pastore, eds. 2003. *Sourcebook of Criminal Justice Statistics 2002*. Washington, DC: U.S. Department of Justice, Bureau of Justice Statistics.

Moore, Mark. 1992. "Problem-Solving and Community Policing." In *Modern Policing*, edited by Michael Tonry and Norval Morris (pp. 99–158). Chicago: University of Chicago Press.

Olsen, Mancur. 1965. *The Logic of Collective Action*. Cambridge: Harvard University Press.

Pollock, Joycelyn. 1994. *Ethics in Crime and Justice: Dilemmas and Decisions*, 2d ed. Belmont, CA: Wadsworth.

Quinney, Richard. 1970. *The Social Reality of Crime*. Boston: Little, Brown, and Company.

Reiman, Jeffrey. 1985. "The Social Contract and the Police Use of Deadly Force." In *Moral Issues in Police Work*, edited by Frederick A. Ellison and Michael Feldberg. Savage, Maryland: Rowman & Littlefield Publishers.

Reiss, A. J. 1971. *The Police and the Public*. New Haven: Yale University Press.

Reiss, Albert. 1992. "Police Organizations in the Twentieth Century." In *Modern Policing*, edited by Michael Tonry and Norval Morris (pp. 51–97). Chicago: University of Chicago Press.

Rothmiller, M. 1992. *L.A. Secret Police: Inside the LAPD Elite Spy Network*. New York: Pocket Books.

Stark, Rodney. 2000. *Sociology*, 8th ed. New York: Wadsworth Publishing Company.

Sullivan, Peggy, Geoffrey Alpert, and Roger Dunham. 1987. "Attitude Structures of Different Ethnic and Age Groups Concerning Policing." *Journal of Criminal Law and Criminology*, 78:501–21.

United States Civil Rights Commission. 1982. *Who is Guarding the Guardians?* Washington, DC: U.S. Printing Office.

Walker, Samuel. 1992. *The Police in America*, 2d ed. New York: McGraw-Hill.

Weisheit, Ralph A., David N. Falcone and L. Edward Wells. 1999. *Crime and Policing in Rural and Small-Town America*, 2d ed. Prospect Heights, IL: Waveland Press.

Weitzer, Ronald and Steven A. Tuch. (Forthcoming). "Determinants of Public Satisfaction with the Police." *Police Quarterly*.

SECTION I
Introduction and Historical Overview

As we have discussed in the first article, American police, like many other social institutions, has evolved over time into what it is today. This slow but certain evolution will continue as American policing is influenced by its current and future social environment. Our objective in this section is to provide some historical perspective to our study of the police in America. Of course, we will only be able to scratch the surface in our few selections. Craig Uchida's article, "The Development of the American Police: An Historic Overview," takes us from the colonial period of law enforcement to the present. Dr. Uchida provides us with an in-depth analysis of the changes in emphasis and form that have occurred in policing over this period of time. His article is divided into the various reform movements that have molded and changed police into our modern day departments. It is important to consider that many aspects of what we are now calling community-oriented policing (COP) began in the early years of policing. It is interesting that Sir Robert Peele may be responsible for many aspects of modern law enforcement.

Excerpts from the Bureau of Justice Statistics' *Census of State and Local Law Enforcement Agencies, 2000*, and *LEMAS, 2000*, are included as the third article in this edition. These documents provide up-to-date statistics that are very helpful in analyzing and understanding the police working environment as well as in assessing the current and future needs of law enforcement agencies. It is interesting to note that in each new edition of our book, the updated figures reflect an increasing number of law enforcement officers and agencies. Further, we can expect that the numbers will continue to increase in the future due to our collective concern with protecting ourselves against terrorist activities.

The Development of the American Police
An Historical Overview

Craig D. Uchida

INTRODUCTION

During the past 30 years, scholars have become fascinated with the history of police. A plethora of studies have emerged as a result. Early writings were concerned primarily with descriptions of particular police agencies. Roger Lane (1967) and James F. Richardson (1970) broke new ground in describing the origins of policing in Boston and New York, respectively. Since that time, others have followed suit with narratives of police organizations in St. Louis (Maniha, 1970; Reichard, 1975), Denver (Rider, 1971), Washington D.C. (Alfers, 1975), Richmond (Cei, 1975), and Detroit (Schneider, 1980).

Other authors have focused on issues in policing. Wilbur R. Miller (1977) examined the legitimation of the police in London and New York. Samuel Walker (1977) and Robert Fogelson (1977) concentrated on professionalism and reform of errant police in the nineteenth and twentieth centuries. Eric Monkkonen (1981) took an entirely different approach by using quantitative methods to explain the development of policing in 23 cities from 1860 to 1920.[1]

Prepared especially for *Critical Issues in Policing* by Craig D. Uchida.

Overall these histories illustrate the way in which police have developed over time. They point out the origins of concepts like crime prevention, authority, professionalism, and discretion. In addition, these historical analyses show the roots of problems in policing, such as corruption, brutality, and inefficiency.

The major emphasis of this article is to examine the development of the police since A.D. 900 and more specifically, to determine whether the role of the police has changed in American society over a period of about 300 years. This is not an easy task. The debate over the "true" or "proper" police function is an ongoing one and cannot itself be resolved in an article such as this.[2] However, by describing the various roles, activities, and functions of law enforcement over time, we can at least acquire a glimpse of what the police do and how their activities have varied over time. To do so, we rely on a number of important contributions to the study of the history of police.

The article is divided into eight parts and basically covers the history of law enforcement and its effect on colonial America to the present. Part I examines the English heritage of law enforcement and its effect on colonial America. The colonists relied heavily on the mother country for their ideas regarding community involvement in law enforcement.

Part II examines the problems of urban centers in the eighteenth and nineteenth centuries and turns to the development of the full-time uniformed police in England and America. The preventive approach to law enforcement became central to the police role in both London and American cities. Part III is concerned with police activity in nineteenth-century American cities. Patrol work and officer involvement in corruption are discussed.

In Part IV the reform movement of the Progressive Era is examined. From 1890 to 1920 reformers attempted to implement social, economic, and political change in the cities. As part of city government, police departments were targets of change as well.

In Part V we study a second reform era. From 1910 to 1960 chiefs became involved in a movement to professionalize the police. Part VI covers the riots and disorders of the 1960s and their immediate effect on policing across the country. Part VII discusses the long-term legacy of the 1960s. That is, we examine the developments of the police since 1969 in terms of research and public policy. Lastly, in Part VIII we describe a third reform movement in policing— the development of community oriented policing of the 1980s and 1990s.

I. Communities, Constables, and Colonists

Like much of America's common-law tradition, the origins of modern policing can be linked directly to its English heritage. Ideas concerning community policing, crime prevention, the posse, constables, and sheriffs developed from English law enforcement. Beginning at about A.D. 900, the role of law enforcement was placed in the hands of the common, everyday citizens.

Each citizen was held responsible for aiding neighbors who might be victims of outlaws and thieves. Because no police officers existed, individuals used state-sanctioned force to maintain social control. Charles Reith, a noted English historian, refers to this model of law enforcement as "kin police" (Reith, 1956). Individuals were considered responsible for their "kin" (relatives) and followed the adage, "I am my brother's keeper." Slowly this model developed into a more formalized "communitarian," or community-based police system.

After the Norman Conquest of 1066, a community model was established, which was called frankpledge. The frankpledge police system required that every male above the age of twelve form a group with nine of his neighbors called a tything. Each tything was sworn to apprehend and deliver to court any of its members who committed a crime. Each person was pledged to help protect fellow citizens and, in turn, would be protected. This system was "obligatory" in nature, in that tythingmen were not paid salaries for their work, but were required by law to carry out certain duties (Klockars, 1985:21). Tythingmen were required to hold suspects in custody while they were awaiting trial and to make regular appearances in court to present information on wrong-doing by members of their own or other tythings. If any member of the tything failed to perform his required duties, all members of the group would be levied severe fines.

Ten tythings were grouped into a hundred, directed by a constable (appointed by the local nobleman) who, in effect, became the first policeman. That is, the constable was the first official with law enforcement responsibility greater than simply helping one's neighbor. Just as the tythings were grouped into hundreds, the hundreds were grouped into shires, which are similar to counties today. The supervisor of each shire was the shire reeve (or sheriff), who was appointed by the king.

Frankpledge began to disintegrate by the thirteenth century. Inadequate supervision by the king and his appointees led to its downfall. As frankpledge slowly declined, the parish constable system emerged to take its place. The Statute of Winchester of 1285 placed more authority in the hands of the constable for law enforcement. One man from each parish served a one-year term as constable on a rotating basis. Though not paid for his work, the constable was responsible for organizing a group of watchmen who would guard the gates of the town at night. These watchmen were also unpaid and selected from the parish population. If a serious disturbance took place, the parish constable had the authority to raise the "hue and cry." This call to arms meant that all males in the parish were to drop what they were doing and come to the aid of the constable.

In the mid-1300s the office of justice of the peace was created to assist the shire reeve in controlling his territory. The local constable and the shire reeve became assistants to the justice of the peace and supervised the night watchmen, served warrants, and took prisoners into custody for appearance before justice of the peace courts.

The English system continued with relative success well into the 1700s. By the end of the eighteenth century, however, the growth of large cities, civil disorders, and increased criminal activity led to changes in the system.

Law Enforcement in Colonial America

In Colonial America (seventeenth and eighteenth centuries), policing followed the English systems. The sheriff, constable, and watch were easily adapted to the colonies. The county sheriff, appointed by the governor, became the most important law enforcement agent particularly when the colonies remained small and primarily rural. The sheriff's duties included apprehending criminals, serving subpoenae, appearing in court, and collecting taxes. The sheriff was paid a fixed amount for each task he performed. Since sheriffs received higher fees based on the taxes they collected, apprehending criminals was not a primary concern. In fact, law enforcement was a low priority.

In the larger cities and towns, such as New York, Boston, and Philadelphia, constables and the night watch conducted a wide variety of tasks. The night watch reported fires, raised the hue and cry, maintained street lamps, arrested or detained suspicious persons, and walked the rounds. Constables engaged in similarly broad tasks—taking suspects to court, eliminating health hazards, bringing witnesses to court, and so on.

For the most part, the activities of the constables and the night watch were "reactive" in nature. That is, these men responded to criminal behavior only when requested by victims or witnesses (Monkkonen, 1981). Rather than preventing crime, discovering criminal behavior, or acting in a "proactive" fashion, these individuals relied on others to define their work. Public health violations were the only types of activity that required the officers to exercise initiative.

II. Preventive Police: Cops and Bobbies

The development of a "new" police system has been carefully documented by a number of American and English historians. Sir Leon Radzinowicz (1948–1968), Charles Reith (1956), and T. A. Critchley (1967) are among the more notable English writers. Roger Lane (1967), James F. Richardson (1970), Wilbur R. Miller (1977), Samuel Walker (1977), and Eric Monkkonen (1981) represent a rather diverse group of American historians who describe and analyze a number of early police departments. Taken together these works present the key elements of the activities of the first English and American police systems that used the preventive model.

During the mid- to late 1700s the growth of industry in England and in Europe led to rapid development in the cities. London, in particular, expanded at an unprecedented rate. From 1750 to 1820 the population nearly doubled (Miller, 1977) and the urban economy became more complex and specialized. The Industrial Revolution led to an increase in the number of factories, tenements, vehicles, and marketplaces. With industrial growth came a breakdown in social control, as a crime, riots, disorder, and public health problems disrupted the city. Food riots, wage protests, poor sewage control, pickpockets, burglars, and vandals created difficulties for city dwellers. The upper and middle classes, concerned about these issues sought more protection and preventive measures. The constable-watch system of law enforcement could no longer deal successfully with the problems of the day, and alternative solutions were devised.

Some of the alternatives included using the militia; calling out the "yeomanry" or cavalry volunteers for assistance; swearing in more law-abiding citizens as constables; or employing the army to quell riot situations (Richardson, 1974:10). However, these were short-term solutions to a long-term problem.

Another proposal was to replace the constable-watch system with a stronger, more centralized police force. Henry and John Fielding (magistrates in the 1750s), Patrick Colquhoun (a magistrate from 1792 to 1818), and philosopher Jeremy Bentham and his followers advocated the creation of a police force whose principal object was the prevention of crime. A preventive police force would act as a deterrent to criminals and would be in the best interests of society. But the idea of a uniformed police officer was opposed by many citizens and politicians in England. An organized police force too closely resembled a standing army, which gave government potentially despotic control over citizens and subjects. The proponents of a police force eventually won out, based primarily on the disorder and fear of crime experienced by London residents. After much debate in the early 1800s, the London Metropolitan Police Act was finally approved by Parliament in 1829 (see Critchley, 1967 and Reith, 1956).

The London Metropolitan Police Act established a full-time, uniformed police force with the primary purpose of patrolling the city. Sir Robert Peel, Britain's Home Secretary, is credited with the formation of the police. Peel synthesized the ideas of the Fieldings, Colquhoun, and Bentham into law; convinced Parliament of the need for police; and guided the early development of the force.

Through Peel and his two police commissioners, Charles Rowan and Richard Mayne, the role of the London Police was formulated. Crime prevention was the primary function, but to enforce the laws and to exert its authority, the police had to first gain legitimacy in the eyes of the public. According to Wilbur R. Miller (1977) the legitimation of the London police was carefully orchestrated by Peel and his associates. These men recognized that in order to gain authority police officers had to act in a certain manner or the public would reject them. To gain acceptance in the eyes of the citizen, Peel and his associates selected men who were even-tempered and reserved; chose a uniform that was unassuming (navy blue rather than military red); insisted that officers be restrained and polite; meted out appropriate discipline; and did not allow officers to carry guns. Overall, the London police emphasized their legitimacy as based on *institutional* authority—that their power was grounded in the English Constitution and that their behavior was determined by rules of law. In essence, this meant that the power of the London "bobby" or "Peeler" was based on the institution of the government.

American cities and towns encountered problems similar to those in England. Cities grew at phenomenal rates; civil disorders swept the nation and crime was perceived to be increasing. New York, for example, sprouted from a population of 33,000 in 1790 to 150,000 in 1830. Foreign immigrants, particularly Irish and Germans, accounted for a large portion of the increase. Traveling to America in search of employment and better lifestyles, the immigrants competed with native-born Americans for skilled and unskilled positions. As a result, the American worker saw Irishmen and Germans as social and economic threats.

Other tensions existed in the city as well. The race question was an important one in the northern cities as well as in the southern plantation. In fact, historians have shown that hostility to blacks was just as high in the North as in the South (Litwack, 1961). Those opposed to slavery (the abolitionists) were often met by violence when they attempted to speak out against it.

Between the 1830s and 1870s, numerous conflicts occurred because of ethnic and racial differences, economic failures, moral questions, and during elections of public officials. In New York, 1834 was designated the "Year of the Riots" because so many took place (Miller, 1977). The mayoral election and anti-abolitionist sentiment were the two main reasons for the disorders. Other cities faced similar problems. In Philadelphia, the Broad Street Riot of 1837 involved almost 15,000 residents. The incident occurred because native-born volunteer firemen returning from a fire could not get by an Irish funeral procession. In St. Louis, in 1850 a mob destroyed the brothels in the city in attempt to enforce standards of public decency. To quell most of these disturbances, the local militia was called in to suppress the violence, as the constables and the night watch were ineffectual.

At the same time that the riots occurred, citizens perceived that crime was increasing. Homicides, robberies, and thefts were though to be on the rise. In addition, vagrancy, prostitution, gambling, and other vices were more observable on the streets. These types of criminal activities and the general deterioration of the city led to a sense of a loss of social control. But in spite of the apparent immediacy of these problems, replacements for the constable-watch police system did not appear over night.

The political forces in the large industrial cities like New York, Philadelphia, Boston, and others precluded the immediate acceptance of a London-style police department. City councils, mayors, state legislatures, and governors debated and wrangled over a number of questions and could not come to an immediate agreement over the type of police they wanted. In New York City, for example, while problems emerged in 1834, the movement to form a preventive police department began in 1841, was officially created in 1845, but officers did not begin wearing uniforms until 1853.

While the first American police departments modeled themselves after the London Metropolitan Police, they borrowed selectively rather than exactly. The most notable carryover was the adoption of the preventive patrol idea. A police presence would alter the behavior of individuals and would be available to maintain order in an efficient manner. Differences, however, between the London and American police abounded. Miller (1977), in his comparative study of New York and London police, shows the drastic differences between the two agencies.

The London Metropolitan Police was a highly centralized agency. An extension of the national government, the police department was purposely removed from the direct political influence of the people. Furthermore, as noted above, Sir Robert Peel recruited individuals who fit a certain mold. Peel insisted that a polite, aloof officer who was trained and disciplined according to strict guidelines would be best suited for the function of crime prevention. In addition, the bobbies were encouraged to look upon police work as a career in professional civil service.

Unlike the London police, American police systems followed the style of local and municipal governments. City governments, created in the era of the "common man" and democratic participation, were highly decentralized. Mayors were largely figureheads; real power lay in the wards and neighborhoods. City councilmen or aldermen ran the government and used political patronage freely. The police departments shared this style of participation and decentralization. The police were an extension of different political factions, rather than an extension of city government. Police officers were recruited and selected by political leaders in a particular ward or precinct.

As a result of the democratic nature of government, legal intervention by the police was limited. Unlike the London police, which relied on formal institutional power, the American police relied on informal control or individual authority. That is, instead of drawing on institutional legitimacy (i.e., parliamentary laws), each police officer had to establish his own authority among the citizens he patrolled. The personal, informal police officer could win the respect of the citizenry by knowing local standards and expectations. This meant that different police behavior would occur in different neighborhoods. In New York, for example, the cop was free to act as he chose within the context of broad public expectations. He was less limited by institutional and legal restraints than was his London counterpart, entrusted with less formal power, but given broader personal discretion.

III. Police Activity in the Nineteenth Century

American police systems began to appear almost overnight from 1860 to 1890 (Monkkonen, 1981). Once large cities like New York, Philadelphia,

Boston, and Cincinnati had adopted the English model, the new version of policing spread from larger to smaller cities rather quickly. Where New York had debated for almost ten years before formally adopting the London style of policing, Cleveland, Buffalo, Detroit, and other cities readily accepted the innovation. Monkkonen explains that the police were a part of a growing range of services provided by urban administrations. Sanitation, fire, and health services were also adopted during this period and the police were simply a part of their natural growth.

Across these departments, however, differences flourished. Police activity varied depending upon the local government and political factions in power. Standards for officer selection (if any), training procedures, rules and regulations, levels of enforcement of laws, and police-citizen relationships differed across the United States. At the same time, however, there were some striking similarities.

Patrol Officers

The nineteenth century patrolman was basically a political operative rather than a London-style professional committed to public service (Walker, 1977). Primarily selected for his political service, the police officer owed his allegiance to the ward boss and police captain who chose him.

Police officers were paid well but had poor job security. Police salaries compared favorably with other occupations. On average in 1880, most major cities paid policemen in the neighborhood of $900 a year. Walker (1977) reports that a skilled tradesman in the building industry earned about $770 a year, while those in manufacturing could expect about $450 a year. A major drawback, however, was that job security was poor, as their employment relied on election day events. In Cincinnati, for example, in 1880, 219 of the 295 members of the force were dismissed, while another 20 resigned because of political change in the municipal government. Other departments had similar turnover rates.

New officers were sent out on patrol with no training and few instructions beyond their rulebooks. Proper arrest procedures, rules of law, and so on were unknown to the officers. Left to themselves, they developed their own strategies for coping with life in the streets.

Police Work

Police officers walked a beat in all types of weather for two to six hours of a 12-hour day. The remaining time was spent at the station house on reserve. During actual patrol duty, police officers were required to maintain order and make arrests, but they often circumvented their responsibilities. Supervision was extremely limited once an officer was beyond the station house. Sergeants and captains had no way of contacting their men while they were on the beat, as communications technology was limited. Telegraph lines linked district stations to headquarters in the 1850s, but call boxes on the beat

were not introduced until late in the nineteenth century, and the radio and
motorized communications did not appear until the 1900s (Lane, 1980).
Police officers, then, acted alone and used their own initiative.

Unfortunately, little is known about ordinary patrol work or routine
interactions with the public. However, historians have pieced together trends
in police work based on arrest statistics. While these data have their limitations, they nonetheless provide a view of police activity.

Monkkonen's work (1981) found that from 1860 to 1920 arrests declined
in 23 of the largest cities in the United States. In particular, crimes without
victims (vice, disturbances, drunkenness, other public order offenses) fell dramatically. Overall, Monkkonen estimated that arrests declined by more than
33 percent during the 60-year period. This trend runs contrary to "commonsense notions about the crime and growth of industrial cities, immigration
and social conflict" (p. 75). Further analysis showed that the decline occurred
because the police role shifted from one of controlling the "dangerous class"
to one of controlling criminal behavior only. From 1860 to 1890, Monkkonen
argues, the police were involved in assisting the poor, in taking in overnight
lodgers, and in returning lost children to their parents or orphanages. In the
period of 1890 to 1920, however, the police changed their role, structure, and
behavior because of external demands upon them. As a result, victimless
arrests declined, while assaults, thefts, and homicide arrests increased
slightly. Overall, however, the crime trend showed a decrease.

Police Corruption and Lawlessness

One of the major themes in the study of nineteenth-century policing is
the large-scale corruption that occurred in numerous departments across the
country. The lawlessness of the police—their systematic corruption and non-
enforcement of the laws—was one of the paramount issues in municipal politics during the late 1800s.

Police corruption was a part of a broader social and political problem.
During this period, political machines ran municipal governments. That is,
political parties (Democrats and Republicans) controlled the mayor's office,
the city councils and local wards. Municipal agencies (fire departments, sanitation services, school districts, the courts, etc.) were also under the aegis of
political parties. As part of this system, political patronage was rampant.
Employment in exchange for votes or money was a common procedure.
Police departments in New York, Chicago, Philadelphia, Kansas City, San
Francisco, and Los Angles were filled with political appointees as police
officers. To insure their employment, officers followed the norms of the political party, often protecting illicit activities conducted by party favorites.

Corrupt practices extended from the chief's office down to the patrol
officer. In New York City, for example, Chief William Devery (1898–1901)
protected gambling dens and illegal prize fighting because his friend, Tim
Sullivan (a major political figure on the Lower East Side) had interests in

those areas. Police captains like Alexander "Clubber" Williams and Timothy Creeden acquired extensive wealth from protecting prostitutes, saloonkeepers, and gamblers. Williams, a brutal officer (hence, the nickname Clubber), was said to have a 53-foot yacht and residences in New York and the Connecticut suburbs. Since a captain's salary was about $3,000 a year in the 1890s, Williams had to collect from illegal enterprises in order to maintain his investments.

Because police officers worked alone or in small groups, there were ample opportunities to shake down peddlers and small businesses. Detectives allowed con men, pickpockets, and thieves to go about their business in return for a share of the proceeds. Captains often established regular payment schedules for houses of prostitution depending upon the number of girls in the house and the rates charged by them. The monthly total for police protection ranged between $25 and $75 per house plus $500 to open or reopen after being raided (Richardson, 1970).

Officers who did not go along with the nonenforcement of laws or did not approve of the graft and corruption of others found themselves transferred to less-than desirable areas. Promotions were also denied; they were reserved for the politically astute and wealthy officer (promotions could cost $10,000 to $15,000).

These types of problems were endemic to most urban police agencies throughout the country. They led to inefficiency and inequality of police services.

IV. Reform, Rejection, and Revision

A broad reform effort began to emerge toward the end of the nineteenth century. Stimulated mainly by a group known as the Progressives, attempts were made to create a truly professional police force. The Progressives were upper-middle-class, educated Protestants who opposed the political machines, sought improvements in government, and desired a change in American morality. By eliminating machine politics from government, all facets of social services, including the police, would improve.

These reformers found that the police were without discipline, strong leadership, and qualified personnel. To improve conditions, the Progressives recommended three changes: (1) the departments should be centralized; (2) personnel should be upgraded; and (3) the police function should be narrowed (Fogelson, 1977). Centralization of the police meant that more power and authority should be placed in the hands of the chief. Autonomy from politicians was crucial to centralization. Upgrading the rank-and-file meant better training, discipline, and selection. Finally, the reformers urged that police give up all activities unrelated to crime. Police had run the ambulances, handled licensing of businesses, and sheltered the poor. By concentrating on fighting crime, the police would be removed from their service orientation and their ties to political parties would be severed.

From 1890 to 1920 the Progressive reformers struggled to implement their reform ideology in cities across the country. Some inroads were made during this period, including the establishment of police commissions, the use of civil service exams, and legislative reforms.

The immediate response to charges of corruption were to create police administrative boards. The reformers attempted to take law enforcement appointments out of the hands of mayors and city councilmen and place control in the hands of oversight committees. The Progressives believed that politics would be eliminated from policing by using this maneuver. In New York, for example, the Lexow Committee, which investigated the corrupt practices of the department, recommended the formation of a bipartisan Board of Police Commissioners in 1895. Theodore Roosevelt became a member of this board, but to his dismay found that the commissioners were powerless to improve the state of policing. The bipartisan nature of the board (two Democrats and two Republicans) meant that consensus could not be reached on important issues. As a result, by 1900 the New York City police were again under the influence of party politics. In the following year the Board of Commissioners was abolished and the department was placed under the responsibility of a single commissioner (Walker, 1977). Other cities had similar experiences with the police commission approach. Cincinnati, Kansas City, St. Louis, and Baltimore were among those that adopted the commission, but found it to be short-lived. The major problem was still political—the police were viewed as an instrument of the political machine at the neighborhood level, and reformers could not counter the effects of the Democratic or Republican parties.

Civil service was one answer to upgrading personnel. Officers would be selected and promoted based on merit, as measured by a competitive exam. Moreover, the officer would be subject to review by his supervisors and removal from the force could take place if there was sufficient cause. Civil service met with some resistance by officers and reformers alike. The problem was that in guarding against the effects of patronage and favoritism, civil service became a rigid, almost inflexible procedure. The civil service exam measured abstract knowledge rather than the qualities required for day-to-day work, and civil service procedures were viewed as problematic. Eventually, the program did help to eliminate the more blatant forms of political patronage in almost all of the large police departments (Walker, 1977).

During this 30-year period, the efforts of the Progressive reformers did not change urban departments drastically. The reform movement resulted, in part, in the elimination of the widespread graft and corruption of the 1890s, but substantive changes in policing did not take place. Chiefs continued to lack power and authority, many officers had little or no education, training was limited, and the police role continued to include a wide variety of tasks.

Robert Fogelson (1977) suggests several reasons for the failure of reform. First, political machines were too difficult to break. Despite the efforts by the Progressives, politicians could still count on individual supporters to undermine the reforms. Second, police officers themselves resented the Progressives' interventions. Reformers were viewed by the police as individuals who knew little about police work and officers saw their proposals for change as ill-conceived. Finally, the reforms failed because the idea of policing could not be divorced from politics. That is, the character of the big-city police was interconnected with policy-making agencies that helped to decide which laws were enforced, which public was served, and whose peace was kept (Fogelson, 1977). Separating the police completely from politics could not take place.

V. THE EMERGENCE OF POLICE PROFESSIONALISM

A second reform effort emerged in the wake of the failure of the Progressives. Within police circles, a small cadre of chiefs sought and implemented a variety of innovations that would improve policing generally. From about 1910 to 1960 police chiefs carried on another reform movement, advocating that police adopt the professional model.

The professional department embodied a number of characteristics. First, the officers were experts; they applied knowledge to their tasks and were the only ones qualified to do the job. Second, the department was autonomous from external influences, such as political parties. This also meant that the department made its own rules and regulated its personnel. Finally, the department was administratively efficient, in that it carried out its mandate to enforce the law through modern technology and businesslike practices. These reforms were similar to those of the Progressives, but because they came from within the police organizations themselves, they met with more success.

Leadership and technology assisted the movement to professionalize the police. Chiefs like Richard Sylvester, August Vollmer, and O. W. Wilson emphasized the use of innovative methods in police work. Samuel Walker (1977) notes that Sylvester, the chief of the Washington, D.C. police, helped to establish the idea of professionalism among police chiefs. As president of the International Association of Chiefs of Police (IACP), Sylvester inculcated the spirit of reform into the organization. He stressed acceptance of technological innovations, raised the level of discussion among chiefs to include crime control ideas, and promoted professionalism generally.

The major innovator among the chiefs was August Vollmer, chief of the Berkeley, California, police. Vollmer was known for his promising work in developing college-level police education programs, bicycle and automobile patrol, and scientific crime detection aids. His department was the first to use forensic science in solving crimes.

Vollmer's emphasis on the quality of police personnel was tied closely to the idea of the professional officer. Becoming an expert in policing meant having the requisite credentials. Vollmer initiated intelligence, psychiatric, and neurological tests by which to select applicants. He was the first police chief to actively recruit college students. In addition, he was instrumental in linking the police department with the University of California at Berkeley. Another concern of Vollmer dealt with the efficient delivery of police services. His department became the first in the nation to use automobiles and the first to hire a full-time forensic scientist to help solve crimes (Douthit, 1975).

O. W. Wilson, Vollmer's student, followed in his mentor's footsteps by advocating efficiency within the police bureaucracy through scientific techniques. As chief in Wichita, Kansas, Wilson conducted the first systematic study of one-officer squad cars. He argued that one-officer cars were efficient, effective, and economical. Despite arguments from patrol officers that their safety was at risk, Wilson claimed that the public received better service with single-officer cars.

Wilson's other contributions include his classic textbook, *Police Administration*, which lays out specific ideas regarding the use of one-man patrol cars, deployment of personnel on the streets, disciplinary measures, and organizational structure. Later in his career, Wilson accepted a professorship at U. C. Berkeley where he taught and trained law enforcement officers. In 1947 he founded the first professional School of Criminology.

Other chiefs contributed to the professional movement as well. William Parker changed the Los Angeles Police Department (LAPD) from a corrupt, traditional agency to an innovative, professional organization. From 1950 to his death in 1966, Parker served as chief. He was known for his careful planning, emphasis on efficiency, and his rigorous personnel selection and training procedures. His public relations campaigns and adept political maneuvers enabled him to gain the respect of the media and the community. As a result, the LAPD became a model for reform across the country.

Technological changes also enabled the police to move toward professionalism. The patrol car, two-way radio, and telephone altered the way in which the police operated and the manner in which citizens made use of the police. Motorized patrol meant more efficient coverage of the city and quicker response to calls for service. The two-way radio dramatically increased the supervisory capacity of the police. Continuous contact between sergeant and police officer could be maintained. Finally, the telephone provided the link between the public and the police. Though not a new invention, its use in conjunction with the car and two-way radio meant that the efficient response to calls for service would be realized.

Overall, the second reform movement met with more success than the Progressive attempt, though it did not achieve its goal of professionalization. Walker (1977) and Fogelson (1977) agree that the quality of police officers greatly improved during this period. Police departments turned away the ill-educated individual, but at the same time failed to draw college graduates to their ranks. In terms of autonomy, police reformers and others were able to reduce the influence of political parties in departmental affairs. Chiefs obtained more power and authority in their management abilities, but continued to receive input from political leaders. In fact, most chiefs remained political appointees. In terms of efficiency, the police moved forward in serving the public more quickly and competently. Technological innovations clearly assisted the police in this area, as did streamlining the organizations themselves. However, the innovations also created problems. Citizens came to expect more from the police—faster response times, more arrests, and less overall crime. These expectations, as well as other difficulties, led to trying times for the police in the 1960s.

VI. RIOTS AND RENEWAL

Policing in America encountered its most serious crisis in the 1960s. The rise in crime, the civil rights movement, anti-war sentiment, and riots in the cities brought the police into the center of a maelstrom.

During the decade of the 1960s crime increased at a phenomenal rate. Between 1960 and 1970 the crime rate per 100,000 persons doubled. Most troubling was the increase in violent crime—the robbery rate almost tripled during these ten years. As crime increased, so too did the demands for its reduction. The police, in emphasizing its crime fighting ability, had given the public a false expectation they had created. As a result, the public image of the police was tarnished.

The civil rights movement created additional demands for the police. The movement, begun in the 1950s, sought equality for black Americans in all facets of life. Sit-ins at segregated lunch counters, boycotts of bus services, attempts at integrating schools, and demonstrations in the streets led to direct confrontations with law enforcement officers. The police became the symbol of a society that denied blacks equal justice under the law.

Eventually, the frustrations of black Americans erupted into violence in northern and southern cities. Riots engulfed almost every major city between 1964 and 1968. Most of the disorders were initiated by a routine incident involving the police. The spark that initiated the riots occurred on July 16, 1964, when a white New York City police officer shot and killed a black teenager. Black leaders in the Harlem ghetto organized protests demanding disciplinary action against the officer. Two days later, the demonstrators marched on precinct headquarters, where rock throwing began. Eventually, looting and burning erupted during the night and lasted two full days. When the riot was brought under control one person was dead, more than 100 injured, almost 500 arrested, and millions of dollars worth of property destroyed. In the following year, the Watts riot in Los Angeles led to more devastation. Thirty-four persons died, a thousand were injured, and 4,000 arrested. By 1966, 43 more riots broke out across the country, and in 1967 violence in Newark and Detroit exceeded the 1965 Watts riot. Disorders engulfed Newark for five days, leaving 23 dead, while the Detroit riot a week later lasted nearly seven days and resulted in 43 deaths with $40 million in property damages.

On the final day of the Detroit riot, President Lyndon Johnson appointed a special commission to investigate the problem of civil disorder. The National Advisory Commission on Civil Disorders (The Kerner Commission) identified institutional racism as the underlying cause of the rioting. Unemployment, discrimination in jobs and housing, inadequate social services, and unequal justice at the hands of the law were among the problems cited by the commission.

Police actions were also cited as contributing to the disorders. Direct police intervention had sparked the riots in Harlem, Watts, Newark, and Detroit. In Watts and Newark the riots were set off by routine traffic stops. In Detroit a police raid on an after-hours bar in the ghetto touched off the disorders there. The police thus became the focus of the national attention.

The Kerner Commission and other investigations found several problems in police departments. First, police conduct included brutality, harassment, and abuse of power. Second, training and supervision was inadequate. Third, police-community relations were poor. Fourth, the employment of the black officers lagged far behind the growth of the black population.

As a means of coping with these problems in policing (and other agencies of the criminal justice system) President Johnson created a crime commission and Congress authorized federal assistance to criminal justice. The president's crime commission produced a final report that emphasized the need for more research, higher qualifications of criminal justice personnel, and greater coordination of the national crime-control effort. The federal aid program to justice agencies resulted in the Office of Law Enforcement Assistance, a forerunner of the Law Enforcement Assistance Administration (LEAA).

VII. THE LEGACY OF THE 60s

The events of the 1960s forced the police, politicians, and policy makers to reassess the state of law enforcement in the United States. For the first time, academics rushed to study the police in an effort to explain their problems and crises. With federal funding from LEAA and private organizations researchers began to study the police from a number of perspectives. Sociologists, political scientists, psychologists, and historians began to scrutinize different aspects of policing. Traditional methods of patrol development, officer selection, and training were questioned. Racial discrimination in employment practices, in arrests, and in the use of deadly force were among the issues closely examined.

In addition, the professional movement itself came into question. As Walker notes, the legacy of professionalization was "ambiguous" (Walker, 1977:167). On one hand, the police made improvements in their level of service, training, recruitment, and efficiency. On the other hand, a number of problems remained and a number of new ones emerged. Corruption scandals continued to present problems. In New York, Chicago, and Denver systematic corruption was discovered. Political parties persisted in their links to policing.

The professional movement had two unintended consequences. The first involved the development of a police subculture. The second was the problem of the police-community relations. In terms of the subculture, police officers began to feel alienated from administrators, the media, and the public and turned inward as a result. Patrol officers began to resent the police hierarchy because of the emphasis on following orders and regulations. While this established uniformity in performance and eliminated some abuses of power, it also stifled creativity and the talents of many officers. Rather than thinking for themselves (as professionals would) patrol officers followed orders given by sergeants, lieutenants, or other ranking officers. This led to morale problems and criticism of police administration by the rank and file.

Patrol officers saw the media and the public as foes because of the criticism and disrespect cast their way. As the crime rate increased, newspaper accounts criticized the police for their inability to curtail it. As the riots persisted, some citizens cried for more order, while others demanded less oppression by the police on the streets. The conflicting message given to the patrol officers by these groups led to distrust, alienation, and frustration. Only by standing together did officers feel comfortable in their working environment.

The second unintended consequence of professionalism was the problems it generated for police-community relations. Modern technology, like the patrol car, removed the officer from the street and eliminated routine contact with citizens. The impersonal style of professionalism often exacerbated police-community problems. Tactics such as aggressive patrol in black neighborhoods, designed to suppress crime efficiently, created more racial tensions.

The problems called into question the need for and effectiveness of professionalism. Some police administrators suggested abandoning the movement. Others sought to continue the effort while adjusting for and solving the difficulties. For the most part, the goal of professionalization remains operative. In the 1970s and 1980s, progressive police chiefs and organizations pressed for innovations in policing. As a result, social science research became an important part of policy-making decisions. By linking research to issues like domestic violence, repeat offenders, use of deadly force, training techniques, and selection procedures, police executives increased their ability to make effective decisions.

VIII. FROM REACTIVE TO PROACTIVE: COMMUNITY POLICING STRATEGIES

As a result of the problems of the 1960s and 1970s, a third wave of reform of police operations and strategies began to emerge—community-oriented policing.

Community policing came to light as an idea and philosophy in response to the communication gap between police and community and because of research studies that questioned police tactics and strategies. A new paradigm, which incorporated the "broken windows" theory, proactive policing, and problem-oriented policing shaped the community policing reform era.

Researchers began to question some of the basic premises of law enforcement. They found that randomly patrolling an area of a city does not deter crime (Kelling, et al., 1974). Other researchers found that detectives could not solve crime by simply gathering evidence from crime scenes—they needed witnesses and other information to assist them (Greenwood, Chaiken and Petersilia, 1977). Researchers also found that rapid response to calls for service does not always result in the apprehension of offenders (Spelman and Brown, 1984).

Police strategists recognized that simply reacting to calls for service limits the ability of law enforcement to control crime and maintain order. Police on patrol cannot see enough to control crime effectively—they do not know how to intervene to improve the quality of life in the community. The reactive strategy used during the professional era no longer was effective in dealing with complex problems in the 1980s and 1990s. Instead, Herman Goldstein (1979) and James Q. Wilson and George Kelling (1982) called for police to engage in proactive work and problem-oriented policing. A whole body of work from police researchers, strategists, and reformers laid the groundwork for the community policing movement.

Defining Community Policing

Community policing has a number of different definitions (Maguire, et al., 1997). For some, community policing means instituting foot patrols and bicycle patrols, getting out of patrol cars, and a host of other activities that are designed to bring police officers closer to the communities they serve. For others, it means order maintenance, cleaning up tattered neighborhoods, and fixing "broken windows" (Wilson and Kelling, 1982). For many agencies, community policing is simply implementing a series of community-relations programs, including Drug Abuse Resistance Education (DARE), Neighborhood Watch, and a variety of others.

Most supporters of community policing view it as a new philosophy of policing. In its ideal sense, it means changing the traditional definition of policing from one of crime control to one of community problem-solving and empowerment (Goldstein, 1990; Wilson and Kelling, 1982). In addition to redefining the police mission, a practical shift to a community policing strategy means changing the "principal operating methods, and the key administrative arrangements of police departments" (Moore, 1992:103). Three integral dimensions are consistently highlighted:

1. engaging and interacting with the community;

2. solving community problems; and

3. adapting internal elements of the organization to support these new strategies (Bayley, 1994).

In its ideal sense, community policing promises to fundamentally transform the way police do business. Reformers argue that police should not be so obsessed with routine "people-processing" activities (e.g., making arrests or filling out reports) but should focus instead on "people-changing" activities (Mastrofski and Ritti, 2000). These include building up neighborhoods, designing custom solutions to local problems, forging partnerships with other community agencies, and a variety of other non-routine police activities.

The Effects of Federal Funding

The Violent Crime Control and Law Enforcement Act of 1994 (Crime Act) gave a tremendous financial boost to the community policing movement. Under Title I, known as the "Public Safety Partnership and Community Policing Act of 1994," Congress and the Clinton Administration determined that 100,000 additional officers, new technology, and innovative programs should be provided to law enforcement agencies throughout the nation, with a particular emphasis on the implementation of community policing. Title I authorized the expenditure of $8.8 billion over six years for use in three primary approaches—hiring new officers for community policing, acquiring technology and hiring civilians to free up time for officers to engage in community policing, and implementing new programs. A new agency, called the Office of Community Oriented Policing Services (COPS Office) was formed within the Department of Justice specifically to distribute grants and carry out the statutory mandates of Title I (see Roth et al., 2000; Gest, 2001).

From 1995 to 2003, the COPS Office provided more than $6.9 billion to nearly 13,000 state and local law enforcement agencies to hire over 118,000 officers, deputies, and troopers. The COPS Office provided law enforcement agencies with an array of community policing training and technical assistance resources. In addition, new programs were developed and funded, including the use of problem-solving partnerships in schools, community-based efforts to combat domestic violence, and advancing community policing through demonstration centers.

As a result of these funds, by 1999 over 60 percent of municipal police agencies had developed a strategic plan that incorporated community policing principles (Hickman and Reaves, 2001). Almost all of the largest police agencies in the country had full-time community policing officers working the streets. In 1997 about 4 percent of all local police officers served as community policing officers. By 1999, the percentage had increased to 21 percent. In jurisdictions with 500,000 or more people, the percentage of full-time sworn personnel increased from 1.4 percent in 1997 to 24.1 percent in 1999.

In addition to the changes in strategic plans and the increase in officers on the street, independent evaluators found that the COPS Office programs accelerated the transition of community policing in three important ways. First, they stimulated a "national conversation about community policing and provided training and technical assistance to agencies." Second, hiring monies and innovative policing grants allowed chief executives to add community policing programs without cutting back other programs. Third, the funds created an incentive for agency executives to adopt community policing (Roth et al., 2000:23).

CONCLUDING REMARKS

With the onset of a new millennium, American police agencies face new challenges. The terrorist attacks on the World Trade Center and the Pentagon changed the way in which law enforcement collectively thinks about public safety and security. Priorities for training, equipment, strategies, and funding have transformed policing once again—this time focusing on homeland security. Time will tell us about the hows and whys of this transformation.

This article has examined the history of American police systems from the English heritage through the last years of the twentieth century. Major emphasis has been placed on the police role, though important events that shaped the development of the police have also been discussed. As can be seen through this review, a number of present-day issues have their roots in different epochs of American history. For example, the idea of community policing can be traced to the colonial period and to medieval England. Preventive patrol, legitimacy, authority, and professionalism are eighteenth and nineteenth century concepts. Riots, disorders, and corruption are not new to American policing, similar events occurred in the nineteenth century. Thus, by virtue of studying history, we can give contextual meaning to current police problems, ideas, and situations. By looking at the past, present-day events can be better understood.

Notes

[1] This list of police histories is by no means a comprehensive one. A vast number of journal articles, books, and dissertations have been written since those cited.

[2] A number of scholars have examined the "police function." Among the most well-known are Wilson (1968), Skolnick (1966), Bittner (1971), and Goldstein (1977). Each of these authors prescribes to a different view of what the police should and should not do.

References

Alfers, Kenneth G. 1975. "The Washington Police: A History, 1800–1866," Ph.D. dissertation, George Washington University.

Bayley, D. 1994. *Police for the Future*. New York: Oxford University Press.

Bittner, Egon. 1970. *The Functions of the Police in Modern Society.* Chevy Chase, MD: National Institute of Mental Health.

Cei, Louis B. 1975. "Law Enforcement in Richmond: A History of Police Community Relations, 1737–1974," Ph.D. dissertation, Florida State University.

Critchley, T. A. 1967. *A History of Police in England and Wales*. Montclair, NJ: Patterson Smith.

Douthit, Nathan. 1975. "August Vollmer: Berkeley's First Chief of Police and the Emergence of Police Professionalism," *California Historical Quarterly* 54 Spring: 101–124.

Fogelson, Robert. 1977. *Big-City Police*. Cambridge, MA: Harvard University Press.

Gest, Ted. 2001. *Crime and Politics: Big Government's Erratic Campaign for Law and Order.* New York: Oxford University Press.

Goldstein, Herman. 1977. *Policing a Free Society*. Cambridge, MA: Ballinger Press.

———. 1979. "Improving Policing: A Problem-Oriented Approach." *Crime and Delinquency* 25: 236–58.

————. 1990. *Problem-Oriented Policing.* New York: McGraw-Hill.

Greenwood, P. W., J. M. Chaiken, and J. Petersilia. 1977. *The Criminal Investigation Process.* Lexington, MA: D.C. Heath.

Hickman, Matthew J. and Brian A. Reaves. 2001. *Community Policing in Local Police Departments, 1997 and 1999.* Washington, DC: Bureau of Justice Statistics, U.S. Dept. of Justice, NCJ 184794.

Kelling, George T., T. Pate, D. Dieckman, and C. Brown. 1974. *The Kansas City Preventive Patrol Experiment: Final Report.* Washington, DC: Police Foundation.

Klockars, Carl. 1985. *The Idea of Police.* Beverly Hills, CA: Sage Publications.

Lane, Roger. 1967. *Policing the City: Boston, 1822–1285.* Cambridge, MA: Harvard University Press.

————. 1980. "Urban Police and Crime in the Nineteenth-Century America," in Michael Tonry and Norval Morris, eds., *Crime and Justice: An Annual Review of Research, Volume 2.* Chicago: University of Chicago Press.

Litwack, Leon. 1961. *North of Slavery.* Chicago: University of Chicago Press.

Maguire, Edward R., Joseph B. Kuhns, Craig D. Uchida, and Stephen M. Cox. 1997. "Patterns of Community Policing in Nonurban America," *Journal of Research in Crime and Delinquency,* Vol. 34 No. 3, August: 368–394.

Maniha, John K. 1970. "The Mobility of Elites in a Bureaucratizing Organization: The St. Louis Police Department, 1861–1961," Ph.D. dissertation, University of Michigan.

Mastrofski, S. and R. Ritti. 2000. "Making Sense of Community Policing: A Theoretical Perspective." *Police Practice and Research Journal* 1(2): 183–210.

Miller, Wilbur R. 1977. *Cops and Bobbies: Police Authority in New York and London, 1830–1870.* Chicago: University of Chicago Press.

Monkkonen, Eric H. 1981. *Police in Urban America, 1860–1920.* Cambridge: Cambridge University Press.

Moore, M. H. 1992. "Problem-solving and Community Policing," in Michael Tonry and Norval Morris, eds., *Modern Policing: Crime and Justice, an Annual Review of Research.* Chicago: University of Chicago Press.

Radzinowicz, Leon. 1948–1968. *History of the English Criminal Law, Volume 1–4.* New York: MacMillan.

Reichard, Maximillian I. 1975. "The Origins of Urban Police: Freedom and Order in Antebellum St. Louis," Ph.D. dissertation, Washington University.

Reith, Charles. 1956. *A New Study of Police History.* Edinburgh.

Richardson, James F. 1970. *The New York Police: Colonial Times to 1901.* New York: Oxford University Press.

————. 1974. *Urban Police in the United States.* Port Washington, NY: Kennikat Press.

Rider, Eugene F. 1971. "The Denver Police Department: An Administrative, Organizational, and Operational History, 1858–1905," Ph.D. dissertation. University of Denver.

Roth, Jeffrey, A., Joseph F. Ryan, Stephen J. Gaffigan, Christopher S. Koper, Mark H. Moore, Janice A. Roehl, Calvin C. Johnson, Gretchen E. Moore, Ruth M. White, Michael E. Buerger, Elizabeth A. Langston, and David Thacher. 2000. *National Evaluation of the COPS Program—Title I of the 1994 Crime Act.* Washington, DC: National Institute of Justice.

Schneider, John C. 1980. *Detroit and the Problems of Order, 1830–1880.* Lincoln: University of Nebraska Press.

Skolnick, Jerome. 1966. *Justice Without Trial: Law Enforcement in Democratic Society.* New York: John Wiley and Sons.

Spelman, William and Dale Brown. 1984. *Calling the Police: Citizen Reporting of Serious Crime*. Washington, DC: U.S. Government Printing Office.

Walker, Samuel. 1977. *A Critical History of Police Reform: The Emergence of Professionalism*. Lexington, MA: D.C. Heath and Company.

Wilson, James Q. 1968. *Varieties of Police Behavior: The Management of Law and Order in Eight Communities*. Cambridge, MA: Harvard University Press.

Wilson, James Q. and George Kelling. 1982. "Broken Windows: The Police and Neighborhood Safety." *Atlantic Monthly* 249: 29–38.

Census of State and Local Law Enforcement Agencies, 2000 and LEMAS, 2000—Highlights

Brian A. Reaves & Matthew J. Hickman

CENSUS, 2000

To ensure an accurate sampling frame for its Law Enforcement Management and Administrative Statistics (LEMAS) survey (excerpts of which appear on pp. 60–68), BJS periodically sponsors a census of state and local law enforcement agencies. The 2000 census included state and local agencies employing the equivalent of least one full-time officer with general arrest powers. This report summarizes the findings of the census, which was co-sponsored by COPS.

As in 1992 and 1996, the 2000 census collected data on the number of sworn and nonsworn personnel, including both full-time and part-time employees. Data were collected from agencies that employed at least one sworn officer or the part-time equivalent at the time of the census. The reference period for all data is the pay period that included June 30, 2000.

Census of State and Local Law Enforcement Agencies, 2000, excerpted from *Bureau of Justice Statistics Bulletin*, October 2002, NCJ 194066. Available online http://www.ojp.usdoj.gov/bjs/pub/pdf/csllea00.pdf. Law Enforcement Management and Administrative Statistics, 2000, excerpted from *Bureau of Justice Statistics*, March 2004, NCJ203350. Available online http://www.ojp.usdoj.gov/bjs/pub/pdf/lemas00.pdf

As of June 2000, state and local governments in the United States operated 17,784 full-time law enforcement agencies—those that employed at least one full-time sworn officer with general arrest powers or the equivalent in part-time officers.

The total included 12,666 general purpose local police departments, 3,070 sheriffs' offices, the 49 primary state law enforcement agencies, 1,376 state and local agencies with a special geographic jurisdiction or special enforcement responsibilities, and 623 county constable offices in Texas.

Overall, these state and local law enforcement agencies employed 1,019,496 persons on a full-time basis. This total included 708,022 full-time sworn personnel (69%) and 311,474 nonsworn (or civilian) personnel (31%). These agencies also had about 99,000 part-time employees, including nearly 43,000 part-time sworn personnel.

Type of agency	Number of full-time state and local law enforcement agencies, June 2000
Total	17,784
Local police	12,666
Sheriff	3,070
Primary state	49
Special jurisdiction	1,376
Texas constable	623

STATE AND LOCAL LAW ENFORCEMENT AGENCIES

By type of agency, general purpose local police departments were the largest employer with 565,915 full-time employees as of June 2000 (table 1). Of this total, 440,920, or 78%, were sworn personnel with general arrest powers. Sheriffs' offices accounted for 293,823 full-time employees, of which 164,711 (56%) were sworn officers.

The 49 primary state law enforcement agencies operating in each state except Hawaii employed 87,028 persons full time. Of these employees, 56,348, or 65%, were full-time sworn personnel.

Agencies with a special geographic jurisdiction or special enforcement responsibilities employed 43,413 full-time sworn personnel and had 69,650 full-time employees overall. (See table 14 for types of special jurisdictions.)

From June 1996 to 2000, the number of full-time state and local law enforcement employees in the United States increased about 97,500, or 10.6% (figure 1, p. 44). The number of full-time sworn personnel was up about 44,500, an increase of 6.7%. Civilian employment rose 53,000, or 20.5%.

Compared to 1992, full-time employment in 2000 was up 173,000, or 20.4%. This included about 100,000, or 16.4%, more sworn personnel, and 73,000, or 30.7%, more civilians.

In June 2000 there were 362 full-time state and local law enforcement employees per 100,000 residents nationwide, an increase of 5.9% from 1996, and 9.6% more than in 1992. This included 252 sworn personnel per 100,000 residents, an increase of 2.4% from 1996 levels, and 6.3% from 1992. The ratio of nonsworn personnel per 100,000 residents increased 19.4% from 1992 to 2000, including a 15.1% rise from 1996 to 2000.

	Full-time state and local law enforcement employees per 100,000 residents		
	2000	1996	1992
Total	362	342	330
Sworn	252	246	237
Nonsworn	111	96	93

Table 1   Employment by state and local law enforcement agencies, by type of agency and employee, June 2000

	State and local law enforcement employees					
	Full-time			Part-time		
Type of agency	Total	Sworn	Nonsworn	Total	Sworn	Nonsworn
Number of employees						
Total	1,019,496	708,022	311,474	99,731	42,803	56,928
Local police	565,915	440,920	124,995	62,110	27,323	34,787
Sheriff	293,823	164,711	129,112	22,737	10,300	12,437
Primary state	87,028	56,348	30,680	817	95	722
Special jurisdiction	69,650	43,413	26,237	13,583	4,667	8,916
Texas constable	3,080	2,630	450	484	418	66
Percent of employees						
Total	100%	69.4%	31.6%	100%	42.1%	57.8%
Local police	100%	77.9%	22.1%	100%	44.0%	56.0%
Sheriff	100	56.1	43.9	100	45.3	54.7
Primary state	100	64.7	35.3	100	11.6	88.4
Special jurisdiction	100	62.3	37.7	100	34.4	65.6
Texas constable	100	85.4	14.6	100	86.4	13.6

State and Local Sworn Personnel

Sixty percent of full-time state and local sworn employees were assigned to patrol duty on a regular basis (figure 2, p. 44). About in 1 in 7 sworn personnel were assigned to investigative duties (15%). Approximately 1 in 9 primarily performed duties related to jail (6%) or court (5%) operations. Duties of other state and local law enforcement officers, but not broken down here, included administration, training, and technical support.

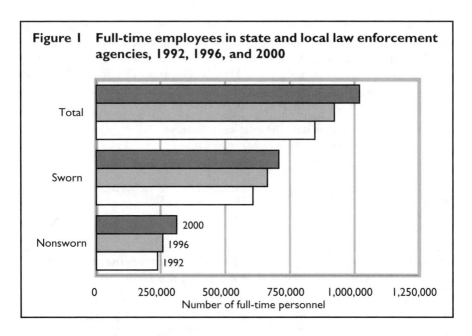

Figure 1 Full-time employees in state and local law enforcement agencies, 1992, 1996, and 2000

Number of full-time personnel

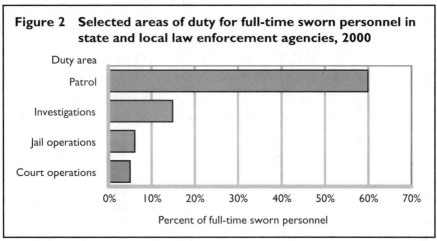

Figure 2 Selected areas of duty for full-time sworn personnel in state and local law enforcement agencies, 2000

Percent of full-time sworn personnel

Size of Agencies

As of June 2000, of the 17,784 state and local law enforcement agencies operating, 1,032, or 6%, employed 100 or more full-time sworn personnel (table 2). This included 77 agencies with 1,000 or more officers.

The majority of agencies employed fewer than 10 full-time officers (52%), and nearly a third, about 5,600 in all, employed fewer than 5 (31%). These smaller agencies included 1,907, 11% of agencies overall, with just 1 full-time officer and 231, 1% of all agencies, with only part-time officers.

Table 2   State and local law enforcement agencies, by size of agency, June 2000

Number of full-time sworn personnel	Agencies	
	Number	Percent
All sizes	17,784	100%
1,000 or more	77	0.4%
500–999	83	0.5
250–499	203	1.1
100–249	669	3.8
50–99	1,177	6.6
25–49	2,237	12.6
10–24	4,124	23.2
5–9	3,623	20.4
2–4	3,453	19.4
1	1,907	10.7
0	231	1.3

Although state and local agencies with 100 or more full-time sworn officers accounted for just 6% of all agencies, they employed 63% of all state and local full-time sworn personnel (table 3, p. 46). The 77 agencies with 1,000 or more officers accounted for 220,512, or 31.1%, of all full-time sworn personnel.

The 77 largest agencies rarely used part-time sworn officers, accounting for just 0.3% of all such personnel nationwide. Nearly half (47%) of part-time sworn personnel were employed by agencies with fewer than 10 full-time officers, and about two-thirds (69%) worked for agencies with fewer than 25 full-time officers.

State-by-State Comparisons

Texas (1,800) had the most full-time state and local law enforcement agencies (table 4, p. 47). The total included 623 county constable offices. Pennsylvania (1,166) had the next highest number of agencies, followed by Illinois (886) and Ohio (845).

California had the most full-time state and local law enforcement employees, about 116,000. Other states with 50,000 or more employees included New York (94,863), Texas (80,535), Florida (68,165), and Illinois (52,769). States with fewer than 2,000 employees included Vermont (1,459) and North Dakota (1,755).

Nationwide, there were 362 full-time state and local law enforcement personnel per 100,000 residents. The District of Columbia (859), Louisiana (527), and New York (500) had the most. West Virginia (229), Kentucky (237), and Vermont (240) had the least.

California (73,762) had the most full-time sworn personnel employed by state and local agencies, followed closely by New York (72,853). Next were Texas (51,478), Illinois (39,847), and Florida (39,452). Vermont (1,034) had the fewest officers.

After the District of Columbia (693), the ratio of full-time sworn personnel per 100,000 residents was highest in Louisiana (415). The next highest ratios were in New York (384), New Jersey (345), and Illinois (321). The lowest ratios were in Vermont (170) and West Virginia (174). Nationwide, the ratio was 252 per 100,000.

The per capita ratio of uniformed officers whose regular duties included responding to calls for service were highest in the District of Columbia (357 per 100,000 residents), New York (240), and Wyoming (200). It was lowest in Oregon (104) and Washington (108). The overall ratio for the nation was 151 per 100,000.

Table 3   State and local law enforcement employees, by size of agency, June 2000

| Full-time sworn personnel | Type of employee | | | | | |
| | Full-time | | | Part-time | | |
	Total	Sworn	Nonsworn	Total	Sworn	Nonsworn
Number of employees						
All sizes	1,019,496	708,022	311,474	99,731	42,803	56,928
1,000 or more	305,828	220,512	85,316	11,749	113	11,636
500–999	89,683	57,464	32,219	4,261	541	3,720
250–499	103,624	71,082	32,542	4,614	1,147	3,467
100–249	152,245	100,549	51,696	10,687	3,328	7,359
50–99	119,034	80,964	38,070	9,313	3,102	6,211
25–49	110,137	77,068	33,069	13,696	5,210	8,486
10–24	91,861	64,068	27,793	18,445	9,295	9,150
5–9	32,673	24,233	8,440	12,825	8,491	4,334
2–4	12,314	10,175	2,139	10,089	7,963	2,126
1	2,087	1,907	180	2,775	2,409	366
0	10	0	10	1,277	1,204	73
Percent of employees						
All sizes	100%	100%	100%	100%	100%	100%
1,000 or more	30.0%	31.1%	27.4%	11.8%	0.3%	20.4%
500–999	8.8	8.1	10.3	4.3	1.3	6.5
250–499	10.2	10.0	10.4	4.6	2.7	6.1
100–249	14.9	14.2	16.6	10.7	7.8	12.9
50–99	11.7	11.4	12.2	9.3	7.2	10.9
25–49	10.8	10.9	10.6	13.7	12.2	14.9
10–24	9.0	9.0	8.9	18.5	21.7	16.1
5–9	3.2	3.4	2.7	12.9	19.8	7.6
2–4	1.2	1.4	0.7	10.1	18.6	3.7
1	0.2	0.3	0.1	2.8	5.6	0.6
0	—	0.0	—	1.3	2.8	0.1

— Less than 0.05%

Table 4   State and local law enforcement agencies and employees, by state, June 2000

	Number of Agencies	Full-time employees					
		Total		Sworn personnel		Responding to calls	
		Number	Per 100,000 residents	Number	Per 100,000 residents	Number	Per 100,000 residents
U.S. total	17,784	1,019,496	362	708,022	252	425,427	151
Alabama	424	16,062	361	10,655	240	7,287	164
Alaska	95	2,151	343	1,348	215	1,031	164
Arizona	135	20,595	401	11,533	225	6,889	134
Arkansas	356	9,207	344	6,157	230	4,066	152
California	517	115,906	342	73,662	217	40,349	119
Colorado	248	15,237	354	10,309	240	5,815	135
Connecticut	125	10,277	302	8,327	245	5,143	151
Delaware	43	2,257	288	1,774	226	1,151	147
District of Columbia	3	4,914	859	3,963	693	2,041	357
Florida	383	68,165	427	39,452	247	24,264	152
Georgia	561	31,282	382	21,173	259	12,393	151
Hawaii	7	3,731	308	2,914	241	1,722	142
Idaho	122	4,522	349	2,749	212	1,732	134
Illinois	886	52,769	425	39,847	321	23,728	191
Indiana	495	17,969	296	11,900	196	7,249	119
Iowa	400	7,600	260	5,333	182	3,769	129
Kansas	353	10,343	385	6,563	244	4,265	159
Kentucky	382	9,589	237	7,144	177	4,800	119
Louisiana	343	23,573	527	18,548	415	7,639	171
Maine	139	3,638	285	2,367	186	1,721	135
Maryland	146	20,272	383	15,221	287	9,024	170
Massachusetts	351	23,593	372	18,082	285	11,784	186
Michigan	565	29,654	298	21,673	218	13,456	135
Minnesota	460	12,677	258	8,606	175	5,748	117
Mississippi	333	10,163	357	6,562	231	4,416	155
Missouri	586	20,459	366	13,630	244	8,749	156
Montana	126	2,958	328	1,760	195	1,344	149
Nebraska	237	4,776	279	3,486	204	2,296	134
Nevada	62	7,918	396	5,252	263	2,959	148
New Hampshire	195	3,268	264	2,542	206	1,736	140
New Jersey	551	37,387	444	29,062	345	16,343	194
New Mexico	135	6,324	348	4,456	245	2,792	153
New York	517	94,863	500	72,853	384	45,462	240
North Carolina	491	26,101	324	18,903	235	11,070	138
North Dakota	129	1,755	273	1,293	201	944	147
Ohio	845	36,863	325	25,082	221	15,689	138
Oklahoma	449	11,376	330	7,622	221	5,129	149
Oregon	178	10,683	312	6,496	190	3,573	104
Pennsylvania	1,166	33,427	272	26,373	215	17,648	144
Rhode Island	51	3,390	323	2,688	256	1,636	156
South Carolina	258	13,046	325	9,741	243	5,973	149
South Dakota	170	2,468	327	1,708	226	1,201	159
Tennessee	367	22,148	389	14,494	255	9,296	163
Texas	1,800	80,535	386	51,478	247	28,831	138
Utah	129	6,346	284	4,179	187	2,545	114
Vermont	65	1,459	240	1,034	170	796	131
Virginia	327	25,842	365	20,254	286	9,900	140
Washington	256	15,513	263	9,910	168	6,367	108
West Virginia	229	4,148	229	3,150	174	2,387	132
Wisconsin	512	18,010	336	13,237	247	8,290	155
Wyoming	81	2,287	463	1,477	299	989	200

LOCAL POLICE DEPARTMENTS

As of June 2000, there were 12,666 general purpose local police departments operating in the United States. Municipal governments operated the vast majority of these agencies. The remainder were county, tribal, or regional (multi-jurisdictional) police.

	Number	
Types of general purpose local police, 2000	Agencies	Full-time officers
Municipal	12,409	412,921
County	52	25,202
Tribal	171	2,303
Regional	34	494

Note: Tribal category excludes agencies operated by the Bureau of Indian Affairs, a Federal agency that provides law enforcement service in some tribal areas.

As of June 2000, full-time employment by local police departments was up about 44,000, or 8.4%, compared to June 1996 (figure 3). The number of full-time sworn personnel increased about 30,000, or 7.3%. The number of civilian employees in local police departments rose about 14,000, or 12.6%.

Compared to 1992, the number of full-time local police employees in 2000 was up by about 87,000, or 18.2%. This included about 66,000, or 17.7% more sworn personnel and about 21,000, or 20.1%, more civilian personnel.

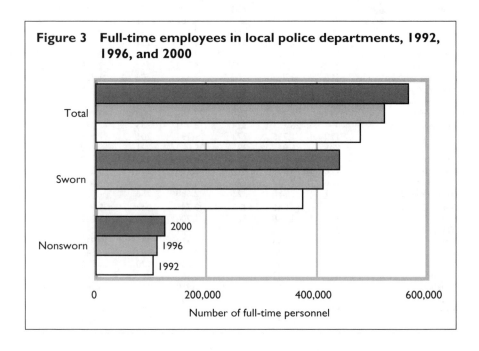

Figure 3   Full-time employees in local police departments, 1992, 1996, and 2000

Number of full-time personnel

Size of Local Police Departments

A total of 567, or 4.5%, of local police departments employed 100 or more full-time sworn personnel (table 5). Included in these larger agencies were 47 with 1,000 or more officers. In contrast, 56.2% of departments employed fewer than 10 full-time officers. Included among these smaller agencies were 1,366 (10.8%) that employed only 1 full-time officer, and 199 (1.6%) that relied solely on part-time officers.

Table 5   Local police departments, by size of agency, June 2000

| | Agencies | |
Number of full-time sworn personnel	Number	Percent
All sizes	12,666	100%
1,000 or more	47	0.4%
500–999	37	0.3
250–499	100	0.8
100–249	383	3.0
50–99	756	6.0
25–49	1,479	11.7
10–24	2,740	21.6
5–9	2,665	21.0
2–4	2,894	22.8
1	1,366	10.8
0	199	1.6

Agencies with fewer than 10 full-time officers employed about 6% of all full-time local police officers (table 6). About three-fifths (61%) of all full-time local police officers worked in an agency with 100 or more officers, and nearly half (48%) worked for an agency with at least 250 officers.

The 47 departments with 1,000 or more officers employed 34.2% of all full-time local police officers. These agencies employed just 0.3% of all part-time sworn personnel, but 27% of part-time civilian personnel.

Functions of Local Police Officers

Nearly all local police officers were working in the area of law enforcement operations. About 65% of full-time officers primarily performed patrol duties, while 16% primarily handled criminal investigations (figure 4, p. 51). Other primary duty areas included administration, training, and technical support. About 2% had regularly assigned court-related (1.4%) or jail-related (0.8%) duties.

Table 6   Local police employees, by size of agency, June 2000

	Type of employee					
	Full-time			Part-time		
	Total	Sworn	Nonsworn	Total	Sworn	Nonsworn
Number of employees						
All sizes	565,915	440,920	124,995	62,110	27,323	34,787
1,000 or more	195,050	150,958	44,092	9,587	79	9,508
500–999	34,394	25,733	8,661	1,449	41	1,408
250–499	46,432	35,152	11,280	1,954	99	1,855
100–249	73,357	56,021	17,336	4,852	610	4,242
50–99	67,143	51,927	15,216	5,990	1,479	4,511
25–49	64,845	51,103	13,742	6,834	2,415	4,419
10–24	53,083	42,551	10,532	10,492	5,654	4,838
5–9	20,932	17,657	3,275	8,959	6,579	2,380
2–4	9,201	8,452	749	8,399	7,116	1,283
1	1,471	1,366	105	2,460	2,189	271
0	7	0	7	1,134	1,062	72
Percent of employees						
All sizes	100%	100%	100%	100%	100%	100%
1,000 or more	34.5%	34.2%	35.3%	15.4%	0.3%	27.3%
500–999	6.1	5.8	6.9	2.3	0.2	4.0
250–499	8.2	8.0	9.0	3.1	0.4	5.3
100–249	13.0	12.7	13.9	7.8	2.2	12.2
50–99	11.9	11.8	12.2	9.6	5.4	13.0
25–49	11.5	11.6	11.0	11.0	8.8	12.7
10–24	9.4	9.7	8.4	16.9	20.7	13.9
5–9	3.7	4.0	2.6	14.4	24.1	6.8
2–4	1.6	1.9	0.6	13.5	26.0	3.7
1	0.3	0.3	0.1	4.0	8.0	0.8
0	—	0.0	—	1.8	3.9	0.2

— Less than 0.05%

The Largest Local Police Departments

As of June 2000 the New York City Police Department (NYPD) was the nation's largest local police department—and its largest law enforcement agency of any kind—with 53,029 full-time employees, including 40,435 sworn officers (table 7, p. 52). Twenty-three NYPD officers were killed in the line of duty as a result of the terrorist attacks of September 11, 2001.

Other cities with police forces of more than 5,000 full-time officers included Chicago (13,466), Los Angeles (9,341), Philadelphia (7,024), and Houston (5,343). In 2000 about 1 in 11 full-time local police officers nationwide worked for the NYPD, and about 1 in 6 worked for one of the five largest forces.

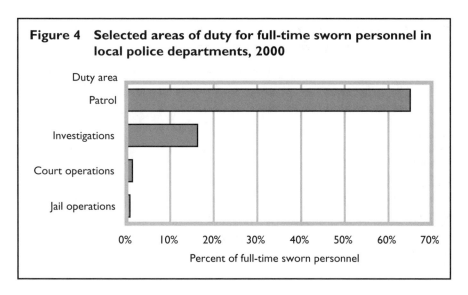

Figure 4   Selected areas of duty for full-time sworn personnel in local police departments, 2000

The largest county police departments in the U.S. included the Nassau County (NY) Police with 3,038 full-time officers, the Miami-Dade (FL) Police (3,008), and the Suffolk County (NY) Police (2,564).

From June 1996 to 2000, the NYPD reported the largest change in number of officers of any state or local police department. During this period, the nation's largest police force expanded by 3,622 officers.

By percent change, the local police departments with the largest increases were those serving in Memphis (34.1%), Las Vegas (27.8%), New Orleans (24.0%), Austin (20.9%), and Newark (20.0%). Decreases in force size occurred in Pittsburgh (10.2%), Honolulu (9.5%), St. Louis (8.7%), Suffolk County (6.6%), and Milwaukee (5.1%).

(See the BJS Special Report, *Police Departments in Large Cities, 1990–2000*, NCJ 175703 for more information on the Nation's largest municipal police agencies.)

State-by-State Comparisons

As of June 2000 Pennsylvania had the most full-time general purpose local police departments (1,015). Next were Texas (737), Illinois (729), and Ohio (712). Other states with more than 400 local police departments included New Jersey (484), Michigan (450), Missouri (449), and Wisconsin (417). Excluding the District of Columbia, Hawaii (4) had the least local police departments, followed by Nevada (28) and Delaware (33).

Local police departments in the State of New York had 74,737 full-time employees, more than in any other state. California was second with 52,541. Other states with more than 25,000 full-time local police employees were Texas (40,321), Illinois (34,382), Florida (29,922), and New Jersey (25,114).

Table 7   Fifty largest local police departments, by number of full-time sworn personnel, June 2000

City or county	Full-time sworn, 2000	Percent change, 1996–2000
New York (NY)	40,435	9.8%
Chicago (IL)	13,466	1.7
Los Angeles (CA)	9,341	3.8
Philadelphia (PA)	7,024	9.8
Houston (TX)	5,343	0.8
Detroit (MI)	4,154	6.4%
Washington (DC)	3,612	0.7
Nassau Co. (NY)	3,038	1.0
Baltimore (MD)	3,034	3.4
Miami-Dade Co. (FL)	3,008	6.5
Dallas (TX)	2,862	–0.1%
Phoenix (AZ)	2,626	7.9
Suffolk Co. (NY)	2,564	–6.6
San Francisco (CA)	2,227	11.4
Las Vegas-Clark Co. (NV)	2,168	27.8
Boston (MA)	2,164	3.0%
San Diego (CA)	2,022	1.8
Milwaukee (WI)	1,998	–5.1
Memphis (TN)	1,904	34.1
San Antonio (TX)	1,882	0.5
Cleveland (OH)	1,822	5.4%
Honolulu Co. (HI)	1792.0	–9.5
Baltimore Co. (MD)	1,754	14.3
Columbus (OH)	1,744	0.8
New Orleans (LA)	1664.0	24.0
Jacksonville-Duval Co. (FL)	1,530	9.8%
Denver (CO)	1,489	4.3
St. Louis (MO)	1,489	–8.7
Atlanta (GA)	1,474	0.0
Newark (NJ)	1,466	20.0
Charlotte-Mecklenberg Co. (NC)	1,442	12.1%
Prince Georges Co. (MD)	1,431	16.3
San Jose (CA)	1,408	9.9
Seattle (WA)	1,261	1.9
Kansas City (MO)	1,253	6.8
Nashville-Davidson Co. (TN)	1,249	10.6%
Fort Worth (TX)	1,196	2.0
Fairfax Co. (VA)	1,163	9.0
Austin (TX)	1,144	20.9
Miami (FL)	1,110	9.7
El Paso (TX)	1,057	8.0%
Indianapolis (IN)	1,045	5.4
Pittsburgh (PA)	1,036	–10.2
Cincinnati (OH)	1,030	7.5
Montgomery Co. (MD)	1,019	8.5
Oklahoma City (OK)	1,011	0.2%
Portland (OR)	1,007	2.4
Tampa (FL)	939	5.6
Buffalo (NY)	928	3.3
Tucson (AZ)	928	11.4

Four states had fewer than 1,000 full-time local police employees: Vermont (735), North Dakota (844), Wyoming (907), and Montana (983).

After the District of Columbia (781), New York ranked highest among the states in terms of local police employees per 100,000 residents, with 394. Other states with 250 or more local police employees per 100,000 residents included New Jersey (298), Illinois (277), Hawaii (276), Massachusetts (263), and Rhode Island (262).

New York (58,588) was the only state with more than 50,000 full-time local police officers. California ranked second with 37,674 officers. The other states with more than 15,000 full-time local police officers were Texas (30,525), Illinois (27,452), New Jersey (21,046), Florida (21,035), Pennsylvania (18,913), and Ohio (16,956).

In terms of full-time police officers per 100,000 residents, New York (309) was second only to the District of Columbia (631). Other states with 200 or more local police officers per 100,000 residents included New Jersey (250), Illinois (221), Massachusetts (218), Hawaii (215), and Rhode Island (205).

SHERIFFS' OFFICES

In June 2000 sheriffs' offices had about 36,000 more full-time employees than in 1996, an increase of 14.0% (figure 5). This included an increase of about 12,000, or 7.7%, in sworn personnel, and an increase of about 24,000, or 23.2%, in nonsworn employees.

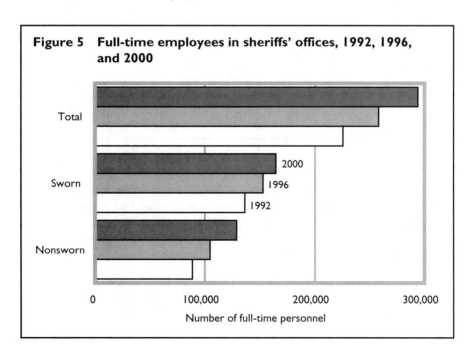

Figure 5   Full-time employees in sheriffs' offices, 1992, 1996, and 2000

Compared to 1992, sheriffs' offices in 2000 had 68,000, or 30.4%, more full-time employees. Civilian employment rose by about 40,000, or 45.4%, during this time, while the number of sworn personnel increased by approximately 28,000, or 23.2%.

These increases, which are larger than those for local police, were influenced to some extent by the fact that about 4 in 5 sheriffs' departments are responsible for jail operations. The Nation's jail inmate population in June 2000 was 20% larger than in June 1996, and 40% larger than in June 1992. (See the BJS Bulletin, *Prison and Jail Inmates at Midyear 2000*, NCJ 185989).

Size of Sheriffs' Offices

As of June 2000, of the 3,070 full-time sheriffs' offices operating nationwide, 323, or 10.5%, employed at least 100 full-time sworn personnel (table 8). This included 12 agencies with 1,000 or more full-time sworn personnel. About a third (32.5%) of sheriffs' offices employed fewer than 10 full-time sworn personnel, and 25 agencies (0.8%) had just 1 full-time officer.

Table 8   Sheriffs' offices, by size of agency, June 2000

Number of full-time sworn personnel	Agencies	
	Number	Percent
All sizes	3,070	100%
1,000 or more	12	0.4%
500–999	27	0.9
250–499	78	2.5
100–249	206	6.7
50–99	311	10.1
25–49	515	16.8
10–24	923	30.1
5–9	658	21.4
2–4	315	10.3
1	25	0.8

The 12 sheriffs' offices employing 1,000 or more sworn personnel accounted for about a sixth of full-time sheriffs' employees (table 9). Sixty-two percent of full-time sheriffs' office personnel worked for an agency with 100 or more employees, including 64% of sworn personnel.

Functions of Sheriffs' Deputies

Nearly all sheriffs' offices are responsible for responding to citizen calls for service. As of June 2000, 41% of sheriffs' deputies were regularly assigned to patrol duty (figure 6, p. 56). Another 12% were assigned to investigative duties.

Table 9   Sheriffs' employees, by size of agency, June 2000

Full-time sworn personnel	Type of employee					
	Full-time			Part-time		
	Total	Sworn	Nonsworn	Total	Sworn	Nonsworn
Number of employees						
All sizes	293,823	164,711	129,112	22,737	10,300	12,437
1,000 or more	49,810	28,817	20,993	1,625	34	1,591
500–999	31,037	18,152	12,885	1,417	455	962
250–499	45,671	27,274	18,397	2,111	791	1,320
100–249	56,430	31,170	25,260	2,883	1,371	1,512
50–99	40,422	21,586	18,836	2,811	1,457	1,354
25–49	32,554	17,758	14,796	3,987	2,243	1,744
10–24	27,435	14,391	13,044	4,932	2,556	2,376
5–9	8,563	4,518	4,045	2,269	1,036	1,233
2–4	1,873	1,020	853	664	326	338
1	28	25	3	38	31	7
Percent of employees						
All sizes	100%	100%	100%	100%	100%	100%
1,000 or more	17.0%	17.5%	16.3%	7.1%	0.3%	12.8%
500–999	10.6	11.0	10.0	6.2	4.4	7.7
250–499	15.5	16.6	14.2	9.3	7.7	10.6
100–249	19.2	18.9	19.6	12.7	13.3	12.2
50–99	13.8	13.1	14.6	12.4	14.1	10.9
25–49	11.1	10.8	11.5	17.5	21.8	14.0
10–24	9.3	8.7	10.1	21.7	24.8	19.1
5–9	2.9	2.7	3.1	10.0	10.1	9.9
2–4	0.6	0.6	0.7	2.9	3.2	2.7
1	—	—	—	0.2	0.3	0.1

— Less than 0.05%

In addition to handling calls for service, about four-fifths of sheriffs' offices operate 1 or more jails, and nearly all have court-related responsibilities such as the serving of process and court security. In 2000, 24% of full-time sheriffs' deputies were assigned to jail-related duties, while 17% primarily performed court-related duties. In this latter category, about three-fifths of officers were assigned to court security, and two-fifths to serving process.

The Largest Sheriffs' Offices

As of June 2000 the largest sheriff's office in the nation, the Los Angeles County Sheriff's Department, employed 8,438 full-time sworn personnel (table 10, p. 57). Twenty-seven percent of that agency's full-time sworn personnel were assigned to patrol, and 8% to criminal investigations. Nearly half were assigned to jail operations (27%) or court security (18%).

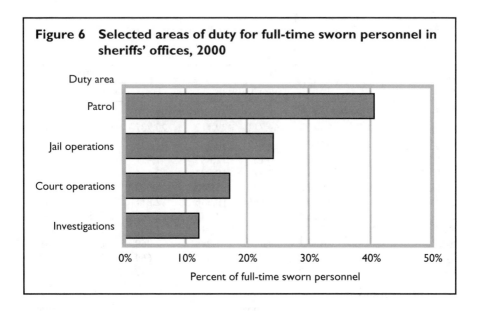

Figure 6   Selected areas of duty for full-time sworn personnel in sheriffs' offices, 2000

The second largest sheriff's office, with 5,309 full-time sworn personnel, was the Cook County (IL) Sheriff's Office. Most of the officers in that agency were assigned to duties related to jail or court operations.

Overall, 9 of the 25 largest sheriffs' offices, including 6 of the 10 largest, were in California. All but one of these agencies had deputies with regular patrol assignments. In addition, all had sworn personnel who primarily performed jail-related duties, and all but one had sworn personnel assigned to court-related duties.

Another 5 of the 25 largest sheriffs' offices were in Florida. All of these agencies had at least 48% of their deputies assigned to patrol operations; however, only the Palm Beach County Sheriff's Office also operated a jail.

Of the three major categories of law enforcement, jail operations, and court operations, 13 of the 25 largest sheriffs' departments had the largest number of sworn personnel assigned to law enforcement, and 12 had the largest number assigned to jail duties.

State-by-State Comparisons

As of June 2000, 3,070 sheriffs' offices were operating full time. Texas (254) had the most. Except for a few who are appointed, sheriffs are elected officials.

California (45,706), Florida (33,303), and Texas (23,621) had the most full-time sheriffs' employees. Other states with 10,000 or more full-time sheriffs' employees included Illinois (13,501), Georgia (12,990), Louisiana (12,745), North Carolina (10,457), New York (10,208), and Ohio (10,199).

Louisiana had the most sheriffs' employees per capita with 285 per 100,000 residents. Other states with more than 150 per 100,000 included

Florida (208), Wyoming (196), Idaho (171), Montana (162), and Georgia (159). Nationwide, there were 104 full-time sheriffs' office employees per 100,000 residents.

States with the most full-time sworn personnel employed by sheriffs' offices were California (25,361), Florida (14,770), Texas (11,133), and Louisiana (10,329). Other states with 5,000 or more full-time sworn personnel included Illinois (9,073), Georgia (7,703), Virginia (7,382), North Carolina (6,140), New York (6,018), and Ohio (5,366).

Sheriffs' offices employed 59 full-time sworn personnel per 100,000 residents nationwide. States that had the highest ratio per 100,000 residents: Louisiana (231), Wyoming (117), and Virginia (104).

Table 10 Twenty-five largest sheriffs' offices, by number and function of full-time sworn personnel, June 2000

County or equivalent	Full-time sworn personnel	Percent of officers by primary duty area				
		Patrol	Investi-gations	Jail operations	Court security	Process serving
Los Angeles Co. (CA)	8,438	27%	8%	27%	18%	0%
Cook Co. (IL)[a]	5,768	9	3	58	26	4
Harris Co. (TX)	2,584	26	12	60	0	1
Orange Co. (CA)	1,770	40	8	42	0	0
San Diego (CA)	1,553	49	13	7	16	3
San Bernardino Co. (CA)	1,421	33%	15%	29%	10%	1%
Sacramento Co. (CA)	1,372	42	11	32	9	1
Broward Co. (FL)	1,310	73	27	0	0	0
Riverside Co. (CA)	1,286	58	16	16	8	2
Orange Co. (FL)	1,211	48	10	0	8	5
Palm Beach Co. (FL)	1,074	64%	23%	0%	9%	5%
Hillsborough Co. (FL)	1,030	65	18	0	0	2
Alameda Co. (CA)	909	15	2	48	16	1
Nassau Co. (NY)	899	0	0	95	0	3
Pinellas Co. (FL)	860	52	25	0	20	3
Wayne Co. (MI)	821	14%	5%	58%	14%	1%
Oakland Co. (MI)	800	41	8	48	3	1
Ventura Co. (CA)	796	33	16	25	11	1
San Francisco Co. (CA)	777	0	2	64	9	1
Monroe Co. (NY)	777	31	3	52	13	1
Fulton Co. (GA)	774	0%	1%	74%	25%	0%
Calcasieu Par. (LA)	730	19	7	33	3	4
E. Baton Rouge Par. (LA)	712	18	10	41	4	3
Orleans Par. (LA)	685	6	2	82	6	4
Jefferson Par. (LA)	681	41	29	0	0	0

[a] Data for Cook County are estimates based on prior years' responses.

As of June 2000, sheriffs' offices nationwide had nearly 66,000 full-time officers assigned to respond to calls for service. States with the most were California (9,033), Florida (8,294), and Texas (4,095). Sheriffs' offices employed 23 such personnel per 100,000 residents nationwide. The highest ratios were in Wyoming (61), Florida (52), Louisiana (52), and Montana (51).

PRIMARY STATE LAW ENFORCEMENT AGENCIES

In June 2000, the 49 primary state law enforcement agencies had 87,028 full-time employees. This was about 3,300, or 3.9%, more than in 1996 (figure 7). There were 56,348 full-time sworn personnel in 2000. This was about 1,800, or 3.2%, more than in 1996. Civilian employment rose by approximately 1,500, or 5.2%, during this period.

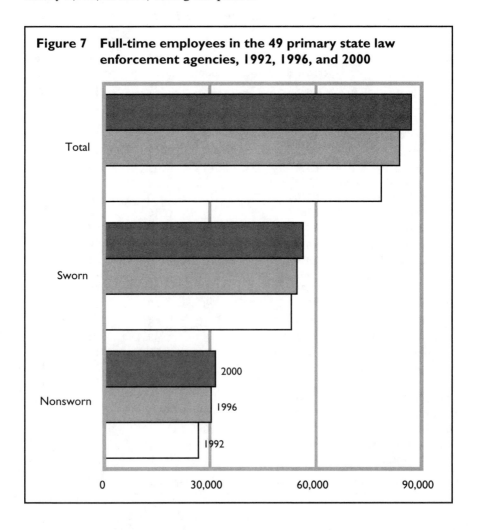

Figure 7   Full-time employees in the 49 primary state law enforcement agencies, 1992, 1996, and 2000

Compared to 1992, overall employment in 2000 was up by about 8,500, or 10.8%. This included increases of about 5,100, or 19.9%, in nonsworn employees, and of about 3,400, or 6.4%, in sworn personnel.

In 2000, 69% of the full-time sworn personnel in state law enforcement agencies were patrol officers and 11% were investigators. Less than 1% were assigned to court-related duties.

Seventeen agencies employed 1,000 or more full-time sworn officers, and 34 employed at least 500 such officers. The largest, the California Highway Patrol, had 9,706 full-time employees including 6,678 full-time sworn personnel. The next largest were the Texas Department of Public Safety (7,025 and 3,119) and the Pennsylvania State Police (5,694 and 4,152).

The smallest agencies in terms of sworn personnel were the North Dakota Highway Patrol (126), the Wyoming Highway Patrol (148), and the South Dakota Highway Patrol (153).

SPECIAL JURISDICTION AGENCIES

In June 2000, nearly 1,400 state and local law enforcement agencies with special geographic jurisdictions or special enforcement responsibilities were operating in the United States. These agencies had 43,413 full-time sworn personnel.

About two-thirds (68%) of full-time sworn personnel primarily handled patrol duties, while 17% were criminal investigators. Approximately 1% were responsible for court-related duties.

The 11,319 full-time police officers serving public 4-year and 2-year colleges and universities accounted for more than a fourth of all sworn personnel serving special jurisdictions. Another 3,219 were police officers for public school districts. Agencies serving state capitols and other government buildings employed about 1,100 sworn personnel.

Agencies enforcing laws related to fish and wildlife conservation employed 7,935 full-time officers, and those responsible for parks and recreation areas about 3,200.

Agencies responsible for mass transit systems employed 2,627 sworn personnel officers, and those serving airports, nearly 2,500. Agencies serving multiple types of transportation facilities employed about 1,700 officers, with the Port Authority of New York-New Jersey Police (1,238), the largest of these forces.

The Port Authority Police are responsible for policing the facilities owned and operated by the Port Authority, including the LaGuardia, Kennedy, and Newark Airports, the Lincoln and Holland Tunnels, the George Washington and Staten Island Bridges, the PATH train system, the Port Authority Bus Terminal, and the Port Newark and Port Elizabeth Marine Terminals.

At the time of the 2000 census, the World Trade Center was also under Port Authority Police jurisdiction. Thirty-seven Port Authority Police officers were killed in the line of duty as a result of the World Trade Center attacks of September 11, 2001.

Other categories of special jurisdiction agencies that accounted for 500 or more full-time sworn personnel included county and city investigative agencies (1,838), state alcohol enforcement agencies (1,287), medical facility police (978), port facility police (940), state investigation bureaus (692), and public housing police (673).

State-by State Comparisons

Texas (185) and California (117) had the most state and local agencies serving special jurisdictions. Other states with 50 or more agencies included Pennsylvania (85), New York (66), and Illinois (54).

About 40% of the nearly 70,000 full-time state and local law enforcement employees serving special jurisdictions were in California (7,953), Texas (6,488), New York (4,970), Pennsylvania (4,469), or New Jersey (4,385). Other states with 2,500 or more employees included Maryland (3,250), Ohio (3,026), Florida (2,802), and Georgia (2,589).

New York (4,135), Texas (4,071), and California (3,949) had the most full-time sworn personnel serving special jurisdictions. Eight other states had 1,000 or more: Maryland (2,255), New Jersey (2,247), Florida (1,989), Pennsylvania (1,880), Georgia (1,692), Virginia (1,385), Ohio (1,378), and Illinois (1,233). States with fewer than 100 included Vermont (55), New Hampshire (76), Nebraska (83), Oregon (92), and Wyoming (99).

The District of Columbia (61) had the most sworn personnel serving special jurisdictions per 100,000 residents. Maryland (43), South Dakota (36), and Alaska (35) had the next highest ratios.

LEMAS, 2000—HIGHLIGHTS

The 2000 LEMAS survey is expected to be instrumental in assessing the state of law enforcement as it exists today in the United States. Furthermore, the results of the survey will provide law enforcement agencies an opportunity to assess their progress relative to that of comparable jurisdictions.

Based on the 2000 Law Enforcement Management and Administrative Statistics survey, more than 800 state and local law enforcement agencies with 100 or more full-time sworn personnel are described in the LEMAS report. Included among these larger law enforcement agencies are 501 municipal police departments, 222 sheriffs' offices, 32 county police departments, and the 49 primary state law enforcement agencies. Collectively, these agencies employed approximately 402,000 full-time sworn personnel, including 241,000 uniformed officers assigned to respond to calls for service. Topics covered include personnel, expenditures and pay, operations, community policing, policies and programs, equipment, and computerization. We present the highlights of this coverage.

PERSONNEL

On average, larger municipal police departments employed 22 full-time sworn personnel per 10,000 residents. County police departments and sheriffs' offices employed an average of 11 and 10 officers per 10,000 residents, respectively. State law enforcement agencies employed an average of 2 officers per 10,000 residents.

From 1996 to 2000 the median percentage increase in number of full-time sworn personnel was higher in county police departments (11%) and sheriffs' offices (10%) than in municipal police (5%) or state agencies (5%). Sheriffs' offices had an 18% median increase in civilian personnel, compared to 7% for municipal and county police, and 10% for state law enforcement agencies.

Seventy-two percent of the sworn personnel in state law enforcement agencies were uniformed officers assigned to respond to calls for service, compared to 61% in county and municipal police departments, and 47% in sheriffs' offices. The latter had more officers handling duties related to jail operations (19%), court security (8%), and process serving (4%) duties.

Fourteen percent of the officers in larger municipal police departments and sheriffs' offices were women, as were 12% of county police officers. Women accounted for 6% of the officers in state agencies. From 1990 to 2000, the average percentage of female officers increased for each type of agency except sheriffs' offices.

In 2000, 32% of the officers in larger municipal police departments were members of a racial or ethnic minority, compared to 23% in county police departments, 22% in sheriffs' offices, and 16% in state agencies. For each agency type, the average minority percentage was higher in 2000 than 1990.

Nearly all larger law enforcement agencies used background investigations, criminal record checks, driving record checks, medical exams, and personal interviews to screen officer recruits. State agencies (94%) and county police departments (90%) were more likely to use credit history checks than municipal police (79%) or sheriffs' offices (73%). County police (97%) were the most likely to use drug tests and state agencies (76%) the least likely. State agencies were the most likely to use written aptitude (92%) and physical agility (90%) tests and sheriffs' offices (65% and 59%) the least likely.

About 1 in 3 state agencies had a college requirement for new officers, with 12% requiring a 2-year degree and 2%, a 4-year degree. About 1 in 4 municipal and county police departments had a college requirement, with about 1 in 10 requiring a degree. In 6% of county police departments and 2% of municipal police departments, a 4-year degree was required. About 1 in 7 sheriffs' offices had a college requirement, including 6% that required a 2-year degree. Overall, larger law enforcement agencies were about twice as likely to have a college requirement in 2000 as in 1990.

The median number of academy training hours required for new officers was higher in state law enforcement agencies (960) and county police depart-

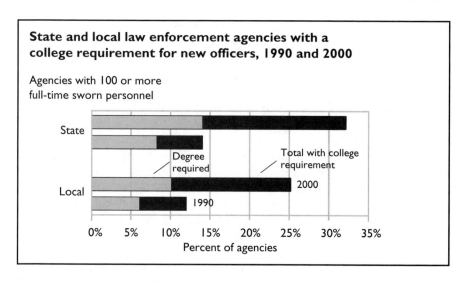

State and local law enforcement agencies with a college requirement for new officers, 1990 and 2000

Agencies with 100 or more full-time sworn personnel

ments (896), than in municipal police departments (720) or sheriffs' offices (640). The median number of field training hours required was slightly higher in municipal police departments (520) than for other agency types (480).

BUDGET AND PAY

Sheriff's offices and state agencies had annual operating budgets of about $108,000 per officer, compared to $90,237 for county police and $83,638 for municipal police. From 1990 to 2000, inflation-adjusted operating costs per officer rose 38% for state agencies, 30% for sheriffs' offices, 27% for county police, and 21% for municipal police.

In 2000 median annual per resident operating costs were $173 for municipal police, $112 for county police, $85 for sheriffs' offices, and $25 for state agencies. Compared to 1990, inflation-adjusted operating costs per resident were up 25% for municipal police, 120% for county police, 30% for sheriffs' offices, and 25% for state agencies.

In 2000 average starting salaries for entry-level officers ranged from $33,233 in municipal police departments to $29,280 in sheriffs' offices. Compared to 1990, inflation-adjusted starting salaries were up 5% in state agencies, municipal police departments, and sheriffs' offices, but unchanged in county police departments.

In 2000 nearly three-fourths of municipal police departments (72%) authorized collective bargaining for officers compared to about half of county police departments (52%) and state agencies (51%). Sheriffs' offices (42%) were less likely to allow collective bargaining for officers.

About two-thirds of municipal police departments (68%) and about half of sheriffs' offices (51%) offered education incentive pay to officers. State agencies (27%) and county police departments (20%) were less likely to offer it. A majority of each type of agency had a tuition reimbursement program for officers: municipal police (73%), county police (70%), state agencies (65%), and sheriffs' offices (59%).

Operations

In 2000, 35% of larger sheriffs' offices were using foot patrol on a routine basis compared to 5% in 1993, and 57% were using bicycle patrols, up from 9% in 1993. Similar increases were observed for county police (31% to 58% for foot patrol, 38% to 84% for bicycle patrol), and municipal police (47% to 74% for foot patrol, 40% to 92% for bicycle patrol). Among state law enforcement agencies, 29% were using bike patrol and 18% were using foot patrol in 2000, compared to 0% for both in 1993.

In 2000 nearly all larger local law enforcement agencies (93%) participated in an enhanced 9-1-1 emergency telephone system where the location of callers could be identified automatically. In 1990, 57% of these agencies were part of such a system. Among state agencies, about half participated in an enhanced 9-1-1 system in 2000 compared to about a third in 1990.

Ninety-one percent of sheriffs' offices performed search and rescue operations during 2000, as did 77% of county police departments and 71% of state agencies. Municipal police (43%) were less likely to handle this function.

County police (97%) were the most likely to perform special weapons and tactics (SWAT) operations; however most municipal police departments (89%), sheriffs' offices (88%), and state agencies (84%) did so as well.

State law enforcement agencies (91%) and county police departments (82%) were more likely to operate a training academy than sheriffs' offices (52%) or municipal police departments (41%).

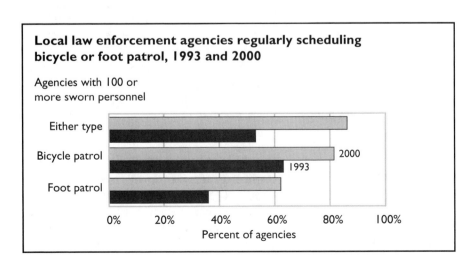

Local law enforcement agencies regularly scheduling bicycle or foot patrol, 1993 and 2000

Agencies with 100 or more sworn personnel

Either type

Bicycle patrol — 2000 / 1993

Foot patrol

0%   20%   40%   60%   80%   100%

Percent of agencies

A majority of county police (89%), municipal police (79%), and sheriffs' offices (69%) had a full-time drug enforcement unit. Thirty-seven percent of state agencies had one. About 4 in 5 local agencies had officers assigned full-time to a multi-agency drug task force, compared to about 1 in 5 state agencies.

Nearly all larger sheriffs' offices handled court-related functions such as court security (98%) and process serving (98%). Less than a third of other agency types performed these functions.

Ninety-one percent of sheriffs' offices operated a jail, compared to 34% of municipal police departments and 13% of county police departments. No state agencies were responsible for this function.

COMMUNITY POLICING

In 2000 a majority of larger county (69%) and municipal (59%) police departments had a written community policing plan. Less than half of sheriffs' offices (43%) and state agencies (35%) had one. For each agency type, the percentage with a written plan was about the same as in 1997.

About two-thirds of larger municipal (68%) and county (66%) police departments had a full-time community policing unit. A majority of sheriffs' offices (57%) also had such a unit, but just a fourth of state agencies did. These percentages were also similar to 1997.

In 2000 nearly all municipal (95%) and county (94%) police departments had sworn personnel designated as full-time community policing officers compared to about 4 in 5 agencies in 1997. Eighty-eight percent of sheriffs' offices had community policing officers in 2000 compared to 66% in 1997. About twice as many state agencies had full-time community policing officers in 2000 (53%) as in 1997 (27%).

More than three-fourths of municipal (79%) and county (76%) police departments trained all new officer recruits in community policing methods during 2000, about the same proportion as in 1997. From 1997 to 2000, the percentage of sheriffs' offices providing such training increased from 49% to 61%, and state law enforcement agencies, from 41% to 47%.

From 1997 to 2000 the percentage of larger local law enforcement agencies that encouraged patrol officers to engage in problem-solving projects increased slightly, from 55% to 58%. Among state agencies the increase was from 22% to 31%. In both survey years, about 1 in 3 local agencies and 1 in 5 state agencies included problem-solving projects in the criteria used for evaluating the performance of patrol officers.

In the 12-month period ending June 30, 2000, 72% of municipal police departments conducted a citizen police academy, as did 52% of county police departments, 47% of sheriffs' offices, and 18% of state agencies.

Nearly 2 in 3 local agencies upgraded technology to support their community policing efforts during this period, including 71% of municipal police departments. About 2 in 5 state agencies upgraded technology for this purpose.

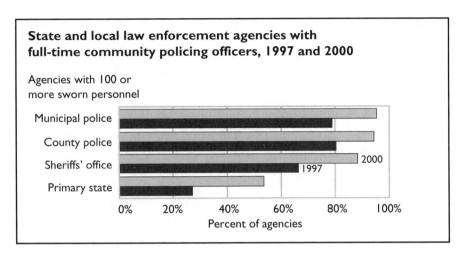

State and local law enforcement agencies with full-time community policing officers, 1997 and 2000

Agencies with 100 or more sworn personnel

During the year ending June 30, 2000, most larger local law enforcement agencies met regularly with neighborhood associations (89%), school groups (79%), business groups (69%), domestic violence groups (64%), other local public agencies (62%), senior citizen groups (59%), advocacy groups (54%), and youth service organizations (54%). A majority of state agencies met regularly with school groups (65%) and local public agencies (57%).

About half of larger local agencies surveyed citizens on their satisfaction with services, and two-fifths conducted a survey of citizen perceptions of crime-related problems. About a fourth conducted surveys of personal crime experiences or crime reporting. About a third of state agencies surveyed citizens about their satisfaction with agency services. Less than a fifth conducted surveys on the other topics.

Evaluating program effectiveness was the most common use of survey data for both local (44%) and state (31%) agencies. Thirty-seven percent of local agencies used survey data as a source of information for patrol officers.

POLICIES AND PROGRAMS

Larger local law enforcement agencies operated a variety of full-time special units to address youth and family problems. For example about 3 in 4 county police departments (79%), sheriffs' offices (76%), and municipal police departments (71%) had a special unit for drug education in schools.

A majority of county police departments had full-time units for child abuse (62%), juvenile crime (62%), and gangs (55%). About half had units for youth outreach (50%), domestic violence (48%), and missing children (48%).

Nearly half of municipal police departments had full-time units for domestic violence (48%), gangs (48%), and child abuse (46%). More than two-fifths of sheriffs' offices had units for child abuse (48%), juvenile crime

(46%), domestic violence (42%), and gangs (41%). Among state agencies, the most common types of units were those for drug education in schools (39%) and missing children (31%).

A majority of larger local agencies also had units for internal affairs (79%), community crime prevention (70%), crime analysis (61%), and research and planning (54%). Most state agencies had internal affairs (84%), and research and planning (76%) units. About half had crime analysis units (47%).

Nearly all larger law enforcement agencies had written policies pertaining to deadly force, conduct and appearance, nonlethal force, and off-duty employment. About 7 in 10 had a policy on the maximum number of work hours allowed for officers.

Local agencies were about 4 times as likely to have a restrictive type (73%) of pursuit driving policy (one based on specific criteria such as offense type or maximum speed) as a judgmental type (19%) (one that leaves pursuits up to the officer's discretion). State agencies were nearly as likely to have a judgmental pursuit policy (45%) as a restrictive one (51%).

EQUIPMENT

As of June 2000, state law enforcement agencies operated 103 cars per 100 officers, compared to 98 cars per 100 officers in 1990. Local agencies also increased their car-to-officer ratio during this period: County police went from 71 to 79 cars per 100 officers, municipal police from 47 to 59, and sheriffs' offices from 55 to 68.

In 2000, 98% of larger local law enforcement agencies and all 49 primary state law enforcement agencies authorized semiautomatic sidearms for officers. In 1990, 85% of local agencies and 80% of state agencies authorized semiautomatics.

From 1990 to 2000 the percentage of larger local law enforcement agencies requiring all regular field/patrol officers to wear body armor increased from 21% to 50%. The percentage of state law enforcement agencies requiring that armor be worn increased from 12% in 1990 to 37% in 2000.

Nearly all larger local law enforcement agencies authorized the use of batons (97%) and pepper spray (91%) in 2000. In 1990, 77% of local agencies authorized the use of impact devices and 71% the use of chemical agents. Among state agencies, nearly all authorized batons (98%) and pepper spray (96%) in 2000. In 1990, 65% allowed impact devices and 61%, chemical agents.

Nearly all (94%) state agencies used video cameras in at least some patrol cars in 2000. Among local agencies more than half of sheriffs' offices (54%) and about two-fifths of county (42%) and municipal (39%) police departments used in-car video cameras.

A majority of state law enforcement agencies (58%) and county police departments (55%) used infrared (thermal) imaging equipment in 2000.

Forty-seven percent of sheriffs' offices and 38% of municipal police departments used this type of equipment.

Nearly all (94%) state law enforcement agencies used tire deflation spikes in 2000, as did about two-thirds of sheriffs' offices (66%). About half of county (52%) and municipal (47%) police departments used such devices.

COMPUTERS AND INFORMATION SYSTEMS

In about four-fifths of larger state and local law enforcement agencies, patrol officers were using in-field computers or terminals during 2000. From 1990 to 2000, the percentage of state agencies using car-mounted computers or terminals rose from 14% to 59%, and among local agencies, from 19% to 68%.

Officers had direct access via in-field computer to vehicle and driving records in more than three-fifths of local agencies in 2000, compared to about half in 1997. Access to this information was available in 53% of state agencies in 2000, compared to 37% in 1997.

About 3 in 8 state and local agencies provided at least some officers with in-field access to criminal history information during 2000, compared to about 3 in 10 agencies in 1997. In 2000, 45% of local agencies provided officers with in-field access to calls for service information compared to 27% in 1997. In state agencies, the percentage rose only slightly—from 12% to 14%.

In 2000, 78% of state and local agencies used paper forms to submit criminal incident reports to the agency's central information system, compared to 86% of local agencies and 90% of state agencies in 1997. The decline in the use of paper reports was accompanied by increases in the use of computer media, data downloads, telephone lines, and wireless transmissions.

From 1990 to 2000 the percentage of larger local law enforcement agencies with exclusive or shared ownership of an Automated Fingerprint Identi-

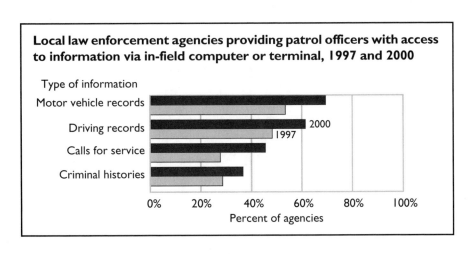

Local law enforcement agencies providing patrol officers with access to information via in-field computer or terminal, 1997 and 2000

fication System (AFIS) increased from 29% to 42%. For state agencies the increase was from 27% to 61%.

Seventy-four percent of local agencies were using digital imaging for mug shots in 2000 compared to 51% in 1997. Similar increases were seen in the use of digital imaging for fingerprints (44% to 65%) and suspect composites (34% to 52%). Among state agencies, 35% were using digital imaging for fingerprints in both 2000 and 1997. During this period, their use of digital imaging for mug shots rose from 14% to 29% of agencies, and for suspect composites, from 14% to 20%.

During 2000 most larger law enforcement agencies used computers for Internet access (87%), records management (86%), dispatch (85%), crime analysis (80%), crime investigations (75%), personnel records (71%), crime mapping (63%), automated booking (56%), interagency information sharing (55%), and fleet management (52%).

A majority of state agencies used computers for Internet access (96%), personnel records (92%), records management (86%), fleet management (74%), in-field report writing (71%), interagency information sharing (71%), crime analysis (63%), crime investigations (59%), dispatch (59%), and resource allocation (57%).

In 2000 about 9 in 10 local agencies had computerized files on arrests (91%), calls for service (90%), and incident reports (88%). More than 7 in 10 had computer files on stolen property (77%), traffic accidents (75%), alarms (74%), traffic citations (71%), and warrants (71%). More than half had computer files on criminal histories (63%) and traffic stops (51%).

Among state agencies, about 3 in 4 had computerized files on traffic accidents (76%) and traffic citations (74%). A majority had files on arrests (63%), incident reports (63%), calls for service (59%), fingerprints (55%), and criminal histories (51%).

SECTION II
Selection, Training, and Socialization

As a result of the trend for increasing accountability of police departments and public oversight of policy making, issues of officer selection, training, and socialization have moved into the forefront of police research. Because of the labor-intensive nature of police work, the most significant investment police departments make is in the recruitment, selection, and training of their personnel. The readings in this section provide students with a working knowledge of issues involving police personnel and of the images the police project as a result of their socialization into the world of policing.

Our first selection, "Law Enforcement Training: Changes and Challenges" by Allison Chappell, Lonn Lanza-Kaduce, and Daryl Johnston, discusses the origin and history of selection and training in police agencies. In addition, the authors discuss the fact that as policing changes there is a need for selection and training to adjust to meet the new demands. The authors question whether police agencies are flexible enough to adjust to the current demands. More specifically they question whether law enforcement agencies will be able to adjust their selection and training to meet the new requirements imposed upon officers charged with community-based and problem-solving policing.

Professor Laure Weber Brooks presents an up-to-date review of the current research on police discretionary behavior, emphasizing the factors that affect police officers' behavioral choices. She notes that it is a collection of "rules of thumb" learned on the job through a combination of formal and informal socialization and training that best accounts for the officers' behavioral choices.

The third article in this section, by Peter Manning, explores how the mass media (television in particular) create dramatic images of the police and how these images affect how the police view themselves. Manning demonstrates how the police are affected by and responsive to the larger society around them.

In the final article in this section, Wesley Jennings and Edward Hudak discuss law enforcement's role in taking responsibility for mentally ill citizens through their power and authority to protect the safety and welfare of the community, in addition to their *parens patriae* obligations to protect individuals with disabilities. They review what officers should and should not do when managing encounters with mentally ill citizens.

Law Enforcement Training
Changes and Challenges

Allison T. Chappell, Lonn Lanza-Kaduce, & Daryl H. Johnston

INTRODUCTION

The purpose of this article is to introduce students to some of the challenges confronting law enforcement training, especially in light of some recent trends in policing. The article is premised on a presupposition: reciprocal relationships exist among society, policing, and law enforcement training. As society changes, policing adjusts; as policing changes, training shifts. With a lot of careful effort and a little luck, the new training will improve policing so that society is better served.

American policing has gone through three recognizable eras (Kelling and Moore 1988). The political era, which lasted through the early twentieth century, was characterized by officers who walked on foot and knew citizens well. Officers had unlimited discretion and limited supervision, which led to widespread allegations of corruption and other abuses of power. The reform era became dominant in the twentieth century when society reacted strongly against that corruption. The reforms resulted in police agencies that were bureaucratic, legalistic organizational structures with strict policies and procedures to limit officer discretion and enhance supervision. Technological advances placed officers in patrol cars with radio dispatch so that they could respond to calls for service quickly and efficiently. The relationship of the

Prepared especially for *Critical Issues in Policing* by Allison T. Chappell, Lonn Lanza-Kaduce, and Daryl H. Johnston.

police to communities suffered as officers were removed from foot patrols, and officers policed from a distance. Riots and racial conflict during the 1960s eventually led to the community era in an effort to improve police-community relations. Heightened concerns for the community and problem solving merged in community-oriented policing (COPS) (see Kelling and Moore 1988). By 1997, most police departments serving 100,000 or more people and sheriff's offices serving 250,000 or more residents had personnel assigned to COPS (Bureau of Justice Statistics 2000).

We are still in the transition from the reform era to the community era. Training, in particular, has been slow to adapt to community policing (or COPS). The transition is especially difficult given the conflicting values and practices between traditional (or reform) policing and current policing. For example, while traditional policing emphasizes strict enforcement of the law, COPS emphasizes building relationships between police and community/ neighborhood residents in order to work together to prevent crime and solve problems (Trojanowicz and Bucqueroux 1990). Without proper training, officers will be less likely to understand the philosophy of COPS and how to translate the philosophy into effective practice (King and Lab 2000).

Training has also evolved. In the political era, officers often learned how to police from senior personnel in the department because no formal training was required. Systematic recruit training in police academies was one of the reforms instituted during the twentieth century. August Vollmer, a pioneering police leader and scholar, is credited with introducing education to policing. In Berkeley, California, he recruited college graduates to law enforcement and publicized the importance of doing so. This led to increased emphases on recruit training and education nationwide. The trend was slow to catch on, however. As recently as 1965, only approximately 15 percent of police departments provided or required training. In 1967, The President's Commission on Law Enforcement and Administration of Justice published its *Task Force Report on the Police*, which called for states to establish minimum selection, training, and education standards for all law enforcement personnel. States now certify law enforcement officers who pass standardized examinations.

Although recruit training in special academies is typical, training requirements are determined by each state (Marion 1998) and are not uniform. Training data from the 430 largest U.S. municipal police departments in 1993 showed that wide variation in practice remained—some departments required no hours of training while others required over 2,500 hours (Alpert and Dunham 1997; Department of Justice 1993).

Training can occur for recruits who are entering law enforcement (often referred to as basic training), for rookies (field training officer or FTO programs), and for existing officers and administrators through advanced and in-service training. Training can also occur through traditional academic degree programs. Recruit training is generally performed in designated facilities that are referred to in different ways (e.g., training academies, institutes of public safety, criminal justice training centers). Some large law enforcement agencies operate their own academies and pay for the training of their recruits. More often training centers are linked with institutions of higher education, especially those geared toward vocational training like community colleges. Law enforcement agencies will sometimes sponsor their recruits as they go through training at the local community college training center. Other prospective officers pay for their own training in hopes of being recruited after they complete training and become certified.

TRAINING CHALLENGES

The function of law enforcement training, whether geared toward traditional policing or COPS, seems obvious. Training should improve performance. What is less obvious is how do accomplish this. The challenge is double-edged in several important ways.

1. Curriculum and Delivery Challenges

Police training is double-edged in that it needs to impart skills (e.g., driving, use of weapons, defensive tactics, report writing, arrest techniques, first aid and first response techniques) and knowledge bases (e.g., law, race relations, interpersonal communication, mental illness, drug and alcohol effects, terrorism) (Marion 1998). As society changes, training will change. New topics will be added and/or the coverage of topics will change. For example, Florida now requires 40 hours of in-service diversity training for sworn officers every four years.

The majority of traditional police recruit training consists of the technical and mechanical aspects of acquiring skills (Birzer 1999) due to concerns about safety. Recruits spend 90 percent of their training time on firearms, driving, first aid, self-defense, and other use-of-force tactics even though only 10 percent of their job duties will put them in positions where they need to use these skills (Germann 1969; Mayhall et al. 1995). Veteran officers—police insiders—frequently are the instructors for skills training. They may also be "drafted" to cover academic subjects like diversity and communications, areas that may stretch their expertise. "Subject matter experts" from law enforcement ranks are also frequently used for in-service training.

Some jurisdictions base their basic or recruit training on a Job Task Analysis (JTA). The reason for this is to ensure that training reflects the demands of the job. However, JTA reflects what has traditionally been done on the job and not necessarily what needs to be learned to do the job better.

The shift in policing toward community relations, problem solving, and COPS heightens the need for improved knowledge bases and additional skills but does not diminish the need for traditional skills (Bradford and Pynes 1999; Buerger et al. 1999). For example, recruits would be ill served if training in officer safety were shortchanged. COPS training augments the curriculum by including topics on human diversity, special populations (such as the elderly, mentally ill), "assessing situations," public speaking, ethics and integrity, proactive or "coactive" problem solving, crime prevention, stress management, domestic violence, and community building (see Palmiotto et al. 2000). Recent developments in policing have led to more training and education in a wider range of knowledge. Those knowledge bases require more reliance on expertise that lies outside of law enforcement. Given the limited time for training, skills areas and knowledge bases compete for priority. As policing changes, either training priorities shift or training hours are increased. For example, some curricula, in the aftermath of September 11, incorporate lessons on weapons of mass destruction and terrorism.

The various types of curriculum content have implications for how instruction is delivered. A vocational, hands-on model seems more appropriate for teaching and enhancing skills than for imparting and developing the knowledge bases, which usually are pursued via academic materials and classroom instruction.

Traditional training in subject areas like law and communications builds on the pedagogical approach used when teaching children. The pedagogy is teacher-centered and structured, and it relies heavily on a lecture format (often referred to by trainees as "talking heads"). This style emphasizes mastery, obedience, and discipline and supports the narrow focus on law enforcement that characterizes traditional policing. One challenge facing training is to incorporate alternative learning models more suited to adults (Birzer 2003; Glenn et al. 2003).

Training for COPS can be more effective if it uses adult learning or andragogy. Andragogy centers on the learner rather than the instructor, emphasizes interactions, and integrates life experiences into training (Birzer 2003; Knowles 1980). The instructor takes on the role of "facilitator" and helps to develop critical thinking, judgment, and creativity in the learner (Birzer and Tannehill 2001). Andragogy is based on "empowerment" and teaches recruits to be self-directed and to work through problems to solve them. This approach runs counter to the quasi-military, top-down style that predominates in traditional policing.

2. Occupational Socialization, Recruitment Challenges, and Informal Lessons

Post-secondary education and occupational training are forms of secondary socialization. Several police scholars have investigated the occupational socialization process. We will focus on the first two stages that Van Maanen (1973) uses to characterize the process: choice/pre-entry (which includes self-selection and screening by agencies) and introduction (which includes both formal and informal lessons at the training academy).

The pre-entry stage (also known as "anticipatory" [Bennett 1984]) occurs prior to starting the academy. In this stage, applicants begin to view themselves in the police role based on real or imagined perceptions (via media, friends, relatives, and police officers whom they know or have had contact with). Academy instructors must work with the skills, knowledge, and values that the recruits bring with them to the academy (Bennett 1984; Van Maanen

1973). In other words, training is double-edged in that it is not independent of other trends both in and out of policing. Recruits self-select, while agencies and academies screen. People most interested in law enforcement have historically not been the "best" students in traditional classrooms. They are probably attracted to police training because they want to hone their skills in driving, shooting, and defensive tactics more than acquire knowledge about crime causation, diversity, and law. Agencies and academies that are looking for new recruits create job announcements and advertising in ways that encourage certain types of applicants to apply. Applications to both academies and agencies can contain questions to screen who is selected. Historically, recruits were selected based on physical attributes (height, weight, strength). Military service has been a recruitment focus since Peele's original police force.

To the extent that COPS emphasizes different activities, recruitment may need to change to screen for different skills and characteristics. Trends in society, however, may constrict the pool of candidates. Retirements, economic fluctuations, pay scales, the juvenile and drug records of young people, and the war against terrorism conjoin to affect the supply of potential recruits and the demand for them. When the recruit pool is limited, training has to be adjusted to match the level of the recruits—even if that means pitching the material at the eighth-grade level. As policing develops and requires more professionalism and deeper knowledge of a broader array of subjects, training demands may outstrip the abilities of many potential recruits.

During the introduction stage of police socialization, recruits are exposed to a mix of formal (official) and informal lessons—and the two kinds of lessons are not necessarily complementary. Recruits receive formal instruction in the training curriculum; they are taught about departmental rules and regulations and other fundamentals (Lundman 1980). They also receive informal training in the attitudes and beliefs about the occupation through war stories and experiencing the quasi-military authority arrangements (see Langworthy and Travis 2003; Van Maanen 1973). Recruits learn roles, attitudes, and beliefs from training staff, experienced officers, and peers at the academy.

Newcomers to all organizations will identify with the work group to some degree. Observers argue that few organizations instill the same degree of occupational identification as do the police (Britz 1997; Van Maanen 1978). Skolnick (1966/1994) reports that the strength of the organizational culture in a police department is so salient that, regardless of personal differences, individuals adopt the beliefs and definitions of the department. In the academy, the recruits learn that their peer group will support them and that they should support their fellow officers.

What is learned informally may not comport with the formal training instruction. We should expect a gap between formal and informal lessons (just as we can expect a gap between law on the books that recruits learn and law as it is practiced on the streets). Indeed, some lessons may be contradictory. For example, despite formal instruction in diversity, informal lessons may be sexist or racist (Marion 1998). While such contradictory informal messages are detrimental to traditional policing, they are devastating to COPS.

During the introduction stage, recruits have their first contact with the police subculture and the discipline and strict obedience that are required of them. The informal content includes lessons about the police subculture (see Alpert and Dunham 1997). The traditional recruit curriculum converges with the classic ideals perpetuated by that subculture, such as an emphasis on crime fighting, making arrests, and getting "a good pinch." This stage also exposes recruits to the "police personality," characterized by secrecy, isolation, and cynicism (Skolnick 1966/1994; Westley 1970). The police personality will develop more fully when recruits hit the streets as rookies. The police personality complicates efforts to use experts outside law enforcement as instructors—isolated cynical officers are less likely to accept outside messengers. This especially complicates in-service training, but the orientation also filters down to recruit training.

Neither the crime fighting ideal of the police subculture nor the attributes of the police personality correspond well with the demands of COPS. COPS officers will need to gravitate toward problem solving and community building rather than high-profile arrests. They will need to be accepted into the community and accepting of community input rather than isolated, apart, and suspicious. They will need to be more democratic and less authoritarian in their orientation than traditional officers.

3. Legal Protection and Failure to Train

Training cuts two ways in another sense—it both enhances what officers can do and protects officers and agencies, to a degree, in the event that something bad happens. The terminology used in training academies underscores the protective function of training. The skills (driving, firearms, defensive tactics, officer safety, and first responder) are lumped together and designated to be "high liability areas." The concern about lawsuits should not be taken lightly (see Ross 2000). Under some circumstances, the trainees can sue trainers and the public can sue officers and agencies for failure to train.

Del Carmen and Smith (2001) review the liability of law enforcement under state (e.g., tort) and federal law (e.g., Section 1983 of the Civil Rights Act). Although failure to train can give rise to both state and federal lawsuits, the law makes it difficult for plaintiffs to prevail. For example, trainees are frequently presumed to assume some risk of injury during training unless the instructors have intentionally or recklessly conducted the training. (See, for example, Hamilton v. Martinelli and Associates 2003; Stone and Berger 2004.) Qualified immunity may help protect law enforcement from some claims by citizens as long as actions were taken within the scope of employment and were not egregious. Del Carmen and Smith (2001:191) highlight two steps that departments need to take to help protect against liability: "(1) a pre-employment training program must be in place; and (2) the training program must focus on the skills needed in policing. . . ." We would only add that as policing changes, training needs to keep pace, which raises the prospect that negligent hiring (both of instructors for teaching and of rookies who attended academies with inadequate training that are behind the times) may complicate liability. Supervisors who know or should know about officers who are inadequately trained can also be liable (Ross 2000).

There are several interrelated implications to the double-edged reality that training is designed both to help officers perform well and to protect against lawsuits when they do not. Standardization of training is functional for liability reasons, but training in knowledge areas may be difficult to standardize. For example, learning to shoot a firearm is fairly standard, while learning to communicate with a hostile murder suspect will present unique challenges each and every time. The knowledge areas for policing are not conducive to standardized textual treatments. Teaching law illustrates the point. Rather than memorizing statutes, law students are trained to think like lawyers so they can analyze fact patterns within and across cases and fit facts with legal precepts. Police officers have to do very much the same thing, but in "real time," during ongoing encounters. Yet, their training in law under traditional academy approaches is text driven and mechanical and not case or scenario based. Arguably, traditional academy law training does not prepare recruits to apply the law well.

One function of standardized training is to establish a customary practice so that officers know (and can be presumed to follow) standardized procedures. Plaintiffs suing law enforcement have a more difficult time attributing bad outcomes to officer errors or omissions if officers are adequately trained and have established routines or customary practices. Plaintiffs have the burden of proof to show that those practices were not followed—the operating presumption favors law enforcement. Even if bad consequences can be attributed to officers, "good faith" mistakes are protected by qualified immunity so plaintiffs frequently must prove some kind of egregious error. That is harder to do if officers have been trained and supervised adequately. Agencies that do not train or are negligent in their training have a harder time defending the actions of their officers when things go wrong. Agencies can distance themselves more easily from rogue officers if customary training and routine supervision is in place. The reform or legalistic era of policing during the twentieth century restricted the discretion of field officers and increased supervision for good reasons. The decentralization of authority and the increased autonomy of decision making for COPS officers raise legitimate concerns about new legal liabilities that need to be anticipated in training.

Certification and licensure are ways to establish the adequacy of training. The process, however, encourages standardized certification examinations. Standardized examinations protect agencies against claims of inadequate training and also help defend against discrimination claims when candidates fail the exams. To the extent that COPS relies on mastery of more knowledge areas that are not easily standardized, COPS presents challenges for examinations and certifications.

Academies need a high "pass" rate, and they can "teach to the test" to get that pass rate if everything is standardized. Recruit training is expensive, so agencies that operate their own academies must make sure their trainees pass certification or they will bear the cost. Where agencies sponsor recruits to attend academies, they also want success or they bear the cost. Agencies want to recruit from academies that have a good track record for screening and training recruits. Regardless of the source of recruits or funding, academies have an institutional interest in their graduates having high pass rates.

Given these pressures, we should not be surprised if trainers "teach to the test." We offer an anecdote to illustrate the way in which this affects police behavior. One of the authors was researching courthouse records and was surprised to see so many police arrest charges for "principal in the first degree"—a relatively obscure legal concept and a charge that the prosecutors always changed before formal charges were issued. The author later observed the delivery of the law section of a traditional academy recruit session. Students were memorizing the legal definition of principal in the first degree via a straight lecture format. Sometime later, the same researcher observed a state meeting where "subject matter experts" were reworking the certification examination. Projected on the overhead was a question about "principal in the first degree." The instructors taught about principal in the first degree, and the certification test covered it. The recruits learned the concept by rote, but did not know how to apply it in practice as was evidenced by the prosecutors' decisions to change the formal charges. Teaching to the test did not enhance performance.

A NEW ACADEMY TRAINING APPROACH

The fact that COPS is being adopted so widely means that training will likely adapt. Some places are already making changes. For example, the state of Florida has adopted a new academy curriculum called Curriculum Maintenance System (CMS),[1] which expressly incorporates COPS into a scenario-based approach. The Los Angeles Police Department (LAPD) has also moved toward new academy training, which was the focus of a recent RAND Corporation analysis (Glenn et al. 2003). We use that analysis to illustrate the wave of the future as training incorporates COPS into its courses and delivery.

LAPD's new policing philosophy recognizes that training must reflect as closely as possible the actual working conditions for which recruits are being prepared (Fyfe 1996). Learning content is not enough; trainees must also be able to digest and interpret material and synthesize it with practical skills. Only this more sophisticated training will enable officers to adapt to the ever-changing demands of their jobs and to improvise in unpredictable situations in the field. Glenn et al. (2003) present four elements fundamental to successful training and consider how each is incorporated into the training experience at LAPD: contextualized learning, integration of topics throughout the curriculum, scenario building, and debriefing.

1. Contextualize the Learning

Contextualized learning is an adult learning principle that seeks to tie new information to existing knowledge bases and real-life situations. It integrates new information with existing knowledge. Based on the assumption that training should mimic reality, it better prepares recruits for the real-life situations they will eventually encounter. Simulated real-life incidents (scenarios) are useful because they may require the recruit to integrate many knowledge bases with an emergency tactical situation. In real-life situations, police officers are often confronted with a multitude of issues in a single citizen contact. It is unlikely that officers will be able to perform a traffic stop, for example, without also having to use communication, law, and officer safety lessons. The approach frames new information in the context of what is already known. It recognizes that recruits need to be trained the same way that they will eventually do their jobs, and that a relationship exists between skills and knowledge. That relationship calls for a critical problem-solving synthesis that changes from context to context and, therefore, runs counter to the standardization preferred in traditional training.

2. Integrate Key Topics throughout the Curriculum

Integration of key topics, also known as "threading," means that selected important themes will be discussed in relation to each substantive topic or module (i.e., woven throughout the curriculum). For example, communications lessons (or diversity training or officer safety) can be reinforced in arrest scenarios, in crowd control exercises, and in community relations material. Skills and knowledge must be integrated in the field, so training should not cover subject areas only in distinct, separate units. Integration helps recruits learn to draw connections among multiple subject areas, which facilitates mastery over the curriculum and prepares recruits for problem-solving challenges when they enter the field. Recruits will be in a better position to deal with unique contexts and help develop appropriate responses to a neighborhood's problems.

3. Build the Scenario

Scenarios allow the recruit to apply contextualized learning and topic integration by grounding instruction in the "known" while introducing the "new." Scenarios help align a curriculum with the main tenets of adult learning: learning by doing, reflecting real life, and making the learning interactive and self-directed (Glenn et al. 2003). Scenarios inherently require the integration of topics. They transform abstract knowledge into understandable, practical, and applicable skills. Scenarios give recruits the opportunity to practice applying what they have learned. Instructors and other police officers put together unique and surprising scenarios that encourage the recruits to "think on their feet" in unexpected situations to find workable, and perhaps even creative, solutions.

4. Conduct a Thorough Debriefing (after the scenario)

Consistent and structured debriefings are important to solidify learning. Because scenarios are unstandardized and involve open-ended interactions, instructors need to tie everything together in the end and review lessons. The debriefing also informs recruits about how they have performed and how they can improve. Recruits have an opportunity to discuss and reconsider their performance, and use their experience as a springboard for further learning. This reflection is important for adult learning. It prepares recruits for the feedback loop that is an inherent part of problem-solving models like SARA. SARA is an acronym which stands for *s*canning for problems, *a*nalyzing the factors that contribute to problems, *r*esponding in ways that can alleviate problems, and *a*ssessing the results (Eck and Spelman 1987).[2]

TRAINING CHALLENGES REVISITED

The way in which LAPD has incorporated threading, scenarios, contextualization, and debriefing into training mirrors what the authors have experienced in Florida while observing CMS recruit training and continuation training of officers at a Regional Community Policing Institute (RCPI). These new curricula and improved delivery methods address many of the challenges that confront law enforcement training.

1. Curriculum and Delivery Challenges

Glenn et al. (2003) observed a complete transformation in the way that LAPD recruit training was delivered. For the most part, instead of using standardized lecture-only techniques, the LAPD academy implemented adult learning principles that included scenarios and debriefing. The authors also observed this in the CMS training (Florida). In fact, one Florida training center adds 40 hours of scenario training to the required CMS curriculum. Even with that addition, recent recruits wanted more scenarios, more instructors to perform scenarios, and the scenarios to be spread throughout the instruction. In the words of one recruit: "Scenario training was awesome, very real-life!"

Overall, both LAPD and the Florida academy did a good job of using adult learning techniques. These techniques helped to keep the recruits alert and involved in their learning. This should better prepare them for law enforcement work in the field.

Glenn et al. (2003) report that the LAPD academy balanced the acquisition of skills with learning other subjects. The same can be said of our observations of the CMS curriculum in Florida. In fact, the first 194 hours of CMS training deal with knowledge areas rather than the acquisition of skills. Knowledge bases, such as law and diversity, were well integrated into most of the modules, including those focusing primarily on skill building. Scenarios helped to pull both skills and knowledge bases together in an integrated and synthesized fashion. For example, instructors encouraged recruits to use information learned in diversity and interpersonal communication in a module on defensive tactics.

2. Occupational Socialization, Recruitment Challenges, and Informal Lessons

The first stage of occupational socialization is preentry and refers to screening and self-selection of recruits, something that Glenn et al. (2003) did not discuss in their review of LAPD training. Our own experience in Florida indicates that academy personnel are sensitive to recruitment realities. They are concerned that the abilities of many of their new recruits may not be sufficient to excel, given the demands of the new curriculum. We argue here that academies and police administrators need to consciously examine how to recruit the kinds of candidates who will excel in the new training and make the best COPS officers. We think the new COPS philosophy of policing calls for different types of recruits.

In fact, some police administrators are interested in developing police selection centers to support regional police academies and agencies in the identification and selection of the best applicants for the discipline. Using minimum standards set by the state's licensing body, a selection center uses techniques based in industrial/organizational psychology to match job tasks with the skills, knowledge, and abilities of the applicants. Advances within selection centers will focus on research on the discipline's needs in community policing and provide law enforcement agencies with access to new data technology and interpersonal skills of the recruit candidate.

The introduction stage of police socialization occurs at the academy. Both the LAPD evaluation and our own observations of training in Florida reveal that the new curricula introduce recruits to COPS and thread lessons relevant to the philosophy and practice of COPS throughout the various modules and areas of instruction. Not only has the content changed but the delivery also has consciously incorporated adult learning practices that require students to analyze, integrate, and apply lessons through scenarios. The formal socialization is indeed different from traditional training.

Despite the best efforts of the instructors, the informal lessons and messages still present a challenge to training. While the curriculum urges recruits to work coactively with the community to solve problems and build trust, the informal lessons still convey an "us vs. them" mentality. Although COPS calls for the gathering of accurate information to build knowledge about specific areas in order to problem solve, the informal message is to fight crime and make arrests.

There is a divergence between the police subculture and the COPS curriculum. Instructors, almost all of whom came of age in traditional policing, are "teaching" COPS formally but are often informally sending different signals (for example, when they share "war stories" and experiences with recruits).

Van Maanen (1973) suggests that war stories are delivered differently from formal lessons. The authority relations become more egalitarian, recruits are able to relax, laugh, and join in the exchange. In other words, the instructor becomes more of a facilitator, where learning occurs through interactions that integrate life experiences. The informal lessons in war stories may be better learned by adult recruits than the formal curriculum.

The informal messages may be so salient that they may counteract the formal curriculum. The new policing training may not be fully effective until the COPS philosophy is fully integrated into the operating environments of police agencies, their organizational goals, and the larger police culture. Even if recruits adopt favorable attitudes toward COPS and problem solving in the academy, attitudes may dissipate if they are not consistently and continuously reinforced. Haarr (2001) warns that traditional subcultural values of police can override what recruits have learned in the academy. Academy personnel have impressed upon us the need to have field-training officers who are knowledgeable about COPS so that the lessons learned in the academy will be reinforced in the field.

3. Legal Implications

By integrating COPS into training, the new curricula expects officers to have a broader knowledge base and to be able to apply that knowledge to help solve a variety of problems in the community. The knowledge and its eventual application are less standardized. The training encourages creative analyses and the practice of COPS requires more autonomy for field officers. Supervisors will not be able to apply hard and fast parameters to manage COPS officers. We are concerned about how COPS and the new training deal with legal liability issues. For example, if COPS officers take the lead to clean up a trashy, weedy vacant lot and enlist community volunteers, but they proceed without taking due care to protect the volunteers from injury, will tort liability ensue? How do academies adequately train for the unstandardized contingencies that problem solving entails? How do administrators exert supervision in a way that encourages creative problem solving without increasing the risk of legal liability?

AUTHORITY RELATIONS AS A CORE CONCERN FOR TRAINING IN THE TWENTY-FIRST CENTURY

Running through much of the preceding discussion is a theme that is critical to law enforcement but that is not always explicit. Policing is premised on authority relations, and successful policing depends on how well those authority relations are managed. Authority relations have to be managed both between officers and citizens (where the officers are the authorities) and between officers and their supervisors and administrative "brass" (where the officers are the subjects of authority).

Training recognizes these authority relations, but only to a degree. Formal lessons on arrest and law establish police authority and address how it can be asserted. Lessons about chain of command, supervision, and agency procedures and policies teach recruits and officers about their position in the authority structure of their organizations.

Some of the training lessons on authority are extracurricular. Van Maanen (1973) describes how recruits are subordinated to others during training. They must wear specific uniforms, use special "recruit" parking, and stand at attention when "real" officers and civilians pass by. Trainees learn the importance of group cohesion and solidarity; they are punished and rewarded as a group. In keeping with the quasi-military style adopted by police, academies reproduce some features of boot camp. As in boot camps, the importance of recruits' individual identities are diminished so that a shared occupational identity can emerge.

In some rare circumstances, officers need to operate in the face of danger as a unit and automatically obey commands for the good of all. Most police work, however, does not pose combatlike challenges. Officers find themselves in different authority relations depending on the circumstances. A display of authority and implicit threat of coercion may be effective in an arrest situation. Empathy and active listening may work best when interviewing a traumatized victim to gather evidence. Deference may be the key when interacting with a supervising sergeant or in court.

One criminologist, Austin Turk (1969, 1982) has explicitly addressed authority relations. He argues that conflict is inherent in authority relationships and that authority relations are the central problem for order maintenance (Lanza-Kaduce and Greenleaf 1994). The key is to understand how to manage authority relations to enhance compliance and minimize overt conflict and resistance. The organization and sophistication of those who have authority and those who are subject to authority can alter the balance between order and conflict. Research supports Turk's basic argument that authority relations can be managed to decrease conflict (Greenleaf and Lanza-Kaduce 1995).

The implications are important for training. For example, officers who can communicate and use language better can defuse potential conflicts more easily, obtain better information from witnesses, prepare better cases for prosecutors, and interact more easily with their supervisors. Modern training recognizes the importance of communications sophistication in de-escalating conflict, and in managing incidents or calls for service. Currently, training often includes lessons in verbal judo as an alternative to an overt use of force. The sophisticated officer who is sensitive to cultural differences because of diversity training can also manage authority relations better. Ironically, these subjects are the ones that some trainees resist most, even though they provide some of the most useful tools in the field.

Turk also posits that people generally defer to authority. Two of the reasons are that we learn norms of deference (including that we should defer to the police) and that we understand differences in power. Lanza-Kaduce and Greenleaf (2000) extended this argument and researched resistance by citizens to the police. When broader social norms of deference regarding age and race reinforced the official authority of police officers, people were more likely to defer. Because people have been socialized to defer to authorities who are older and white rather than to authorities who were young and non-white, older white officers have fewer problems with resistance from citizens, according to their research. The training implications are important. Authority relations will be especially complicated for recruits (who are not only less experienced and less sophisticated but who are also young). The situation is compounded for minority recruits who will face the highest probability of resistance in their encounters with the public once they enter the field. We argue that training needs to deal directly with such complicated authority relations so officers can manage them better. One training activity that may be useful in dealing with this issue is role playing.

COPS further complicates the challenge presented by authority relations. COPS officers still have to be trained to deal with potential resistance from suspects in police-citizen encounters. In those situations, the lines of authority are clear. When COPS officers *partner* with citizens to identify and seek problem-solving solutions, when police officers work within their own organizations, and when they seek assistance from outside service providers to implement solutions, the lines of authority blur.

Three of the salient themes in the new COPS paradigm are: community involvement, problem solving, and organizational decentralization (see Oliver 1998). Each entails important shifts in authority relations for which officers need to be prepared.

1. Community Involvement

A sense of community cannot be imposed; it must be homegrown. The telling feature of community for COPS, the sense of shared interest, needs to be identified by those who live and work in a geographical area. COPS officers can help move the process along but do not "own" a neighborhood's problems. In COPS, the role of law enforcement officers needs to shift to reflect this more "democratic" take on policing. Are they trained well enough to interact with residents as partners? Are they sensitive to community issues and concerns? Can they facilitate community building?

Working with communities involves sorting through competing values and ideas while knowing what is feasible and workable in that context. Not all neighborhoods will have citizens with sophisticated knowledge and skills to assist with the solutions, leaving the officers carrying more of the load. COPS officers need skills in leadership, communications, interpersonal relations, diversity awareness, and a variety of other areas to assist in problem solving. The reconfiguration of power/authority relations in COPS requires officers to be trained differently from traditional models. The very subjects that officers have historically trivialized (e.g., social issues, communications) are central to their new roles. Arguably these subjects need more emphasis and more time during training. In fact, the list of "soft" subjects probably needs to increase. Palmiotto, Birzer, and Unnithan (2000), for example, explicitly include a subject heading for "social/economical/political make-up of community" in their list of recommended classes.

Expertise, rather than the symbols of power and coercion, will be the basis for partnerships in community outreach. Well-trained COPS officers will be able to lead in positive ways—ways that citizens will support and endorse rather than resent. COPS officers will not contribute to community involvement if they "throw their weight around" or play the authority card too heavy-handedly.

2. Problem Solving

Officer leadership is especially important to problem solving. Typically, problems and solutions are unique (or at least have dimensions that are unique) to a particular neighborhood. The COPS philosophy is premised on the notion that informal social controls (those exerted by citizens who have a stake in their own neighborhoods) will be more effective over the long term than traditional police reactions to incidents, like arrests. This is one of the important lessons of the "broken windows" model (Wilson and Kelling 1982) that informs COPS to solve quality of life issues. Training will need to focus on both skills for motivating community involvement and on the problems communities are likely to face, such as drugs, alcohol, domestic violence, speeding, noise, delinquency, and gangs.

COPS officers will have to learn how to identify and support community defined priorities. Residents may be able to identify problems but not fully appreciate which factors maintain the undesirable state of affairs. For example, residents concerned primarily with burglary may not have the luxury of ignoring vice crimes and so-called victimless crimes that send crime-promoting signals and attract additional criminality. COPS officers may need to educate residents and forge consensus through problem solving about workable solutions. But COPS officers cannot do so if they are ill-prepared in subjects of crime causation and prevention (e.g., COMPSTAT, crime mapping, routine activities theory). Training will have to be open to outside expertise, and training centers will have to find ways to break down the traditional resistance to outsiders.

Traditional policing that emphasizes top-down authority relations, where police have "ownership" over crime problems, needs to give way to community involvement and partnerships. Success will depend on training that teaches and demonstrates how to share power and authority, how to gather information and suggestions, how to work through conflict to build consensus, and how to cooperate and coordinate with others. The new demands of the job require a shift in the paradigm of police training that must be introduced in academies for recruits, reinforced by field training officers as recruits go onto the job, and repeated during in-service training.

3. Organizational Decentralization

The success of COPS officers in working with residents to define and solve community problems rests on whether the authority relations in law enforcement organizations can evolve in ways that permit bottom-up problem solving and top-down support for the efforts. COPS requires decentralization of authority in law enforcement organizations (Oliver 1998). Supervisors must work with COPS officers to identify time and resources to assist officers in their coordination with the community in the problem solving model. The profession cannot remove supervision and policy regulations in ways that increase corruption and abuse. Policies and supervision, however, will have to adjust for COPS to work well, and members of law enforcement organizations will need to establish different patterns of authority.

The COPS philosophy calls for a hybrid system to deal with the various problems in neighborhoods (Chappell and Lanza-Kaduce 2004). Other kinds of organizations have faced similar challenges. Some, like many technology firms, have adopted what is called a matrix organization in order to increase effectiveness.

Matrix organizations are based on a web of relationships (Mee 1964). They rely on team management and adopt a grid structure that integrates resources from different sectors rather than impose a top-down hierarchical structure (Kolodny 1979). These organizations concentrate on particular sources, projects, or divisions, so lines of authority converge at a lower level in the organization (Daft 1992). Matrix organizations have dual reporting relationships; an employee may have to answer to a quality manager and a financial manager (a COPS officer has to answer to a supervisor and the community). They emphasize flexibility and adaptability to ever-changing conditions. Their success rests on problem solving, conflict management, and communication skills. Employees have to value a diversity of opinions, as well as how to move from reactive to proactive behavior.

The parallels with COPS are striking. Effective community policing requires building relationships within the neighborhood, between the neighborhood and law enforcement, and with other service providers. Resources need to be found and integrated to focus on addressing community issues. COPS officers need to facilitate working teams that concentrate on particular agreed-upon problems, and they must have the autonomy and support from both the community and the police agency to do so. They need to be flexible and proactive, rather than just reactive to crime.

The question we pose is whether law enforcement training, for existing officers and administrators, or for recruits, is anticipating these organizational changes. Other organizations have successfully made the transition, a transition that can be facilitated by training that helps employees understand the new structure and learn how to operate effectively within it. The success of COPS depends on learning a new way to organize and conduct law enforcement—new patterns of authority relationships. The COPS philosophy may have outstripped both the traditional organizational structure of law enforcement and the training regimen. The lag may doom the promise of COPS unless training can adjust quickly to help mesh the democratic community-based philosophy with field practices that are supported by a new organizational structure and philosophy.

Notes

[1] Florida Department of Law Enforcement's Criminal Justice Standards and Training Commission's CMS application-based law enforcement basic recruit training curriculum.

[2] Other problem-solving models also have a feedback loop. For example, the Royal Canadian Mounted Police (RCMP) use the CAPRA model and Florida Department of Law Enforcement's new CMS curriculum uses SECURE (which stands for Safety, Ethics, Community, Understanding, Response, and Evaluation) to blend crisis management, routine investigation, and long-term problem solving.

References

Alpert, Geoffrey P. and Roger G. Dunham. 1997. *Policing Urban America*. Prospect Heights, IL: Waveland Press.

Bennett, Richard. 1984. Becoming blue: A longitudinal study of police recruit occupational socialization. *Journal of Police Science and Administration* 12 (1): 47–58.

Birzer, Michael L. 1999. Police training in the 21st century. *FBI Law Enforcement Bulletin*.

Birzer, Michael L. 2003. The theory of andragogy applied to police training. *Policing: An International Journal of Police Strategies and Management* 26 (1): 29–42.

Birzer, Michael L. and Ronald Tannehill. 2001. A more effective training approach for contemporary policing. *Police Quarterly* 4 (2): 233–252.

Bradford, David and Joan E. Pynes. 1999. Police academy training: Why hasn't it kept up with practice? *Police Quarterly* 2 (3): 283–301.

Britz, Marjie T. 1997. The police subculture and occupational socialization: Exploring individual and demographic characteristics. *American Journal of Criminal Justice* 21 (2): 127–146.

Buerger, M.E., A.J. Petrosino, and C. Petrosino. 1999. Extending the police role: Implications of police mediation as a problem-solving tool. *Police Quarterly* 2: 125–149.

Bureau of Justice Statistics. 2000. *Local Police Departments 1997*. Washington D.C.: Department of Justice.

Chappell, Allison T. and Lonn Lanza-Kaduce. 2004. Integrating Sociological Research with Community-Oriented Policing: Bridging the Gap between Academics and Practice. Annual Meeting of the Southern Sociological Society, Atlanta, GA.

Daft, Richard L. 1992. *Organization Theory and Design*. 4th ed. New York: West.

Del Carmen, Rolando and Michael R. Smith. 2001. Police Civil Liability and the Law. Pgs 181–198 in Roger G. Dunham and Geoffrey P. Alpert (eds.), *Critical Issues in Policing*, 4th ed. Prospect Heights, IL: Waveland Press.

Department of Justice, Bureau of Justice Statistics. 1993. Law Enforcement and Administrative Statistics Survey (LEMAS). Ann Arbor, MI: Interuniversity Consortium for Political and Social Research.

Eck, John E. and William Spelman. 1987. Who ya gonna call? The police as problem busters. *Crime & Delinquency* 33: 53–70.

Fyfe, James J. 1996. Training to reduce police-civilian violence. In William A. Geller and Hans Toch (eds.), *Police Violence: Understanding and Controlling Police Abuse of Force*. New Haven: Yale University Press.

Germann, A.C. 1969. Community policing: An assessment. *Journal of Criminal Law and Police Science* 60: 89–96.

Glenn, Russell W., Barbara R. Panitch, Dionne Barnes-Proby, Elizabeth Williams, John Christian, Matthew W. Lewis, Scott Gerwehr, and David W. Brannan. 2003. *Training the 21st Century Police Officer: Redefining Police Professionalism for the Los Angeles Police Department*. Santa Monica, CA: RAND.

Greenleaf, Richard G. and Lonn Lanza-Kaduce. 1995. Sophistication, organization, and authority-subject conflict: Rediscovering and unraveling Turk's theory of norm resistance. *Criminology* 33: 565–586.

Haarr, Robin N. 2001. The making of a community policing officer: The impact of basic training and occupational socialization on police recruits. *Police Quarterly* 4 (4): 402–433.

Hamilton v. Martinelli and Associates. 2003. 110CA4 102.

Kelling, G. and M. Moore. 1988. From political to reform to community: The evolving strategy of police. In J. Greene and S. Mastrofski (eds.), *Community policing: Rhetoric or reality*. New York: Praeger.

King, William R. and Steven P. Lab. 2000. Crime prevention, community policing, and training: Old wine in new bottles. *Police Practice and Research* 1 (2): 241–252.

Knowles, M.S. 1980. *The Modern Practice of Adult Education: From Pedagogy to Andragogy.* New York: Cambridge.

Kolodny, Harvey F. 1979. Evolution to a matrix organization. *The Academy of Management Review* 4/4: 543–553.

Langworthy, Robert and Lawrence Travis. 2003. *Policing in America. A Balance of Forces,* 3rd ed. Upper Saddle River, NJ: Prentice Hall.

Lanza-Kaduce, Lonn and Richard G. Greenleaf. 1994. Police-citizen encounters: Turk on norm resistance. *Justice Quarterly* 11: 605–623.

Lanza-Kaduce, Lonn and Richard G. Greenleaf. 2000. Age and race deference reversals: Extending Turk on police-citizen conflict. *Journal of Research in Crime and Delinquency* 37: 221–236.

Lundman, Richard J. 1980. *Police and Policing: An Introduction.* New York: Holt, Rinehart and Winston.

Marion, Nancy. 1998. Police academy training: Are we teaching recruits what they need to know? *Policing* 21 (1): 54–75.

Mayhall, P.D., T. Barker, and R.D. Hunter. 1995. *Police Community Relations—and the Administration of Justice.* Englewood Cliffs, NJ: Prentice Hall.

Mee, John F. 1964. Ideational items: Matrix organization. *Business Horizons* 7: 70–72.

Oliver, Willard M. 1998. *Community-Oriented Policing: A Systemic Approach to Policing.* Upper Saddle River, NJ: Prentice Hall.

Palmiotto, Michael J., Michael Birzer, and N. Prabha Unnithan. 2000. Training in community policing: A suggested curriculum. *Policing: An International Journal of Police Strategies and Management* 23 (1): 8–21.

President's Commission on Law Enforcement and Administration of Justice. 1967. *Task Force Report on the Police.* Washington D.C.: U.S. Government Printing Office.

Ross, Darrell L. 2000. Emerging trends in police failure to train liability. *Policing: An International Journal of Police Strategies and Management* 23 (2): 169–193.

Skolnick, Jerome. 1966/1994. *Justice without Trial.* New York: John Wiley and Sons.

Stone, Michael P. and Marc J. Berger. 2004. Police trainers cannot be held civilly liable for trainees' injuries during training. *The Law Enforcement Trainer* January/February: 24–28.

Trojanowicz, R. and B. Bucqueroux. 1990. *Community Policing: A Contemporary Perspective.* Cincinnati, OH: Anderson Publishing.

Turk, Austin. 1969. *Criminality and Legal Order.* Chicago: Rand McNally.

Turk, Austin. 1982. *Political Criminality: The Defiance and Defense of Authority.* Newbury Park, CA: Sage.

Van Maanen, John. 1973. Observations on the making of policemen. *Human Organization* 32: 407–418.

Van Maanen, John. 1978. The asshole. In Victor Kappeler (ed.), *The Police and Society.* Prospect Heights, IL: Waveland Press.

Westley, W.A. 1970. *Violence and the police: A sociological study of law, custom, and morality.* Cambridge, MA: MIT Press.

Wilson, James Q. and George L. Kelling. 1982. Broken windows. *Atlantic Monthly* 249 (3): 29–38.

Police Discretionary Behavior
A Study of Style

Laure Weber Brooks

INTRODUCTION

The exercise of discretion by police has been the focus of an enormous amount of research. The issues of how police spend uncommitted time, how quickly they respond to calls for assistance, and what police do when handling a call for service have all received attention. While all police officers exercise some discretion, not all exercise the same levels of discretion. There are many factors which affect the degree of leeway an officer has in determining outcomes. Officers may develop response styles and these styles may affect not only police perceptions, but they may also predispose the officer to act in certain ways. Additionally, levels of discretion are contingent on the flexibility that police departments allow their officers, by policy, in handling day to day calls for service. When organizational rules are strict, less discretion is afforded to police. Conversely, when rules are vague or lax, officers are allowed, or perhaps forced, to make their own decisions on how to conduct themselves.

Much research attention has been paid to the examination of what factors affect police discretionary behavior. To explain this behavior, research has focused primarily on the characteristics of the situation in which police act (Engel, Sobol, and Worden, 2000; Terrill and Mastrofski, 2002; Engel, 2003; Novak, Frank, Smith, and Engel, 2002; McCluskey, Mastrofski, and

Prepared especially for *Critical Issues in Policing* by Laure Weber Brooks.

Parks, 1999; Mastrofski, Reisig, and McCluskey, 2002; Mastrofski, Snipes, Parks, and Maxwell, 2000; Terrill and Reisig, 2003; Riksheim and Chermak, 1993; Klinger, 1994; Lundman, 1994; Klinger, 1996; Worden and Shepard, 1996; Worden, 1989; Friedrich, 1977; Smith and Visher, 1981; Ericson, 1982; Black, 1980). Other discretionary factors which have received scholarly attention include: characteristics of the police organization (Mastrofski, Ritti, and Hoffmaster, 1987; Crank, 1993; Riksheim and Chermak, 1993; Wilson, 1968; Smith, 1984; Brown, 1981; Mastrofski, 1981; Sherman, 1983), characteristics of the environment or neighborhood in which the police work (Crank, 1993; Terrill and Reisig, 2003; Klinger, 1997; Riksheim and Chermak, 1993; Rossi, et al., 1974; Smith, 1986; Nardulli and Stonecash, 1981; Ostrom et al., 1977; Brown, 1981; Mastrofski, 1981; Smith and Klein, 1984), and characteristics of the officer involved in the encounter (Crank, 1993; Brooks, Piquero, and Cronin, 1993; DeJong, 2003; Terrill and Mastrofski, 2002; Riksheim and Chermak, 1993; Friedrich, 1977; Bloch and Anderson, 1974; Worden, 1989; Brown, 1981; Brooks, 1986). Taken together, the research concerning these four dimensions (situational, organizational, environmental, and officer) provide us with information on the determinants of police behavior.

With the advent of community policing, which has as a basic tenet the recognition that law enforcement behavior is not always the best way to handle social problems, scholars have speculated about how police discretion may be influenced by this movement. Mastrofski, Worden, and Snipes (1995) studied the determinants of police discretion in a police department which had implemented community policing. They explored the possibility that, due to the focus on community preferences and less on legal requirements that community policing encourages, officers might tend to rely less on legal variables (strength of evidence, seriousness of offense, the preference of the victim, etc.) and more on extralegal variables (suspect and victim characteristics). They found, though, that legal variables actually showed a much stronger effect on the arrest decision than did the extra-legal ones, however, this depended on the officer's attitude about community policing. Officers who were supportive of community policing were more selective in making arrests and tended to rely less on legal variables, than were officers who were not supportive of community policing. Overall, the more positive the officers were toward community policing, the less likely they were to effect an arrest. These researchers concluded that pro-community policing officers arrest more selectively and rely less on legal variables, but show no greater reliance on extra-legal variables to guide their arrest decision than officers who are not pro-community policing.

Novak, Frank, Smith, and Engel (2002) in comparing beat and community officers, found no significant direct influence of type of officer assignment on arrest decisions. However, in a study examining citizens' preference, Mastrofski, Snipes, Parks, and Maxwell (2000) found that officers with a strong proclivity for community policing were more responsive to requests by citizens. It has also been speculated that in the spirit of community policing, police administrators may demand that officers take a zero tolerance approach toward crime and thus increase police arrest behavior (Nowicki, 1998). Unfortunately, as Nowicki (1998) points out, a zero tolerance policy goes against community empowerment, problem solving, exercise of discretion, and the involvement of the community, which are all basic tenets of community policing.

This article will commence with a discussion of the definition of police discretion in order to present a clear picture of the focus of this research, while discussing both the benefits and the problems associated with police discretion. Next, attention will turn to the role of police in society. Third, a discussion of police orientations or styles of policing is presented. Finally, this article will conclude with a discussion of research findings concerning the determinants of police behavior.

POLICE DISCRETION

At least some discretion is exercised in every aspect of the police task. Some discretionary actions involve very subtle and perhaps minor decisions, while others involve blatant and important ones. Police discretion exists when officers have some leeway or choice in how to respond to a situation. The fewer the rules about handling incidents and situations, the more discretion officers have. Discretion involves both action and inaction (Davis, 1968; Ericson, 1982). Not doing something may be equally as important as doing something. Discretion involves both having the power to decide which rules apply to a given situation and whether or not to apply these rules (Ericson, 1982). Both of these decisions have potentially important implications for the community and for the police department.

Police discretion has been justified on many grounds including: the existence of vague laws, limited resources, community alienation, the need to individualize the law, and the fact that many violations are minor in nature. The exercise of police discretion poses some difficulties, such as: unequal treatment of citizens, interference with due process, a reduction in deterrent effects, and the hidden or unreviewable nature of many discretionary decisions. Police discretion exists at both the individual level (patrolling strategies, decisions to arrest, stop and frisk, write a report, etc.) and at the administrative or departmental level (manpower levels, allocation of personnel and resources, policies, training, etc.).

Police departments are being both encouraged and perhaps compelled to enact clear policies regulating officer actions. As Alpert and Fridell (1992) aptly point out, the purpose of departmental policy is to reduce officer or individual discretion, as well as to help officers prepare for situations they may confront. Clearly, some officer decisions, such as the decision to arrest, how to patrol, and to stop and frisk should be made with a significant amount of individual discretion, while others, such as the use of deadly force and continuing a police pursuit, are certain candidates for a reduced amount of discretion.

THE POLICE ROLE

To understand the behavior of police, we need to first clarify the functions of police or the police role in society. The appropriate role of police is an area where there is some dissension among scholars. Scholars generally agree that, in practice, police have multiple functions, many of which involve situations where no crime has occurred. While some scholars disagree that police response to such matters should be an appropriate police function, most would concur that they do represent a substantial portion of police activity (Goldstein, 1977; Nardulli and Stonecash, 1981; Scott, 1981; Reiss, 1971; Mastrofski, 1983). Thus, scholars not only recognize the existence of the law enforcement role of police, but also the order maintenance component of policing. While this noncriminal component is referred to in different terms in the police literature and all do not agree on the exact nature of these noncriminal activities, most recognize there is a distinction between traditional law enforcement response and this noncriminal dimension. However, for certain situations (such as arrest for domestic violence), the distinction between law enforcement and order maintenance behavior is less clear. Of major importance is the recognition that the police task is one most accurately described as dealing with many different types of problems (Goldstein, 1979).

With the advent of community policing, the police role has changed somewhat. Community policing, which is generally expected to include creative problem solving, community partnership and empowerment, decentralization, flexible responses, supportive environments, and risk taking behavior on the part of police (Greene, 1998; Skogan, 1998), requires more of our officers than before. It is clear then, that police in our society have multiple functions to perform. Additionally, the exercise of discretion depends on many factors. One important factor concerns the development of styles or orientations. This issue is discussed in the following section.

ORIENTATIONS OF POLICE OR STYLES OF POLICING

Given the wide discretion of police and their multiple functions, many of which are noncriminal, it is interesting to consider how these discretionary judgments are made. In view of suggestions made in previous research, we can no longer ignore the role that attitudes, orientations, or styles of policing play (Brown, 1981; Smith and Klein, 1984; Berk and Loseke, 1981; Brooks, 1986). Wilson (1968:38) contends that police make judgments about situations and individuals, and practice distributive justice. They evaluate the moral character of victims and suspects, and these judgments determine action. Worden (1995:50) argues that a police officer's belief system is "comprised of beliefs, attitudes, values, and other 'subjective outlooks.'" Others have also suggested that the exercise of police discretion is structured by the officer's belief system (Werthman and Piliavin, 1967). Police develop indicators which are used to determine behavior. Past experience leads police to make conclusions concerning suspiciousness, crime proneness, and the moral character of certain types of individuals (Werthman and Piliavin, 1967).

Police develop styles of policing which affect their discretionary behavior (Chatterton, 1983; Wilson, 1968; Brown, 1981). Some have argued that certain types of police departments encourage different styles of policing (Wilson, 1968). For example, in a "legalistic" police department, law enforcement activities are emphasized over order maintenance behavior (Wilson, 1968). In the same vein, Chatterton (1983) argues that an individual officer's style of policing affects the outcome of encounters. He argues that some officers are overzealous and are preoccupied with arrest while others operate on the premise that "doing justice" is the underlying goal of policing.

Brown (1981), Muir (1977), and Ericson (1982) have been advocates of the need to consider police attitudes or orientations in our understanding of police discretionary behavior. Brown (1981) argues that to understand what determines the routine choices that patrol officers make, we need to examine the beliefs that officers hold toward their job, the law, and the events and people they confront in the daily course of their occupation. Police do not react to each incident as though it were unique, rather they generalize. They fashion a coherent set of beliefs or orientations which guide their behavior. The belief system they develop structures their perceptions and definitions of order, and thereby provides the norms and standards that influence their discretionary behavior. Brown (1981:26) contends that the exercise of discretion requires the use of beliefs and values or an "operational style." According to Brown, the decision to act is partly the result of a succession of choices that the patrol officer has made prior to the actual encounter (such as decisions on the appropriateness of service or order maintenance activities, crime control preoccupation, utilization of time, etc.). These decisions or attitudes shape discretionary choices, although Brown argues that action is not totally based on beliefs but also on other factors such as organizational and environmental characteristics.

Ericson (1982:25) contends that officers develop a "recipe of rules" which guide their behavior. This recipe of rules is essentially a collection of rules-of-thumb learned on the job which mediate actual events, police departmental rules, and legal codes. The community, the law, and the policing organization provide the officer with rules, and these rules provide the officer with a sense of order—what the officer perceives as appropriate conduct (Ericson, 1982:26). This sense of order may affect not only the ultimate outcome of encounters, but also the process by which police achieve their outcome. This process involves the interaction between police and citizens, both as complainants and suspects.

It is clear from this review of the literature that many scholars believe that attitudes can play a role in police discretionary behavior. Many suggest that police officers act on the basis of predispositions or overall orientations and these predispositions provide an interpretive framework in which the situational cues are evaluated. Predispositions supply the officer with a repertoire of possible behavior and, from this collection, the officer selects an appropriate response to a specific situation. While there exists intuitive support for the connection between police attitudes and behavior, little empirical research has been conducted to examine this issue and the few studies which have addressed this have reported disappointing results (Crank, 1993; DeJong, 2003; Terrill and Mastrofski, 2002; Worden, 1989). The next section reviews previous research to identify what factors affect police discretionary behavior.

PREDICTORS OF POLICE BEHAVIOR

Much research has focused on determining what factors predict police behavior. While most of the attention has been paid to situational characteristics, however, research has also examined the situation, the police organization, the neighborhood, and the officer. Each level will be discussed in turn.

Organizational Variables

Organizational variables deal with characteristics of the police department in which the officer works and would include such factors as how bureaucratic and/or professional a police agency is, the size of the police department, whether the department rotates their officers among different areas, and supervision levels. Research examining organizational variables and their effect on police behavior has been minimal in recent years. A recent review of the literature has concluded that: organizational variables have largely been ignored in the study of police service behavior, organizational variables do appear to influence police use of force, and the effect of organizational variables on police arrest behavior is unresolved (Riksheim and Chermak, 1993).

The word "bureaucracy" has been used rather loosely in the police literature, but there does appear to be some consensus of the characteristics that bureaucratic police departments share. Bureaucratic police departments are thought to have a high degree of vertical differentiation (a tall rank structure), in which efficiency, discipline, and productivity are stressed (Bittner, 1970:52–62; Manning, 1977:193–197).

Skolnick (1966:11), in his case study of two police departments, contends that the degree to which a police department is organized around the military model with its stress on regulations, hierarchy, and obedience, determines the officer's "conception of order." He argues that in militaristic police departments, police members will have a rigid conception of order and routinism. Officers from these departments will be so concerned with following the rules and regulations that they will feel compelled to follow them to the letter in order to avoid punishment and this rigid conception of order may result in an emphasis on crime control behavior (Skolnick, 1966:11).

Police departments may also be classified on the basis of professionalism. Professional police organizations have been characterized in many different ways, but are thought to be agencies in which education, service, and citizen respect are central (Goldstein, 1977:2–3). Professional departments may have tall or shallow rank structure but generally have wide ranges of specialty units. These specialty units (such as various crime prevention, police-community relations, etc.) are thought to express the department's commitment to service and positive police-community relations. Professional police departments may be identified by various factors such as college incentive pay, community relations training, and percent of officers who are college educated (Smith and Klein, 1984; Swanson, 1978).

Smith's (1984) research is one of the few attempts to clarify the issues of bureaucracy and professionalism in police departments. Smith (1984) finds, when examining discretionary decisions by type of police organization, there are differences in factors that affect the decision to arrest. He finds that increasing the degree of bureaucracy in professional departments, results in a shift from conciliatory to punitive responses by police, at least in settling interpersonal disputes. Smith and Klein (1984) find that the probability of arrest increased as departments became more bureaucratic and more professional.

The size of a police department relates to how bureaucratic it is and some research has examined the effect of an agency's size on police discretionary behavior. Mastrofski, Ritti, and Hoffmaster (1987) found that officers in the larger, more bureaucratic police agencies were much less likely to arrest than were officers from the smaller departments. Contrary to Brown's (1981) findings, Mastrofski, Ritti, and Hoffmaster (1987) found that as department size and level of bureaucracy increased, the willingness of officers to make DUI arrests, decreased. They argue that this may be the result of the fact that small police departments may be easier to control by supervisors and that discretion in large police agencies is less accountable. It may be that large police departments are expected to have less effective controls on their members (due to the numerous members in the department), less group stability, and fewer and less effective links to the community—all of which detract from a service style of policing (Mastrofski, 1981).

How frequently police departments rotate their officers may also influence how officers behave. Departments which frequently rotate their personnel into different beats, shifts, or units inhibit close relations with community members (Brown, 1981:58; Murphy and Pate, 1977:39). Mastrofski (1981) argues that an officer's continued presence in a neighborhood increases the likelihood of repeated contact with citizens and helps officers develop empathy through an understanding of problems. He argues that this understanding will result in fewer instances of force and arrest. Murphy and Pate (1977:39, 225) use the phrase "stranger policing" to refer to jurisdictions which frequently rotate their officers. Davis (1978:135) discusses the "territorial imperative" which occurs when officers become protective of their area and their residents. This theme is central to the concept of community policing.

Neighborhood Variables

Prior research has identified several neighborhood or environmental variables which appear to be related to police discretionary behavior. They include: racial composition of a neighborhood, socio-economic status of an area, and the neighborhood crime rate. Some researchers have utilized a rate reflecting neighborhood "disadvantage" which includes variables relating to socio-economic status, race, and the percentage of female-headed households (Terrill and Reisig, 2003; Novak, Frank, Smith, and Engels, 2002; Mastrofski, Reisig, and McCluskey, 2002).

Research has found that in poor neighborhoods and neighborhoods where the proportion of black residents was high, there was more of a demand for police intervention (Walker, 1991; Nardulli and Stonecash, 1981). This was due to the increased number of "happenings" in these areas, as well as a belief in the appropriateness of calling the police in these areas (Nardulli and Stonecash, 1981:86–88). Similar results were found with respect to low socioeconomic status neighborhoods. Research examining the relationship between neighborhood socio-economic status and arrest, finds that these variables are significant predictors of this discretionary decision (Riksheim and Chermak, 1993; Smith, 1984; Smith and Klein, 1984; Smith, 1986) with the general finding being that higher arrest rates occur in poorer areas. It has also been argued that police are more likely to listen to a preference for arrest in a high socio-economic status neighborhood than in a poorer one (Smith and Klein, 1984). Additionally, police respond differently to the settlement of disputes depending on the socioeconomic status of a neighborhood. Regardless of whether or not a preference for arrest was expressed, as the percentage of households below the poverty level increased, so did the probability of arrest (Smith and Klein, 1984).

Research examining how the crime rate of a neighborhood affects police discretionary behavior have resulted in mixed findings (Riksheim and Chermak, 1993). Perceptions of crime risk and the potential for danger to police may affect how police behave, and may appear to justify a coercive or aggressive police response in the minds of police (Mastrofski, 1981; Bayley and Mendelsohn, 1969). Klinger (1997) suggests that as crime increases in a neighborhood, police resources become scarce and officers must respond less vigorously (fewer arrests and reports, and less thorough investigations). Some research has indicated that the neighborhood crime rate may influence officer attitudes (Brooks, Piquero, and Cronin, 1994).

Terrill and Reisig (2003) found that police officers were significantly more likely to use higher levels of force when they encountered suspects in disadvantaged neighborhoods, i.e. those neighborhoods with higher percentages of homes below the poverty level, unemployment, female-headed households, and African Americans. They also found that higher levels of force are used in neighborhoods with higher homicides rates, independent of suspect characteristics such as suspect resistance and several officer characteristics (age, education, and training). They found evidence to support the finding noted by Smith (1986) that police "do act differently in different neighborhood contexts". Mastrofski, Reisig, and McCluskey (2002) found that police were significantly more likely to behave disrespectfully in disadvantaged neighborhoods, but argued that suspect behaviors are the most powerful predictors of police disrespect.

Situational Variables

Situational variables have received most of the research attention in terms of their effect on police discretionary behavior and involve characteristics of the encounter between the citizen(s) and the police. They include such variables as the characteristics of both the suspect and the complainant, the type of call for service or crime involved, and the visibility of the encounter.

One of the most frequently examined situational variables has been the race of the suspect and the results found in research are mixed. Some fairly recent research has found that nonwhite suspects are more likely to be arrested and/or to be treated more punitively by police (Powell, 1990; Terrill and Mastrofski, 2002; Smith and Visher, 1981; Smith and Davidson, 1984; Brooks, 1986), but other studies report no effect (Klinger, 1996; Smith and Klein, 1983; Smith, 1984). A recent study by Mastrofski, Reisig, and McCluskey (2002) found that in one city, minority suspects experienced disrespect from police less often than white suspects. They do acknowledge that this may be a result of a clear policy of the Police Chief in that city to curtail police abuse in that department. Engel (2003) found that nonwhite suspects were more likely to be noncompliant and to show all types of resistance toward police, with the exception of physical aggression. Some research on deadly force finds that blacks are disproportionately shot more often than are whites, however this may be due to an overrepresentation in serious crime (Geller and Karales, 1981; Fyfe, 1980), while other research reports no racial effect on deadly force decisions (Blumberg, 1981).

Early research found gender differences in police treatment of suspects and complainants, but recent research is somewhat mixed. Some research has found that either no gender differences occur or that they are less prominent than previously thought (Klinger, 1996; Smith and Visher, 1980; Smith and Visher, 1981; Krohn, et al., 1983; Visher, 1983; Smith and Davidson, 1983; Smith and Klein, 1983; Smith, 1984), but others suggest gender differences do occur with females being more likely to be treated forcefully or to be arrested (Terrill and Mastrofski, 2002; Novak, Frank, Smith, and Engel, 2002). Some research has found that female suspects act more disrespectfully towards officers than male suspects (Engel, 2003).

It is generally supported in the literature that individuals in the lower socio-economic strata receive harsher treatment by police (Black, 1971; Reiss, 1971; Black and Reiss, 1967; Friedrich, 1977; Lundman, 1974; Terrill and Mastrofski, 2002; Black, 1980; Riksheim and Chermak, 1993). It is important to note that these general findings may be related to the race and demeanor of the suspect and the complainant.

Research is also somewhat mixed regarding the effect of a citizen's age on police discretionary behavior. Some research finds that young suspects are more likely to be arrested, less likely to comply with police, more likely to be the recipients of deadly force by police, and/or that older complainants were more likely to be taken seriously (Sherman, 1980; Terrill and Mastrofski, 2002; Novak, Frank, Smith, and Engel, 2002; McCluskey, Mastrofski, and Parks, 1999; Friedrich, 1977), while other research indicates that suspect age is not an important predictor of police behavior (Klinger, 1996; Smith and Visher, 1981; Smith and Davidson, 1983; Smith, 1984; Visher, 1983).

The demeanor, or attitude, of the suspect and the complainant have received considerable attention, especially recently, in the research literature. The general finding has been that disrespectful or uncooperative citizens are more likely to be treated punitively (arrested, targets of force, less often accommodated as complainants) (Black and Reiss, 1970; Black, 1971; Brooks, 1986; Piliavin and Briar, 1964; Friedrich, 1977; Engel, Sobol, and Worden, 2000; Novak, Frank, Smith, and Engel, 2002; Smith and Visher, 1981; Ericson, 1982; Black, 1970; Sherman, 1980; Visher, 1983; Smith, 1986; Smith, 1987). A hostile attitude may signify a threat to an officer's control or a challenge to their authority. However, questions concerning the measurement of demeanor have been raised (Klinger, 1994). Klinger (1994) argues that previous studies examining the effect of suspect demeanor on police behavior have been flawed due to the failure to properly measure "demeanor". Specially, he argues that previous research may have included illegal conduct by the suspect in their demeanor measure and that previous research does not control adequately for the suspect's behavior during the entire encounter (before police arrive, toward police during the encounter, and toward others during the encounter). He finds that when these two problems are corrected, that demeanor does not significantly affect arrest, except in the case of extreme hostility (Klinger, 1994; Klinger, 1996) and suggests that there may be implications for findings concerning other extra-legal variables as well. Several scholars responded to this argument and reanalyzed data sets with new measures of demeanor. Lundman (1994) did find that the effects of demeanor depended on how demeanor was measured, while Worden and Shepard (1996) concluded that their research provides no evidence that previous research findings were flawed due to an improper measurement of demeanor. Terrill and Mastrofski (2002), when using an expanded view of force, found that officers were more coercive toward disrespectful suspects than they were to respectful ones.

Research has been fairly consistent in the finding that when a complainant expresses a preference for arrest, an arrest is more likely to occur (Black, 1971; Black, 1970; Friedrich, 1977; Smith and Visher, 1981; Visher, 1983; Novak, Frank, Smith, and Engel, 2002; Smith, 1987; Worden, 1989; Brooks, 1986). The degree of relational distance or the degree of intimacy between suspects and complainants seems to be related to police behavior, as well.

Research indicates that as relational distance decreases or intimacy increases, police are less likely to take official action (Black, 1971, 1970; Friedrich, 1977; Smith and Visher, 1981). It may be that police believe that taking official action against a suspect who is in a relationship with the complainant may cause future problems or they may feel that it is not part of police responsibility. Mastrofski, Snipes, Parks, and Maxwell (2000) found an interaction between officer characteristics and responsiveness to citizen requests with male, less experienced officers who had a proclivity toward community policing, to be significantly more likely to give citizens what they request.

Characteristics of the encounter itself have received attention in the study of police discretionary behavior. Generally, research indicates that the more serious the offense that police encounter, the more likely a harsher disposition will be the result (Wilson, 1968; Ericson, 1982; Black, 1971; Piliavin and Briar, 1964; Smith and Visher, 1981; Brooks, 1986; Visher, 1983; Sherman, 1980; Smith and Klein, 1983; Smith, 1984).

Police, with the many demands on their time, may have to prioritize and choose to take action when dealing with serious crimes. However, most research has found that the presence of injuries was not an important determinant of arrest (Smith and Klein, 1984; Worden and Pollitz, 1984). Some research has found that when an encounter is visible (public) or when others were present (including supervisors), that police would be more likely to either write a report, make an arrest, or use force (Friedrich, 1977; Brooks, 1986; Reiss, 1971; Smith and Visher, 1981; Smith and Klein, 1983; Smith, 1984). Police may behave aggressively or officially when encounters are visible to others due to a belief that they must appear in control.

Officer Characteristics

Researchers have examined characteristics of the police officer (i.e. experience, race, gender, attitudes, etc.) to determine how they may influence what police do. Overall, these characteristics have not been found to exert strong influences on police discretionary behavior (Riksheim and Chermak, 1993) however some significant findings do emerge.

Some research has shown that less experienced officers perform more "work" (are more aggressive, stop and frisk more often, arrest more often) but more experienced officers engage in higher quality work and/or are less likely to engage in a legalistic manner (Friedrich, 1977; Sherman, 1980; Crank, 1993), while other research has found no relationship between individual officer experience and arrest behavior (Smith and Klein, 1983; Worden, 1989). Some research has suggested a connection between officer experience and certain officer attitudes (i.e. cynicism, role definition, perception of the public, perception of support by the criminal justice system) which may relate to discretionary behavior (Brooks, Piquero, and Cronin, 1993; Canter and Martensen, 1990; Hayeslip and Corder, 1987). As noted previously, some research has found a connection between officer experience and responsiveness to citizen preference (Mastrofski, Snipes, Parks, and Maxwell, 2000). Other recent research has found that encounters with officers who have less experience and less education result in increased levels of police force (Terrill and Mastrofski, 2002).

It has been assumed that the level of education of an officer affects police behavior, and the advent of police professionalism has definitely incorporated this premise. It has been argued that college educated officers learn things that are independent of what is taught in their curriculum, in addition to the course work which improves their work performance (Goldstein, 1977). The research, however, has resulted in findings which suggest that there is no effect of individual education on police behavior (Worden, 1989, 1990; Smith and Klein, 1983; Crank, 1993), but there may be a negative effect on arrest if officer education is measured at the departmental level (Smith and Klein, 1983). Some research has also suggested a link between officer education and certain attitudes (attitudes toward legal restrictions, attitudes toward discretion, perceptions of ethical conduct, cynicism, attitudes toward the community, solidarity, use of force, role) which may in turn influence police behavior (Shernock, 1992; Worden, 1990; Canter and Martensen, 1990; Hayeslip and Cordner, 1987; Brooks, Piquero, and Cronin, 1993).

The race of an officer has been examined in terms of its effect on police behavior. Early research reported a link between officer race and arrest behavior (Sherman, 1980), however more recent research finds no such effect (Worden, 1989; Smith and Klein, 1983). Some research concerning race and the use of force have reported racial differences. In general, the deadly force literature concludes that black officers are overrepresented in police shootings of citizens, although most researchers note that this relationship is most likely due to differential deployment of black officers in high crime areas and to the higher rate of black officers residing in these areas (Geller and Karales, 1981; Fyfe, 1978). There is some evidence that race may play a role in officer attitudes which may influence their behavior (Brooks, Piquero, and Cronin, 1993).

Generally, recent research has indicated that the gender of an officer exerts no influence on police behavior (Worden, 1989) while some earlier research found that females were less likely to make arrests, use deadly force, and be involved in deadly force situations (Sherman, 1980; Horvath, 1987; Grennan, 1978). Research has also suggested that officer attitudes may be related to gender (Dorsey and Giacopassi, 1986; DeJong, 2003; Brooks, Piquero, and Cronin, 1993). Unfortunately, there has been little empirical work examining police attitudes and their influence on police discretionary behavior, and the research which has been done on this issue have yielded disappointing results. As indicated previously, many scholars have speculated that attitudes influence behavior, however, few researchers have been able to actually demonstrate this link. Job dissatisfaction has been found to be related to police behavior, with high levels of job dissatisfaction associated with less legalistic and order maintenance behaviors, and police professionalism and attitudes toward street justice being unrelated to either behaviors (Crank, 1993). Some research has found that crime-control oriented officers are more likely to use force, but less likely to use the arrest sanction, than are officers who did not espouse this philosophy (Brooks, 1986). There has been some indication that attitudes may influence proactivity in traffic enforcement, but these attitudes play a very small role (Worden, 1989). Additionally, research has suggested that police prejudice may affect an officer's use of force (Friedrich, 1989). Overall, it seems apparent that attitudes contribute little to our understanding of police behavior (Worden, 1989; Terrill and Mastrofski, 2002; Smith and Klein, 1983; Riksheim and Chermak, 1993), however, it has been suggested that maybe the more fundamental attitudes held by police officers would do better in explaining police discretionary behavior, than the specific occupational attitudes typically examined in research (Worden, 1989). Certain police officer attitudes have been found to relate to other officer attitudes (Worden, 1995; Brooks, 1986), but additional research needs to clarify the presumed attitude-behavior link.

CONCLUSIONS

Since police exercise so much discretion, it is important to understand the factors which affect their discretionary choices. It appears as though organizational, situational, neighborhood, and officer characteristics all may play some part in the decisions that police make. While much research has focused on the determinants of police behavior and much has been learned in the process, there is still a great deal that is unexplained. As researchers use more sophisticated designs and methods, it becomes apparent that the study of police discretionary behavior is a complicated endeavor. Adopting a community policing philosophy in police departments would seem to influence the discretionary choices that police officers make and future research might do well to explore this issue. Additionally, while attitudes of police officers appear to contribute little to our understanding of police behavior, more attention should be paid to this area.

References

Alpert, G., and L. Fridell. 1992. *Police Vehicle and Firearms: Instruments of Deadly Force.* Prospect Heights, IL: Waveland Press.

Bayley, D. H., and H. Mendelsohn. 1969. *Minorities and the Police.* New York: Free Press.

Berk, S. F., and D. Loseke. 1981. "Handling Family Violence: Situational Determinants of Police Arrest in Domestic Disturbances." *Law and Society Review* 15(2).

Bittner, E. 1970. *The Functions of Police in Modern Society.* Rockville, MD: National Institute of Mental Health.

Black, D. 1971. "The Social Organization of Arrest." *Stanford Law Review* 23: 1087–1111.

———. 1980. *The Manners and Customs of Police.* New York: Academic Press.

Black, D., and A. Reiss. 1967. *Studies of Crime and Law Enforcement in Major Metropolitan Areas Vol. 2, Field Surveys III.* Section I: "Patterns of Behavior in Police and Citizen Transactions." Washington, D.C.: Government Printing Office.

———. 1970. "Police Control of Juveniles." *American Sociological Review* 35: 63–77.

Bloch, P., and D. Anderson. 1974. *Policewomen on Patrol: Final Report.* Washington, D.C.: Police Foundation.

Blumberg, M. 1981. "Race and Police Shootings: An Analysis in Two Cities." In *Contemporary Issues in Law Enforcement*, J. J. Fyfe (ed.). Beverly Hills: Sage.

Brooks, L. W. 1986. "Determinants of Police Officer Orientations and Their Impact on Police Discretionary Behavior." Unpublished Ph.D. Dissertation. Institute of Criminal Justice and Criminology, University of Maryland.

Brooks, L. W., A. Piquero, and J. Cronin. 1993. "Police Officer Attitudes Concerning Their Communities and Their Roles: A Comparison of Two Suburban Police Departments." *American Journal of Police* 12: 115–139.

———. 1994. "'Workload' Rates and Police Officer Attitudes: An Examination of 'Busy' and 'Slow' Precincts." *Journal of Criminal Justice* 22.

Brown, M. K. 1981. *Working the Street: Police Discretion and the Dilemmas of Reform.* New York: Russell Sage Foundation.

Canter, P., and K. Martensen. 1990. "Neiderhoffer Revisited—Comparison of Selected Police Cynicism Hypotheses." Paper presented to the 1990 American Society of Criminology Annual Meetings in Baltimore, Maryland.

Chatterton, M. 1983. "Police Work and Assault Charges." In *The Police Organization*, M. Punch (ed.). Cambridge: The MIT Press: 194–221.

Crank, J. P. 1993. "Legalistic and Order-Maintenance Behavior among Police Patrol Officers: A Survey of Eight Municipal Police Agencies." *American Journal of Police* XII: 103–126.

Davis, E. M. 1978. *Staff One: A Perspective on Effective Police Management.* Englewood Cliffs, NJ: Prentice-Hall.

DeJong, C. 2003. "Gender Differences in Officer Attitude and Behavior: Providing Comfort to Citizens." An Unpublished Paper. School of Criminal Justice, Michigan State University.

Dorsey, R., and D. Giacopassi. 1986. "Assessing Gender Differences in the Levels of Cynicism among Police Officers." *American Journal of Police* 5: 91–112.

Engel, R. S. 2003. "Explaining Suspects' Resistance and Disrespect toward Police." *Journal of Criminal Justice* 31: 475–492.

Engel, R. S., J. J. Sobol, and R. E. Worden. 2000. "Further Exploration of the Demeanor Hypothesis: The Interaction Effects of Suspects' Characteristics and Demeanor on Police Behavior." *Justice Quarterly* 17: 235–258.

Ericson, R. 1982. *Reproducing Order: A Study of Police Patrol Work.* Toronto: University of Toronto Press.

Friedrich, R. J. 1977. "The Impact of Organizational, Individual, and Situational Factors on Police Behavior." Ph.D. Dissertation. Department of Political Science, University of Michigan.

Fyfe, J. J. 1978. "Shots Fired: An Examination of New York City Police Firearms Discharges." Ph.D. Dissertation. School of Criminal Justice, State University of New York at Albany.

———. 1980. "Geographic Correlates of Police Shootings: A Microanalysis." *Crime and Delinquency* 17: 101–113.

Geller, R., and K. Karales. 1981. *Split Second Decisions: Shootings of and by the Chicago Police.* Chicago Law Enforcement Study Group.

Goldstein, H. 1977. *Policing a Free Society.* Cambridge: Harvard University Press.

———. 1979. "Improving Policing: A Problem Oriented Approach." *Crime and Delinquency* 25: 236–258.

Greene, J. "The Road to Community Policing in Los Angeles: A Case Study." In *Community Policing: Contemporary Readings*, 2/E, Geoffrey Alpert and Alex Piquero (eds.). Prospect Heights, IL: Waveland Press.

Grennan, S. 1987. "Findings on the Role of Officer Gender in Violent Encounters with Citizens." *Journal of Police Science and Administration* 15: 78–85.

Hayeslip, D., and G. Cordner. 1987. "The Effects of Community-Oriented Patrol on Officer Attitudes." *American Journal of Police* 6.

Horvath, F. 1987 "The Police Use of Deadly Force: A Description of Selected Characteristics of Intrastate Incidents." *Journal of Police Science and Administration* 15: 226–238.

Klinger, D. A. 1994. "Demeanor or Crime? Why 'Hostile' Citizens Are More Likely to Be Arrested." *Criminology* 32: 475–493.

———. 1996. "More on Demeanor and Arrest in Dade County." *Criminology* 34: 61–82.

———. 1997. "Negotiating Order in Patrol Work: An Ecological Theory of Police Response to Deviance." *Criminology* 35(2): 277–306.

Krohn, M., J. Curry, and S. Nelson-Krueger. 1983. "Is Chivalry Dead? An Analysis of Changes in Police Dispositions of Males and Females." *Criminology* 21: 395–416.

Lundman, R. J. 1994. "Demeanor or Crime? The Midwest City Police-Citizen Encounter." *Criminology* 32: 631–656.

Manning, P. 1977. *Police Work: The Social Organization of Policing.*Cambridge: The MIT Press.

Martin, D. 1976. *Battered Wives*. San Francisco: Glide Publications.

Mastrofski, S. 1981. "Policing the Beat: The Impact of Organizational Scale on Patrol Officer Behavior in Urban Residential Neighborhoods." *Journal of Criminal Justice* 9: 343–358.

———. 1983. "The Police and Noncrime Services." In *Evaluating Performance of Criminal Justice Agencies*, G. Whitaker and C. D. Phillips (eds.). Beverly Hills: Sage.

Mastrofski, S. D., M. D. Reisig, and J. D. McCluskey. 2002. "Police Disrespect toward the Public: An Encounter-Based Analysis." *Criminology* 40: 519–552.

Mastrofski, S. D., R. Ritti, and D. Hoffmaster. 1987. "Organizational Determinants of Police Discretion: The Case of Drinking-Driving." *Journal of Criminal Justice* 15: 387–402.

Mastrofski, S. D., J. B. Snipes, R. B. Parks, and C. D. Maxwell. 2000. "The Helping Hand of the Law: Police Control of Citizens on Request." *Criminology* 38: 307–342.

Mastrofski, S. D., R. E. Worden, and J. B. Snipes. 1995. "Law Enforcement in a Time of Community Policing." *Criminology* 33: 539–563.

McCluskey, J. D., S. D. Mastrofski, and R. B. Parks. 1999. "To Acquiesce or Rebel: Predicting Citizen Compliance with Police Requests." *Police Quarterly* 2: 389–416.

Muir, W. K. 1977. *Police: Streetcorner Politicians*. Chicago: University of Chicago Press.

Murphy, P. V., and T. Pate. 1977. *Commissioner*. New York: Simon and Shuster.

Nardulli, P. F., and J. M. Stonecash. 1981. *Politics, Professionalism, and Urban Services: The Police*. Cambridge: Oelgeschlager, Gunn, and Hain.

Novak, K. J., J. Frank, B. W. Smith, and R. S. Engel. 2002. "Revisiting the Decision to Arrest: Comparing Beat and Community Officers." *Crime and Delinquency* 48: 70–98.

Nowicki, D. 1998. "Mixed Messages." In *Community Policing: Contemporary Readings*, 2/E, Geoffrey Alpert and Alex Piquero (eds.). Prospect Heights, IL: Waveland Press.

Ostrom, E., R. B. Parks, and G. Whitaker. 1977. *The Police Services Study*. Bloomington: Workshop in Political Theory and Policy Analysis, Indiana University.

Piliavin, J., and S. Briar. 1964. "Police Encounters with Juveniles." *American Journal of Sociology* 70: 206–214.

Powell, D. D. 1990. "A Study of Police Discretion in Six Southern Cities." *Journal of Police Science and Administration* 17: 1–7.

Reiss, A. 1971. *The Police and the Public*. New Haven: Yale University Press.

Riksheim, E. C., and S. M. Chermak. 1993. "Causes of Police Behavior Revisited." *Journal of Criminal Justice* 21: 353–382.

Rossi, P., R. Berk, and B. Eidson. 1974. *The Roots of Urban Discontent: Public Policy, Municipal Institutions, and the Ghetto*. New York: John Wiley and Sons.

Scott, E. J. 1981. *Calls for Service: Citizen Demand and Initial Police Response*. Washington, D.C.: National Institute of Justice.

Sherman, L. 1980. "Causes of Police Behavior: The Current State of Quantitative Research." *Journal of Research in Crime and Delinquency* 17: 69–100.

———. 1983. "Reducing Police Gun Use: Critical Events, Administrative Policy, and Organizational Change." In *Control in the Police Organization*, M. Punch (ed.). Cambridge: The MIT Press.

Shernock, S. 1992. "The Effects of College Education on Professional Attitudes among Police." *Journal of Criminal Justice Education* 3: 71–92.

Skogan, W. 1998. "Community Policing in Chicago." In *Community Policing: Contemporary Readings*, 2/E, Geoffrey Alpert and Alex Piquero (eds.). Prospect Heights, IL: Waveland Press.

Skolnick, J. 1966. *Justice without Trial: Law Enforcement in a Democratic Society*. New York: John Wiley & Sons.

Smith, D. A. 1984. "The Organizational Aspects of Legal Control." *Criminology* 22: 19–38.

———. 1986. "The Neighborhood Context of Police Behavior." In *Crime and Justice: An Annual Review of Research* Vol. 8, A. J. Reiss and M. Tonry (eds.). Chicago: University of Chicago Press.

———. 1987. "Police Response to Interpersonal Violence: Defining the Parameters of Legal Control." *Social Forces* 65: 767–782.

Smith, D. A., and L. A. Davidson. 1984. "Equity and Discretionary Justice: The Influence of Race on Police Arrest Decisions." *Journal of Criminal Law* 75: 234–249.

Smith, D. A., and C. Visher. 1980. "Sex and Involvement in Deviance/Crime: A Quantitative Review of the Empirical Literature." *American Sociological Review* 45.

———. 1981. "Street Level Justice: Situational Determinants of Police Arrest Decisions." *Social Problems* 29: 167–178.

Smith, D. A., and J. R. Klein. 1983. "Police Agency Characteristics and Arrest Decisions." In *Evaluating Performance of Criminal Justice Agencies*, G. D. Whitaker and C. D. Phillips (eds.). Beverly Hills: Sage.

Smith, D. A., and J. Klein. 1984. "Police Control of Interpersonal Disputes." *Social Problems* 31: 468–481.

Swanson, C. 1978. "The Influence of Organization and Environment on Arrest Policies in Major U.S. Cities." *Policy Studies Journal* 7: 390–318.

Terrill, W., and S. D. Mastrofski. 2002. "Situational and Officer-Based Determinants of Police Coercion." *Justice Quarterly* 19: 215–248.

Terrill, W., and M. D. Reisig. 2003. "Neighborhood Context and Police Use of Force." *Journal of Research in Crime and Delinquency* 40: 291–321.

Visher, C. A. 1983. "Gender, Police Arrest Decisions, and Notions of Chivalry." *Criminology* 21: 5–28.

Walker, S. 1991. *The Police in America*, Second Edition. New York: McGraw-Hill.

Werthman, C., and I. Piliavin. 1967. "Gang Members and the Police." In *The Police: Six Sociological Essays*, David Bordua (ed.). New York: John Wiley & Sons.

Wilson, J. Q. 1968. *Varieties of Police Behavior.* Cambridge: Harvard University Press.

Worden, R. E. 1989. "Situational and Attitudinal Explanations of Police Behavior: A Theoretical Reappraisal and Empirical Assessment." *Law and Society Review* 23: 667–711.

Worden, R. E. 1990. "A Badge and a Baccalaureate: Policies, Hypotheses, and Further Evidence." *Justice Quarterly* 7: 565–592.

———. 1995. "Police Officers' Belief Systems: A Framework for Analysis." *American Journal of Police* 14: 49–81.

Worden, R. E., and A. A. Pollitz. 1984. "Police Arrests in Domestic Disturbances: A Further Look." *Law and Society Review* 18: 105–119.

Worden, R. E., and R. L. Shepard. 1996. "Demeanor, Crime, and Police Behavior: A Reexamination of the Police Services Study Data." *Criminology* 34: 83–105.

Policing and Reflection

Peter K. Manning

This article explores the consequences of reflexivity on policing.[1] Reflexivity is defined as the anticipatory shaping of action choices by imagining the response of the other. This "imagining" is shaped by the self's beliefs about others' anticipated reactions (Cullum-Swan, personal communication). Although reflexivity can be considered at the role level, it is also a correlate of framing (Goffman, 1974: 76) in the sense that once framed, an activity orchestrates expectations, but reflecting on action is also a structural property of modern societies (Giddens, 1991). Here, I explore television's role in reflexivity to suggest the importance of reflexivity to theorizing police.

MASTER TRENDS

Modern society is both reflective and reflecting. It is shaped by consideration and modification of decisions in light of their anticipated consequences. This process of reflection and consideration is central to social organization when social integration is partially determined by negotiation and social construction of meanings, and where stranger-stranger interaction is the mode. Clearly, the mass media play a central role in modern consciousness and should significantly shape systematic interpretive social theory. Unfortunately, current models of interaction and communication are derived from the assumptions of early twentieth century social psychology—the ideas of William James, G. H. Mead, and Charles Cooley.

Reprinted with permission of Academy of Criminal Justice Sciences, from the *Police Forum*, 6(4) (Oct. 1996): 1–5.

Mass media, especially television, must be dragged into modern theorizing because our sources of information and sensibilities are increasingly mediated. The media amplify the relevance of imagery, heighten reflexivity, and create seductive, alternative, often layered or laminated, social realities. Mass media create and authoritatively reify social forms, alter and reshape boundaries between the private and the public, personal and impersonal, and modify and mix communicational genres. Media events (those either created wholly by the media, or amplified and disseminated by them) compete profoundly with socialization and personal experience for salience in shaping worldviews. Media present mini-realities fabricated from fragments of actual events, fantasies, gossip, recreations, simulations, infotainments, altered and distorted imagery and self-conceptions, combining at times, cartoons, graphics, and human figures. Importantly, forms of electronically created reality, virtual reality, cyber- and hyper-space, and hypertexts, that simulate interpersonal relations by facilitating visual, computer-based, media connections between people, compete for relevance, time and intimacy, with embodied interpersonal relations. Electronically mediated communication via bulletin boards, e-mail, hypertexts, and Faxes, *simulates* the intimacy of personal private communication but does not require the use of a personal identity, real address, or even a socially legitimated self. Internet transactions are communications between electronically activated addresses, some of which may be false, mere numbers, or misrepresentations. This depersonalizes communication and mitigates authorship and obligation.

As this litany suggests, social control, whether by third parties, formal agencies of social control or informal sanctions, is matter of symbolizing consequences of behavior. When the imagery of control is conveyed electronically, social control works through distant surveillance and society resembles Bentham's panopticon, social control takes new forms and varieties.

In short, the self and other, ideas spawned nearly 100 years ago by philosophers, are now bound together in a symbolic threesome that includes the media. Given these changes in society and social control processes, re-thinking policing and other forms of social control is imperative. Television holds preeminent place in mediating experience. First, a quick overview of the sources of television's power (Manning, 1996).

SOME CONSEQUENCES OF TELEVISION'S PERSPECTIVE

Television's power comes from its counterintuitive presentation of time and space unfolding before the viewer's eyes. Violating the logic of causality, it represents itself as presenting the present, or the now, immediately. Watching television is an engaging experience that combines the real, the might be real, the surreal and the fantastic. Because it is a frame, it connects domestic life and the external world in marvelous complexity.

Its affect on personal relations is most striking when it seeks the immediate and thrusts itself into personal space, showing reactions to disasters, serial murders, or grand accomplishments. It also mimics the immediate, showing people's reactions to the aggressive intrusion of cameras, video crews, lights, microphones, and the interviewer.

The immediate fabrication of realities is television's forte. Television is a commercial industry that seeks to commodify visual pleasures. Interaction results between television's institutional biases, program structure and content and viewers' perceptions, producing reflexivity (seeing self as media sees self and others) in terms of television's perspective and a selectively induced blindness to other aspects of social structure. Here are some generalizations about the effects of television on the shape of experience.

Television provides a kind of meta-reading, or interpretations of interpretations, of experience. While local experience is both shaped by television and reduced in importance by it (Meyrowitz, 1986: Ch.6), overall local knowledge and experience are declining in importance in socialization. Television's eye and perspective compete with other knowledge. Recall that television produces and reproduces a special kind of distant and ironic perspective on much of social life. Television displays image assemblages or a pastiche that is often ironic and anti-authoritarian. Recycling views of the police on sit-coms, excessive parodies of violence in films; police knowledge and taste on *Cops*; *Hard Copy* and *America's Most Wanted* and on cartoons, it both caricatures authority and exaggerates its importance. Television "re-enacts" police-public scenes, conflating hypothetical dialogue, possible scenarios, real people and actors, tapes of actual voices and re-created dialogues, calling these "reality shows" (*Detroit Free Press* 14 July, 1991).

Television amplifies some emotions, and is lodged in the self. Television is framed apart from everyday life yet is deeply grounded in it. Television is rooted in the emotional preconditions and predispositions of modern life, and reproduces experiences meaningful to the viewer's self. Television is a powerful projective source from which emotions are read and read-off (Goffman, 1959: Ch 1). Television seems to produce a seductive electronic place, not exclusively the world of the floating *simulacra* (symbols without clear referents), or even Baudrillard's hyperreality (1990), but an active source of experience. Television, in some dialogue with viewers' readings, produces redundant, cybernetic, emotional, and expressive communication that provides a kind of "back channel" self-affirmation.[2]

POLICING AND MEDIA

The dominant explanation for the behavior of the police is a sociocultural theory. Assuming that policing is shaped by a single subculture arising from the interaction of a risky and dangerous working environment, the need to assert authority and apply violence, and the social isolation of officers (Skolnick,

1967), the experience of the urban patrolman is thus caricatured. Modifications of this view, and theories of policing based on the centrality of violence (Bittner, 1992), omit the effects of police views of themselves as an aspect of their conduct and decisions (Kappeler, Sluder and Alpert, 1994). The conflict between internal rules, regulations, policies and procedures and external audiences' expectations is a powerful source of police dilemmas that puts segments of police at risk differentially. Information technology has segmented policing and given rise to a middle management cadre. The high politics of policing, relations with the power elites in a community, elected officials, and significant minority groups, is made more salient by the community policing reform movement.

Unfortunately, theories of policing heretofore discuss the media only in the context of managing them or their role in amplifying scandals. Mass media, especially television, sets public expectations, amplifying scandal and police crimes, misconduct, and rule-violation, as well as amplifying the symbolic connection of the police to the law and the moral structure of society.

Real policing appears on the news, recreations of policing on *Emergency 911*, dramatizations of policing on *Cops*, fantasies surround police in feature films, and officers discuss and reflect on policing in talk shows, features and interview programs. The media eyes policing dramatically, as news, as feature material, and as an exciting source of probative "investigative journalism" and scandalous misconduct. Media reshow and reshow police-dominated scenes, looping them back into consciousness. The O.J. Simpson trial saturated even the most avid viewer with repeated film snippets. These salient amplification loops serve to punctuate and encourage police focus on *symbolic violence*, that is, maintaining the imagery of vertical and horizontal ordering consistent with the conventional wisdom (Manning, 1997), and to give credence to their role in communications work generally (Ericson, forthcoming). The police see themselves as we do: as at least in part a product of mass media imagery. Let us now rehearse the logic of police reflexivity.

THE LOGIC OF POLICE REFLEXIVITY

Police Work (1977) argued, following Hughes (1958), that metaphorically the police claim a mandate to assert binding moral definitions of the nature of the risks they are permitted to take. An occupational culture grows up around the routine risks and mistakes (Hughes, 1958). Given this mandate, that is if a negotiated legitimacy is granted, they will seek a license to practice, to be paid and rewarded for their social role. The mandate and license are thus matters negotiated in the arena of public opinion, and reflect transactions between significant and powerful audiences and the police. The mandate expands and contracts reflecting the tasks society expects and rewards, and in connection with similar dynamics of other competing occupations. Critical in this expansion and contraction process are scandals and public events that display for public scrutiny practices normally concealed and kept well backstage.

Risk plays a central role in policing, but "risk" is in part objective and in part a social construction. The work involves periodic high risk situations in which the probability of making an error is high, and police in the past were well-protected by common-law tradition (in liability and torts), case law, and criminal law, against prosecution for their judgments. The police culture reflects, responds to, and incorporates routine risks and solutions thereto. The occupational culture is a social creation that mystifies, dramatizes, and elevates the ideological notion that policing is essentially risky, violent crime control. Risk is also avoided by officers; both risk avoidance and risk-seeking are commonly seen. Consider the viability of the advice: "keep low, don't rock the boat"; emphasis upon "covering your ass" (having a ready excuse or account for any detected error or lying about it) and the fear of capricious discipline. Patrol officers find risk in not only in citizen encounters, but also in the possible consequences of errors, given the punitive and rule-focused character of the police-bureaucracy, and the inherent conservatism of senior officers. Evidence from our recent COPS-funded research suggests that many patrol officers resist "community policing" because it alters their role repertoires and significant audiences, and seek job protection in union contracts.

The media add a new and growing level of risk because of their access to police records (through the Freedom of Information Law). Television's (since 1974 with the introduction of hand-held video cameras) ability to respond quickly to events is awesome. The combination of mobile units for monitoring images and sound, satellites for world-wide transmission, small hand-held television cameras, citizen access to 911 and emergency numbers via cellular phones, the commonality of citizen-owned video cameras, and computers and faxes that send and receive images digitally all reduce the lag between event and coverage, even world-wide coverage, to minutes. Local news formats including routine on the scene reporting, the emphasis on the banal, titillating and commercial, and emergent journalistic ethics that emphasize, especially since Watergate, anti-authoritarian and anti-institutional biases, all contribute to the police as a cynosure. Police, in turn, employ media officers, attending training schools and Management Institutes on media management, issue press releases and videos, and use the media to convey their accomplishments. These structural conditions tend to both amplify and reduce protection for police risk-taking.

POLICE EVENTS AND REFLECTIONS

Television has subtle effects on policing and vice-versa, but these effects are not well known. I speculate here on the kinds of events that shape policing and those relevant to a communicational theory of policing. The number of media-amplified incidents involving the police since the widespread dissemination of the video of the Rodney King beating is remarkable. Here are some observations:

1. The police self is shaped by mass media, pop culture versions of the self, particularly those televised, while television's police reflect partially and in a systematically distorted fashion police views of themselves policing.

2. Media revelations of scandal and malfeasance create media issues arising from the media, sustained by the media, and amplified by the media. These revelations are looped, and stimulate a media-reaction cycle. The first indications are responded to by "containment moves" by police, attempts to maintain the original police framing of an event (Goffman, 1974). Police actions are seen as "damage control," rather than response to the problem (Chan, 1996), and the media continue to make counter-counter-containment moves.

3. The significant others of police are not only embodied others in co-presence, but may be television figures, celebrities, and media heroes: Clint Eastwood as Harry Callahan, Jack Lord as Steve McGarrett of *Hawaii 5-0*, figures on *Adam 12*, and *Dragnet* (sanitized renditions of the LAPD) as well as the anti-heroes on *Hill Street Blues, NYPD Blue* and *Homicide*. These figures are evoked by cliché, shorthand phrases, such as "Make my day," and "Just the facts, Ma'am."

4. Police life choices and selves are shaped by abstracted typifications and stereotypes seen on "Infotainment" programs (combining "information" and "entertainment") such as *True Stories of the Highway* Patrol, *Cops* and *America's Most Wanted*. These programs, like *Rescue 911*, are *simulations* of policing, combining written scripts, commentary, reflections, and interviews with film of working police. These shows contain scenes stylishly edited by skilled television producers, cut from hours of film and censored by officers and administrators in the host police departments (Hallett and Powell, 1995).

5. Police see themselves as international figures. Both the relative salience and number of mass media figures shaping experience are expanded by cable, mass satellite distribution of television and movies, and international cable channels that broadcast in indigenous languages. The beating of Rodney King was shown internationally within hours of its appearance on a Los Angeles television station.

6. The police are active in live scenes, nightly news and in emergency situations, now frequently covered quickly by television. The media are also "on the scene," televising brutal and tragic events live—suicides, murders and violent assaults, natural and human-caused disasters (hurricanes, floods, tornadoes, earthquakes and explosions) and human-caused tragedies such as terrorist bombings and hostage situations. Police and other agents of control (soldiers, firefighters, EMS technicians and ambulance drivers), are typically asked to explain what happened, what is happening, or what will happen.

7. Media cover assiduously axial media events, events created by their actions, such as showing the Rodney King beating, the sequel of the Rodney King beating, the riots after the acquittal of LAPD officers Koon and Powell (convicted later of beating Rodney King), and the O.J. Simpson trial of February-September, 1995 (Manning, 1996, Goodwin, 1995). Axial media events are real-world events transformed using television's code so that the line between personal experience, audience experience, and politics is blurred and reduced. Political, moral and personal meanings are conflated in a series of brief repeated images.

8. Axial media events become interwoven tightly with actual events and shape policing. This is almost the essential feature of a media "scandal." For example, an LAPD detective, Mark Fuhrman, testifies in the Simpson trial, says he has not used "nigger" in ten years, and subsequently is found to be a liar. This raises questions about the credibility of other evidence he has presented. The media publicize his perjury. Chief Willie Williams of the LAPD, interviewed on *Good Morning America*, minimizes racism in the force, says it is being dealt with, and announces that the LAPD are investigating Fuhrman's previous cases (*GMA* Aug. 30, 1995). Two LAPD detectives appear on *GMA* (March 1, 1996) and *Geraldo* on CNBC (April 22, 1996) defending their actions.

9. One media makes "news" of other media's stories. These media loops are often highly embedded. The Fuhrman story is written about in the newspapers and news magazines. Television reporters interview officers in the LAPD and elsewhere about their reactions to the media reactions to Fuhrman's televised remarks. These were played from a tape and shown on graphics on the screen before the interviews. The media promote complex intertextuality (using one text within another) and stimulate reflexivity. The *Washington Observer* (August, 31 1995) claimed that "The Fuhrman tapes are the missing sound track for the Rodney King beating."

10. Real events, e.g., the AFT-FBI raid on the Waco compound of Koresh and his followers in April, 1993, become the basis for television movies in matter of months. Media sitcoms and action stories are converted into TV shows and movies; movies are converted into TV shows, movies scripts made into books. LAPD officers see themselves portrayed in re-runs of Jack Webb Productions (*Adam 12* and *Dragnet*). Webb had been advised by LAPD Chiefs Davis and Parker and sought to portray the LAPD as they urged (Gates, 1993). Chief Gates played himself and another chief in two televised dramas.

11. The justice system uses videos to prove and prosecute. Videos were used in the prosecution of Marion Barry for drug use; the FBI's ABSCAM operation to trap corrupt politicians, and in the Simpson

trial. They are used to improve efficiency e.g., faxing accident reports to citizens, videoing bookings for transmission to the jail to reduce paperwork (in Lansing, Michigan).

12. Media is claimed by media to shape police behavior. A reduction in baton beatings, and the use of taser guns, is reported after the Rodney King events (*Newsweek* September 4, 1995). William Bratton resigns or is fired by the mayor as police commissioner, according to *Newsweek* (April 7, 1996), because he was taking too much media attention away from Mayor Giuliani.

13. Videos of police misconduct become the basis for national news, e.g., the high speed chase and beating of fleeing immigrants by the Riverside County, California Sheriff's Department (March, 1996); the videoed brutalizing of a black women by a state patrolman in South Carolina after she had not stopped when he had signaled to stop (from an unmarked car) (April, 1996).

14. Police engage in media-publicity contests. A few days after the videos of the South Carolina State Trooper screaming at and dragging the black motorist out of her car appeared, the Director of Public Safety in South Carolina appeared on *Good Morning America* (April 23, 1996). He provided a video that he narrated showing a state patrol officer standing beside a car talking to a stopped motorist. He was suddenly grazed by the rear view mirror of a passing truck. The director praised the officer, citing him as an example of the high quality of police in South Carolina: "The officer showed courage and determination, got in his car, pursued the motorist, was verbally assaulted but arrested him with the help of citizens. He followed proper procedures . . . did not lose his cool."

15. Videos in turn are used to protect and defend police actions. The Lansing, Michigan Police Department filmed a raid of an illegal drinking establishment that consisted of shadowy scenes of officers booking suspects, because a woman present claimed harassment. Lansing police released to the press a video of the jailing of a man who subsequently died in custody (MSU State News 14 March 1996).

In these ways, media create and sustain police selves, reflect on those selves and interweave the real and imaginary in their renditions of police work. Police find the media monitoring their behavior, e.g., news helicopters filmed the chase of immigrants in Riverside County, and supervisors review film from car-mounted cameras. Police selectively use electronic and visual technology for defense and containment of media scrutiny. Police counter media definitions with their own media technology. Visual forms of social control shape policing internally and externally. This means at the very least that media working and effects, their simulacra (and its commodification), are relevant to constructing theories of police behavior in the late nineties.

Notes

[1] The concept of reflexivity is widely used and cited in the social sciences. e.g., Sewell, 1992, Luhmann 1990, Giddens 1991, and G. H. Mead, 1934.

[2] Television is not all of a piece. It shows films of ballet, classical theatre and concerts; "live" coverage of games, news conferences and disasters, live on film debates in the British Parliament, the U.S. Senate and House, highly stylized news, religious ceremonies, and advertising and promotional programs for real-estate selling, fortune hunting, etc., created genres such as "rockumentaries," "docudramas," and "fact-based dramas," and reshown (films of) all of the above. It combines genres, innovatively shaping them, and embedding one within the other, e.g., showing news clips of past sports events at the half-time of a televised game and employing a round-table talk-show format to discuss them. As a result, it is laminated "internally" with meaning.

References

Baudrillard, Jean. 1990. *Selected Writings* edited by Mark Poster. Palo Alto: Stanford University Press.

Bittner, E. 1992. *Aspects of Police Work*. Boston: Northeastern University Press.

Chan, J. 1996. "Changing Police Culture." *British Journal of Criminology* 36:109–34.

Ericson, Richard. Forthcoming. *Policing the Risk Society*. University of Toronto Press. forthcoming.

Gibbs, Jack. 1989. *Control*. Urbana: University of Illinois Press.

Giddens, A. 1991. *Modernity and Self-Identity*. Palo Alto: Stanford University Press.

Goffman, E. 1974. *Frame Analysis*. New York: Basic Books.

Goffman, E. 1959. *The Presentation of Self in Everyday Life*. Garden City: Doubleday Anchor.

Goodwin, C. 1995. "Professional Vision." *American Anthropologist* 96:606–33.

Hallett, M. and D. Powell. 1995. "Backstage with 'Cops': The Dramaturgical Reification of Police Subculture in American Infotainment." *American Journal of the Police*.

Hughes, E. C. 1958. *Men and Their Work*. Glencoe, IL: Free Press.

Kappeler, V., R. Sluder and G. Alpert. 1994. *Forces of Deviance*. Prospect Heights, IL: Waveland Press.

Luhmann, N. 1990. *The Risk Society*. Berlin: deGruyter/Aldine.

Lyon, D. 1995. *The Surveillance Society*. Minneapolis: University of Minnesota Press.

Manning, Peter K. 1977. *Police Work*. Cambridge, MA: MIT Press.

Manning, Peter K. 1996. "Dramaturgy, Politics, and the Axial Event." *The Sociological Quarterly* 37: 261–78.

Manning, Peter K. Forthcoming, 1997. "Media Loops." In Donna Hale and Frankie Bailey, eds., *Popular Culture, Crime and Justice*. Belmont, CA: Wadsworth.

Mead, G. H. 1934. *Mind, Self and Society*. Chicago: University of Chicago Press.

Meyrowitz, J. 1986. *No Sense of Place*. New York: OUP.

Sewell, William, Jr. 1992. "A Theory of Structure: Duality, Agency and Transformation." *American Journal of Sociology* 98: 1–29.

Skolnick, J. 1967. *Justice Without Trial*. New York: Wiley.

Police Response to Persons with Mental Illness

Wesley G. Jennings & Edward J. Hudak

Prior to the 1960s the mentally ill were virtually "warehoused" in large state psychiatric hospitals in abject living conditions and with little emphasis placed on their treatment (Perez, Leifman, & Estrada, 2003). The nineteenth century marked the beginning in British and American construction of a variety of "welfare institutions," such as insane asylums, workhouses, and prisons designed to provide custodial care for the mentally ill. The housing of these individuals was well intended and developed from a genuine concern for the well-being and safety of the mentally ill. However, the underlying motive was to protect the public from real or perceived abnormal behavior. Little time elapsed before these institutions became severely overcrowded. They quickly became characterized by their inhumane living conditions and for their insensitive treatment of the mentally ill. This reality combined with the growing concern for the mentally ill, the increased availability of revolutionary psychotropic medications (e.g., Thorazine), the economic cost associated with their institutionalization, and state legislative restrictions on involuntary commitment, permissible length of stay, and community mental health centers contributed to an era of immense social reform during the second half of the twentieth century (Aderibigbe, 1997; Murphy, 1989). These driving factors became the foundation for what is known as the *deinstitutionalization movement* and resulted in a paradigmatic shift in treatment of the mentally ill from "long-term psychiatric hospitalization to more independent living environments" (Krieg, 2001, p. 367).

Prepared especially for *Critical Issues in Policing* by Wesley G. Jennings and Edward J. Hudak.

The principal humanitarian, treatment-focused, and fiscally efficient determinants that fueled the deinstitutionalization movement have since contributed to the displacement of the mentally ill from within the mental health system and into the criminal justice system. Over the past five decades, the number of mentally ill institutionalized in state psychiatric facilities has markedly declined, from approximately 560,000 in 1955, to fewer than 60,000 today (National Association of State Mental Health Program Directors Research Institute, 2000). Comparatively, there are now more people with mental illnesses institutionalized in our nation's jails and prisons than in all the state psychiatric hospitals combined (Sigurdson, 2000). Roughly one out of every 15 individuals in United States' jails suffers from a major mental disorder, such as a major depressive disorder, schizophrenia, or bipolar disorder (Steadman, Deane, Morrissey, Westcott, Salasin, & Shapiro, 1999; Walsh & Holt, 1999). The dynamic changes in public policy regarding the mentally ill mean that a fairly significant segment of the population needs a specialized response on behalf of the police. The purpose of this article is to begin with a brief overview of the impact of both deinstitutionalization and of the criminalization of the mentally ill on law enforcement. We will then examine police interactions with citizens, specifically, the level of discretion police exercise and the training to equip them for dealing with persons who suffer from mental illness. The article concludes by proposing specific policy modifications for law enforcement departments to better enable their development of a more specialized and individualized response in future encounters with the mentally ill.

THE IMPACT OF DEINSTITUTIONALIZATION

According to Lamb and Bachrach (2001, p.1039), deinstitutionalization comprises three procedural processes: (1) the release of mentally ill individuals from psychiatric hospitals to alternative placement in the community, (2) the diversion of new psychiatric hospital admissions to alternative facilities, and (3) the development of special services for the noninstitutionalized mentally ill. There is little controversy regarding the "success" of the first two processes. The occupancy of state hospital beds has drastically declined since its height of 339 per 100,000 in 1955. As of 1998, there were only a 57,151 occupied state hospital beds for the 275 million persons living in the United States (21 per 100,000). However, the adequacy and availability of quality care for the mentally ill varies substantially. The improved care and services range from facilitating the mentally ill's ability to realize a relative degree of normalcy in their routine activities, achieve greater satisfaction with their life circumstances, and promote positive development to what is more often the case, where community-based care for the mentally ill is either grossly inefficient or absent (Lamb & Bachrach, 2001).

In order to understand fully the impact of deinstitutionalization on law enforcement agencies and their personnel it is important first to identify the

labeled as a "criminal," as opposed to being directed to suitable treatment resources. This label virtually ensures that such individuals are significantly more likely to be arrested in subsequent cases of disorderliness (Teplin, 2000). The initial arrest, therefore, is typically the precursor of a perpetual cycle that shuttles mentally ill citizens between jail and the streets (Perez et al., 2003). In order to understand this revolving door hypothesis, it is essential to understand the nature of the interactions between the police and the mentally ill and the options that the responding officer has to deal with said situation.

POLICE INTERACTIONS WITH CITIZENS AND THE MENTALLY ILL

Wilson (1968) developed a typology that placed calls for police intervention into four distinct categories: (1) police-invoked law enforcement, (2) police-invoked order maintenance, (3) citizen-invoked law enforcement, and (4) citizen-invoked order maintenance. Police-invoked law enforcement is a proactive, legally sufficient, and officer-initiated response. Officers' decisions to act are based solely on their knowledge, perceptions, and personal assumptions about the mentally ill. Given that a substantial portion of the mentally ill are homeless and, as a result of deinstitutionalization, are forced to live on the streets, it follows that they are much more likely to be the recipients of police-invoked intervention. This is due in combination to their visibility, their behaviors, and their disproportionate concentration in urban environments (Murphy, 1989; Patch & Arrigo, 1999; Wilson, 1968).

Police-invoked order maintenance refers to situations where the officer perceives a need to intervene to allay some sort of social disturbance. Public drunkenness and disorderly conduct are the crimes most commonly associated with this type of intervention (Brown, 1981; Wilson, 1968). Citizen-invoked law enforcement is the type of intervention that is initiated when a citizen makes a complaint. The officer, who is frequently forced to act within what amounts to considerable departmental constraints, usually resolves these instances. In such situations, officers make an attempt to "satisfy" all the parties involved, including the citizen who filed the complaint, the officer's departmental supervisors, and the general public. The fourth type of intervention, citizen-invoked order maintenance, is relatively devoid of departmental influences because the situations necessitating this type of intervention are isolated events and cannot be anticipated by the officer (e.g. loud music, marital squabbles that prompt neighbor complaints) (Patch & Arrigo, 1999, p. 29; Wilson, 1968).

Encounters between law enforcement and the mentally ill follow patterns relatively similar to all police calls for service. The greatest number come during the evening shift, followed by the day shift; the fewest come during the night shift. However, the mentally ill tend to be most vulnerable and responsible for an increased number of calls for service during the night and weekend hours, as well as on public holidays. This is primarily because this is the time when their primary service resources (e.g., mental health agencies) are unavailable (Murphy, 1989).

Additionally, police encounters with the mentally ill tend to occur in several key locations, with the individuals displaying a similar pattern of behavior. The majority of police contact with the mentally ill occurs either at or near the individual's place or residence. The most common location is in the street, but incidents also occur in halfway houses, mental health agencies, and public buildings. The behaviors that most frequently characterize the mentally ill during their encounters with law enforcement include bizarre or unusual behavior, confused thoughts and actions, aggressiveness, destructive or violent behavior, and/or attempted suicide. Furthermore, mentally ill citizens are typically unattached, lacking social support mechanisms (most notably family support), diagnosed as psychotic (primarily schizophrenic), difficult to manage (in denial about illness), and have alcohol or drug abuse dependency problems (Murphy, 1989).

Lewis, Lurigio, and Riger (1994) followed a random sample of persons with mental illness out of a state psychiatric hospital in Chicago, Illinois, for a period of twelve months. Their findings showed a 20 percent recidivism rate, measured by re-arrest one year after their release. Perhaps the more provocative finding is that 75 percent of all the crimes committed by the former patients were either city ordinance violations (e.g., trespassing, public drunkenness) or property crimes (e.g., theft, burglary). However, upon further analysis, their findings revealed that the former patients who were re-arrested upon follow-up were characterized as having extensive and serious criminal and hospitalization histories.

In a similar study using arrest data, Lurigio and Lewis (1987) categorized the criminal histories of persons with mental illness into three groups: (1) crimes were a by-product of their mental illness (e.g., disturbing the peace, trespassing, intoxication, expressing symptoms of mental disorder in public), (2) crimes were committed for survival purposes (e.g., shoplifting, theft, prostitution), or (3) serious crimes were associated with their manifestation of severe mental illness and alcohol and drug dependency problems (e.g., assault, rape, robbery). Wilson's (1968) proposed typology of police-citizen interactions and the specific characteristics that describe the typical encounters between the police and the mentally ill (Lurigio & Lewis, 1987; Murphy, 1989) underscore the extent of the role that the public, the officer, and the mentally ill have in determining the officer's level of discretion and response. The public (i.e., the citizen) has the right to voice its concern or file a formal complaint to the police requesting a response to a situation involving a person with mental illness. The nature of this type of complaint is variable, as is the degree of authenticity that can be attached to it (people can and do lie). However, a perceived and reported public threat necessarily demands a police response. Additionally, the behavior and demeanor of the officer and the person with mental illness is also situationally specific.

POLICE DISCRETION WITH THE MENTALLY ILL

Generally, an officer has three possible choices upon encountering an irrational person creating a social disturbance. The officer's first response option is to transport the person to a mental hospital. This alternative is usually employed whenever the mentally ill individual is either a danger to him- or herself or to others, or lacks the ability to protect him- or herself from victimization. The officer's second alternative is to make an arrest. This decision may appear to be the most severe. However, to many officers it is preferable as it at least ensures that the individual would be provided with treatment; often the individual is either *not dangerous enough* to satisfy the strict hospital criteria for admission or is defined as *too dangerous* by the hospital's standards. The officer's third alternative, which is generally the least invasive and most preferred option, is to informally resolve the problem. However, responsibility for the subject's continued conduct can fall squarely on the officer in today's litigious society. At first glance each option may appear to be distinct and clear; however, the officer exercises a great deal of discretion when determining which response is appropriate in any given situation (Patch & Arrigo, 1999; Teplin, 2000, p. 9).

Bittner's seminal study on police discretion (1967) found that in encounters with the mentally ill, officers were reluctant to make psychiatric referrals unless an individual was perceived to be violent or a potential harm to him-/ herself or someone else. Otherwise, in the majority of police encounters with the mentally ill, the officer chose the more informal alternative of "calming" the individual down. Since Bittner's (1967) study there have been a host of other researchers who have addressed the factors involved in an officer's decision to arrest a mentally ill individual rather than transport him or her to a mental hospital. These determining factors include the level of the social disturbance, the strictness of legal requirements for involuntary commitment, the willingness of mental health facilities or state hospitals to accept intoxicated patients, the relative complexity of admission procedures, the length of waiting periods in the emergency room, and an officer's perception that there are no other viable community alternatives (i.e., a "mercy booking") (Durham, 1989; Gillig, Dumaine, Stammer, & Hillard, 1990; Laberge & Morin, 1995; Ogloff & Otto, 1989; Teplin, 1984). Regardless of the initial justification for the decision to either arrest or refer a person with mental illness to the state hospital, officers exercise a great deal of discretion and authority in determining which system, either criminal justice or mental health, is employed, and by which means, either arrest or civil commitment, the mentally ill citizen will be processed (Patch & Arrigo, 1999).

POLICE TRAINING

Most police departments in the early 1980s made attempts to incorporate specialized approaches and specific training curricula in how to deal more effectively with the mentally ill. A recent national study by Deane, Steadman, Borum, Veysey, and Morrissey (1999) found that as many as 88 percent of law enforcement agencies have some sort of training related to mental illness. Although the training has been proven to change officers' attitudes towards the mentally ill, to enhance their knowledge of mental health related issues, and to improve their relationships with mental health professionals, the content and quality of the training has not yet been quantitatively evaluated (Godschlax, 1984; Hails & Borum, 2003; Murphy, 1989).

Deane et al. (1999, p. 100) administered a survey in 1996 to the police departments in the 194 cities in the United States with a population of 100,000 or more to determine the prevalence of specialized responses in dealing with the mentally ill. The researchers found that 96 of the 174 departments that responded to the survey did not have any procedure in place for dealing with the mentally ill. The 78 departments that indicated the presence of specialized response strategies were categorized into one of the three following models:

1. *Police-based specialized police response*—This strategic response involves sworn officers who have special mental health training who can provide crisis intervention services and act as liaisons with the mental health system.

2. *Police-based specialized mental health response*—This strategic response utilizes mental health consultants hired by the police department. The consultants are not sworn officers, but they provide on-site and telephone consultations to the sworn officers in the field.

3. *Mental-health-based specialized mental health response*—This strategic response is a combination of any other type of response and includes departments that rely solely on mobile crisis teams. The teams are part of the local community's mental health service system and provide a response to any special needs at the site of an incident.

Hails and Borum (2003) conducted a similar study in an attempt to update the findings from the 1996 survey (Deane et al., 1999). Their questionnaire was administered and responded to by a total of 84 of the 135 medium- and large-sized police departments that were surveyed. The researchers arrived at a similar conclusion to Deane et al. (1999). They found that very little attention and training, especially with new recruits and veteran law enforcement officers, was directed towards understanding and dealing with the mentally ill. This is alarming due to the amount of media coverage, community tension, and legal liability that arises from situations where the police use deadly force against mentally ill individuals (Hails & Borum, 2003).

Despite the relative national inattention to the need for training officers in dealing with the mentally ill, several model programs do exist. Steadman et al. (2000) conducted an analysis of three different study sites, each representing one of Deane et al.'s (1999) previously identified models for emergency response to the mentally ill. The Birmingham Police Department (Birmingham, Alabama) employs the *police-based specialized police response* model. The department utilizes community service officers to assist police officers with incidents involving the mentally ill. These community service officers are civilians, with some degree or professional training in social work or a related field, who provide twenty-four-hour coverage, seven days a week (including holidays).

The Memphis Police Department (Memphis, Tennessee) deploys the *police-based specialized mental health response* model. The department utilizes a crisis intervention team comprised of specially trained officers to deal with situations involving the mentally ill. The officers on this team receive 40 hours of specialized training from mental health professionals, family advocates, and mental health consumer groups and are issued crisis intervention team medallions for immediate identification. Once a member of the crisis intervention team arrives on the scene, he or she is automatically designated as the officer in charge. This Memphis model has since been replicated with success in Waterloo, Iowa; Portland, Oregon; Albuquerque, New Mexico; and Seattle, Washington.

The Knoxville Police Department (Knoxville, Tennessee) utilizes the *mental-health-based specialized mental health response* model. The department has a mobile crisis unit that responds to calls from the community, as well as telephone calls and referrals from the jail, regarding situations with the mentally ill.

Steadman et al. (2000) found that the Memphis response model had the most active procedures for referring the mentally ill to the appropriate mental health resources, and in almost 75 percent of the mental disturbance calls the mentally ill were transported to the psychiatric facility as opposed to the local jail. The Birmingham community service officers were able to resolve almost two-thirds of the mental disturbance calls without the use of coercion or civil commitment. The Knoxville mobile crisis intervention unit effectively linked almost three-fourths of the mentally ill they encountered with the necessary treatment services and only 5 percent of the incidents resulted in an arrest.

This said, these three programs were not without their flaws. The findings indicated that they were frequently delayed and that their response times were lengthy, especially on nights and weekends. This was due primarily to the limited number of trained staff and attendance at other similar assignments. This shortcoming affected violent and potentially violent police encounters with the mentally ill. However, despite these limitations, the authors regard these innovations as an overall success. Overall, when looking at the aggregate arrest rate for the three cites, only 7 percent of the mental disturbance calls resulted in an arrest and more than half of the mentally ill individuals were either transported to or directed to appropriate treatment services. Perhaps the most salient finding was that the officers were able to facilitate a resolution that enabled the individual to remain in the community without the additional impact of sanctions from the criminal justice system (Steadman et al., 2000). These findings have significant implications for departmental and public policy.

POLICY IMPLICATIONS

The fact that the mentally ill are being criminalized is a dual indictment of the failure of the mental health system and the criminal justice system, neither of which is effectively and appropriately dealing with persons with mental illnesses (Teplin, 2000). The reality of the situation is that neither system has proven itself able to manage mental health crises alone (Wolff, 1998). An integrated and collaborative effort between both systems might therefore prove to be the most beneficial for all parties (i.e., the mentally ill, law enforcement, the courts, corrections, and mental health treatment providers).

The police need to be aware of, and accept, that their primary role in dealing with the mentally ill is law enforcement. Their foremost concern should be ensuring the safety of the individual and the community. Once they have minimized the disturbance, however, their objective should shift to locating and transporting the mentally ill individual to the most appropriate treatment facility. Likewise, the mental health professionals need to realize that their primary role is to assist the officer in conflict resolution and recommend the most beneficial treatment response. The two agencies would therefore benefit from developing an ongoing and reciprocal understanding of the occupational expertise the other possesses (Lamb et al., 2002).

The Criminal Justice/Mental Health Consensus Project was one of the most comprehensive and involved attempts to investigate police responses to persons with mental illness. Its purpose was to develop recommendations, with bipartisan agreement, to enhance the response of the criminal justice and the mental health systems in dealing with persons with mental illness. Stakeholders included state lawmakers, police chiefs, officers, sheriffs, district attorneys, public defenders, judges, court administrators, state corrections directors, community corrections officials, victim advocates, consumers of mental health services, family members, county commissioners, state mental health directors, behavioral health care providers, and substance abuse experts. The final report was released on June 11, 2002 (Council of State Governments et al., 2002), and Thompson et al. (2003) summarized the seven policy statements most germane to mental health professionals and law enforcement agencies in order that they improve their response to the mentally ill:

1. Improve availability of and access to comprehensive, individualized services, when and where they are most needed, to enable persons with mental illness to maintain meaningful community membership and avoid inappropriate criminal justice involvement (mental health).

2. Ensure that people with mental illness who are no longer under the supervision of the criminal justice system maintain contact with mental health services and have support for as long as is necessary (mental health).

3. Provide dispatchers with training to determine whether mental illness may be a factor in a call for service, and use that information to dispatch the call to the appropriate responder (law enforcement).

4. Develop procedures that require officers to determine whether mental illness is a factor in the incident, and whether a serious crime has been committed, while ensuring the safety of all parties involved (law enforcement).

5. Establish written protocols that enable officers to implement an appropriate response based on the nature of the incident, the behavior of the person with mental illness, and available resources (law enforcement).

6. Document accurately police contacts with people whose mental illness was a factor in an incident to promote accountability and to enhance service delivery (law enforcement).

7. Collaborate with mental health partners to reduce the need for subsequent contacts between people with mental illness and law enforcement.

CONCLUSION

As noted by Hails and Borum (2003), understanding the problems regarding traditional police responses to persons with mental illness has resulted in the provision of a better service to the community. Unfortunately, when officers and agencies are not prepared and mistakes are made, lawsuits claiming negligence or deliberate indifference to these citizens are often filed.

In situations where time permits, properly trained officers or specialists can assist and provide a specialized response. These respondents are often part of a team and can react when called upon for assistance. In a barricaded suspect scenario, for example, or in a situation where a citizen needs help, these crisis intervention teams or trained individuals can provide much needed assistance to those in difficulty.

Unfortunately, and quite often, officers face real and immediate threats from mentally ill individuals, and it is this threat to the officer or to a citizen that becomes critical and more important than dealing with the mental illness itself. When an individual, whether mentally ill or not, pulls a weapon on an officer, it is clear that the weapon, and not the mental illness, is the most serious threat and must be dealt with for the safety of all those in the area, including the subject as well as the responding officer.

Additionally, officers would do well to realize that dealing or negotiating with a mentally ill person requires a more specialized and directed response than is generally employed in similar threatening situations involving a nonmentally ill individual. For example, people with mental illnesses may be more apt to respond to and cooperate with an officer who recognizes the issues germane to their life circumstances. The officer needs to be aware of how to best respond to the individual's threatening behavior in a nonconfrontational and/or nonadversarial manner. Any immediate or aggressive action taken by the officer may inadvertently increase the mentally ill individual's confusion and thereby intensify any antisocial behavior. In an excellent review of the issues, Murphy (1989, chapter four, pp. 9–10) has provided suggestions for officers should they find themselves in such a situation.

What officers **should** do when managing an encounter with a mentally ill person:

1. Gather as much information as possible before arriving on the scene.
2. Check for any weapons that could be perilous to the officer.
3. Be discreet and avoid attracting attention.
4. Be calm, avoid excitement, and portray a take-charge attitude.
5. Remove as many distractions or upsetting influences from the scene as possible—this includes bystanders and disruptive friends or family members.
6. Gather as much information as possible from helpful witnesses, family members, and friends.

What officers **should not** do when managing encounters with the mentally ill:

1. Do not become [excited] or allow excitement, confusion, or upsetting circumstances. These may frighten the person, inhibit communication, and increase the risk of physical injury to the officer, the subject, or bystanders.
2. Do not abuse, belittle, or threaten. Such actions may cause the person to become alarmed and distrustful.
3. Do not use inflammatory words such as "psycho" or "nut house."
4. Do not lie to or deceive the person. This can also cause the person to be distrustful. It may also limit any chances for successful mental health treatment and make any future management of the person by officers more difficult. It can also endanger the safety of other officers.
5. Do not cross-examine the person with a flurry of close-ended (e.g., "yes" and "no") questions. Instead, the person should be asked questions that allow him [/her] to explain the problems that are bothering him [/her].
6. Do not dispute, debate, or invalidate the person's claims. Do not agree or disagree with the person's statements. Rather, legitimize the person's feelings. For example, if the person claims a waitress is poisoning his/her food, the officer should say: "You believe that other people are trying to kill you?"

7. Do not rush the person or crowd his [/her] personal space. Do not touch the person unless you are prepared to use force. Any attempt to force an issue may quickly backfire in the form of violence.

8. Avoid being a "tough guy." Tough methods will usually frighten the person and cause a defensive reaction and possibly violent behavior.

9. Do not let the person upset or trick you into an argument. Ignore any attacks on your character, personal appearance, or profession, as these will undermine your ability to communicate and will also provide the person with ammunition for future attacks.

Although these suggestions are not exhaustive and do not ensure a non-combative resolution in all situations, they remain useful and serve to offer some guidance in dealing with the mentally ill.

This article has illustrated the profound impact that the process of *deinstitutionalization* has had on the treatment available to the mentally ill, and the duties and responsibilities of law enforcement. The ensuing and seemingly inevitable criminalization of the mentally ill has further exacerbated their plight. Not only do they suffer from often debilitating illnesses but they are also labeled "criminal," often as a direct result of their illness.

In the midst of a mental health crisis, there is no disputing the existence of a genuine threat to the officer and any individuals in the vicinity. It is therefore the officer's duty to take appropriate action to protect himself/herself and those in harm's way, be it the mentally ill person or an innocent bystander. Police departments need to implement ongoing training for their officers to help them recognize the signs of mental illness, training that would include education on the different types and symptoms of various mental illnesses. For example, a situation involving a suicidal individual or a paranoid schizophrenic certainly requires a more immediate and cautious response than a situation involving an individual displaying only mild symptoms of depression. However, a misdiagnosis can and occasionally does have dire consequences: knowing when to act and when to stand back are therefore equally important and are decisions that become far easier to make with comprehensive training. Although characterizing police officers as "street-corner psychiatrists" is often viewed negatively, officers must nonetheless be provided with the necessary tools so that they can best deal with situations involving the mentally ill. Without proper training, and through no fault of their own, police officers run the risk of mishandling situations and increasing the risk of injury to themselves, to the public, and also to those citizens who stand to benefit the most from such measures, the mentally ill themselves.

References

Abramson, M. L. (1972). The criminalization of mentally disordered behavior: Possible side effects of a new mental health law. *Hospital and Community Psychiatry, 23,* 101–105.

Aderibigbe, Y. A. (1997). Deinstitutionalization and criminalization: Tinkering in the interstices. *Forensic Science International, 85,* 127–134.

Ainsworth, P. (1995). *Psychology and policing in a changing world.* New York, NY: John Wiley & Sons.

Arboleda-Florez, J., & Holley, H. L. (1988). Criminalization of the mentally ill: Initial detention. *Canadian Journal of Psychiatry, 33,* 87–95.

Bittner, E. (1967). Police discretion in emergency apprehension of mentally ill persons. *Social Problems, 14*(2), 278–292.

Brown, M. K. (1981). *Working the street.* New York, NY: Russell Sage Foundation.

Council of State Governments, Police Executive Research Forum, Pretrial Services Resource Center, Association of State Correctional Administrators, Bazelon Center for Mental Health Law, & the Center fro Behavioral Health, Justice, and Public Policy. (2002). *Criminal Justice/ Mental Health Consensus Project.* New York, NY: Council of State Governments.

Deane, M., Steadman, H., Borum, R., Veysey, B., & Morrissey, J. (1999). Emerging partnerships between mental health and law enforcement. *Psychiatric Services 50*(1), 99–101.

Durham, M. L. (1989). The impact of deinstitutionalization on the current treatment of the mentally ill. *International Journal of Law and Psychiatry, 12*(2), 117–131.

Gillig, P. M., Dumaine, M., Stammer, J. W., & Hillard, J. R. (1990). What do police officers really want from the mental health system? *Hospital and Community Psychiatry, 41,* 663–665.

Green, T. M. (1997). Police as frontline mental health workers: The decision to arrest or refer to mental health agencies. *International Journal of Law and Psychiatry, 20*(4), 469–486.

Godschlax, S. (1984). Effect of a mental health educational program upon police officers. *Research in Nursing and Health, 7,* 111–117.

Hails, J., & Borum, R. (2003). Police training and specialized approaches to respond to people with mental illnesses. *Crime & Delinquency, 49*(1), 52–61.

Husted, J. R., Charter, R. A., Perrou, M. A. (1995). California law enforcement agencies and the mentally ill offender. *Bulletin of the American Academy of Psychiatry and Law, 23,* 315–329.

Krieg, R. G. (2001). An interdisciplinary look at the deinstitutionalization of the mentally ill. *The Social Science Journal, 38*(3), 367–380.

Laberge, D, & Morin, D. (1995). The overuse of criminal justice dispositions: Failure of diversionary policies in the management of mental health problems. *International Journal of Law and Psychiatry, 18*(4), 389–414.

Lamb, H. R., & Bachrach, L. L. (2001). Some perspectives on deinstitutionalization. *Psychiatric Services, 52*(8), 1039–1045.

Lamb, H. R. & Weinberger, L. E. (2001). *Deinstitutionalization: Promise and problems.* San Francisco, CA: Jossey-Bass.

Lamb, H. R., Weinberger, L. E., & DeCuir, W. J. (2002). The police and mental health. *Psychiatric Services, 53*(10), 1266–1271.

Lewis, D. A., Lurigio, A. J., & Riger, S. (1994). *The state mental patient and urban life: moving in and out of the institution.* Springfield, IL: Charles C. Thomas.

Lurigio, A. J., & Lewis, D. A. (1987). *Toward a taxonomy of the criminal mental patient.* Evanston, IL: Manuscript prepared for Northwestern University, Center for Urban Affairs and Policy Research.

Murphy, G. R. (1989). *Managing persons with mental disabilities: A curriculum guide for police trainers.* Washington, D.C.: Police Executive Research Forum.

National Association of State Mental Health Program Directors Research Institute. (2000). Closing and reorganizing state psychiatric hospitals: 2000. Retrieved January 21, 2004, from www.rdmc.org/nri/SH_RPT.pdf.

Ogloff, R. P., & Otto, R. K. (1989). Mental health interventions in jail. In K. P. Heyman (ed.), *Innovations in clinical practice.* Sarasota, FL: Professional Resource Exchange.

Patch, P. C., & Arrigo, B. A. (1999). Police officer attitudes and use of discretion in situations involving the mentally ill. *International Journal of Law and Psychiatry, 22*(1), 23–35.

Perez, A., Leifman, S., & Estrada, A. (2003). Reversing the criminalization of mental illness. *Crime & Delinquency, 49*(1), 62–78.

Ruiz, J. (1993). An interactive analysis between uniformed law enforcement officers and the mentally ill. *American Journal of Police, 12*(4), 149–177.

Sigurdson, C. (2000). The mad, the bad, and the abandoned: The mentally ill in prisons and jails. *Corrections Today, 62*(7), 70–78.

Steadman, H. J., Deane, M. W., Borum, R., & Morrissey, J. P. (2000). Comparing outcomes of major models of police responses to mental health emergencies. *Psychiatric Services, 51*(5), 645–649.

Steadman, H. J., Deane, M. W., Morrissey, J. P., Westcott, M. L., Salasin, S., & Shapiro, S. (1999). A SAMHSA research initiative assessing the effectiveness of jail diversion programs for mentally ill persons. *Psychiatric Services, 50*(12), 1620–1623.

Teplin, L. A. (1984). Managing disorder: Police handling of the mentally ill. In L. A. Teplin (ed.), *Mental health and criminal justice* (pp. 157–175). Beverly Hills, CA: Sage Publications.

Teplin, L. A. (2000). Keeping the peace: Police discretion and mentally ill persons. *National Institute of Justice Journal* (July 2000), 8–15.

Teplin, L. A., & Pruett, H. (1992). Police as street-corner psychiatrist: Managing the mentally ill. *International Journal of Law and Psychiatry, 15*(2), 139–156.

Thompson, M. D., Rueland, M., & Souweine, D. (2003). Criminal justice/Mental health consensus: Improving responses to people with mental illness. *Crime & Delinquency, 49*(1), 30–51.

Walsh, J., & Holt, D. (1999). Jail diversion for people with psychiatric disabilities: The sheriff's perspective. *Psychiatric Rehabilitation Journal, 23*(2), 153–160.

Wilson, J. Q. (1968). *Varieties of police behavior: The management of law and order in eight communities.* Cambridge, MA: Harvard University Press.

Wolff, N. (1998). Interactions between mental health and law enforcement systems: Problems and prospects for cooperation. *Journal of Health Politics, Policy, and Law, 23,* 133–174.

SECTION III
Management and Organization

The purpose of policing, beyond protecting life, is to control crime and maintain order, which involves the unique ability to use force to conduct daily activities. As a result of this authority, several methods have been developed by which administrators can organize and manage police departments. The articles chosen for this section describe potential conflicts that must be controlled in a fair and impartial manner. Unlike conflicts in other organizations, those faced by the police can result in violence, injury, or death.

In the first selection, "How Police Supervisory Styles Influence Patrol Officer Behavior," Robin Shepard Engel addresses the question of how much a field supervisor's style of supervision influences officers' performance. She uncovers four supervisory styles that have different impacts on officers' behaviors, such as use of force, problem solving, and proactivity.

In the next selection, Eve and Carl Buzawa describe the historical and current trends in police response to domestic violence. They trace the changes that have occurred in how the police respond to and perceive calls concerning domestic abuse. Their article provides an excellent overview of the problems relating to domestic violence.

In a new selection to the book, Meghan Stroshine discusses the role of information technology innovations in policing. She describes the profound changes information technology has made in computer-aided dispatch, record keeping, crime mapping and analysis, and operations, in addition to how police administrators use IT to enhance management, accountability, and personnel/resource allocations.

In the next article, Sam Walker explains how police agencies are using early intervention (EI) systems to improve accountability to themselves and to the communities they serve. These are data-based programs for identifying officers with problems and providing the basis for intervention to correct those problems before they develop into a serious incident such as a lawsuit, citizen complaint over excessive force, or some other public crisis. Early intervention systems are growing in popularity but are still in the early stages of development and need to address some difficult yet important issues.

The next selection is about Compstat, an emerging police managerial strategy that uses technology to structure a goal-oriented management process, and its use as a management tool. William Walsh provides the reader with an understanding of the evolution of this new management paradigm and an assessment of the organizational changes it requires.

Another innovation in policing is the use of geographic information systems (GIS). Professor Will Pelfrey explains GIS and the many ways it can assist in understanding crime patterns and help plan police responses to them. GIS allows police agencies to compare layers of crime data with census information, identify vulnerable areas of a city, and develop geographic profiles of crime patterns and individual criminals.

How Police Supervisory Styles Influence Patrol Officer Behavior

Robin Shepard Engel

Does field supervision of patrol officers matter? Chances are that personal experience, common sense, and intuition would elicit a quick "yes" from most police administrators and managers. But does street-level evidence justify that viewpoint?

The answer is a qualified yes, according to recent field research. Research findings not only confirm that view but also shed light on how frontline supervisory styles can influence such patrol officer behavior as making arrests, issuing citations, using force, and engaging in community policing.

The study involved field observations of and interviews with sergeants and lieutenants who directly supervised patrol officers in the Indianapolis, Indiana, Police Department and the St. Petersburg, Florida, Police Department. The research is based on data from the Project on Policing Neighborhoods (POPN), a 2-year research project sponsored by the National Institute of Justice that broadly examined policing issues, especially the effects of community policing initiatives on police and the public (see "The Project on Policing Neighborhoods").

The most important finding was that style or quality of field supervision can significantly influence patrol officer behavior, quite apart from quantity of supervision.[1] Frontline supervision by sergeants and lieutenants can influence some patrol officer behavior, but the study found that this influence varies according to the style of supervision. An "active" supervisory style—

NIJ Research for Practice, June 2003, NCJ 194078.

involving leading by example—seems to be most influential despite potential drawbacks. Indeed, active supervisors appear to be crucial to the implementation of organizational goals.

This report in NIJ's Research for Practice series addresses three principal questions:

- What are the four supervisory styles identified by the research?
- How do those styles influence patrol officer behavior?
- What are the implications for departmental policy and practice?

Exhibit 1 Characteristics of 81 supervisors

Characteristics	Minimum	Maximum	Mean
Supervisor age (years)	31	70	44
Years of experience as a supervisor	1	33	10
Percentage of supervisors who were female			15
Percentage of supervisors who were nonwhite			15
Percentage of supervisors who held a 4-year college degree			51
Amount of training* in community policing	1	5	4
Amount of knowledge† about community policing	1	3	2
Amount of training in supervision, management, leadership	1	5	4
Amount of knowledge about supervision, management, leadership	1	3	1

Note: 17 lieutenants and 64 sergeants.
* Amount of training: 1 = none, 2 = less than 1 day, 3 = 1–2 days, 4 = 3–5 days, 5 = more than 5 days.
† Amount of knowledge: 1 = very knowledgeable, 2 = fairly knowledgeable, 3 = not very knowledgeable.

FRONTLINE SUPERVISORY STYLES

The study's field observations and interviews identified four main supervisory styles: traditional, innovative, supportive, and active. Supervisor characteristics include personal features such as age as well as level of training and experience (see exhibit 1). Each of the four styles encompasses about 25 percent of the 81 field supervisors (see exhibit 2). In general, none of the four supervisory styles was found to be ideal. Each style has benefits and drawbacks. (See "Study Methodology.")

The active style of supervision emerged as having the most influence over patrol officers' behaviors. Officers with active supervisors were more likely than those with other types of supervisors to use force and spent more time on self-initiated activities, community policing activities, and problem solving.

Exhibit 2 Distribution of supervisory styles, in percent

	Traditional	Innovative	Supportive	Active
Gender				
Male (n = 69)	22	30	25	23
Female (n = 12)	50	8	17	25
Race				
White (n = 69)	26	26	25	23
Nonwhite (n = 12)	25	33	17	25
Location				
Indianapolis lieutenants (n = 17)	12	35	24	29
Indianapolis sergeants (n = 39)	18	28	26	28
St. Petersburg sergeants (n = 25)	48	20	20	12
Total (N = 81)	26	27	23	23

Note: Each percentage is the proportion of field supervisors associated with the style noted in the far left column. Thus, traditional supervisors constituted 26 percent of all 81 supervisors, 22 percent of 69 male supervisors, etc.

Traditional Supervisors

Traditional supervisors expect aggressive enforcement from subordinates rather than engagement in community-oriented activities or policing of minor disorders. They are more likely than other types of supervisors to make decisions because they tend to take over encounters with citizens or tell officers how to handle those incidents.

Traditional sergeants and lieutenants are highly task oriented and expect subordinates to produce measurable outcomes—particularly arrests and citations—along with paperwork and documentation.

Less inclined toward developing relationships, traditional supervisors give more instruction to subordinates and are less likely to reward and more likely to punish patrol officers. The traditional supervisor's ultimate concern is to control subordinate behavior.

Traditional supervisors are more likely to support new policing initiatives if they are consistent with aggressive law enforcement. More than 60 percent of these supervisors "agree strongly" that "enforcing the law is by far a patrol officer's most important responsibility," compared with 14 percent of innovative supervisors, 11 percent of supportive supervisors, and 11 percent of active supervisors. Along with their no-nonsense approach to policing, traditional supervisors strictly enforce rules and regulations and adhere to the chain of command.

Innovative Supervisors

Innovative supervisors are characterized by a tendency to form relationships (i.e., they consider more officers to be friends), a low level of task orientation, and more positive views of subordinates. These supervisors are considered innovative because they generally encourage their officers to embrace new philosophies and methods of policing. Innovative supervisors are defined by their expectations for community policing and problem-solving efforts by subordinates. For example, 96 percent of these supervisors reported that they "agree strongly" that "a good patrol officer will try to find out what residents think the neighborhood problems are," compared to 48 percent of traditional supervisors, 68 percent of supportive supervisors, and 68 percent of active supervisors.

One goal of innovative supervisors is to help subordinates implement community policing and problem-solving strategies by coaching, mentoring, and facilitating. They are less concerned with enforcing rules and regulations, report writing, or other task-oriented activities than traditional supervisors.

Unlike traditional supervisors, innovative supervisors generally do not tell subordinates how to handle situations and do not take over the situations themselves. They are more likely to delegate decision making. They spend significantly more time per shift dealing with the public or other officers than other supervisors do (15 percent compared with 9 percent).

Supportive Supervisors

These supervisors support subordinates by protecting them from discipline or punishment perceived as "unfair" and by providing inspirational motivation. They often serve as a buffer between officers and management to protect officers from criticism and discipline. They believe this gives their officers space to perform duties without constant worry of disciplinary action for honest mistakes.

In some cases, supportive supervisors do not have strong ties to or positive relations with management. They may attempt to shield patrol officers from the police administration. Thus, some supervisors classified as supportive may function more as "protectors" than "supporters."

Of supportive supervisors, 68 percent reported that "protecting their officers from unfair criticism and punishment" is one of their most important functions, compared with 10 percent of traditional supervisors, 5 percent of innovative supervisors, and no active supervisors.

The protective role adopted by some supportive supervisors can be a problem, however. Other research has found that shielding officers from accountability mechanisms within the department can lead to police misconduct.[2]

Supportive supervisors are less concerned with enforcing rules and regulations, dealing with paperwork, or ensuring that officers do their work. They may encourage officers through praise and recognition, act as counselors, or display concern for subordinates' personal and professional well-being. The study found that supportive supervisors praise or reward subordinate officers significantly more often during an average shift (3 times per shift) than do other supervisors (2 times per shift).

Active Supervisors

Active supervisors embrace a philosophy of leading by example. Their goal is to be heavily involved in the field alongside subordinates while controlling patrol officer behavior, thus performing the dual function of street officer and supervisor.

Almost all active supervisors (95 percent) report that they often go on their own initiative to incidents that their officers are handling, compared to 24 percent of traditional supervisors, 55 percent of innovative supervisors, and 68 percent of supportive supervisors.

Active supervisors also give importance to engaging in patrol work themselves. They spend significantly more time per shift than other supervisors on general motor patrol (33 percent compared with 26 percent) and traffic encounters (4 percent compared with 2 percent). These supervisors attempt to strike a balance between being active in the field and controlling subordinate behavior through constant, direct supervision. Supervisors with an active style are characterized by directive decision making, a strong sense of supervisory power, and a relatively positive view of subordinates.

Although active supervisors believe they have considerable influence over subordinates' decisions, they are less likely to encourage team building, coaching, or mentoring. One possible explanation for this is that they are reluctant to become so involved that they alienate subordinate officers. A fine line separates an active supervisor from being seen as overcontrolling or micromanaging.

IMPACT OF SUPERVISORY STYLE ON PATROL OFFICERS

What impact does supervisory style have on patrol officer activities? The study examined the influence of 64 sergeants' supervisory styles on the behavior of 239 patrol officers, having identified the sergeant-supervisor of each officer. The study's findings focus on how likely officers were to make arrests, issue citations, and use force as well as how much time per shift they allocated to community policing activities, administrative duties, and personal business.

Arrests and Citations

Supervisory style did not affect the likelihood that patrol officers would make arrests or issue citations in either traffic or nontraffic situations. In nontraffic encounters, however, the mere presence of a field supervisor, regardless of style, significantly influenced officer behavior; the longer a supervisor was present, the more likely patrol officers were to make an arrest.

Use of Force

Patrol officers with active supervisors were twice as likely to use force[3] against suspects as officers whose supervisors employ other styles. In addition, active supervisors themselves used force against suspects more often than other types of supervisors. The mere presence of a supervisor at the scene, however, did not have a significant influence on police use of force.

Self-Initiated Activities

Patrol officers with active supervisors spent more time per shift engaging in proactive (self-initiated) activities than officers with other supervisors. The former spent 15 percent of their time per shift being proactive, in contrast to 14 percent, 13 percent, and 11 percent for officers under supportive, traditional, and innovative supervisors, respectively. Proactivity excludes time spent on dispatched or supervisor-directed activities, general patrol, traveling to a location, personal business, and administrative activities.

Community Policing and Problem Solving

Officers with active supervisors spent more time per shift engaging in problem solving and other community-policing activities than officers with other types of supervisors. Officers under active supervision spent 11.3 percent of their time per shift on problem solving, compared with 10.7 percent for officers with supportive supervisors, 9.4 percent for those with traditional supervisors, and 8.0 percent for officers with innovative supervisors. Although differences between these percentages seem small, they can produce substantial differences in the amount of time spent on community policing by an entire patrol force over the course of a year.

At first glance it appears contradictory that officers with innovative supervisors spent the least amount of time on community policing and problem solving. This finding suggests that simply having an innovative supervisory style does not necessarily translate into more innovative activities from subordinates. Possibly, innovative supervisors may be more inclined to encourage community-building tactics, while active supervisors may encourage more aggressive enforcement, which may lead active supervisors and their subordinates to be more engaged with problem solving and other citizen interactions.

Administrative Activities

Patrol officers with active supervisors spend significantly less time per shift on administrative tasks. Officers under active supervision spent 13 percent of their time dealing with administrative matters, compared with 19 percent for patrol officers with traditional supervisors and 17 percent for those with innovative or supportive supervisors.

Community Policing in Field Training and Supervision

Although not part of POPN research, a study conducted by Robin N. Haarr Ph.D., under NIJ grant 96-IJ-CX-0060, also looked at influences on patrol officer behavior, particularly new recruits. This research also found that field supervisors have crucial influence, although in a different context.[a]

A separate study of how police recruits are taught community policing principles provides some guidance for police managers on how field training and actual policing experience may supersede academy training in influencing the attitudes and beliefs of new officers.

The 3-year study surveyed police recruits at four intervals[b] during their training and first year on the job. It focused on academy "reform training"[c] designed to change recruits' attitudes positively toward community-oriented policing and problem-solving policing.

The research found that academy reform training often proved ineffective because it was not followed up during field training, and factors contradicting academy training[d] dominated recruits' actual policing experiences.

The study also found that recruits' beliefs about the nature of policing were firmly established before training even begins:

> The best predictors of attitude change were by far the attitudes that recruits brought with them to the academy. In other words, police recruits are not empty vessels to be filled with new attitudes and values related to policing.[e]

Nonetheless, academy reform training did influence recruits' beliefs about police work before field training. But the study found "little evidence of a formal and/or systematic approach to incorporating community policing and/or problem-solving training into the field training process."[f] Thus, community policing principles— already on shaky ground because of recruits' previously held beliefs—often appeared to be academic:

> It seems unreasonable to expect police recruits to continue their commitment to community policing and problem-solving policing principles and practices if they leave the training academy and return to a police agency that does not require its officers to engage in community policing or problem-solving activities.[g]

It falls to police leadership, the study concluded, to set the tone for community policing. When supervisors and the organization practice community-oriented and problem-solving policing, recruits will too. The study recommends that academy-taught principles be' coupled more closely with field training and actual police practices.

Notes

[a] Haarr, R. N., *The Impact of Community Policing Training and Program Implementation on Police Personnel*, final report for the National Institute of Justice, grant number 96-IJ-CX-0060, Washington, DC; National Institute of Justice, 2000, NCJ 190680.

[b] Surveys were administered on the first day at the academy, near the last day at the academy, 12 weeks later (near the end of field training), and at the end of 1 year on the job.

[c] "Reform training" is defined as "training designed to alter an officer's perception of the world and/or police work. . . . In the case of community policing training, the goal is to replace outdated attitudes and beliefs about policing with new attitudes and beliefs that are consistent with community policing and problem-solving policing philosophies and strategies." (Haarr, *The Impact of Community Policing Training end Program Implementation on Police Personnel*, pp. 3–4.)

[d] Such as shift, coworkers' attitudes, and precinct location.

[e] Haarr, p. v.

[f] Ibid., p. 176.

[g] Ibid., p. 175.

Personal Business

Supervisory style has little effect on the time patrol officers spend conducting personal business (nonwork-related encounters and activities, including meal and restroom breaks). Overall, officers spent 16 percent of their time on personal business.

IMPLICATIONS FOR POLICY AND PRACTICE

Collectively, the research findings indicate that supervisory styles affect some types of subordinate behavior. Police administrators are encouraged to consider supervisory style in setting department goals and training.

Compared with other styles, an active supervisory approach appears to wield the most influence over patrol officer actions. The findings suggest that to best influence their patrol officers' behavior, field supervisors must lead by example—the hallmark of an active style.

One clear implication of the research is that police administrators and managers would be well-advised to direct and train field supervisors to become more involved and set an example of the behavior they expect from subordinates. (For discussion of a different study that examined supervisory practices and officer training, see "Community Policing in Field Training and Supervision.")

An active supervisory style, however, has potential problems. Leading by example can be positive or negative, depending on the example set. As noted previously, for instance, active supervisors and their subordinates are more likely to use force against suspects.

One reason why active supervisors might promote greater use of force and proactivity (which could expose the officer to greater risk if things go wrong) is that by taking precisely the risks that he/she wants the officer to take, the active supervisor demonstrates that "if it's safe for Sarge, then it's safe for me, too."

Supervisory styles influenced only those officer behaviors that are hardest to monitor and measure, such as use of force, problem solving, and proactivity. Conversely, supervisory styles did not significantly affect officer behaviors that are relatively easy to monitor and measure, such as making arrests and issuing citations. One reason may be that supervisors have more influence in situations where patrol officers have the most discretion. Perhaps the less certain the task and the less visible its performance, the more opportunity a sergeant may have to define the duties of subordinates, who may appreciate such clarification of their roles.

Another possible explanation is that such easily measured officer activities as arrests and citations may be most influenced by policy guidelines from higher ranking officials. This effect is likely to be relatively uniform regardless of field supervisors' styles. Thus, the place to look for supervisory influence over these activities may be at the district or departmental level, not the field supervisory level.

Leading by example is an effective frontline supervisory tool only if the example supports departmental goals. For instance, many officers at both sites had received relatively little training in community policing and were skeptical about its worth. Sergeants who practiced an active supervisory style supplemented training deficiencies while building the self-confidence of subordinate officers.

These findings strongly suggest that police administrators are more likely to achieve departmental goals if they align them with supervisory practice and encourage field supervisors to "get in the game."

Study Methodology

This study used data collected for the POPN multimethod study of police patrol in the Indianapolis, Indiana, and St. Petersburg, Florida, police departments, which were implementing community policing at the time of the study.

The core methodology was systematic social observation of patrol officers in the field. Trained observers accompanied officers on their work shifts and took field notes. Officers assigned to each of the 24 study beats were observed for approximately 240 hours. Researchers observed more than 5,700 hours of patrol work during the summer of 1996 in Indianapolis and the summer of 1997 in St. Petersburg. From their field notes, observers prepared narratives and coded data items about officer activities.

Researchers also interviewed patrol officers and frontline supervisors about their personal characteristics, training and education, work experience, perceptions of their beats, attitudes toward the police role, and perceptions of their department's implementation of community policing and problem solving. Participation was voluntary and confidential. To encourage candid responses to potentially sensitive questions about the quality of supervision, officers were not asked for their supervisors' names. Officers were matched with sergeants through other information.

Review of prior research identified 10 attitudinal dimensions that potentially shape supervisors' styles:
- How they make decisions.
- How they distribute power.
- The extent to which they attempt or avoid exerting leadership.
- The priority they place on aggressive enforcement.
- The priority they attach to community policing and problem solving.
- How they view subordinates.
- Whether they engage in inspirational motivation.
- Haw task oriented they are.
- Whether they focus on building friendships and mutual trust with subordinates.
- Whether they focus on protecting subordinates from unfair criticism and punishment.

Factor analysis of these dimensions revealed the four individual supervisory styles: traditional, innovative, supportive, and active.

Notes

[1] "Quantity" is used here in the sense of amount of supervision, i.e., the number of supervisors, the amount of interaction between supervisors and subordinates, and time spent on supervised encounters between patrol officers and citizens. This study is unique in its focus on the quality and style—as well as quantity—of patrol officer supervision.

[2] For example, see Christopher Commission, *Report of the Independent Commission on the Los Angeles Police Department*, Los Angeles Independent Commission on the Los Angeles Police Department, 1991; Mollen Commission to Investigate Allegations of Police Corruption, *Commission Report*, New York: The Mollen Commission, 1994; Skolnik, J.H., and J.J. Fyfe, *Above the Law: Police and the Excessive Use of Force*, New York: Free Press, 1993; and Kappeler, V.E., R.D. Sluder, and G.P. Alpert, *Forces of Deviance: Understanding the Dark Side of Policing*, 2d edition, Prospect Heights, IL: Waveland Press, 1998.

[3] Use of force includes firm grip or nonpain restraint, pain compliance (hammerlock, wristlock, finger grip, carotid control, bar arm lock), impact or incapacitation (striking with body or weapon, mace, taser), or drawing or discharging a firearm.

Bibliography

Engel, R., "Patrol Officer Supervision in the Community Policing Era," *Journal of Criminal Justice* 30(1) (January/February 2002): 51–64.

Engel, R., "Supervisory Styles of Patrol Sergeants and Lieutenants," *Journal of Criminal Justice* 29(4) (July/August 2001): 341–355.

Engel, R., "The Effects of Supervisory Styles on Patrol Officer Behavior," *Police Quarterly* 3(3) (September 2000): 262–293.

Bergner, L., "Building Teamwork Among Officers," *Law Enforcement Trainer* 12(6) (November/ December 1997): 10–12.

Haarr, R., "Making of a Community Policing Officer: The Impact of Basic Training and Occupational Socialization on Police Recruits," *Police Quarterly* 4(4) (December 2001): 402–433.

Mastrofski, S., R. Parks, A. Reiss, Jr., and R. Worden, *Policing Neighborhoods: A Report from St. Petersburg*, Research Preview, Washington, DC: U.S. Department of Justice, National Institute of Justice, July 1999, NCJ 184370.

Mastrofski, S., R. Parks, A. Reiss, Jr., and R. Worden, *Policing Neighborhoods: A Report from Indianapolis*, Research Preview, Washington, DC: U.S. Department of Justice, National Institute of Justice, July 1998, NCJ 184207.

Mastrofski, S., R. Parks, and R. Worden, *Community Policing in Action: Lessons from an Observational Study*, Final Report to the National Institute of Justice, 1998.

Office of Community Oriented Policing Services Web site, www.usdoj.gov/cops/

Weisburd, D., and R. Greenspan, et al., *Police Attitudes Toward Abuse of Authority: Findings From a National Study*, Research in Brief, Washington, DC: U.S. Department of Justice, National Institute of Justice, May 2000, NCJ 181312.

Traditional and Innovative Police Responses to Domestic Violence

Eve S. Buzawa & Carl G. Buzawa

In 1993 we acknowledged that few areas of policing have exhibited as much change and remain as controversial as does the police response to domestic violence. Surprisingly, as of this date, the controversies over the proper police response remain unresolved.

What is not surprising is that continuing controversies coupled with the inherent vagaries of achieving change may have further increased the variations in street-level performance. Mandatory and proarrest legislative reforms have resulted in markedly different policies and practices even when departments operate under the same statutory framework or "official" policies read similarly. This is often the result of differences in how individual departments respond to new legislative mandates as well as how officers within departments comply with legislative mandates for which they may not personally agree. In this article, we will explore both the continuing themes of police response and the dynamics of change.

TRADITIONAL POLICING: A CONTINUING THEME?

Reform of police action in domestic assault cases has been a recurrent theme for over 20 years. For a variety of reasons that we will explore in this

Prepared especially for *Critical Issues in Policing* by Eve S. Buzawa and Carl G. Buzawa.

article most departments have dramatically changed officer behavior. However, in many cases the traditional police response to domestic violence is still practiced at the street level by many departments and individual officers today. The traditional police response has several characteristics: few domestic violence cases were formally addressed by the criminal justice system—the majority being "screened out"; police avoided intervention in most cases; and there was a strong, sometimes overwhelming, bias against making arrests.

Victim Screening of Cases

Researchers know that historically only a minority of domestic assaults resulted in the dispatch of police officers. This was partially due both to screening by victims and potential witnesses. While estimates varied widely, research generally confirmed that historically less than 10 percent of domestic violence incidents were ever reported to the police. Even at present, most research finds calls to the police regarding domestic violence remain at rates of no more than 30–50 percent in most communities.

Furthermore, those incidents that were reported to the police did not truly reflect the scope of domestic violence. For example, nonparticipant callers usually had their own motivations (i.e., quieting noisy altercations rather than stopping actual violence). As a result, violence among acquaintances or strangers, being more likely to be committed in public, was far more likely to be observed than those involving married or cohabiting adults. Neighbors tended not to report such occurrences since family disputes were often viewed as being an inevitable part of a "problem family" and/or an expected, annoying, or at times even entertaining, neighborhood distraction. Moreover, when domestic violence was reported, it was more likely to be in lower socioeconomic neighborhoods where the close proximity of living made these situations more observable to outsiders and where there was a tradition of calling the police.

Reporting victims presented their own bias; far fewer middle- and upper-income victims of spouse abuse referred domestic violence cases, due in part to the social distance between the police and these communities (the police being associated by the middle classes with crime control and the "lower classes"), the shame at involving the police in family problems, and the reality of economic dependence of women without their own careers. Hence, while domestic violence appears to exist in all classes, even if more commonly in lower classes (Moore, 1997), violence in the higher economic groups was more likely to be handled by doctors, the clergy, or other family members.

Severity of injury may also affect victim reporting. Their need for immediate medical attention may necessitate victims or witnesses to seek assistance (Bachman and Coker, 1995; Felson et al., 1999). Since injuries are estimated to occur in less than 3 percent of domestic assaults on women and .5 percent of domestic assaults on men, female victims are more likely to seek police assistance. However, Pierce and Spaar (1992) examined police and emergency room cases in Boston and reported that the most severe cases of violence resulted in demands for medical rather than police assistance. These "medical" cases were not customarily reported to the police. Clearly, the net effect was that traditionally police-citizen encounters were a rarity, being relegated to a small minority of potentially reportable incidents.

Police Screening

Of equal significance to victim screening, police often reduced their domestic assault caseloads even further by making explicit decisions to avoid intervention. In addition, departments' standard operating procedures often did not prioritize such calls. For example, dispatcher call screening and the "neutral technology" of call prioritization effectively excluded cases. This resulted in many assaults, even those constituting a felony by anyone's definition, to be recategorized as minor "family trouble calls." Consequently, the caller was discouraged from demanding a police response and instead was diverted out of the system. The caller would be referred to social service agencies or incorrectly told that the police could not provide assistance for "marital" conflicts.

If police intervention was still requested, dispatch according to standard operating procedures would occur only when time permitted, often hours later. One study found, in a sample of cases, over two-thirds of domestic violence cases were thus "solved" without dispatch of officers. While formally condemned, this practice was unofficially accepted and well documented. It is important to recognize the context of this practice: while the police might be singled out for their failure to protect victims of crime, this truly represented a reflection of the then pervasive lack of societal concern. For many decades, and for many people today, domestic violence was "known" to be a problem of the "lower classes" and minority groups, so no one cared enough to devote scarce resources. The police could—and did—minimize their response to domestic violence victims without fear of adverse consequences.

Why Did the Police Avoid Intervention?

Research exploring police attitudes consistently shows that most police officers, regardless of individual or department characteristics, dislike responding to domestic violence calls. Several reasons explain this reluctance: former organizational impediments to adequate performance; lack of sufficient/sophisticated training; cynicism as to efficacy of the response, a belief that such calls are not "real" policing; and finally, somewhat overemphasized worries over officer safety.

Organizational Impediments. While no longer a factor, until successive waves of reform legislation were enacted in the 1970s and early 1980s, virtually all states limited police arrest powers in cases of misdemeanor assaults, including domestic violence cases. Domestic violence assaults—absent homicide—were typically termed misdemeanors—regardless of extent of victim injury or assailant use of weapons. Unless police actually witnessed the incident, they could not make a warrantless arrest, which severely limited responses. Due to this restriction on responding to misdemeanor assaults, few arrests and little effective action could be taken since most offenders retained enough self-control to avoid continuing to batter the victim in the officer's presence. As a result, many police believed that their role was peripheral, restricted to a perfunctory, service-oriented call (to separate the parties) rather than investigate a crime.

Another major organizational impediment to effective action, at least for large police departments, was that most information systems did not effectively inform responding officers of an offender's prior history of assault. Because police record systems were not well organized or computerized, large departments, serving communities where the officers did not typically know the families, often had little ability to differentiate between first offenders and hard-core recidivists—unlike the "rap sheets" distributed for repeat offenders for felonies and certain other offenses. As a result, big city departments tended to treat such offenses as an isolated occurrence.

Finally, the number and distribution of these calls posed a significant challenge to police resources. Apart from traffic and code enforcement actions, and even with the voluntary victim screening described above, domestic violence calls often constituted the single largest category of criminal complaints in many cities. Making this even worse, domestic violence typically occurs during the weekend evenings when other calls—including substance abuse related offenses, such as drunk driving, bar fights, gang incidents, loud parties; crimes including breaking and entering, robberies; and certain other assaults—put major organizational demands on police time.

Lack of Training. Independent of organizational and legal issues, police also were not well trained to cope with domestic violence incidents. In many cases, police were profoundly ignorant of the proper methods of handling domestic violence cases. In fact, in one sample, over 50 percent of the officers did not even know probable cause requirements for domestic violence related assault (Ford and Burke, 1987).

Police Attitudes. It has long been known that police are cynical toward the public and the long-term impact of their intervention, particularly in social service type calls (Manning, 1988, 1997; Gaines, Kappeler, and Vaughn, 1999; Kappeler, Blumberg, and Potter, 2000). This attitude is especially relevant to domestic violence cases. Responses to traditional law enforcement and even code violations demand certain fairly routinized behavior in conformity with police and prosecutors' needs to develop and preserve evidence for a crime. In contrast, the skill of handling a dynamic and potentially volatile intervention among intimates requires both specialized skills and a willingness to expend considerable effort. Neither is especially likely if the officer is cynical and believes no positive outcome likely.

Officers often quickly decide that, from their perspective, not all victims give a complete or honest account of the situation, thus reinforcing police tendencies to be wary and skeptical. This leads officers to define their role in domestic violence cases not in terms of "enforcing the law" but in terms of "handling the situation." Class issues reinforce such cynicism. Much research has shown that when police confront members of the lower economic classes or minorities of any class, they often tend to act in a bureaucratic, impersonal, authoritarian fashion and are unlikely to show compassion toward victims. When interviewed, many officers, even those who wish to perform service tasks, often readily state that violence is a "normal part of the lives of the lower class." The implication is that domestic problems are a logical outgrowth of this environment. Defining such behavior as "normal" in the participants' lives means that the officers are less willing to aggressively intervene and are more inclined to "manage" disputes to avoid more "serious" public breaches of peace. From this perspective, an officer would far prefer temporarily restoring order to attempting a resolution to the underlying conflict and/or responding to the situation as a criminal incident.

General police cynicism is compounded by specific feelings toward intimate partner violence. Risking overgeneralization, many officers believe that responding to any domestic violence call as a criminal incident is inappropriate. There are also still some officers who believe they should not even be the agency contacted for any type of intervention. These officers may feel uncomfortable with social-work tasks and prefer to deal only with "real" crime. They prefer a self-image of a "crime fighter" where acts of heroism and/or "significant arrests" might distinguish the officer for promotion.

Fear of Injury. To this day, police view responding to "domestics" as being particularly dangerous. Many officer deaths and serious injuries have occurred during family violence calls. Anecdotal evidence of unprovoked attacks by offenders and "unappreciative" victims are legion.

This is explainable—almost no other source of injury is as unpredictable or as personally outrageous as being assaulted when responding to a call for help in a domestic case. Resistance might be expected from an offender whose "power" is being externally challenged. However, officers say that when they try to interview the victim, whom they came to help, the person often "turns" against them or, at best, shows no interest in pressing charges.

For many years, the FBI reinforced such beliefs by publishing annual reports to "show" that "disturbance calls" were among the most common sources of officer death. However, this has been seriously questioned. A 1988 report sponsored by the National Institute of Justice found rates of police injury were overstated by three times in prior FBI reports due to the then current practice of lumping together all "disturbance" calls (e.g., including "domestics" with gang fights, bar brawls, etc.). When this obvious disparity was removed, the reported rate of officer deaths declined markedly. Other research has supported relatively few incidents of officer injury when responding to domestic violence calls (Hirschel, Dean, and Mills, 1992; Hirschel, Dean, and Lumb, 1994).

Despite the findings above, police to this date emphatically believe that responding to domestic violence cases is very dangerous, especially if they have to make an arrest. The number of officer injuries in domestic violence calls is increasing, as a result of the increased number of these calls reaching police attention. Therefore, it is not surprising that the actual number of police injuries in these situations is high. However, the actual likelihood of injury in these cases has not necessarily increased.

Are Police Less Likely to Arrest for Domestic Assault than Nondomestic Assault?

Viewed in isolation and without knowledge of past practices, one might suppose a high rate of arrest for cases of domestic assault. After all, there is a known victim, usually with an apparent, often severe, injury. Since the offender is known, apprehension is relatively straightforward. Instead, the closer the relationship between victim and offender, the less likely an arrest will be made.

There are varied reasons for their reluctance to arrest. Police departments generally discourage arrests for certain offenses since they force a further diversion of scarce resources, including not only the extra time spent by the officer, including making a court appearance, but also by booking sergeants and lock-up personnel. In the past, it was difficult to organizationally justify an arrest as it involved a low-status misdemeanor with relatively poor chances of conviction.

Many victim advocates have argued that the failure to arrest in domestic violence cases simply validates the claim that police do not care about female victims of violence (Lerman, 1981; Stanko, 1989; Ferraro, 1989; Mills, 1999; Coker, 2000). Police researchers note the inherent difficulties faced in responding to domestic violence calls and making arrests, especially in the context of increasing demands on police with decreasing resources (Manning, 1997; Buzawa and Buzawa, 2003). Organizationally, past societal and consequently legal definitions of domestic violence as a misdemeanor impacted on the police interpretation of appropriate priorities in making arrests. In addition, police continue to respond to demands that they focus on the "epidemic" of drugs, drunk driving, street violence, and other public disorder offenses, and now they are also confronted with political pressure to handle threats of international and domestic-based terrorism.

The above analysis also assumes implicitly that police departments disproportionately fail to make domestic violence arrests; however, this assumption has itself been debated. In addition, the issue may not be whether an assault is nondomestic or domestic but the circumstances under which the assault occurs, that is, situational factors. In support of this, Elliott (1989) reported that a review of studies indicated that there were not significant differences in arrest rates between domestic and nondomestic assaults. The primary reason for this lack of difference was the failure to respond to nondomestic assaults rather than proactive arrest practices for domestic assault. Other researchers have also reported that nondomestic assault is treated lightly and variations are affected by situational characteristics (Faragher, 1985; Oppenlander, 1982; Smith, 1986).

Unfortunately, the above studies address all domestic assaults rather than contrasting domestic assaults with nondomestic assaults. Since nondomestic assaults often involve friends or acquaintances, and depending on the state's legal definition, relatives as well, distinctions may be blurred. The importance of this is suggested by research showing that while there is no difference between domestic and nondomestic assault, there *are* differences when spousal assault cases are separated out.

Current research continues to find variation in actual police practices, despite an overall increase in arrest rates. Fyfe, Klinger, and Flavin (1997); Buzawa, Austin, and Buzawa (1995); and Sheptcyki (1993) all reported that domestic assaults were treated more leniently than other assaults. Felson and Ackerman (2001) also found this to be the case when domestic assaults were compared to assaults by identifiable strangers but believed it explainable based on the greater presence of witnesses in stranger assault and the reluctance of many victims in intimate assaults to sign complaints. This conclusion contrasts with research by Hotaling and Buzawa (2001) that reported higher rates of arrest for domestic assaults (77 percent) compared to nondomestic assaults (36 percent). This was true both for assaults involving physical force (39 percent vs. 52 percent) and even for assaults where there was only a threat (59 percent vs. 26 percent).

Preliminary analysis of all assaults from the National Incident-Base Reporting System (NIBRS) database for the year 2000 revealed 577,862 cases of assault in 2,821 police departments from 19 states reported to the police that year. Overall 37 percent of the assaults resulted in the arrest of an offender. Domestic violence cases were *more* likely than nondomestic violence cases to result in the arrest of an offender. While 49.9 percent of intimate partner cases and 44.5 percent of other domestic cases resulted in the arrest of at least one offender, only 35.0 percent of the cases in which the victim and offender were strangers, and 29.9 percent of the nondomestic cases in which the victim and offender knew each other, ended up with the arrest of at least one offender (Hirschel, Buzawa, Faggiani, Reuland, and Pattavina, 2003).

The Role of Victim Preference. Despite frequent official protestations to the contrary, rarely is the criminal justice system victim oriented (Fattah, 1999). This is partially due to an overall belief by key agencies such as the police and prosecutors' office (as a generalized group) that their primary mission is to protect society as a whole from crimes against the public order, not necessarily to provide assistance to a particular victim (Fagan, 1996). Unfortunately, neither a punishment model nor a deterrent model by itself necessarily operates in a manner that empowers, or even protects, many victims of domestic violence. Attempts to integrate victim needs and interests into criminal justice case processing has been difficult. After all, victim advocates often disagree with the victim's efforts to maintain a relationship with the assailant, believing *they* best understand victim needs. This is compounded by the fact that victim advocates employed by the criminal justice system are expected to ensure victim cooperation in case processing. As a result, victims are often suspicious of victim advocates and hesitant to trust them in representing their interests.

Even the most commonly cited measure of police involvement in domestic violence—arrest rates—limits the importance of other factors that could more accurately measure if victims are actually being helped. While the police response to domestic assault has frequently only been measured by arrest rates, there are a number of other potential services that police might perform for victims, such as informing them of their rights to get a restraining order, taking them and their children to an available shelter, connecting them with a specialized advocacy group, and so forth. These services are usually encouraged or even mandated by statute or departmental policy, but unfortunately they are neither measured nor followed in practice by many departments, resulting in a missed opportunity to evaluate their effectiveness. From the data that *are* available, research has found that performance of these services highly influences victim satisfaction with the police.

We must note that some respected researchers readily argue that a crime fighting approach to domestic violence is preferable given the limitations of the intervening institutions. For example, Fagan (1996) stated that the criminal justice system should primarily focus on the detection, control, and punishment of batterers, with only indirect involvement in the provision of extra services to battered women. He stated that an emphasis on the rights of the victim would too easily conflict with the primary mission of these institutions and inadvertently make it easier for agency personnel to simply marginalize "domestic" cases as disliked "social work" rather than "real crimes."

Even so, we believe the criminal justice system *should* consider the impact of its actions on individual victims. While there are clear societal interests in suppressing domestic violence, the reality is that victims often disproportionately bear the vast majority of "costs" for the offense. In addition, as we later discuss, the enormous burdens are often placed upon victims at each stage of criminal justice processing.

The conflict in goals appears most evident when policies mandating arrest and prosecution of all offenders contradict victim preferences (for further discussion, see Belknap et al., 1999; Buzawa and Buzawa, 2003; Buzawa et al., 1999; Buzawa and Buzawa, 1996; Ford and Regoli, 1993; Mills, 1998; Wuest and Merritt-Gray, 1999). As a result, such policies may result in "victim deterrence." There is now evidence to suggest that victim failure to report new incidents of domestic assault is because an arrest will be made (Buzawa et al., 1999; Buzawa and Hotaling, 2000).

In research involving victim interviews one year following the study incident, Hotaling and Buzawa (2001) reported that there were two identifiable groups of victims that would not contact the police again in the case of a future domestic assault: *those with the least serious* and *those with the most serious* offenders. While the results may at first seem paradoxical, they were readily explained and supported by the data. Victims with first-time offenders who never wanted arrest stated that they believed the police "overreacted" to a "one-time" occurrence. Follow-up interviews and official data validated their beliefs; this was the group by far least likely to reoffend. Victims believed, with apparent justification, that the decision to arrest was inappropriate and unneeded.

When Arrests Have Occurred.   Traditionally, when arrests were made, they were not the result of a reasoned application of textbook law and procedure. In fact, research shows only a weak correlation between the extent of victim injury and other factors usually relevant to police decisions to arrest. Instead, in common with other relatively minor offenses, specific factors predominate in the decision to arrest: how the police and offender interacted, how police perceived the victim's conduct, and police "organizational" issues.

Most studies appear to show that the primary influence of the offender on the officer's decision to arrest is what he does *after* the officer arrives. If disrespectful or still violent in the officer's presence, this implies a threat to the officer's ability to control the situation. Arrest then becomes a vehicle to assert police authority rather than to protect a victim from future assaults or vindicate her rights. The victim also directly or indirectly strongly influences arrest decisions. Her preference was critical since she was in the best position to state her rights and her cooperation was essential to successful prosecution. As a result, some studies have shown that victim preference was a de facto prerequisite to arrest.[1]

Interaction with the victim also affects arrest rates in other, more troublesome ways. Police regularly judge the conduct of the citizens with whom they interact. Their occupationally ambiguous and potentially dangerous environment necessitates this discretion. However, in the context of domestic violence, police may judge the victim's overall conduct as inappropriate. For such cases, the officer might have believed her injuries did not justify an arrest. When the victim lived with her assailant, arrests were less common because the police viewed the victim's conduct as "demonstrating" that she was not really seriously harmed while also limiting the probability that arrest would lead to successful prosecution. Similarly, arrest was unlikely if the victim acted in a manner that in some way offended the officers. Hence, if she was an "unfaithful spouse" or if she attacked the offender, officers seldom made an arrest.

If the victim remained "rational," "undemanding," and very deferential to the police, in short was deemed a "good" woman, they awarded her preferences far more weight in the decision to arrest. Conversely, we found that when the victim was disruptive, intoxicated, or verbally demanding or abusive toward the officers, she was virtually ignored. Finally, a few studies have reported on the impact of organizational factors, which have no relationship to the offense itself and are often unknown to the public. For example, arrests appear less likely to be made during particularly busy periods or at the end of an officer's shift.

Why Has Change Occurred?

After the existence of relatively stable policies of police inaction, profound changes have swept many departments throughout the country. Commencing with pioneer legislation enacted in 1977 in Pennsylvania, all states and the District of Columbia have repeatedly passed domestic violence reforms. Arrests are encouraged for domestic assaults (or even "mandated" in many statutes); new statutory specific "domestic violence" offenses were incorporated into the criminal code and were passed, and protective or restraining orders (TROs) became readily available. While many provisions merely encouraged police action, real impediments were removed. For the first time, most statutes allowed warrantless arrests for domestic violence related assaults even if unwitnessed by police.

However, it would be simplistic to assert that any particular factor itself accounted for the shift in official policies. In part, this change was a logical extension of an overall trend to criminalize deviance. While illegal for many years, domestic violence and many other inappropriate actions had been tacitly tolerated by failure to rigorously enforce laws. As society has become more conservative and punitive toward offenders, efforts to rehabilitate have been discredited while punitive solutions are emphasized. For example, drug-offender and youthful-offender programs have been dropped or not adequately funded in favor of trying addicts as criminals and juveniles as adults. Drunk drivers are being prosecuted at unprecedented rates.

In this context, battered women advocates, policy makers, and researchers have emphasized the criminal context of a domestic assailant's actions and deride as wholly inappropriate or sexist any attempt to mediate family disputes or take actions short of formal arrest. In this climate, it is not surprising that an abortive reform movement of the 1970s emphasizing conflict resolution and offender rehabilitation using specialized "crisis intervention units" was quietly abandoned in favor of arrest-oriented policing.

Punishing domestic offenders was also justified as necessary in order to "deter" future assaults by the same or potential offenders. Deterrence theory suggests that a police action such as arrest may be justifiable even if subsequent conviction is unlikely, if it deters future assaults. Hence, the ability of the police to "shame" the offender or by arrest hold him to public scorn is potentially useful to modify future behavior.

It is interesting that academics, often staunchly liberal in other contexts, and many feminists failed to find anything distressing about using the police in this manner. While the police as an institution are often deeply mistrusted by these same people, they largely endorsed changes that increased police involvement in intimate disputes and family violence. Research was often ignored when results began to suggest such statutes were used far more frequently against minorities and the lower classes than for other offenders and were not against most middle-class, "respectful," or "respectable" white males.

Proarrest policies also addressed concerns of responding to public reaction and legal repercussions for inaction. As a result of publicity, political pressure on the police shifted from the previous model of "let the police decide" to an environment where police decisions were examined to see if they were adequate. Political pressure also became a major factor speeding the adoption of proarrest practices. Lawsuits during the early period of the reforms also proliferated, addressing the more egregious failure of the police to respond appropriately. In fact, the "clarity" of a mandatory arrest policy (where arrests must be made and police discretion is removed) and its resultant ability to be justified in court may, at least partially, explain why police officials embraced such policies.

While the increased criminalization of offenses, political pressure, and fear of lawsuits undoubtedly set the stage for change, the rapidity of official policy change was startling. In our minds, the immediate catalyst for such action was the Minneapolis Domestic Violence Experiment (MDVE) (Sherman and Berk, 1984). This study used an experimental research design to "prove" that arrest was far more effective to deter future violence than merely separation of the parties or officer "mediation."

Despite the limited scope of this research, its lack of a theoretical context of its findings, it was vigorously promoted by its authors and was cited (often incorrectly) by hundreds of departments and subsequent research papers as justifying, even mandating, arrests to "deter" violence. Despite intense publicity and official sponsorship, it took other researchers years to note the incongruity of the Minneapolis results with findings from general criminology and juvenile delinquency studies that simply did not show such deterrent effects of arrest (Elliott, 1989; Dugan, Nagin, and Rosenfeld, 2001; Klein, 1994).

While the first wave of proarrest policies was based on the MDVE's finding of a deterrent effect of arrest, subsequent research has tended to cast doubt on this relationship (Dunford, Huizinga, and Elliott, 1989; Sherman, Smith, Schmidt, and Rogan, 1992; Hirschel, Hutchison, Dean, Kelley, and Pesackis, 1991; Berk, Campbell, Klap, and Western, 1992). The implications of the MDVE Replication Studies and the problems with the use of arrest as a treatment for domestic violence are discussed in detail in Zorza and Woods, 1994; Bowman, 1992; Mills, 1999; Garner and Maxwell, 2000; and Buzawa and Buzawa, 2003.

Although deterrence may exist for a period of time for some groups (Berk et al., 1992; Pate and Hamilton, 1992; Sherman, 1992), the results in several of the studies showed little or no reduction or prevention of continuing violence when arrest was isolated as a single variable (Dunford et al., 1989; Hirschel et al., 1991). Perhaps most disturbingly, in one study the group *most* likely to commit severe beatings in the future (the unemployed with a previ-

basic demographics of the mentally ill. Although it is difficult to ascertain the exact number of persons with mental illness because of the lack of a comprehensive mental health data collection system, some estimates indicate that as many as 1 in 10 persons suffer from some type of mental illness and that there are between 1 and 4 million seriously mentally ill persons in the United States. The mentally ill live in an array of community settings with varying degrees of care and means of support, including private residences, halfway houses or group homes, bed and board homes, nursing homes, single-room hotels, jails and prisons, and homeless shelters (Murphy, 1989). The prevalence of mental illness and the inadequate and often squalid living conditions of the mentally ill lead almost inevitably to the increased involvement of law enforcement agencies.

Officer's Role as "Gatekeeper"

According to Lamb, Weinberger, and Decuir (2002, p. 1266), there are two common-law doctrines that emphasize law enforcement's role in taking the responsibility for persons with mental illness: (1) their power and authority to protect the safety and welfare of the community and (2) their *parens patriae* obligations to protect individuals with disabilities. The public visibility and the 24 hours a day, seven days a week availability of the police contribute to their often unilateral decision making in dealing with persons with mental illness (Lamb et al., 2002). In addition, society's negative attitudes, misperceptions, and general apprehension towards the mentally ill further increase the police's obligation to either recognize the individual's need for treatment and connect him/her with the proper mental health service provider (Husted, Charter, & Perrou, 1995) or determine that the individual's illegal activity warrants an arrest (Arboleda-Florez & Holley, 1988). This assessment procedure places the officer in the position of "gatekeeper" between the mental health system and the criminal justice system (Lamb et al., 2002) and forces a determination that many argue the police are neither trained nor qualified to deliver (Ainsworth, 1995; Bittner, 1967; Green, 1997; Ruiz, 1993).

Criminalization of the Mentally Ill

Abramson first proposed the expression *criminalization of the mentally ill* in 1972. This has been interpreted as meaning that a criminal justice rather than a mental health response has been adopted (Patch & Arrigo, 1999). This refers to the process by which the mentally ill citizens involved in minor criminal offenses such as disturbing the peace, public drunkenness, and trespassing are disproportionately arrested and prosecuted through the county court system (Bittner, 1967; Lamb & Weinberger, 2001; Teplin & Pruett, 1992).

The principal issue that arises from this flawed method of social control is that the criminal justice system was neither intended nor designed to be the initial point of entry into the mental health system (Teplin, 2000). Consequently a number of those individuals suffering from a mental illness are being

ous criminal history of violent crime) became even *more* likely to commit abuse five months after arrest than those not arrested (Sherman, 1992).

Sherman inferred from such data that his earlier MDVE study (even when so rigorously promoted) was limited. He maintained that arrest simply would be ineffective where the suspect had weak social bonds to the community.

Research in general does continue to point out that while some offenders might respond positively to a particular sanction others may react wholly differently.[2] In this context, the replication studies' results are not surprising to many domestic violence researchers and practitioners. It has been established that a victim is in greatest danger in the period immediately following separation from the batterer rather than while the victim is living with the batterer.

Logically, a violent individual who resorts to abuse as part of a generally violent or criminal lifestyle will not be easily deterred by being locked up for a few hours and then released. Rather, he may become even further enraged, placing the victim in greater danger upon release. Similarly, contact with the criminal justice system may not be unfamiliar, and being arrested then shortly released becomes a relatively minor event.

For other offenders, the act of bringing the offender into the purview of the criminal justice system by whatever means (warrantless arrest by the police, arrest subsequent to a warrant, or a simple summons to appear before a court official) may reduce prospects of recidivism. The possible key may be the criminal justice system's ability to mandate rehabilitation. Hence, an arrested person's exposure to counseling to learn to control anger and substance abuse therapy may account for differences in recidivism outcomes seen in some, but not all, studies. At the same time, there does appear to be a population unresponsive to *any* type of intervention. This might necessitate incapacitation as it would for any other type of dangerous offender.

While the foregoing replication studies en masse and individually were subjected to a thorough methodological critique by Bowman (1992), Zorza and Woods (1994), and Garner and Maxwell (2000), they did demonstrate the limited impact of police action taken out of context. Clearly, arrest cannot be considered in isolation from other factors in the criminal justice system. Arrest without long-term involvement does not appear to work for severe abusers. If arrested violators are released without prosecution, they may simply conclude that society simply does not care.

Similarly, prosecutors may decide that they should not use scarce resources if judges fail to treat domestic violence as a serious crime or fail to sentence offenders. In any event, despite the frequent failure to examine the police effort in a systemic context and the lack of agreement as to the ideal police response, virtually all reform legislation and administrative directives now direct police to use arrests more aggressively. Despite profound controversy over the efficacy of such practices when applied without discretion, an increasing number of statutes and police administrative policies now mandate arrest upon the occurrence of certain circumstances or upon violation of expanded protective orders (Hart, 1992; Buzawa and Buzawa, 2003).

Changes in Training

Another area of profound change has been the training given to new officers and in-service personnel. In response to statutory mandates and in recognition that then existent materials were seriously out of date, departments throughout the country rapidly shifted from curricula that emphasized the futility and danger of police intervention to those that stress the essential role of the police within a coordinated program to handle domestic violence.

There is some evidence that real attitudinal change is taking place among those exposed to comprehensive training (Kinsport and Fischer, 1993; Malefyt, Little, and Walker, 1998). However, it is unlikely that the impact of training is consistent nationwide. In most departments, the majority of time devoted to basic training has not increased in duration (Eigenberg, 2001). Further, the amount of time devoted to domestic violence varies considerably from 2 to 30 hours with an average of 10 hours. However, it is interesting to note that 29 states now mandate extensive domestic violence training with 21 of these specifying minimum training standards that could not be covered in the allocated time (Mills, 1997). Further, the quality and impact of in-service training is also problematic, varying tremendously both in frequency and quality (Gaines, Kappeler, and Vaughn, 1999; Eigenberg, 2001).

Many analysts continue to believe that the subculture of policing is highly cynical, maintaining a cohesive, stable, and largely negative view of their mission and the public that they serve. They say that police tend to dismiss out of hand the results of research that contradicts preconceived attitudes and instead rely on "street" experience. If this is true, then despite training, officers may quickly revert to preconceived attitudes and practices that can successfully circumvent legal and organizational requirements. Training may also be overshadowed by: the contradictory pressures of the police organization's paramilitary structure, coupled with the hierarchy's real limits on control of officer conduct on the street; inability to provide rewards for appropriate behavior; and the retrograde informal lessons that many new officers receive often from cynical, hardened training partners.

Finally, while we believe there are real limits to the following analysis, many victim advocates believe that the social structure within American society is patriarchal. Following this logic, unless the criminal justice system remains under continuing pressure, it will inevitably revert to patriarchal norms that diminish crimes against women. The result is despair about affecting long-term attitudinal change, reinforcing the belief that the only way to effect change is through even more political pressure, restrictive laws, and the potential of lawsuits.

Violence Against Women Act

Until 1994, it could reasonably be stated that the federal response to domestic violence was quite limited. While specific federal funding agencies such as the National Institute of Justice, Centers for Disease Control, and several others funded demonstration projects, and experimental and evaluation research, there was little actual legislation that set forth what actions were expected by local law enforcement. This has markedly changed. In 1994, the Violence Against Women Act (VAWA) funded local, state, and Indian tribal governments to develop and strengthen post–law enforcement and prosecution strategies to combat violence against women. In fiscal year 1995, $23.5 million was funded—a drop in the bucket compared to real needs but still welcome recognition of the problem. Additional programs provided for enhancements to data collection between departments (e.g., setting up inter-jurisdictional files on offenders violating protective orders), toll-free hotlines for victims to more effectively seek assistance from police and shelters in rural areas, and direct funding of programs for victims and batterers.

In 2000 the VAWA Reauthorization Act was passed, providing for markedly more funding and "encouraging" more active police response by dangling the prospect of significant grants for training, material support, technology, database development and so forth, for departments that could demonstrate that they were endeavouring to assist victims of domestic violence.

DO REFORMS REALLY WORK AS INTENDED?

Clearly, in many if not most police departments there has been a broadening of the structural role of police in domestic violence cases. Increased support exists for formal organizational changes emphasizing proactive policing, especially the use of arrest. A more activist response in training is evident at the national, state, and local levels.

What is more problematic is the actual change in "street-level" justice. Most research has examined either the classic patterns of police behavior or, if more recently conducted, the "new" policing. The latter, while having far greater potential to break a cycle of violence, has not reached its full potential. Many departments (and certainly individual officers in almost all departments) still believe that the police role in this area should remain limited. Although higher percentages of police than in the past may acknowledge that a crime has been committed, they are deeply frustrated by highly visible failures of their intervention to prevent future assaults.

Even without empirical data, a pattern may be emerging. Most high-level police officials now willingly embrace proarrest policies. However, this is met with various degrees of passive resistance from lower-level supervisors and line personnel. This is not surprising since police administrators historically have often tended to be more progressive (or at least politically responsive) than line personnel. The importance of this dichotomy is that the public often incorrectly assumes street-level behavior reflects the administrative goals and stated policies. In fact, substantial discretion remains with line officers. As such, they can critically obstruct implementing any new policy. Without changes in their attitude, merely imposing new rules sometimes leads to a subversion of policies.

Police literature suggests that in such cases, actual change may be problematic. Official rules, no matter how strict, are difficult to enforce when the usual measure of output—decisions to arrest/not arrest—depends upon an officer's judgment as to proof of injury, probable cause, and defenses such as self-defense. Nonetheless, research now suggests that in many, if not most departments, and regardless of measurement techniques and definitions of the crime chosen, arrest rates have risen. Arrest rates from data collected in the 1970s and 1980s varied from 3 percent (Langley and Levy, 1977), 4 percent (Lawrenz, Lembo, and Schade, 1988), 10 percent (Roy, 1977), 7.5 percent (Holmes and Bibel, 1988), and 13.9 percent (Bayley, 1986). This contrasts with more recent research reporting rates of 30 percent (Robinson and Chandek, 2000) and 34 percent (Buzawa and Hotaling, 2000).

Preliminary findings using NIBRS data for 2,821 police jurisdictions in 19 states confirm this observation. Overall, 37.0 percent of all assault and intimidation incidents to which the police responded resulted in the arrest of an offender. However, 32.3 percent of cases in jurisdictions with discretionary and 33 percent of the cases in states with preferred police arrest powers resulted in an arrest compared to 41.9 percent of the cases in states with mandatory arrest powers resulted in the arrest of an offender (Hirschel, Buzawa, Faggiani, Reuland, and Pattavina, 2003). The question still remains as to why there are still so many cases where no arrest is made in states where there now is legislation or policies that either "presume" or even "mandate" arrest in the case of domestic violence.

Inter-Departmental Variations

Research on the actual response of the criminal justice system to domestic assault continues to report highly inconsistent results. While most police departments have officially instituted proactive arrest-oriented policies, often such efforts receive little encouragement or reinforcement from prosecutors or the judiciary. Even today, truly integrated responses to domestic violence offenders such as those in Santa Barbara County, CA; Quincy District Court, MA; Duluth, MN; Dade County, FL; King County, WA; and San Diego County, CA are more the exception rather than the rule. Further, the *impact* of these programs still needs further research. Results to date have been ambiguous (Davis and Taylor, 1997; Murphy, Musser, and Maton, 1998; Buzawa et al., 1999; Osofsky, 1999).

Clearly there is a proliferation of research on arrests in domestic violence cases with varied findings apparently affected by a huge number of variables such as legislation, policies, community expectations, and officer characteristics. The conclusion to be drawn may simply be that these observed variations are *real;* there is no one consistent set of variables among all departments (Buzawa et al., 1999). In fact, some research has found little variation within departments, but significant variation between different departments. Little attention has been focused on organizational commitment to change and what structural changes are made to ensure compliance.

While many police administrators try to aggressively respond, others display varying levels of commitment at monitoring the implementation of domestic violence policies. Some simply file these policies in their office. Others distribute the policies at the periodic rapid-fire roll calls. Still others discuss them in detail at roll call. Finally, there are departments that mandate strong efforts to ensure that all officers receive in-service training both on the new policy and on their role in intervention. Differences in observed arrest rates may therefore largely reflect different implementation practices and perhaps implicitly serve as an indicator of the officer's perception regarding the policy's overall importance to his/her department's administration.

What is the impact of administrative efforts to increase arrests? Despite some instances of officer resistance to this policy, current research suggests that in proarrest jurisdictions, where administrators strictly enforce policies, there is a marked increase in arrest rates. Arrest data collected for Boulder County in 1994, a jurisdiction that has aggressively enforced a proactive police policy since 1986, indicates that almost three-fourths of cases received a formal police response. In only 20 percent of cases was absolutely no action taken. In addition, extralegal factors appeared to be far less significant than in previous research (Jones and Belknap, 1999).

Intra-Agency Variation in Practices

Even within a particular police department, a variety of organizational, attitudinal, situational, and socio-demographic variables involving victims, offenders, and police impact the decision to arrest even when circumstances of the crime committed would suggest similar treatment. Some research has found biased officer attitudes toward certain types of behavior disproportionately affect the police response to domestic violence when compared to other types of assaults where arrest is more predictable.

For example, research continues to find variation in actual practices among different types of domestic assaults, even within the context of a trend toward increased arrest rates. Fyfe, Klinger, and Flavin (1997) reported that men who assault their wives were treated more leniently than men who commit other assaults. Buzawa and Hotaling (2000) found that while overall arrest rates indicated a more aggressive arrest policy than in the past, variations included a three times greater likelihood of arrest if the offender did not give a good "reason" for the assault or if there was injury (Eigenberg, Scarborough, and Kappeler, 2000). Jones and Belknap, 1999; Klinger, 1995; and Feder, 1998 did not find significant differences among classes of victims.

Even the victim may have a powerful impact in the decision to arrest. Arrest decisions in cases of domestic assault are often motivated by fear of liability, public pressure, or the officer's attitudes toward victims and offenders. This statement is supported by research findings that those victims who conform to societal expectations are more likely to have their offender arrested (Black, 1980).

For example, one recent report found that when an adult female was assaulted, the likelihood of arrest was three times greater than when a child (male or female) or adult male was an assault victim, and a five times greater chance than when a male (child or adult) was the victim. Even more troublesome was that when children were the suspect in a domestic assault, they were eight times more likely to be arrested, regardless of injury to the victim (Buzawa and Hotaling, 2000).

Why do such distinctions exist? It may be that the response of police concerns for liability coupled with public pressure increase the likelihood of an arrest in male against female intimate partner violence cases. In contrast, many officers expect children, especially in poorer neighborhoods, to be assaulted and they have low levels of tolerance for juvenile misconduct. This leads to the anomaly that children are far less likely to have an arrest made when they are assault victims and far more likely to be arrested when they are assault offenders. Therefore, domestic violence laws may markedly increase the number of children drawn into the criminal justice system as *offenders* while largely failing to value them when they are victims.

Limitations in Legal Definitions of Domestic Violence

Domestic violence, more than any other criminal act, includes a very wide range of behaviors and relationships. Unfortunately, criminal codes are typically rather blunt instruments, defining violence as an *individual act,* usually a physical assault or a threat of physical harm. In reality, most researchers now more accurately conceptualize domestic violence as a range of behaviors, some obviously criminal in nature, others more manipulative, which in total are intended to exercise *coercive control.* These include physical, sexual, psychological, and verbal behaviors used to dominate another person. This perspective focuses on the *pattern* of violent and abusive behavior within the relationship rather than on individual acts of perpetrators.

By treating domestic violence primarily as a criminal justice issue, emphasis has largely been placed upon offenders, why they commit violence, and what can deter future violence. Little attention is paid to the needs of victims. From this offender-based perspective, deterrence-based theories of offending and reoffending have predominated policy responses. Not surprisingly, the current strategies rely primarily on tactical issues, including deterrence via certainty of apprehension and arrest, aggressive prosecution through adjudication, and "target hardening" through the issuance of restraining orders. The emphasis of the criminal justice system on the apprehension and processing of offenders has relegated victim-centered approaches to incidental status. They are not often considered important by significant policy makers or activists and are even scarcer in reports of funded research in the area of criminal justice.

Therefore, for the criminal justice system to operate, there needs to be a crime with a defined victim and offender in the context of a criminal statute.

Criminal law relies on purely objective criteria for this determination. There is also an assumption that a person's status is not only identifiable but constant. Unfortunately, there are many violent families where members are both violent and victimized by violence. Further, such acts of violence occur in both public and private settings and at various points in their lives.

When there is difficulty in determining which party is a victim, police face the choice of taking no action, because there is no legally recognizable victim or, paradoxically, arresting both parties. For example, a woman who has been the victim in an ongoing pattern of violence may find that when the police arrive they take interactions out of context and arrest, from a long-term perspective, the "wrong party."

Certainly, the criminal justice system's focus on incidents and the need to establish a victim/offender dichotomy prevents domestic violence from being seen as a type of interaction that is part of a pattern of long-term abuse. This is further complicated by incidents where both parties are injured and each has a long history of calling the police about the other.

Finally, the very statutes in question, domestic violence criminal codes, have inexplicable gaps in coverage. The relationships included under these acts vary state to state, sometimes only including married individuals or, alternatively, including some or all of the following: current and past intimate partners; anyone living in the same residence; children, siblings, any other family members and/or any relative. Researchers and policy makers have seldom addressed relationships *other* than intimate partner violence. When examining relationships between intervention and incidents of domestic violence, this is significant, as research by Maxwell and Bricker (1999) and Buzawa and Hotaling (2000) found 35 percent and 61 percent, respectively, involved present or past intimate partner relationships. Preliminary analysis of the NIBRS data set described earlier found that 36 percent of domestic assaults involved relationships other than intimate partner (Hirschel et al., 2003).

Some troubling evidence shows that well-meaning reform efforts can backfire in terms of the intent of the legislative advocates and in concrete ways actually disadvantage victims. We will briefly review the key claims asserted as possible effects of aggressive police actions.

Is Systemic Intervention the Answer?

As a result of the acknowledged problems of trying to change police behavior in a systemic vacuum, since the 1990s a new service model has been implemented: centralized units of police, prosecutors, and probation departments linked by common procedures and commitments to cope aggressively with the problems presented by domestic abuse. Initially funded by federal grants, "demonstration" or "model" programs were developed in some jurisdictions, such as Quincy, Massachusetts; Duluth, Minnesota; and San Diego and Santa Barbara, California, and then copied by many police departments, prosecutors, and courts eager to adopt the best method to curb domestic violence.

Although each is unique in terms of structure and leadership, they all start with a commitment to organizational excellence by the administrative heads of the affected police, prosecutors' offices, the judiciary, and probation departments. Insistence on following up cases is typically mandated by policy and by actual supervisory practices.

There is also typically an attempt to change attitudes of line officers and caseworkers. As such, an essential component is the development and use, for both pre-service and in-service officers, of modern training programs that emphasize both independent action required of officers and also necessary coordination with other individuals or agencies such as shelters, victim advocates, and prosecutors. Information systems are developed to provide a direct link between offender data, arrest warrants, and outstanding protective orders.

Of perhaps equal importance, the phenomenon of victim-led attrition of criminal cases is directly addressed. Victim support personnel, so-called "victim advocates," are assigned and/or coordinated by special assignment within prosecutors' offices, the police department, and somewhat less formally nongovernmental victim-rights advocates. Although hard-core and repeat offenders are incarcerated, most offenders are routinely sentenced to intensive probation, often with requirements to attend treatment and/or substance abuse programs.

Evaluation of the effects of such programs unfortunately does not lead to automatic conclusion that the programs are always effective. On the one hand, enough research has been published to conclude that such interdepartmental programs do lessen subsequent violence among many offenders who are arrested. They probably also deter many others who now believe they may not only be arrested but also prosecuted to conviction if they abuse their mates.

In addition, many women with whom we have spoken also feel for the first time that society cares about their problems. As a result, they are much less willing to tolerate abuse of themselves or their children. Even agency personnel feel better about their role because of a tangible output and enhanced prospects for a satisfactory outcome.

Finally, as discussed earlier, there is certainly little doubt that such efforts pay off in terms of a dramatic increase in arrest rates of offenders. These arrests occur not only at far higher rates after an initial act of abuse but also for violation of a subsequent restraining order forbidding future abuse or even contact. This is a message of mixed news. In one sense, the police operate in such jurisdictions in the context of a system that refuses to abandon responsibility when faced with a particularly recalcitrant abuser. In short, our implicit assumption is that criminal justice intervention will dramatically affect the cycle of abuse. On the other hand, there is a core of abusers that are not, and apparently will not, be deterred.

In addition, we are concerned that in such jurisdictions there may be unintended consequences to victims, offenders, families, and agencies of efforts to rigorously and proactively implement systemic policies of control. These concerns are bolstered by both empirical evidence and observations arising from research. In one such study conducted by the author it became apparent, from even cursory conversations with key actors in the criminal justice system, that implementation of laws designed to prevent domestic violence had already had substantial consequences, both intended and unintended. Most publicity, as it should, has gone toward the impact that aggressive enforcement has had on certain victims, who are far quicker now to engage the system to stop abuse, and on the larger numbers of violent offenders who have either voluntarily stopped abuse or have been incarcerated (Buzawa et al., 1999).

By every indication, the community became markedly less tolerant of abuse, and agencies now see their efforts being rewarded through highly visible impact on some victims and their families. Although we readily acknowledge that society should and must aggressively intervene in domestic violence cases, we also must explore whether such intervention efforts lead to tertiary problems that may result in unanticipated consequences to the victim, the offender, the intervening agencies, and society in general.

Why Unanticipated Consequences Should Be Expected Even in Model Jurisdictions

A case study may help illustrate the impact and limits of such a program. Along with Professors Hotaling and Byrne and Andrew Klein (at the time, the chief probation officer of the Quincy District Court), one of the authors of this article examined the process and outcomes of domestic violence abuse in the Quincy District Court (QDC). The QDC had been nationally recognized as a model in the Violence Against Women Act for its integrated response. Few jurisdictions have moved more aggressively to intervene in such cases. It was featured on *60 Minutes* and in numerous other television and radio programs and newspaper articles and has won a Ford Foundation "Innovations in State and Local Government Award" for its model domestic abuse program. Courts nationwide currently still attempt to emulate QDC. The records are in fact quite impressive; unlike most departments, Quincy police arrest 75 percent of abusers when called to the scene of an incidence of domestic abuse. Model police crime scene investigations help ensure successful prosecution without requiring excessive victim involvement. The Quincy District Court itself issues 2,000 restraining orders per year in a jurisdiction of only 250,000 inhabitants.

Their district attorney's office has successfully prosecuted 70 percent of domestic violence arrestees. Most offenders are sentenced to probation, which is strictly enforced. Each year, it sends about 100 abusers to the county's House of Correction when they reabuse their victims and/or fail to fulfill their various conditions of probation. Examination of the data in such a "model" setting is informative of the fundamental limits of a system mandating an aggressive criminal justice response. We found and reported that among a certain subset of domestic violence batterers (represented by those

70 percent of batterers who were actually arrested) are a serious group of offenders—exactly the sort of offenders that are not easily deterred from future assaults and even prone to retaliate.

For example, of 277 domestic violence batterers on probation in 1994, 208 were subsequently charged with violating probation. Thirty were sentenced to the House of Correction with an average sentence of three months or less. Excluding defendants held without bail or those unable to meet bail, this represents the majority of QDC domestic violence post-trial commitments. In other words, community-based supervision (probation) is the "going rate" for domestic violence offenses.

We found that domestic violence batterers are the category of offenders most likely to fail *scheduled* drug/alcohol testing, with a noncompliance rate exceeding that of drunk drivers. Clearly, this group does not worry about consequences of failure to comply with court requirements. On a more global basis, the vast majority (80 percent) of male batterers had substantial prior criminal records for unrelated and related crimes.

The number of prior crimes charged against them positively correlated with reabuse over two years. Almost 50 percent of the abusers reabused their victims over two years as measured by new arrests or the issuance of new restraining orders. Reabuse correlated with abuser characteristics, not incident or victim characteristics, including whether or not the victim maintained the restraining order or dropped it before its legal termination date. In fact, we believe that any strategy for intervention presents some threat of unanticipated consequences against victims.

Increase in Dual Arrest Rates. There has been considerable concern over increasing rates of dual arrest as a result of mandatory arrest policies and legislation (Lawrenz et al., 1988; Martin, 1997; Municipality of Anchorage, 2000; Office of the Attorney General, State of California, 1999; Saunders, 1995; Wanless, 1996; Zorza and Woods, 1994). When New York State enacted its mandatory arrest law in 1995, dual arrests were reported to have had similar increases (Haviland, Frye, Rajah, Thukral, and Trinity, 2001). Subsequent research has shown wide variations in dual arrest rates. Where statewide data are available for domestic violence cases, dual arrest rates range as high as 23 percent in Connecticut to as low as 4.9 percent in neighboring Rhode Island (Hirschel and Buzawa, 2002). Using a national data set, Hirschel et al. (2003) reported that 1.9 percent of cases in states with mandatory arrest powers resulted in dual arrests while only 0.7 percent of cases in jurisdictions with discretionary powers, and 0.6 percent of the cases in states with preferred police arrest powers resulted in dual arrests. These patterns were observed when controlling for measures of offense severity, including offense type, victim injury, and presence of a weapon.

Increase in Violence and Harassment. In certain circumstances, intervention has actually provoked further violence against partners. In at least two reported cases, abusers sentenced to jail have subsequently been indicted for trying to hire hit men to harm the abusers' partners while the abusers remained in jail (see *Commonwealth vs. Phillips*, 1994). Another case was reported where an abuser, held without bail in jail for contacting his partner in violation of a restraining order, used jail phones to call her 228 times over the course of his ten-day stay awaiting trial for the original charges (*Boston Globe*, July 10, 1994).

Judicial Intervention Has Itself Been Seized upon as a Weapon. Deterred by criminal court and restraining orders from continuing *physical* abuse of their current partners, there seems to be a growing trend of abusers to seek new vehicles to continue abuse. Child protective agencies and probate courts now often report that abusers, who previously totally ignored their off-spring, suddenly are suing for visitation and custody as a vehicle for abusing, harassing, punishing, and even tracking down partners. Abusers are also reporting former partners to state protective agencies for allegations of child neglect and abuse including, ironically, the victim's failure to protect the child from the abuser's abuse.

Similarly, the number of abusers seeking restraining orders has increased every year as abusers see judicial offense as the best defense. In the 1980s, there were at most only 10 percent males seeking restraining orders. This proportion has grown to 20 percent (Massachusetts Supreme Judicial Court, 1996). In many cases, they are getting *ex parte* orders even if permanent orders are denied after the woman refutes allegations. Although reversed after the initial ten-day period, the effects of temporary orders on the woman and children are unknown. In one homicide case in Lynn, Massachusetts, it was revealed that an alleged murderer had secured two temporary restraining orders against a woman, whom he eventually stalked and shot, wounding her and killing both her brother and new boyfriend (*Boston Globe*, December 13, 1995).

Use of Batterer Treatment Programs to Reinforce Batterer's Behavior. Many treatment programs have reported that batterers form support groups among themselves and exchange ideas about new and more "effective" ways of victimizing the woman. There is some evidence that treatment could actually increase violence against victims (Harrell, 1991). Hence, clinical programs that might be expected to temper violent behavior might instead trigger new (often less sanctioned) forms of intimidation and harassment.

Harassment and Stalking of Victims. Harassment by domestic violence offenders who have left their abused partners is becoming epidemic. One estimate is that up to 80 percent of stalking offenses arise out of domestic violence situations (Buzawa and Buzawa, 2003). In these cases, stalking becomes the best method of abuse for many offenders who are concerned about being prosecuted for actual violent episodes. Hence, in Quincy, a visitation center, established so that abusive men could visit their children without endangering their children's mothers, reported that one of the most common violations of visitation committed by these abusive men is that they illegally extract information from their children about their abused partner's location. Some abusers will even go so far as soliciting a friend to continue their abuse while in jail. Being incarcerated may be perceived by the inmate as insulating himself from further charges of abuse.

Victims Are Stigmatized. Victims of battering have been subjected to differential treatment because of their circumstances; in several cases, women were fired from their jobs because their abusers stalked or harassed them at work, jeopardizing the safety of other employees.

Victims also have greater fears that their children might be taken away from them, especially in states mandating the investigation of all domestic assault cases in which children are present.They are also at greater risk of having their own criminal activities uncovered (e.g., drug-addicted victims) with mandatory arrest policies (Coker, 2000).

In the African American community, the label of victim may create an unwanted stigma. Such victims may see domestic violence as "white feminism and male bashing" (Bent-Goodley, 2001, p. 321).

Displacement to New Victims. Ultimately the goal of effective criminal justice intervention must be the reduction of overall levels of violence, not simply displacement to other less assertive victims. There may be a subset of extraordinarily violent offenders—exactly the offenders most likely to kill or severely injure a victim. Straus (1996) reported that 10 percent of batterers in general fit this high-risk profile. However, they attack their victims on average of 60 times per year compared with five assaults by other batterers.

When these types of batterers are confronted with a victim willing to initiate criminal justice intervention, there is also the possibility that they may simply leave and seek alternate victims who do not disclose abuse. For example, Buzawa et al. (1999) reported that those offenders who reoffend were more than four times as likely to have had multiple restraining orders taken out against them by different victims. Further, anger at criminal justice intervention may result in increased danger, not only to the victim but also to other family, friends, or coworkers. In fact, often batterers go to extraordinary efforts to track victims to shelters, friends' homes, or places of employment.

Unanticipated Consequences for Agencies

Displacement of Resources. An unintended consequence of enhanced enforcement of policies is that agencies may develop various means to limit demands imposed by these well-meaning policies and statutory directives. As noted earlier, stated policies are always considered discretionary and open to interpretation. To understand the consequences, it is critical to know what the stated policy *is* and how it is carried out. In some cases, police may simply ignore proarrest policies. In other departments, police screening of calls may limit organizational demands, even if statutes specify differently.

Although difficult to quantify, strains on resources have inevitably led to a deemphasis by the police, prosecutors, and courts on other crimes. It has been theorized that police may downgrade or increase call screening on other calls to avoid mandatory processing of an assault. Further, laws in certain jurisdictions have increased local jail population. In addition, the violent nature of these new inmates has created new problems for staff at detention centers and jails.

Examining the impact of agency costs solely from the narrowness of an economic perspective parallels the error of focusing on arrest (Institute for Women's Policy Research, 1995). Diversion of resources from other priorities, dissipation of existing initiatives, and demoralization of staff can be far more costly than economic costs. For example, mandatory arrest may raise concerns about contradictions with current community policing initiatives, especially in minority and low-income communities. In these communities efforts have been increased to improve citizen encounters, yet mandatory arrest policies have disproportionate impact there.

Violence against Police and Court Personnel. Violence associated with domestic violence cases has seeped into the courthouse. Court officers now report increased violence inside the courtrooms. A graphic demonstration of this was filmed by PBS at a routine bail hearing on an alleged domestic assault in Quincy in order to obtain background tape for a documentary. They were astounded when the cameraman found himself filming the defendant assaulting a bevy of court officers while screaming to his girlfriend, the alleged victim, "I love you."

Conclusions

Tremendous progress has been made by police agencies in their efforts to respond more effectively to the needs of domestic violence victims. Many officers and departments now actively attempt to intervene. They correctly perceive their job to protect the victim and maintain society's goal to prevent violence. However, it is also an overgeneralization to state that police currently do everything possible to handle this pervasive problem. There are clearly many instances where the police continue to respond, if at all, perfunctorily—with the goal of extracting themselves as quickly as possible.

Research instead should acknowledge and build upon the following observations. There has been an almost unprecedented rapid, profound change in policies on domestic violence. Only a decade or so earlier, most departments had explicit policies or guidelines directing officers to separate parties and exit the premises. Within a relatively short time span, official policies have recognized the official role of the police in stemming violence and have undertaken extensive efforts to change deeper, ingrained practices. Responding to prevailing social science research, federal pressure, lawsuits, and political pressures from the battered women's movement, many departments have undergone at least two policy changes, including initially setting up crisis intervention/mediation-type efforts and now advancing a proarrest policy. These changes have also been reflected in official training materials that now more clearly define the police role in domestic violence intervention. Failure to acknowledge this sets up a "straw man" argument, allowing some writers to continue to critique the police for ideological or political reasons or out of ignorance of real changes.

Nevertheless, it is uncertain how extensive change has been on the street. Studies remain contradictory. Some show major increases in rates of arrest and/or other indices of real change; others indicate an apparent resistance to change. We can understand that this may be very disheartening to advocates for battered women, who see the many failures of police intervention and are still on the firing line, helping victims cope with real crises. Being confronted with unresponsive, uncaring officers or departments not unexpectedly reinforces their negative image of the police.

However, those who study implementation of change will recognize that change occurs sporadically, often organization by organization and in some cases with wide gaps within an organization. Some officers readily change their attitudes and behavior immediately. Others are far more skeptical. Still others will never change their attitudes but are forced by department pressure, or fear of liability, to begin to change. Finally, one might expect a residual category of officers who, until the day they retire, will always treat domestic violence as a low-priority item.

Street-level change appears sporadic, with some departments having "reformed" their policies to comply with legislative intent of revised statutes. However, there are still some key unanswered questions. While the current emphasis is on increasing the use of arrest in cases of domestic assault, *the impact of more aggressive intervention remains unclear. There are some key questions regarding the appropriate role of arrest in cases of domestic assault.*

- Does arrest really deter potential offenders or those arrested from reoffending?

- Does the increased use of arrest really cause a larger number of victims to contact police or are we limiting the numbers of victims to those who want arrest?

Clearly, the possibility of unintended, adverse consequences to the victim and her family, the police, other agencies, and even the abuser should be explored to determine the extent and depth of such consequences and what methods could be pursued to limit negative impacts while preserving the recognized benefits of a proactive response. From this effort, we would anticipate even further growth of integrated programs with a better understanding of the diverse needs of the population of victims and batterers.

We also need to *better address the "costs," economic and otherwise, incurred by police departments* that use arrest widely for domestic assault. Can these aggressive arrest practices be successfully reconciled with competing initiatives of modern police administrators, including community policing (a policy that appears to deliberately make police *less* authoritative), which places an emphasis on responding to public disorder? Does the current emphasis on domestic assault displace resources, or are budgetary increases sufficient to address this?

What makes certain departments change? Is the most effective motive for agency change fear of adverse consequences (e.g., political pressure and/or lawsuits)? If so, are there other methods to affect the behavior of those agencies and officers who, to date, have refused to change? In such cases can a dynamic police executive implement rapid and profound organizational change simply through leadership? Is there a particular training scheme/orientation that is more effective than others at increasing the rate of change?

Can measures of police accountability realistically be increased? Are particular characteristics of police organizations, or of the service population of their respective cities, conducive to rapid or slower rates of change?

Hopefully, the reader is encouraged by the tremendous strides that have been made in recent years. Considerable positive change *has* occurred. However the limitations and repercussions have yet to be satisfactorily addressed.

Notes

[1] Of course, the problem is that a victim's desire to arrest was itself usually *insufficient*. In fact, we found that while victim preferences were very important in Detroit, Michigan, in other departments this was not a factor. A study of Massachusetts departments found that approximately 75 percent of the responding officers could not even *report* what the victim's preferences were, let alone follow them.

[2] Preliminary research in Quincy, Massachusetts (Buzawa, Hotaling, Klein, and Byrne, 1996), indicates that prior criminal record may be the critical variable (as with other offenses), rather than social class or employment. If proven, policy implications may be easier to implement.

References

Bachman, R. and A. L. Coker. (1995). "Police Involvement in Domestic Violence: The Interactive Effects of Victim Injury, Offenders' History of Violence, and Race." *Violence and Victims* 10(2): 91–106.

Bayley, D. H. (1986). "The Tactical Choices of Police Patrol Officers." *Journal of Criminal Justice* 14: 329–48.

Belknap, J., D. L. R. Graham, P. G. Allen, J. Hartman, V. Lippen, and J. Sutherland. (1999, October/November). "Predicting Court Outcomes in Intimate Partner Violence Cases: Preliminary Findings." *Domestic Violence Report* 5: 1–2, 9–10.

Bent-Goodley, T. (2001). "Eradicating Domestic Violence in the African American Community: A Literature Review and Action Agenda." *Trauma, Violence & Abuse: A Review Journal* 2: 316–30.

Berk, S. F., A. Campbell, R. Klap, and B. Western. (1992). "Beyesian Analysis of the Colorado Springs Spouse Assault Experiment." *Criminal Law and Criminology* 83: 170–200.

Black, D. (1980). *The Manners and Customs of the Police.* New York: Academic Press.

Bowman, C. (1992). "The Arrest Experiments: A Feminist Critique." *Journal of Criminal Law and Criminology* 83(1): 201–8.

Buchanan, D. R. and P. A. Perry. (1985). "Attitudes of Police Recruits Towards Domestic Disturbances: An Evaluation of Training." *Journal of Criminal Justice* 13: 561–72.

Buzawa, E. (1979). "Legislative Responses to the Problem of Domestic Violence in Michigan." *Wayne Law Review* 25(3): 859–81.

Buzawa, E. (1988). "Explaining Variations in Police Response to Domestic Violence: A Case Study in Detroit and New England." In G. Hotaling, D. Finkelhor, J. Kirkpatrick, and M. A. Straus (Eds.), *Coping with Family Violence: Research and Policy Perspectives* (pp. 169–82). Newbury Park, CA: Sage Publications.

Buzawa, E. and T. Austin. (1993). "Determining Police Response to Domestic Violence Victims." *American Behavioral Scientist* 36: 610–23.

Buzawa, E., T. Austin, and C. Buzawa. (1995). "Responding to Crimes of Violence against Women: Gender Differences vs. Organizational Imperatives." *Crime & Delinquency* 41, 443–66.

Buzawa, E. and C. Buzawa (Eds.). (1996). *Do Arrests and Restraining Orders Work?* Newbury Park, CA: Sage.

Buzawa, E. and C. Buzawa. (2003). *Domestic Violence: The Criminal Justice Response,* 3rd ed. Newbury Park: Sage Publications.

Buzawa, E. and G. Hotaling. (2000). *The Police Response to Domestic Violence Calls for Assistance in Three Massachusetts Towns.* Washington, DC: Office of Community Policing, U.S. Department of Justice.

Buzawa, E., G. Hotaling, A. Klein, and J. Byrne. (1999). *Understanding, Preventing and Controlling Domestic Violence Incidents: An Evaluation of the Effectiveness of Formal and Informal Deterrence Mechanisms. Final Report.* Washington, DC: National Institute of Justice.

Coker, D. (2000). "Shifting Power for Battered Women: Law, Material Resources, and Poor Women of Color." *U.C. Davis Law Review* 33: 1009–55.

Coker, D. (2001). "Feminism and the Criminal Law: Crime Control and Feminist Law Reform in Domestic Violence Law: A Critical Review." *Buffalo Criminal Law Review* 4: 801–48.

Commonwealth v. Phillips, Worcester Superior Court, April 19, 1994.

Davis, R. C. and B. G. Taylor. (1997). "A Proactive Response to Family Violence: The Results of a Randomized Experiment." *Criminology* 35(2): 307–33.

Dugan, L., D. Nagin, and R. Rosenfeld. (2001). *Exposure Reduction or Backlash? The Effects of Domestic Violence Resources on Intimate Partner Homicide: Final Report.* Washington, DC: U.S. Department of Justice.

Dunford, F. W., D. Huizinga, and D. Elliot. (1989). *The Omaha Domestic Violence Police Experiment: Final Report to the National Institute of Justice and the City of Omaha.* Boulder, CO: Institute of Behavioral Science.

Dutton, D. G. (1986). "Wife Assaulters' Explanations for Assault: The Neutralization of Self Punishment." *Canadian Journal of Behavioral Science* 18(4): 381–90.

Eigenberg, H. M. (2001). *Woman Battering in the United States: Till Death Do Us Part.* Prospect Heights, IL: Waveland Press.

Eigenberg, H. M., K. Scarborough, and V. Kappeler. (1996). "Contributory Factors Affecting Arrest in Domestic and Non-Domestic Assaults." *American Journal of Police* 15(4): 55–77.

Elliott, D. S. (1989). "Criminal Justice Procedures in Family Violence Crimes." In L. Ohlin and M. Tonry (Eds.), *Crime and Justice: A Review of Research* (pp. 427–80). London: University of Chicago Press.

Epstein, S. D. (1987). *The Problem of Dual Arrest in Family Violence Cases.* Meriden, CT: Connecticut Coalition Against Domestic Violence.

Fagan, J. (1996). "The Criminalization of Domestic Violence: Promises and Limits." *NIJ Research Report.* Washington, DC: National Institute of Justice.

Faragher, T. (1985). "The Police Response to Violence against Women in the Home." In J. Pahl (Ed.), *Private Violence and Public Policy* (pp. 16–48). London: Routledge and Kegan Paul.

Fattah, E. A. (1999). "From a Handful of Dollars to Tea and Sympathy: The Sad History of Victim Assistance." In J. M. van Dijk, R. G. H. van Kaam, and J. Wemmers (Eds.), *Caring for Crime Victims: Selected Proceedings of the 9th International Symposium on Victimology.* Monsey, NY: Criminal Justice Press.

Feder, L. (1998). "Police Handling of Domestic Violence Calls: Is There a Case for Discrimination?" *Crime & Delinquency* 44(2): 139–53.

Felson, R. B. and J. Ackerman. (2001). "Arrest for Domestic and Other Assaults." *Criminology* 39: 655–75.

Felson, R. B., S. F. Messner, and A. Hoskin. (1999). "The Victim-Offender Relationship and Calling the Police in Assaults." *Criminology* 37: 931–47.

Ferraro, K. (1989). "Policing Woman Battering." *Social Problems* 36: 61–74.

Ford, D. (1983). "Wife Battery and Criminal Justice: A Study of Victim Decision-making." *Family Relations* 32: 463–75.

Ford, D. (1990). "The Preventive Impacts of Policies for Prosecuting Wife Batterers." In E. Buzawa and C. Buzawa (Eds.)., *Domestic Violence: The Criminal Justice Response.* Westwood, CT: Auburn House.

Ford, D. A., and M. J. Burke. (1987, July). *Victim Initiated Criminal Complaints for Wife Battery: An Assessment of Motives.* Paper presented at the Third National Conference for Family Violence Researchers, Durham, NH.

Ford, D., and M. J. Regoli. (1993). "The Criminal Prosecution of Wife Assaulters: Process Problems, and Effects." In N. Zoe Hilton (Ed.), *Legal Responses to Wife Assault: Current Trends and Evaluation.* Newbury Park, CA: Sage.

Fyfe, J. J., D. A. Klinger, and J. M. Flavin. (1997). "Differential Police Treatment of Male-on-Female Spousal Violence." *Criminology* 35: 455–73.

Gaines, L., V. Kappeler, and J. Vaughn. (1999). *Policing in America,* 3rd ed. Cincinnati, OH: Anderson.

Garner, J. and C. Maxwell. (2000). "What Are the Lessons of the Police Arrest Studies?" In S. Ward and D. Finkelhor (Eds.), *Program Evaluation and Family Violence Research* (pp. 83-114). New York: Haworth.

Harrell, A. (1991). *Evaluation of Court Ordered Treatment for Domestic Violence Offenders (Final Report).* Washington, DC: Urban Institute.

Hart, B. (1992). *State Codes on Domestic Violence: Analysis, Commentary and Recommendations.* Reno, NV: National Council of Juvenile and Family Court Judges.

Hart, B. (1995). "Coordinated Community Approaches to Domestic Violence." Paper presented at the Strategic Planning Workshop on Violence Against Women, National Institute of Justice, Washington, DC (March 31). Reading, PA: Battered Women's Justice Project, Pennsylvania Coalition Against Domestic Violence.

Haviland, M., V. Frye, V. Rajah, J. Thukral, and M. Trinity. (2001). *The Family Protection and Domestic Violence Act of 1995: Examining the Effects of Mandatory Arrest in New York City.* New York: Urban Justice Center.

Hirschel, D. and E. Buzawa. (2002). "Understanding the Context of Dual Arrest with Directions for Future Research." *Violence Against* Women 8(12): 1449–73.

Hirschel, D., E. Buzawa, D. Faggiani, M. Reuland, and A. Pattavina. (2003, July). "Victim-Offender Relationship and the Likelihood of Arrest." Paper presented at the National Institute of Justice, Research and Evaluation Conference in Assault Cases: Using NIBRS to Provide the Answer

Hirschel, J. D., C. Dean, and R. Lumb. (1994). "The Relative Contribution of Domestic Violence to Assault and Injury of Police Officers." *Justice Quarterly* 11: 99–117.

Hirschel, J. D., I. W. Hutchison, C. W. Dean, J. J. Kelley, and C. E. Pesackis. (1991). *Charlotte Spouse Assault Replication Project: Final Report.* Washington, DC: National Institute of Justice.

Hirschel, J. D., I. W. Hutchison, C. W. Dean, and A. Mills. (1992). "Review Essay on the Law Enforcement Response to Spouse Abuse: Past, Present, and Future." *Justice Quarterly* 9(2): 247–83.

Holmes, W. and D. Bibel. (1988). *Police Response to Domestic Violence: Final Report.* Washington, DC: Bureau of Justice Statistics.

Hotaling, G. and E. Buzawa. (2001). *The Nature, Scope and Response to Assault Victimization in Athol and Orange, MA.* Washington, DC: Office of Community Policing, U.S. Department of Justice.

Hutchison, I. W. and J. D. Hirschel. (1998). "Abused Women: Help Seeking Strategies and Police Utilization." *Violence against Women* 4: 436–56.

Institute for Women's Policy Research (1995). Measuring the Costs of Domestic Violence and the Cost Effectiveness of Interventions: An Initial Assessment of the State of the Art and Proposals for Further Research. Unpublished paper.

Isaac, N. (1994). "Men Who Batter, Profile from a Restraining Order Database." *Archives of Family Medicine* 3(1): 50–54.

Jones, D. and J. Belknap. (1999). "Police Responses to Battering in a Progressive Pro-Arrest Jurisdiction." *Justice Quarterly* 16: 249–73.

Kappeler, V., M. Blumberg, and G. Potter. (2000). *The Mythology of Crime and Criminal Justice,* 3rd ed. Prospect Heights, IL: Waveland Press.

Kinsport, K. and K. Fischer. (1993). "Orders of Protection in Domestic Violence Cases: An Empirical Assessment of the Impact of the Reform Statutes." *Texas Journal of Women and Law* 2: 163–276.

Klein, A. (1994). Recidivism in a Population of Court Restrained Batterers After Two Years. Unpublished dissertation. Northeastern University.

Klinger, D. (1995). "Policing Spousal Assault." *Journal of Research in Crime and Delinquency* 32: 308–24.

Langan, P. and C. Innes. (1986). *Preventing Domestic Violence against Women.* Bureau of Justice Statistics. Washington, DC: Department of Justice.

Langley, R. and R. Levy. (1977). *Wife Beating: The Silent Crisis.* New York: Dutton.

Lanza-Kaduce, L., R. Greenleaf, and M. Donahue. (1995). "Trickle Up Report Writing: The Impact of a Pro-arrest Policy for Domestic Disturbances." *Justice Quarterly* (12)3: 525–42.

Lawrenz, F., R. Lembo, and S. Schade. (1988). "Time Series Analysis of the Effect of a Domestic Violence Directive on the Number of Arrests per Day." *Journal of Criminal Justice* 16: 493–98.

Lerman, L. (1981). *Prosecution of Spouse Abuse Innovations in Criminal Justice Response.* Washington, DC: Center for Women Policy Studies.

Loving, N. (1980). *Responding to Spouse Abuse and Wife Beating: A Guide for Police.* Washington, DC: Police Executive Research Forum.

Malefyt, M., K. Little, and A. Walker. (1998). *Promising Practices: Improving the Criminal Justice System's Response to Violence against Women.* Washington, DC: National Institute of Justice.

Manning, P. (1988). *Symbolic Interaction: Signifying Calls and Police Response.* Cambridge: MIT Press.

Manning, P. (1997). *Police Work: The Social Organization of Policing.* Prospect Heights, IL: Waveland Press.

Martin, M. E. (1994). "Mandatory Arrest for Domestic Violence: The Court's Response." *Criminal Justice Review* 19(2): 212–27.

Martin, M. (1997). "Double Your Trouble: Dual Arrest in Family Violence." *Journal of Family Violence* 12: 139–57.

Massachusetts Supreme Judicial Court (1996). *Annual Report of the Massachusetts Court System.* Fiscal Year 1981–1996. Boston: Supreme Judicial Court.

Maxwell, C. and R. Bricker. (1999, March 11). *The Nature of Police and Citizen Interactions within the Context of Intimate and Domestic Conflict and Violence.* Paper presented at the Annual Meeting of the Academy of Criminal Justice Sciences, Orlando, Florida.

Mills, L. G. (1997). "Intuition and Insight: A New Job Description for the Battered Woman's Prosecutor and Other More Modest Proposals." *UCLA Women's Law Journal* 7: 183–99.

Mills, L. G. (1998). "Mandatory Arrest and Prosecution Policies for Domestic Violence: A Critical Literature Review and the Case for More Research to Test Victim Empowerment Approaches." *Criminal Justice and Behavior* 25: 306–18.

Mills, L. (1999). "Killing Her Softly: Intimate Abuse and the Violence of State Inverventions." *Harvard Law Review* 113: 551–613.

Moore, A. (1997). "Intimate Violence: Does Socioeconomic Status Matter?" In A. Cardarelli (Ed.), *Violence between Intimate Partners: Patterns, Causes and Effects.* Needham Heights, MA: Allyn and Bacon.

Municipality of Anchorage. (2000). *Analysis of Police Action and Characteristics of Reported Domestic Violence in Anchorage, Alaska Ten Year Study, 1989–1998.* Anchorage, AK: Author.

Murphy, C., P. Musser, and K. Maton. (1998). "Coordinated Community Intervention for Domestic Abusers: Intervention System Involvement and Criminal Recidivism." *Journal of Family Violence* 13: 263–84.

Office of the Attorney General, State of California. (1999). *Report on Arrest for Domestic Violence in California, 1998.* Sacramento, CA: Author.

Oppenlander, N. (1982). "Coping or Copping Out: Police Service Delivery in Domestic Disputes." *Criminology* 20: 449–65.

Osofsky, J. (1999). "The Impact of Violence on Children." *Domestic Violence and Children* 9: 33–49.

Pate, A. and E. Hamilton. (1992). "Formal and Informal Deterrents to Domestic Violence: The Dade County Spouse Assault Experiment." *American Sociological Review* 57: 691–97.

Peng, Y. and D. C. Mitchell. (2001). *Dual Arrest among Intimate Partners for Family Violence Offenses in Connecticut.* Middletown, CT: Connecticut State Police, Crime Analysis Unit.

Pierce, G. and S. Spaar. (1992). "Identifying Households at Risk of Domestic Violence." In E. Buzawa and C. Buzawa (Eds.), *Domestic Violence: The Changing Criminal Justice Response.* Westwood, CT: Auburn House.

Pierce, G., S. Spaar, and B. Briggs. (1988). *Character of Calls for Police Work.* National Institute of Justice. Washington, DC: Department of Justice.

Robinson, A. L. and M. S. Chandek. (2000). "The Domestic Violence Arrest Decision: Examining Demographic, Attitudinal, and Situational Variables." *Crime & Delinquency* 46(1): 18–37.

Roy, M. (Ed.). (1977). *Battered Women: A Psychosociological Study of Domestic Violence.* New York: Van Nostrand Reinhold.

Sanders, D. (1988). "Personal Violence and Public Order: The Prosecution of 'Domestic' Violence in England and Wales." *International Journal of the Sociology of Law* 16: 359–82.

Saunders, D. G. (1995). "The Tendency to Arrest Victims of Domestic Violence." *Journal of Interpersonal Violence* 10: 147–58.

Sheptycki, J. W. E. (1993). *Innovations in Policing Domestic Violence.* Newcastle upon Tyne: Athanaeum.

Sherman, L. (1992). "The Influence of Criminology on Criminal Law: Evaluating for Misdemeanor Domestic Violence." *Journal of Criminal Law and Criminology* 85(1): 901–45.

Sherman, L. W. and R. A. Berk. (1984). "The Specific Deterrent Effects of Arrest for Domestic Assault." *American Sociological Review* 49: 261–72.

Sherman, L. W., D. A. Smith, J. D. Schmidt, and D. P. Rogan. (1992). "Crime, Punishment, and Stake in Conformity: Legal and Informal Control of Domestic Violence." *American Sociological Review* 57: 680–90.

Smith, D. A. (1986). "The Neighborhood Context of Police Behavior." In A. J. Reiss, Jr., and M. Tonry (Eds.), *Communities and Crime,* Vol. 8 of *Crime and Justice: A Review of Research.* Chicago: University of Chicago Press.

Stanko, E. A. (1989). "Missing the Mark? Police Battering." In J. Hanmer, J. Radford, and B. Stanko (Eds.), *Women, Policing and Male Violence* (pp. 46–49). London: Routledge & Kegan Paul.

Straus, M. A. (1996). "Identifying Research on Criminal Justice Offenders on Domestic Assault." In E. Buzawa and C. Buzawa (Eds.), *Do Arrests and Restraining Orders Work?* Newbury Park, CA: Sage.

Straus, M. A. and R. G. Gelles. (1990). "How Violent are American families? Estimates from the National Family Violence Resurvey and Other Studies." In M. A. Straus and R. J. Gelles (Eds.), *Physical Violence in American Families: Risk Factors and Adaptations to Violence in 8,145 Families* (pp. 49–73). New Brunswick, NJ: Transaction Publishers.

Urban Institute (1996, March 29). *The VAWA Act of 1994: Evaluation of the STOP Block Grants to Combat Violence Against Women.* Washington, DC: The Urban Institute.

Victim Services Agency (1988). *The Law Enforcement Response to Family Violence: A State by State Guide to Family Violence Legislation.* New York: Victim Services Agency.

Wanless, M. (1996). "Mandatory Arrest: A Step towards Eradicating Domestic Violence, but Is It Enough?" *University of Illinois Law Review* 2: 533–87.

Wuest, J. and M. Merritt-Gray. (1999). "Not Going Back: Sustaining the Separation in the Process of Leaving Abusive Relationships." *Violence against Women* 5: 110–33.

Zorza, J. (1994). "Must We Stop Arresting Batterers? Analysis and Policy Implications of New Police Domestic Violence Studies." *New England Law Review* 28: 929–90.

Zorza, J. and L. Woods. (1994). *Analysis and Policy Implications of the New Police Domestic Violence Studies.* New York: National Center on Women and Family Law.

Information Technology Innovations in Policing

Meghan S. Stroshine

> Walking the beat is now a matter of "walking" through the reporting process with a keyboard rather than a nightstick in hand. (Ericson and Haggerty, 1997:395)

As suggested by Ericson and Haggerty (1997), the degree by which policing is being transformed by information technology (IT) innovations is profound. Undoubtedly, the technological advances that have had the most substantial effect on policing occurred early in the twentieth century. The inventions of the automobile, telephone, and two-way radio had dramatic effects on the way police performed their functions. Officers who were once relegated to walking a limited geographical beat with a nightstick in hand now drive vehicles that allow for greater geographical coverage, a more rapid response to calls, but ultimately, less face-to-face contact with the citizenry. The telephone, in combination with the two-way radio, also had a significant impact on the police profession in America. Once restricted to seeking out police officers walking beats in their neighborhoods, citizens are now able to mobilize the police simply by picking up the telephone. Moreover, the telephone served to make police accessible to the public at any time of the day or night, 365 days a year. The two-way radio allowed police departments not only to dispatch officers in response to calls for service, but it also revolutionized police supervision, allowing police supervisors to more closely monitor the actions of their officers.

Prepared especially for *Critical Issues in Policing* by Meghan S. Stroshine.

While the automobile, telephone, and two-way radio had a tremendous impact on American policing early in the twentieth century, one might argue that since the dawn of the information age, we have entered a second major wave of reform in policing: those innovations directly resulting from startling improvements in IT. This article highlights recent IT advances in the areas of communications, record keeping, operations, and administration that are significantly changing the nature of policing in the United States.

COMMUNICATIONS

911/311

After the invention of the automobile, telephone, and two-way radio, the next major advance in policing occurred in the 1960s, when in 1968 the President's Crime Commission argued that a national emergency number was necessary and 911 was adopted by the Federal Communications Commission (FCC) and AT&T (Abt Associates, 2000). In 2000, 89% of local police departments (employing 98% of all officers) used a 911 or a similar emergency telephone system. Today, most (71%) 911 systems are "enhanced," meaning that the systems are capable of pinpointing the number, location, and any special needs of the caller (see Figure 1) (Hickman & Reaves, 2003). By 2005, the FCC will require that wireless services have the technology in place to allow police to identify the location and number of incoming cell phone calls to 911 (McEwen, Spence, Wolff, Wartell, & Webster, 2003).

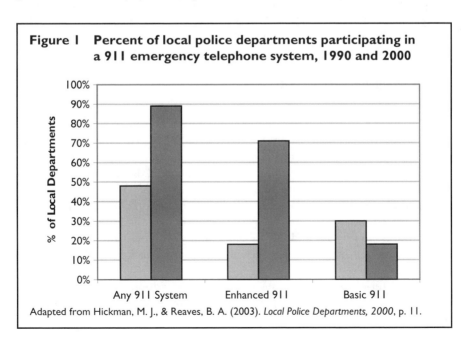

Figure 1   Percent of local police departments participating in a 911 emergency telephone system, 1990 and 2000

Adapted from Hickman, M. J., & Reaves, B. A. (2003). *Local Police Departments, 2000*, p. 11.

Since its introduction nearly 40 years ago, our emergency call system has been remarkably successful—perhaps too successful. While 911 was explicitly designed and marketed for use as an emergency call number, police dispatchers are regularly inundated with nonemergency calls for service, ranging from complaints about unkempt lawns to requests for driving directions. These nonemergency calls for service have created backlogs, inefficiency, and in some cases, death or other tragic consequences when citizens calling for assistance have received busy signals or a delayed response time due to an overload on the emergency call system (Harris, 2003).

In response to this burden on police agencies, several jurisdictions have implemented a three-digit alternative to 911 for nonemergency calls for service (e.g., 311). Baltimore was the first city in the country to adopt a 311 alternative to 911 in 1996, and by 1997, the FCC had designated "3-1-1 as a national, voluntary, non-toll number for nonemergencies" (McEwen et al., 2003). While only 3% of police departments surveyed in 2000 indicated that they had a 311 system in place for nonemergency calls, data from the pilot project in Baltimore demonstrate its effectiveness. During the study period, the volume of calls to 911 was reduced by 25% (Mazerolle, Rogan, Frank, Famega, & Eck, 2001), the average time taken to answer 911 calls was reduced by 50%, and the total number of calls dispatched to police units was reduced by 12% (Harris, 2003).

Another advance in communications technology are auto-dialing systems, also referred to as "reverse 911." This system allows law enforcement agencies to send prerecorded messages to every telephone in a predefined area (e.g., a neighborhood). These messages may contain information about crime trends, suspicious persons, and suggestions for reducing victimization. In addition, some auto-dialing software systems are capable of tracking outcomes after the system is activated, allowing police to gauge the effectiveness of these efforts.

Computer-Aided Dispatch (CAD)

Enhanced 911 systems have been augmented by computer-aided dispatch (CAD) systems. Traditionally, calls for service were handled by dispatching an officer to the scene as quickly as possible. This was not the most efficient use of police resources, however, since not all calls for service merited an emergency response. In fact, one study showed that 50–90% of calls to 911 were, in fact, nonemergency in nature (Harris, 2003). Computer-aided dispatch (CAD) systems now allow for the prioritization of calls by providing an automated means of classifying and prioritizing calls for service. Urgent calls are handled by immediately dispatching an officer to the scene, while calls for which a delayed response will suffice are "stacked" until an officer becomes available.

Computer-aided dispatch systems were first adopted by larger departments across the country (e.g., New York, Boston, Detroit) in the early 1970s with funds made available by the Law Enforcement Assistance Administration (LEAA). In 1990, 40% of police departments across the United States used CAD; by 1999 this figure had grown to 56%, with nearly all departments with dispatch functions serving populations of 50,000 or more residents using it (Hickman & Reaves, 2001).

Internet

There has been a significant increase in the past decade in the number of local police departments who have an Internet home page. In 1999, 18% of all local police departments (employing over 60% of all officers) maintained an Internet home page (Hickman & Reaves, 2001). Police departments can facilitate communication with the public by using their home page in a variety of ways. First, departments can provide a directory of its personnel, including names, phone numbers, and/or e-mail addresses, thereby facilitating the ability of the public to make contact with members of the agency. The Web site can also serve as an important vehicle for the posting and distribution of a wide variety of information, such as crime prevention information, a "most wanted" page, crime maps, and the like. Finally, the Internet may also be used to obtain information from citizens. One national survey found that approximately 6% of departments had features on their Web sites that allowed citizens to submit complaints, commendations, crime reports, and even crime tips online (McEwen et al., 2003).

RECORD KEEPING

In the past, records collected by police departments (e.g., crime incident reports, arrest records, field interview cards) were manually recorded, first with pen and paper and then the typewriter. Technological advances, particularly the invention of the computer, have made possible the more rapid collection, collation, and sharing of this information. "One of the earliest uses of computers in law enforcement was records storage and retrieval" (Craig-Moreland, 2004:300). Since the introduction of computers, data from handwritten or typewritten "hard copies" can be entered into computer databases, which allow for their storage and then retrieval at a later time. In 2000, the majority (60%) of local police departments (employing 85% of all officers) used computers for records management (Hickman & Reaves, 2003). Between 1990 and 1999, the use of computers by law enforcement agencies for maintaining various records increased substantially (Hickman, 2001). Figure 2 provides an indication of the percentage of local agencies in 2000 that maintained computerized records of various types of information.

While the number of local police departments maintaining computerized files has increased, it is still uncommon for departments to use computers to submit crime incident reports to the agency's central records system. In 2000, just 19% of local departments used computers for this purpose. This figure,

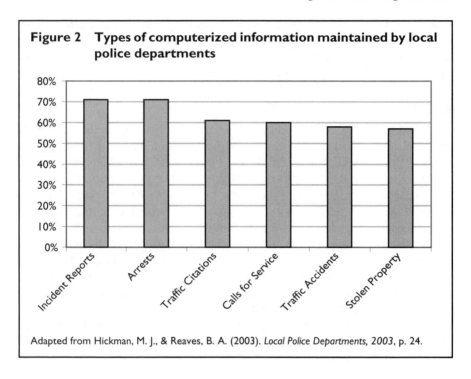

Figure 2   Types of computerized information maintained by local police departments

Adapted from Hickman, M. J., & Reaves, B. A. (2003). *Local Police Departments, 2003*, p. 24.

however, does represent a significant increase from 1997; between 1997 and 2000, the number of local police departments using computers to transmit crime incident reports has more than doubled, from 9% in 1997 to 19% in 2000 (Hickman & Reaves, 2003).

In addition, while computers allow for data storage and retrieval, efficient use of that data is not always the case. As Craig-Moreland (2004) noted,

> . . . most records are organized by case, and accessed by the name of the person for whom the record was created. This hierarchical structure limits access to those who know that key piece of information, making it difficult for officers to search for records by the date or type of an event. (p. 300)

Moreover, in order to allow for the efficient querying and analysis of data, databases must be linked. According to a 2000 survey of local police departments across the country, just 14% maintained linked data files (Hickman & Reaves, 2003).

ANALYSIS OF POLICE DATA

Crime Analysis

O'Shea and Nicholls (2003) state that there are three primary functions of crime analysis:

(1) assess the nature, extent, and distribution of crime in order to efficiently and effectively allocate resources and personnel, (2) identify crime-
suspect correlations to assist investigations, and (3) identify the conditions
that facilitate crime and incivility so that policymakers may make
informed decisions about prevention approaches. (p. 8)

The ability of law enforcement agencies to engage in crime analysis for these
purposes has been greatly enhanced by IT innovations. Computer-aided dispatch (CAD) systems and the computer have had a tremendous impact on
the ability of the police to analyze calls for service. CAD systems automatically collect certain information on every call—type of call, location, date,
and time. Based on this information and other information routinely provided by officers to dispatchers (e.g., time of arrival, time back in service),
officer response time and the time spent at each call can be easily calculated.
When these data sources are linked with others, crime analysts are capable of
identifying "hot spots" of crime, detecting patterns of crime and disorder, and
identifying factors or conditions that may be contributing to crime. According
to a 2000 survey of local police departments, a little over one-third (30%) of
departments used computers for crime analysis (Hickman & Reaves, 2003).

Crime Mapping

Crime mapping, at one time performed by placing "pushpins" in maps
displayed on precinct station walls, is now significantly more sophisticated.
Early manual maps using pushpins allowed for a simple visual representation
of crime. Today, due to computer hardware and software advances, police are
able to create maps that allow for the analysis of data. Crime mapping is
based on Geographic Information Systems (GIS) technology. As defined by
Boba (2001):

A geographic information system (GIS) is a set of computer-based tools
that allow a person to modify, visualize, query and analyze geographic
and tabular data. A GIS is a powerful software tool that allows the user
to create anything from a simple point map to a three-dimensional visual-
ization of spatial or temporal data. (p. 19)

Different types of data may be used with crime mapping, much of which
is regularly collected by law enforcement agencies (e.g., calls for service,
arrests). After beginning with a map, different databases serve as thematic
layers. Maps can be designed to depict different information, utilizing different databases. For example, a map might be designed to depict only the location of burglaries in a city, thus drawing solely on the database that stores this
information. This type of map is a "spot" map, and might be used to assist
police in identifying "hot spots" of crime. A more complex type of map,
referred to as a "thematic map," allows police to access far more information.
For example, by using a thematic map, it would be possible for police to
access several off-screen databases—in addition to the information depicted
on a "spot map." These databases might contain information about victim,

offender, and crime characteristics. With this type of map, analysts are able to manipulate and analyze the data behind the geographical representations on the map.

In 2000, 15% of local police departments, employing 59% of all officers, used computers for crime mapping purposes (Hickman & Reaves, 2003). Many of the departments using crime mapping software and hardware have acquired their technology with the assistance of federal grants, particularly those funded through the office of Community Oriented Policing Services (COPS) and the Making Officer Redeployment Effective (MORE) program (Boba, 2001).

OPERATIONS

Computers in the Field

Police now have the capability to use computers in the field. These computers are often referred to as mobile data/digital terminals (MDTs) or computers (MDCs). The use of in-field computers is still not commonplace; instead, they tend to be used by larger departments. In 2000, 40% of local police departments (employing 75% of all officers) used in-field computers or terminals. This is a significant increase from 1990, when just 5% of local police departments (employing 31% of all officers) used them (Hickman & Reaves, 2003).

Computers in the field can serve a variety of functions. Approximately one-quarter of agencies with in-field computers use them to prepare field reports (23%) or for communications (19%) (Hickman & Reaves, 2003). Field reports prepared using in-field computers may be saved to disk and submitted at a later point at the station house, or, depending on the software used by a particular jurisdiction, submitted online.

Used in conjunction with CAD systems, officers are able to obtain a variety of information about a call for service before ever arriving on the scene, such as the nature of the call, the location of the call, and the history of prior calls for service to the address. Police can also use in-field computers to collect a variety of information about the person(s) and place(s) with whom they come into contact. Figure 3 depicts the various types of information accessible to officers through their in-field computers.

While the effectiveness of officers has undoubtedly been improved by the increased accessibility of various types of data in the field, there has also been an effect on communications. The ability of officers to collect the types of information depicted in Figure 3 has had a significant impact on the demands placed on police dispatchers and the amount of time officers spend on the radio. While officers were once reliant upon dispatchers for information on suspects or driving records, it is now possible to obtain this information without using scarce airtime or bothering dispatchers.

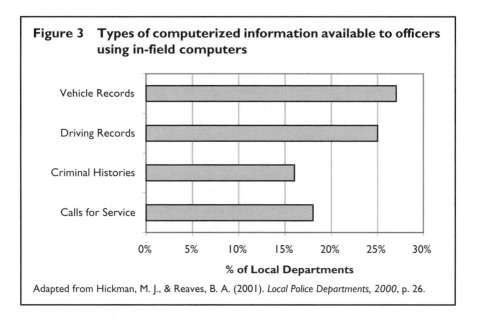

Figure 3   Types of computerized information available to officers using in-field computers

% of Local Departments

Adapted from Hickman, M. J., & Reaves, B. A. (2001). *Local Police Departments, 2000,* p. 26.

ADMINISTRATIVE

IT innovations have had an impact on the ability of police to perform a variety of administrative functions. IT innovations have made an impact in two particular areas: management/accountability and personnel/resource allocation.

Management and Accountability

Technology has aided police managers and supervisors in tracking and monitoring the behavior of subordinate officers. In the past and to a large extent today, subordinate officer behavior has been monitored by supervisors directly, either in-person or over the radio, and by administrators or Internal Affairs (IA) personnel who might take the time to examine an officer's personnel file. Performance evaluations and interventions tended to be reactive and piecemeal. If an officer received a citizen complaint, the situation was largely evaluated as an isolated matter, and any disciplinary action taken was in response to that incident. Today, innovations in computing technology are allowing for the identification of problems in a much more holistic fashion (e.g., taking into account an officer's assignment, activity level, past complaints or commendations), and allowing management to take a variety of preventive and preemptory actions.

Early Warning (EW) systems, also known as Early Intervention (EI) systems, are one such example. Data on officer performance (e.g., use of force, citizen complaints, pursuits, traffic accidents) are either entered into preexisting or new databases, which are then linked. Different software programs are then used systematically to evaluate officer performance, and to identify any area(s) of performance in need of correction. According to Walker (2003):

> the major contribution of an EI system is its capacity to spot patterns of performance and to intervene before problems lead to a serious incident such as a lawsuit, a citizen complaint over excessive force, or some other public crisis involving the department. (p. 8)

A 1999 study conducted by the Police Executive Research Forum (PERF) showed that 27% of local law enforcement agencies serving populations of 50,000 or more residents had an EW/EI system in place; another 12% indicated that they planned on implementing one (Walker, Alpert, & Kenney, 2001). Three case studies were conducted in departments using an EI system (e.g., Miami, Minneapolis, and New Orleans). Results indicated that an EI system can have a substantial effect on officer behavior, with a significant decrease in problem behaviors after supervisory intervention.

Just as EW/EI systems might be conceived of as data-driven systems of behavioral accountability and important management tools, so too might systems such as Compstat and its successors. Compstat is a management tool that was first adopted in 1994 by the New York City Police Department (NYPD) to hold officers and precinct commanders accountable for crime and the quality of life in the city. A critical piece of the Compstat system is the analysis and mapping of data. In fact, Compstat is an abbreviation for "computer comparison statistics" (Walsh, 2001). Each week, maps and statistics of crime in each of the department's 76 precincts are calculated. Compstat meetings, attended by precinct commanders and executive staff, are held as forums in which precinct commanders are held accountable for the crime figures in their precincts. This is also a time that precinct commanders and executives can discuss patterns of crime, high-profile incidents, and the effectiveness of various tactics and strategies being used to combat crime and disorder (Silverman, 1999).

While exact numbers on the prevalence of the Compstat model are unavailable (due to the varying forms of these programs), McDonald (2002) estimates that up to one-third of major cities across the country have adopted this or a similar model. The available research suggests a substantial effect on crime; in New York City, crime statistics for the seven major Index crimes declined by more than 50% between 1993 and 1998 (Silverman, 1999). Other cities (e.g., New Orleans, Minneapolis) have also reported double-digit decreases in reported crime (Walsh, 2001) after the implementation of a Compstat model.

Personnel/Resource Allocation

Traditionally, law enforcement agencies have deployed officers on the basis of the personnel available and workload demands. The extent to which these deployment decisions were based on an in-depth analysis of data, however, varied considerably. The introduction of CAD systems into policing had a significant impact on the ability of administrators to make more informed decisions regarding the allocation of patrol resources. By analyzing CAD data, administrators were able to confirm that some areas, shifts, and days of the week were busier than others, and were able to make resource allocation decisions accordingly.

Today, personnel allocation decisions may also be the result of crime analysis or crime mapping. For example, in departments practicing community or problem-oriented policing, or using a management model similar to Compstat, personnel from multiple units and functions could be deployed in response to a specific problem. In this way, IT innovations are helping police managers to be more flexible and effective in their allocation decisions, adapting to particular situations that may require more personnel.

CHALLENGES AHEAD

There are several challenges ahead for law enforcement. First, law enforcement agencies must learn to fully capitalize on the capabilities of their technology systems. Today, most large departments have computers and maintain computerized files; however, no department has yet to develop and operate a system in which these databases are linked and systematically integrated (Abt Associates, 2000; Manning & Stroshine, 2003). As O'Shea & Nicholls (2003) commented, "The combination of money and improved technology has vastly improved law enforcement's information processing capacity, but this improved capability does not necessarily translate into more complex data analysis" (p. 8).

Second, many departments have computer systems that are outdated. The time that it takes for computer systems to become outdated or obsolete has shortened considerably during the information age, with one innovation replacing the next in short succession. The budgetary crisis of the early twenty-first century is making this a significant problem, with police executives having to do more with less. There simply is not money in the budget to replace entire computer systems or to purchase costly software programs. There is also the issue of sunken costs; police executives and city managers are reluctant to devote large sums of money to replace a system after such a large initial investment.

As a result, many police departments are often forced to backfit various technologies to existing technology systems. Once a primary computer system is up and running in a department, a variety of *ad hoc* changes may made, perhaps the result of purchasing decisions, vendors, trends, and/or failed innovations (Manning & Stroshine, 2003). The result is a series of disparate, unrelated, and often incompatible technologies.

Different software programs utilized by law enforcement agencies in different jurisdictions will also pose a problem of compatibility. While we are increasingly able to recognize the need for greater collaboration and information sharing between agencies, the different technology and software programs being used in those agencies will pose a significant obstacle for the sharing and dissemination of information.

Finally, the police culture is one that is very resistant to change. Even with the capabilities available today, some departments (usually smaller agencies) are reluctant to part ways with old practices, or simply don't have the budget to do so. The ability of most officers to utilize the available technology is also in question. Although it is becoming more and more common that at least some college education is a necessary condition of employment, many forms of data analysis (e.g., crime mapping) require special expertise not readily possessed by most police applicants (or the population at large, for that matter).

These changes must be overcome, however, as the computer and Internet have become major breeding grounds for crime. Beyond the use of computers and the Internet for investigative and administrative purposes, a recent study by Correia and Bowling (2004) cautioned that law enforcement, particularly agencies at the local level, is ill prepared to deal with the burgeoning problem of cyber crime. These scholars suggest that there is hope, however. As they stated, ". . . just as law enforcement has adapted to the automobile, radio, and telephone, so too can they become a formidable foe of the cybercriminal" (p. 294). Clearly, law enforcement has met serious technological challenges in the past, and faces new ones in the future.

References

Abt Associates (2000). *Police Department Information Systems Technology Enhancement Project (ISTEP)*. Washington, DC: Department of Justice, Office of Community Oriented Policing Services.

Boba, R. (2001). *Introductory Guide to Crime Analysis and Mapping*. Washington, DC: U.S. Department of Justice, Office of Community Oriented Policing Services.

Correia, M. E., & Bowling, C. (2004). "Veering toward digital disorder," in *Contemporary Policing: Controversies, Challenges, and Solutions*, eds. in Q. C. Thurman and J. Zhao, pp. 285–298. Los Angeles: Roxbury Press.

Craig-Moreland, D. E. (2004). "Technological challenges and innovation in police patrolling," in *Contemporary Policing: Controversies, Challenges, and Solutions*, eds. in Q. C. Thurman and J. Zhao, pp. 299–303. Los Angeles: Roxbury Press.

Ericson, R. V., & Haggerty, K. D. (1997). *Policing the Risk Society*. Oxford: Oxford University Press.

Harris, E. (2003). 311 for *Non-Emergencies: Helping Communities One Call at a Time*. Washington, DC: U.S. Department of Justice, Community Oriented Policing Services.

Hickman, M. J. (2001). "Computers and information systems in local police departments, 1990–1999." *Police Chief*, 68(1), 50–56.

Hickman, M. J., & Reaves, B. A. (2003). *Local Police Departments, 2000*. Washington, DC: U.S. Department of Justice, Office of Justice Programs, Bureau of Justice Statistics.

Hickman, M. J., & Reaves, B. A. (2001). *Local Police Departments, 1999*. Washington, DC: U.S. Department of Justice, Office of Justice Programs, Bureau of Justice Statistics.

Manning, P. K., & Stroshine, M. S. (2002). "Information technology and policing," in *Encyclopedia of Crime and Justice*, Vol. 3 (pp. 1194–2000), edited by D. Levinson. Great Barrington, MA: Berkshire Reference Works.

Mazerolle, L., Rogan, D., Frank, J., Famega, C., Eck, J. E. (2001). *Managing Citizen Calls to the Police: An Assessment of Non-Emergency Call Systems*, Final Report Submitted to the National Institute of Justice. Washington, DC: Office of Community Oriented Policing Services, U.S. Department of Justice.

McDonald, P. P. (2002). *Managing Police Operations: Implementing the New York Crime Control Model*. Belmont, CA: Wadsworth.

McEwen, T., Spence, D., Wolff, R., Wartell, J., & Webster, B. (2003). *Call Management and Community Policing: A Guidebook for Law Enforcement*. Washington, DC: U.S. Department of Justice, Office of Community Policing Services.

O'Shea, T. C., & Nicholls, K. (2003). *Crime Analysis in America: Findings and Recommendations*. Washington, DC: U.S. Department of Justice, Office of Community Oriented Policing Services.

Silverman, E. (1999). *NYPD Battles Crime: Innovative Strategies in Policing*. Boston: Northeastern University Press.

Walker, S. (2003). *Early Intervention Systems for Law Enforcement Agencies: A Planning and Management Guide*. Washington, DC: U.S. Department of Justice, Office of Community Oriented Policing Services.

Walker, S., Alpert, G. P., & Kenney, D. J. (2001). *Early Warning Systems: Responding to the Problem Police Officer* (Research in Brief). Washington, DC: U.S. Department of Justice, Office of Justice Programs.

Walsh, W. F. (2001). "Compstat: An analysis of an emerging police managerial paradigm." *Policing: An International Journal of Police Strategies and Management*, 24(3): 347–362.

Introduction to Early Intervention Systems

Samuel Walker

THE CONCEPT OF EARLY INTERVENTION

An Early Intervention (EI) system is a data-based management tool designed to identify officers whose performance exhibits problems, and then to provide interventions, usually counseling or training, to correct those performance problems. EI systems have emerged as an important mechanism for ensuring police accountability.[1]

EI systems do more than just focus on a few problem officers. As a 1989 report by the International Association of Chiefs of Police (IACP) explains, an EI system is "a proactive management tool useful for identifying a wide range of problems [and] *not just a system to focus on problem officers.*"[2]

In an EI system, performance data are entered into a computerized database. These data include departmental use-of-force reports, citizen complaints, officer involvement in civil litigation, resisting arrest charges, and other performance indicators. Some current EI systems use a dozen or more performance indicators while others use a smaller number.

An EI system is early in the sense that it helps to identify officer performance problems that do not warrant formal disciplinary action but suggest that an officer is having problems dealing with citizens. The major contribu-

Early Intervention Systems for Law Enforcement Agencies: A Planning and Management Guide. Washington, DC: Office of Community Oriented Policing Services, 2003, ch. 1.

tion of an EI system is its capacity to spot patterns of performance and to intervene before problems lead to a serious incident such as a lawsuit, a citizen
complaint over excessive force, or some other public crisis involving the department. An EI system warns an officer to the extent that it sends an informal but
nonetheless clear message that his or her performance needs improvement.

An EI system is officially separate from the formal disciplinary system. It
is designed to help officers improve their performance through counseling,
training, or coaching. No record of participation in an EI program is placed
in an officer's personnel file, although a separate record of participation is
usually maintained by the internal affairs or professional standards unit. One
or more of the incidents identified by an EI system may warrant formal disciplinary action that is officially recorded, but identification by the EI system
remains separate from the disciplinary process.

EI systems are data-driven mechanisms of accountability, providing systematic data as a basis for performance evaluations of officers. They differ
from traditional performance review systems that rely heavily on subjective
assessments such as "works well with people" or "demonstrates initiative."[3]
The database can identify specific areas of performance that need correcting
(e.g., a pattern of citizen complaints alleging rudeness).

Bob Stewart, former Executive Director of the National Organization of
Black Law Enforcement Executives (NOBLE), says that "If I could choose
only one accountability mechanism, it would be an early intervention system." Stewart has seen police performance problems from several perspectives: he was a police officer in Washington, DC, the chief of police in
Ormond, Florida, and is now a consultant to communities and law enforcement agencies around the country. Based on this long experience, he now
regards EI systems as the single most valuable tool for achieving accountability, primarily because of their capacity to monitor a wide range of officer
activities and to spot performance problems at an early stage.[4]

EI systems are retrospective performance reviews. They do not attempt
to predict officer performance based on background characteristics or other
factors, rather they indicate that current performance levels, while not war-
ranting disciplinary action, still warrant improvement. Past efforts to develop
a methodology for predicting which applicants for police employment will
perform well and which are not likely to perform well have not proven successful.[5] An EI system provides a basis for counseling or warning an officer
that his or her performance needs to improve in the future, and in successful
cases, for documenting that the improvement has occurred.

EI systems are designed to help officers improve their performance. The
names of several EI systems reflect this orientation. The New Jersey State
Police EI system is known as the Management Awareness Program (MAP),
indicating its purpose of assisting management. In this respect, EI systems
represent a significant departure from traditional police disciplinary practices. Law enforcement agencies have been punishment-oriented bureaucracies, with innumerable rules and regulations that can be used to punish an

officer, but with few procedures for either rewarding good conduct[6] or helping officers with problems. Apart from employee assistance programs (EAP)
designed to address substance abuse or family problems, police departments
have done relatively little in a formal way to correct problem behavior.[7] An
EI system helps to identify specific performance problems that need to be
addressed (e.g., a tendency toward verbal abusiveness, frequent charges of
resisting arrest, etc.).

EI systems represent a problem-solving approach to officer performance.
The problem in this instance involves questionable officer performance. The
problem-solving involves identifying officers in need of assistance and providing that assistance through counseling or training. (The EI problem-solving
process is discussed in detail later in this article.) As one commander with EI
system experience explained, his agency's EI system "provides a way for the
department to provide non-disciplinary direction and training before the
officer becomes a liability to citizens, the department, and him/herself"
(*Early Intervention Systems for Law Enforcement Agencies*, p. 78).

EI systems are very similar to COMPSTAT programs. COMPSTAT is
one of the most important innovations in police management. It is a data-
based system designed to help law enforcement agencies respond effectively to
crime and disorder and to hold their managers accountable for their performance.[8] Both EI systems and COMPSTAT programs rely on the analysis of
systematic and timely data—in the case of COMPSTAT the data involve crime
and disorder, with EI systems the data involve individual officer performance.

EI systems are consistent with the basic principles of personnel management and human resource development.[9] Employers recruit, select, and train
employees to effectively serve the goals and objectives of their organizations.
Effective personnel management assumes that employee performance is
assessed and evaluated on a regular basis, and that the organization takes
steps to correct unsatisfactory performance.

Contrary to the expectations of many people, EI systems have not
encountered significant opposition from police unions representing rank and
file officers.[10] To be sure, there has usually been grumbling and fear of the
unknown, but in practice unions have not succeeded in blocking the operation of an EI system once it is in place. The police managers' survey found
that only 16 percent of managers had encountered serious opposition from
police unions (*Early Intervention Systems for Law Enforcement Agencies*, p. 79).
Potential opposition from unions is best overcome by involving union representatives in the planning of an EI system.

EI systems are consistent with the goals of community oriented policing
(COP). Community policing creates demands for responsiveness to community residents and in the process new measures of police performance. The
traditional measures of the crime rate and the clearance rate are no longer
adequate. EI systems have the capacity to quickly document the performance
of officers who are not effectively serving the community and provide a basis
for remedial action by the department.

The available evidence indicates that EI systems are successful in achieving their goals of reducing officer misconduct. An NIJ study of EI systems in three police departments found significant reductions in use-of-force and citizen complaints among officers following EI intervention.[11] Commanders with EI system experience, meanwhile, are able to report specific examples of individual officers whose performance improved as a result of intervention. One commander, for example, has described an officer who had on-the-street problems because of an excessive fear of being struck in the face. Intervention counseling identified the problem, and retraining in tactics helped the officer overcome the problem. Commanders report many other such success stories. In the survey of managers, about half (49 percent) reported that the system has had a positive impact on the on-the-street performance of their officers, while almost a third (28 percent) reported a mixed impact. No commanders reported a negative impact. Generally, managers have had very positive experiences with the impact of their systems of supervision and accountability (*Early Intervention Systems for Law Enforcement Agencies*, p. 76).

Box I   EI Systems: An Overview

- Data-based management information system
- Capacity for identifying and correcting performance problems
- Recommended police accountability "best practice"
- Separate from the formal disciplinary system
- Consistent with the goals of community policing
- Consistent with the process of problem-oriented policing
- Rely on systematic and timely data
- Consistent with the process of COMPSTAT
- Careful planning is needed for development and implementation

---

A WORD ABOUT TERMINOLOGY

Early Intervention

This report uses the term *early intervention*. It does not use the more widely used term *early warning*. *Early warning* has a negative connotation, suggesting that the system is primarily oriented toward discipline. One department with a comprehensive EI system found through interviews with officers that they did not like the phrase *early warning* because of its "big brother" connotation. EI systems are evolving in the direction of more comprehensive personnel assessment systems, for the purpose of examining a broad range of performance issues. For this reason, the more positive *early intervention* term is used here. Other terms are also appropriate. These include *Personnel Perfor-*

mance Index, as used by the Los Angeles County Sheriff's Department, or the *Personnel Assessment System* (PAS), as used by the Phoenix Police Department.

Officers with Performance Problems

This report uses the term *officers with performance problems* rather than the commonly used term *problem officers*. The latter terms unfairly labels officers and suggests that their performance cannot change. The term *officers with performance problems* focuses on behavior without labeling an officer and conveys the message that performance can improve.

A RECOMMENDED BEST PRACTICE IN POLICE ACCOUNTABILITY

EI systems have been recommended by a wide range of organizations as a best practice in police accountability.

- A January 2001 report by the U.S. Department of Justice, *Principles for Promoting Police Integrity*, includes EI systems among its recommended best practices.[12]

- The Commission on Accreditation for Law Enforcement Agencies (CALEA, 2001) has adopted Standard 35.1.15 mandating EI systems for large agencies. The CALEA Standard states that:

  A comprehensive Personnel Early Warning System is an essential component of good discipline in a well-managed law enforcement agency. The early identification of potential problem employees and a menu of remedial actions can increase agency accountability and offer employees a better opportunity to meet the agency's values and mission statement.[13]

The CALEA Standard warns that a department should not be faced with a situation where an officer is alleged to have committed a serious act of misconduct where "there was an escalating pattern of less serious misconduct, which could have been abated through intervention." The Standard suggests but does not require the use of such performance indicators as use-of-force incidents, citizen complaints, and disciplinary actions.

- A 1989 report by the International Association of Chiefs of Police (IACP) (1989:80) recommends EI systems as a means of controlling corruption and building integrity in police departments.[14]

- The U.S. Civil Rights Commission was the first agency to recommend EI systems, in its 1981 report, *Who is Guarding the Guardians?*[15]

- Since 1997, EI systems have been included in consent decrees and memoranda of understandings settling law suits brought by the Civil Rights Division of the U.S. Justice Department under the "pattern or practice" clause of the 1994 Violent Crime Control Act. EI systems are mandated in the agreements related to the Pittsburgh Police Bureau;

the New Jersey State Police; the Metropolitan Police Department of Washington, D.C.; the Los Angeles Police Department; and the Cincinnati Police Department.[16]

The consent decree settling the Justice Department suit against the New Jersey State Police, for example, requires the development of a Management Awareness Program (MAP) for the purpose of "maintaining and retrieving information necessary for the supervision and management of the State Police to promote professionalism and civil rights integrity, to identify and modify potentially problematic behavior, and to promote best practices . . ."[17] The consent decree with the Los Angeles Police Department (LAPD) sets requirements for an EI system, known as TEAMS (Training Evaluation and Management System). The consent decree specifies seventeen categories of data to be collected and entered into the system.[18]

Box 2   EI Systems Recommended By:

- U.S. Department of Justice
- U. S. Civil Rights Commission
- Commission on Accreditation for Law Enforcement Agencies
- International Association of Chiefs of Police

EI SYSTEMS AND OTHER BEST PRACTICES

EI Systems are the centerpiece of an emerging package of best practices designed to enhance police accountability. The other elements in the package of best practices, as recommended by the U.S. Department of Justice report *Principles for Promoting Police Accountability (2001)*, include a comprehensive use-of-force reporting system and an open and accessible citizen complaint system. Data on officer traffic enforcement can also be entered into an EI system and can be used to address the issue of potential racial bias in traffic stops.[19] The EI system is the central repository of data on use-of-force and citizen complaints (and other indicators). In this new paradigm of accountability, particular issues such as use-of-force performance are no longer treated as separate items but are linked to all areas of officer performance in a systematic fashion.

A Vera Institute evaluation of the implementation of a consent decree in Pittsburgh commented that "the early warning system is the centerpiece of the Police Bureau's reforms in response to the consent decree."[20] It is the mechanism by which these performance data become useful to managers committed to enhancing accountability and reducing officer misconduct.[21]

Goals and Impacts of EI Systems

The goals and potential impacts of EI systems are broader than generally understood. When the EI concept originally developed more than twenty years ago, EI systems had a narrow focus on "problem" police officers. The implicit idea was to "catch" the "bad" cops. As EI systems have developed over time, however, police managers increasingly understand that they have broader goals and potential impacts, including individual officers, supervisors, and the department as a whole.

Individual Officers

EI systems have a major focus on individual officers. The goal of the system is to correct the performance of officers who appear to be having performance problems. The NIJ study found that the EI systems investigated did succeed in reducing citizen complaints and officer use of force among officers subject to intervention. . . .

One important change that has occurred is that there is now a broader definition of a "problem" employee. Originally, problem officers were defined primarily as those who frequently used excessive force and received a large number of citizen complaints. Reflecting a broader approach, however, the commander responsible for the Pittsburgh Police Bureau's PARS reports that the system allows them to identify their "top performers" and their "under-performers" as well as their "problem officers." Another police department with a comprehensive system, for example, identified an officer who had made no arrests, no pedestrian stops, and no traffic stops in a given time period. The data also indicated that this officer was working the maximum number of permissible hours of off-duty employment. These indicators allowed the department to take the appropriate corrective action.

The capacity to identify top performers as well as officers with performance problems requires a comprehensive EI system such as the Pittsburgh PARS. Most of the early EI systems are not able to identify under-performers, however, because they do not collect the necessary performance data, such as arrest activity. . . .

Supervisors

An EI system also reorients the role of supervisors in a department. An EI database provides first-line supervisors with documentary evidence of officers' performance and permits both a detailed analysis of individual officers and comparisons among officers. In the survey of police managers . . . one manager reported that the EI system as "A useful tool to involve supervisors and lieutenants in non-traditional models of problem solving. It has served to enhance their management skills and help round out their people interaction skills" (*Early Intervention Systems for Law Enforcement Agencies*, p. 78).

At the same time, however, orienting supervisors to their new role is one of the major challenges facing EI systems. Engaging an officer with performance problems and helping that person to recognize his or her performance problems is a role that many supervisors are reluctant to undertake. Some prefer to define their role as friend and supporter of their officers. Some do not have the skills for the task. Most have not been properly trained for this new role. Supervisor training tends to emphasize the formal disciplinary aspects of the job. The intervention phase of an EI system requires supervisors to be a combination of coach and trainer, providing a delicate mix of support, criticism, and help.[23]

As already mentioned, the Pittsburgh PARS takes a special approach to reorienting the role of supervisors. Sergeants are required to access the system's database and review the performance of officers under their command. In addition, as mentioned earlier, the PARS requires sergeants to conduct "roll-bys" of officers who have been identified by the system. In this way, PARS creates a structured and systematic form of intensive supervision for officers who have been identified as having performance problems. (In this and other systems, a supervisor has a password granting access to all officers under his or her command but no other officers. A district commander at the rank of captain, for example, would have access to the records of all lieutenants, sergeants, and officers in that district.)

Some EI systems record each supervisor's access of the system. Thus, the performance review of a sergeant can include a review of the extent to which he or she accessed the system during the period under review.

An evaluation of the consent decree in Pittsburgh concluded that the department's PARS "marks a sweeping change in the duties of the lowest level supervisors." Supervisors log on to the PARS each day prior to roll call. The screen notifies each supervisor of any critical incident involving an officer under his or her command since the last time that supervisor logged on.[24]

The consent decree regarding the Los Angeles Police Department requires that "on a regular basis, supervisors review and analyze all relevant information in TEAMS II about officers under their supervision . . . ."[25] Additionally, the consent decree requires that "LAPD managers on a regular basis review and analyze relevant information in TEAMS II about subordinate managers and supervisors in their command . . . and that managers' and supervisors' performance in implementing the provisions of the TEAMS II protocol shall be taken into account in their annual personnel performance evaluations."[26] The consent decree involving the Cincinnati Police Department contains a similar requirement that supervisors be evaluated on the basis of "they're to use the risk management system to enhance department effectiveness and reduce risk"[27]

EI systems can also address the problem that, with regular shift changes, sergeants often find themselves responsible for officers who they do not know. As one commander reports, "There is a lot of movement of personnel, so supervisors often do not know the histories of their officers. The EWS report

---

Box 3   Goals and Impacts of EI Systems

The Individual Officer
• Improved Performance
• Higher Standards of Accountability

Supervisors
• Improved Supervisory Practices
• Higher Standards of Accountability as Supervisors

The Department
• Higher Standards of Accountability
• Reduction in Litigation
• Improved Community Relations

---

brings them up to speed in a much more timely fashion" (*Early Intervention Systems for Law Enforcement Agencies*, p. 78).

The San Jose Police Department has taken EI systems to a new level by developing a Supervisor's Intervention Program (SIP) that addresses the performance of supervisors as well as rank and file officers. Whenever the team of officers under a supervisor's command receives three or more citizen complaints within a six-month period, the supervisor is required to meet with his or her chain of command and the head of Internal Affairs. (The San Jose EI system relies only on citizen complaints.) In the first year of the SIP program, four supervisors met the thresholds and were counseled by the department.[28]

Some departments are exploring ways to use their EI system to hold sergeants accountable. The San Jose Police Department, for example, identifies sergeants when officers under their command receive a certain number of citizen complaints. This approach recognizes that many officer performance problems are the result of inadequate supervision.[29]

The Department

An EI system also has the potential for considerable impact on the department as a whole. The system defines standards of conduct and provides a database for measuring officer performance and identifying substandard performance. At the same time, a fully operational system redefines the role of supervisors, giving them specific duties related to supervision of officers with performance problems. And as mentioned in the previous section, the more sophisticated EI systems have the capacity to monitor supervisors' use of the system and to grade their performance accordingly.

Problems identified by the EI system can also lead to changes in departmental policy. The consent decree between the Justice Department and the New Jersey State Police, for example, requires that "Each supervisor shall, consistent with his or her authority, implement any appropriate changes or remedial measures regarding traffic enforcement criteria, training, and enforcement practices for particular units or subunits . . ."[30]

Over the long run, the cumulative effect of the changes in the role of supervisors and changes in departmental policy has the potential for changing the organizational culture of a police department and establishing new standards of accountability. In the police commander survey, one commander explained that over time rank and file officers came to accept the goals of the EI system: "Most no longer believe this system is out to 'get' them, but rather to assist them" (*Early Intervention Systems for Law Enforcement Agencies*, p. 81). A top commander in the Pittsburgh Police Bureau claims that PARS has begun to change the culture within the department. Two impacts are particularly notable. First, the system forces a more intensive form of supervision on the part of sergeants. Second, by identifying officers who are underperforming because they are devoting too much time to off-duty employment, and then correcting that problem, PARS helps to develop a greater commitment by officers to their primary employment.[31]

The positive impact on the organizational culture of a department is not guaranteed, however. If there is little effective use of the EI system—as in failure to conduct meaningful interventions with officers—the impact could easily be negative: reinforcing officer cynicism about the gap between stated ideals and actual practice.

LEARNING FROM THE CORRECTIONS PROFESSION

The corrections profession has already begun to incorporate the EI concept into its accreditation process. The American Correctional Association (ACA) is adopting a "performance-based" approach to accreditation. The indicators for agency performance are essentially the same as those used in law enforcement EI systems. The Performance-Based Standards for Adult Community Residential Services, for example, includes the following standard:[32]

> Number of offenders' grievances filed alleging inappropriate use of force
> in the past 12 months, divided by [the] Average daily offender population
> in the past 12 months.

The approach used by the ACA focuses on the agency, with organizational-level performance measures, while law enforcement EI systems focus on individual officers. There are good reasons for suggesting that the ACA approach is the better of the two. It properly focuses on organizational-level issues of management and supervision where corrective action can prevent future misconduct. The current law enforcement focus on individual officers tends to make scapegoats of a few officers, generate hostility from the rank and file, and ignore important issues of management and supervision.

EARLY INTERVENTION AND COMMUNITY POLICING

EI systems are fully compatible with the goals of community oriented policing (COP). In particular, the community policing movement has created demands for new measures of police performance.[33] Because COP reorients the goals of policing, new measures of are needed for both individual police officers and entire departments. The traditional measures of the crime rate and the clearance rate are no longer adequate.

Traditional police performance measures are inadequate in several regards. They emphasize crime, to the neglect of quality-of-life issues; they fail to take into account perceived community needs; and they fail to reward adequately good police performance.[34] By systematically identifying and attempting to control inappropriate behavior, an EI system can potentially reduce the number of incidents that alienate communities from the police.

One of the basic goals of COP is to establish closer ties to the communities receiving police services. COP places particular emphasis on being more responsive to community concerns about the quality of police services, particularly with respect to racial and ethnic minority communities' concern about excessive force or other forms of inappropriate behavior by officers.

In this regard, Alpert and Moore recommend "the development of statistical evidence on the use of force and the incidence of brutality, discourtesy, and corruption . . ." This is precisely what an EI system does. Indeed, Alpert and Moore's approach suggests that a law enforcement agency's personnel data system should transcend a narrow focus on suspected officers with performance problems and include all current sworn officers.[35]

EARLY INTERVENTION AND PROBLEM-ORIENTED POLICING

EI systems are also consistent with the principles of problem-oriented policing (POP). In this case, the problem is not graffiti or public drunkenness, but those officers with performance problems. As initially formulated by Herman Goldstein, POP holds that law enforcement agencies should desegregate the various aspects of their role and, instead of attempting to address "crime" and "disorder" as global categories, should identify particular problems within each category and develop narrowly tailored responses appropriate to each. In addition, they should develop the appropriate performance measures for each problem.[36]

The POP process of scanning, analysis, response, and assessment (SARA) is, for all practical purposes, the way an EI system operates:

- **Scanning:** review of data in the EI system database

- **Analysis:** identification and selection of potential officers with performance problems

- **Response:** intervention with selected officers
- **Assessment:** post-intervention review of officers' performance

EARLY INTERVENTION AND COMPSTAT

EI systems are very similar to COMPSTAT programs in terms of both purpose and process. Both rely on the analysis of systematic data for the purpose of addressing problems and holding police managers accountable for problems under their command. An evaluation of the Pittsburgh PARS (its EI system) described one key element as modeled after COMPSTAT. The Quarterly COMPSTAT meetings in Pittsburgh involve a review of officers who have been identified by PARS. Area commanders make presentations about any officers under their command who have been identified and conclude with a recommendation regarding formal intervention. After a discussion, the chief of police makes a final decision on what course of action to take.[37]

COMPSTAT is one of the most notable police innovations in recent years, and has been widely adopted across the country. A COMPSTAT program involves a computerized database of timely and systematic data on criminal activity. Analysis of the data provides a means of developing rapid and narrowly targeted responses designed to reduce crime. Regular COMPSTAT meetings are designed to hold police managers accountable by requiring them to describe crime trends in their areas of responsibility and to explain what responses they have developed.

EARLY INTERVENTION AND RISK MANAGEMENT

EI systems can be a key component in a risk management system (RMS).[38] Risk management is a process for reducing an organization's exposure to financial loss due to litigation. In law enforcement, the major civil litigation costs arise from fatal shootings, excessive physical force, and high-speed pursuit incidents. An EI system database can readily identify patterns of individual officers and situations that represent actual or potential risks. It also provides a structured process for correcting those problems and reducing the potential financial risk. In fact, the expanded EI system in the Cincinnati Police Department, as mandated by a memorandum of understanding with the Justice Department, is called the Risk Management System.

EARLY INTERVENTION AND POLICE-COMMUNITY RELATIONS

EI systems represent a potentially effective response to the historic problems of officer misconduct and tensions between law enforcement professionals and the communities they serve. For many decades, alleged police officer misconduct, including misuse of deadly force, use of excessive physical force, and discourtesy, has been a major cause of tensions between the police and racial and ethnic minority communities. Civil rights leaders have alleged that minority citizens are not only the targets of police misconduct at a rate disproportionate to their presence in the population, but that police departments have failed to investigate citizen complaints about misconduct and discipline guilty officers.[39]

To an unfortunate extent, police abuse of citizens has been explained in global terms, typically labeling all police officers with a broad brush. Abusive behavior for example, has been attributed to a general police subculture, with the implicit assumption that certain attitudes and behaviors are common to all officers in all police departments.[40] Other observers have attributed abusive behavior to race, arguing that abuse reflects racist attitudes and behavior on the part of white police officers toward citizens of color.[41] Some observers have attributed overly aggressive or abusive behavior to gender, holding that reflects male norms of behavior.[42] Still other observers have attributed police misconduct to organizational dysfunction, arguing that poor leadership and low standards of professionalism have tolerated many different forms of police officer misconduct.[43]

The great virtue of an EI system is that it can pinpoint specific actions that are creating conflict with the community and the particular officers responsible for them. For example, if there are complaints in one neighborhood about frequent use of force, an EI system can help to confirm or refute the allegations, and if confirmed, identify the officers involved. At the same time, it can help to identify those officers who are engaged in active police work (e.g., a high volume of arrests) without resorting to inappropriate behavior.

Early Intervention and Racial Profiling

A comprehensive EI system has the potential for addressing the issue of racial profiling. The Pittsburgh and Phoenix EI systems collect data on traffic stops, including data on the race and gender of drivers. These data make it possible to identify officers who are stopping a suspiciously high number of racial or ethnic minority drivers. As a discussion paper by Samuel Walker argues, an EI system solves many of the problems associated with interpreting traffic stop data. Rather than use resident population data, as many reports do, an EI system permits comparisons among officers working similar assignments.[44]

In a predominantly Latino neighborhood, for example, it is to be expected that a high percentage of all stops would involve Latino drivers. The EI system database can help identify officers who are stopping far more Latino drivers than their peers. The data alone would not prove that racial profiling exists. Rather, it would be the starting point for supervisory review that would determine whether or not an officer's activities involve racial or ethnic bias. The peer officer comparison approach . . . is the methodology currently used in the Pittsburgh PARS.[45]

In one department, the EI system identified an officer who had a practice of stopping female drivers for questionable purposes. The department received a formal citizen complaint from one female driver who alleged that the officer made improper sexual advances during a traffic stop. A review of the EI database revealed a very high rate of traffic stops of female drivers. Combined with the original complaint, these data were sufficient to cause a formal departmental intervention.

Using peer officers as the comparison group solves the most vexing problem with regard to the analysis of traffic stop data. Most current data collection efforts use the racial and ethnic composition of the resident population as the baseline or denominator.

ONE SIZE DOES NOT FIT ALL DEPARTMENTS

There is no single model for EI systems. The outline of the basic components of a system described above represents a single framework. Each department can develop an EI system appropriate to its needs. These needs will vary significantly according to the size of the department.[46]

Medium-sized and small agencies do not need as complex and sophisticated a system as do large departments. Most of the available information about EI systems at present, however, is derived from large law enforcement agencies. Consequently, at this time it is not possible to specify the exact needs of medium-sized and small departments. Developing those needs is on the list or priorities for future research and program development. . . .

A WORK IN PROGRESS

Although EI systems are increasingly popular and have been recommended by a wide range of professional groups, they are far more complex than is generally realized. They require making a number of difficult choices regarding their design, and once operational require close, ongoing administrative attention.

EI systems are in a state of continuing development. There is no solid consensus regarding a single best way to operate a system. Local police departments have found that they need to continually revise and fine-tune their EI systems. As one police manager explains, "this is a new practice that may, and has, changed over time. It continues to evolve." Another explains that an EI system "needs to continuously evolve and expand" (*Early Intervention Systems for Law Enforcement Agencies*, p. 84).

Additionally, our understanding of EI systems is experiencing a paradigm shift. First, they are no longer seen only as a means of identifying officers with performance problems, but instead are recognized as an effective data-based tool for general personnel assessment. Second, instead of focusing exclusively on rank and file officers they are seen as a tool for promoting the accountability of supervisors.

Conclusion

Early Intervention systems are an important new tool for police accountability. They are data-based programs for identifying officers with performance problems and providing the basis for departmental intervention to correct those problems.

EI systems have emerged as a recommended best practice in police accountability. They have been recommended by a wide range of professional associations. In addition, EI systems are consistent with the goals of both community policing and problem-oriented policing.

Although they are growing in popularity, EI systems are still in the early stages of development. Departments are still wrestling with a number of difficult and important issues. These issues are addressed in the remaining chapters of this report.

Notes

[1] Samuel Walker, Geoffrey P. Alpert, and Dennis Kenney. 2001. *Early Warning Systems: Responding to the Problem Police Officer*. Research in Brief. (Washington, DC: National Institute of Justice, 2001). Available on the Web at www.ncjrs.org. NCJ 188565.

[2] International Association of Chiefs of Police, *Building Integrity and Reducing Drug Corruption in Police Departments* (Washington, DC: Government Printing Office, 1989), p. 80.

[3] Frank Landy, *Performance Appraisal in Police Departments*. (Washington, DC: The Police Foundation, 1977).

[4] Bob Stewart, Comments, Focus Group Session, Nebraska State Patrol, June 9, 2003.

[5] Gary Stix, "Bad Apple Picker: Can A Neural Network Help Find Problem Cops?" *Scientific American* (December 1994): 44–45. Bernard Cohen and Jan M. Chaiken, *Police Background Characteristics and Performance* (Lexington, MA: Lexington Books, 1973).

[6] Herman Goldstein, *Police Corruption* (Washington, DC: The Police Foundation, 1975).

[7] It is significant, for example, that a recent National Institute of Justice (NIJ) publication on developing programs to deal with law enforcement officer stress includes a section on "Selecting Target Groups" but contains no reference to specific performance indicators such as are commonly used in EI systems. Peter Finn and Julie Esselman Tomz, *Developing a Law Enforcement Stress Program for Officers and Their Families* (Washington: Government Printing Office, 1997), pp. 23–26. Available on the Web at www.ncjrs.org. NCJ163175.

[8] David Weisburd, Stephen Mastrofski, Ann Marie McNally, and Rosann Greenspann, *Compstat and Organizational Change: Findings from a National Survey* (Washington, DC: The Police Foundation, 2001). Eli B. Silverman, *NYPD Battles Crime: Innovative Strategies in Policing* (Boston: Northeastern University Press, 1999).

[9] Robert L. Mathis and John H. Jackson, *Human Resource Management*. Michael Poole and Malcolm Warner, *The IEBM Handbook of Human Resource Management* (London: International Thomson Business Press, 1998).

[10] One large city on the West Coast the union demanded that the EI system be subject to collective bargaining or meet and confer. The issue remained unresolved at the time this report was written. Nonetheless, this remains the only known case of union opposition to date.

[11] Walker, Alpert, and Kenney, *Early Warning Systems: Responding to the Problem Police Officer*.

[12] U.S. Department of Justice, *Principles for Promoting Police Integrity* (Washington, DC: Department of Justice, 2001). Available on the Web at www.ncjrs.org, NCJ # 186189.

[13] Commission on Accreditation for Law Enforcement Agencies, Standard 35.1.15. "Personnel Early Warning System" (2001). Commission on Accreditation for Law Enforcement Agencies, *Standards for Law Enforcement Agencies*, 4th ed. (Fairfax, VA: CALEA, 1999). www.calea.org.

[14] International Association of Chiefs of Police, *Building Integrity and Reducing Drug Corruption in Police Departments*.

[15] U. S. Commission on Civil Rights, *Who is Guarding the Guardians?* (Washington DC: The United States Commission on Civil Rights, 1981).

[16] The various consent decrees and memoranda of understanding, along with other related documents, are available at www.usdoj.gov/crt/split.

[17] *United States v State of New Jersey*, Consent Decree (1999), Parag. 40. Available at www.usdoj.gov/crt/split.

[18] *United States v Los Angeles*, Consent Decree (2000), Section II. Available at www.usdoj.gov/ crt/split.

[19] Department of Justice, *Principles for Promoting Police Integrity*.

[20] Robert C. Davis, Christopher Ortiz, Nicole J. Henderson, Joel Miller and Michelle K. Massie, *Turning Necessity into Virtue: Pittsburgh's Experience with a Federal Consent Decree* (New York: Vera Institute of Justice, 2002), p. 37. Available at www.vera.org.

[21] Samuel Walker, "The New Paradigm of Police Accountability: The U.S. Justice Department 'Pattern or Practice' Suits in Context," *St. Louis University Public Law Review*, XXII (No. 1, 2003): 3–52.

[22] Walker, Alpert, and Kenney, *Early Warning Systems: Responding to the Problem Police Officer*.

[23] Early Intervention System State of the Art Conference, Report (Omaha, 2003). Available at www.policeaccountability.org.

[24] Davis, et al., *Turning Necessity into Virtue*, pp. 44 (quote), 43.

[25] *United States v City of Los Angeles*, Consent Decree, Sec. II, Para. 47.

[26] The Los Angeles and other consent decrees are available on the U.S. Department of Justice Web site: www.usdoj.gov/crt/split.

[27] *United States v Cincinnati*, 2002: Sec. VII. 62. i.

[28] San Jose Independent Police Auditor, *2001 Year End Report* (San Jose: Independent Police Auditor, 2002), pp. 48–49.

[29] This program is described in Special Counsel Merrick J. Bobb, *16th Semiannual Report* (Los Angeles: Special Counsel, 2003), pp. 79–80.

[30] *United States v. State of New Jersey*.

[31] Unpublished Remarks. Early Intervention State of the Art Conference (2003).

[32] American Correctional Association, *Performance-Based Standards for Adult Community Residential Services*, 4th ed. (Lanham, MD: American Correctional Association, 2000), Appendix B, p. 82.

[33] Timothy N. Oettmeier and Mary Ann Wycoff, *Personnel Performance Evaluations in the Community Policing Context* (Washington, DC: The Police Foundation, 1997).

[34] Geoffrey Alpert and Mark H. Moore, "Measuring Police Performance in the New Paradigm of Policing," Bureau of Justice Statistics, *Performance Measures for the Criminal Justice System* (Washington, DC: Government Printing Office, 1993), pp. 109–140.

[35] Ibid.

[36] Herman Goldstein, "Improving Policing: A Problem-Oriented Approach," *Crime and Delinquency*, 25 (1979): 236–258. Tara O'Connor, Shelley and Anne C. Grant, eds., *Problem-Oriented Policing* (Washington: Police Executive Research Forum, 1998).

[37] Davis, et al., *Turning Necessity into Virtue*, pp. 45–47.

[38] Carol Archbold, "Innovations in Police Accountability: An. Exploratory Study of Risk Management and Police Legal Advising." (March 2002). Available at www.policeaccountability.org.

[39] National Advisory Commission on Civil Disorders, *Report* (New York: Bantam Books, 1968). NAACP, *Beyond the Rodney King Story* (Boston: Northeastern University Press, 1995). Human Rights Watch, *Shielded From Justice: Police Brutality and Accountability in the United States* (New York: Human Rights Watch, 1998).

[40] William A. Westley, *Violence and the Police* (Cambridge: MIT Press, 1970).

[41] The argument is implicit in the long-standing recommendations that police departments diversify their workforces and actively recruit more racial and ethnic minority officers. See, for example, National Advisory Commission on Civil Disorders, *Report*, 315.

[42] Catherine H. Milton, *Women in Policing* (Washington: The Police Foundation, 1970).

[43] This view is central to the movement for police professionalism and the reform proposals that dominated the professionalization from about 1900 to the present. Samuel Walker, *A Critical History of Police Reform* (Lexington, MA: Lexington Books, 1977).

[44] On using peer officers to evaluate officers' performance, see Special Counsel, *16th Semiannual Report*, p. 74.

[45] Samuel Walker, Internal Benchmarking for Traffic Stop Data: An Early Intervention Approach. Discussion Paper. Omaha, NE, 2003. Available at www.policeaccountability.org.

[46] Early Intervention State of the Art Conference, *Report*.

Compstat
An Analysis of an Emerging Police Managerial Paradigm

William F. Walsh

Police departments in New York City, New Orleans, and Minneapolis have reported double-digit decreases in reported crime since they instituted a new organizational management process entitled Compstat.[1] Compstat is a goal-oriented strategic management process that uses computer technology, operational strategy and managerial accountability to structure the manner in which a police department provides crime-control services. The development of this process has been attributed to the innovative strategies and the dynamic management processes developed under former New York City police commissioner William Bratton and carried on by his predecessor Howard Safir (Bratton and Knobler, 1998; Maple and Mitchell, 1999; Safir, 1997; Silverman, 1999). In 1996, Compstat won the prestigious Innovations in American Government Award from the Ford Foundation and the John F. Kennedy School of Government at Harvard University. Presently, an increasing number of municipal and state police agencies and county sheriffs departments are replicating the Compstat management process in their organizations.[2] The rapid adaptation of Compstat indicates that it is an emerging police organizational management paradigm. The purpose of this article is to analyze this paradigm and the change it brings to police organizational management.

Reprinted with permission of Emerald Journals, from *Policing: An International Journal of Police Strategies & Management*, (24)3 (2001): 347–362.

THE PARADIGM SHIFT

Contemporary law enforcement administration is engaged in a challenging and exciting period of redefinition. This process began in the 1980s with the foot patrol experiments in Newark, New Jersey (Pate et al., 1986), Flint, Michigan (Trojanowicz and Banas, 1985), and New York City (Farrell, 1988); the development of Problem-Oriented Policing in Newport News, Virginia (Eck and Spelman, 1987), Baltimore County Maryland (Cordner, 1986), and London, UK (Hoare et al., 1984); and Neighborhood Oriented Policing in Houston (Brown and Wycoff, 1987). It is exemplified by a period of examination, reflection, and experimentation that involves a variety of managerial and operational strategies. These strategies are designed to use organizational resources in new ways to meet public safety needs. However, they are also redefining the internal and external relationship within and between police departments and the communities they serve (Geller and Swanger, 1995; Sparrow et al., 1990).

This process of operational experimentation is challenging the core beliefs and attitudes of many police managers about what constitutes effective policing (Eck and Rosenbaum, 1994; Moore and Stephens, 1991). As might be expected, there exists a debate regarding what is the appropriate way for police managers to direct their organization's service delivery function. Some administrators favor the traditional bureaucratic professional model with its emphasis on efficiency and organizational control that has dominated policing for most of the last century (Goldstein, 1990). Others believe that community and/or problem-oriented policing is a more appropriate way of addressing the needs of our diverse communities and public safety. Advocates of this position claim that community policing has emerged as the dominant strategy of modern policing (Trojanowicz and Bucqueroux, 1990; Peak and Glensor, 1999), while others question the ability of community policing strategies to achieve their objectives (Greene and Mastrofski, 1988; Safir, 1997; Skogan, 1990). Lastly, there are those that believe crime prevention, order maintenance, and community safety are the products of integrated problem solving, strategy development, and intense managerial oversight of the entire organizational process (Bratton and Knobler, 1998; Kelling and Coles, 1996; Maple and Mitchell, 1999, Safir, 1997; Silverman, 1999).

As a result of this debate, the taken-for-granted commonsense rules and perspectives about the way that police organizations should be managed are being tested from within and without the profession. It may be said that policing is in the middle of what organizational theorists call a "paradigm shift," a period in which external demands, unanswered questions, and operational experimentation are challenging the established beliefs of the profession (Barker, 1991; Kuhn, 1970). It is during such a period that established beliefs prove insufficient to address current problems and new strategies are tested. Strategies are organizational game plans designed by managers to successfully respond to demands, achieve objectives, and insure proper performance by organizational personnel (Thompson and Strickland, 1998). Managers create organizational strategies to exert leadership and shape in a coordinated productive manner the way their organizations respond to environmental (internal and external) demands. According to this perspective the crafting, implementing and execution of operational strategies are critical management functions worthy of analysis.

EVOLUTION OF COMPETING OPERATIONAL STRATEGIES

The debate over police strategies is a direct outgrowth of the historical development of professional policing. However, this strategic shifting is not the creation of any one theorist, practitioner, or management philosophy. It is a direct result of the historical development of the police function in Western society and the offspring of centuries of searching for ways to create safe and secure communities.

The organizational development of municipal policing can be traced to the *Vigiles* of Rome (Kelly, 1973), fourteenth-century Paris, France, and Dublin, Ireland, 1786 (Palmer, 1988). However, it was the establishment of the London Metropolitan Police Force in 1829 that created the strategic model upon which all future municipal police forces were to be based (Fyfe et al., 1997). The administrative guidance of this department was based on a centrally managed, military style, hierarchical rank structure and mission statement (Peel's principles of law enforcement) that directed the officers to lawfully carry out their crime preventive services based on public need and cooperation (Critchley, 1973; Lee, 1901). The success of the London Metropolitan Police established administrative control through a centralized bureaucratic management structure and foot patrol by uniform officers as the primary organizational strategies for municipal policing throughout the nineteenth and early twentieth centuries. In the nineteenth century American municipal governments created decentralized, administratively weak, partisan, politically dominated police departments that utilized foot patrol to provide social welfare and safety related services as well as law enforcement (Reppetto, 1978; Richardson, 1974).

In America, a movement to reform municipal government emerged in the latter half of the nineteenth century that sought to establish a politically free, impersonally administered, tightly disciplined, rational, legal bureaucratic police organization similar to that created in London in 1829 (Reppetto, 1978). This reform movement failed but the concept of a politically free, strong administrator who would use the power of the chief's office to create change and successfully control the police organization was not lost on the police reformers that emerged in the early twentieth century. The police administrators who led this reform sought to create a neutral, tightly controlled, apolitical efficient police. They based their mandate upon law, scientific investigation, and a vision of police administration that is grounded in the principles of bureaucratic management (Goldstein, 1990; Johnson, 1981; Kelling and Moore, 1988; Wilson, 1989).

As a result, municipal policing during the period between 1930 to 1970 was dominated by a bureaucratic management control system known as the "Professional Model" that focused on internal efficiency and controlling crime as the primary mission of policing. This rigid, top-down system sought to control patrol officer discretion and centralized the management of day-to-day operations in the hands of the department's executive staff. Its primary focus was with the how to or means of policing instead of the end product or goals of police action (Goldstein, 1990).

The technological developments of the automobile, telephone, and radio during this same period gradually led to the radio directed patrol car replacing foot patrol as the principal police service delivery strategy (Fyfe et al., 1997; Peak and Glensor, 1999). For most of the twentieth century, police administrators believed that the most effective and efficient means of achieving crime prevention and control was visible random preventive patrolling by uniformed officers in radio directed patrol vehicles (Fyfe et al., 1997). The random-preventive patrol strategy requires that the majority of a department's police officers be assigned to patrol cars that roam their community's streets continuously at all times, observing and waiting for assignment (Sherman, 1986; Wilson and McLaren, 1977). The adoption of 911 emergency telephone systems in many cities beginning in the 1960s facilitated the accessibility of patrol services to the public. This increased the workload demand of patrol officers to such extent that rapid response by motorized patrol units became the dominant operational strategy (Sparrow et al., 1990). As a result, an organizational imperative evolved based upon the technical skills and values associated with responding to and recording incidents instead of preventing or solving the problems or conditions that created the incidents (Goldstein, 1990).

Thus, in the second half of the twentieth century, policing became dominated by a service delivery strategy that was based upon three strategic cornerstones: random patrol, rapid response to calls for service, and reactive follow-up investigation of crime (Cordner and Sheehan, 1999). The objectives of these three strategies are to deter and control crime; provide immediate aid to people in distress; and to deliver nonemergency services (Eck and Rosenbaum, 1994). However, research has failed to support their effectiveness at crime prevention and control (Greenwood et al., 1977; Kelling et al., 1974; Spelman and Brown, 1984).

The emergence of community policing in the last quarter of the twentieth century challenged the dominant operational strategies and management practices of policing. Today, the term community policing has become commonplace in the media, political discussions, academic texts, and households across this nation. However, community policing does not constitute a single organized program or strategy. Instead, it is described as a philosophy that is based on the rationale that the police must involve the community in a practical way in their mission and community problem solving (Trojanowicz and Bucqueroux, 1990). It encourages police departments to experiment with a variety of programs that engage the community in crime prevention and problem solving activities. Eck and Rosenbaum (1994, p. 5) note that the range of approaches to community policing is indicative of the flexibility of the concept as well as the difficulty of defining what it is.

Encouraged by federal funding, many police departments decentralized a portion of their patrol resources into community-oriented operations such as community resource officers, neighborhood foot beats, and substations. The primary objective of this decentralization is to put officers in direct contact with citizens and communities. Ideally, community policing is a bottom-up strategy that places emphasis on the police officer's ability to use information, judgment, wisdom, and expertise in working with neighborhood residents to fashion solutions to community problems. Community policing encourages police departments to use a variety of directed patrol tactics that are designed to meet the security and safety needs of specific neighborhoods. Consequently, it seeks to turn patrol from a reactive to a proactive function.

As such, community policing constitutes a major redefinition not only of patrol operations but also of the mission, function, and administrative practices of policing. At the very least, it requires the empowerment of patrol officers and operational supervisors who are responsible for developing solutions to community problems. It also demands that police administrators actively engage their external environment and assess the threats and opportunities they are facing in order to respond to them appropriately. Thus, community policing represents a significant shift in organizational power and control from administration to operations; from closed to open organizations (Peak and Glensor, 1999). This power shift requires a new flexible leadership style to emerge in organizations that have traditionally engaged in centralized command and control management (Moore and Stephens, 1991). The traditional police management culture emphasizes adherence to internal rules, procedures, and efficiency rather than effectiveness (Goldstein, 1990). There is a serious question as to the willingness of some police administrators to support this reform movement and the shift in power that it requires (Sadd and Grinc, 1996).

In fact, community policing represents a philosophy that is the antithesis of police cultural norms (Weatheritt, 1988). In many police departments community policing is the responsibility of an organizational sub-unit not the whole department. For example, 65 percent of departments serving 50,000 or more residents indicate that they have a, full-time community-policing unit (Reaves and Goldberg, 2000, p. 16). However, research has found that the process of organizational change needed to support this philosophy and make community-oriented strategies work, is often incomplete (Zhao et al., 1995). Many managers are unwilling to support empowerment of line officers because operationally the strategy is dependent on the lowest, often less experienced members of the patrol division who are ill-prepared to address complex community problems (Safir, 1997). Community policing for all its support by the national government has never fully achieved what its advocates hoped it would. Today, almost every specialized program developed by a police department is labeled community policing. While many police departments claim they are engaged in some form of community policing, the majority of them are still bureaucratically structured and delivering their services based upon the strategies of the professional model.

COMPSTAT—MANAGERIAL SYNTHESIS

Compstat is a goal-oriented strategic management process that builds upon the police organizational paradigms of the past and blends them with the strategic management fundamentals of the business sector. At the core of the Compstat process is a strong executive team who are centrally managing their organization's service delivery functions. However, this team is using information gathering and processing technology, flexible operational strategy, and managerial accountability to prevent and control crime and police communities. At the core of the Compstat process is a computerized information dissemination system, which is expected to process, map, and analyze weekly crime and disorder statistics. This information is then sent to operational managers in a timely fashion, usually once a week. These operational managers are empowered and held accountable to focus, manage, and direct their organizational sub-unit's problem-solving process towards addressing the crime and disorder issues associated with this data. This empowerment of the operational commanders to select their own tactics allows Compstat to blend the traditional command managerial oversight responsibility with the flexibility of the operational strategies suggested by community policing and problem-oriented policing (Safir, 1997; Silverman, 1999).

The New York City Police Department began conducting weekly crime control strategy meetings in January 1994 as a means to increase the flow of information between the agency's executives and the commanders of their operational units as well as to ensure the accountability of this process. The primary focus of these meetings is incidents of crime and quality of life enforcement information in each precinct (Silverman, 1999). Commissioner William Bratton designed these Compstat meetings as a way to make his 76 precinct commanders and their officers accountable for crime in New York City (Bratton and Knobler, 1998). These meetings enabled the executive staff to identify and discuss patterns and high profile incidents, review tactics and results on a face-to-face basis with operational commanders while at the same time cutting out the communication barriers inherent in large bureaucratic organizations (Silverman, 1999).

Bratton decided that the primary responsibility for day-to-day operations would reside with his precinct commanders and was determined to discover which of them would adopt a results-oriented strategy to reduce crime in their command (Bratton and Knobler, 1998). This process eventually created four levels of Compstat. At level one, the law enforcement executive empowers, then in Compstat meetings, interviews and evaluates the precinct commander as to his or her operational strategies and outcomes. This forces the commander to analyze problems and develop a plan to attack crime conditions and measure results prior to the meetings. At the meetings the plans, tactics, and results become the heart of the communication exchange between the executive staff and their commanders. At the next level down, operational commanders empower, interview, and assess their sub-unit commanders at command level meetings regarding their strategies and outcomes. They and their subcommanders are held accountable for the results they achieve and the resources they use to achieve them. Next, the sub-unit commanders empower, interview, and assess their sergeants as to their strategies and how they are deploying their resources to address crime conditions in the areas for which they accountable. At the lowest level, the sergeants are communicating and working with their officers to define strategy and develop crime control measures for specific street-level conditions (Bratton and Knobler, 1998, p. 239).

The Compstat process when employed in this fashion establishes accountability at all managerial levels under the direction of the executive staff and focuses the entire organization on the department's mission. Thus, Compstat by involving the whole organization goes way beyond the incremental structural changes that occurred during the adaptation of community policing but retains an organizational leadership style similar to that established by Sir Robert Peel during the police reform of 1829 and the professional reform movement of 1930–1970.

During the first operational year of the Compstat process, Bratton replaced three-fourths of his precinct commanders because of their inability to rise to the demands of this managerial system (Heskett, 1996). However, since he and his predecessor Howard Safir instituted and maintained this operational strategy, NYPD's crime statistics from 1993 to 1998 for the seven major index offenses show an overall decline of 50.05 percent. During this same period New York City dropped from a position of 114th to 163rd in the ranking of the 200 most dangerous U.S. cities with population above 100,000 (Silverman, 1999, p. 7).

Bratton and his leading strategist, Deputy Commissioner Jack Maple, created Compstat to turn a dysfunctional department into a functional one (Bratton and Knobler, 1998; Maple and Mitchell, 1999). It has been replicated and has resulted in crime rate reductions with similar statistical results in New Orleans, Minneapolis, Philadelphia, Newark, New Jersey, and several other cities. At the heart of this process is a new managerial perspective that is based on the belief that the police can and should control crime and improve the livability of neighborhoods not just react to it.

Bratton and Knobler (1998, p. 224) identified four principles that form the basis of the Compstat process. These are as follows:

(1) accurate and timely intelligence;

(2) rapid focused deployment of personnel and resources;

(3) effective tactics;

(4) relentless follow-up and assessment.

Accurate and Timely Intelligence

Underlying this principle is the belief that if the police are to effectively respond to crime and community needs, officers at all levels of the organization must have accurate knowledge of when particular types of crimes are occurring, how and where the crimes are being committed, and who are the criminals.

According to this principle, operational managers, supervisors, and officers, investigators, and special unit officers should receive, gather, and disseminate timely and accurate crime information. This information serves as the foundation for crime analysis, strategy development, and outcome evaluation. The strategic management concepts of teamwork and organizational systems thinking are stressed between operational commanders, crime analysts, investigators, supervisors, and officers. They are expected to work together to make intelligence gathering and its distribution effective. This information processing system in effect turns the police department into what Senge (1990) describes as a learning organization: an organization that becomes effective because it assesses, evaluates, and adapts its responses to the needs of its environment.

Rapid Focused Deployment of Personnel and Resources

This Compstat principle departs from the traditional managerial perspective that creates organizational subdivisions into competing power centers fighting over limited resources. Instead, it envisions the department as made up of one large team focused on the primary organizational mission. Compstat empowers operational commanders with the authority to use an array of personnel and other necessary resources to achieve their objectives. The empowered operational commander is in effect playing a role similar to the football quarterback. He or she "calls the plays" by coordinating the efforts of line and support staff personnel to achieve strategic objectives. At the Compstat meetings operational commanders can ask for additional resources needed to achieve their objectives. Also, the executive staff can shift resources from one commander to the other as tactical needs dictate.

Effective Tactics (Managerial Strategy)

Organizations using the Compstat process develop a strategic management system that uses organizational strategy to unite executive, operational commanders and officers' decisions and actions into a coordinated and compatible pattern. As such Compstat is both proactive (intended) and reactive (adaptive). Thus, strategy developed as part of this process can be a combination of planned actions or on-the-spot reactions to changing unanticipated conditions. Strategy is the process by which an organization responds to a variety of environmental conditions such as crime, disorder, citizen demand, public safety, and/or training of employees. Strategy makers must consider the critical managerial issue of how to achieve performance objectives in light of the organization's situation and resources. Objectives are the ends, and strategy is the means of achieving them. Under Compstat, the police organization is not deciding to remain committed to one service delivery strategy or the other. Instead, managers shape and reshape organizational strategy as events transpire and operational demands change.

This principle requires operational commanders to develop tactics (strategy) that will achieve the desired results of crime reduction and community order. Tactics are created after studying and analyzing the crime mapping and incident information provided by the department. Tactics are expected to be comprehensive, flexible, and adaptable to the shifting crime trends that are identified and then monitored. The Compstat process provides information that enables an executive staff to identify where their operational commanders' tactics should be developed, and to track the progress of tactics that are created and implemented. Under Compstat operational commanders are held accountable for:

- the quality of their plans;
- the quality of their efforts toward crime reduction;
- their managerial oversight of operations; and
- results (Safir, 1997).

Relentless Follow-up and Assessment

As in any problem-solving endeavor, an ongoing process of follow-up and assessment is essential to ensure that the desired results are actually being achieved. To be successful, Compstat demands that the executive staff as well as operational commanders constantly follow up on what is being done by their personnel, and assess results of their strategies. This is accomplished through the Compstat meetings where the executive staff and operational personnel communicate directly to each other on a regular basis. As a result, evaluation is ongoing and an instant feedback process is created for the assessment of tactical responses. These meetings provide the executive staff means to assess what worked and what failed, enabling them to better construct and implement effective responses for similar problems in the future. The follow-up and assessment process enhances managerial accountability and effectiveness because it lets agency executives and commanders at all levels assess their results and change tactics and deployment based on what they see and know.

Strategic Management

In the business sector, strategic management is defined as the art and science of formulating, implementing, and evaluating cross-functional strategies that enable an organization to respond to the demands of its environment and achieve its objectives (Thompson and Strickland, 1998). At the executive level, it focuses on integrating organizational elements such as information gathering, computer information systems, sub-units, and staff support systems to achieve the organization's mission. At the unit level, it constitutes the managerial integration of information, strategy, operational tactics, personnel, and strategy evaluation in order to achieve objectives. This is a proactive instead of a reactive approach to organizational administration.

Thompson and Strickland (1998, p. 3) identify the five basic tasks of strategic management as follows:

(1) forming a strategic vision of what is the basic mission and function of an organization in order to provide long-term direction, establish how the organization will achieve its mission, and infuse the organization with a sense of purposeful action;

(2) setting objectives—converting the strategic vision into specific performance outcomes for the organization to achieve;

(3) crafting a strategy to achieve desired outcomes;

(4) implementing and executing the chosen strategy efficiently and effectively; and

(5) evaluating performance and initiating corrective adjustments in vision, long-term direction, objectives, strategy, or implementation in light of actual experiences, changing conditions, new ideas, and new opportunities.

Taken together, it may readily be observed that these components are the defining characteristics of the Compstat process. Emerging out of this process is a new organizational management paradigm for policing that involves changes in: vision, mission, values, goals, engagement, empowerment, accountability, outcomes, and evaluation. This new organizational paradigm provides policing with a leadership style grounded in the traditions of the past while at the same time incorporating the organizational strategies of the present. Executives as strategic leaders centrally direct their departments while proactively developing and implementing an organizational direction that allows their department to initiate and reshape its activities to meet the demands of its operational environment. Simply put, Compstat is something new from something old. It is an overarching management process that allows the retention of positive elements of the past, i.e. strong executive leadership, while at the same time creating an organization flexible enough to respond to the dynamic changing environment faced by the police departments of today.

IMPLICATIONS FOR POLICING

It is too early to tell if Compstat can sustain the claims of its supporters that it is responsible for falling crime rates. Research and evaluation are just beginning to assess this process. However, its adaptation by police departments at the local and state level is moving forward rapidly. The success of this organizational strategy depends upon a variety of factors that must all be present to insure success, any one of which if missing can destroy its effectiveness. Caution must be exercised in the rush to adapt Compstat without carefully considering the change process associated with this organizational transformation. This analysis will examine these changes using the Compstat principles as the basis for this analysis.

The gathering of *accurate and timely intelligence* requires that police organizations actively engage their external environment in a structured and meaningful way. This will necessitate the training of officers in information gathering techniques beyond that demanded by current police report taking. Operational commanders will be required to reach out and communicate with community leaders and associations to obtain information about community concerns and conditions. The executive staff will need to assess their organization's current level of technology. Organizational information systems will need to be carefully evaluated and reprogrammed to provide information analysis in a timely and usable fashion for operational commanders. The technology to do this is easily attainable but it is not found in many police departments. Purchasing the appropriate software and reprogramming systems that have been used mostly for information storage will require a higher degree of technical sophistication than presently found in many departments and an additional expenditure of funds to purchase the appropriate software.

The *rapid focused deployment of personnel and resources* will require the full use of a department's internal and external assets. Compstat is the creation of the largest police department in the USA with 38,000 sworn officers. It has an infinitely larger resource base to draw from than Hickory, North Carolina, with its 126 sworn officers, which has also adopted the Compstat process. In many police departments, managerial use of police personnel is closely controlled by contractual agreements and by strong adversarial unions, which dictate staffing levels for patrol shifts. These agreements do not permit the flexible use of personnel required by the Compstat process.

Ideally, while this concept envisions the police department as one large team focused on its primary mission, the demand for results expected from operational commanders contains the antithesis of this concept. Compstat has the potential of enhancing competition between commanders as they work to achieve their objectives within a limited organizational resource base. Instead of working for the overall good of the team the department can be turned into competing power centers focused on individual instead of team objectives.

The development of *effective tactics* by operational commanders will require training in advanced analytical and problem-solving skills beyond that which most police managers are currently receiving. The development of tactics requires an understanding and knowledge of cause-and-effect relationships. Crafting strategy in the Compstat process is an exercise in outside-in strategic thinking. Operational commanders will be responsible for moving beyond the mere execution of tasks to solving larger and more complex problems. At minimum, they must be empowered and given the latitude by the executive staff to make operational changes to achieve the desired results. They will need to be evaluated on knowing when to do the right thing at the right time (Serge, 1990; Quinn et al., 1996; Walsh, 1998). This will necessitate major changes in police managerial development and culture.

Traditional police bureaucratic managers are cautious by nature. They usually focus most of their time and energy inwardly, solving internal problems and taking care of daily administrative duties. In traditional bureaucratic police organizations this is what is expected of them and what they receive rewards for (Osborne and Gaebler, 1993). It will be a major challenge to get these police managers to keep their strategies closely matched to the environmental drivers of changing incidents of crime and social disorder, changing needs of specific communities, special events, external political initiatives, and projected future demands. At minimum, rewards systems and managerial promotion systems will need to reflect the attributes of this new leadership role (Osborne and Plastrik, 1997).

Compstat demands the establishment of managerial accountability through *relentless follow-up and assessment*. However, police organizations with their civil service protected employees are vastly different organizations than the business corporations that are managed by strategic management. If a department has three operational managers all of whom are tenured civil service captains what happens if one of them is unable to fulfill the demands of the Compstat process? This presents a major question for organizational executives wishing to adopt this process. What do you do with the managerial failures?

Bratton addressed this problem by downsizing one managerial level of NYPD between the executive staff and the operational precincts. He abolished divisional commands and placed the inspectors and deputy inspectors assigned to these units in command of precincts. These are appointed ranks that serve at the pleasure of the police commissioner. If they failed to meet their command leadership requirements they could be demoted back to their civil service rank of captain and removed from command by order of the commissioner. Following Bratton's example, the 648-officer Louisville, Kentucky, Police Department, when it transitioned to a full Compstat model, placed appointed majors in command of operational districts. Similar to New York City, if these individuals failed to perform properly, they faced the possibility of removal or demotion by the chief of police. It remains to be seen if this becomes a standard managerial response to the tenured position problem.

In addition, results and outcomes can become code words for a process that has the potential to evolve into a statistically driven numbers game. Measurement criteria must be carefully selected and outcome measures agreed upon before this process is implemented. Strict oversight must be maintained because the demand for accountability and the potential competitiveness of this process can result in ethical dilemmas for a department. Both the New York City and Philadelphia Police Departments have found operational commanders falsifying statistics. However, if the focus of this process shifts to only statistics and not long-term community impact on crime and disorder it will violate what its creators envisioned and replicate the mistakes of the past.

Lastly, during Bratton's first two years in office civilian complaints against his officers had risen almost 50 percent. Allegations that the police had performed illegal searches had risen 135 percent and excessive force complaints were up 61.9 percent (Buntin, 1999). It seems that the more officers engage in quality-of-life arrests the more civilian complaints can be expected. It remains to be seen if this is an anomaly restricted to New York City. As other departments adapt this process, time and research will confirm or deny this result. However, it is a consideration for any executive command staff that wishes to adapt this process.

CONCLUSION

Compstat is not a quick fix to control crime or lower the crime rate. Creating more responsive and effective police organizations will require organizational changes that demand more than quick adaptation and limited structural changes. It will necessitate major reengineering of police organizations, changes in managerial culture and re-training of police personnel especially at the supervisory and managerial levels—all of which will take significant time and resources to achieve. Whether this process has a long-term effect on crime rates remains to be empirically established. However, since it is evolving into a new paradigmatic direction for police organizational management it should be subjected to ongoing independent analysis. Only through testing and analysis will we come to understand if Compstat is the appropriate direction that policing management should take to govern their departments and provide services in the future.

Notes

[1] NYPD termed the word "Compstat" which is shorthand for "computer comparison statistics."

[2] For example, Indianapolis, Indiana; Louisville, Kentucky; Boston, Massachusetts; Baltimore City, Maryland; Prince George's County, Maryland; Newark, New Jersey; New Orleans, Louisiana; Broward, Orange, and Polk County Sheriff's Offices, Florida; Seattle, Washington; Los Angeles, California; Hickory, North Carolina; Philadelphia, Pennsylvania; Illinois and Delaware State Police.

References

Barker, J. (1991), "Discovering the Future: The Business of Paradigms" 2nd ed., videotape, Charterhouse Learning Corp, Burnsbille, MN.

Bratton, W. and Knobler, P. (1998), *Turnaround: How America's Top Cop Reversed the Crime Epidemic*, Random House, New York, NY.

Brown, L. P. and Wycoff, M. A. (1987), "Policing Houston: reducing fear and improving police service," *Crime and Delinquency*, Vol. 33, pp. 71–89.

Buntin, J. (1999), *Assertive Policing, Plummeting Crime: Epilogue: Crime Falls, Doubts Arise*, John F. Kennedy School of Government, Cambridge, MA.

Cordner, G. W. (1986), "Fear of crime and the police: an evaluation of a fear-reduction strategy," *Journal of Police Science and Administration*, Vol. 14, pp. 223–33.

Cordner, G. W. and Sheehan, R. (1999), *Police Administration*, 4th ed., Anderson, Cincinnati, OH.

Critchley, T. A. (1973), *A History of Police in England and Wales*, 2nd ed. Patterson Smith, Montclair, NJ.

Eck, J. and Rosenbaum, D. (1994), "The new police order: effectiveness, equity, and efficiency in community policing," in Rosenbaum, D. (Ed.), *The Challenge of Community Policing: Testing the Promise*, Sage, Thousand Oaks, CA, pp. 3–23.

Eck, J. and Spelman, W. (1987), "Who ya gonna call? The police as problem-busters," *Crime & Delinquency*, Vol. 33, pp. 31–52.

Farrell, M. (1988), "The development community patrol officer program, community oriented policing in the New York city police department," in Greene, J. and Mastrofski, S. (Eds.), *Community Policing: Rhetoric or Reality*, Praeger, New York, NY, pp. 73–88.

Fyfe, J, Greene, J., Walsh, W., Wilson, O. W. and McLaren, R. (1997), *Police Administration*, 5th ed., McGraw-Hill, New York, NY.

Geller, W. and Swanger, G. (1995), *Managing Innovation in Policing: The Untapped Potential of the Middle Manager*, Police Executive Research Forum, Washington, DC.

Goldstein, H. (1990), *Problem-Oriented Policing*, McGraw-Hill, New York, NY.

Greene, J. and Mastrofski, S. (Eds.) (1988), *Community Policing: Rhetoric or Reality*, Praeger, New York, NY.

Greenwood, P., Chaiken, J. and Petersilia, J. (1977), *The Criminal Investigation Process*, D.C. Heath, Lexington, MA.

Heskett, J. (1996), *NYPD New*, Harvard Business School, Boston, MA.

Hoare, M., Stewart, G. and Purcell, C. (1984), *The Problem Oriented Approach: Four Pilot Studies*, Metropolitan Police, Management Services, London.

Johnson, D. (1981), *American Law Enforcement: A History*, Forum Press, St. Louis, MO.

Kelling, G. and Coles, C. (1996), *Fixing Broken Windows: Restoring Order & Reducing Crime in Our Communities*, The Free Press, New York, NY.

Kelling, G. and Moore, M. (1988), "The evolving strategy of policing," *Perspectives on Policing*, National Institute of Justice and Harvard University, Washington, DC, No. 4.

Kelling, G., Pate, T., Dieckman, D. and Brown, C. (1974), *The Kansas City Preventive Patrol Experiment: A Technical Report*, Police Foundation, Washington, DC.

Kelly, M. (1973), "The first urban policeman," *Journal of Police Science and Administration*, Vol. 1; pp. 56–60.

Kuhn, T. (1970), *The Structure of Scientific Revolutions*, 2nd ed., University of Chicago Press, Chicago, IL.

Lee, M. (1901), *A History of Police in England*, Methuen, London.

Maple, J. and Mitchell, C. (1999), *The Crime Fighter: Putting the Bad Guys Out of Business*, Doubleday, New York, NY.

Moore, M. and Stephens, D. (1991), *Beyond Command and Control: The Strategic Management of Police Departments*, Police Executive Research Forum, Washington, DC.

Osborne, D. and Gaebler, T. (1993), *Reinventing Government—How the Entrepreneurial Spirit is Transforming the Public Sector*, Penguin, New York, NY.

Osborne, D. and Plastrik, P. (1997), *Banishing Bureaucracy: The Five Strategies for Reinventing Government*, Addison-Wesley, Reading, MA.

Palmer, S. (1988), *Police and Protest in England and Ireland 1780–1850*, Cambridge Press, New York, NY.

Pate, A., Wycoff, M., Skogan, M. W. and Sherman, L. (1986), *Reducing Fear of Crime in Houston and Newark: A Summary Report*, Police Foundation, Washington, DC.

Peak, K. and Glensor, R. (1999), *Community Policing and Problem Solving: Strategies and Practices*, Prentice-Hall, Upper Saddle River, NJ.

Quinn, J., Anderson, P. and Finkelstein, S. (1996), "Managing professional intellect: making the most of the best," *Harvard Business Review*, March-April, pp. 71–80.

Reaves, B. and Goldberg, A. (2000), *Local Police Departments 1997*, U.S. Department of Justice, Office of Justice Programs, Washington, DC.

Reppetto, T. (1978), *The Blue Parade*, The Free Press, New York, NY.

Richardson, J. (1974), *Urban Police in the United States*, National University Publications, Port Washington, NY.

Sadd, S. and Grinc, R. (1996), "Implementation challenges in community policing: innovative neighborhood-oriented policing in eight cites," *Research in Brief*, National Institute of Justice, Washington, DC.

Safir, H. (1997), "Goal-oriented community policing: the NYPD approach," *The Police Chief*, December, pp. 31–58.

Senge, P. (1990), *The Fifth Discipline: The Art & Practice of The Learning Organization*, Doubleday, New York, NY.

Sherman, L. (1986), "Policing communities: what works?" in *Communities and Crime*, Reiss, A. Jr. and Tonry, M. (Eds.), The University of Chicago Press, Chicago, IL, pp. 343–86.

Silverman, E. (1999), *NYPD Battles Crime: Innovative Strategies in Policing*, Northeastern University Press, Boston, MA.

Skogan, W. (1990), *Disorder and Decline: Crime and the Spiral of Decay in American Neighborhoods*, Free Press, New York, NY.

Sparrow, M., Moore, M. and Kennedy, D. (1990), *Beyond 911: The New Era of Policing*, Basic Books, New York, NY.

Spelman, W. and Brown, D. (1984), *Calling the Police: Citizen Reporting of Serious Crime*, Government Printing Office, Washington, DC.

Thompson, A. Jr. and Strickland, A. III. (1998), *Strategic Management Concepts and Cases*, Irwin McGraw-Hill, New York, NY.

Trojanowicz, R. and Banas, D. (1985), "Job satisfaction: a comparison of foot patrol versus motor officers," *Community Policing Series No. 2*, Michigan State University, National Neighborhood Foot Patrol Center, East Lansing; MI.

Trojanowicz, R. and Bucqueroux, B. (1990), *Community Policing. A Contemporary Perspective*, Anderson, Cincinnati, OH.

Walsh, W. (1998), "Policing at the crossroads: changing directors for the new millennium," *International Journal of Police Science & Management*, Vol. 1 No. 1, pp. 17–25.

Weatheritt, M. (1988), "Community policing rhetoric or reality," in Greene, J. and Mastrofski, S. (Eds.), *Community Policing: Rhetoric or Reality*, Praeger, New York, NY, pp. 153–76.

Wilson, J. (1989), *Bureaucracy, What Government Agencies Do and Why They Do It*, Basic Books, New York, NY.

Wilson, O. W. and McLaren, R. (1977), *Police Administration*, 4th ed., McGraw-Hill, New York, NY.

Zhao, J., Turman, Q. and Lovrich, N. (1995), "Community-oriented policing across the U.S.: Facilitators and impediment to implementation," *American Journal of Police*, Vol. 1, pp. 11–28.

Further Reading

Banner, D. and Gagne, T. (1995), *Designing Effective Organizations: Traditional and Transformational Views*, Sage, Thousand Oaks, CA.

Bolmam, L. and Deal, T. (1991), *Reframing Organizations: Artistry, Choice, and Leadership*, Jossey-Bass Inc., San Francisco, CA.

Brodeur, J. (1998), *How to Recognize Good Policing: Problems and Issues*, Sage, Thousand Oaks, CA.

Drucker, P. (1966), *The Effective Executive*, Harper & Row, New York, NY.

Mintzberg, H., Ahlstrand, B. and Lampel, J. (1998), *Strategy Safari: A Guided Tour through the Wilds of Strategic Management*, The Free Press, New York, NY.

Ogle, D. (Ed.) (1991), *Strategic Planning for Police*, Canadian Police College, Ottawa.

Rosenbaum, D. (Ed.) (1994), *The Challenge of Community Policing: Testing the Promise*, Sage, Thousand Oaks, CA.

Geographic Information Systems
Applications for Police

William V. Pelfrey Jr.

INTRODUCTION

In the new millennium, American law enforcement agencies have been asked to increase their efficiency and productivity with dwindling resources. One of the tools that police can use to facilitate a more efficient and effective response is a geographic information system (GIS). A GIS is a software package that links data sets (like arrest reports, census information) with computerized base maps to tell the police where crime occurs most frequently. A recent survey suggests about 13 percent of all police departments regularly use geographic information systems and many more agencies are integrating them into their routine (National Institute of Justice, 1999). Using a GIS has two key benefits for police agencies. First, by deploying officers in a more intelligent fashion, police agencies will have more officers available for proactive work (such as problem solving). Second, by identifying crime patterns and inferring where crime is likely to develop, police can engage in preventive work to reduce their future workload.

To take advantage of a geographic information system's capabilities, an agency must develop the appropriate layers of data, obtain base maps of the city or region, and make sure the people who will use them can understand and process the information. Next, maps can be developed to serve a variety

Prepared especially for *Critical Issues in Policing* by William V. Pelfrey Jr.

of purposes: describing crime patterns, linking crime to various factors or correlates, or predicting future crime patterns. This article will describe the process of developing maps, including data requirements, software options, and layer assembly, and will then consider some of the ways these programs can benefit police agencies.

CRIME MAPPING PROCESS

Electronic maps are usually developed within one of several software frameworks. An individual obtains a data set (for example, all the arrests made by the Gotham Police Department in 2003) then imports those data into a mapping program. When the data are overlaid with streets, city boundaries, and landmark maps, the operator can print out any of a variety of map types. The process of obtaining the right data, cleaning the data, and mapping the results can be somewhat daunting the first time, but once the infrastructure for data handling is in place, it is easily updated from month to month or year to year with new data. Some agencies have officers who are trained to implement and use these systems while other agencies hire consultants and trainers to develop the basic system and train officers to use them. There are several important steps in the process of developing these electronic maps.

Data Collection

The first, and most important, piece of the mapping puzzle is the data. For law enforcement agencies, the most common data sets are *arrests, offenses,* and *calls for service.* Most large to medium sized police departments have a computer system which works in conjunction with dispatchers to track calls for service, commonly called a CAD (Computer Aided Dispatch). Every time an individual calls for police assistance with a problem, a line of data gets created. These calls for service files can be complicated: Philadelphia, a city of approximately 1.5 million residents, annually generates 3.5 million or more calls for service. Many of these calls are redundant, which means several people call in the same event. For example, eight people may call in a gun shot at the corner of 1st and Main streets. A good dispatcher will code all these calls as a single event. Unfortunately, proper coding does not always occur. A single gunshot could be coded as an assault, attempted murder, discharging a firearm, possession of a firearm, or several other charges. At this point the offense file becomes most useful.

The offense files are based on police reports that are usually handwritten and then entered into a computer (although many police departments are now equipping officers with laptops and data are simply downloaded). When the officer arrives on the scene of the gunshot, he or she will create a report describing what happened, names of witnesses, details about the offender and the victim, and the resolution of the event.

The final, and smallest, data set is the arrest file. This spreadsheet presents details of all individuals arrested for crimes within a given district, precinct, or city. A common line of data in an arrest file would contain an event code number; date, time, location of the offense and of the arrest; arresting officer's badge number, name; offender's address; age, sex, and race of the offender; the charges for which the arrest is being made; and any extenuating circumstances of the arrest (possession of weapons or drugs). For a single event, the gun shot on 1st and Main, there may be seven or eight calls for service, at least one offense report, and one or more arrest reports. All of these are assembled into data sets that can be mapped for future use.

A number of other data sets are available to law enforcement agencies to provide depth and meaning to a simple map of crime. Census information presents much more than just the number of people in a city or county. The census collects a host of information on income, education, employment, number of people in a dwelling, whether people rent or own (a good indicator of the stability of a neighborhood), race, sex, and age breakdown of a community, and even how far people travel to get to work. These data are broken down by census tract (which usually contains between 2,500 to 8,000 people) and can be specified down to the city block level, although with less information. A police analyst could add census information to crime information to determine what area characteristics are most related to crime and use that information to develop preventive programs or assign officers. More information on these topics can be found at the census Web site: www.census.gov.

These data sets are all very interesting but are of limited use, from a GIS perspective, without a frame of reference. Maps of the county, the city, the streets, and the important geographic features (lakes, rivers, valleys, even street lights) are an absolute necessity to geographic information systems. Most maps of these types are available from geographic clearinghouses like universities, city planning groups, or even utility companies. For small or relatively new cities, maps of the city and all the streets may not yet exist and must be created on the computer. These files are not easy to generate but, once available, need only be updated occasionally. As cities change street names, build or close roads, and change geographic features (e.g. damning a stream into a lake), maps must be updated. A common way to develop or update maps relies on global positioning systems (GPS). A GPS links to satellites and uses a triangulation process to provide precise latitude and longitude coordinates. An exciting option for this process lies in Orthophotos. A plane with a photographic system can fly over a city and take detailed photos that are then scanned into a computer and converted to a database. These photos can aid in keeping data sets current or in enhancing the level of detail of existing map sets.

Data sets are limited only by the creativity of the analysts and available resources. Databases frequently used by police departments include: lists of all pawnshops, bars, liquor stores, hospitals, fire departments, subway entrances, churches, convenience stores, parking lots, and many other sites.

Sitting down with a phone book and a spreadsheet program may be the only step required to develop these databases. In other cases, particularly for illicit venues (a shot house, crack house, prostitution den, etc.) data collectors may have to find these locations to determine where these places actually are. After these data sets are collected they can prove very valuable to law enforcement agencies.

Data Reduction

While collecting the data sets is the first step in developing a geographic information system, the geographic portion has not yet emerged. The second step in the process is data reduction. This means the data sets have to be reduced to a manageable, geographically useful dataset. The key step in this stage is geocoding. Geocoding refers to assigning a geographic reference point to a bit of data. A person may be able to give directions using landmarks (go down past the Big Deal grocery store and turn left at the hot dog stand), but maps work best with latitude and longitude figures. To convert data points into information a mapping program can handle, each address has to be assigned a latitude and longitude code. This can be done by hand with a global positioning system if one only has a few addresses (i.e. all the movie theaters of a city) but for big groups of data, like all the houses in a city, driving to each address and recording the "lat" and "long" figures would take years. Instead, analysts acquire a list of all the addresses and run a geocoding program. The program "knows" where the street is and estimates where the address is on that block. For example, a geocoding program knows the latitude and longitude figures for Broad Street. The program knows odd number addresses are on the east side and even addresses are on the west side. The program knows the 1400 block is between 14th and 15th streets, which also have set latitude and longitude figures. The program would then take an address and estimate where it is on the street. The address 1450 Broad Street would be placed in the middle of the block on the west side and assigned a latitude and longitude code. Once the program repeats this process for every home, building, and business address a database is produced that combines addresses with a geographic reference point. A mapping program can then tie these geographic reference points to known reference points (the streets, the borders of the city or county) and place the address on a computerized map. This base map of all the addresses can then be tied to a data set of crimes, such as homicides, and the location of all the homicides for a given year can be mapped.

While this process may sound simple, in practice it is much more complicated. The old adage of "garbage in, garbage out" pervades the geocoding process. Addresses with a single typo are enough to throw a geocoding program into a tailspin. Coding a mugging as 131 Main Street is very different than the actual location of 1311 Main Street. Many cities have streets with similar, or sometimes identical, names. Atlanta, Georgia, has dozens of streets named Peachtree. King Street can be on the opposite side of town from King Avenue. Many of these quirks have to be corrected or smoothed out by hand to develop an accurate base map of the city with streets, landmarks, and addresses.

Once the base map is assembled, data sets can be compared to the base map. All the auto thefts for the month of August can be listed in a data set, and then mapped onto the base map. Each auto theft may appear using a symbol of a little car sitting on top of an address. Address matching is the process of assigning an address to each event, or auto theft. Every little letter and number has to be just right or the map can misrepresent the event.

It is important to remember that every piece of information carries significant weight. An error entering a social security number can prevent authorities from identifying a repeat offender. A typo in the name column can do the same. My name could be entered as William Pelfrey, William V. Pelfrey, Jr., Will Pelfrey, W. Pelfrey, Bill Pelfrey, or the dreaded Willy Pelfrey. These are all reasonable permutations of my name and a computer might not tie any of them to my arrest record.

Layer Assembly

The first two steps of the crime mapping process have occurred: data sets have been collected and have been converted into geocoded spreadsheets. These data sets must now be matched to existing or newly created maps of the city, street databases, and other templates. This is usually done within a mapping software package. These programs take spreadsheets of data and link them with maps to generate maps with data points of an event (i.e. a map of homicides) or some other descriptor of events (i.e. maps of hot spots of drug activity). Two of the most commonly used programs are: ArcGIS and MapInfo. Each is marketed on a detailed Web site demonstrating how the software functions.

It is best to think of these maps as layers. Imagine a series of transparencies with pieces of information on each one. These transparencies can be layered on top of each other to produce different maps or coverages. The first transparency has an outline of the city. The second transparency might have an outline of all the major streets. The third transparency might have labels of these streets. A fourth transparency might describe the major geographic landmarks (rivers, forests, etc.). With these base maps, different datasets of information can be layered on top. A map of all the drunken driving accidents may be the next layer. Another map of all the bars may be interesting. A final layer of all the DUI checkpoints used by the police might also be brought up. Clearly, these different layers can get complicated and cluttered. The mapping program allows the user to turn different layers on or off as they wish. If all the layers on the computer screen become too confusing, the analyst might turn off the street names layer, or use a less detailed layer of geographic features. A good mapping program, matched with a skilled user who has access to many datasets and coverages can produce brilliant maps and answer (or sometimes raise) hundreds of questions.

Map Production

The simplest map is much like the police pin maps of the old days. The mapping software places a colored dot or a symbol at a location. This point represents some offense, crime, or arrest. Most mapping programs come with their own set of predefined symbols (a skull equals a homicide, a syringe equals a drug offense, and so on). These symbols are usually tied back to the original data set so clicking on a skull will bring up that line of data (indicating how the victim died, whether anyone has been arrested for the offense, and the age, race, or sex of the victim or offender).

However, an analyst has many other options that can provide significantly greater depth of information. Mapping all the incidences of an event, perhaps all the burglaries in a city, would produce a single giant blur of symbols. Aggregating information and mapping the concentrations, perhaps across census tracts or police districts, provides less detail but is much more intelligible. A color range (bright red to dark red) or different colors (red equals high, blue equals average, green equals low) can produce a thematic map of an area that is informative and easily understood. These chloropleth maps often resemble a weather map that uses different colors to define the level of precipitation.

Another option is to use graduated circles to represent an event. A small circle may mean a small number of events (1 to 5 larcenies) and four progressively larger circles mean progressively higher rates of the event. Varying the colors of these graduated circles allows the analyst to plot different types of crimes. For example, one could plot three common crimes using three different colors, each of which has three different ranges. Green circles could equal burglary, red could equal larceny, and yellow could equal robbery, and each color could come in three size ranges (small, medium, or large) to represent the frequency of the event. Alternatively, the three different colors could represent years. Robberies from 1997 could be in green, robberies from 1998 in red, and robberies from 1999 could be blue. Yet another option uses contour maps, which look like topographic maps, and trace different grades of crime throughout a city. Different software packages have their own set of maps and mapping tools that analysts can use to determine the most appropriate map style to convey their information.

Ethical Issues

There are important ethical issues in the mapping and geocoding process. The most important of these issues concerns the victim's right to privacy. As the level of specificity of crime and offense information increases, the possibility of embarrassment and secondary victimization by the media or general public likewise increases. If a map of all the rapes or sexual assaults in a city were released to the media, victims would be victimized a second time by the publication of such a list. Even diffusing the information by describing rapes at the block level instead of the address level could be problematic. On many blocks there are no more than a dozen residences. If a teenage female had been sexually assaulted, it would be a simple matter for a reporter to determine which of these residences was home to a teenage female.

A second ethical issue concerns the problem of aggregating data. Crime reports may indicate the Riverfront District of Gotham city has a high rate of robberies. The robberies may in fact be isolated in a small portion of the Riverfront District but such a report could scare tourists and consumers from the entire district. This error is known as the geographic fallacy—generalizing the problems within a region to all the locations or individuals within that region. The South Side may have a high number of drug arrests but that does not mean everyone in the South Side is a drug dealer or user.

Reports of aggregated crime figures may hurt business or land values in an area, however, extremely specific reports of crime may compromise victims' privacy. While law enforcement has a responsibility to make the public aware of crime in their city and neighborhood, the police must tread a careful line to insure the privacy of victims is not violated.

Role of Hypotheses in Map Production

At this stage in the crime mapping process an analyst has collected and assembled data sets and is now prepared to generate some very interesting and useful maps. Simply printing out all the possible combinations of maps is unrealistic. Intelligent questions have to be formulated that link events or locations to each other. These hypotheses are based on one of several factors. *Experience* or *common sense* may suggest that certain things tend to co-exist— such as parking lots and thefts from autos. A *theory* may indicate some relationship between factors is likely to exist. For example, routine activities theory suggests criminals will commit crimes near their travel patterns so main roads and bus routes see high levels of victimization. Once the hypothesis is formed, data can be arranged into coverages or layers to answer the question. If an analyst hypothesized that there was a relationship between reports of mail theft and the location of check-cashing businesses, data could be assembled to answer that question empirically. While maps have tremendous descriptive uses, formulating intelligent hypotheses can significantly extend the capabilities of geographic information systems.

Uses of Crime Maps

The process of developing crime maps is sometimes tedious, but once created, these maps have any number of applications. Maps can describe events, help identify patterns, suggest a relationship between factors, and be used for projective analysis.

Descriptive Component

The most common use of crime maps is to describe crime for a given area. Using points, graduated circles, or chloropleth maps, analysts can arm officers and supervisors with detailed descriptions of the crime for their district or precinct. Buslik and Maltz suggest that officers who have spent a significant amount of time assigned to a single beat usually feel like they know their beats well: "who the bad actors are, what to watch out for, how and when things happen" (1997:121). In Joseph Wambaugh's classic police tale, *The Blue Knight* (1973), Officer Bumper Morgan knows the bad guys so well he can complete the boxes in an arrest report from memory, having arrested the same people over and over. But police officers only work their beat during a given shift and during a set schedule of days. Thus, no one officer truly knows what happens on a beat all the time. A descriptive map can show the locations, times, and suspect description to an officer who might not have been on duty when the offense happened but may have knowledge about the offender or area.

Identification of Patterns

An observant officer or analyst who views a series of descriptive maps is likely to start looking for patterns. Crime maps are especially useful in this endeavor. By layering offenses from different periods of time, one can conduct trend analysis. Considering how offenses change during the seasons can provide important information regarding resource allocation and manpower distribution. If robberies in city parks significantly increase during the summer (as more pedestrians spend time outside) then assigning more officers to these regions during the summer and fewer in the winter should be the natural outcome.

Identifying patterns of crime has important accountability implications. District and precinct commanders are, to some degree, held responsible for the crime in their district. As patterns of crime develop, police chiefs want to know what their district commanders are doing to resolve these problems. One of the best examples of this accountability process exists in New York City through the Compstat program. The Computerized Statistics program began in 1994 and has been replicated or adopted in many law enforcement departments (Harries, 1999). In Philadelphia, the process is known as "The Inquisition" (Pelfrey and Greene, 1997). District commanders attend a weekly or bi-weekly meeting where crime maps of their district are projected on a screen. A police administrator then identifies the crime patterns existing in that district and asks the district commander how they are handling that particular problem. Other district commanders can offer advice about programs that have succeeded or failed to address that particular problem. Thus district commanders are held accountable for crime in their area and they are given a series of possible solutions to the problem so they do not have to "reinvent the wheel" in every police district. If a district commander fails to adequately address the problem, he or she may be replaced by someone who will try a different tack. Compstat and similar procedures force the police to make data-driven decisions and be more efficient with their resources.

Another pattern identification approach is the mapping of *hot spots*. A hot spot is a small area, address, or region of a city or county that has an unusual concentration, or a clustering, of a particular crime. Crime maps often present hot spots as an ellipse around a region, a brightly colored street block, or a symbol over an address. These hot spots signal officers to focus their attention on that area or indicate a need for some program or initiative to resolve the problem. With the current law enforcement emphasis on problem oriented policing, the hot spot approach has significant merit. Identification of hot spots, followed by a well conceived program or intervention that is then evaluated empirically is consistent with the notion of problem oriented policing described by Goldstein (1979, 1990).

It is important to note that there are limitations with the hot spot approach. Concentrations of people tend to be hot spots. Places where calls for service are clustered represent hot spots. These could include bars, bus stops, apartment buildings, or pay telephones (Sherman and Weisburd, 1995). The process of drawing hot spots is sometimes misleading and inaccurate—hot spots may not fit the descriptive method used to present them (i.e. shading of a single block or an ellipse). Despite these limitations the hot spot approach represents a valuable tool for law enforcement agencies in the identification of crime patterns.

The identification of patterns is not limited to the local level. Broader, macro-level research has been conducted, which specifies the relationship of various factors (such as socio-economic status and racial diversity) to the occurrence of homicide across the entire United States. These analyses (Baller et al., 2001; Messner et al., 1999) use county level, homicide data and investigate regional patterns of violence. They noted, for example, that the South tends to have higher rates of homicide than most other parts of the country (Baller et al., 2001). They also suggest that a spillover effect may occur: that is, in urban areas with high violence rates, surrounding counties may experience higher rates of violence than one would otherwise expect (Messner et al., 1999). While these macro-level studies may not be particularly useful to local law enforcement, they are invaluable to researchers who are attempting to define the causes and correlates, and subsequently the *predictors*, of crime.

Interaction of Factors

One of the most common uses of geographic information systems by law enforcement departments is to identify factors that are related to the production, or prevention, of crime. There are many obvious examples of correlated factors that most departments have already explored—the locations of bars and drunk driving accidents, thefts and the locations of pawn shops, abandoned houses and drug markets. There are other factors related to crime that agencies can identify and subsequently address.

Where and how people travel can influence crime rates. Studies addressing the routes students use when they walk to school indicated a need for "safe corridors" for children. Police can consider where assaults or drug sales occur within or around a school and then take specific steps to address these problems.

Defining important interactions of factors is not limited to crime issues. These analyses can be conducted to assist officers in the prevention of problems, especially traffic accidents. Reviewing data on drunk driving usually suggests problem locations within cities and can signal a need for DUI checkpoints or strict enforcement of drunk driving laws. Police officers can also assist businesses in addressing or identifying security concerns and possible remedies for these problems. By first identifying high larceny and theft areas, then suggesting locations of lights, alarms, and secure access points, police can deter criminals and cut down on crime rates.

Projective Analysis

The two primary uses of geographic information systems for law enforcement agencies have been in the areas of describing crime problems or patterns and considering factors that are highly correlated in the production of crime. The next step for law enforcement and researchers lies in the area of predicting crime. These projective, or inferential, analyses estimate where crime is likely to occur based on a series of factors. For example, if we know that drug sales are likely to increase as the number of rental properties increase in an area (as home owners move out and slum lords take over), once a certain threshold has been passed, police can begin to pay special attention to an area to *prevent* the expected increases in drug sales. By identifying a series of factors that are related to the production of crime, analysts can help law enforcement deter the development of problem areas.

This type of work is exemplified by the research of George Rengert (1998). He suggested that analysts could predict where drug markets would develop based on the presence of a fence. Fences buy stolen property and are necessary for the drug users who steal property, sell it to the fence, and then use the cash to purchase drugs. If the locations of fences are known, one can predict where property crimes may occur and where drug sales are likely to happen. These pieces of information can help police maintain a watch over fences to deter the development of drug markets.

Geographic Profiling

A unique and progressive use of crime mapping has been defined by Kim Rossmo, a Canadian police detective and scholar (2000). He uses a technique called Criminal Geographic Targeting (CGT) based on theories from environmental criminology and routine activities theory. Rossmo suggests that serial criminals are likely to commit their crimes in a specific pattern, which can then be analyzed to predict where they live. Based on a distance decay function simulating the journey to the crime, a probability is assigned to each point and the offender's residence is projected. There are four steps to the model:

- Map boundaries are drawn that delineate hunting area.
- Distances along a grid from every point on the map are calculated.
- Distances are then used in as independent variables in an equation.
- Figures are combined to generate a probability that a point represents offender's residence.

This technique does not produce specific addresses of offenders. Instead, it identifies neighborhoods from which the offenders probably traveled to commit their crimes. Those areas that are defined as high probability neighborhoods are then exposed to increased patrol, surveillance, and investigation. Rossmo has found this technique to be effective in the apprehension of serial criminals and now teaches it to other law enforcement groups.

CONCLUSIONS

Geographic Information Systems have come a long way since the police pin maps of earlier decades. Police agencies can now compare layers of crime data with census information, identify vulnerable areas of a city, and develop geographic profiles of criminals. Geographic Information Systems have many more uses than could be described in this article. Some agencies are using them to map the locations of paroled sex offenders to make sure they are not close to a target population (e.g. a playground or nursery school). Some police agencies are mapping zoning restrictions and using these zoning laws as a way to close problematic bars and businesses. A GIS can be used to evaluate existing police programs and determine whether crime-fighting programs have displaced crime to other areas of a city.

As the public demand for more efficient police services increases, police managers must become innovators. Police chiefs and sheriffs can no longer rely on a reactive style of policing—they must become proactive in identifying and preventing crime. A key tool in the drive for improved police services is the geographic information system. If agencies are willing to allocate funds and personnel to the development of GIS, they will see a significant return on their investment.

Works Cited

Baller, R. D., L. Anselin, S. F. Messner, G. Deane, & D. Hawkins. (2001). Structural covariates of U.S. County homicide rates: Incorporating spatial effects. *Criminology, 39,* 561–590.

Buslik, M. and M. D. Maltz. (1997). Power to the people: Mapping and information sharing in the Chicago Police Department. In D. Weisburd and T. McEwen (Eds.) *Crime Mapping and Crime Prevention*. Monsey, NY: Criminal Justice Press.

Goldstein, H. (1979). Improving policing: A problem-oriented approach. *Crime and Delinquency, 25*, 236–258.

Goldstein, H. (1990). *Problem Oriented Policing, Second Edition*. New York: McGraw Hill.

Harries, K. (1999). *Mapping Crime: Principle and Practice*. Washington DC: U.S. Department of Justice.

Messner, S. F., L. Anselin, R. D. Baller, D. F. Hawkins, G. Deane, & S. E. Tolnay. (1999). The spatial patterning of county homicide rates: An application of exploratory spatial data analysis. *Journal of Quantitative Criminology, 15*, 423–450.

National Institute of Justice. (1999). *The Use of Computerized Crime Mapping by Law Enforcement: Survey Results*. Washington DC: U.S. Department of Justice.

Pelfrey, Jr. W. V. and J. R. Greene. (1997). *Final Report: Temple University-Philadelphia Police Department Locally Initiated Collaboration on Community Policing*. Submitted to National Institute of Justice.

Rengert, G. F. (1998). *The Geography of Illegal Drugs*. Boulder, CO: Westview Press.

Rossmo, D. K. (2000). *Geographic Profiling*. Boca Raton, FL: CRC Press.

Sherman, L. and D. Weisburd. (1995). General deterrent effects of police patrol in crime "Hot Spots": A randomized, controlled trial. *Justice Quarterly, 12*, 4, 625–649.

Wambaugh, J. (1973). *The Blue Knight*. Boston: Little, Brown, and Co.

SECTION IV
Police Deviance
Corruption and Controls

There has always existed a concern about the control of the powers granted by the government to use force. Where power exists, there also exists the potential to abuse that power. Police corruption requires only two elements: opportunity and greed. This section covers traditional areas as well as newly defined areas of police corruption and the control of potential abuses.

In the first selection, "Breeding Deviant Conformity," Victor Kappeler, Richard Sluder, and Geoffrey Alpert describe how the real and exaggerated sense of the danger inherent in police work affects how the police picture the world and nurture a police subculture. This police subculture enforces many postulates that influence what are deemed as acceptable and unacceptable behaviors of police officers.

In their article, Professors Rojek, Decker, and Wagner have provided us with an examination of the process that is initiated when a civilian issues a complaint against a police officer. They suggest that the police have failed to meet the challenge presented by citizen complaints. Perhaps, when citizens complain, and police administrators respond, it is akin to shutting the barn door after the horse escapes. One way to discover police behaviors that require more administrative oversight is to examine information included in complaints made about the police by citizens.

In the next selection of this section, "Ethics and Law Enforcement," Joycelyn Pollock discusses the many ethical dilemmas that police officers frequently face. She also discusses various ways the police can resolve these ethical dilemmas, such as utilizing the Code of Ethics for Law Enforcement (IACP), traditional ethical rationales, or some other ethical guidelines.

In the final selection, Lori Fridell and Michael Scott discuss how law enforcement agencies perceive and respond to the problem of racially biased policing, such as racial profiling of citizens. They argue that this complex and challenging problem is not new, but law enforcement has never been better situated to address these issues. In fact, progressive chiefs and sheriffs across the nation are acknowledging the problem and implementing initiatives to create critically needed change.

Breeding Deviant Conformity
The Ideology and Culture of Police

Victor E. Kappeler, Richard D. Sluder, & Geoffrey P. Alpert

> Man is not just an individual, he belongs to the whole; we must always take heed of the whole, for we are completely dependent on it.
>
> —Theodor Fontane(1819–1898)

While it is important to understand the structural and organizational explanations of police deviance, it is equally important to consider the processes that shape the character of police. Police are selected based on demonstrated conformity to dominant social norms and values. Those who become police officers bring to the occupation the perceptual baggage and moral standards common to the working middle class. Police learn a distinct orientation to their occupational role through formal and informal learning exchanges. In essence, police are selected, socialized, and placed into a working environment that instills within them an ideology and shared culture that breeds unprecedented conformity to the traditional police norms and values.

In this article, police ideology is examined by focusing on the processes that shape the cultural and cognitive properties of police officers. The article illustrates that police selection techniques, while premised on equity of treatment, limit the diversity of the police and contribute to an occupational culture and working ideology conducive to the exploitation of certain segments of society. Similarly, the methods by which police are trained reinforce the ideology and its application in the performance of police tasks. The occupational

Forces of Deviance: The Dark Side of Policing, 2/E. Prospect Heights, IL: Waveland (1998), pp. 83–108. Reprinted with permission.

culture of policing is given extensive treatment to develop an understanding of how police internalize norms and values in adjusting to the profession.

Perspectives on the Development of Police Character

Before exploring the ideological and cultural attributes of the police, it is instructive to examine some of the different perspectives theorists and researchers have used to gain a better understanding of the character and behavior of the police as an occupational group. At the risk of oversimplification, one of three general perspectives or paradigms are commonly selected: psychological, sociological, or anthropological. In the sections that follow, the psychological and sociological perspectives of police character are discussed first to demonstrate the difference between researchers' perspectives on the police and to show the complexity of understanding police character. The anthropological perspective of police character is then given extensive treatment because it allows for the integration of research findings from the other areas and provides a broad framework for understanding both police character and behavior.

The Psychological Paradigm of Police Character

Many researchers adopt a psychological orientation to the study of police character. At one extreme, theorists taking this perspective limit their examination of the police to individual officers and attempt to understand how individual personality shapes behavior. According to this view, each person has a core personality that remains static throughout life (Adlam, 1982). Although events, experiences, and social situations change, an individual's basic personality is thought to stay the same. Behavior is structured by preexisting personality traits that are fixed early in life and remain intact.

When this fixed perspective of personality is applied to the police, researchers tend to focus on the personality characteristics exhibited by people who are attracted to the police occupation. Persons with certain personalities enter law enforcement and behave in distinct ways (Rokeach, Miller, & Snyder, 1971). Often this approach is limited to an examination of the personality structures of police recruits (see Burbeck & Furnham, 1985; Hannewicz, 1978). Theorists adopting this perspective think that people with certain personality characteristics are attracted to careers in law enforcement; those with other personality characteristics choose alternative career paths. From this perspective, researchers are inclined to examine the theorized "police personality." This perspective and research orientation has been referred to as a *predispositional model* of police behavior (Alpert & Dunham, 1997).

The predispositional model has led some to conclude that police recruits are more authoritarian than people who enter other professions. The *authoritarian personality* is characterized by conservative, aggressive, cynical, and rigid behaviors. People with this personality have a limited view of the world and see issues in terms of black and white. For the authoritarian personality, there is little room for the shades of gray that exist in most aspects of social life. People are either good or bad, likable or unlikable, friends or enemies. People with this psychological make-up are said to be conservative, often having "knee jerk" reactions to social issues. Some have labeled these people as "reactionary conservatives" because they seem to react instinctively in a conservative manner regardless of the merit of their position and often without reflecting on the consequences of their acts. It is thought that people with these personality traits have a dislike of liberal values, sentiments, and ideals. The authoritarian personality is also characterized by a rigid view of the world that is not easily changed; they are, in essence, defenders of the *status quo*. People with an authoritarian personality are thought to be submissive to superiors but are intolerant toward those who do not submit to their own authority (Adorno, 1950). John J. Broderick (1987) has done an excellent job of capturing how the term authoritarian is used in discussions of the police.

> Those who . . . use it are usually referring to a person who has great respect for power and authority and strongly adheres to the demands of his or her own group. This person is also submissive to higher authority and hostile toward outsiders who do not conform to conventional standards of behavior. The characteristics of willingness to follo.w orders and respect for authority might seem to be virtues when possessed by police officers, but in the sense used here, the term authoritarian means an extreme, unquestioning willingness to do what one is told and an extremely hostile attitude toward people who are different than oneself. (p. 31)

While Broderick rejected the notion that police are more authoritarian than people who go into other occupations, there is research to support the authoritarian police character. Recently, research from this perspective has focused on positive personality characteristics of the police, but it still captures the basic idea that police are conformists with personalities that more closely resemble the characteristics of military personnel than those from other occupations. Carpenter and Raza (1987) found that police applicants differ from other occupational groups in several significant ways. First, these researchers found that police applicants, as a group, are psychologically healthy, "less depressed and anxious, and more assertive in making and maintaining social contacts" (p. 16). Second, their findings indicated that police are a more homogeneous group of people and that this "greater homogeneity is probably due to the sharing of personality characteristics which lead one to desire becoming a police officer" (p. 16). Finally, they found that police were more like military personnel in their conformance to authority.

The psychological perspective of police and its conclusion that people attracted to law enforcement are more authoritarian than their counterparts who go into other occupations have been called into question by researchers who adopt a different perspective of police behavior (Bayley & Mendelsohn,

1969). Researchers who take a more social psychological perspective see personality as developmental and, therefore, subject to change given differential socialization and experience (Adlam, 1982). Instead of assuming that personality is fixed, these researchers see personality as dynamic and changing with an individual's life experience. Essentially, researchers adopting this alternative orientation feel that personality cannot be divorced from the experience that shapes it. Researchers like Bahn (1984) and Putti, Aryee and Kang (1988) often focus on the role police perform in society and how training influences personality. From this perspective, researchers study the effects of police training, peer group support, and the unique working environment—all of which are thought to influence and shape police character and behavior. Many of these researchers, however, still view behavior from an individualistic level focusing on a single officer's unique experiences and the development of individual personalities. This limited view of the police character has been questioned by researchers adopting a sociological perspective.

The Sociological Paradigm of Police Character

Several studies have rejected the concept of an individualistic socialization process in favor of a group socialization model (Stoddard, 1995). Arthur Niederhoffer (1967), David H. Bayley and Harold Mendelsohn (1969), as well as other social scientists, have rejected the notion that police have certain personality characteristics that might predetermine their behavioral patterns. Instead, they and others adopt the perspective that behavior is based on group socialization and professionalization. *Professionalization* is the process by which norms and values are internalized as workers learn their occupation (Alpert & Dunham, 1997; Gaines et al., 1997). It is maintained that just as lawyers and physicians learn their ethics and values through training and by practicing their craft, so do the police. Exposure to a police training academy, regular in-service training, and field experience all shape occupational character. Police learn how to behave and what to think from their shared experiences with other police officers.

From this perspective, many researchers find that rookie police officers just beginning their careers are no more authoritarian than members of other professions who come from similar backgrounds (Broderick, 1987). This proposition, however, does not conflict with the notion that citizens who are selected to become police officers are very conservative and homogenous. This perspective of police behavior assumes police learn their occupational personality from training and through exposure to the unique demands of police work (Skolnick, 1994). If officers become authoritarian, cynical, hard, and conservative, it is not necessarily because of their existing personalities or because of their pre-occupational experiences. Rather, the demands of the occupation and shared experiences as law enforcement officers shape their development.

Research findings support the position that recruit and probationary officers are profoundly affected by their training and socialization. The socialization process experienced by the police affects their attitudes and values. Richard R. Bennett (1984) studied police officers from several departments and found that while recruit and probationary officers' values are affected by the training process, there was little support for the idea that police personalities were shaped by their peers in the department. This however, may be explained by the fact that new officers often do not become true members of the department until they are accepted by their peers and granted membership and acceptance into the police occupational culture. Others maintain that the full effect of the police socialization process is not felt during this initial "setting in" phase and may not develop until later in a police career (Bahn, 1984). Similarly, Joseph Putti and his colleagues (1988) stated their findings on police values "could be interpreted to mean that complete socialization into an occupational subculture is a function of time" (p. 253). While it is not known to what extent other reference groups shape personality in older officers, it seems that—at least initially—new police officers' values are shaped as they are trained for the demands of law enforcement and as they become accepted into the occupation.

The Anthropological Paradigm

The most dramatic change in the police social character occurs when officers become part of the occupational culture. The term *culture* is often used to describe differences among large social groups. Social groups differ in many aspects, and people from different cultures have unique beliefs, laws, morals, customs, and other characteristics that set them apart from other groups. These attitudes, values, and beliefs are transmitted from one generation to the next in a learning process known as socialization. Cultural distinctions are easy to see when one compares, for example, cultures of Japan and the U.S. Both of these countries have laws, language, customs, religions, and art forms that are different from the other. These differences provide each group with unique cultural identities.

There can also be cultural differences among people who form a single culture or social group. People who form a unique group within a given culture are called members of a *subculture*. The difference between a culture and a subculture is that members of a subculture, while sharing many values and beliefs of the larger culture, also have a separate and distinct set of values that set them apart. Clearly, police share cultural heritage with others in the United States—they speak the same language, operate under the same laws, and share many of the same values. There are, however, certain aspects of the police occupational subculture that distinguish the police from other members of society. The police are set apart from other occupational groups and members of society by their unique role and social status. Therefore, some scholars have adopted a *culturalization* perspective of the police as a unique occupational subculture.

THE POLICE WORLDVIEW

The concept of *worldview* refers to the manner in which a culture sees the world and its own role and relationship to the world (Benedict, 1934; Redfield, 1952, 1953). This means that various social groups, including the police, perceive situations differently from other social or occupational groups. For example, lawyers may view the world and its events as a source of conflict and potential litigation. Physicians may view the world as a place of disease and illness. For the physician, people may become defined by their illness rather than their social character. The police process events with similar cognitive distortion. The police worldview has been described as a working personality. According to Jerome H. Skolnick (1994), the police develop cognitive lenses through which to see situations and events—distinctive ways to view the world.

The way the police view the world can be described as a "we/they" or "us/them" orientation. The world is seen as composed of insiders and outsiders—police and citizens. Persons who are not police officers are considered outsiders and are viewed with suspicion. This "we/they" police worldview is created for a variety of reasons: the techniques used to select citizens for police service; the normative orientation police bring to the profession; an exaggeration of occupational danger; the special legal position police hold in society; and the occupational self-perception that is internalized by people who become police officers.

Before citizens can become police officers they must pass through an elaborate employment selection process. In order to be selected for employment, police applicants must demonstrate that they conform to a select set of middle-class norms and values. Police selection practices, such as the use of physical agility tests, background investigations, polygraph examinations, psychological tests, and oral interviews, are all tools to screen out applicants who have not demonstrated their conformity to middle-class norms and values. Many of the selection techniques that are used to determine the "adequacy" of police applicants have little to do with their ability to perform the real duties associated with police work (Cox, Crabtree, Joslin, & Millet, 1987; Gaines et al., 1997; Holden, 1984; Maher, 1988; Paynes & Bernardin, 1992). Often, these tests are designed merely to determine applicants' physical prowess, sexual orientation, gender identification, financial stability, employment history, and abstinence from drug and alcohol abuse.

If police applicants demonstrate conformity to a middle-class life style, they are more likely to be considered adequate for police service. The uniform interpretation of psychological tests, based on middle-class bias, tends to produce a homogeneous cohort. As one researcher has noted "the usefulness of psychological testing for police officer selection is, at best, questionable . . . no test has been found that discriminates consistently and clearly between individuals who will and who will not make good police officers" (Alpert, 1993, p. 100).

In part due to the traditional police selection process, the vast majority of people in policing have been (Kuykendall & Burns, 1980; Sullivan, 1989) and are today (Maguire et al., 1996), middle-class white males. The data in Table 1 show that even in cities where minority citizens are the majority, few municipal police departments employ personnel representative of the communities they serve in terms of race or gender.

A consequence of the police personnel system is that it selects officers who are unable to identify with groups on the margins of traditional society. The police process people and events in the world through cognitive filters that overly value conformity in ideology, appearance, and conduct. This conformist view of the world, derived from a shared background, provides police a measuring rod by which to make judgments concerning who is deviant and in need of state control (Matza, 1969) and what is "suspicious" (Skolnick, 1994) and in need of police attention. The shared background of the police provides a common cognitive framework from which police process information and respond to events.

This homogeneous group of police recruits experiences formal socialization when it enters the police academy. The police academy refines the cohort again by weeding out those recruits who do not conform to the demands of paramilitary training. Police recruits soon learn

> that the way to "survive" in the academy . . . is to maintain a "low profile," by being one of the group, acting like the others. Group cohesiveness and mutuality is encouraged by the instructors as well. The early roots of a separation between "the police" and "the public" is evident in many lectures and classroom discussions. In "war stories" and corridor anecdotes, it emerges as a full blown "us-them" mentality. (Bahn, 1984, p. 392)

Some have argued that the paramilitary model of police training and organization is inconsistent with humanistic democratic values. It demands and supports "employees who demonstrate immature personality traits" (Angell, 1977, p. 105) and creates dysfunctional organizations (Argyris, 1957). The encouraged traits closely resemble attributes of the authoritarian personality. In short, police are further differentiated from the public and become more homogeneous in their worldview through formal training.

As Skolnick (1994) has noted, danger is one of the most important facets in the development of a police working personality. The relationship between the "real" dangers associated with police work and the police perception of the job as hazardous is complex. While police officers perceive their work as dangerous, they realize that the chances of being injured are not as great as their preoccupation with the idea of danger. Francis T. Cullen, Bruce G. Link, Lawrence F. Travis, and Terrence Lemming (1983) have referred to this situation as a paradox in policing. Their research in five police departments found that

> even though the officers surveyed did not perceive physical injury as an everyday happening, this does not mean that they were fully insulated

Table I   Minority Citizens and Police in Select Cities and Departments[*]

City	Citizens Population	Citizens Minorities	Police Employees	Police Minorities	Females
Compton, CA	90,454	98.5%	126	75.4%	7.1%
Laredo, TX	122,899	94.4%	188	98.4%	5.9%
East Orange, NJ	73,552	93.8%	245	56.7%	3.3%
Inglewood, CA	109,602	91.5%	206	35.5%	5.8%
Brownsville, TX	98,962	90.7%	144	41.1%	5.6%
Hialeah, FL	188,004	89.1%	315	40.0%	9.2%
Miami, FL	358,548	87.8%	1,110	64.7%	12.1%
Gary, IN	116,646	85.9%	208	74.0%	12.5%
Camden, NJ	87,492	85.6%	291	11.0%	2.4%
El Moune, CA	106,209	84.8%	113	24.0%	8.8%
Newark, NJ	275,221	83.5%	1,260	42.0%	3.0%
Detroit, MI	1,027,974	79.3%	4,595	53.5%	20.0%
McAllen, TX	84,021	78.1%	162	87.0%	4.3%
Santa Ana, CA	293,742	76.9%	382	29.6%	3.9%
Paterson, NJ	140,891	75.5%	352	27.0%	3.1%
Honolulu, HI	365,272	74.5%	1,781	80.4%	8.3%
El Paso, TX	515,342	73.6%	738	63.8%	6.4%
Washington, D.C.	606,900	72.6%	4,506	67.9%	18.5%
Pomona, CA	131,723	71.8%	172	13.9%	2.9%
Oakland, CA	372,242	71.7%	661	44.6%	7.0%
Atlanta, GA	394,017	69.7%	1,560	54.2%	12.9%
Hartford, CT	139,739	69.5%	443	30.1%	7.0%
Richmond, CA	87,425	69.4%	179	45.2%	5.0%
Oxnard, CA	142,216	67.7%	145	25.6%	4.1%
New Orleans, LA	496,938	66.9%	1,397	40.1%	12.0%
Birmingham, AL	265,968	64.2%	706	36.0%	18.0%
Mount Vernon, NY	67,153	64.2%	176	22.2%	6.3%
San Antonio, TX	935,933	63.8%	1,576	43.8%	5.7%
Jersey City, NJ	228,537	63.4%	918	13.4%	2.8%
Los Angeles, CA	3,485,398	62.7%	8,295	37.5%	12.5%
Trenton, NJ	88,675	62.5%	358	16.8%	2.2%
Chicago, IL	2,783,726	62.1%	11,837	30.4%	13.0%
Baltimore, MD	736,014	61.4%	1,540	27.7%	10.9%
Salinas, CA	108,777	61.2%	132	19.0%	3.0%
Elizabeth, NJ	110,002	60.3%	296	13.5%	4.7%
West Covina, CA	96,086	59.6%	109	14.7%	5.5%
Wilmington, DE	71,529	59.5%	259	34.3%	6.9%
Houston, TX	1,630,553	59.4%	4,104	26.3%	9.6%
Harrisburg, PA	52,376	59.3%	154	29.8%	11.7%
Monroe, LA	54,909	57.1%	125	21.6%	10.4%
Richmond, VA	203,056	57.0%	646	27.4%	9.4%
New York, NY	7,322,564	56.8%	25,655	23.8%	12.8%
Jackson, MS	196,637	56.6%	350	37.1%	5.4%
Stockton, CA	210,943	56.4%	242	10.3%	16.9%
Memphis, TN	610,337	56.390	1,382	32.2%	14.6%
Albany, GA	78,122	56.290	189	41.9%	12.7%
Corpus Christi, TX	257,453	56.2%	367	46.0%	6.0%
Port Arthur, TX	58,724	54.9%	108	17.6%	2.8%
Pinebluff, AR	57,140	54.5%	111	18.0%	4.5%

[*] Cities with populations greater than 50,000 where minorities are the majority. Municipal police employing 100 or more sworn officers. Compiled by authors from: US Census, 1990; Bureau of Justice Statistics (1992). Law Enforcement Management and Administrative Statistics, 1990: Data for Individual State and Local Agencies with 100 or More Officers. Washington, DC: US Department of Justice.

against feelings of danger. Hence . . . it can be seen that nearly four-fifths of the sample believed that they worked at a dangerous job, and that two-thirds thought that policing was more dangerous than other kinds of employment. (p. 460)

The disjuncture between the potential for injury and the exaggerated sense of danger found among police officers is best explained in the remarks of David Bayley (1976) who observes:

The possibility of armed confrontation shapes training, patrol preoccupations, and operating procedures. It also shapes the relationship between citizen and policeman by generating mutual apprehension. The policeman can never forget that the individual he contacts may be armed and dangerous; the citizen can never forget that the policeman is armed and may consider the citizen dangerous. (p. 171)

An inordinate amount of attention and misinformation concerning the dangers of police work is disseminated to police recruits at police academies. Police instructors are generally former street enforcement officers; their occupational experiences and worldview have been filtered through the cognitive framework described earlier. Thus, much of the material presented to new police officers serves to reinforce the existing police view of the world rather than to educate police recruits or to provide appropriate attitudes, values, and beliefs (Cohen & Feldberg, 1991; Delattre, 1989; Murphy & Caplan, 1993).

Even though well intended, police instructors' ability to educate is restricted because most police training curricula overemphasize the potential for death and injury and further reinforce the danger notion by spending an inordinate amount of time on firearms skills, dangerous calls, and "officer survival." The training orientation often resembles preparation for being dropped behind enemy lines on a combat mission. This is not to dismiss the possibility of danger in police work. Certainly, police are killed and injured in the line of duty, but these figures remain relatively small (FBI, 1997; Kappeler et al., 1996) in comparison to the time spent indoctrinating recruits with the notion that the world is a dangerous place—especially if you are a police officer.

As Table 2 shows, police training is dominated by an attempt to develop the practical rather than the intellectual skills of recruits. In addition to the substantial amount of time spent on the skills associated with officer safety, a large block of time is spent indoctrinating police on the basic elements of criminal law and the techniques to be used to detect criminal behavior. Little time is spent on developing an understanding of constitutional law, civil rights, or ethical considerations in the enforcement of the law. As the table indicates, police instructors evaluate student performance by weighting certain areas more heavily than others. Differential importance is given to the use of firearms, patrol procedures, and how to use force in arresting and restraining citizens. These three areas are seen as the most critical functions by instructors and are given greater emphasis in scoring the performance of recruits in the police academy.

Table 2   Typical Law Enforcement Basic Training Program

Topic	Hours Spent	Percent of Time	Weight
Administration	24.5	6.13	(—)
Introduction to Law Enforcement	20.5	5.00	1.00
Firearms (skills development)	56.5	14.10	2.00
Vehicle Operation (pursuit driving)	25.5	6.40	1.00
First Aid/CPR	16.0	4.00	.50
Accident Investigation	15.0	3.80	.50
Criminal Law (statutes)	55.5	13.80	1.00
Patrol Procedures (crime detection)	50.0	12.50	2.00
Criminal Investigation	19.0	4.80	.50
Specific Investigations (street crime)	31.0	7.80	1.00
Arrest and Restraint/Physical Fitness	67.5	16.90	2.00
Practical Performance Exercises	19.0	4.75	1.00

Police vicariously experience, learn, and relearn the potential for danger through "war stories" and field training after graduation from the police academy (see Kraska & Paulsen, 1997). The real and exaggerated sense of danger inherent in police work contributes greatly to the police picture of the world. As a result, the police may see citizens as potential sources of violence or as enemies. Citizens become "symbolic assailants" to the police officer on the street (Skolnick, 1994). The symbolic assailant is further refined in appearance by taking on the characteristics of marginal segments of society (Harris, 1973; Piliavin & Briar, 1964). The image of the symbolic assailant takes on the characteristics of the populations police are directed to control (see Sparger & Giacopassi, 1992). To the officer in southern Texas, the young Hispanic man becomes the potential assailant; in Atlanta, the poor inner-city black man becomes a source of possible injury; and in Chinatown, the Asian becomes the criminal who may resort to violence against the police.

Symbolic assailants, however, are not limited to those persons who pose a threat to the officer's physical safety, nor are they identified solely in terms of race or ethnicity. Jennifer Hunt's (1985) field study of police practice in one large urban police department found that officers also perceive certain types of citizens' actions as symbolic threats. She remarks that while

> [f]ew officers will hesitate to assault a suspect who physically threatens or attacks them . . . [v]iolations of an officer's property such as his car or hat might signify a more symbolic assault on the officer's authority and self, justifying a forceful response to maintain control. (p. 328)

She also found that some of the female officers she observed resorted to the use of force when their authority was explicitly denied by insults or highly sexualized encounters.

The element of danger and the symbolic assault are recurring themes in police culture. A survey in 1997 documented an enormous increase in the use of police paramilitary units (PPUs). The survey reported that these units were employed routinely in situations where there was the perception of a high potential for assault or danger. Most often these units are deployed in drug raids, street sweeps, or in dense urban areas seen by the police as constituting a high potential for danger. Police perceive these situations as inherently dangerous and have even extended the use of tactical units to serving what once were thought of as routine search and arrest warrants. Likewise many of these units are used precisely for their symbolic or shock value. In urban areas, officers conduct "jump outs"—numerous officers exiting vehicles simultaneously and creating an enormous display of fire power.

Peter Kraska and Derek Paulsen (1997) describe the sense of "hyper-dangerousness" in tactical units and remark that

> the military weapons, tactics, training, and drug-raids generate an intense feeling of "danger" among the officers. There exists of course a universal fear of being victim of violence among regular police officers. . . . However, the preoccupation with danger in this special operations team, and the fear of being a victim of violence, is heightened. All the PPU officers expressed an extreme fear of the worst happening to them, emphasizing the "real possibility" that every call-out could end in tragedy. . . . The perception of danger and death serves to create a military-like camaraderie among PPU officers. Just as the fear of danger involved in the PPU is more intense than in normal policing, the camaraderie formed is also more intense. Officers emphasize that they must rely on fellow officers more, and their close bonding functions to protect each other's "backsides." (p. 263)

Emphasizing danger fosters the "we/they" worldview and focuses police attention on selective behaviors of certain segments of society. Research into the police culture over the course of thirty years has documented the changing nature yet sustained presence of danger and symbolic assailants as central themes in police culture. Perhaps the greatest change in this aspect of police culture is the growing abstraction of who and what constitutes symbolic danger.

Skolnick (1994) has noted the importance of authority vested in the police as another important characteristic in the development of the police working personality. The law shapes and defines interactions between people and grants social status to members of society (Black, 1970, 1976). The police, by virtue of their social role, are granted a unique position in the law. Police have a legal monopoly on the sanctioned use of violence (Bittner, 1995a; Bordua & Reiss, 1967; Reiss, 1971; Westley, 1995) and coercion (Bittner, 1995a; Westley, 1995) against other members of society. The legal sanctions that prevent citizens from resorting to violence are relaxed for police officers. Police often resort to coercion to accomplish their organizational goals of controlling crime and enforcing the existing social order. This legal distinction between citizens and police sets officers apart from the larger culture and other occupations.

Since the primary tools used by the police are violence and coercion, it was easy for the police to develop a paramilitary model of training and organization (Bittner, 1995b). In this model, likeness of dress, action and thought is promoted; homogeneity of appearance, ideology, and behavior is emphasized. The military model reinforces the "we/they" worldview of the police; it allows officers to see themselves as a close-knit, distinct group and promotes a view of citizens as "outsiders and enemies" (Sherman, 1982; Westley, 1956). The strength of this conditioning is evident in the alienation felt by officers promoted to positions of management or by those who leave the profession. These individuals often feel isolated from their reference group when their organizational or occupational standing changes (Gaines et al., 1997).

Finally, the police worldview is intensified by the perception of policing as the most critical of social functions. As the process of socialization and culturalization continues, police begin to believe and project for the public the image that they are the "thin blue line" that stands between anarchy and order. "Brave police officers patrol mean streets" and are on the front lines of a war for social order and justice. The war for social order is seen by the police as so important that it requires sweeping authority and unlimited discretion to invoke the power of law—through the use of force if necessary.

Criticality of Police Function and Abuse of Authority

". . . On January 24, 1991 two inmates of the Coahoma County Jail, Alonzo Wilson and Eddie Wilkins, attempted to escape while leaving church services which were conducted in the conference room on the first floor. They attempted to make their escape by breaking through glass doors at the front of the jail, but were seized by officers while the attempt was in progress. Wilson and Wilkins were shackled hand and foot and were then taken into the conference room where church services had been held. They were at that time fully controlled by the officers, and there were no further escape attempts. All of the other inmates were locked in their cells or secured behind locked doors.

"When the escape attempt occurred, Sheriff Thompson was not at the jail, but was at the courthouse approximately one block away. When he learned of the escape attempt he immediately went to the jail and found Wilson and Wilkins secured in the conference room. . . . An investigation of the escape attempt was promptly begun, and it was learned that plans for the escape had involved at least one other inmate and that the escape plan called for the glass front doors of the jail to be broken with a metal bar which the conspiring inmates had secreted somewhere in the jail. However, the bar was not used by Wilson and Wilkins in their abortive attempt.

"Sheriff Thompson questioned Wilson and Wilkins in the conference room in an effort to obtain information which might lead officers to weapons and implements, including the metal bar. . . . That interrogation was not productive. Accordingly, Sheriff Thompson obtained a length of coaxial cable approximately three to three and one-half feet long. . . . According to Sheriff Thompson he used this length of cable in an attempt to 'coerce' Wilson and Wilkins into revealing where the metal bar was secreted and was thereby able to extract from them the information that it was upstairs in the jail. According to Thompson, in the process of 'coercing' them he struck Wilson and Wilkins on the buttocks with the cable 'a couple of times each.'

". . . Sheriff Thompson had them taken to their third floor cell and there proceeded to interrogate the five occupants of the cell. . . . Thompson asked the occupants of the cell to surrender the metal bar or brace, but they did not respond. He ordered his deputies to search the cell, and that search produced a steel rod and a length of coaxial cable similar to that which Thompson had used to 'coerce' information from Wilson and Wilkins. However, the bar or brace which was the principal object of the search was not found.

"Thompson then required the five inmates in the cell to remove all clothing from the lower parts of their bodies, including trousers and underwear, and 'applied' the cable to their lower bodies. The only substantial evidentiary dispute centers on the number of blows struck and the severity of those blows. Thompson's testimony was that he 'applied' the cable to each of the five inmates 'a couple of times each.' He also testified that at his direction Deputy Sheriff Tony Smith 'applied' the cable to two of the inmates. According to Thompson the force used was not sufficient to injure the inmates or to raise welts. . . . Alonzo Wilson testified that he was struck nine or ten times in the downstairs conference room and was whipped again in the third floor cell, both by Sheriff Thompson and Deputy Smith. He testified that all five of the inmates in the cell were crying after the whipping and that his right hip was bleeding and discolored. A photograph taken the next day, January 25, 1991, shows raised and discolored areas on Wilson's right hip, which he described as welts and sores caused by the whipping. On January 25, Wilson was seen by the jail doctor, who gave him a lotion to apply to his hip.

"The whipping of the five inmates with the coaxial cable led to discovery of the metal bar in the shower of the cell, and to information that a shank, a type of homemade knife, had been passed out of the cell to another inmate. The metal bar was retrieved from the shower, but the shank was never found.

"Sheriff Thompson testified that he has approximately seventeen years experience in law enforcement, eight and one-half years as a deputy sheriff in Coahoma County. He further testified that this was the only occasion on which he had used such a method to elicit information from an inmate. He also testified that under the same circumstances he would do the same thing again, although it would be as a last resort. . . . In the opinion of the sheriff, he [has] the authority to authorize the use of force, including the use of force to obtain information when it is deemed necessary to jail security. He recognized, however, that it is not appropriate to use force to obtain a confession or to solve a crime. Sheriff Thompson emphasized that he used the cable strictly for the purpose of coercing information concerning the location of the metal bar, which he deemed to be a threat to jail security because of its potential for use as a weapon or a tool for escape. In the opinion of Sheriff Thompson, as long as such an item remained in the jail it constituted a threat to the officers, as well as other inmates. While, in the sheriff's view, the presence of the metal bar in the jail constituted a security emergency which justified his use of force, he admitted that he had in the past received other reports of weapons in the jail and had never resorted to such tactics to obtain information concerning those weapons."

Source: Cohen v. Coahoma County, Miss., 805 F.Supp. 398 (N.D.Miss. 1992).

The police believe in the goodness of maintaining order, the nobility of their occupation, and the fundamental fairness of the law and existing social order. Accordingly, the police are compelled to view disorder, lawbreaking, and lack of respect for police authority as enemies of a civilized society.

> They are thus committed ("because it is right") to maintain their collective face as protectorates of the right and respectable against the wrong and the not-so-respectable. . . . Thus, the moral mandate felt by the police to be their just right at the societal level is translated and transformed into occupational and personal terms and provides both the justification and legitimation for specific acts of street justice. (Van Maanen, 1995, pp. 313–314)

If law, authority, and order were seen as fostering inequity or injustice, the police self-perception would be tainted and the "goodness" of the profession would be questioned by the public. Police could no longer see themselves as partners in justice but rather partners in repression—a role most police neither sought nor would be willing to recognize. Police who begin to question the goodness of the profession, the equity of law, or the criticality of maintaining the existing social order often quit or are forced out of the occupation for other careers, further solidifying the police social character of those who remain.

The Spirit of Police Subculture

The concept of *ethos* encompasses the distinguishing character, sentiments, and guiding beliefs of a person or institution. When this term is applied to the police subculture, three general ideas surface. First, the police value an *ethos of bravery.* Bravery is a central component of the social character of policing. As such, it is related to the perceived and actual dangers of law enforcement. The potential to become the victim of a violent encounter, the need for support by fellow officers during such encounters, and the legitimate use of violence to accomplish the police mandate all contribute to a subculture that stresses the virtue of bravery. The bravery ethos is so strong among police that two authors have remarked,

> Merely talking about pain, guilt or fear has been considered taboo. If an officer has to talk about his/her personal feelings, that officer is seen as not really able to handle them . . . as not having what it takes to be a solid, dependable police officer. (Pogrebin & Poole, 1991, p. 398)

The military trappings of policing, organizational policies such as "never back down" in the face of danger, and informal peer pressure all contribute to fostering a sense of bravery. "Reprimand, gossip and avoidance constitute the primary means by which police try to change or control the behavior of co-workers perceived of as unreliable or cowardly" (Hunt, 1985, p. 322).

It is common for training officers to wait until a new recruit has faced a dangerous situation before recommending the recruit be given full status in the organization. Peer acceptance usually does not come until new officers have proven themselves in a dangerous situation. More than anything else, training officers and others in the police subculture want to know how probationary officers will react to danger—will they show bravery?

The importance of bravery in criminal justice occupational groups was highlighted in James Marquart's participant study of the prison guard subculture. Following a confrontation that required the use of force, Marquart (1986) found that:

> The fact that I had been assaulted and had defended myself in front of other officers and building tenders raised my esteem and established my reputation. The willingness to fight inmates was an important trait rewarded by ranking guards. Due to this "fortunate" event, I earned the necessary credibility to establish rapport with the prison participants and allay their previous suspicions of me. I passed the ultimate test—fighting an inmate even though in self-defense—and was now a trustworthy member of the guard subculture. (p. 20)

An *ethos of autonomy* is also evident in the police subculture. As the first line of the criminal justice process, police officers make very authoritative decisions about whom to arrest, when to arrest, and when to use force. To this extent the police are the "gatekeepers" to the criminal justice system (Alpert & Dunham, 1997). Police officers cling to their autonomy and the freedom to decide when to use force. The desire for autonomy often exists despite departmental, judicial, or community standards designed to limit the discretion of street enforcement officers. Personally defined justice, reinforced by subcultural membership, can lead to abuses of discretion. Any attempt to limit the autonomy of the police is viewed as an attempt to undermine the police authority to control "real" street crime and not as an attempt on the part of citizens to curb police abuses of authority.

A third ethos evident in police subcultures is the *ethos of secrecy*. William Westley (1995, p. 298), a leading scholar on policing, noted that the police "would apply no sanction against a colleague who took the more extreme view of the right to use violence and would openly support some milder form of illegal coercion." Similar conclusions were reached by William J. Chambliss and Robert B. Seidman (1971) in their consideration of police discretion. The police code of secrecy is often the result of a fear of loss of autonomy and authority as external groups try to limit police discretion and decision-making ability. A second factor supporting the development of a code of secrecy is the fact that policing is fraught with the potential for mistakes. Police feel they are often called upon to make split-second decisions that can be reviewed by others not directly involved in policing. This "split-second syndrome" rationalization, however, has been used by the police "to provide after-the-fact justification for unnecessary police violence" (Fyfe, 1997, p. 540). The desire to protect one's coworkers from disciplinary actions and from being accused of making an improper decision can promote the development of a code of secrecy. John Crank (1998) observed that the veil of secrecy emerges from the practice of police work from the way in which everyday events conspire against officers. . . . It is a cultural product, formed by an environmental context that holds in high regard issues of democratic process and police lawfulness, and that seeks to punish its cops for errors they make. (p. 226)

The police code of secrecy is also a product of the police perception of the media and their investigative function. Some researchers suggest that police officers are very concerned with the manner in which the media report their actions (Berg, Gertz, & True, 1984). Coupled with a police perception of the media as hostile, biased, and unsupportive, this contributes to friction in police-media relations and to increased police secrecy.

However, it is sometimes mandatory for officers to refrain from making media releases, having public discussion, or commenting on current criminal investigations. Media Information Restrictions (Section 6.9) in Illinois prohibit a police department from releasing the name of an officer under investigation unless there has been a criminal conviction or a decision rendered by the Police Board. Police unions say these restrictions protect innocent officers from bogus claims, but they also provide police with protections not available to other citizens. In addition, they reinforce the wall of silence. By state law, police internal investigations are off-limits to the public and subject to only minimal review by a civilian oversight board. This is often interpreted by the media, citizens, and others as a self-imposed censorship of information. Perceptions of this nature can promote the separation of the public and the police and create the impression of a secret police society.

Cultural Themes in Policing

The concept of *themes* in a culture is related to the "dynamic affirmations" (Opler, 1945) maintained by its members. Themes help to shape the quality and structure of the group's social interactions. Themes are not always complementary to one another; however, they do occasionally balance or interact. This fact becomes readily apparent in studying the police subculture's dominant themes of social isolation and solidarity.

Isolation is an emotional and physical condition that makes it difficult for members of one social group to have relationships and interact with members of another group. This feeling of separateness from the surrounding society is a frequently noted attribute of the police subculture in the United States (Cain, 1973; Harris, 1973; Manning, 1995a; Reiss & Bordua, 1967; Sherman, 1982; Skolnick, 1994; Westley, 1956, 1970, 1995). Social isolation, as a theme of police subculture, is a logical result of the interaction of the police worldview and ethos of secrecy. The self-imposed social isolation of the police from the surrounding community is well documented.

Persons outside the police subculture are viewed somewhat warily as potential threats to the members' physical or emotional well-being, as well as to the officer's authority and autonomy. According to James Baldwin (1962) and Jerome H. Skolnick (1994), police impose social isolation upon themselves as a means of protection against real and perceived dangers, loss of personal and professional autonomy, and social rejection. Rejection by the community stems, in part, from the resentment which sometimes arises when laws are enforced (Clark, 1965). Since no one enjoys receiving a traffic ticket or being arrested and no one enjoys being disliked, the police tend to look inward to their own members for validity and support. Therefore, the police often self-impose restrictions on personal interactions with the community.

Bruce Swanton (1981) examined the topic of police isolation. He pointed out that two primary groups of determinants promote social isolation. Swanton maintained that these determinants were either self-imposed by the police or externally imposed upon the police by the community. Self-imposed police determinants generally concerned work-related requirements of the police profession. These represent structurally induced determinants created by the organization and the police subculture. The most important of these include: administrative structures, work structures, and personality structures.

Swanton found that the traditional view of police work—enforcing the law, detecting, and apprehending criminals—created a sense of suspiciousness in police officers. This suspiciousness led to a false belief that positive community interactions or kindness from citizens were designed to compromise the officer's official position. A further deterrence to the maintenance of relationships with members of the general community outside the police subculture is the ambiguity evident in the police officer's on-duty and off-duty status. Swanton noted that the long and often irregular working hours—a result of shift schedules and possible cancellation of days off or vacations—coupled with the community's perception of police work as socially unattractive contribute to the police officer's sense of isolation. Swanton's (1981) publicly initiated determinants of isolation include:

> suspicion that police compromise their friendships with higher loyalty to their employer; resentment at police-initiated sanctions or the potential thereof; attempts at integration by those wishing to curry favor, which are resented by others; and personality of police perceived as socially unattractive, thereby reducing the motivation of nonpolice to form close relationships with them. (p. 18)

Charles Bahn (1984) summarized the problem using a different perspective of the police.

> Social isolation becomes both a consequence and a stimulus. . . . Police officers find that constraints of schedule, of secrecy, of group mystique, and of growing adaptive suspiciousness and cynicism limit their friendships and relationships in the nonpolice world. (p. 392)

The second theme evident in the police subculture is *solidarity* (Banton, 1964; Harris, 1973; Skolnick, 1994; Stoddard, 1995; Westley, 1956, 1970, 1995). Traditionally, the theme of police solidarity and loyalty was seen as the result of a need for insulation from perceived dangers and rejection by the community. Michael Brown (1981) has noted the importance of loyalty and solidarity among the police. Consider his interpretation of one police officer's remarks.

> "I'm for the guys in blue! Anybody criticizes a fellow copper that's like criticizing someone in my family; we have to stick together." The police culture demands of a patrolman unstinting loyalty to his fellow officers, and he receives, in return, protection: a place to assuage real and imagined wrongs inflicted by a (presumably) hostile public; safety from aggressive administrators and supervisors; and the emotional support required to perform a difficult task. The most important question asked by a patrolman about a rookie is whether or not he displays the loyalty demanded by the police subculture. (p. 82)

Theodore N. Ferdinand (1980), however, has noted that solidarity and loyalty change in proportion to an officer's age and rank. He maintained that police cadets have the least amount of solidarity and line officers have the greatest amount of solidarity. Ferdinand noted that until the age of forty, much of a police officer's social life is spent within the confines of the police subculture. However, solidarity declines as police move into higher ranks in the department. Indeed, we saw earlier that members of the police administrative hierarchy are frequently categorized by line officers with nonpolice members of the community as threatening to the welfare of the subculture.

Police solidarity, therefore, may be said to be an effect of the socialization process inherent to the subculture and police work. New members are heavily socialized to increase their solidarity with the group, and those who move away from the subculture, either through age or promotion, are gradually denied the ties of solidarity. This cohesion is based in part on the "sameness" of roles, perceptions, and self-imagery of the members of the police subculture.

Postulates of Police Culture

Postulates are statements which reflect the basic orientations of a group (Opler, 1945). Postulates are the verbal links between a subculture's view of the world and the translation of that view into action. Because postulates and cultural themes may conflict, the degree to which they complement one another and are integrated is said to indicate the homogeneity and complexity of a culture. Postulates, then, are statements—expressions of general truth or principle that guide and direct the actions of subcultural members. These statements reveal the nuances of a subculture to a greater degree than do ethos or themes. Postulates act as oral vehicles for the transmission of culture from one generation to the next and reinforce the subcultural worldview.

Postulates basic to an understanding of the police subculture have been collected and arranged into an informal code of police conduct. Elizabeth Reuss-Ianni (1983), drawing from the research of many others (Manning, 1997; Rubinstein, 1973; Savitz, 1971; Skolnick, 1994; Stoddard, 1995; Westley, 1956, 1995), identified several of these postulates (also see Reuss-Ianni &

Ianni, 1983) to demonstrate the conflict between administrators and line officers. Reuss-Ianni's work is important because it illustrates the influence that line officers have on the total organization. Her work shows that despite administrative efforts to produce organizational change, substantive change is difficult to attain without the collective efforts of group members. In the case of the police, Reuss-Ianni recognized the importance of informal work groups and the influence those groups have on structuring social relationships both in and outside the police subculture. Hence, postulates are important in shaping not only the attitudes, values, and beliefs of police officers but also in shaping a shared understanding of unacceptable behaviors.

Postulates Shaping the Ethos of Secrecy and the Theme of Solidarity.
The first group of postulates identified by Reuss-Ianni (1983, pp. 14–16) contribute to the ethos of secrecy that surrounds much of police work. This secrecy has many functions, three of which are especially important to the study of police deviance. First, the public is denied knowledge of many police activities because, in the eyes of the police, they have no "need to know." While it may be prudent to restrict access to certain types of sensitive information in law enforcement, the veil of secrecy that shields police from the public has the effect of minimizing public scrutiny of police activities and behaviors. Secondly, many of the postulates identified by Reuss-Ianni are guideposts which keep officers from relaying too much information to police supervisors. Line officers support these postulates as necessary protections to insulate themselves from punishment or challenges to their autonomy. Because police administrators are perceived as applying sanctions situationally and erratically, line officers develop postulates that bring predictability to their working world. Finally, perhaps the most important function is providing line officers with a sense of solidarity. As the Mollen Commission's (1994) investigation of the New York City Police Department found:

> These aspects of police culture facilitate corruption primarily in two ways. First, they encourage corruption by setting a standard that nothing is more important than the unswerving loyalty of officers to one another—not even stopping the most serious forms of corruption. This emboldens corrupt cops and those susceptible to corruption. Second, these attitudes thwart efforts to control corruption. They lead officers to protect or cover up for others' crimes—even crimes of which they heartily disapprove. (pp. 51–52)

The discussion in chapter 11 of the assault on Abner Louima provides a chilling illustration of the corruption facilitated by these postulates. Some of the postulates reinforcing the ethos of secrecy and the theme of police solidarity include:

- *"Don't give up another cop."* As perhaps one of the most important factors contributing to secrecy and to a sense of solidarity, this postulate admonishes officers to never, regardless of the seriousness or nature of a case, provide information to either superiors or nonpolice that would cause harm to a fellow police officer. Reuss-Ianni notes that this postulate implicitly informs a police officer that abiding by this canon and never giving up another cop means others "won't give you up."

• *"Watch out for your partner first and then the rest of the guys working that tour."* This postulate tells police officers they have an obligation to their partners first, and then to other officers working the same shift. "Watching out," in this context, means that an officer has a duty not only to protect a fellow officer from physical harm, but also to watch out for their interests in other matters. If, for example, an officer learns that another member of his or her squad is under investigation by an internal affairs unit, the officer is obligated to inform the officer of this information. As with the postulate listed above, the implicit assumption here is that if you watch out for fellow police, they will also watch out for you.

• *"If you get caught off base, don't implicate anybody else."* Being caught off base can involve a number of activities, ranging from being out of one's assigned sector to engaging in prohibited activities. This postulate teaches officers that if they are discovered in proscribed activities, they should accept the punishment, not implicate others. This postulate insulates other police officers from punishment and reduces the possibility that organized deviance or corruption will be uncovered.

• *"Make sure the other guys know if another cop is dangerous or 'crazy.'"* Police are caught in a double-bind if they become aware that one of their fellow members is unstable or presents a safety hazard. The secrecy dictum prohibits a line officer from informing police supervisors of another officer's instability; at the same time, an officer has an obligation to watch out for his or her peers. In order to deal with such a contradiction, this rule of behavior tells an officer that there is an obligation to let other police know of potential safety risks but not to take formal action against another officer. This postulate allows "problem" officers to continue to operate within the profession and reduces the chances that they will be detected by the agency administration or the public. It does, however, allow informal sanctions of exclusion to be imposed.

• *"Don't get involved in anything in another cop's sector."* Reuss-Ianni notes that in older, corrupt departments, this dictum advised officers not to try to hedge in on another police officer's illegal activities. In essence, this rule informed police that officers "owned" certain forms of corruption in their sector. Today, this postulate teaches officers that they are to stay out of all matters in other officers' sectors. This rule of territoriality is believed necessary because officers are responsible for activities in their respective beats. This postulate serves to limit the spread of information making it easier for officers to deny knowledge of deviance, which in turn makes deviance appear to be a mere aberration.

- *"Hold up your end of the work; don't leave work for the next tour."* These postulates teach officers that if they neglect their work responsibilities, two results are likely to occur. First, other officers must cover for those who shirk their responsibilities. Second, malingerers call attention to everyone on a shift. Thus, there are pressures for all officers to carry their own weight to avoid being detected for deviance. If, however, an officer fails to follow this edict, other officers are expected to "cover" for the officer and to deflect attention away from the group.

- *"Don't look for favors just for yourself."* This dictum admonishes officers not to "suck up" to superiors. In essence, this rule tells officers that their primary responsibilities are to their peers and that attempts to curry favors with superiors will meet severe disapproval. This postulate prevents line officers from developing relationships with superiors that might threaten the safety of the work group.

Postulates Supporting Police Isolationism. Reuss-Ianni (1983, pp. 14–16) identified several postulates that teach new officers that nonpolice simply do not understand the true nature of police work. These statements reinforce the notion that there are vast differences between police and citizens—who will never be able to understand the unique problems inherent in policing. In John Van Maanen's (1995) typology of how the police characterize outsider views of their occupation, these citizens are classified as "know nothings" (p. 309). This we/they worldview increases police isolation from citizens.

- *"Protect your ass."* As perhaps one of the most important postulates leading to a sense of isolation, this rule teaches police to be wary of everyone including citizens and superiors. At the simplest level, the rule informs police that anyone who wants to cause trouble for an officer probably can; it teaches police that others cannot be trusted. Officers must be vigilant and take all steps necessary to protect themselves from any possible threat. While threats include the possibility of physical harm, they also include the possibility of disciplinary action by superiors and the potential for citizens to complicate the lives of police by filing complaints, making allegations, or uncovering deviance.

- *"Don't trust a new guy until you have him checked out."* Rookie police and officers who are new to a work group are not accorded status automatically. Instead, outsiders are treated cautiously until information about them can be obtained—until they have "proven" themselves. In some cases, rookie officers are "tested" to determine if they can be trusted. Those officers having a history with the department are checked out through the "grapevine" and are often intentionally placed in situations to see if they can be trusted.

- *"Don't talk too little or too much; don't tell anybody more than they have to know."* The themes of "don't talk too much," and "don't reveal more than necessary" inform new police officers that others including citizens and supervisors are not to be trusted. These dictates reinforce the notion that "loose lips sink ships" and that there is no need to provide others with information beyond the minimum required. Information can be distorted or used in other ways that are potentially harmful. At the same time, the dictate "don't talk too little" lets new police officers know that excessive silence or introversion will be seen as suspicious behavior by other officers. As Reuss-Ianni notes, the extremes of talking too much or too little are both viewed as suspicious behaviors by fellow officers. This postulate directs officers to maintain communications with the work group but to limit their exposure to administrators and citizens.

- *"Don't trust bosses to look out for your interests."* This maxim informs new police officers that when forced to make a choice, managers and administrators will look out for their own best interests rather than those of the officer. Whether true or not, this idea has the effect of further distancing officers from their superiors. Since line officers are taught that they cannot depend on either citizens or superiors, they are forced to align themselves with the only group left for protection—fellow police.

Postulates Indicative of the Ethos of Bravery.   David H. Bayley and Egon Bittner (1997) have noted that a crucial part of a police officer's job is to take charge of situations and people. Taking charge, in this sense, involves developing a "presence" to handle incidents. In essence, this means that officers must be poised to take control regardless of the situation. Yet, it is crucial not to appear too ready, since overeagerness can escalate situations. In one officer's words, "Always act . . . as if you were on vacation." At the same time, however, "One must be keyed up but not 'choke'" (p. 28). Reuss-Ianni (1983, p. 16) identified two postulates that strongly suggest new officers must always, above all else, show bravery in the performance of police work.

- *"Show balls."* The police characterize their work as dangerous and fraught with hazards. This postulate counsels police that they are never to back down from a situation; backing down signals weakness. All police are harmed by the cowardice of an individual officer. Officers must have fortitude to control situations. When the authority of a single officer is challenged, the authority of the entire police group is challenged and must be addressed. While this is especially true for incidents that occur in view of the public, it is also important for an officer never to back down from a situation where other officers are present.

- *"Be aggressive when you have to, but don't be too eager."* This postulate reflects the idea that while officers should always be alert, they should not go out of their way to seek trouble. This is partly because overeagerness, or having a "chip" on one's shoulder, will only bring unneeded complications. In a sense, the maxim, "If you look for trouble, it will find you," applies here. Therefore, challenges to authority must be met and dealt with, but they should not be sought out. Police are to avoid acting in ways that cause the group to undergo unnecessary scrutiny. However, this postulate also reminds an officer to meet a challenge or confrontation as aggressively as necessary to handle it effectively.

Through exposure to these and other postulates, new generations of police officers combine their experiences and perceptions of the world—all of which are filtered through the unique perspective of police officers' eyes. With these "truths," officers develop a belief system which dictates acceptable and unacceptable behavior. These postulates serve as reinforcers of the police worldview and act as part of the socialization process for members of the police occupation. Through these postulates, officers are taught the necessity for secrecy and solidarity among the ranks, and the belief that police are different and isolated from larger society. Violations of these canons may lead to immediate sanctions from fellow subculture members, frequently resulting in expulsion from the security of the group. It is ironic that police who violate the precepts of the subculture are doubly isolated—first from the community by nature of the occupation and later by the police subculture for violation of its informal norms of conduct. Police officers who do not conform to the postulates of the work group become outcasts who have been stripped of the benefits of group membership.

Summary

Many approaches have been used to explain the unique character of the police. Scholars who endorse the psychological paradigm suggest that police character may be explained by one of two approaches. Personality theorists suggest that people with certain personality types—such as those who are authoritarian—are attracted to police work. Seen in this light, police character is a reflection of the unique personality characteristics of those who enter and remain in police work. An alternative social-psychological explanation for police character posits that the police working environment shapes the personality, character, and behavior of individual officers. Those who adopt this perspective believe that experiences such as recruit training and relationships with coworkers shape personality and, therefore, the behavior of individual officers.

The sociological paradigm rejects the idea that personality characteristics alone predetermine police character. Instead, this paradigm suggests that police character is molded and shaped by occupational experiences. That is, police character is determined by the police working environment. Socialization experiences—including academy and on-the-job training—are responsible for the development of police values and ethics.

The anthropological paradigm offers perhaps the most complete explanation for the development of police character. The occupational culture provides police with a unique working personality. This working personality includes the development of a worldview that teaches police to distinguish between insiders and outsiders (i.e. police/nonpolice)—in other words, those who are okay versus those who must be watched.

This we/they perspective instills in officers a perpetual concern for the element of danger in their work. The police working personality reinforces the notion of "differentness" in three ways. First, police are taught that they are vested with the unique power to use force and violence in carrying out legal mandates. Second, the paramilitary nature of police work isolates police from others in society. Finally, police are indoctrinated with the idea that they are the "thin blue line" between anarchy and order.

Three guiding beliefs define the police ethos. The social character of policing is shaped by a reverence for bravery, autonomy, and secrecy. The police subculture stresses these sentiments and teaches new officers the value of adopting these attitudes—and the consequences of not conforming.

Cultural themes are also a part of the police culturalization process. In this case, cultural themes are fairly specific rules of behavior that shape police interactions. A dominant cultural theme in policing is the idea that police are socially isolated from the rest of society. A second important cultural theme extols the need for police solidarity.

Finally, several postulates of the police culture were reviewed. Postulates are specific statements that guide and direct the actions of subcultural members. Postulates that reinforce the need for police secrecy and solidarity include instructions never to "give up" another cop and to watch out for other police, especially one's partner. Postulates that support police isolationism instruct police to "protect your ass" by being wary of everyone; not to trust new officers until they have proven themselves; and not to trust supervisors to look out for an officer's best interests. Postulates also instruct officers on the ethos of bravery: never back down and be aggressive but not overeager in handling situations.

References

Adlam, K. R. (1982). The police personality: Psychological consequences of becoming a police officer. *The Journal of Police Science and Administration, 10*(3), 347–348.

Adorno, T. W. (1950). *The authoritarian personality.* New York: Harper.

Alpert, G. P. (1993). The role of psychological testing in law enforcement. In R. G. Dunham & G. P. Alpert (Eds.), *Critical issues in policing: Contemporary readings* (2nd ed., pp. 96–105). Prospect Heights, IL: Waveland Press.

Alpert, G. P., & Dunham, R. G. (1997). *Policing urban America* (3rd ed.). Prospect Heights, IL: Waveland Press.

Angell, J. E. (1977). Toward an alternative to the classical police organizational arrangements: A democratic model. In L. K. Gaines & T. A. Ricks (Eds.), *Managing the police organization.* St. Paul, MN: West.

Argyris, C. (1957, June). The individual and organization: Some problems of mutual adjustment. *Administrative Science Quarterly,* 1–24.

Bahn, C. (1984). Police socialization in the eighties: Strains in the forging of an occupational identity. *Journal of Police Science and Administration, 12*(4), 390–394.

Baldwin, J. (1962). *Nobody knows my name.* New York: Dell.

Banton, M. (1964). *The policeman in the community.* New York: Basic Books.

Bayley, D. H. (1976). *Forces of order: Police behavior in Japan and the United States.* Berkeley: University of California Press.

Bayley, D. H., & Bittner, E. (1997). Learning the skills of policing. In R. G. Dunham & G. P. Alpert (Eds.), *Critical issues in policing: Contemporary readings* (3rd ed., pp. 114–138). Prospect Heights, IL: Waveland Press.

Bayley, D. H., & Mendelsohn, G, (1969). *Minorities and the police: Confrontation in America.* New York: The Free Press.

Benedict, R. (1934). *Patterns of culture.* Boston: Houghton Mifflin.

Bennett, R. R. (1984). Becoming blue: A longitudinal study of police recruit occupational socialization. *Journal of Police Science and Administration, 12*(1), 47–57.

Berg, B. L., Gertz, M. G., & True, E. J. (1984). Police-community relations and alienation. *Police Chief, 51*(11), 20–23.

Bittner, E. (1995a) The capacity to use force as the core of the police role. In V. E. Kappeler (Ed.), *The police & society: Touchstone readings* (pp. 127–137). Prospect Heights, IL: Waveland Press.

Bittner, E. (1995b). The quasi-military organization of the police. In V. E. Kappeler (Ed.), *The police & society: Touchstone readings* (pp. 173–183). Prospect Heights, IL: Waveland Press.

Black, D. (1970). Production of crime rates. *American Sociological Review, 35,* 733–748.

Black, D. (1976). *The behavior of law.* New York: Academic Press.

Bordua, D. J. & Reiss, A. J., Jr. (1967). Law enforcement. In P. Lazarsfeld, W. Sewell, & H. Wilensky (Eds.), *The uses of sociology.* New York: Basic Books.

Broderick, J. J. (1987). *Police in a time of change* (2nd ed.). Prospect Heights, IL: Waveland Press.

Brown, M. K. (1981). *Working the street: Police discretion and the dilemmas of reform.* New York: Russell Sage.

Burbeck, E., & Furnham, A. (1985). Police officer selection: A critical review of the literature. *Journal of Police Science and Administration, 13*(1), 58–69.

Bureau of Justice Statistics (1992). *Law enforcement management and administrative statistics, 1990: Data for individual state and local agencies with 100 or more officers.* Washington, DC: U.S. Department of Justice.

Cain, M. E. (1973). *Society and the policeman's role.* London, England: Routledge and Kegan Paul.

Carpenter, B. N., & Raza, S. M. (1987). Personality characteristics of police applicants: Comparisons across subgroups and with other populations. *Journal of Police Science and Administration 15*(1), 10–17.

Chambliss, W. J., & Seidman, R. B. (1971). *Law, order and power.* Reading, MA: Addison-Wesley.

Clark, J. P. (1965). Isolation of the police: A comparison of the British and American situations. *Journal of Criminal Law, Criminology and Police Science, 56,* 307–319.

Cohen, H. S., & Feldberg, M. (1991). *Power and restraint: The moral dimension of police work.* New York: Praeger.

Cox, T. C., Crabtree, A., Joslin, D., & Millet, A. (1987). A theoretical examination of police entry-level uncorrected visual standards. *American Journal of Criminal Justice, 11*(2), 199–208.

Crank, J. P. (1998). *Understanding police culture.* Cincinnati, OH: Anderson.

Cullen, F. T., Link, B. G., Travis, L. F., & Lemming, T. (1983). Paradox in policing: A note on perceptions of danger. *Journal of Police Science and Administration, 11*(4), 457–462.

Delattre, E. J. (1989). *Character and cops: Ethics in policing.* Washington, DC: American Enterprise Institute for Public Policy Research.

Ferdinand, T. H. (1980). Police attitudes and police organization: Some interdepartmental and cross-cultural comparisons. *Police Studies, 3,* 46–60.

Fyfe, J. J. (1997). The split-second syndrome and other determinates of police violence. In R. G. Dunham & G. P. Alpert (Eds.), *Critical issues in policing: Contemporary readings* (3rd ed., pp. 531–546). Prospect Heights, IL: Waveland Press.

Gaines, L. K., Kappeler, V. E., & Vaughn, J. B. (1997). *Policing in America* (2nd ed.). Cincinnati: Anderson.

Hannewicz, W. B. (1978). Police personality: A Jungian perspective. *Crime and Delinquency, 24*(2), 152–172.

Harris, R. (1973). *The police academy: An insider's view.* New York: John Wiley.

Holden, R. (1984). Vision standards for law enforcement: A descriptive study. *Journal of Police Science and Administration, 12*(2), 125–129.

Hunt, J. (1985). Police accounts of normal force. *Urban Life, 13*(4), 315–341.

Kappeler, V. E., Blumberg, M., & Potter, G. W. (1996). *The mythology of crime and criminal justice* (2nd ed.). Prospect Heights, IL: Waveland Press.

Kraska, P. B., & Kappeler, V. E. (1997). Militarizing American police: The rise and normalization of paramilitary units. *Social Problems, 44*(1), 1–18.

Kraska, P. B. & Paulsen, D. J. (1997). Grounded research into U.S. paramilitary policing: Forging the iron fist inside the velvet glove. *Police and Society, 7,* 253–270.

Kuykendall, J., & Burns, D. (1980). The black police officer: An historical perspective. *Journal of Contemporary Criminal Justice, 1*(4), 103–113.

Maguire, K., Pastore, A. L., & Flanagan, T. J. (Eds.). (1996). *Sourcebook of criminal justice statistics, 1995.* Washington, DC: U.S. Government Printing Office.

Maher, P. T. (1988). Police physical agility tests: Can they ever be valid? *Public Personnel Management Journal, 17,* 173–183.

Manning, P. K. (1995). The police: Mandate, strategies and appearances. In V. E. Kappeler (Ed.), *The police & society: Touchstone readings* (pp. 97–125). Prospect Heights, IL: Waveland Press.

Manning, P. K. (1997). *Police work: The social organization of policing* (2nd ed.). Prospect Heights, IL: Waveland Press.

Marquart, J. (1986). Doing research in prison: The strengths and weaknesses of full participation as a guard. *Justice Quarterly, 3*(1), 20–32.

Matza, D. (1969). *Becoming deviant.* Englewood Cliffs, NJ: Prentice-Hall.

Mollen Commission. 1994. *The City of New York Commission to Investigate Allegations of Police Corruption and the Anti-Corruption Procedures of the Police Department: Commission Report.* New York: City of New York.

Murphy, P. V., & Caplan, D. G. (1993). Fostering integrity. In R. G. Dunham & G. P. Alpert (Eds.), *Critical issues in policing: Contemporary readings* (2nd ed., pp. 304–324) Prospect Heights, IL: Waveland Press.

Niederhoffer, A. (1967). *Behind the shield: The police in urban society.* Garden City, NY: Anchor Books.

Opler, M. E. (1945). Themes as dynamic forces in culture. *The American Journal of Sociology, 51,* 198–206.

Paynes, J., & Bernardin, H. J. (1992). Entry-level police selection: The assessment center is an alternative. *Journal of Criminal Justice, 20,* 41–52.

Piliavin, I., & Briar, S. (1964). Police encounters with juveniles. *American Journal of Sociology, 70,* 206–214.

Pogrebin, M. R., & Poole, E. D. (1991). Police and tragic events: The management of emotions. *Journal of Criminal Justice, 19,* 395–403.

Putti, J., Aryee, S., & Kang, T. S. (1988). Personal values of recruits and officers in a law enforcement agency: An exploratory study. *Journal of Police Science and Administration, 16*(4), 249–265.

Redfield, R. (1952). *The primitive worldview.* Proceedings of the American Philosophical Society, *96,* 30–36.

Redfield, R. (1953). *The primitive world and its transformations.* Ithaca, NY: Cornell University Press.

Reiss, A. J. (1971). *The police and the public.* New Haven: Yale University Press.

Reiss, A. J., & Bordua, D. J. (1967). Environment and organization: A perspective on the police. In D. J. Bordua (Ed.), *The police: Six sociological essays.* New York: John Wiley.

Reuss-Ianni, E. (1983). *Two cultures of policing.* New Brunswick, NJ: Transaction Books.

Reuss-Ianni, E., & Ianni, F. A. J. (1983). Street cops and management cops: The two cultures of policing. In M. Punch (Ed.), *Control in the police organization.* Cambridge: MIT Press.

Rokeach, M., Miller, M. G., & Snyder, J. S. (1971). The value gap between the police and the policed. *Journal of Social Issues, 27*(2), 155–177.

Rubinstein, J. (1973). *City police.* New York: Farrar, Straus and Giroux.

Savitz, L. (1971). The dimensions of police loyalty. In H. Hahn (Ed.), *Police in urban society.* Beverly Hills: Sage.

Sherman, L. W. (1982). Learning police ethics. *Criminal Justice Ethics, 1*(1), 10–19.

Skolnick, J. H. (1994). *Justice without trial: Law enforcement in a democratic society* (3rd ed.). New York: Macmillan.

Sparger, J. R., & Giacopassi, D. J. (1992). Memphis revisited: A reexamination of police shootings after the Garner decision. *Justice Quarterly, 9,* 211–225.

Stoddard, E. R. (1995). The informal code of police deviancy: A group approach to blue-collar crime. In V. E. Kappeler (Ed.), *The police & society: Touchstone readings* (pp. 185–206). Prospect Heights, IL: Waveland Press.

Sullivan, P. S. (1989). Minority officers: Current issues. In R. G. Dunham & G. P. Alpert (Eds.), *Critical issues in policing: Contemporary readings* (pp. 331–345). Prospect Heights, IL: Waveland Press.

Swanton, B. (1981). Social isolation of police: Structural determinants and remedies. *Police Studies, 3,* 14–21.

Van Maanen, J. (1995). The asshole. In V. E. Kappeler (Ed.), *The police & society: Touchstone readings* (pp. 307–328). Prospect Heights, IL: Waveland Press.

Westley, W. A. (1956). Secrecy and the police. *Social Forces, 34*(3), 254–257.

Westley, W. A. (1970). *Violence and the police: A Sociological study of law, custom and morality.* Cambridge: MIT Press.

Westley, W. A. (1995). *Violence and the police.* In V. E. Kappeler (Ed.), *The police & society: Touchstone readings* (pp. 293–305). Prospect Heights, IL: Waveland Press.

Addressing Police Misconduct
The Role of Citizen Complaints

Jeff Rojek, Scott H. Decker, & Allen E. Wagner

INTRODUCTION

The rule of law constrains the behavior of public agencies in American society. In no other case is this more apparent than for law enforcement agencies. The police are constrained by a variety of factors as they endeavor to go about their job. Perhaps it is the irony that the police sometimes act outside the law as they enforce the law, which makes police misconduct particularly troublesome in a democratic society. From a more pragmatic perspective, the police are dependent upon citizen cooperation to fulfill their crime control mandate. Absent such cooperation, the identification and apprehension of criminal suspects becomes a nearly impossible task, and misconduct undermines citizen cooperation.

One only need look at the national news media over the past couple of years to find cases of misconduct that question police legitimacy. In 1998, a New York City police officer was convicted of sexually assaulting a Haitian immigrant with an object. The Los Angeles Police Department experienced one of its worst cases of police misconduct stemming from officer corruption in a divisional gang unit (LAPD, 2000). Citizen complaints of officer misconduct, however, rarely rise to this level of seriousness or media coverage. The day-to-day cases of officer misconduct examined by police review systems range from complaints about an officer's attitude to complaints of excessive

Prepared for *Critical Issues in Policing* by Jeff Rojek, Scott H. Decker, and Allen E. Wagner.

use of force. Nonetheless, the review of this wide range of complaints is an important function of a civilian law enforcement agency.

This article examines the process by which a civilian complaint against the police emerges and is resolved. The first half of this article gives discussion to the role of the police and how misconduct arises within this context. Included in this discussion is an overview of the explanations for this misconduct. The latter half of the article is then directed at the citizen complaint process, acknowledging some of the pitfalls in this effort.

THE POLICE ROLE AND COMPLAINTS

Herman Goldstein cautions that "anyone attempting to construct a workable definition of the police role will typically come away with old images shattered and a new-found appreciation for the intricacies of police work" (1977:21). While definitions of the police role are divergent, the following list provided by former F.B.I. Director J. Edgar Hoover represents an often cited framework (Niederhoffer, 1969:7):

1. protection of life and property;

2. preservation of the peace;

3. prevention of crime;

4. detection and arrest of violators of the law;

5. enforcement of laws and ordinances; and

6. safeguarding the rights of individuals.

This list of police goals (or one similar) has been taught to recruit officers for at least a generation, and no one seriously doubts their foundation in the law. But the goals, laudable as they are, do not accurately reflect the vagaries of the police role.

What, then, is the role? Walker (1983:56–57) posits that, however one defines role, it is complex and ambiguous and leads to conflict within the individual officer and between the police and the public. Such conflicts often lead to the filing of a complaint against the police. Clearly, the diffuse and often contradictory roles of the police precipitate many police-citizen misunderstandings. Different expectations regarding the police role, differences that stem in part from the discretion exercised by officers, lead to citizen complaints.

The multifaceted nature of police discretion is best exemplified by Bittner's (1990) discussion of police working in skid row areas. The enforcement of minor offenses on skid row is often overridden by the desire to maintain the peace. In summation of skid row practices, Bittner states:

> The basic routine of keeping the peace on skid row involves a process of matching the resources of control with situational exigencies. The overall objective is to reduce the total amount of risk in the area. In this, practicality plays a considerably more important role than legal norms. Pre-

cisely because patrolmen see legal reasons for coercive action much more widely distributed on skid row than could ever be matched by interventions, they intervene not in the interest of law enforcement but in the interest of producing relative tranquility and order on the street. (1990:55)

Though the situational application of the law by police officers often has an internal logic, to the outsider it can often look arbitrary, and perhaps abusive.

This "discretionary" aspect of police work is sometimes at the cutting edge of dissonance between the police (indeed, individual police officers) and the public. Consider the citizen; the public has its own definition and expectations of the police role. Like police work, these expectations vary from community to community, individual to individual. Essentially, the general public believes that the police should enforce the law, prevent crime, and maintain order. But, as Ward points out, "a group of drug addicts might have different expectations than the local Chamber of Commerce with regard to the way policemen institute searches" (1975:215).

The officer, therefore, must learn to react to the situation and the individuals involved, keeping in mind the expected gains or losses. The officer must determine which of several options are open and then choose between one or more alternatives that may be at variance with the expectations of some of those concerned, including other police officers. Crank (1998:29) underscores this variation in expectations when he observes, "Line officers are not presented with a single monolithic environment in which they conduct their work, but instead confront a series of environments, each with its own particular expectations of the police." It can be easily observed that the ambiguous nature of the police role almost invites criticism. Perez (1994:36) notes, "police malpractice, in a real sense, is created by several dynamics that impact these average men and women who are trying to accomplish their multiple, 'impossible tasks.'"

Police Misconduct

In 1903, a New York City police commissioner turned judge noted that his court had seen numerous citizens with injuries received when the police effected their arrest. He felt that many of them had done nothing to deserve an arrest, but most of them had made no complaint. Said the judge, "If the victim complains, his charge is generally dismissed. The police are practically above the law" (Reiss, 1970:57). Almost seventy years later, Germann observes that "police attitudes for the most part, indicate no responsibility for unnecessary or illegal police violence, or abuses of police authority" (1971:418).

The key word is "authority." The laws of most states, coupled with department regulations, usually define the extent to which force may be used by a police officer in the performance of official duties. In addition to articulating the proper circumstances for police use of force, legal codes and department policies give vague boundaries to the authority of police to intervene in the lives of citizens. However, as noted above, police work unfolds in a dynamic environment that is often filled with ambiguity of the proper police role. The coexistence of formal regulations and the uncertainty of police work often results in a struggle between department accountability and officer autonomy, which Crank (1998:234–236) calls the "paradox of accountability." Police agencies, as well as legislative bodies, attempt to develop more accountability through elaborate rules that provide guidelines for police conduct. However, police officers will attempt to insulate themselves from a formal accountability system that cannot account for the dynamic and uncertain nature of their work. The result is Crank's paradox, where the department attempts to increase its control over police conduct, and officers further distance themselves from department accountability in an attempt to develop self-protection. This paradox provides difficult environment for a police department that seeks to provide accountability to its constituency.

Some Definitions of Police Misconduct

A variety of definitions of police misconduct have been developed. Field observers, working on a project for the Center of Research on Social Organization (CRSO) in the late 1960s, were given several guidelines to assist them in determining when police use of force was judged to be unnecessary or improper.

1. If a policeman physically assaulted a citizen and then failed to make an arrest; proper use involves an arrest.
2. If the citizen being arrested did not, by word or deed, resist the policeman; force should be used only if it is necessary to make an arrest.
3. If the policeman, even though there was resistance to the arrest, could easily have restrained the citizen in other ways.
4. If a larger number of policemen were present and could have assisted in subduing the citizen in the station, in lockup, and in the interrogation rooms.
5. If an offender was handcuffed and made no attempt to flee or offer violent resistance.
6. If the citizen resisted arrest, but the force continued even after the citizen was subdued (Reiss, 1970:64).

Stark notes that a set of guidelines was also prepared by the International Association of Chiefs of Police (IACP). While the IACP directions were longer and more legalistic in appearance than were those given the CRSO observers, they were similar in content (1972:57).

The unnecessary or excessive use of force by the police (both of which fit under the label of "physical abuse"), especially when a citizen is seriously injured, is often considered the most serious of these complaints. But, there are other abuses that, while they don't physically injure anyone, might be termed degrading, dehumanizing, or humiliating. Police departments around the country record these types of complaints under a variety of terms such as verbal abuse, discourtesy, harassment, improper attitude, and ethnic slur.

By the same token, Reiss (1970:59–62) discovered that citizens objected to, and complained about:

1. the way police use language (not necessarily the words they select);
2. the habit police officers have of "talking down" to them; and
3. the "harassing" tactics of the police—the indiscriminate stopping and searching of citizens on foot or in cars, commands to go home or to "move on."

In 1968, the National Advisory Commission on Civil Disorders (the Kerner Commission) reported the finding of similar abuses. While it noted that verbal abuse or discourtesy in urban areas was more likely to be directed at whites, such tactics were particularly distressing to blacks. Said the commission report, "In nearly every city surveyed, the Commission heard complaints of harassment of interracial couples, dispersal of social street gatherings, and the stopping of (blacks) on foot or in cars without obvious basis. These, together with contemptuous and degrading verbal abuse, have great impact in the ghetto . . ." (1968:299–322).

Reiss (1970:59) summarizes the ways in which police have traditionally dealt with certain citizens, particularly those in the lower class:

1. the use of profane and abusive language;
2. commands to move on or get home;
3. stopping and questioning people on the street or searching them and their cars;
4. threats to use force if not obeyed;
5. prodding with a nightstick or approaching with a pistol; and
6. the actual use of physical force or violence itself.

These acts articulated by Reiss are consistent with what Perez (1994:21) labels "police malpractice." Perez notes that these actions represent the common complaints received by police agencies, which he categorizes as use of excessive force and abuse of discretion. In fact, it is this second category, abuse of discretion, that represents the large portion of citizen complaints (Dugan and Breda, 1991:168). Perez (1994:25) notes that such acts as verbal abuse, harassment, discrimination, and failure to take action are representative of the abuse of discretion. This behavior on the part of police officers frequently results in citizen attempts at redress. Such redress often takes the form of a complaint.

Previous Studies in Police Misconduct

The President's Commission on Law Enforcement and Administration of Justice reported that earlier studies had shown that physical abuse was a significant problem. Said the commission:

> The National Commission on Law Observance and Enforcement (the Wickersham Commission), which reported to President Hoover in 1931, found considerable evidence of police brutality. The President's Commission on Civil Rights, appointed by President Truman, made a similar finding in 1947. And, in 1961, the U.S. Civil Rights Commission concluded that "police brutality is still a serious problem throughout the United States." (1967:193)

The commission stated that it did not feel that physical abuse was as serious a problem as in the past, saying "the few statistics . . . suggest small numbers of cases involving excessive use of force" (1967:193). Black and Reiss submitted a research study to the same commission. It was based upon seven weeks of observations of police-citizen interactions in Boston, Chicago, and the District of Columbia. The research was not particularly focused on physical abuse but on other forms of police abuse. The Black and Reiss (1967:35–107) study found that: (1) police tend to be hostile toward antagonistic citizens, offenders, and intoxicated persons (in some instances) during field interrogations; (2) permission of citizens was seldom requested before personal searches were made of subjects; searches were determined to be unnecessary as often as 86 percent of the time; and (3) black citizens objected the least to personal searches, were less apt to be taken to the station house and released without charge, and were less discriminated against, when antagonistic, than whites, at least in radio dispatch situations.

In 1971, Reiss addressed the subject of excessive force. This study determined that: (1) more than three-quarters of the cases involving excessive force took place in a patrol car, precinct station, or public place (primarily the streets); (2) almost all victims were offenders or suspects and were young, lower-class males from any racial group; and (3) persons regarded by the police as deviant offenders (drunks, homosexuals, drug addicts), or who were perceived (by the officer) to have defied the officer's authority, were the most likely victims of undue force (1971:1).

Reiss noted the disparity between his findings and popular opinion that black citizens are the primary victims of physical abuse. He suggested that, even though white officers might be prejudiced toward blacks, they did not discriminate in the use of excessive force. It was Reiss's contention that the police culture more readily explained the use of force than did prejudice (1971:76).

Studies conducted after Reiss, however, show that nonwhite citizens, especially blacks, *are* more often the victims of police misconduct. Hudson, in his study of complaints investigated by the Philadelphia Police Advisory Board, found that police encounters with nonwhite citizens more frequently led to altercations than did police encounters with white citizens. Nonwhite citizens also constituted 70 percent of the principal complainants in Hudson's study (1970:187). Wagner found that blacks constituted slightly more than two-thirds of those who filed complaints against the police (1980:249). Decker and Wagner determined that black complainants were more likely to have been injured in an incident that precipitated a complaint against the police and were also more likely to be arrested than their white counterparts (1982:116–117). Decker and Wagner also found that the incident which prompted the complaint was more likely to have occurred in police custody and out of public view, if the complainant was black (1985:111).

Studies by Lersch and Mieczkowski (1996:39) found that minority citizens are disproportionately represented among complainants. While minority citizens consisted of only 22.2 percent of the population studied by Lersch and Mieczkowski, they accounted for 50.5 percent of complaints. However, they found that minority officers disproportionately accounted for complaints by minority citizens. Minority officers represented 15 percent of the department's personnel, yet they accounted for 35 percent of complaints by minority citizens. Using the same data set, Lersch (1998:96) found that when controlling for complaint type, minority citizens had the same likelihood as whites of having their complaints sustained by police internal affairs divisions.

Causes of Police Misconduct

In addition to documenting its prevalence, research on police misconduct also attempted to explain the reason for its occurrence. Explanations of misconduct range from the individualistic "bad apples" approach to the institutional "police culture" perspective. Each of these frameworks has found support in the police literature.

Bad Apples.   The bad apple analogy states that a few bad apples can ruin the entire barrel, suggesting that the rest of the apples in the barrel are otherwise good. In the case of police departments, the analogy suggests that the majority of police misconduct can be isolated to a small group of problem-prone officers. This approach has found some statistical support. For example, the Christopher Commission (1991) found that 183 of the department's more than 8,000 officers had four or more allegations of excessive use of force or improper tactics in a four-year period, and 44 officers had six or more allegations.

Consistent with the notion of concentrated misconduct, Lersch and Mieczkowski (1996:32) found that 35.5 percent of complaints about misconduct in a large southeastern police department was accounted for by 7.3 percent of the department's sworn personnel. These officers each had five or more complaints. Further, 46 percent of the officers did not receive a single complaint over the same three-year examination period. However, the bad apple theory cannot explain all misconduct, or even the modal category. Almost two-thirds of the complaints examined by Lersch and Mieczkowski were attached to officers not classified as problem prone.

Police Culture.   Some researchers have suggested that misconduct can more readily be explained by the "police culture," which represents that various informal rules develop among officers. Chevigny observed that "police recruits are much like other young men of similar background; it is police mores and police role that make them adopt police attitudes" (1969:137), and "the challenge to police authority continues as a chief cause of force in all urban police departments" (1969:60). Similarly, Niederhoffer asserted, "At first impression it would appear that above all other groups the police ought to be tied to the law, but because they learn to manipulate it, the law can become nothing more than a means to an end" (1969:97). What each of these assertions allude to is that police culture supports the subversion of official rules and thus represents the cause of misconduct.

Recent literature on police culture has moved away from the deterministic approach of past scholars, however. Crank (1998:14) notes that police culture is a complex mixture of various themes, which unfold in the environmental context of police work. The culture develops out of the various exchanges and experiences that officers are exposed to in their day-to-day work environment. Police culture is a set of informal norms that develop in an occupation of uncertainty. As Crank (1998:94) observes, "What is often overlooked is the mediating influence of police culture on the relationship between unpredictable encounters and police administration. Officers deal with the unknown on a daily basis, and develop broad cultural adaptations to unknown situations." This perspective suggests that police culture is more than a basis for subverting formal regulations. It is not to say that such cultural themes as danger, morality, or solidarity cannot lead to misconduct. However, these themes of police culture are more commonly the basis for addressing the multiple and uncertain tasks of police work. As a result, these informal cultural adaptations will always exist to some extent as long as officers are asked to fulfill an undefined role. Thus, the informal norms that emerge among officers does not solely contribute to misconduct, and as a result it cannot be simply isolated and removed.

A review of police behavior and misconduct show that complaints are based on a variety of explanations. The actions that prompt citizen complaints can be a result of a mistake or the intended subversion of formal regulations. Nonetheless, in order for police agencies to provide accountability and an image of legitimacy, they must provide a process that allows citizens to file complaints about conduct they believe is improper or unjust. Such a process allows for the correction of behavior deemed undesirable or the dismissal of those who are unable to perform adequately the tasks required of police officers.

FILING A COMPLAINT

When a breakdown in the management of a police-citizen encounter has occurred, the citizen may file a complaint. Russell, in his study in England and Wales, found that those citizens who did decide to file a complaint against the police did so only after giving consideration to one or more of the following:

1. the citizen was advised that he might well succeed in his complaint;

2. he was able and prepared to make the effort to complain in the belief that justice would be done;

3. he believed that by complaining a policeman might be deterred from misbehaving in the future and that the result could only be in the public interest; and

4. the complaining citizen does not believe that any effort will be made by the officer or his associates to seek revenge (1978:54).

Conversely, Russell found the following to be the reasons why citizens did not file a complaint:

1. the advice of significant others;

2. the apathy of the potential complainant;

3. the apprehensiveness of the citizen;

4. the fatalistic approach that no effective action will be taken by the police;

5. the belief that police work is sufficiently difficult and hazardous without making it more so; and

6. an unawareness of the complaint procedure (1978:52–53).

These reasons were used by Russell to form the following typology of individuals who fail to report misconduct.

The Advised

The advice not to complain against the police may be given by a professional (i.e., attorney, social worker) or another governmental agency based upon the facts given to the individual about the potential complaint. The advisor, perhaps more knowledgeable than the citizen, might "explain away" the basis for the citizen's feeling that the officer was not properly conducting himself or herself. Also a "significant other," such as a friend or relative, might advise that he or she had previously filed a complaint and received no satisfaction. The advice of this individual (not to bother to file a complaint) contributes to the fatalistic posture described below.

The Apathetic

Russell's survey of citizens disclosed that 14 percent were "apathetic potential complainants" who "could just not be bothered to become involved in the detailed procedures of making a complaint" (1978:52). The apathetic citizen has no other reason than a lack of desire to make a complaint.

Bayley and Mendelsohn found the same to be true in their study of complaints in Denver. They discovered that there was a minority of persons in Denver who just didn't want to take the time to complain. "People simply did not want to be bothered; the complaint was not as important as the time they would have to devote to it" (1969:132).

The Apprehensive

Apprehensive citizens indicated that they feared reprisals, whether by personal violence or extralegal means, which deterred them from filing a complaint. The 1967 President's Commission on Law Enforcement and Administration of Justice learned that such apprehensiveness was sometimes well founded. The commission noted that in one large eastern city "the police department used to charge many of those who filed complaints of police misconduct with filing false reports with the police" (1967:195). More recently, the police have begun filing civil suits for libel and/or slander against complainants whose complaints are not substantiated by the police department investigation or who have filed civil suits against the police and lost. While the police argue that they are within their rights in suing a complainant, others feel that they are simply nuisance suits to harass and intimidate not only the present complainant but potential complainants as well.

The National Advisory Commission on Criminal Justice Standards and Goals also expressed knowledge of the problem when it asserted that "personal fear of reprisal or harassment, complex and cumbersome filing procedures, and the highlighted possibility of criminal prosecution for making a false report are three conditions that can discourage the public from making even valid complaints" (1973:471). Reiss asserted that, "many citizens are reluctant to complain against agencies that hold power over them and could respond with punitive action" (1971:190).

The Fatalistic

Russell described the fatalistic person as "those citizens who do not utilize the complaint process because they believe that no effective action will be taken by the police" (1978:53). The potential complainant who believes that nothing will really be done by the police dominated the literature. Bayley and Mendelsohn, for example, stated:

> The evidence very clearly shows that people, regardless of ethnicity, do not complain against the police automatically when they feel aggrieved. People commonly accept what is done to them without trying to buck the system. . . . Willingness to complain seems to be a function of what happens to people and what they expect to be able to gain from it, and these factors are not class-specific. (1969:130)

The Public Spirited

Russell's survey located a group of citizens who believed that the police have a difficult and hazardous job and that they would only make it more difficult by filing a complaint. This notion is not indicated in other literature.

The Unaware

In contrast to the "Public Spirited," instances of potential complainants who either did not know how to initiate the complaint process or did not know that such a process existed are not unusual. The President's Commission commented that "the mechanics of receiving complaints often tends to discourage potential complainants from taking any action. Some procedures are so little known, so complex, or so hard to pursue that the ordinary citizen either gives up or never tries in the first place" (1967:196). Repeating a recommendation of the National Advisory Commission on Civil Disorders some three years earlier, the National Advisory Commission on Criminal Justice Standards and Goals warned that this might be the result of a misunderstanding by the public, and "if this is the case, it is incumbent on the police agency to educate the public in these areas" (1973:471).

Police Accountability and the Citizen Complaint Process

The citizens of a democratic society should have the right to make complaints about the actions of public officials acting in their official capacity. Further, police officers should be no less accountable for their actions than the mayor or any other employee of a political subdivision. Establishing a process that provides such accountability can have both positive and negative aspects.

Positive Aspects of Citizen Complaints

Police administrators should look upon citizen complaints as a barometer of police performance. Police officers have little supervision as they go about their duties, and fellow police officers are not likely to report their colleagues' misconduct. Citizens can provide the police department with valuable information about how well the department is performing.

The United States Commission on Civil Rights believes that citizen complaints also provide another useful function, acting as "important indicators of public perception of the agency" (1981:50). Police departments, says the commission, can use information obtained through citizen complaints to improve the public image and community relations of the department as they strive to provide better service to the community.

The complaint system has also found a fiscal basis in recent years. The paying out of large sums of money in liability lawsuits stemming from police officer misconduct has become increasingly more common (del Carmen, 1993:87–90). Such court findings against the police not only damage department images of legitimacy but also affect the future funding of police departments and services provided by local government entities. The ability to identify problem officers via a complaint process, in order to provide them with additional training or to terminate those who are most problematic, can reduce future exposure to liability.

Negative Aspects of Citizen Complaints

Making a complaint often takes a great deal of time and effort. The citizen may not know where to go to make the complaint. Even if he or she *does* know where to make the complaint, several obstacles exist.

First, the complainant may discover that there are no complaint procedures established for that police department; the citizen may, at best, be introduced to a ranking officer who will listen to the complaint but will take no formal action. (One of the authors will long remember the comment made to him by a member of a rural police department that "we don't accept complaints.") Second, the complainant may be required to go to the police department, a seemingly simple requirement that may actually be a hardship or an impossibility for the poor, disabled, or busy. Third, the citizen who goes to the police department to make a complaint against an officer may be greeted with any number of reactions. The literature is rich with evidence of the close-knit police fraternity. Accordingly, the complainant may be treated with courtesy and respect or may meet with intimidation, threats, and hostility. Caiden and Hahn point out, for example, that some departments require that the citizen complete a complaint form that states that the complainant is subject to prosecution for making false statements if the information is not substantiated (1979:171). Finally, the complainant may discover that the police department has an arbitrarily assigned "statute of limitations" on citizen complaints; the complaint will not be accepted if it is made after a certain length of time following the precipitating incident.

The citizen who overcomes the obstacles to the process and files a formal complaint then learns, if it wasn't previously known, that the complaint will be investigated by officers of that police department. Whether the investigators will be one of the accused officer's supervisors or a member of an internal affairs unit, the complainant comes face-to-face with the reality that the police department is investigating itself, a fact that the complainant may find, at the least, disheartening. Whether the concern of the citizen that police investigating police will prove fruitless is justified or not, the police department must recognize that suspicion and take steps to avoid even the appearance that the investigation is anything but impartial.

All of these considerations, both positive and negative, are best addressed within the framework of a formal, written citizen complaint procedure.

ESTABLISHING A PROPER CITIZEN COMPLAINT PROCESS

In its 1981 report to President Ronald Reagan, the United States Commission on Civil Rights (1981:v–vi) listed several reasons for "the continuous, thoughtful examination" of police conduct. "Police officers possess awesome powers . . . protection of civil rights demands close examination of the exercise of police authority . . . police officers exercise their powers with wide discretion and under minimal supervision . . . a single occurrence or a perceived pattern of discriminatory and unjustified use of force can have a powerful, deleterious effect on the life of the community." Finally, the commission noted:

Thus, there is ample reason for studying police conduct even without further justification. However, the volume of complaints of police abuse received by the Commission has increased each year, and the nature of the alleged abuse has become more serious. *Patterns of complaints appear to indicate institutional rather than individual problems.* (1981:vi, italic added)

The International Association of Chiefs of Police (IACP) contributed its voice to a similar endeavor, publishing a detailed manual of rules and procedures for the management of effective police discipline. The lengthy IACP publication began with a sample policy statement that police departments might adopt. The model statement called for: "the establishment of a system of complaint and disciplinary procedures . . ." and "the prompt receipt, investigation and disposition of complaints regarding the conduct of members and employees of the Department . . ." (1976:40). The IACP policy statement also recognized the importance of citizen complaints in the management of a police department when it stated: "The Police Department welcomes from the people of the community constructive criticism of the Department and valid complaints against its members or procedures" (1976:40–41).

The Police Executive Research Forum (PERF) began its model police misconduct policy statement by asserting that "the purpose of this policy is to improve the quality of police services" (1981:1). PERF then listed three positive outcomes that could be accomplished:

1. through the provision of meaningful and effective complaint procedures, citizen confidence in the integrity of police increases and this engenders community support and confidence in the police department;

2. disciplinary procedures permit police officials to monitor officers' compliance with departmental procedures;

3. the third purpose is to clarify rights and ensure due process protection to citizens and officers alike (1981:1).

All three of the documents, those of the U.S. Civil Rights Commission, the International Association of Chiefs of Police, and the Police Executive Research Forum, are remarkably similar. These similarities include:

1. the publication and distribution by the police department of written rules and regulations guiding the conduct of officers as they perform the various duties required of them;

2. an emphasis on the importance of proper supervision as a means of reducing and controlling police misconduct;

3. the establishment of an internal affairs unit (or individuals in a small department) with written guidelines on conducting an internal investigation;

4. the creation of a citizen complaint system, one that: is not intimidating, is accessible, and accepts anonymous complaints;

5. the education of the public about the disciplinary process and how complaints against the police may be filed;

6. the use of complaint forms for recording citizen complaints and for forming the basis for an investigation (one copy would go to the accused officer); the Civil Rights Commission recommended, in addition, the use of bilingual forms;

7. a prompt investigation of the complaint; and

8. equally prompt notification of the complainant and the accused officer as to the results of the investigation and what channels of appeal are open.

THE STRUCTURE OF THE POLICE REVIEW PROCESS

Much of the debate about citizen complaints against the police has focused on the structure of responses to such complaints. There is considerable evidence that police and citizens desire different structures to deal with such complaints. And there is also evidence to indicate that the structure, responsibility, jurisdiction, and staffing of such review boards have a significant impact on their decisions.

West (1988) noted that any determination about what form the complaint process should take must consider all actors. While the system must, he says, be thorough and impartial, it must also be equally acceptable "to the officers themselves, to members of the public, and to those elected political officials who are charged with the responsibility of ensuring that police agencies are effectively and efficiently managed" (101–102). Dugan and Breda (1991:171) asserted that the way that a police agency deals with criticism "will determine whether criticism is a positive management tool or a basis for low morale, cynicism, and nonprofessional behavior." We turn our attention now to the various structural aspects of the complaint process, and their impact on the process.

The review of police conduct is a complex process. There are both formal and informal controls on police behavior, subjecting it to review from a variety of different sources. Most important in the review process are the reviews that come from criminal justice institutions, including, most directly, courts, prosecutor's office, and police administration. It is obvious that each of these are entrusted with the formal responsibility of review of police procedures, policies, and actions, many on a daily basis. Even the potential for review by one or more of these agencies exerts a control on police behavior. In addition to these formal agencies entrusted with an oversight function, there are many groups and institutions, external to the justice system, that perform a similar function. Notable among these are the media. Newspapers, radio, and television are all actively engaged in reviewing police conduct through news reports and editorials. As such, their "reviews" of police behavior are likely to have a widespread impact, perhaps greater than those conducted within the criminal justice system.

The review of police conduct provided by these external groups is significant, but it tends to lack the focus of those formally entrusted with the direct responsibility of oversight of allegations of police misconduct. The central issue in the consideration of the formal structure of the process is the extent to which citizens are involved. The level of involvement by citizens in the formal police review process varies significantly. It is this level of involvement that distinguishes the several formal procedures now in use by police departments.

Traditionally, the police review process excluded citizens from the process altogether. In their review of the administrative structure of police complaint procedures in the 1960s, Beral and Sisk (1964) found that the model in which only police were involved predominated. This was true into the 1980s, as the research of Terrill (1982) and Kerstetter (1985) indicated; they estimated that perhaps as many as 80 percent of all administrative structures were composed of only police officers.

Walker and Bumphus (1991) have shown, however, that since 1986 there has been an increase in the number of cities involving citizens at some stage of the complaint review process. They found that investigations of police misconduct in 18 cities (36%) were solely internal, that is, had no citizen involvement. Another 6 cities (12%) had minimal civilian involvement; usually the complainant was given the opportunity to appeal the final disposition to a board that includes nonsworn personnel. The remaining 26 cities (52%) provided for greater involvement of citizen review.

Several arguments exist to support the police-only model. First is the expertise brought to a review process. Police officers are well versed in matters of law and police procedure and, it is argued, are thus in the best position to render informed and competent decisions regarding citizen complaints (Walker, 2000). Supporters of this model also argue that the process lacks credibility among police officers when it includes citizens. The effectiveness of the process is enhanced when police are the sole arbiters in the process, and thus outcomes are likely to have more significant consequences. Further arguments include the well-accepted notion that bureaucracies and public sector organizations are responsible for solving their own problems. Citizen involvement in the process is evidence of the inability of the police organization to deal effectively with the shortcomings or misbehavior of its members. While this list is not an exhaustive one,[1] it provides the major arguments presented in support of review structures that include only police personnel.

The other major structural alternative includes citizens in some part of the review process. It should be noted that the review process is a truncated one involving many different decision points. Prominent among those are the receipt of complaints, evaluation, investigation, adjudication, and disciplinary recommendations. There is considerable variation among those structures that allow citizen input as to what stages of the process that input is allowed. Kerstetter and Rasinski (1994) say, however, that their study of the Minneapolis Police Department underscores the value of even modest civilian participation in the process. We will examine each of the structures that allow citizen input, beginning with the least amount of involvement and stretching along a continuum to those that have full citizen involvement at each stage.

The structure allowing for the least amount of input by citizens is that which includes citizens who are employees of the police department in a nonsworn capacity. Typically, models that utilize this approach involve these "police-civilians" in the earlier stages of the complaint process (i.e., the receipt and/or investigation of complaints), reserving the latter stages (adjudication and assignment of penalties) to police personnel.

The remaining three models all involve citizens from outside the police department. They do, however, vary considerably as to the extent of that citizen involvement. Kerstetter (1985) has identified these models, which he refers to as the civilian monitor, civilian input, and civilian review complaint structures. Each progressively involves citizens to a greater extent.

The first of the models, the *monitor*, is the weakest of the three, allowing citizen input into the complaint review process only after the complaint has been reviewed and a punishment determined within the police structure. Under this model, citizens provide a review of police decisions after the fact. The opportunity to have an impact on the process and outcome of any individual complaint is minimal. The next structure, *input*, allows citizen participation at the earliest stages of the complaint review process. In particular, citizen input is used at the stages of receipt and investigation of the complaint. However, the remaining stages (adjudication and punishment) are handed over to the police agency. The final model, *review*, is the strongest of the three in that citizens are involved in all of the meaningful stages of the complaint process, receipt, investigation, adjudication, and punishment.

In the first national survey of civilian review procedures in the United States, Walker and Bumphus (1991) found that 32 of the 50 largest cities had instituted civilian review procedures.[2] They observed that 17 of the 32, over half of the total, have been established only since 1986.

Walker and Bumphus found no two agencies whose civilian review procedures were identical. Thus, they divided the 32 systems along two general criteria:

1. who does the initial investigation of a citizen complaint; and

2. who reviews the investigative report and makes a recommendation for action (1991:1).

They call the models that emerged Classes I, II, and III.

Class I: (a) Initial investigation and fact-finding by nonsworn personnel; (b) Review of investigative report and recommendation for action by nonsworn person or board consisting of a majority of nonsworn persons.

Class II: (a) Initial investigation and fact-finding by sworn police officers; (b) Review of investigative report and recommendation for action by a nonsworn person or board that consists of a majority of nonsworn persons.

Class III: (a) Initial investigation and fact-finding by sworn officers; (b) Review of investigative report and recommendation for action by sworn officers; (c) Opportunity by the citizen who is dissatisfied with the final disposition of the complaint to appeal to a board that includes nonsworn persons (1991:1).

Walker and Bumphus (1991:3) note that the three classes are similar to Kerstetter's three models: Class III is "similar" to Kerstetter's "civilian monitor;" Class II is "similar" to "civilian input;" and Class I "is the same" as "civilian review."

As a result of their survey, Walker and Bumphus classified 12 (37.5%) of the 32 police agencies as Class I; 14 (43.7%) as Class II; and 6 (18.7%) as Class III. Thus, almost half of the 32 police departments with civilian review procedures have included some civilian input in the process.

While the Walker and Bumphus survey did not measure the effectiveness of civilian review procedures, the authors noted (1991:1) that, "the spread of civilian review represents a new national consensus on civilian review as an appropriate method of handling citizen complaints about police misconduct."

There are many dilemmas that emerge as a result of this consideration of the structure of the complaint review process. The clearest distinction between structures can be made between those that include meaningful citizen participation and those that do not. An issue of primary significance to the resolution of complaints—credibility—cuts both ways. West (1988:108) observes that those who favor external review argue that a closed system, where police investigate the police, is contrary to "the rules of natural justice." Those opposed to external review say that such review threatens police morale and professionalism. It seems imperative that citizen involvement be integrated into the police structure, but in such a way as to preserve the ability of the police to monitor themselves. Kerstetter (1985) has argued that the emphasis on the resolution of complaints should not be on punishment, but rather on conciliation, compensation, training, and assistance. Such a call is consistent with the emerging mediation models of citizen complaint resolution. Walker and Kreisel (1996) found that of 65 police departments they observed having some form of citizen review, 12 had some form of mediation available. Walker and Kreisel further state that at the present time there has been little evaluation of the effectiveness of the mediation approach.

The reintegrative or mediation approach, whatever merits its may have, ignores the obvious dilemma that in many departments a serious problem exists with many officers and indeed with the prevailing norms regarding citizen treatment. These problems may require solutions of a punitive nature, rather than the reintegrative ones recommended by Kerstetter.

A final reactive system must be included. A number of police departments have been the subject of external scrutiny, often in the form of commissions or investigations by the U.S. Justice Department. The Christopher Commission Report (1991) resulted from the beating of Rodney King and made several recommendations for changing police practice and culture. In

Chicago, the Commission on Police Integrity (1997) examined police corruption following citizen complaints and formal investigations of misconduct. Such reports can be viewed as a form of reactive, external control of police departments, as they carry both the force of public opinion and political will. Another form of reactive, external institutional control of the police is the consent decree. A number of U.S. cities, notably, Cincinnati, Pittsburgh, and Los Angeles, have entered into such decrees with the U.S. Justice Department. These decrees represent an extreme form of the role that police complaints about police misconduct can play, as they invoke federal investigations and ultimately agreements about specific aspects of police behavior that must be implemented by the agency and then monitored by the Justice Department.

PROACTIVE EFFORTS IN MANAGING MISCONDUCT

Our discussion of the response to police misconduct to this point has focused on reactive efforts, where agencies do not take corrective action until they receive a citizen complaint regarding an officer's behavior. Given the recognition in the policing literature that often a small number of officers account for a disproportionate number of complaints (e.g., Christopher Commission, 1991; Lersch and Mieczkowski, 1996), it stands to reason that a more proactive approach could pay dividends in reducing the total number of future complaints. Such an approach represents a risk management orientation that seeks to address hazards that increase an organization's exposure to loss or otherwise negative events (Head and Horn, 1991). In the context of officer misconduct, the hazards are officers who have routinely displayed problematic behavior (i.e., frequent improper use of force incidents, harassing citizens, etc.). Just such a proactive approach, referred to as "early warning systems," has slowly emerged within police departments over the past twenty-five years.

The typical early warning system is composed of a three-step process (Walker, Alpert, and Kenney, 2001). First, potentially problematic officers are identified through monitoring of a number of conduct indicators (e.g., citizen complaints, firearms-discharge reports, use of force reports, civil litigation, resisting arrest incidents, and pursuits and vehicular accidents). Second, officers who have a number of these indicators within a given period of time are diverted for intervention. The intention of the intervention process is to provide an informal corrective action to improve the officer's performance rather than applying the punitive responses found in the more reactive complaint process discussed above. Thus, the common intervention techniques include counseling from a supervisor or training in a related area where the officer is deficient (e.g., communication or decision-making skills). Third, once the intervention is applied the officer continues to be monitored. The monitoring provides feedback on the effectiveness of the intervention efforts and identifies the possible need to take stronger corrective action for those officers who are not responsive. (See Walker, Alpert, and Kenney in this volume for a more extensive discussion of early warning systems.)

A recent survey of law enforcement agencies has found that early warning systems are becoming more common, with 27 percent of the agencies that serve populations of 50,000 or more having such a process (Walker, Alpert, and Kenney, 2001). Further, a case study conducted in three of these agencies found that officer complaints were dramatically reduced for individuals who had received some form of intervention. For example, in the Minneapolis and New Orleans police departments the average number of citizen complaints for officers who went through the process dropped more than 60 percent in the year that followed the intervention. Although these findings are based on a limited number of agencies, they suggest that comprehensive efforts to address officer misconduct should include this proactive process.

CONCLUSION

This article has examined police misconduct and its review through the citizen complaint process. The nature of police work, particularly the enforcement aspect of the role, is adversarial by nature. Such interactions are likely to generate disagreement and hostility. That complaints eventuate from such interactions is not surprising. Campaigns to recruit more sensitive or less aggressive police officers would appear to have little if any effect in reducing citizen complaints. The evidence presented in this article suggests that the informal culture that develops among police officers has a contributing role in misconduct. Most commentators have pointed to the role of the police culture in shaping the actions that are most likely to result in citizen complaints. However, this article acknowledges that police culture often represents legitimate norms that allow officers to conduct their day-to-day activities in an uncertain environment. This creates a difficult situation in which a police department must find a way to curb norms that foster misconduct yet allow officers the flexibility to address the variety of situations they confront. The failure to do so may result in the greater application of formal controls on officers, which will in turn influence officers to become more evasive to accountability procedures.

Traditionally, police departments addressed citizen complaints through some form of internal review system. Claims that the internal review process was too lenient on officers prompted the creation of various levels of civilian input in the complaint resolution process. The assumption was that civilian input would create a process of greater officer and agency accountability. However, some observers have suggested that a civilian process tends to be more lenient on officers than the internal review system. There has been no empirical evaluation to support or deny this claim. Nonetheless, this position questions whether the goal of the complaint process is to project an image of legitimacy to the citizenry or to provide greater accountability to formal regulations. It is reasonable to assert that both of these are desirable goals (see Walker, 2000 for both perspectives on citizens review).

This article has presented various models of complaint response, and none of these have proven to be the perfect answer. Whatever the model chosen by a police agency, it is important that a citizen complaint process must address allegations of misconduct in a way that guarantees both due process for officers and accountability to the public. The process also has to be viewed as legitimate in order to instill confidence on the part of the citizenry. A society that places a high value on democracy and the preservation of civil rights requires some level of civilian participation in the control of law enforcement agencies. An adequate citizen complaint process plays an integral role in fostering citizen support for the institution of policing. Such support is necessary to the overall function of police agencies.

Notes

[1] For a more exhaustive list, see Terrill (1982), and International Association of Civilian Oversight of Law Enforcement (IACOLE) (1989).

[2] The number of cities with civilian review procedures was listed as thirty in the original report. It was updated to thirty-two cities in a February 1992 addendum.

References

Bayley, David H. and Harold Mendelsohn (1969), *Minorities and the Police,* New York: The Free Press.

Beral, Harold and Marcus Sisk (1964), "The Administration of Complaints by Civilians Against the Police," *Harvard Law Review,* Vol. 77.

Bittner, Egon (1990), *Aspects of Police Work,* Boston, MA: Northeastern University Press.

Black, Donald J. and Albert J. Reiss, Jr. (1967), "Patterns of Behavior in Police and Citizen Transactions," *Field Surveys III, Studies in Crime and Law Enforcement in Major Metropolitan Areas,* Vol. 2, Washington, DC: U.S. Government Printing Office.

Caiden, Gerald and Harlan Hahn (1979), "Public Complaints Against the Police," in Ralph Baker and Fred A. Meyer, Jr. (eds.), *Evaluating Alternative Law-Enforcement Policies,* Lexington, ME: Lexington Books.

Chevigny, Paul (1969), *Police Power,* New York: Vintage Books.

Christopher Commission (1991), Report of the Independent Commission on the Los Angeles Police Department, Los Angeles, California.

Commission on Police Integrity (1997), Report of the Commission on Police Integrity, Presented to the City of Chicago, Chicago, IL.

Crank, John (1998), *Understanding Police Culture,* Cincinnati, OH: Anderson.

Decker, Scott H. and Allen E. Wagner (1982), "Race and Citizen Complaints Against the Police: An Analysis of Their Interaction," in Jack R. Green (ed.), *The Police and the Public,* Beverly Hills, CA: Sage Publications.

——— (1985), "Black and White Complainants and the Police," *American Journal of Criminal Justice,* Vol. 10, No. 1.

del Carmen, Rolando V. (1993), "Civil Liberties in Law Enforcement: Where Are We and Where Should We Go From Here?" *American Journal of Police,* Vol. 12, No. 4.

Dugan, John R. and Daniel R. Breda (1991), "Complaints About Police Officers: A Comparison Among Types and Agencies," *Journal of Criminal Justice,* Vol. 19, No. 2.

Germann, A. C. (1971), "Changing the Police—The Impossible Dream?," *The Journal of Criminal Law, Criminology and Police Science,* Vol. LXII (September).

Goldstein, Herman (1977), *Policing a Free Society,* Cambridge, MA: Bailinger Publishing Company.

Head, G. and S. Horn (1991), *Essentials of Risk Management: Volume 1,* Malvern, PA: Insurance Institute of America.

Hudson, James R. (1970), "Police-Citizen Encounters That Lead to Citizen Complaints," *Social Problems,* Vol. 18, No. 2, 179–193.

International Association of Chiefs of Police (1976), *Managing for Effective Police Discipline,* Gaithersburg, MD: International Association of Chiefs of Police, Inc.

International Association of Civilian Oversight of Law Enforcement (IACOLE) (1989), *Compendium of International Civilian Oversight Agencies,* Evanston, IL: IACOLE.

Kerstetter, Wayne A. (1985), "Who Disciplines the Police? Who Should?" in William A. Geller (ed.), *Police Leadership in America: Crisis and Opportunity,* Chicago: American Bar Foundation.

Kerstetter, Wayne A. and Kenneth A. Rasinski (1994), "Opening a Window into Police Internal Affairs: Impact of Procedural Justice Reform on Third-Party Attitudes," *Social Justice Research,* Vol. 7, No. 2 (March).

Lersch, Kim M. (1998), "Predicting Citizen Race in Allegations of Misconduct Against the Police," *Journal of Criminal Justice,* Vol. 26, No. 2.

Lersch, Kim M. and Tom Mieczkowski (1996), "Who are the Problem-Prone Officers? An Analysis if Citizen Complaints," *American Journal of Police,* Vol. 15, No. 3.

Los Angeles Police Department (2000), Board of Inquiry Report into the Rampart Area Corruption Incident, *LAPD Online,* http://www.lapdonline.org/whats_new/boi/boi_report.htm.

National Advisory Commission on Civil Disorders (1968), *Report of the National Commission on Civil Disorders,* New York, NY: Bantam Books.

National Advisory Commission on Criminal Justice Standards and Goals (1973), *Police,* Washington, DC: U.S. Government Printing Office.

Niederhoffer, Arthur (1969), *Behind the Shield: The Police in Urban Society,* Garden City, NY: Anchor Books.

Perez, Douglas W. (1994), *Common Sense about Police Review,* Philadelphia, PA: Temple University Press.

Police Executive Research Forum (1981), *Police Agency Handling of Officer Misconduct: A Model Policy Statement,* Washington, DC: Police Executive Research Forum.

President's Commission on Law Enforcement and Administration of Justice (1967), *Task Force Report: The Police,* Washington, DC: U.S. Government Printing Office.

Reiss Jr., Albert J. (1970), "Police Brutality-Answers to Key Questions," in Michael Lipsky (ed.), *Law and Order Police Encounters,* New Brunswick, NJ: Aldine Publishing Co.

——— (1971), *The Police and the Public,* New Haven, CT: Yale University Press.

Russell, Ken (1978), *Complaints Against the Police: A Sociological View,* Glenfield, Leicester, England: Milltak Limited.

Stark, Rodney (1972), *Police Riots,* Belmont, CA: Wordsworth Publishing Company, Inc.

Terrill, Richard J. (1982), "Civilian Review Boards," *Journal of Police Science and Administration,* Vol. 10, No. 4.

U. S. Commission on Civil Rights (1981), *Who is Guarding the Guardians? A Report on Police Practices,* Washington, DC: U.S. Government Printing Office.

Wagner, Allen E. (1980), "Citizen Complaints Against the Police: The Complainant," *Journal of Police Science and Administration,* Vol. 8, No. 3.

Walker, Samuel (1983), *The Police in America,* New York: McGraw-Hill Book Company.

Walker, Samuel and Vic W. Bumphus (1991), *Civilian Review of the Police: A National Survey of the 50 Largest Cities,* Omaha, NE: Center for Public Affairs Research.

Walker, Samuel and Betsy W. Kreisel (1996), "Varieties of Citizen Review: The Implications of Organizational Features of Complaint Review Procedures for Accountability of the Police," *American Journal of Police*, Vol. 15, No. 3.

Walker, Samuel (2001), *Police Accountability: The Role of Citizen Oversight,* Belmont, CA: Wadsworth.

Walker, Samuel, Geoffrey P. Alpert, & Dennis J. Kenney (2001), *Early Warning Systems: Responding to the Problem Police Officer.* Research in Brief. Washington, DC: National Institute of Justice.

Ward, Richard H. (1975), "The Police Role: A Case of Diversity," in George G. Killinger and Paul F. Cromwell Jr. (eds.), *Issues in Law Enforcement,* Boston, MA: Holbrook Press.

West, Paul (1988), "Investigation of Complaints Against the Police: Summary Report of a National Survey," *American Journal of Police,* Vol. 7, No. 2.

Ethics and Law Enforcement

Joycelyn M. Pollock

> You are a police officer, riding "one-man" patrol. You observe a car weaving erratically and, suspecting intoxication, pull over the driver. The driver fails a breathalyzer, in fact he is over double the legal limit. However, he is also your father. What would you do?

In the situation above, clearly the choice is whether to arrest or deal with the stop informally by taking your father home or calling to have someone come and get him. For many people, this is not perceived as an ethical dilemma because they would never even consider arresting their father. For others, duty to the law versus loyalty to one's father creates a troubling choice. An ethical dilemma can be defined as a difficult decision either because the right thing to do is not obvious, or because the right thing to do is difficult or is contrary to some other value or interest.

In this article we will look at ethics and law enforcement. First, we explore the concept of a dilemma and describe some of the types of dilemmas that exist in law enforcement. Dilemmas may occur in two major areas of ethical decision making, which will be called *"day-to-day ethics"* and *"noble cause ethics."* Second, we will discuss police corruption and look at some of the explanations that have been proposed to explain police deviance and corruption. Finally, we examine some of the proposals that seek to improve ethical decision making in law enforcement.

Prepared especially for *Critical Issues in Policing* by Joycelyn M. Pollock.

ETHICAL DILEMMAS

Police officers face myriad dilemmas during the course of their careers (Heffernan and Stroup 1985). Of course, they are not the only professionals who face difficult decisions. Individuals in every profession encounter their own particular types of ethical dilemmas. Doctors are tempted to prescribe unneeded drugs by huge incentives offered by pharmaceutical companies; lawyers face ethical dilemmas when their clients want them to pursue cases with no legal merit or suborn perjury; and business leaders are often tempted to engage in unethical or even illegal practices to improve the profitability of their company. However, the ethical dilemmas faced by law enforcement professionals are different from others because officers are public servants. Public servants typically have authority over others and/or make decisions that should contribute to the "public good." They have a great deal of power, and we expect them to wield this power fairly and without favor or prejudice (Delattre 1989a).

Most of us do not expect to be judged in our professional lives by the decisions we make in our private lives. To have an extramarital affair is a private matter, although when it involves a coworker or client, it becomes an ethical issue. Drinking is ordinarily a private matter unless it affects the way one performs on the job. We are not particularly interested in the sexual peccadilloes of our plumber, nor do we care about his gambling or drinking habits outside of the job. Public servants, however, are subjected to a high degree of scrutiny even in their private lives (Delattre 1989b). The private behavior of politicians, judges, and other public servants concerns us. Why? Probably because we suspect that the decisions made regarding private behavior also affect, in some way, their role as a public servant. Police officers fall into this group of people who are held to a higher standard of behavior. Public service is, after all, a choice the individual makes, and the power we entrust to public servants is quite awesome.

Part of the reason that public servants are held to a higher standard is that they make decisions for and about the rest of us. Cohen and Feldberg (1991) discuss how the police officer's authority comes from the "social contract." Complete freedom is given up in return for guaranteed protection. Police power is part of this *quid pro quo*—we give the police power to protect us, but we also recognize that this power can be used against us. We accept that power, but only when we trust that the police use it fairly, objectively, and democratically. In the day-to-day decisions of policing, there are temptations to abuse the power entrusted to them. The ethical police officer never forgets that his or her authority and power is a public trust.

Day-to-Day Ethics

Discretion and Decision Making. Discretion can be defined as the power to make a decision. Officers make dozens of decisions every day

(Cohen 1985). In some instances there is a clearly "right" course of action, either because of law, policy, or consequence. In other instances, however, there is no decision that is clearly right. This may be because law or policy does not cover such a circumstance or because law or policy results in an effect that doesn't seem just or fair. In some situations police officers temper the law with "street justice." Police do not arrest or ticket in all situations that they could. Most of us, in fact, have probably been the grateful recipients of an officer's discretionary power to ticket or not. Use of discretion is guided by personal ethics rather than a mechanistic application of the law. In the situations below, many officers ignore the formal law to arrive at a result that they feel is more "just." Other officers, however, would enforce the law "by the book" as they were trained to do.

> An officer responds to a shoplifting call and finds a 70-year-old lady being held for stealing batteries for her hearing aid. She is on a fixed income and can't afford them.

> A very poor woman is stopped for not having child seats for her two children. Since she can't afford the child seats to begin with, she certainly can't afford the ticket for not having them, yet she broke the law.

In some situations, there is no clear legal response called for. In these circumstances, officers could rightfully argue that they have no role since there is no illegality involved, or they could perceive their role more broadly and help to solve problems. What is their ethical duty?

> An officer responds to a disturbance call and finds that a drunken father is trying to remove his son and daughter-in-law and their kids from his home. They refuse to leave and argue that he is drunk and will change his mind tomorrow.

> An officer responds to a call in a housing project to discover a distraught mother who has just chased a rat away from her newborn baby.

> An elderly woman constantly calls the station reporting burglaries or noises on her porch. The fact is that she is lonely and scared since the neighborhood has changed around her and she has no close friends or neighbors to check in on her.

The scope of a law enforcement officer's duty is a complicated issue and one we keep redefining. Community policing efforts have dramatically redefined the officer's role. Duty may be defined by the organization, but each individual officer also shapes and personalizes his or her own parameters of duty. To not do what one is paid to do is an obvious ethical transgression, but beyond that, there are nuanced answers for how much an officer is or should be expected to do given the complicated and difficult situations they encounter.

We expect police to utilize their discretion in an ethical manner, but what does that mean? Clearly, when officers discriminate on the basis of race, sex, or any other unfair categorizations, they are using their discretionary power in an unethical way (Cohen 1986, 1987). Kappeler, Sluder, and Alpert

(1994:176–184) discuss the case of Konerak Sinthasomphone (one of Jeffrey Dahmer's victims) as an example of a violation of the ethical obligation of officers to protect and serve all citizens equally. Sinthasomphone, a young Laotian man, attempted to escape from Dahmer's apartment and was found naked and incoherent on the street. Neighbors called police, but evidently because the officers thought he was Dahmer's homosexual lover, they brought the young man back to Dahmer. Shortly after the officers left, Dahmer killed him. The officers' treatment of this victim was arguably influenced by his race and/or apparent sexual orientation. It certainly seems unlikely that a young woman in a similar state would be returned to her captor.

Many argue that police officers treat minority citizens differently. This is certainly the perception in the minority community (Cole 1999, Walker, Spohn and DeLone 2000). African Americans have significantly more negative interactions with police, and many report disrespectful language or swearing by police officers (Weitzer, 1999). Crank (1998) argues that racism is "endemic" in police departments.

Racial profiling and pretext stops can be analyzed under legal criteria but are also ethical issues. Crank (2003:242) reports that in New Jersey, 73 percent of police stops were of African Americans even though they made up only 14 percent of all motorists. In Volusa County, Florida, 70 percent of stops and 80 percent of searches after stops were directed toward African Americans or Latinos, though these groups made up only 5 percent of drivers. When young, black men are stopped frequently for little or no reason, the perceived harassment inevitably poisons the relationship between the community and the police department.

Gratuities. Gratuities can be defined as something given because of one's role or position as a matter of policy, while a gift may be defined as an item of value given to an individual as an individual. Sometimes it is not clear whether something is being offered as a gift or gratuity.

> An officer, new to his beat, stops at a convenience store. The clerk refuses to accept payment for his cold drink, even though the officer argues that he would prefer to pay. The clerk, now upset, accuses the officer of trying to be "better than the others" and says he will tell the officer's supervisor.

> An officer stops to help a motorist on the side of the freeway. The officer drives the individual to his home, which is only a short distance away, and, in appreciation, the man offers the officer $5.00 for breakfast.

In the first situation, the clerk was offering something simply because of the officer's uniform. In the second situation, the person helped was offering a gift to a particular officer because of a kind act over and above the officer's duty. Arguments for gratuities include the idea that such social interchanges cement public relations and help officers with their networking. Another argument supporting the taking of gratuities is that some citizens are more frequent "consumers" of police services and so should expect to "pay more."

Arguments against gratuities include the idea that there is an expectation of different or "special" service when gratuities are a store policy. Officers may patrol differently or make decisions because of them, and this is unfair (Kania 1988, Pollock 2003).

Even the second situation, which may be defined as a gift, raises ethical flags. Some would argue that it would be unethical for the officer to accept what is, in essence, a tip and, in fact, rules in most departments strictly prohibit it. The officer is a public servant and we do not expect to have to pay extra for public service, especially for those public servants who have discretionary power over us. Litigants do not give a judge a tip for a good decision, and residents do not give city council members tips for a vote to pave their street or the zoning commissioner a tip for pushing through an exemption application. Why shouldn't such people get tips? Because we want their decision making to be completely free of bias and they should not be influenced by anything other than the law and the public good. On the other hand, this was not a situation where an officer was making a decision over the individual and, in fact, went beyond his legal duty. Should this situation be analyzed differently? Most ethicists would say no because it would lead to a slippery slope where officers might expect tips in more situations when interacting with the public.

In a more sophisticated analysis, we would want to look at motivation and intent on the part of the officer and the giver (Kania 1988). Typically, however, departmental rules cannot be written by taking into account "good intentions." A departmental rule manual cannot have a rule that states gratuities are acceptable as long as the giver and receiver do so with "good intentions" but are unacceptable otherwise. Therefore, most departments have official policies prohibiting gratuities entirely, yet informal departmental policies often accept the taking of gratuities to lesser or greater extents and punishes only those who abuse the practice.

Other Issues. In addition to issues of discretion, duty, and discrimination, officers make many other decisions that can be judged under ethical criteria. Many of these decisions are no different from those of other workers, such as calling in sick to go to the beach, or lying on overtime reports or expense accounts. In some jurisdictions, courtroom duty involves extra pay and is known as a "gravy train" if an officer is so inclined. Other dilemmas involve protecting oneself. For example, having an accident in a patrol car requires a report to be written, but the officer will be sanctioned even if the accident was minor or not his or her fault. It is tempting to ignore the accident and hope that the damage will be ignored or someone else will be blamed. Lying to stay out of trouble begins before kindergarten and often never ends.

These examples of lying are not qualitatively different from any individual in any occupation or profession who might lie for self-gain or lie to stay out of trouble. Only the circumstances are unique to law enforcement. There is another kind of lying, however, that occurs uniquely in law enforcement and criminal justice settings (Klockars 1984). Some officers lie about probable cause to get a warrant, or lie on the witness stand to ensure a conviction. This type of lying arguably is done not for self-gain but rather to secure the interests of justice. This is discussed by many authors, and we will borrow Crank and Caldero's (2000) "noble cause corruption" concepts to discuss the issues involved.

Noble Cause Ethics

In an early discussion of police practices, Klockars (1983) asked whether it was ethically acceptable for a police officer to inflict pain on a suspect in order to acquire information that would save an innocent victim (with due credit to Clint Eastwood's *Dirty Harry* movie). This discussion has been elaborated upon by others, most notably by Crank and Caldero (2000) who proposed that such practices as "testilying" and coercion are not caused by selfishness but by "ends-oriented thinking." The "noble cause" of police officers is crime fighting or, as Crank and Caldero put it, "a profound moral commitment to make the world a safer place to live" (2000:9).

The discussion of "noble cause corruption" draws heavily from Herbert Packer's (1968) two models of law enforcement—crime control and due process. The crime control model operated under certain principles, including the idea that repression of criminal conduct is the most important function of law enforcement, efficiency as a top priority, and an emphasis on speed and finality. Under this model a failure of law enforcement signaled a breakdown of order. The due process model, on the other hand, operated under the principles that efficiency was less important that eliminating error, and the protection of the process of law was more important than any end result of conviction. Under this model there is a recognition that the coercive power of the state is sometimes subject to abuse, and that must be guarded against by due process.

"Noble cause" corruption is a type of wrongdoing that stems from a crime control orientation. It is a type of "means-end" thinking in that the *end* of crime control justifies the *means*, even if the means is otherwise unethical or illegal. Therefore, police officers may feel compelled to lie either while testifying or to support a warrant request, use physical coercion during an interrogation, ignore exculpatory evidence if they feel they have the right guy in custody, overlook criminal acts of an informant, and/or plant or manufacture evidence. What sets apart these acts from other ethical issues is that they are done for arguably good motives. The trouble is that many activities that might be categorized under the label of noble cause corruption are neither ethical nor effective. One of the problems with means-end thinking is that one can never know the outcome of any decision so if one bends the law to achieve a good result, what might happen is a bad result and a broken law. When an individual trades his or her personal judgment for the law's protection, it is usually a poor trade for the rest of us. In the sections that follow, we will examine how noble cause corruption may emerge.

Undercover Investigation. Carter (1999:316) discusses the phenomena of police officers who go undercover and become socialized to the drug culture. They may adapt norms conducive to drug taking. Elements of police work that lead to drug use include: the exposure to a criminal element, relative freedom from supervision, and the uncontrolled availability of contraband. The large amounts of money that is present in the drug trade and the perception that it is "just drug money" may even lead to some officers stealing evidence or robbing drug dealers.

In undercover operations, lying is a necessity and is perfectly legal (Skolnick 1982, Marx 1985, 1992). Undercover officers lie about who they are; informants lie and are lied to; suspects are lied to on the street and in the interrogation room. In undercover investigation there is a continuum of deception that starts with a simple buy-bust scenario where an officer lies about wanting to buy drugs. At the other end of the continuum are the most elaborate and profound deception scenarios where officers engage in fairly intimate relationships in order to gather information on suspects. These are the most problematic, and some ethicists have remarked that the end rarely justifies the means in these cases of trust violation (Schoeman 1985, 1986, Sherman 1985b, Pollock 2003). Another problem with lying at the investigative phase is that it sometimes leads to a temptation to lie at the trial stage of the prosecution. The officer may see no difference if the "end justifies the means."

Interrogation. Skolnick and Leo (1992) present a typology of deceptive interrogation techniques. The following is a brief summary of their descriptions of these practices:

1. Calling the questioning an interview, questioning in a non-custodial setting, and telling the suspect that he is free to leave (thus eliminating the need for Miranda warnings).
2. Presenting Miranda warnings in a way designed to negate their effect (mumbling or by using a tone suggesting that they are unnecessary).
3. Misrepresenting the nature or seriousness of the offense.
4. Using manipulative appeals to conscience through role playing or other means.
5. Misrepresenting the moral seriousness of the offense.
6. Making promises beyond the power of the police to offer.
7. Misrepresenting identity by pretending to be lawyers or priests.

The Supreme Court has basically approved of many types of lying during interrogation. Again, the argument is that the end (gaining a confession) outweighs the harm or evil of lying. Therefore, police are taught various tricks of interrogation including pretending that a crime partner is "rolling over" on the defendant, pretending that they have found overwhelming physical evidence at the crime scene, and so on. Most people don't have a problem with these examples. However, police also threaten female defendants that they will lose their children if they don't cooperate, or promise to put the word out on the street that the defendant is a snitch. Are these as defensible? The question is whether the coercion used (whether physical or mental) would be enough to make an innocent person confess. What about telling a suspect that his relatives in Mexico will be harmed if he doesn't confess? This evidently happened in the Danziger and Ochoa case in Texas. Ochoa confessed and implicated Danziger, not because he was guilty, but because he was afraid of what might happen if he didn't confess. The trouble was that both men were innocent and have been exonerated by D.N.A. evidence and the confession of another. They served twelve years in prison for a crime they didn't commit (Hafetz 2002).

The Central Park jogging case is another example where the tactics of zealous interrogators resulted in a confession from innocent suspects (Getlin 2002). The teenage boys who were originally interrogated and confessed during their interrogation turned out to be innocent, and the attack was actually committed by a single individual who has since confessed. Can innocent people be coerced to confess to a crime they didn't commit? It happens and is likely to continue to happen when officers use extreme and coercive techniques (Tanner 2002).

Testilying and Evidence Manufacturing. An example of what can happen when police and prosecutors are more interested in convictions than justice occurred in Tulia, Texas. In this small town, 43 people were arrested after an undercover drug operation. The police officer who gathered evidence was hired from outside the town and targeted mostly African Americans. Convictions were obtained almost solely on his testimony with no corroborating evidence. After an investigation by the ACLU and NAACP, it was discovered that the officer had lied and there was ample exculpatory evidence in many cases that should have alerted the prosecutor and the officer's superiors to the problem. In the zeal to obtain convictions, however, this evidence was ignored. The scandal resulted in a special gubernatorial pardon for all convicted, but not before many had served many months in jail and/or prison (Herbert 2002, Pollock 2003). The loss of credibility and public trust that has occurred as a result of this operation far outweighs any possible gain from any drug convictions that might have occurred.

Cover-ups and Whistleblowing. In these situations, the conflict is between loyalty to one's friend/colleague and loyalty to the organization or to one's own integrity (Wren 1985, Ewin 1990). If one had no loyalty to friends, there would be no dilemma in turning them in; if one had no integrity or loyalty to the organization, there would be no inclination to do anything at all about the wrongdoing of a friend. Officers experience conflict only when they are loyal and also honest. These examples might be categorized as noble cause corruption because the officers involved believe what they are doing is right and that the end of maintaining a loyal front is worth protecting those who did wrong.

The most awesome example of a cover-up is the Abner Louima case in New York in which a Haitian man, arrested for a dispute at a bar, was anally assaulted by Officer Justin Volpe in the station house. The incident was witnessed by at least one other officer and others were implicated in the cover-up. It was only when others were threatened with criminal action that they cooperated with prosecution efforts. Volpe is now in prison for the assault, but the question why some officers would cover up such a heinous act lingers.

POLICE DEVIANCE AND CORRUPTION

Deviance and corruption are not necessarily the same. Police deviance is behavior engaged in by only a small number of officers. Police corruption, on the other hand, may be endemic to a division or an organization. Barker (1978) asked fifty officers in a small police department how many of their number participated in the following types of misconduct. Their responses are in parentheses after the behavior listed: sleeping on duty (39.6 percent), engaging in sex on duty (31.8 percent), police brutality (39.2 percent), perjury (23 percent), and drinking on duty (8 percent). Since Barker's study is quite dated, the results must be interpreted with caution.

Klockars, et al. (2004) report on a more recent study of police officers. In their measurement of integrity, they asked officers to rank the seriousness of a number of hypotheticals involving wrongdoing. They also asked if the officer would report the behavior and what level of discipline would probably result. Although the rank order of the hypotheticals were the same across the many departments surveyed, there were differences in the level of seriousness ascribed, as well as willingness to report. For instance, in a hypothetical involving excessive force, less than 10 percent would definitely not report in one department whereas over 40 percent would definitely not report the incident in another department. Similar differences were found in all hypotheticals between these two departments (Klockars, et al. 2004:280). Another finding was that the officers' perceptions of seriousness correlated with the level of discipline they expected would be the result of each incident.

Some police departments seem to have a consistent history of corruption. Wide-scale investigations and exposés occurred in 1894, 1913, 1932 (the Wickersham Commission), 1949 (the Kefauver Commission), 1972 (the Knapp Commission), and 1993 (the Mollen Commission), with the most recent scandal being the Abner Louima case (Rothlein, 1999). In 1973, the Knapp Commission detailed their findings of corruption within the New York City Police Department. The terms "grass eaters" and "meat eaters" were used to describe New York City police officers who used their position to engage in corrupt practices. Taking bribes, gratuities, and unsolicited protection money was the extent of the corruption engaged in by "grass eaters," who were fairly passive in their deviant practices. "Meat eaters," on the other hand, participated in shakedowns, "shopped" at burglary scenes, and engaged in more active deviant practices. The Mollen Commission, investigating New York City Police Department corruption twenty years later in 1993, concluded that meat eaters were engaged in a qualitatively different kind of corruption in more recent times. More than just cooperating with criminals, the corrupt cops were active criminals themselves, selling drugs, robbing drug dealers, and operating burglary rings.

The Ramparts scandal in Los Angeles is another example where a group of officers engaged in a variety of unethical and illegal activities including illegal use of force, vandalism, evidence planting, and theft. More bizarre allegations included stories of "killing" parties to celebrate shootings, spreading ketchup to imitate blood at crime scenes, spraying graffiti such as "LAPD rules" on searched premises, and handing out plaques for killing gang members. Over 40 convictions were overturned after the scandal broke (Jablon 2000).

Quite a bit of academic literature exists that discusses the prevalence, origin, and reasons for the existence of such activities (Murphy and Moran 1981, Barker and Carter 1991 and 1999, Murphy and Caplan 1993, and Souryal 2004). Gaines and Kappeler (2003:388) discuss a number of scandals and offer information regarding the number of officers involved. For instance, in 1996, ten Chicago officers were involved in extortion, robbery, and sale of drugs. Forty-four Cleveland officers were implicated in a protection racket in 1998. About 100 officers were implicated in the Miami river rats scandal in the 1980s where officers were involved in robberies of drug dealers. At least one homicide occurred as well (Dorschner 1993; also see Rothlein 1999, Crank and Caldero 2000:162). Chicago police officers have been accused of "shaking down" Polish immigrants and robbing suspected drug dealers (who turned out to be FBI agents). This group of officers evidently joined forces with a street gang in order to control the cocaine trade. Brutality charges and other corruption charges have also been recently leveled against Chicago officers (Babwin 2001). In New Orleans, eleven officers were involved in a protection racket that included murder in 1994, and the list goes on. Carter (1999) discusses drug use and other forms of corruption related to drugs. He found that up to 20 percent of officers in one city used marijuana and other drugs while on duty.

Kraska and Kappeler (1995) discuss sexual misconduct, including harassment and assault. They looked at 124 cases of police sexual misconduct, including 37 sexual assaults by on-duty officers. These authors challenged earlier studies that indicated sexual misconduct of officers occurred most often when women traded sexual favors for lenient treatment. This study's authors concluded that norms in a police department that ignored or condoned the exchange of sex for favored treatment opened the door to officers who used more aggressive tactics to coerce sex from citizens.

Kraska and Kappeler (1995:93) propose a continuum of sexual invasion that ranges from some type of invasion of privacy to sexual assault. This range of behavior includes: viewing a victim's photos or videos for prurient purposes, field strip searches, custodial strip searches, illegal detentions, deception to gain sex, provision of services for sex, sexual harassment, sexual contact, sexual assault, and rape. Even the most innocuous of contacts between female citizens and officers, where officers might ask a woman he has stopped for a date, involves issues of power and coercion. The authors report that police in their study described how they routinely went "bimbo hunting," which involved sexual harassment of women out drinking (1995:104).

Illegal use of force has been examined by a number of authors including Skolnick and Fyfe (1994), Doyle (2000), and Nelson (2000). Cohen and Feldberg (1991) also explore the misuse of police authority. Even with the notoriety of the Rodney King episode and the extreme public reaction to the spectacle of that use of force, incidents involving officers' abusive behavior toward motorists continues to occur. It may be that this pattern is so ingrained in some police departmental cultures that it remains relatively unaffected. Los Angeles seems to be such a department. Rothlein (1999) writes that the Christopher Commission reported that LAPD management was responsible, to some extent, for the brutality exhibited by the Rodney King incident in that there was an apparent failure to punish or control those who had repeated citizen complaints of violence. Further, there was a culture that encouraged the use of force, an ineffective citizen complaint system, with no civilian oversight. In other words, leadership did not exist that actively discouraged or sanctioned the excessive use of force. Even with such scrutiny and criticism, the department was exposed to disgrace again after the Ramparts Division scandal hit the news. Skolnick and Fyfe (1994) discuss the culture of LAPD as one where the use of violence was tolerated, even encouraged. The result has been civil rights cases—in 1990, for instance, Los Angeles paid out over $11 million in civil rights cases for excessive force violations (Skolnick and Fyfe, 1994:3).

EXPLANATIONS FOR POLICE DEVIANCE AND CORRUPTION

There are a variety of explanations for the presence of corruption in police organizations. Some point to weaknesses in the recruiting and training practices (Dorschner 1993). Some point to the police subculture, and some to more systemic elements of policing that set the groundwork for a network of corruption to exist (Johnston 1995).

Individual

The "rotten apple" explanation of police deviance and corruption is that individual officers are either already deviant when they enter policing or become so after they join. There is no failsafe method to eliminate dishonest officers from an applicant pool, although psychological testing continues to improve the hiring process. Once hired, some officers may be tempted by the opportunities unique to policing. Officers are also exposed to a fairly steady diet of deviance. After years of policing, many officers become convinced that everyone is crooked and so they might as well profit from wrongdoing as well.

The slippery slope explanation is that some officers start down the path of deviance by relatively minor transgressions and then proceed to more serious misconduct in a slow but steady progression (Sherman 1982, 1985a; Malloy 1982). Because most officers engage in their share of minor transgressions, they are unable to point fingers at those who commit serious violations. Individuals who follow rules to the letter are threatening to the rest of the force and are dealt with accordingly in the informal subculture. Rationalizations used by officers who engage in corruption include: "The public thinks that every cop is a crook, so why try to be honest?" "The money is out there; if I don't take it, someone else will." "I'm only taking what's rightfully mine." "If the city paid me a decent wage, I wouldn't have to get it on my own." (Murphy and Moran 1981).

Organizational

Organizational explanations of police deviance and corruption point to either the police subculture, management and administration, or both. The parameters and elements of the police subculture have been described by many authors. Muir (1977:191) described some elements of the informal police code: "Cover your men," "Keep a cool head," and "Don't backdoor it" (a prohibition against certain gratuities). Reuss-Ianni (1983:14) presented a very inclusive list, including the following principles: "watch out for your partner first and then the rest of the guys working that tour," "don't give up another cop," "show balls," "don't get involved in anything in another guy's sector," "if you get caught off base, don't implicate anybody else," "don't trust a new guy until you have checked him out," and "protect your ass."

The police "subculture," like all subcultures, has been described as holding contrary, even anti-ethical, values to the formal organization. Larry Sherman (1982) described the subculture's values as including loyalty to colleagues, the idea that the public is the enemy, acceptance of the use of force, belief in the right to employ discretion, and a protective use of the truth. Scheingold (1984) elaborated on the values of the subculture, mentioning cynicism (everyone is a crook), the use of force (acceptable whenever a threat is perceived, even a threat to one's respect), and the idea that police are victims themselves (of poor pay, stigma, and lack appreciation on the part of the public). Crank (1998) discussed a number of "themes" of policing. These themes are not values *per se*, but rather elements of police work and/or shared perceptions of police officers. The themes include: coercive territorial control, force, illicit coercion, importance of guns, suspicion, danger, uncertainty, "maintaining the edge," seduction of excitement, and crime (he argues policing teaches some officers how to be criminals), solidarity, and masculinity.

The subculture of policing obviously doesn't support the worst forms of deviance such as drug dealing and theft, but what the culture does do is create an atmosphere where individuals come to feel that the law does not apply to them. Many citizens criticize officers who drive too fast, park in the road and block traffic, leave restaurants without paying, give "professional courtesy" to fellow officers who have broken traffic laws, and otherwise let it be known that even though they enforce laws, they don't have to follow them. The culture creates an "us-versus-them" attitude that fosters the blue curtain of secrecy, even for the more deviant members of the profession.

Most agree that the strongest correlate to the level of dishonesty among employees is the level of dishonesty among administrators. If there is wide-scale corruption in a police department, inevitably that corruption has reached high levels of management that protected and even encouraged dishonesty on the part of the rank and file. What is also true though is that even honest administrators and managers can foster and encourage corruption when they do nothing about it. In most wide-scale corruption scandals there was an attempted cover-up from high in management ranks. There is a aversion to "airing dirty laundry" in law enforcement that influences decisions to curtail investigations of dirty cops and keep evidence of corruption under wraps. Ironically, this often results in worse publicity in the long run.

Societal

Much of what is defined as unethical on the part of officers is supported by the public itself. If the "end" of catching criminals becomes more important than the "duty" of protecting the sanctity of the law, then unethical actions are sure to follow because anything can be justified. If we accept unethical practices when they benefit us, then we can hardly cry out when unethical practices flourish and spread to other behavioral decisions. For instance, requesting different treatment from officers because of who we are, accepting unethical means for removing street people and vagrants, agreeing that violating constitutional rights to catch drug dealers is acceptable, and offering gratuities so officers will frequent our place of business all encourage a type of policing that ignores the equal protection of law.

When police departments emphasize crime control over community relations, there are consequences. In New York City, the implementation of a zero tolerance mandate toward petty crime and street people has supposedly contributed to the city's dramatic decline of crime. Others point out that citizen complaints against police have gone up 75 percent in the four-year period between 1995 and 1999 (Greene 1999:176). Even downtown merchants who were thrilled with the effects of the crackdown are now feeling the effects of the pervasive police influence. Some complain that police are "harassing" them by enforcing trivial ordinances (such as placement and size of window signs or sidewalk sales). Minorities perceive police harassment, and the relationship between NYPD and the minority community has been strained to the breaking point.

Historically some police have been responsible for harassing and brutalizing labor union organizers in the early part of the twentieth century, and civil rights demonstrators in the 1950s and 1960s (Fogelson 1977, Crank 2003, Skolnick and Fyfe 1994, Nelson 2000). Today, many in the black community feel that police have been given *carte blanche* to keep order by any means necessary, even if it means violating the rights of black citizens. Certainly the public does not seem to care if drug dealers' civil liberties are violated. The trouble is that once those protections are removed from one group, it becomes easier to ignore due process protections for everyone.

IMPROVING ETHICAL DECISION MAKING IN LAW ENFORCEMENT

The Code of Ethics for Law Enforcement promulgated by the International Association of Chiefs of Police was written in 1956 and updated in 1991. It is an "aspirational" code, meaning that it promotes the model of a perfect police officer, one that mere mortals can only aspire to. It is interesting that the Code has made few changes over the last twenty years, but one change that has been made has been to add the phrase "I will cooperate with all legally authorized agencies and their representatives in the pursuit of justice." This phrase brings into bold relief the dilemma of the officer who must choose between loyalty to colleagues and loyalty to the organization. There may be no issue more problematic in the application of the Code to day-to-day decision making by individual officers. Critics of the Code contend that it is so far removed from the everyday behavior practices of police officers that it has become irrelevant (Johnson and Copus 1981; Swift, Houston and Anderson 1993; Davis 1991). Officers may hear it once during their academy training and never have occasion to hear or read it again, much less use it as a model for conduct.

Officers themselves typically identify several standard elements important to being a "good officer." These elements include: *legality* (enforcing and upholding the law), *service* (protecting and serving the public), *honesty and integrity* (telling the truth, being honest in action), *loyalty* (to other police officers), and the *Golden Rule* (treating people with respect or the way one would like to be treated) (Pollock and Becker 1996). These elements seem to be universal with those officers who are committed to doing their best. They are not all that different from principles to live by in one's private life as well.

The question is how to create a situation wherein all officers in a division or department try to uphold those standards of behavior. Carter (1999) identified leadership from the chief's office, management and supervision, supervisory training, organizational control and information management, internal auditing of the use of informants, internal affairs, drug enforcement units having audit controls and turnover of staff, better evidence handling, early warning systems, and training and discipline. Hunter (1999) discusses decertifying officers who have committed serious misconduct, community policing, college education, enhanced discipline, civilian review boards, and training. These answers fall into three general categories: better selection, better training, better enforcement, and better management.

Figure 1   Law Enforcement Code of Ethics

As a law enforcement officer, my fundamental duty is to serve the community; to safeguard lives and property; to protect the innocent against deception, the weak against oppression or intimidation and the peaceful against violence or disorder; and to respect the constitutional rights of all to liberty, equality and justice.

I will keep my private life unsullied as an example to all and will behave in a manner that does not bring discredit to me or to my agency. I will maintain courageous calm in the face of danger, scorn or ridicule; develop self-restraint; and be constantly mindful of the welfare of others. Honest in thought and deed both in my personal and official life, I will be exemplary in obeying the law and the regulations of my department. Whatever I see or hear of a constitutional nature or that is confided to me in my official capacity will be kept ever secret unless revelation is necessary in the performance of my duty.

I will never act officiously or permit personal feelings, prejudices, political beliefs, aspirations, animosities or friendships to influence my decisions. With no compromise for crime and with relentless prosecution of criminals, I will enforce the law courteously and appropriately without fear or favor, malice or ill will, never employing unnecessary force or violence and never accepting gratuities.

I recognize the badge of my office as a symbol of public faith, and I accept it as a public trust to be held so long as I am true to the ethics of police service. I will never engage in acts of corruption or bribery, nor will I condone such acts by other police officers. I will cooperate with all legally authorized agencies and their representatives in the pursuit of justice.

I know that I alone am responsible for my own standard of professional performance and will take every reasonable opportunity to enhance and improve my level of knowledge and competence.

I will constantly strive to achieve these objectives and ideals, dedicating myself before God to my chosen profession . . . Law Enforcement.

http://www.theiacp.org/documents/index.cfm?fuseaction=document&document_id=95

Selection

The process of selecting the appropriate individuals for hire in law enforcement is one that continues to be improved. Psychological testing is now fairly standard and helps, to some extent, weed out those who are not qualified to take on the responsibilities of the role. The MMPI and other tests, however, do not adequately measure one's moral development, nor do they accurately predict how the individual will respond to ethical dilemmas. Higher education continues to be debated as a requirement of hire. There are studies on both sides of the argument, but no one has proven that education insulates someone from unethical decisions. Thus, those who examine the applicant pool continue to look at past experience and use "gut instinct" to determine the best among those who pass the preliminary battery of tests. It is possible that better tests will be developed, but they do not exist today.

Training

The police subculture and the Code of Ethics are sometimes in conflict. Academy and in-service training attempt to thwart some of the most negative aspects of the subculture, but often with limited success. The Field Training Officer (FTO) will start his or her training by first telling the rookie, "forget everything you learned in the academy. . ." Academy training may be considered irrelevant and separate from the real world of policing. In-service classes may also be considered irrelevant—something to get through either by sleeping or maintaining the mere appearance of compliance. Old guard officers describe younger officers as the "New Breed" or the "New School" if they earnestly employ the lessons learned from the Code and Ethics classes in academies and in-service. In their eyes, these officers "sell out" other officers and do it for themselves so they will not get into trouble. Most police officers will admit that the "blue curtain" is still a potent force.

Many departments have instituted ethical training as part of the academy training and/or as an in-service class. Various models have been proposed (Pollock-Byrne 1988, Swift, Houston and Anderson 1993, Kleinig 1990, Sherman 1981). Martinelli (2000) proposes a course that is grounded in the actual discipline cases of each law enforcement agency. He argues that some of the law enforcement code provisions are ambiguous to officers and need explanations—such as keeping one's private life "unsullied." Officers may not realize that they can receive departmental sanctions for their behavior in their private life. These types of classes explain the disciplinary process and attempt to improve decision making by giving officers more information about why certain behaviors are sanctioned.

Another model of training utilizes the philosophical underpinning of an applied ethics class. Ordinarily this would include a section on ethical systems. An ethical system is an approach to resolving a problem. Most people employ egoism, religion, utilitarianism, or some form of deontological ethics (which involves doing one's duty and respecting others' rights) when deciding upon a course of action. Egoism, according to most ethicists, is not an acceptable rationale for resolving ethical dilemmas. Police officers also tend to employ one or the other of these systems, or some combination, with utilitarianism perhaps being the most common one intuitively applied by criminal justice professionals (Swift, Houston and Anderson 1993, Pollock 2003). Officers quickly grasp the essential elements of each of the systems and can utilize them to resolve ethical dilemmas.

Ethical formalism demands, first of all, that one do one's duty. All of us have a multitude of duties based on our roles. We may be students, teachers, police officers, probation officers (professional roles); mothers, fathers, daughters, sons, brothers, sisters (familial roles); and, of course, all of us are citizens. All of these roles have duties attached to them. The duties are categorical—one must do them regardless of external reward or consequences. If everyone lived up to his or her duties, it would be a perfect world. The second part of ethical formalism is to abide by the "categorical imperative," which is

---

Figure 2   Ethical Systems

Religion

What is good is that which conforms to God's will.

How do we know God's will?

- Bible or other religious documents
- Religious authorities
- Faith

Ethical Formalism (deontological ethics)

What is good is that which conforms to doing one's duty and the categorical imperative.

What is the categorical imperative?

- Act in such a way that one would will it to be a universal law.
- Treat each person as an end and not as a means.

Utilitarianism

What is good is that which results in the greatest benefit for the greatest number.

Act utilitarianism "weighs" the benefits of act for just those people and just that incident.

Rule utilitarianism "weighs" the benefits after determining the consequences of making that behavior a rule for the future.

Egoism

What is good is that which results in the greatest benefit for me.

Enlightened egoism, however, may reciprocate favors and be practiced by a "good" person (because it benefits the self to be nice to others).

---

basically acting in a way that you would want everyone to act and treating each person as an end and not as a means.

Utilitarianism defines good as that which benefits the many. Most of us resolve ethical issues using some elements of utilitarianism in our thinking. We intuitively understand that the individual is less important than the majority. Utilitarianism is consequentialist, meaning that it looks to the end, not the means to determine "goodness." "Bad" means may result in a "good" end and therefore be redefined as "good" under utilitarianism. Utilitarianism is often used as a justification for means-end thinking, the kind that was previously mentioned as supporting "noble cause corruption." This ethical system is difficult to apply, however, in that there is a need to predict consequences. Is lying to gain a conviction "good" because we get one criminal off the street? Or is it "bad" because it results in a loss of credibility for police? We would have to have a crystal ball to predict the consequences of each behavior decision in order to apply utilitarianism accurately. Ethical formalism (or other deontological systems) needs no such prediction to determine goodness, since the definition of goodness lies in the essential nature of the action (for example, lying is bad because it violates the police officer's duty to uphold the law and it also violates the categorical imperative).

Religion is used by many as an ethical system. Christianity's most obvious application to many ethical dilemmas is the Golden Rule. Egoism is also a consequentialist system but its measurement is more simple—what is good is that which benefits oneself. We all use egoism in many behavioral choices. In training, the goal is to get officers to at least recognize egoistic rationalizations when they use them. There are other ethical systems, but these four probably represent the thinking patterns of most individuals.

Another approach to training ignores the philosophical basis and utilizes a more simple form of decision analysis. These are three step or question formats that can help an individual decide if his or her course of action raises ethical red flags. For instance, the "front-page test" asks how would you feel if your action appeared on the front page of the newspaper? If you would not like such exposure, then your action should be examined more closely. Another question is related to the first: "How will you feel about your action when looking back on it?" Again, if you are not proud of your action or there are questionable ethics involved, you would probably want to forget the action. A final question is an application of the Golden Rule or universalism: "Would you consider your action fair if you were each of the other parties involved?" Another way of saying it is, "Did you treat others the way you would want to be treated?" These questions are sometimes overlooked when making day-to-day decisions. Thoughtful policing involves being sensitized to the ethical nature of decision making.

Monitoring and Enforcement

All departments have some version of internal affairs and an internal discipline process (Prenzler and Ransley 2002). Some departments take monitoring and investigation a step further. "Integrity testing" is using undercover officers to offer temptations to unsuspecting officers to see if they will commit illegal or unethical acts. There are tests, for instance, where a wallet is turned in to see if officers would take money from the wallet (Marx 1991). It is reported that almost 30 percent of officers have failed to turn in found money (Prenzler and Ronken 2001:322). New York City has utilized "integrity testing" since the late 1970s, after the Knapp Commission exposed widespread corruption. "Field associates" were recruited straight from academies to investigate suspected officers (Reuss-Ianni 1983:80).

Needless to say, most police officers have very negative attitudes about integrity testing. Spokesmen argue, "testing raises serious issues regarding privacy, deception, entrapment, provocation and the legal rights of individuals" (Prenzler and Ronken 2001:323–324). There is a widespread belief that it is unfair and overly intrusive and detrimental to morale. Officers hate the idea that an officer who pretends to be a friend may, instead, be someone who is trying to obtain evidence that they are doing wrong. It is the same argument, of course that is used to criticize undercover operations. Specifically, critics argue that the use of undercover operations may undermine the fabric of social relations by reducing a level of trust.

There seems to be a growing belief that police departments have proven themselves to be incapable of policing themselves, and that what is needed is some outside oversight. Civilian review boards have been created in several cities to monitor and review the investigation and discipline of officers who have complaints filed against them. There are many models that exist for the idea of civilian review, and no one model has been reported to be more effective or better than any other. Prenzler and Ronken (2001) argue that it is difficult to analyze the success of such bodies because a high level of complaints may mean that there is greater trust in the process rather than a spike in misconduct.

Management

If management is corrupt, then it is obvious that the whole department will have problems. However, the more common case is that management does not necessarily engage in corruption, but encourages it by poor or ill-conceived management practices. Previously mentioned was the practice of covering up the wrongdoing of individual officers. While the intent may be to protect the department, the effect is to broadcast a message to the rank and file that wrongdoing will be ignored or protected. When the honest officer isn't supported, the dishonest officer wins. The research of Klockars et al. (2000, 2004) showed that the discipline practices of management had a direct bearing on how serious officers perceived various forms of wrongdoing.

Crank and Caldero (2000:159; also see Crank 1998:230) argue that management practices may impose pressures that lead to noble cause corruption. Criteria for promotion, arrest quotas, administrative directives and other elements may pressure the individual officer to lie or otherwise subvert the formal values of law enforcement in order to get arrests and convictions. If management emphasizes crime control over due process, then noble cause corruption is bound to follow.

CONCLUSION

Police departments probably represent the communities they police. Cities torn by racial strife will also have a police department that plays racial politics. Communities where corruption is endemic among local politicians rarely escape similar corruption in their police departments. Communities that turn a blind eye to police violence (as long as it is visited upon less desirable groups) will probably have a police department marked by brutality.

Today, we are in a new era of policing where the challenge is not only crime but also terrorism. Greater fear engenders a climate where means-end thinking flourishes. When the "end" is combating terrorism many are willing to look the other way regardless of the "means" used. Law enforcement absorbs these messages and acts accordingly. In the United States, the trend toward community policing has been replaced with themes of a nationalized police force, reduced civil liberties, and zero tolerance. There has been resistance to the nationalization of police because of the origins of this country and the legacy of distrust of centralized power, yet today it seems more of a possibility (Stuntz 2002).

A "rights based" model of policing recognizes the police as servants to the public good. Although crime control is important, protection of civil liberties is the fundamental mission. This concept is more prevalent in Europe and the United Nations Code of Conduct for Law Enforcement Officials is a good example of this premise: "In the performance of their duty, law enforcement officials shall respect and protect human dignity and maintain and uphold the human rights of all persons" (Article 2, reported in Kleinig, 1999). Neyroud and Beckley (2001:62) describe Police Standards in the United Kingdom as reflecting an emphasis on human rights, including standards that discuss human dignity and human rights and integrity, impartiality, proportional force and personal liability for wrongdoing.

The "end" of catching terrorists is incredibly more persuasive than the "end" of catching garden-variety criminals. Prevention of terrorist attacks has changed the balance between crime control and due process, and many are willing to give up their rights in order for government to protect them from terrorism. Some, however, argue that it is a false argument to weigh privacy or any civil liberties against security. Alderson (1998:23), writing before the attack on the World Trade Towers, presents a prescient argument against the "end" of security as a justification for taking away liberties:

> I acknowledge that liberty is diminished when people feel afraid to exercise it, but to stress security to unnecessary extremes at the price of fundamental freedoms plays into the hands of would be high police despots. Such despots are quick to exploit fear in order to secure unlimited power.

Since European police have had more experience dealing with terrorism, it is interesting that the trend there evidently has been to move toward a rights-based model of policing. British police, for instance, have had their share of "noble cause" corruption in dealing with Irish terrorists, Spain has dealt with Basque terrorists, and so on. What may be the case is that "the end justifies the means" thinking by law enforcers leads inevitably to violations of civil liberties and fear, and this official oppression always leads to more bitterness and disenfranchisement, and ultimately, more unrest and terror.

Individual officers will continue to be the decision makers in the multitude of situations where they must choose between two or more courses of behavior. They must hold themselves accountable for their own individual behavior. It is possible to be a "good" person and a "good" police officer when one takes time to define the terms, is aware of the ethical nature of decision making, and has the courage to live up to one's own principles.

Bibliography

Alderson, J. (1998) *Principled Policing: Protecting the Public with Integrity*. Winchester, MA: Waterside Press.

Babwin, D. (2001) "In Chicago, Allegations Plague Police Department," *Austin American Statesman*, Sunday, April 22, 2001: A26.

Barker, T. (1978) "An Empirical Study of Police Deviance Other Than Corruption," *Journal of Police Science and Administration* 6, 3: 264–274.

Barker, T. and D. Carter (1991) *Police Deviance*. Cincinnati, OH: Anderson Publishing Company.

Barker, T. and D. Carter (1999) "Fluffing Up the Evidence and Covering Your Ass: Some Conceptual Notes on Police Lying." In L. Gaines and G. Cordner (eds.), *Policing Perspectives*, pp. 342–351. Los Angeles: Roxbury.

Carter, D. (1999) "Drug Use and Drug-Related Corruption of Police Officers." In L. Gaines and G. Cordner (eds.), *Policing Perspectives*, pp. 311–324. Los Angeles: Roxbury.

Cohen, H. (1985) "A Dilemma for Discretion." In W. Heffernan and T. Stroup (eds.), *Police Ethics: Hard Choices in Law Enforcement*, pp. 69–83. New York: John Jay Press.

———. (1986) "Exploiting Police Authority," *Criminal Justice Ethics* 5, 2: 23–31.

———. (1987) "Overstepping Police Authority," *Criminal Justice Ethics* 6, 2: 52–60.

Cohen, H. and M. Feldberg (1991) *Power and Restraint: The Moral Dimension of Police Work*. New York: Praeger Publishing.

Cole, D. (1999) *No Equal Justice: Race and Class in the American Criminal Justice System*. New York City: The New Press.

Crank, J. (1998) *Understanding Police Culture*. Cincinnati, OH: Anderson Publishing Company.

Crank, J. (2003) *Imagining Justice*. Cincinnati, OH: Anderson Publishing Company.

Crank, J. and M. Caldero (2000) *Police Ethics: The Corruption of Noble Cause*. Cincinnati, OH: Anderson Publishing Company.

Davis, M. (1991) "Do Cops Really Need a Code of Ethics?" *Criminal Justice Ethics* 10, 2: 14–28.

Delattre, E. (1989a) *Character and Cops: Ethics in Policing*. Washington, DC: American Enterprise for Public Policy Research.

——— (1989b) "Ethics in Public Service: Higher Standards and Double Standards," *Criminal Justice Ethics* 1, 2: 179–283.

Doyle, A. (2000) "From the Inside Looking Out: Twenty-Nine Years in the New York Police Department." In J. Nelson (ed.), *Police Brutality*, pp. 171–189. New York: W.W. Norton & Co.

Dorschner. J. (1993) "The Dark Side of the Force." In R. Dunham and G. Alpert (eds.), *Critical Issues in Policing* (2nd ed.), pp. 254–275. Prospect Heights, IL: Waveland Press.

Ewin, R. E. (1990) "Loyalty and the Police," *Criminal Justice Ethics* 9, 2: 3–15.

Fogelson, R. (1977) *Big City Police*. Cambridge, MA: Harvard University Press.

Gaines, L. and V. Kappeler (2003) *Policing in America*. Cincinnati, OH: Anderson Publishing Company.

Getlin, J. (2002) "DA Suggests Overturning Convictions in Jogger Case," *Austin American Statesman*, Dec. 6, 2002: A16.

Greene, J. (1999) "Zero Tolerance: A Case Study of Police Policies and Practices in New York City," *Crime and Delinquency* 45, 2: 171–187.

Hafetz, D. (2002) "Their Innocence Proved, Men Sue," *Austin American Statesman*, Nov. 8, 2002: B1.

Heffernan, W. and T. Stroup (1985) *Police Ethics: Hard Choices in Law Enforcement*. New York: John Jay Press.

Herbert, B. (2002) "In Tulia, Justice Has Gone Into Hiding," *Austin American Statesman*, Aug. 13, 2002: A9.

Hunter, R. (1999) "Officer Opinions on Police Misconduct," *Journal of Contemporary Criminal Justice* 15, 2: 155–170.

Jablon, R. (2000) "L.A. Confronts Police Scandal That May Cost Tens of Millions," *Austin American Statesman*, Feb. 19, 2000: A18.

Johnson, C. and G. Copus (1981) "Law Enforcement Ethics: A Theoretical Analysis." In F. Schmalleger and R. Gustafson (eds.), *The Social Basis of Criminal Justice: Ethical Issues for the 80's*, pp. 39–83. Washington, DC: University Press.

Johnston, M. (1995) "Police Corruption." In D. Close and N. Meier (eds.), *Morality in Criminal Justice*, pp. 37–85. Belmont, CA: Wadsworth.

Kania, R. (1988) "Police Acceptance of Gratuities," *Criminal Justice Ethics* 7, 2: 37–49.

Kappeler, V., K. Sluder and G. Alpert (1994) *Forces of Deviance: Understanding the Dark Side of Policing*. Prospect Heights, IL: Waveland Press.

Kleinig, J. (1990) "Teaching and Learning Police Ethics: Competing and Complementary Approaches," *Journal of Criminal Justice* 18: 1–18

Kleinig, J. (1999) "Human Dignity and Human Rights: An Emerging Concern in Police Practice." In G. Lynch (ed.), *Human Dignity and Police: Ethics and Integrity in Police Work*. Springfield, IL: Charles C. Thomas.

Klockars, C. (1983) "The Dirty Harry Problem." In C. Klockars (ed.), *Thinking About Police: Contemporary Readings*, pp. 428–438. New York: McGraw Hill.

———. (1984) "Blue Lies and Police Placebos," *American Behavioral Scientist* 27, 4: 529–544.

Klockars, C., S. Ivkovic, W. Harver and M. Haberfeld (2000) "The Measurement of Police Integrity," *NIJ Research in Brief*. Washington, DC: US Dept. of Justice.

Klockars, C., S. Ivkovic and M. Haberfeld (2004) *The Contours of Police Integrity*. Thousand Oaks, CA: Sage Publications.

Kraska, P. and V. Kappeler (1995) "To Serve and Pursue: Exploring Police Sexual Violence against Women," *Justice Quarterly* 12, 1: 85–111.

Malloy, E. (1982) *The Ethics of Law Enforcement and Criminal Punishment*. Lanham, NY: University Press.

Martinelli, T. (2000) "Combating the Charge of Deliberate Indifference Through Police Ethics Training and a Comprehensive Risk Management Policy." Presented at the 2000 Annual Meeting of the Academy of Criminal Justice Sciences, New Orleans, LA.

Marx, G. (1985) "Who Really Gets Stung? Some Issues Raised by the New Police Undercover Work." In F. Elliston and M. Feldberg (eds.), *Moral Issues in Police Work*, pp. 99–129. Totawa, NJ: Rowman & Allanheld.

———. (1991) "The New Police Undercover Work." In C. Klockars and S. Mastrofski (eds.), *Thinking About Police: Contemporary Readings,* pp. 240–258. New York: McGraw-Hill.

———. (1992) "Under-the-covers Undercover Investigations: Some Reflections on the State's Use of Deception," *Criminal Justice Ethics* 11, 1: 13–25.

Muir, W. 1977. *Police: Streetcorner Politicians.* Chicago: University of Chicago Press.

Murphy, P. and D. Caplan (1993) "Fostering Integrity." In R. Dunham and G. Alpert (eds.), *Critical Issues to Policing* (2nd. ed.), pp. 304–327. Prospect Heights. IL: Waveland Press.

Murphy, P. and K. Moran (1981) "The Continuing Cycle of Systemic Police Corruption." In F. Schmalleger and R. Gustafson (eds.), *The Social Basis of Criminal Justice: Ethical Issues for the 80's*, pp. 87–109. Washington, DC: University Press.

Nelson, J. (ed.) (2000) *Police Brutality.* New York: W.W. Norton & Company.

Neyroud, P. and A. Beckley (2001) *Policing, Ethics and Human Rights.* Devon, England: Willan Publishing.

Packer, H. (1968) *The Limits of the Criminal Sanction.* Stanford, CA: Stanford University Press.

Pollock, J. (2003) *Dilemmas and Decisions: Ethics in Crime and Justice.* Belmont, CA: Wadsworth/ITP.

Pollock, J. and R. Becker (1996) "Ethical Dilemmas in Police Work." In M. Braswell, B. McCarthy and B. McCarthy (eds.), *Justice, Crime and Ethics,* pp. 83–103. Cincinnati, OH: Anderson Publishing Company.

Pollock-Byrne, J. M. (1988) "Teaching Criminal Justice Ethics," *The Justice Professional* 3, 2: 283–97.

Prenzler, T. and J. Ransley (2002) *Police Reform: Building Integrity.* Sydney, Australia: Hawkins Press.

Prenzler, T. and C. Ronken (2001) "Models of Police Oversight: A Critique," *Policing and Society* 11: 151–180.

Reuss-Ianni, E. (1983) *Two Cultures of Policing: Street Cops and Management Cops.* New Brunswick, NJ: Transaction Books.

Rothlein, S. (1999) "Policy Agency Efforts to Prevent Abuses." In G. Lynch (ed.), *Human Dignity and the Police: Ethics and Integrity in Police Work,* pp. 15–27. Springfield, IL: Charles C. Thomas.

Scheingold, S. (1984) *The Politics of Law and Order.* New York: Longman.

Schoeman, F. (1985) "Privacy and Police Undercover Work." In W. Heffernan and T. Stroup (eds.), *Police Ethics: Hard Choices in Law Enforcement,* pp. 133–153. New York: John Jay Press.

———. (1986) "Undercover Operations: Some Moral Questions About S.804," *Criminal Justice Ethics* 5, 2: 16–22.

Sherman, L. (1981) *The Teaching of Ethics in Criminology and Criminal Justice.* Washington, DC: Joint Commission on Criminology and Criminal Justice Education and Standards. LEAA.

———. (1982) "Learning Police Ethics," *Criminal Justice Ethics* 1, 1: 10–19.

———. (1985a) "Becoming Bent: Moral Careers of Corrupt Policemen." In F. Elliston and M. Feldberg (eds.), *Moral Issues in Police Work,* pp. 253–273. Totawa. NJ: Rowman & Allanheld.

———. (1985b) "Equity against Truth: Value Choices in Deceptive Investigations." In W. Heffernan and T. Stroup (eds.), *Police Ethics: Hard Choices in Law Enforcement,* pp. 117–133. New York: John Jay Press.

Skolnick, J. (1982) "Deception by Police," *Criminal Justice Ethics* 1, 2: 40–54.

Skolnick, J. and R. Leo (1992) "Ideology and the Ethics of Crime Control," *Criminal Justice Ethics* 11, 1: 3–13.

Skolnick, J. and J. Fyfe (1994) *Above the Law: Police and the Excessive Use of Force.* New York: Free Press.

Souryal, Sam (2004) *Ethics in Criminal Justice: In Search of the Truth.* Cincinnati, OH: Anderson Publishing Company.

Stuntz, W. (2002) "Terrorism, Federalism, and Police Misconduct," *Harvard Journal of Law and Public Policy* 25, 2: 665–680.

Swift, A., J. Houston and R. Anderson (1993) "Cops, Hacks and the Greater Good," Academy of Criminal Justice Sciences Conference, Kansas City, Missouri.

Tanner, R. (2002) "Central Park Case Puts Focus on Confessions," *Austin American Statesman*, Dec. 7, 2002: A9.

Walker, S., C. Spohn and M. Delone (2000) *The Color of Justice*. Belmont, CA: Wadsworth Publishing.

Weitzer, R. (1999) "Citizens' Perceptions of Police Misconduct: Race and Neighborhood Context," *Justice Quarterly* 16, 4: 819–846.

Wren, T. (1985) "Whistle-Blowing and Loyalty to One's Friends." In W. Heffernan and T. Stroup (eds.), *Police Ethics: Hard Choices in Law Enforcement*, pp. 25–47. New York: John Jay Press.

Law Enforcement Agency Responses to Racially Biased Policing and the Perceptions of Its Practice

Lorie Fridell & Michael Scott

The vast majority of law enforcement officers—of all ranks, nation-wide—are dedicated men and women committed to serving all citizens with fairness and dignity. They are concerned both with racially biased policing and the perceptions of its practice, but addressing each of these involves complex issues and challenges. The issues involved in "racial profiling" and racially biased policing are not new—they are the latest manifestation of a long history of sometimes tense, even volatile, police-minority relations. This need not be viewed, however, as proof of the problem's intractability. Police are more capable than ever of effectively detecting and addressing police racial bias. In the past few decades, there has been a revolution in the quality and quantity of police training, the standards for hiring officers, the procedures and accountability regarding police activity, and the widespread adoption of community policing.

In this article, we will set forth the specific challenges facing law enforcement agencies and discuss various options for addressing them.

Originally published as "Responding to Racially Biased Policing and the Perceptions of Its Practice" by the Cultural Diversity and the Police Project conducted by the John Jay College of Criminal Justice, in conjunction with the Bureau of Justice Assistance.

CONCEPTUALIZING RACIALLY BIASED POLICING: DEFINITIONS, ISSUES, AND MANIFESTATIONS

Definition of the Issue

The discussion of terminology and definition has advanced over the several years that this topic has been at the forefront of policing issues. There has been increased recognition on the part of law enforcement practitioners, scholars, and other stakeholders that "racial profiling," as originally defined, does not fully encompass the important issues. That is, they recognize that "racial profiling" has been defined so restrictively that it does not fully capture the concerns of both police practitioners and citizens. Racial profiling is frequently defined as law enforcement activities (e.g., detentions, arrests, searches) that are initiated *solely* on the basis of race. Central to the debate on terminology and definitions is the word "solely." In the realm of potentially discriminatory actions, this definition likely references only a very small portion. Even a racially prejudiced officer likely uses more than the single factor of race when conducting biased law enforcement. For example, officers might make biased decisions based on the neighborhood and the race of the person, the age of the car and the race of the person, or the gender and the race of the person. Activities based on these sample pairs of factors would fall outside the most commonly used definition of racial profiling.

Moreover, one could interpret the common definition of racial profiling to exclude activities that are legally supportable in terms of reasonable suspicion or probable cause, but are nonetheless racially biased. Because the traditional definition only prohibits actions based *solely* on race, it does not encompass decisions based on reasonable suspicion or probable cause *plus* race. That is, this definition could be interpreted to exclude, for instance, officers' pulling over black traffic violators and not white *because* of race, or citing Hispanic, but not white, youth for noise violations *because* of race/ethnicity. Such disparate treatment would not necessarily be encompassed by a definition that referred to actions based "solely" on race, because the officers would have acted on the basis of reasonable suspicion or probable cause, as well as race.

Further, during the course of focus groups held around the country by staff of the Police Executive Research Forum (PERF), it became clear that the term "racial profiling" hampered national and local discussions of the problem. This was most clearly exemplified in focus groups composed of both police and citizens. Staff noted that most *citizens* were using the term "racial profiling" to discuss *all* potential manifestations of racial bias in policing. The *police* participants were likely to define "racial profiling" quite narrowly—as law enforcement activities (particularly vehicle stops) based *solely* on race. The citizens claimed that "racial profiling," as they defined it, was widespread. In contrast, the police, using their more narrow definition were frequently quite adamant that police activities based solely on race were quite rare. These contrasting, but unspoken, definitions led to police defensiveness and citizen frustration.

As mentioned above, the concerns of law enforcement practitioners and citizens are clearly broader than the use of race as a sole criterion for police decision making. Our language and actions should reflect this broader concern. The PERF report adopted the term "racially biased policing" which occurs "when law enforcement inappropriately considers race or ethnicity in deciding with whom and how to intervene in an enforcement capacity." The various policy models discussed below articulate more precisely when the use of race/ethnicity might be "inappropriate."

Reality versus Perception

The topic of racially biased policing actually breaks down into two challenges for the executives of law enforcement agencies (e.g., chiefs, sheriffs): (1) personnel's racially biased policing conduct, and (2) citizens' perceptions of racially biased policing. We are unable in some contexts or within individual incidents to determine whether racially biased policing is real or perceived; the executive should commit to address both even if they cannot be fully disentangled. While racially biased policing is the misuse of race/ethnicity to make law enforcement decisions, the counterpart is the perception on the part of citizens that race/ethnicity is being used inappropriately in police decision making.

Potential Manifestations

Within both of these subtopics—actual and perceived racially biased policing—the executive needs to think about and respond to the various ways they might manifest. Specifically, the executive needs to think about (1) how to deal with "bad apples," (2) how to guide well-meaning officers, and (3) how to identify and fix institutional practices that contribute to the problems. That is, an executive needs to attend to the possibility of current or future problems of biased policing that result from the actions of a few "bad apples" among his/her personnel, the unintentional biased activities on the part of well-meaning officers, and/or department policies and practices that *inadvertently* (we hope, anyway) reflect bias.

The "bad apples" are the small minority of racist officers who act on their biases with impunity. These personnel are a great challenge to executives. Policy and training are not likely to impact on these officers; for the most part, their actions are already contrary to the existing policies of the agency and the training they have received. The greatest hopes for impacting on the behavior of these practitioners are close and effective supervision, an early warning system, and accountability through discipline or dismissal. There may be additional problem officers that, while they may not be conducting racially biased policing, treat citizens in such a negative and disrespectful manner as to give rise to the perceptions of it. Again, this calls upon measures in the form of effective supervision, early warning, and accountability.

In stark contrast to these bad apples, the vast majority of police personnel are well-meaning individuals who are dedicated to serving all citizens with fairness and dignity. Despite their good intentions, however, their behaviors may still manifest racially biased policing or give rise to the perceptions of it. It is likely that many of these officers are not fully cognizant of the extent to which race/ethnicity are used in their decision making (something that is equally true of individuals in other professions) or fully cognizant of the behaviors that may give rise to citizen perceptions of bias. These officers need policy to provide them with guidance on the circumstances in which race/ethnicity are or are not appropriate factors in the decisions they make and training that conveys that policy and facilitates their analytical understanding of racially biased policing. They need to be informed about their actions that citizens perceive as biased. Also important are effective supervision and an agency reward structure that reinforces behaviors consistent with the executive's commitment to impartial law enforcement and the dignified treatment of all citizens.

An executive needs to consider that racial bias is not the result of either intentional or unintentional deviation from agency policy or standards, but instead is the result of adherence thereto. Executives need to review policies, enforcement strategies, deployment, reward structures, and other operational administrative practices to ensure that they do not reflect biases and communicate openly and constructively with residents who express concern about the disparate impact of police activities.

RESPONDING TO REAL AND PERCEIVED RACIALLY BIASED POLICING

A law enforcement executive should consider responses/reforms within these areas:

- institutional practices and priorities,
- accountability and supervision,
- recruitment and hiring,
- education and training,
- minority community outreach,
- policies prohibiting racially biased policing, and
- data collection.

We will review potential responses within all of these areas.[1]

Institutional Practices and Priorities

Many of the potential response areas below focus on trying to remove bias from incident-level decision making by individual officers; we discuss how to hire impartial officers (or, at least, hire officers who are attuned to their own biases), guide officers with policy and training, supervise them, and so forth. Biased policing or perceptions of biased policing, however, may occur, not because individuals are working *outside* of agency parameters but *within* them. That is, there may be institutional policies and practices that produce biased policing or perceptions of its practice—even unintentionally. As such, an important early step for any department committed to addressing racially biased policing should include an "audit" of all operational and administrative practices that might result in disproportionate negative impacts on racial/ethnic minorities *and* that cannot be justified by race-neutral factors.

An assessment of how operational strategy might contribute to racially biased policing might begin by having personnel challenge some of the assumptions underlying conventional police strategy which emphasizes criminal and traffic enforcement as the primary means to control crime and disorder. The expectation with the conventional strategy is that numerous stops, searches, citations, and arrests will yield reductions in crime, disorder, and accidents. Under certain conditions, and with adequate community input and support, intensive criminal and traffic enforcement may be justified and sensible. But sometimes, intensive criminal and traffic enforcement (particularly if they are the only strategies in place to address particular problems) fall short of the desired effects, and instead, only worsen the relationship between police and the minority community.

Racial bias does not manifest itself the same way in every jurisdiction. Thus, it might make sense in one jurisdiction to explore how racial bias might play out in police efforts to interdict illegal drug shipments along major highways, but not make sense to do so in a jurisdiction where drug trafficking is not a major concern. In some jurisdictions, the potential for racially biased policing might manifest itself most prominently in how police handle problems associated with disorderly youth, gangs, migrant workers, or any number of concerns. There may be particular units in the department that—as a result of their mandate—are at greater risk than others for manifestations of bias.

Agencies should also review patterns of deployment for signs of over- or under-policing that cannot be explained by relevant and reasonable factors related to effective policing (such as calls for service). For instance, the primary author recently facilitated a focus group with citizens on the topic of racially biased policing. The perceptions of this group were that their police department *under*-policed their areas because the residents were predominantly minority (and low income). In contrast, another city is being sued on the charge that they over-police racial/ethnic minorities in their undercover drug enforcement efforts. In both of these examples, the first step for the agency would be to conduct an assessment to determine whether their deployment patterns reflect relevant, race-neutral factors such as general calls for service, citizen complaints of drug trafficking, and so forth. Agency practices may, in fact, result in *disparate impact* on racial/ethnic groups. However, disparate impact is not necessarily biased policing. The key to an assessment is to ensure that operational strategies and allocations of resources are not influenced by racial biases, but rather reflect reasonable and rational factors that facilitate effective policing for all citizens. Disparate impact, however, may lead to citizens' *perceptions* of bias that need to be heard and addressed constructively in public forums.

Another aspect of analyzing agency practices is to review reward structures to determine if they result in increased minority stops and/or searches. Reward structures include all those activities that are recorded and/or counted and that can have a positive job-related impact on the employee (e.g., be considered in merit raises and/or promotion). While the rewarded activity will most certainly be neutral with regard to race, it may interact with employees' stereotypes to produce an inappropriate negative impact on racial/ethnic minorities. For example, positive departmental reinforcements for weapons arrests or for drug seizures might lead officers to be particularly aggressive in their weapons and drug stops. Officers may link these crimes to racial/ethnic minority citizens, producing a disproportionate amount of detentions that may exceed their actual representation among offenders of these crimes. This type of finding could result in changes to the reward structure[2] or might be addressed through training and education as described more fully below.

Agencies can promote some of the aspects of community and problem-oriented policing that are directly relevant to the issue of racial bias. One important principle of community policing is the emphasis placed on having police personnel develop a comprehensive knowledge of the area to which they are assigned—whether a beat, a sector, or a district. Essential to this understanding is getting to know, not only the general demographics of the area—including which residents can be expected to be where, and when—but also, to the extent possible, getting to know the particular routines in an area, including which individuals normally are in certain places at certain times.

Knowing many citizens by face and name improves officers' abilities to differentiate between suspicious and nonsuspicious people on a basis other than race. Getting to know the community's law-abiding citizens helps police overcome stereotypes based on characteristics such as race. For example, the more young black males officers know by face and name, the less likely they will be to view all young black males as suspects or potential threats.

Also consistent with the principles of community and problem-oriented policing is actively soliciting community input about crime and disorder problems, what priority each should have, and how they might best be addressed. These conversations can reveal possible manifestations of racial bias or the perceptions of its practice and also allow police to convey their priorities, concerns, and issues regarding crime and disorder in the neighborhoods. These forums also provide the opportunity to explain that particular policies that produce disparate impact are, in fact, based on race-neutral principles and are in place to serve the public safety objectives of community residents. Garnering community support, especially minority community support, for police actions can go a long way toward reducing perceptions of racial bias.

Finally, agency executives should explore possible racial bias or the perceptions of it as it relates to the internal operation of the police agency itself. If there is racial mistrust and tension among police personnel, it is highly likely that some of that mistrust and tension will show in their attitudes and conduct toward the public. For instance, if racial bias is tolerated within the agency, some officers might conclude it will be tolerated in police-citizen interactions as well. Alternatively, officers who feel aggrieved by racial bias within the agency might take out their frustrations on citizens. These outcomes are not inevitable, but a climate of racial mistrust and tension within the agency, at a minimum, inhibits its efforts to discuss and address police racial bias on the streets.[3]

Accountability and Supervision

Police accountability and supervision are important factors in reducing or eliminating bias in policing. The tasks of policing are most often performed by single officers or pairs of officers operating independently and without immediate institutional oversight or independent observers. Under these circumstances, effective supervision to ensure accountability is a great challenge.

Sergeants, lieutenants, and captains wield by far the most powerful influence over the day-to-day activities, attitudes, and behaviors of street personnel. Top management must clearly convey to these supervisory personnel the expectations that the agency has for them, which is to prevent and detect actions that reflect racially biased policing or the behaviors that promote citizen perceptions of its practice. The first-line supervisor has the responsibility to spot-check officer performance in a variety of circumstances, observing the style of verbal communication and quality of discretionary decision making and enforcement action. The supervisor must be alert to any pattern or practice of possible discriminatory treatment by individual officers or squads (through observation, information from fellow officers, or close review of complaints) and be willing and able to take appropriate action in response to inappropriate behavior.

In-car video cameras should be considered if resources permit. This technology has the potential to suppress inappropriate behavior, increase supervisors' ability to observe behaviors, and document proper or improper officer actions in defense or support of later allegations. The introduction of video cameras should be accompanied by a policy that sets forth standards for supervisors' periodic review of officer tapes to enable detection of problem behavior.

Many progressive law enforcement agencies are implementing record systems with decision-prompting mechanisms called "early warning systems." These systems collect occurrence data on a broad selection of individual performance indicators, not only from public complaints, but other elements of an officer's performance from disciplinary actions, vehicle collisions, absenteeism reports, performance appraisals, personal problems, and training results. Any employee activity that could signal the presence of stress, dysfunctional behavior, or a training need becomes the subject of record. To provide for balance and equity, data collection could include positive inputs such as commendations, letters of appreciation, and awards.

Supervisors should take advantage of annual and periodic performance appraisals to recognize and promote professional, unbiased behavior. The appraisal instrument should provide an opportunity to grade officers on their communication skills, ability to carry out duties absent of bias, and ability to demonstrate tolerance and respect for individual rights in enforcing the law.

Recruitment and Hiring

Recruiting and hiring policies and practices have the potential to reduce racially biased policing and citizen perceptions that an agency is biased in two basic ways: (1) by hiring officers who can police in an unbiased manner, and (2) by establishing a police workforce that reflects the racial demographics of the community the agency serves. Good police officers carry out their duties with fairness, integrity, diligence, and impartiality. They respect basic individual rights and civil liberties. They know how to communicate effectively and respectfully to people of any race, culture, or background. They make the effort to understand the culture, language, mores, and customs of whatever population they are policing, and to get others to understand their own perspective. They look for ways to resolve disputes and address chronic community problems without creating or aggravating racial tensions. They do not rely solely on their arrest powers to establish their authority. They exercise their professional discretion thoughtfully and judiciously. They understand why some communities distrust the police as an institution, and work hard to earn their trust. They reject racial and cultural stereotypes, recognizing how unfair, inadequate and even dangerous they are to effective policing. They have the self-confidence and courage that is sometimes needed to reject the biased attitudes and behavior they may find among some fellow police officers.

Most police officers today have these qualities, and it is in no small measure because of how they police that there is not greater tension between the police and citizens in many communities. Police agencies must seek to recruit and hire more applicants who have, and can further develop, these qualities. To recruit and hire such applicants, however, is no simple matter. It calls not only for making judgments about applicants' racial attitudes, but also for predicting how applicants would act on these attitudes while working in the highly autonomous and discretionary environment of street policing.

It is important to bear in mind that few, if any, people are totally free of bias in one form or another. Most people stereotype others whom they don't know in some, usually benign, way. The search for unbiased police officers is not the search for the saintly and pure, but rather a search for well-intentioned individuals who, at a minimum, are willing to consider and challenge their own biases and make a conscious effort not to allow them to affect their decision making as officers.

In the search for unbiased police officers, staff must consider applicants' own statements on matters involving race and what background investigations might reveal about applicants' character, reputation, and documented history. Applicant interviews, whether conducted by community members or police staff, might include questions that reveal applicants' understanding and attitudes about race relations and police-community relations. Asking the questions alone signals to applicants that their attitudes about race are important to the police agency and that the agency will not tolerate biased policing. Applicants will sometimes admit to harboring attitudes and opinions that one might expect they would keep to themselves. While not foolproof, if one wants to know about applicants' racial attitudes and biases, there is no better place to start than by asking them directly.

Background investigations should explore many facets of applicants' lives, including clues about how they feel and act toward members of other racial and cultural groups. It is especially important to look for applicants who have some experience interacting with members of other races and cultures, and to assess how well they have done so.

A police agency whose officers reflect the racial demographics of the community they serve fulfills several important purposes in reducing racial bias and/or the perceptions of its practice. First, it conveys a sense of equity to the public, especially to minority communities. Second, it increases the probability that, as a whole, the agency will be able to understand the perspectives of its racial minorities and communicate effectively with them. Third, it increases the likelihood that officers will come to better understand and respect various racial and cultural perspectives through their daily interactions with one another.

Executives must communicate to their recruiting staffs their commitment to a diverse workforce and devote the resources necessary to achieve that goal. Police recruiters themselves should reflect the community's racial and cultural makeup and the recruitment messages should appeal not merely to potential applicants' desire for the adventure of policing or the wages and benefits offered, but also to a spirit of fairness, justice, and racial equality. To counter mistrust of police agencies, recruitment messages can promote policing as an opportunity to serve society in ways that can truly advance justice and racial harmony. Some methods for recruiting minority applicants are (1) recruiting at historically black colleges and universities, (2) recruiting through military channels, (3) recruiting with the help of current minority police officers, (4) recruiting through the religious community, and (5) recruiting people who want to change careers.

Police executives should periodically audit their agency's personnel recruitment and hiring process to gauge the fairness of each aspect of the selection process and whether the process as a whole, or at any stage, disproportionately disqualifies minority applicants. If there is evidence of disparate impact, the agency should explore the reasons for it and determine if remedies exist that will not compromise hiring standards. As a case in point, PERF staff recently visited a coastal community and learned that their greatest loss of minorities (including bilingual applicants) during the hiring process was a result of their high swimming standards. We also learned that the agency responded to just three or four incidents per year that might require swimming skills. While reasonable minds can certainly differ regarding whether the swimming standard is necessary, this recognized disparate impact, at the very least, calls for a serious cost-benefit analysis of the standard.

Education and Training

Education and training can play critical roles in reducing actual and perceived racial bias in policing. Police executives should be clear, however, about what such programs can realistically accomplish. They can convey new information, provide and refine critical skills, encourage compliance with policies and rules, facilitate dialogue, and/or convey a commitment to addressing the problem. They are unlikely to alter individuals' fundamental beliefs and biases. These programs must be of high quality to be effective. Education and training programs relating to racial bias in policing should be carefully monitored and evaluated to ensure they are credible to the participants and cover the issues in sufficient breadth and depth. They should be developed and presented in a genuine spirit of professionalism in which police executives commit themselves to helping their personnel understand and deal more effectively with an extraordinarily complex matter. These programs should not convey an accusatory tone; they should engage personnel in discussion, rather than preach to them.

Considerations of racial bias in policing should be woven into many education and training courses and should target all police personnel, including command officers.

Topics to be addressed should include the following:

- *Protection of Individual Rights:* Discussions of racial bias in policing should begin by having police personnel reflect on the core mission and values of policing. The founding principles of modern policing should be revisited, as should the mission and value statements adopted by the trainees' own agencies. Personnel should understand that the protection of civil rights and liberties is a central and affirmative part of the police mission, not an obstacle to effective policing. In this vein, they should understand the fundamental purpose and underpinnings of our nation's constitution, particularly the Bill of Rights.

- *Evidence of Racial Bias and the Perceptions of Racial Bias:* Education and training programs should present what evidence exists about the forms and dimensions of racial bias in policing and the extent of citizen perceptions of its practice. Trainers could present public opinion and sur-

vey data on perceptions of racial bias, as well as statistical data from
quality research on such things as police stops, searches, and arrests.

- *Effects of Racially Biased Policing on Individual Citizens, Police and the Community:* Police personnel should consider how the level of public trust in the police affects their ability to carry out their duties. Specifically, they should consider how public support for police policies and initiatives is eroded, how the flow of information from citizens to police is inhibited, and how police officers themselves are placed at greater risk because of mistrustful citizens who might harm or fail to assist them. Personal testimonials from minorities who have suffered from the effects of racial profiling or other forms of racial bias in policing can be effective in personalizing the problem and emphasizing the real harm caused to real people.

- *Key Decision Points at Which Racial Bias in Policing Can Occur:* Racially biased policing can occur at the incident level or be reflected in strategies or policies. A discussion of the key decision points at which racial bias in policing can occur reflects the possibility that practitioners are not always cognizant of the extent to which race/ethnicity enters into the decisions they make. Training for line officers should focus on the activities with the potential for bias at the incident level while training for supervisors, mid-managers, and command staff should reflect on strategic-level decisions and policy. Line officers should reflect on the potential for bias in decisions such as whom to contact or detain to investigate suspicions, deciding what attitude to adopt during contacts, deciding how long a stop will last, deciding whom to search or from whom to request consent to search, and deciding how dangerous suspects are and what level of force is necessary to control them. Some high-risk, strategic-level activities and policies were mentioned in the section on Institutional Practices and Priorities. Police personnel should consider what factors they rely on to make such decisions, and how suspects' race/ethnicity may or may not affect their decisions.

- *Policy on Racially Biased Policing:* The discussion regarding the key decision points at which racial bias in policing can occur, should go hand in hand with training on department policy. A subsequent section of this article recommends two policy options for executives to consider. The adoption of either of these should be accompanied by training in their implementation.

- *The Ineffectiveness of Racial Profiling:* Police personnel should also be informed about what the research reveals about using race/ethnicity to predict criminality. Studies have demonstrated that race/ethnicity is not a useful predictor of criminality, either as a sole factor or in combination with other factors.[4] Police personnel should understand that not only are there legal and moral concerns about targeting minorities for suspicion of criminality, but also that doing so is not an effective crime control strategy. Furthermore, false predictions erode public trust in and support for the police.

* *Steps to Reduce Perceptions of Racial Bias:* Education and training should also address ways to minimize the likelihood that police actions will be perceived as racially biased. Training should highlight how police can deal with people, including suspects, in ways that minimize the likelihood for misunderstanding, conflict, hostility, and violence.

Minority Community Outreach

Both the incidents and the perceptions of racially biased policing lead to mistrust of police. Relying as they do on resident input, support, and compliance, the police cannot function effectively where tensions are prevalent. Outreach to all residents, but particularly to minority communities is an important component of any departmental strategy to respond to racially biased policing and the perceptions of its practice. Departments should reach out to minority communities on the specific topic of racially biased policing and institute methods for building and sustaining, at a more general level, mutually respectful and trusting relationships.

Police practitioners should be willing to discuss racially biased policing and the perceptions thereof with community residents. Constructive dialogue between the police and citizens can lead to an agreement that racially biased policing likely occurs to some unknown degree within the jurisdiction, but perceptions may not always reflect the scope and nature of the problem. With this understanding in place, police and citizens can begin to collaborate to develop ways to address the issues. A jurisdiction-level task force comprised of police and citizens can take the lead—analyzing the problems and formulating interventions. These discussions can and should also take place within smaller geographical areas. Lieutenants and sergeants can develop task forces or arrange for focus groups within districts or beats to hear the concerns of citizens and focus on area-level issues. A key aspect of this dialogue is listening to what citizens have to say—allowing them to voice their frustrations or even anger. This process is key to initiating dialogue and constructive joint development of solutions.

Effective outreach, however, involves more than police-citizen engagement on the topic of race. Police departments should have long-term, sustained programs for reaching out to minority communities. While some outreach programs focus on making police accessible and approachable or improving minorities' perceptions of police, departments should also initiate concerted efforts to engage minorities in dialogue and decisions about department operations. Trust between the police and the community is built through long-term engagement. The police gain respect by consistently demonstrating respect for citizens. Giving up absolute control and allowing citizens to participate in decision making affecting how they are policed ensures a shared responsibility between police and the community. Police department efforts to provide significant means for community input into operational and policy decisions are the backbone of community engagement. Improved relations between police and minorities will increase officers' ability to provide high quality police services to all the residents in their jurisdiction and produce mutual trust, respect, and shared responsibility for public safety.

Policies Prohibiting Racially Biased Policing

According to the definition provided above, racially biased policing occurs when law enforcement inappropriately considers race or ethnicity in deciding with whom and how to intervene in an enforcement capacity. There are significant differences of opinions as to when it is and is not appropriate to consider race or ethnicity, and these views are reflected in the various policies that have been adopted around the nation to address racially biased policing.

It is critically important for an agency executive to be sure that his/her personnel are provided with guidance as to the appropriate use of race/ethnicity in making decisions. A key way to convey this guidance is in policy (supported by training). Executives shouldn't assume that all of their personnel use race/ethnicity the same way and should be concerned that their use may be broader than what the executive believes is just. In focus groups held around the country, it became clear to PERF staff that practitioners at all levels—line officers, command staff, and executives—have very different perceptions regarding the circumstances in which officers can consider race/ethnicity. Participants discussed when officers can use race/ethnicity as one factor in the "totality of the circumstances" to establish reasonable suspicion or probable cause. We found many differences of opinion among line officers and command staff, even within agencies, on this point. Some believed that officers should not use race/ethnicity to justify law enforcement intervention except when specified as part of a suspect's description. Others—when provided with hypothetical examples—clearly revealed an on-the-street use of race/ethnicity as a general indicator or predictor of criminal activity.

Most of the policies that have been adopted by agencies nationwide are what we call "anti-racial profiling" policies. They are distinguished by the use of the words "sole" or "solely," such as in *"the race or ethnicity of an individual shall not be the sole factor in determining the existence of probable cause . . . or in constituting a reasonable and articulable suspicion"* (Connecticut Public Act No. 99-198). Some agencies have adopted policies that direct personnel "not to discriminate." Neither of these policy models provides sufficient guidance on the use of race/ethnicity to make law enforcement decisions. Without clear parameters, some officers will, and do (as indicated by the focus group data), use race/ethnicity as a general indicator of criminal activity, to help justify, for instance, detentions of citizens. In this environment of minority citizen mistrust of law enforcement, agencies should set forth written policy parameters on the use of race/ethnicity to justify law enforcement intervention. Without clear guidance in both policy and training, law enforcement executives risk having line personnel inappropriately intrude on citizens' freedom based on those officers' personal biases as opposed to objective criteria.

Much more meaningful guidance can and should be afforded line personnel and there are two policy models that can fulfill this purpose: the "suspect specific model" and the PERF report policy. Both of these policies attempt to distinguish between the appropriate, or legally relevant, use of race/ethnicity in making decisions and the inappropriate use of race/ethnicity—when that usage is based on stereotypes and/or biases. Both of these policies place significant restrictions on the use of race/ethnicity in making law enforcement decisions; the suspect-specific model is more restrictive than the PERF report model.

The suspect-specific policies generally read as follows: *Officers may not consider the race or ethnicity of a person in the course of any law enforcement action unless the officer is seeking to detain, apprehend, or otherwise be on the lookout for a specific suspect sought in connection with a specific crime who has been identified or described in part by race or ethnicity.* The key to this model is that the set of identifiers—which includes reference to race/ethnicity—must be linked to a particular suspect that is being sought for a particular crime. Thus, if reliable witnesses describe a convenience store robber as 5' 8" tall, lean, long-haired, and Asian, Asian can be considered along with the other demographics and with other evidence in developing reasonable suspicion to detain or probable cause to arrest.

As mentioned above, the suspect-specific model is the most restrictive that we have identified. The PERF report policy encompasses the suspect-specific provision, but allows for additional uses of race/ethnicity beyond the circumstances involving a "specific suspect" and a "specific crime." The PERF model has both 4th and 14th Amendment provisions. The 4th Amendment[5] provision is what distinguishes the PERF report model from the suspect-specific model and will receive the most attention here. It reads: "*Officers shall not consider race/ethnicity to establish reasonable suspicion or probable cause except that officers may take into account the reported race/ethnicity of a potential suspect(s) based on trustworthy, locally-relevant information that links a person or persons of a specific race/ethnicity to a particular unlawful incident(s)*" (Fridell et al., 2001:52).

Pursuant to the 4th Amendment provision, the PERF report policy disallows race/ethnicity used as a general indicator for or predictor of criminal behavior; it disallows the use of racial or ethnic stereotypes in making law enforcement decisions. It allows for the use of race/ethnicity when those demographics are legally relevant descriptors.

Reflecting the 14th Amendment guarantee of equal protection[6] in all law enforcement activities, the PERF report policy states that "*Except as provided above [referencing the 4th Amendment provisions], race and ethnicity shall not be motivating factors in making law enforcement decisions*" (Fridell et al., 2001:52). The 4th Amendment provisions are insufficient by themselves. Even if officers meet the 4th Amendment mandates of law and policy, they could still be biased in deciding, for instance, *which lawbreakers* they will arrest or let go or *which citizens* to treat with respect and dignity. We need the second provision reflecting the general principle of equal protection.

Together, the 4th and 14th Amendment provisions prohibit racially biased policing. They will prompt officers to carefully consider their motives for engaging citizens, and tightly circumscribe their use of race/ethnicity in making enforcement decisions.

There are two important similarities between the two policies that must be highlighted. First of all, neither policy permits the use of race/ethnicity as the *sole* factor for law enforcement decision making. These policies, instead, reference when it is acceptable to use race/ethnicity as *one* factor among multiple factors in establishing reasonable suspicion or probable cause. Secondly, these policies rely on *descriptions* of actual suspects as opposed to *predictions* of who may be involved in crime. As Harris (2002:152) states: "What must *not* be allowed is using race or ethnic appearance, alone or in combination with other factors, to stop a particular person based on a *prediction* that he or she is more likely to be involved in crime."

Data Collection

Since "racial profiling" has become a national issue, many jurisdictions have started collecting data on the race/ethnicity of citizens stopped and/or searched by the police. It is interesting that data collection became known early on as *the way* for police agencies to respond, with very little attention given to other ways agencies might address both racially biased policing and perceptions thereof (e.g., training, recruitment/hiring, supervision).[7]

The agencies involved in data collection require officers to report information on each targeted stop. Most agencies are collecting data for just traffic-related stops or for all vehicle stops (traffic-related stops and crime-related stops of vehicles). The information collected by officers includes the race/ethnicity of the driver and other information about the driver (e.g., age, gender) and the stop (e.g., reasons for the stop, disposition of the stop, whether a search was conducted, outcome of the search).[8]

There are arguments for and against collecting this police-citizen contact data. On the positive side, collecting police-citizen contact data helps agencies convey a commitment to unbiased policing and builds trust with the community. Data collection conveys important messages to both the community and agency personnel: that biased policing will not be tolerated and that officers are accountable to the citizens they serve. This has been the impetus for many agencies around the country that have adopted data collection systems.

Two major arguments—one for data collection and one against—go head to head and center on the ability of social science to turn the data that are collected into valid and meaningful assessments of whether racially biased policing is occurring. On the one hand—supporting data collection—is the argument, articulated by Ron Davis of NOBLE that "You cannot manage what you don't measure." He (among others) argues that much of management within police departments is based on information. We use information such as reported crime, calls for service, and complaints to make decisions regarding the allocation of resources, training needs, and so forth. Similarly, "[p]roper data collection, utilizing credible benchmarks . . . provides an organizational 'snap shot' . . . [which] assists administrators in identifying institutional and systemic problems" (Davis, 2001:1).

Challenges to this position reflect the concern that police-citizen contact data do not yield valid information regarding the nature and extent of racially biased policing and are therefore of questionable utility as a management tool. That is, there are legitimate questions as to whether the data collected on police stops can tell us whether those stops are based on police racial/ethnic bias. The challenge is in developing the "benchmarks," to which Captain Davis refers, to determine whether racially biased policing is indicated by, for instance, the fact that 25 percent of an agency's traffic stops are of Hispanics. Developing the right benchmark is critical to making data collection efforts worthwhile, and yet this process poses many challenges.

To draw definitive conclusions regarding police-citizen contact data that indicate disproportionate engagement of racial/ethnic minorities, we need to be able to identify and disentangle the impact of race from legitimate factors that might reasonably explain individual and aggregated decisions to stop, search, and otherwise engage people. In an attempt to rule out alternative factors, agencies strive to develop comparison groups against which to evaluate their police-citizen contact data. Agencies strive to develop comparison groups ("benchmark" groups) that most closely reflect the demographic makeup of groups at risk of being stopped by police *assuming no bias.* For example, a department collecting data on traffic stops would, ideally, want to compare the demographics of those stopped by police for a traffic violation with the demographics of those people legitimately at risk of a stop, taking into consideration numerous factors, including, but not limited to, driving quantity, driving quality, and driving location.[9]

Many agencies that are collecting data are analyzing their data using very weak benchmarks. For instance, many agencies are conducting "census benchmarking," whereby the analyst compares the demographic profile of drivers stopped by police to the U.S. Census Bureau demographic profile of jurisdiction residents. This is a very poor benchmark because the group of people who reside in a jurisdiction does not necessarily reflect the group of people who are at legitimate risk of being stopped by police. Possible variations across racial/ethnic groups in terms of driving quantity, quality, and location are not considered with this method. In the many jurisdictions that use census information to benchmark their data, the authors either irresponsibly draw conclusions regarding whether racial bias exists, or more responsibly, indicate that no conclusions can be drawn.

Researchers and practitioners are still struggling to identify methods for developing valid comparison groups. As yet, there is no consensus on what might be the most the cost-effective and valid benchmark(s). Some jurisdiction teams are comparing the demographic profiles of persons stopped with the demographic profiles of licensed drivers, people involved in vehicle accidents, or persons observed to be driving in the jurisdiction. In jurisdictions with cameras that record the license plates of vehicles running red lights (a "color-blind" form of enforcement), the demographic profile of the owners (unfortunately, not the *drivers,* necessarily) of those vehicles can be compared with the profile of persons stopped by police. Similarly, radar stops can be a color-blind form of enforcement allowing agencies to compare the demographic profile of citizens stopped with radar to the demographic profile of citizens stopped without radar. Jurisdictions can also rely on internal comparisons—comparing the profiles of people stopped by individual officers or units to the corresponding data for other officers or units that are "matched" in terms of their assignments (e.g., beat, shift). Resident surveys can be used to collect data, not only on the extent to which residents are stopped by police but also on the nature and extent of their driving. Corresponding to the data that police collect on their own activities, the survey could solicit information from the respondents regarding the frequency and nature of their encounters with the police. Corresponding to benchmarking efforts for department-collected stop data, such a survey could ask the residents about the nature (e.g., speed, passing behavior, driving violations), location (e.g., interstate highways, around their neighborhood) and amount of their driving.

Many agencies involved in data collection are hiring an independent researcher or research group to assist in the analysis/interpretation of the data. This can promote the quality of the social science methodology in those agencies that lack advanced research units and, importantly, increase the credibility of the results. Further, many agencies are involving citizens in planning and implementing their data collection efforts. By including influential citizens on a police-citizen task force an agency can again enhance the credibility of the effort and educate these citizens as to the challenges of analyses so that they can, in turn, educate their peers through the media or other forums.

CONCLUSION

In this article, we have discussed the complex and challenging issue of racially biased policing and outlined how law enforcement can address both the real and perceived manifestations of it. As mentioned in the introduction, the issue of "racial profiling" is not new. We, instead, have a new label for the longstanding tensions between police and minority communities. But, as also conveyed above, law enforcement has never been better situated to address these issues. This is a new era of policing—one characterized by new tools and skills for dealing with complex and highly charged issues. Reflecting this changed profession, progressive chiefs and sheriffs across the nation are acknowledging the problems of racially biased policing and widespread perceptions of its practice and implementing initiatives to bring about critically needed, constructive change.

Notes

[1] The reader is invited to refer to the relevant chapters in the PERF report entitled "Racially Biased Policing: A Principled Response" (Fridell et al., 2001) for more depth on all topics.

[2] For instance, rewarding search efficiency (percent of searches that result in hits), instead of total volume of contraband discovered.

[3] With PERF's Assistance, the Kansas City (MO) Police Department conducted surveys and focus groups of personnel to assess concerns regarding racial bias and racial tensions in the agency.

[4] See, in particular, Kennedy (1997) and Harris (2002).

[5] "The right of the people to be secure in their persons, houses, papers and effects against unreasonable searches and seizures shall not be violated; and no warrant shall issue, but upon probable cause, supported by oath or affirmation, and particularly describing the place to be searched, and the persons or things to be seized."

[6] "[N]o State shall make or enforce any law which shall . . . deny to any person within its jurisdiction the equal protection of the laws."

[7] It is likely that this attention to data collection was spawned by the several prominent early court cases—including *State v. Pedro Soto* against the new Jersey State Troopers and *Wilkins v. Maryland State Police*—for which data were important aspects of the evidence and/or settlement.

[8] For discussions of which stops to target and what data elements to collect, see Ramirez et al., 2000 and Fridell et al., 2001.

[9] For more information on the conceptual challenges of benchmarking and the various methods used to create benchmarks, see Fridell 2004.

References

Davis, R. (2001). *Racial Profiling: What Does the Data Mean. A Practitioner's Guide to Understanding Data Collection and Analysis.* Unpublished manuscript.

Fridell, L., R. Lunney, D. Diamond, and B. Kubu with M. Scott and C. Laing (2001). *Racially Biased Policing: A Principled Response.* Washington, DC: PERF (Available in its entirety on the PERF website at www.policeforum.org).

Fridell, Lorie (2004). *By the Numbers: A Guide to Analyzing Race Data From Vehicle Stops.* Washington, DC: PERF. (Available on the PERF website at www.policeforum.org.)

Harris, D. (2002). *Profiles in Injustice: Why Racial Profiling Cannot Work.* New York: The New Press.

Kennedy, R. (1997). *Race, Crime and the Law.* New York: Pantheon Books.

State v. Pedro Soto 734 A. 2d 350 (N.J. Super. Ct. Law. Div. 1996).

Ramirez, D., J. McDevitt, and A. Farrell (2000). *A Resource Guide on Racial Profiling Data Collection Systems: Promising Practices and Lessons Learned.* Washington, DC: U.S. Department of Justice.

Wilkins v. Maryland State Police et al., Civil No. MJG-93-468 (D. Md. 1993).

Section V
Minorities in Policing

Historically the majority of police officers have been white males. Although the proportion of officers who are members of minority groups (e.g., African Americans and women) has been increasing, it is still quite low and a cause of concern to many, including community members who see the need for the police to be more representative of the populations they serve. One approach to resolving this problem is to recruit more African Americans and women (as well as members of other minority groups) into police work. Unfortunately, there has not been a great deal of research or literature directed toward the problems faced by minority officers or toward the impact of hiring those officers. Yet, the calls for community-based policing strategies, which emphasize the integration of the formal control system of the police with the informal control system of the community, require minority participation in policing. Further, the values of affirmative action, equal opportunity, and involvement of minorities encourage the hiring and advancement of minorities in law enforcement. This section includes two articles that address the issues of how blacks and women interact within the institution of policing.

Professor Chris Cooper presents some important suggestions for the study of police. His ideas focus on the Afrocentric perspectives on the history of policing in the United States and how the current customs and practices are interpreted by African Americans. His article presents a view of policing that is not readily available and deserves critical attention. He argues that the personal and collective experiences of black people with police officers gives African Americans a reality different from that of white Americans.

Susan Martin examines the changes in the status of women in police work, the nature of the resistance of male officers to having women on the force, and the research and policy issues related to women who choose police work. She concludes that the most blatant barriers to the recruitment of women in police work have fallen, and women are entering the profession in increasing numbers. However, female officers are still underrepresented and face discriminatory treatment that limits their career mobility and options for advancement.

An Afrocentric Perspective on Policing

Christopher Cooper

> As a U.S. Marine, I was told that I was green, hence to discard my black-
> ness. As a black policeman in America, there were many times when it
> was suggested that I disregard recognizing that I didn't look like most
> other officers—we were all supposed to be blue. As a scholar, there are
> just as many, if not more, times that I am reminded by my colleagues that
> to champion causes of people of color is to jeopardize tenure and publi-
> cation possibilities. I choose to notice my societal position as a black man
> in America. To discard it is to avoid realizing and challenging the injus-
> tices that come with my societal position. The same people who tell you
> to forget who you are, are the same people who will not let you forget
> who you are.
>
> —The author

The Afrocentric perspectives on the history of policing in the United
States, the policing institution, and its day-to-day practices differ from the
perspectives held by many people not of African descent. This article presents
the "other side," the way that people of color see policing in the United
States. It bolsters its points by reliance on empirical data and attention to factual information and events.

In the twenty-first century, black people are unavoidably intertwined
with the institution of U.S. policing. The reasons lie with crime problems in

Prepared especially for *Critical Issues in Policing* by Christopher Cooper.

some black communities that prompt police–black citizen interaction, with racism in the form of police officers who choose not to have a good relationship with people of color, and with officers singling out people because of their skin color (racially discriminatory policing). These phenomena have meant that scholarly discourse on policing, police programs, initiatives, and strategy are often about or directed at black people and often imposed on black people (i.e., community policing in many jurisdictions). No other racial group in U.S. society is as much the focus, and at the nucleus, of policing policy. Under these conditions, an open-minded person would think that black people would be invited to proffer their perspectives on policing their communities; that black scholars (Ph.D.s) with sociological and criminological expertise would be included by their white colleagues in research efforts to identify causes and solutions and ultimately to make recommendations to policy makers.

The situation is quite to the contrary. Black people are often objects of policing, and the experts in the black community are treated by many of their white colleagues with disdain. It is white police scholars who assert that they know what is best for policing black communities. Case in point, an entire industry, criminal justice, has been built around analyzing the social interactions (e.g., police–black citizen) and day-to-day lives of black and brown people. Whether it is classroom instruction concerning policing black communities or a panel established to make recommendations regarding police–black citizen relations, the players are seldom if ever black. Black social scientists are available, and the black community is available—available to function as integral parts of society in discussions on policing and policy making around policing.

The black social scientists are prepared to present their perspective on U.S. policing. What they have to say about policing has merit, but seldom are there mainstream outlets welcoming the Afrocentric perspective on policing. Scholarly work concerning policing written by African Americans having an Afrocentric perspective, if published at all, is most often found in the black press or in black scholarly journals. This article's presence in a mainstream publication is unusual. Hopefully, its appearance indicates that some positive changes are coming from the scholarly policing field.

This article presents the Afrocentric perspective on three policing phenomena that adversely impact black communities. The first is an Afrocentric perspective on status-quo police scholars: how they perpetuate racism and exacerbate poor police–minority relations. Most importantly, the status-quo police scholars deny the existence of racism and have misquoted policing history (by presenting a Eurocentric perspective). The second perspective is the use of race by some police officers as a factor in deciding whether or not to use deadly force. In instances of interactions with persons of color, such decisions can lead to dispensing with protocol, as in "shooting first and asking questions later." The third and final perspective calls attention to how black people are often excluded, by the media, police administrations, and government from discourse and decision-making processes regarding policing of their communities. These three perspectives combine to present the reader with the other side of the story.

THE PERSPECTIVE OF THE POLICE SCHOLARS

Police scholars are usually social scientists with doctorate degrees. Many are academicians, while others are a combination of practitioner and academician. Most of those who study and write about U.S. policing are white males. There are legitimate concerns by people of color that this is a scholarship lacking racial and ethnic diversity.

The words conservative, status quo, mainstream, and traditional best describe the majority of police scholars. Sadly, the status-quo mainstream scholars have the podium. What they have to say about policing in the United States is taken seriously and given great weight by policy researchers and much of the lay populace. In this way, these scholars influence and shape the perception of policing in the United States for many Americans. For example, they influence judges, prosecutors, and the public about what constitutes the crime of police brutality versus a mere mistake.

Often, scholars convey information about the police in the form of scientific research. The social scientists who analyze phenomena do so with an objective of ameliorating conditions and alleviating problems. In the end, they give their findings to policy makers in the form of recommendations. The public receives the findings in lay terms (e.g., via the newspaper or a television news program) and is supposed to add the new information to what it believes it already knows about policing.

The problem lies with the fact that from an Afrocentric perspective, the status-quo police scholars (especially those who undertake historical analyses) are not truthful concerning policing in the United States. Much like the history lessons of the past, which did not divulge that Native Americans occupied North America when Christopher Columbus arrived, the police scholars present a Eurocentric perspective of policing in the United States. It excludes mention of people of color, the events, epidemics, tragedies, and triumphs to which black people were and are connected.

The Hidden History

With few exceptions, the status-quo police scholars do not address the fact that early policing was for the purpose of maintaining slavery—black people were policed by organized police long before these scholars say formal policing was established (Dulaney, 1996). The brutality of the police during the slavery era is sometimes denied or mitigated by the status-quo scholars. As an example, Monkkonen (1981) asserts that reports of Southern police in the 1860s being repressive and brutal are the result of sentiments that reflect an anti-Southern bias (p. 198, n96). He likened the observers of police brutality to people who would have said that they had witnessed brutality even if they had not.

With the abolition of slavery, the police establishment embarked on a new style of class control. This included enforcing segregation and championing white supremacy,[1] but a reader would not learn this from twenty-first century, status-quo policing textbooks and lecture instruction. Rather, the status-quo or Eurocentric version (e.g., Carte and Carte, 1975) reveals a period of varying police functions, such as giving shelter to the homeless and garbage collection, and the resultant identity crisis of the vocation. Not far behind is discourse on the realization that policemen needed uniforms and that corrupt behavior by many of them spawned major "clean house" initiatives in 1884, 1890, and 1894, to name just a few (Fogelson, 1977). What the reader is not told by most Eurocentric writers, for example, is how blacks were often excluded from becoming police officers and that in many communities the Ku Klux Klan and police were either complicit or one and the same.

The policing literature places emphasis and significance on the police reform movement—the period in U.S. history in which, according to the Eurocentric perspective, the policing establishment is said to have gotten a moral and professional conscience. The corrupt establishment was called to task by innovators from within the ranks as well by a concerned external populace. Much of the Eurocentric police literature describes the reform era as an epiphany. We are to believe that the people rose up, realized the pathetic character of the policing establishment, then called for law and order to be taken seriously and administered equally. No doubt the reform movement was a pivotal moment in removing politics from policing and upgrading the establishment's status. However, its inattention to racial injustice makes the reform movement also a pivotal point of increased intolerance. Why the recent policing literature (post–civil rights era of the twentieth century, and the twenty-first century) conveniently leaves out the racial issues that were intertwined with the police reform movement is baffling. The policing establishment was concerned with defining its mandate and with maintaining segregation laws.

To this day, in classroom instruction, the Eurocentric heroes of policing are individuals who made their mark in the reform movement era: August Vollmer, Bruce Smith, Herbert Jenkins, and William Parker, to name a few. The movement's leaders are portrayed as benevolent and having had few faults. Their motives are said to have been for the good of all people. In reality, they were often upper-class men attempting to protect upper-class interests (Fogelson, 1981). The Afrocentric perspective is that the reformers had a primary, glaring fault—not paying attention to social justice as it applied to all people. The criminal justice student wouldn't learn this fact from the typical police history textbook published by Eurocentric police scholars.

Sparrow, Moore, and Kennedy (1990) are among the many policing scholars who have written and published about the history of policing in the

United States. From their work, the reader would know how political patronage could land an individual a police position but would find no mention of how the reformers shirked their responsibility to society by not addressing racially discriminatory policing. It is not sufficient to argue that blacks did not meet the higher educational standards put in place by the reform movement. Many blacks who satisfied the educational criteria applied to police agencies but were not hired because they were black (Dulaney, 1996, p. 65).

The reform era of policing, in particular, provided the stage for race-based, violent, and brutal behavior by police officers, including lynch mobs comprised of police officers and officers who hunted and shot black people like animals. Violence by police officers would in large part give way to some of the most serious race riots that the United States has ever experienced (e.g., Watts and Newark). Yet, the mainstream literature scarcely mentions that police provoked the rioting.[2] The race riots that rocked the nation were spawned by one standard of policing for whites and another for blacks. They were propelled by horrific police brutality from dogs set on people because they were black to jail-house beatings of people of color because they were black. It only makes sense that there would be poor police–community relations following the civil rights era riots. Moreover, the provocation by police that led to most of the race riots is referenced by police scholars of color (e.g., Alex, 1976; Cooper, 1980; Dulaney, 1996) and a few white scholars (e.g., Fogelson, 1977).

The late Arthur Niederhoffer (1969), police sociologist, included issues of race in his brief discussion of the history of U.S. policing in his work, *Behind the Shield*. He called attention to occupational issues of black police officers and how officers abridged the civil rights of black and Puerto Rican people. Niederhoffer was an anomaly in the police scholarly field in 1969 and would be in the early twenty-first century because he revealed a connection to policing and the John Birch Society (among other things). He referenced a November 8, 1965, *New York Times* article announcing that the former chief of the Salt Lake City police department (a reform and professionalization era chief) was scheduled to be a keynote speaker at a John Birch Society function (in spite of the society's white supremacist views and support of racial segregation).[3]

In a 1982 issue of *Atlantic Monthly*, police scholars Wilson and Kelling published "Broken Windows."[4] The article is held in the highest esteem by conservative police academia. For good reason, many students of color find the article racially offensive. From an Afrocentric perspective, the article is condescending and reflects narrow-mindedness. Recall that the article is largely based on Kelling and Wilson's (two white men) observations and study of how black people felt about, and interacted with, police officers assigned to foot patrol in Newark housing projects in the 1970s. For example, the authors assert that although "the neighborhoods were predominantly black and the foot patrolmen were mostly white, this 'order maintenance' function of the police was performed to the general satisfaction of both parties" (p. 30). This statement is problematic for obvious reasons. In the twenty-

first century, black citizen–white police relations are incredibly strained. At
the time of Kelling and Wilson's observations, relations were worse or equal
to the current climate. They chose to imply that black people were not astute
enough to be suspicious of racial hostility from the police or that the police–
citizen relationship was tense. This same argument was posited in the slavery
era by proslavery observers. They described slave masters and slaves in close
physical proximity as having a peaceful coexistence.

Most patronizing and racially insensitive is that "Broken Windows" (and
a subsequent article by Mark Moore and George Kelling, entitled, "To Serve
and Protect: Learning from Police History" [1983]) suggests that the policing
of yesteryear was so wonderful and beneficial that the United States should
restore the "good ol' days," or the reform model. From an Afrocentric perspective, police scholar Samuel Walker (1984) is correct when he calls attention to how the authors not only misinterpreted police history but also were
not truthful in describing the past. Walker adds, "the tradition of policing
cited by Wilson, Kelling, and Moore never existed."[5] McNamara (1982), in
an article with a fitting title, "Dangerous Nostalgia for the Cop on the Beat,"
bolsters Walker's position in pointing out that the good old days were not all
that good.

A more recent reminder of the status-quo position and its insensitivity
are the remarks from a professor of criminal justice about a conservative Web
site for police officers operated by a Chicago police officer. Although the Web
site included racial slurs and sexual innuendoes, the professor said he found
the site "more positive than negative" because it allows police to vent.[6]

On Contributions by Black Police

There were black police officers prior to the Civil War (Dulaney 1996),
but that is a fact not easily found in the status-quo literature or passed on to
college students studying criminal justice. In most publications, the tremendous contributions of black people to policing are not mentioned at all or are
mentioned in passing. Instead, people like Darryl Gates, the former Los
Angeles police chief, are often praised. To people of color, Gates was known
for the terror that he imposed on communities of color; his name conjures
memories of random sweeps of black and Mexican people and the most cruel
and sadistic police brutality.[7] Yet this man was described (shortly before the
Rodney King incident) by Harvard University professors (police scholars)
Sparrow, Moore, and Kennedy "as a pioneering police chief" who had
"pointed the way forward" (1990, p. ix). In complimenting "progressive"
police departments, the authors described Gates as handsome, honest, and
professional. They described him as "the epitome of the reform police chief
and his department a shining example of the best in reform policing" (p. 60).

The Eurocentric perspective on Gates's tenure is completely distinguishable from the Afrocentric perspective. King's beating was not an aberration of
Gates's reign. Atypical was that the beating was videotaped. It is likely that

Gates's tyranny would have continued had the country not seen the brutality. The infamous Mark Fuhrman served under Gates's watch. In 1994, by his own admission, Fuhrman told how he and other members of the police department beat people mercilessly because they were black, planted evidence on people because they were black, and routinely referred to black people as "niggers."[8] Presently, the Los Angeles Police Department is in the midst of what could turn out to be the largest police scandal in U.S. history. Dubbed the "Rampart scandal," it includes admissions by police officers that they sought Latino victims because they were people of color, planted evidence on them, and filed countless false police reports about them, some of which were to cover for police officers who had committed murder (Cohen, 2000). Not surprisingly, the LAPD faces a federal civil rights suit alleging a "pattern and practice" of abuse and racial discrimination and the possibility of federal oversight for the department. By June 2000, eighty-one criminal cases brought by officers of the Rampart Division had been overturned (Murr, 2000). The truth of how the Los Angeles Police Department operates (and has always operated) is finally subject to unfiltered public view. In fact, the multiple lawsuits against the LAPD may result in the agency being considered an ongoing criminal enterprise subject to RICO statues for the recovery of damages.

In contrast to the publicity given to flawed reform initiatives and out-of-control police departments like the LAPD, contributions to policing by black people have been underreported. Accomplishments of black police executives include team policing established in Newark by Hubert Williams. Lee Brown was instrumental in bringing community policing to New York City. Sadly, he never received the support from his middle managers that was needed to make it a success (Dulaney, 1996). To Brown's credit, his community-policing model has been replicated by other jurisdictions.

The fact that the accomplishments of black police executives are reported primarily in Afrocentric publications calls attention to denial and bigotry within policing academia. It is status-quo work that is accepted for publication, even though it presents an inaccurate portrayal of the history of policing in the United States. Many phenomena (e.g., how black officers are often physically harmed by white officers in the twenty-first century) worthy of presentation, and of social utility to black people, are censored or simply not published. Equally guilty are the journal editors and reviewers who allow writing that contains falsehoods to be published or who oppose publication of Afrocentric manuscripts, alleging that the writing is scientifically invalid (something that black authors often hear concerning their research from close-minded peer reviewers; commonly, it is an accusation that the black author has misinterpreted policing history).

On Police Brutality

The mainstream, status-quo, twenty-first-century police scholar bristles at notions that police brutality could be a widespread problem. He/she sees policing as having followed a steady progression of improvement over time. For example, review of the policing literature shows that the Knapp Commission (1973) investigation into police corruption in New York City reduced corruption there and had reverberations nationwide. There is a false sense of confidence that contributes in some part to the Eurocentric position that police brutality could not in fact be widespread in the twenty-first century following a "clean house" investigation of such magnitude. While financial crimes (e.g., shakedowns) by police have declined, the same cannot be said for police brutality.

When research on police brutality has been conducted, status-quo (Eurocentric) methods are suspect. An example of one such method is the use of police reports without other corroboration. Police scholars know that police reports alone yield invalid information; therefore, one can assume that researchers who use reports do so knowing that the documents produce scientifically invalid research.[9] For other researchers, it is their naiveté (sometimes from not having had police experience before becoming academicians) that causes them to fail to realize that an officer can write a police report in any way that he or she chooses. The authoritative version is often shaped so that illegal use of force is masked. Reports are written to mitigate the use of force and/or to deny its very occurrence.[10] In spite of these obvious shortcomings, many of those charged with informing the public (e.g., academicians) concerning the extent of such a serious social concern continue to champion this methodological method. As a result, many acts of police brutality are not recorded in status-quo police scholarly research.[11]

Status-quo police scholarship discourages attention, especially from policy makers, on police brutality. These academicians assert that incidents of police brutality are mere aberrations—the "rotten apple theory"[12] (notwithstanding all of the evidence and common sense that shows the theory to be a falsehood). As an example, Kelling (1997/1999) commented about the Abner Louima[13] case: "The assault and torture of Abner Louima by New York City police officers . . . was an appallingly deviant act, not representative of the New York City Police Department, of policing generally, or of good order-maintenance tactics," (p. 48).

To prove their position that brutality is rare, the scholars raise an argument that arouses suspicions that they are contradicting themselves. They point to the difficulty in collecting data about the extent of police brutality. Essentially, the scholars take a position that if you "can't quantify it, it doesn't exist." This is absolute ignorance of the fact that a great deal of physical police brutality is never reported. Furthermore, they are seldom willing to give credence to self-reports from victims and other nonpolice sources. These are sources that from an Afrocentric perspective are very reliable—and indicative of an epidemic of police brutality. For example, data derived via content analysis (e.g., analyzing periodicals), when coupled with other empirical data, are extremely helpful. Content analyses findings present a strong case for a scientifically generalizable pattern and conclusions about police practices. Other examples include reliance on existing data. These secondary analyses include figures kept by the Department of Justice (Civil Rights Division) based on the number of complaints received by it. Additional sources of information for gauging the extent of police brutality are the many civil lawsuits alleging police brutality. Most significant are those for which a jurisdiction settles out of court.[14]

In an effort to deny the existence of the systemic problem of police brutality in the United States, status-quo scholars write off a large chunk of police brutality as good faith—not criminal—mistakes. For example, Fyfe (1995) argues that many instances are examples of excessive or unnecessary force, not police brutality. He claims the harm and excessive physical punishment are the result of "ineptitude or carelessness and occurs when well meaning officers prove incapable of dealing with situations they encounter" (p.163). Said another way, Eurocentric scholars attribute the harm to the victim as the result of well meaning officers incapable of dealing with situations they encounter.

Because of the influence of mainstream policing literature on policy making and the criminal justice system, it is not uncommon that defense attorneys representing police officers charged with police brutality call upon scholars championing the good-faith-mistake position as expert witnesses. Court characterizations of police brutality as noncriminal and mere mistakes perpetuate an unwillingness of fact finders to find officers guilty of police brutality. The acquittal of the officers who killed Amadou Diallo (discussed later in this article) is an example of this phenomenon. The state of affairs (as well as race relations in the United States) will not change anytime soon as long as the powerful mainstream police academic lobby is able to persuade fact finders (judge or jury) to choose mistake over crime.

Even worse, a number of scholars (e.g., Stoddard, 1968; Fyfe, 1982, 1995) place blame for the behavior on macrophenomena. Officers are said to have guns that fire too quickly, supervisors who don't supervise, and a police subculture, or an administration, that is so powerful that it takes away an individual officer's ability to function on his/her own volition. A notion that more training is the solution rather than better pre-employment screening further insults the reality that human beings participating in police work possess free agency. From an Afrocentric perspective, it is racially offensive to hear from police administrators and scholars that horrific acts (e.g., sodomization of Abner Louima) are indicative of a need for more training. It seems more prudent to realize that many individuals hired as police officers should not have been hired because of their racial bias or lack of respect for human life. To suggest that training is to blame or that it is the panacea for police brutality is to disavow the seriousness of "individualistic" racial intolerance and its ingrained mind-set character.

The problem with placing blame on macrophenomena is that it prompts people (prosecutors and jurors for example) to allow individual officers to escape responsibility for their actions. Research by Brown (1981) among others, as well as common sense, show that U.S. police officers are not robots but possess extensive autonomy, notwithstanding the influences of their subculture.

RACE AND USE OF DEADLY FORCE

When making a decision to use deadly force, the problem is that for many police officers the race of the "other" is an impacting factor. Race prompts an officer's fears, or race prompts his/her aversions, or race prompts him/her to marginalize another's self-worth. An officer's fear can cause indifference, reckless acts, or irrational interactions with a member of a racial group. This is one possible explanation of why police officers killed Amadou Diallo. Aversion can be another impetus for an officer's behavior. The officer manifests his or her racial hatred, very often with physical violence. Marginalization (treating a person's self-worth as insignificant) explains a police officer knowingly using unnecessary violence on a person: the officer has marginalized the person because of that person's race. These race-based impetuses (except fear in some cases, although still acting with depraved indifference to human life) increase the likelihood of shooting when you know that you don't have to shoot, but shooting anyway because you know that your actions will be justified.

Many police–black citizen interactions have a connection to racial profiling, since it is the race of the citizen that prompts the officer to confront the citizen in the first place. All of the aforementioned impetuses for deadly force are equally impetuses for why an officer engages in racial profiling.

Whether race was the factor that motivated the officer to behave the way that he/she did is the million-dollar question. As fast as some will argue that race was not a factor, they should, as quickly, consider the possibility that race was involved. Problematic for people of color is the Eurocentric presumption that race could *never* have been the reason why an officer used deadly force. Such denial happens within hours (or a short time thereafter) of the use of deadly force by a white police officer against a person of color. The denial is always based on automatic, unquestionable deference for the authoritative (police) version of what happened—and preconceived notions held about a particular racial group. Additionally, it is "white privilege" that stands in the way of many white people realizing the Afrocentric version of what happened on the "scene." Moreover, where blacks are unwilling to pay automatic deference to an authoritative version, many whites, on the other hand, have no such problem.[15]

Again and again, lay people of color—supported by their own personal experiences, research findings of scholars of color, and expertise in the minority community—show how a police officer's actions were motivated by race. This conclusion is an understanding that all human beings carry sociological baggage. Within that baggage may be stereotypical or adverse perceptions about particular racial groups, for example. The Afrocentric perspective is that many individuals who have in their baggage race-based fear and animus are hired as police officers (to the detriment of visible minorities). This is a deserving indictment, indicative of inadequate recruitment and screening processes of many police departments. These departments have shirked their responsibility to use methods (and there are many) to determine the applicant's mind-set—essentially, to probe what he or she has in his or her sociological baggage concerning race. So, people of color have a right to be offended by a white professor's assertion about the shooting death of a black policeman by his white colleagues: "Even if these officers were both awful racists, it wouldn't matter. [What matters is] whether their conduct was objectively reasonable based on the totality of circumstance" (Breton, 2000, p. 8A).

This typical Eurocentric conclusion influences prosecutorial decisions about police brutality and the likelihood of criminal convictions when cases are prosecuted. It fails to take into account race-based fear and aversion manifested by the officer via recklessness and depraved indifference to human life (both of which are elements of crimes such as second-degree murder). Both the fear and aversion are unreasonable, but the aversion is especially a catalyst for the actions of the officer. The legal test is not whether a reasonable white police officer who has issues about black people would have shot. The test is whether a reasonable police officer in similar circumstances would have shot. But this is the Afrocentric perspective,[16] not the way that the status-quo scholars see things. This is why a white law professor says it should not matter if the officers were awful racists when it should. Although *Scott v. U.S.* (1978) is not a criminal case, the Court's holding gives direction to the thinking needed in assessing race-based police brutality: "Of course, in assessing the credibility of an officer's account of the circumstances that prompted the use of force, a fact finder may consider, along with other factors, evidence that the officer may have harbored ill will toward the citizen" (139, n. 13).

All human beings carry stereotypical notions. In determining an individual's fitness to be a police officer, the following measurements are important: the degree from the norm that his/her stereotypical perceptions extend and or deviate; the manner (reasonable versus unreasonable) in which he/she reacts to his/her sociological baggage; the ability to remain objective in the face of stereotypical perceptions; and the degree of ease with which he or she can dispel stereotypical notions. For critics to say, for example, that both black and white police officers are equally likely to mistake an undercover black officer for a suspect is, unfortunately, true. However, the critics fail miserably when they do not recognize the high likelihood that black officers would not shoot the suspect. The data show that black officers are *not* responsible for friendly fire that has wounded or killed black police officers. Even if it should happen one day, the sheer number of friendly-fire incidents involving white against black is overwhelming. These criteria should call attention to the dynamics of the social interaction between black plain-clothes cops and black uniformed cops as opposed to white–black cop interaction.

Shootings and Lowered Threshold

Is there a "shoot first, ask questions later" policy (a police subcultural norm) that applies when the citizen is black? The evidence certainly supports such a conclusion. One example taken from the vast evidence available is the recorded radio transmissions received by the Christopher Commission (1992) investigating police brutality by the Los Angeles Police Department following the Rodney King riots. One officer says to another: "If you encounter these Negroes shoot first and ask questions later." The commission goes on to say that "officers also used the communications system to express eagerness to be involved in a shooting incident" (pp. 4–5).

Said another way, the issue is whether some police officers dispense with protocol when interacting with people of color. From an Afrocentric perspective, many do. In other words, a white police officer sees a lone black man holding a gun. The man does not know of the officer's presence, hence the man is not threatening the officer. Instead of shouting to the man "police, drop the weapon" (or something to that effect) as protocol would require, the officer commences gunfire. If this sounds unbelievable in the post–*Tennessee v. Garner* (1985) era, there are countless such cases in communities of color. Of course, there is almost always a dispute between police and black citizens and blacks and whites as to whether protocol was ignored.

One such case is the death of Cornel Young, Jr. at the hands of his fellow police officers. It was a cold January night in 2000 when an off-duty Young (required by law to act when he observed a crime) attempted to apprehend a gun-toting suspect outside of a diner in Providence, Rhode Island. As Young was closing in on the suspect, he was shot to death by two white Providence police officers, who said they mistook their colleague for a suspect. Soon after, the two officers would tell a wild story of having instructed their fellow officer to drop his weapon six to seven times, but that he refused.[17]

In controversy are several things, one of which is whether the officers dispensed with protocol. Many black police officers, based on having been the victims of friendly fire (or "friendly" beatings) at the hands of fellow officers, coupled with their knowledge of police subcultural norms that encourage shooting blacks first and then asking questions, believe that the facts of the Young case do not give rise to a dispute.[18] For them, the officers dispensed with protocol. A grand jury in declining to indict the Providence officers held that the officers did not violate protocol. Notwithstanding acknowledgment that the grand jury proceedings were secret, the grand jurors obviously believed the officers when they said that they repeatedly ordered Young to drop his weapon and that Young refused.[19] Further, they accepted an authoritative (police) version that Young placed the officers in a position in which they feared for their lives. The Afrocentric perception is that Young's life was marginalized by the officers. After all, the officer who fired rounds at Young from within approximately fifteen feet had been Young's classmate in the academy. Additionally, the two men had worked together in a unit car for two weeks.[20]

Consider the statements of a white law school professor[21] who was asked about the actions of the two white police officers several days after the shooting. "They were doing their job. If they felt this guy was threatening the other people with a gun, their job is to protect people from the threat of harm" (Mingis, 2000, p. 1A). Unless new evidence emerges, she said, "there's no question in my mind that these officers would not be held liable for anything here" (Breton, 2000, p. 8A). On February 12, 2000, approximately 14 days following Young's death, a Providence Police Department official, Lieutenant Timothy M. Lee, said in a television interview that he believed the two white officers who shot Officer Young would be exonerated. The black community responded, appropriately, with anger. Finally realizing that the statement was presumptuous and racially offensive, the Providence Police Department issued a statement regarding Lee's statement: "The Providence Police Department regrets and specifically disavows any and all statements tending to express an opinion regarding the outcome of this case and is committed to a fair and impartial investigation" (Sabar, 2000, 1A).

People of color find the authoritative (police) version of the Young case suspicious because of many prior similar cases in which the police versions are almost identical. The officers who killed Young asserted the same thing that other white police officers who have killed black police officers (and people in general) have asserted: "I told him to drop the gun and he disobeyed my command." All of the authoritative reports regardless of the venue (from New York City to Los Angeles to Washington, D.C.) read almost identically (Duggan, 1995).

The Afrocentric perspective is that some police officers dispense with use of deadly force protocol via not shouting a command(s) or shouting a command(s) contemporaneously with firing their weapons. The latter is the likely explanation of how a Providence police officer died in a pool of his own blood one cold January night. Why Young died had everything to do with how his colleagues perceived black men (as dangerous) and the amount of policy they felt should be afforded to black men confronted by the police.

Police officers are in numerous situations in which they do not shoot, although the rules of deadly force allow them to shoot. There is evidence that many officers don't use the discretion that is expected of a police officer. Instead, they shoot according to the minimum criteria allowed for use of deadly force, knowing that the shooting will probably be ruled justified. Consider domestic calls-for-service (and the author can speak from considerable experience with such calls when he was a police officer). A cop with more than a month on the street knows that a woman who is abused by her boyfriend, husband, or another male may grab a knife to defend herself from her attacker. Seven out of ten times, she will drop the knife if the officers give her a chance—they don't need to shoot her! But many officers do. Decisions to punish or prosecute police officers usually don't consider that the officer did not have to shoot (McGriff, 1999).

Officers learn very early on in their police tenure that they will be exonerated when they state that their subjective state of mind was that they feared for their lives (or something to that effect). Officers are just as aware (as are civilians) that police officers are seldom if ever prosecuted for police brutality; if they are prosecuted, they are seldom convicted. Officers know that the prosecutor's investigations into use of deadly force rarely second guess what the officer says was his/her state of mind at the time. Even more problematic, officers know that the norms of the police subculture mean that fellow police officers are not supposed to "sell them out" (Reuss-Ianni, 1982). So, some officers, when dealing with people of color, shoot at the mere flicker of a green light from the deadly force policy. In many cases, this is abuse of the furtive gesture rule—a slight harmless movement by a citizen is known to be harmless by the officer, but the officer shoots since he/she knows that he/she can describe the movement as threatening.

This raises the issue of police shootings of black people who were not involved in criminal activity and did not initiate contact with the police. Two recent cases illustrate the concerns of people of color. First, Amadou Diallo was shot and killed February 4, 1999; the police say he refused their commands and then reached for what they say they believed was a gun. From an Afrocentric perspective, it is questionable whether he reached for anything. If he did reach for something, it was his wallet. Of particular importance is the fact that Diallo was approached by the police although he had not committed a crime. The police say that they wanted to ask him questions. A criminologist testified at the trial of the police officers who shot Amadou Diallo that the officers simply made a mistake. Following the trial, several jurors said that they were persuaded by the testimony (see Barry, 2000 and Barry and Waldman, 2000).

Another example was Patrick Dorismond, shot and killed March 16, 2000. He was hailing a taxi on a New York City street when he was approached by an undercover police officer posing as a drug user. The officer asked Dorismond where he could buy marijuana. Dorismond told the officer he could not assist him and continued to look for a taxi. A scuffle ensued when the officer became offended by Dorismond's rebuffing him. The officer's partner, standing nearby, shot Dorismond in the chest at point blank range (Alpert, 2000).

While black people know that many black victims of police gunfire were not criminals or committing a felony, the Eurocentric perspective believes otherwise. As an example, Fyfe (1982) states "there is little to support the contention that Blacks are shot disproportionately in relatively trivial and nonthreatening situations" (p. 190). This denial is contradicted by case after case.

There seems to be an unwritten criminal justice system rule that black victims of police brutality should know the protocol for interacting with the police (e.g., hands placed on the steering wheel; do not reach for anything unless instructed; etc.) This is an offensive and constitutionally invalid requirement. The Afrocentric perspective is that a person of color who does not know the protocol can expect that he or she may be harmed or even killed. Case in point, Latanya Haggerty, killed June 4, 1999, by a Chicago police officer. She was described by the Chicago Office of Corporation Council as causing her own death, because she did not behave as a suspect.[22] Had the unarmed, terrified Haggerty followed the expected protocol of exiting the vehicle when told to do so, she would be alive today.[23]

In an episode of the popular sitcom, *Fresh Prince of Bel-Air*, savvy, street-conscious, African-American Will Smith was visiting his cousin in a posh California community far away from urban Philadelphia. Smith was a passenger in a vehicle pulled over by the police. Without direction from the officer, Smith stepped outside of the automobile and assumed a spread-legged position at the rear of the vehicle. Smith's elitist cousin, Carlton, is baffled and unaware of the motivation for Smith's behavior. Carlton's not recognizing the unwritten rule is similar to Latanya Haggerty's tragic unawareness of the consequences of not responding in the "expected" manner or to Amadou Diallo, if the position is taken that Diallo wanted to show the officers his identification as is customarily done in the country in which he was raised.

There are many situations in which black people follow the unwritten rule and are shot and killed anyway. On Christmas Day, 1997, NYPD Officer Michael Davitt, who in fourteen years as a police officer had been involved in approximately eight shootings, shot and killed Michael Whitfield, an unarmed black man. Whitfield ran and hid in a grocery store when he saw police because he was afraid there was a warrant out for his arrest for not having paid child support. He was following police instructions coming out from behind a set of boxes with his arms outstretched when Davitt shot and killed him. Davitt was not terminated by the police department or charged criminally (McFadden, 1997).

In citizen–police interaction, body movements that are accepted from whites are not allowed for blacks. An otherwise harmless body movement by a person of color is suspicious, described as a furtive gesture. Furtive gestures by people of color are what many white officers say caused them to respond with gunfire. In response to learning of a death of a black person over a harmless gesture, the Eurocentric scholars and many prosecutors shirk their duty by classifying the use of force as a mistake. So, it is a gesture by a black person that warrants suspicion and use of deadly force, but that same movement by a white person invites no similar reaction. Something to consider: the Bronx district attorney who prosecuted the officers who killed Amadou Diallo, Robert Johnson, was black. How likely is it that a white district attorney would have brought charges against the officers?

For those cases of police brutality against black victims that make it to trial, stereotypical perceptions of minorities lead fact finders to blame the police brutality on the victim. Both Rodney King and Amadou Diallo, for example, were misrepresented as superhuman. King was said to have resisted with unbelievable strength; therefore, it was argued, the force was commensurate. Diallo was said to have contributed to his death by his body movements. Further, the defense characterized Diallo as remaining standing after a volley of bullets, so forty-one bullets were said to have been needed to "bring him down" and to protect the police and the "public." These xenophobic characterizations are often followed by problematic instructions to juries by the judge—problematic since they are riddled with victim-blaming suppositions. What should be judged a crime is reduced to a mistake or "terrible" happening. Avoidable, says the judicial system, had the victim not contorted his body, had not been recalcitrant, and had submitted to the police inquiry without questioning authority.

Investigations of Police

In the twenty-first century, police officers who patrol in a racially discriminatory manner have learned to conceal racial epithets. Police officers are cognizant of their speech because of the consequences of revealing racist attitudes; they know that epithets satisfy the elements of a hate crime. It is therefore difficult (but not impossible) for investigators and prosecutors to show that the officer engaged in behavior because of a racial aversion, for example.

Problematic is that even if the officers' actions were prompted by the race of the citizens, investigations into use of deadly force seldom if ever explore for race-based phenomena. Typically, investigations into use of deadly force by police involve a forensics analysis (e.g., ballistics) and eliciting the subjective state of mind of the officer at the time of the situation, according to the officer him/herself. What the officer declares was his or her subjective state of mind is almost always accepted without further inquiry. This is the principal problem. In every case, the officer will state, "I feared for my life" or something to that effect. Sadly, it is the script learned in the police academy (the author also learned it when he began police work but, like some other officers, rejected it as a universal). In some cases, the officer is being truthful, but in others the officer is to be doubted. But we won't find out if we don't fully investigate the officer's sociological baggage.

From an Afrocentric perspective, consideration must be given to the role that the norms of the police subculture play in a use of deadly force situation. A firm, conceptual understanding of the police literature and police subculture can offer a great deal of insight as to what happened on a scene. Both enable an investigator to ask the right questions and to know when to be suspicious of the answers.

Although the policing literature has its biases and problems as noted throughout this article, the policing literature has documented a great deal about the way that day-to-day police duties are performed and why particular actions occur (e.g., see Reuss-Ianni, 1982). Specifically, the literature has documented the inner workings of the police subculture. Take, for instance, the subcultural norm that "if you run from the poe-lice you get fucked-up."[24] (The videotaped beating of Thomas Jones by Philadelphia police in July 2000 is a vivid example of this phenomenon.[25]) When an investigator and/or prosecutor is faced with a case in which the victim/defendant says that a police officer kicked him in the face as he lay prone on the ground or that he ran out of fear after he saw a police car, the investigator or prosecutor should possess a willingness to investigate further. Police officers learn early in their career that people who run from the police are to be abused. To accept at face value the officer's account that the victim is lying, in the face of overwhelming documentation that there is a subcultural norm that calls for "street justice" when you run from the police, is to commit a more serious injustice and to demonstrate utter indifference coupled with ignorance of pragmatic reality. Even United States Supreme Court justices, in *Illinois v. Wardlow*,[26] acknowledge that minorities often run from the police—not because they committed a crime but because they have credible reasons to fear an encounter with police.

Cops talk with each other about how they take the legal use of force right to the edge. As a cop you learn how to create situations that are legally indecipherable (see Crank, 1998, p. 65), such as intentionally placing yourself in front of an automobile so a fear of loss-of-life claim can be made. For investigators and prosecutors to get a clear sense of what happened at scenes where an officer said that the victim tried to run him or her over, they need to consider this phenomenon.[27] It is a pattern that an investigator will recognize if he/she looks at similar cases and examines police subcultural norms. Having discovered the pattern, he/she can see if the code dictated when and in what manner force was likely employed in the situation under investigation. No doubt, no two scenes are alike; however, pattern and practice (based on past scenes) suggest what questions to ask and what suspicions to maintain.

Other subcultural norms include "dead men tell no tales." Once you have shot and wounded a man, you are supposed "to put a cap in him"—otherwise he will sue you or file a complaint against you (the officer) littered with falsities. This norm is relevant to an investigator's toolbox, since a common problem with prosecuting police officers for "bad shootings" is that of being able to rebut effectively the officer's explanation as to why he or she shot a person. In this regard, the police subculture has a script already prepared to handle bad shootings. It includes, first and foremost, asserting that you feared for your life or something to that effect. It is followed by one of these primary assertions: (1) he tried to run me over with his car; (2) he pointed a gun at me; (3) he lunged at me with a knife. There is a cartoon that is passed out in police locker rooms that is referred to as the "Police Shooting Report Checklist," which includes the aforementioned choices.

Consider perhaps the most popular script and falsity: "he tried to run me over." In December 1998, a Pittsburgh police officer was arrested and charged with the murder of Deon Grimmitt, an unarmed black male. The officer, who was alleged to belong to a white supremacist group, became upset when Mr. Grimmitt slowed down his vehicle to observe the police making an arrest. The officer asserted that he wanted to question Grimmitt about his interest and that when he approached the automobile, Grimmitt tried to run him over. The autopsy revealed that Grimmitt had been shot in the head through a side window. Even with this information, the officer was acquitted at trial. In 1999 Louisville police shot Rudolph Desmond, an African American, as he sat inside an incapacitated automobile. Yet, the officers, who were white, said Desmond attempted to run them over. In Saint Louis in June 2000, two white police officers approached two black men in a vehicle. The officers shot and killed both men and claimed that the victims tried to run them over. In July 2000, a white Omaha police officer shot and killed George Bibbins, an unarmed black man who took police on an eight-minute car chase. Bibbins was shot as he sat inside the vehicle after it crashed into a telephone pole.

These cases are just the tip of the iceberg of an epidemic of officers shooting—not because they are justified, but because they know they can most likely get away with it. In the Louisville case, some law enforcement personnel publicly expressed doubt about the officers' claims.[28] In the Omaha case, the police chief, who is white, stated publicly that he couldn't pinpoint a reason why the officer shot George Bibbins. The chief stated, "As we indicated, there are concerns about what happened. We can't put our finger on the justification."

The fact that "he tried to run me over" claims sometimes make it to a grand jury is not much solace to communities of color. Many prosecutors act as gatekeepers to protect officers from prosecution for police brutality. They intentionally present facts to grand juries in such a way that the grand jurors will find that the officers acted properly. In other words, the rash of grand jury declinations to indict in police brutality cases in the United States where the officers are white and the victims are black or Latino is indicative of many prosecutors who "throw the fight."

It is not by accident or simply the result of rehearsal that the testimony of the officers indicted for killing Amadou Diallo was virtually identical (whether you believe that the officers acted properly or improperly in the shooting). *New York Times* reporters Dan Barry and Amy Waldman (2000) wrote "prosecutors have . . . encountered a blue wall . . . [in] which officers used almost identical language to defend their actions" (p. B1). Familiarity with the subculture socialization process should alert the investigator not just to what the defendant officer will say at trial but also to what really happened at the scene. The Code provides trial preparation long before any action takes place. Because many prosecutors know little to nothing about the premeditation for police brutality that the police subculture provides, they are not aware of the need to be suspicious. There are prosecutors who do know about and accept the premeditation perversion, yet do nothing, while others refuse to believe that it exists. The result is unchecked, egregious human rights violations.

STAKEHOLDERS EXCLUDED

There is no other racial group in the United States that has been policed as long as and as much as people of African descent (cf., Dulaney 1996). Initially, it was the phenomenon of organized policing to maintain slavery. Over time, it became policing of black people and those classes considered unpopular for the benefit of the upper-middle, wealthy, and elite classes (Niederhoffer, 1969; Fogelson, 1981). It has always been the contention of the wealthy that the police may use whatever means necessary to keep the unpopular classes from interrupting the "flow" of their quality of life. This explains how a bombing of a church by the Ku Klux Klan in 1968 in which four children were killed ("Six Dead . . . ," 1963) did not shock many Americans who were not of color. Or that a California sheriff's deputy, Jeffrey Coates, in 1999 candidly told a journalist that he has one traffic-stop protocol for whites and another for black and Latino males. He says that he orders black or Latino males out of their automobiles and has them place their hands on the roof of the police cruiser; however, whites receive the mainstream treatment, no need to exit the automobile or stand hunched over. Even worse, the deputy killed a black man in 1998, admits to racial profiling, and like other officers in his unit, wears a "Grim Reaper" tattoo on his ankle—this is the insignia worn by white police officers signifying membership in a white supremacist gang (Goldberg, 1999). The fact that Coates is still employed by the Los Angeles Sheriff's Department is appalling to black and Latino people, but apparently to few white people.

The lack of concern expressed by whites about illegal and brutal policing practices in black communities has meant that the burden of raising awareness and pushing for change (justice) has been undertaken almost entirely by black police organizations, black elected officials, and scholars who are people of color.[29] Racial profiling, for example, now has a national forum not because of efforts by white policy researchers or police department self-analysis, but because of efforts by people of color themselves. This fact contributes to why black people are unavoidably connected to just about every facet of U.S. policing, both internal and external. One would think and expect that black people would have a role in the creation and implementation of police policy. Yet, black people are routinely excluded from discussion about these matters by: (1) white scholars, (2) media outlets, and (3) government.

The status-quo scholars hold themselves out to the media and policy makers as authorities on what is best for policing black communities. It is not uncommon to see a talk-show panel of all white people talking about police–black community relations on the heels of a violent encounter between a white police officer and a black citizen. In some cases, under pressure, the media will concede and invite a black panelist. Unfortunately, they often invite a black panelist who is an authority on certain subject matter but not necessarily on that which is the focus of the news television program. This discredits Afrocentric concerns and positions. For example, black clergy are experts who rightfully and often spearhead battles for social justice. However, it is disingenuous to include them with a white police scholar (Ph.D.) on a program about policing phenomena from a scientific or research perspective. By all appearances, it is media that are either indifferent (because of "racial privilege") or maliciously trying to portray an image of black "position/perspective" ineptness. If a person were to step off of a spaceship, never having been to earth, on the heels of a violent encounter between a white police officer and a black person, that alien would never know that there is one black Ph.D. or expert in this country, since typically the guests (experts) selected by the media are almost always white.[30]

Scholars of color are often excluded by their status-quo colleagues in discourse (e.g., debates, studies, dialogue) concerning police tragedies involving black victims. Consider that status-quo scholars are often given the authority and responsibility to form the commissions, and other investigatory or oversight bodies, that are concerned with policing phenomena. They decide who is appointed and who is not appointed or who will be appointed as a consultant and who will not. In some cases, commission appointments are not the responsibility of the status-quo scholars, but their influence is felt. Not surprisingly then, commissions and committees established to investigate poor community relations between black residents and the police (e.g., the Christopher Commission) are almost always headed by whites and comprised of whites. The Select Commission on Race and Police-Community Relations in Providence, established in 2000 on the heels of Cornel Young's death, is among the few commissions truly representative of all the people affected by an issue.[31]

Many white scholars deserve criticism because they do not take responsibility for calling media attention to the lack of racial diversity on a panel, for example. Status-quo reluctance to advocate for inclusion is most evident in the refusal to acknowledge how privilege[32] has enabled status-quo scholars to be the focus of the media or government in the establishment of a commission. They refuse to alert the media and policy makers to the need for black voices in talking about policing phenomena affecting black people.

Publishing also deserves criticism. This is evident by a vast amount of published work on policing black communities, little of which is written by black people. Publishing companies appear to be indifferent to the need for publications written by blacks on the subject of policing.

CONCLUSION

When talking about policing in the United States, there are two very different audiences. What white citizens find implausible or hard to believe is everyday experience for black people. Hence, it was no surprise to black people to learn in 1992 that a New Orleans Police officer had a mother of two murdered because she filed a complaint against him for police brutality. Fortunately, the officer's telephone call to the "hit man" was tape-recorded by federal law enforcement officers who were investigating the officer pursuant to another matter (Nossiter, 1994). Without incontrovertible evidence (the tape recording), the tendency to believe officer denials might well have allowed him to escape punishment. The officer is presently awaiting execution for the murder.

It is the personal and collective experiences of black people with police officers and other people of color that enables these minorities to understand without the aid of videotaped footage, or knowledge of a victim's feces on a broken broomstick (the Louima case), or hearing a tape-recorded call to a hit man that a law enforcement officer committed an inhumane act of brutality. Few visible minorities in the United States can speak of not having experienced nor having been an eyewitness to a police action that many white people would claim the police would never do.

Consider the outlandishness of blanket statements by some police administrators that their officers don't engage in racial profiling or that their officers would never behave in a racially discriminatory manner. These statements are made by people who do not spend eight hours a day riding around with their police officers, yet they make assertions that suggest that they know their officers' every move. It was refreshing to people of color when two New Jersey state troopers explained how they regularly engaged in racial profiling. Governor Christine Todd Whitman was left with no choice but to acknowledge the Afrocentric perspective. She retracted her statements that racial profiling didn't happen in New Jersey.[33]

The reality is that policing is just one microcosm in the scheme of life. In life there is racism. Some of those who choose to manifest their biases are police officers. It is not so far-fetched that a police officer would shoot and kill a man simply because the man is a person of color. From an Afrocentric perspective, there is more than enough reason in twenty-first-century United States for status-quo scholars to refrain from giving automatic deference to authoritative versions of encounters between black people and the police. For the Eurocentric/status-quo scholar not to consider seriously that the system may have erred greatly in hiring an officer who acted out of racial animus is to display the highest level of "white privilege" and ignorance.

Notes

[1] cf. Dulaney, 1996.

[2] Fogelson, a historian rather than a police sociologist, presents an Afrocentric perspective. He says of race riots that gripped the nation in the 1960s, ". . . some of the blue-ribbon commissions appointed to look into the disorders issued reports that placed much of the blame on the local police" (Fogelson, 1977, p. 240).

[3] While Niederhoffer can be categorized as friendly to people of color by his exposition of police work phenomena, there are times when his opinions show otherwise.

[4] The article is reprinted in this volume, article 20.

[5] Article 21 in this collection.

[6] Van Slyke and Gordo. 1999. The Web site is www.PONetwork.com.

[7] Serrano, 1991; Tobar and Connell, 1991.

[8] See Marriott, 1995. Marriott writes, "Mark Fuhrman has expressed his racial hatred so bluntly that he may become a foil for the racism of others."

[9] Reasons include that policy makers who commissioned the research do not want to know the extent of police brutality.

[10] cf. Troutt, 1999; Prial, 1987.

[11] Chevigny's 1969 findings that many officers will legitimatize their actions in police reports via reporting falsely are still timely. He called attention to the practice of catchall offenses (e.g., resisting arrest and disorderly conduct) for which citizens are charged following having been brutalized. This author (Cooper) learned early on in his police tenure that officers who brutalized people were supposed to find something to charge them with in order to justify the beating. Often that charge was disorderly conduct.

[12] Defined as only a few aberrant police officers who engage in police brutality.

[13] See Kappeler, et al., 1998, pp. 272–275 for a discussion of this case.

[14] cf. Sontag and Barry, 1997.

[15] See June 17, 1999, Quinnipiac College Polling Institute Poll, which found that whites and minorities are sharply divided in their views of police brutality.

[16] and, the perspective of other people of color.

[17] See Marion Davis, 2000; Rockoff, 2000, "Officer."

[18] See Rockoff, 2000, "Grand jury."

[19] Since normally a prosecutor can get a grand jury to do whatever he or she wants it to do, one can safely assume that the prosecutor(s) in the Young case did not desire that the officers be indicted.

[20] See Rockoff, 2000, "How it all happened."

[21] Why Karen Blum was interviewed is puzzling, since she has never been a police officer and she is not a police scholar.

[22] See Lithty and Wilson, 1999; Lithty, 1999.

[23] The shooter of Haggerty was a black female officer. This tragedy has no indications that it was connected to race-based fear, animus, or marginalization, rather, the perception by the officer that Haggerty should have known "how the game is played," because she was black.

[24] As a rookie, the author remembers having to witness these violent attacks. These were vicious attacks that were almost always followed by a false arrest for disorderly conduct. It wasn't long before I started pulling officers off of people.

[25] See Cooper, 2000. Recall that the police said that Jones fled from officers and shot an officer. It turned out that Jones fled, but he did not shoot an officer, rather an officer shot another officer in the hand.

[26] *Illinois v. Wardlow*: No. 98–1036 (full opinion not yet in print); see dissent opinion by Justice Breyer.

[27] See McGriff (1999) for a report on the *Hood* case in which the Philadelphia P.D. said that its officer had lied.

[28] See Zambroski, et al, 2000. In this case, the nine-page police investigation noted numerous instances in which the officers who killed Rudolph committed tactical errors. When asked if the shooting could have been avoided, the lead investigator said, "One could come to that conclusion." A grand jury was convened and voted along racial lines. Since there were fewer blacks than whites, the grand jury voted not to indict. Even with the incriminating report, the officers were given medals of valor for shooting Rudolph.

[29] E.g., The National Black Police Association (NBPA) advocates for black police officers and represents the interests of the black community with regard to policing issues.

[30] The media must take some blame, for it is not uncommon for them to seek out white expertise when they know of qualified black people. The author is reminded of hearing so many times from the media that they didn't know where to find an African American to participate in the panel discussion.

[31] See Karen Davis, 2000, p. A1.

[32] That of being Caucasian or Caucasian in appearance for others.

[33] See Peterson, 1999; Peterson writes: "Gov. Christine Todd Whitman and her Attorney General conceded today for the first time that some state troopers singled out black and Hispanic drivers on the highway" (p. 1A).

References

Alex, N. (1976). *New York cops talk back: A study of a beleaguered minority.* New York: John Wiley & Sons.

Alpert, L. I. (2000, March 25). Funeral of Patrick Dorismond ends in violence. *Associated Press.*

Barry, D. (2000, February 27). Diallo Legacy: Myriad Questions About Tactics for Policing Streets. *New York Times*, p. A1.

Barry, D., & Waldman, A. (2000, February 22). Erecting a blue wall of silence. *New York Times*, p. B1.

Breton, T. (2000, February 8). Experts: Criminal charges against officers unlikely. *Providence Journal*, p. 8A.

Brown, M. (1981). *Working the street: Police discretion and the dilemmas of reform.* New York: Russell Sage Foundation.

Carte, G. E., & Carte, E. H. (1975). *Police reform in the United States: The era of August Vollmer, 1905–1932.* Berkeley: University of California Press.

Chandler, G. F. (1974). *The policeman's art as taught in the New York State School for Police.* New York: AMS Press.

Chevigny, P. (1969). *Police power: Police abuses in New York City.* New York: Vintage.

Cohen, A. (2000, March 6). Gangsta cops: As the LAPD scandal keeps growing, a city asks itself, how could the police have gone so bad? *Time Magazine*, pp. 30–34.

Cooper, C. (2000, July 21). Entrenched subculture is at root of police brutality and bias cases. *Philadelphia Inquirer*, p. A27.

Cooper, C. (1995, October 6). The O. J. Simpson trial and rotten apples: Academics are to blame for the neglect of police racism unmasked by the O. J. Simpson trial. *Times Higher Education Supplement* (London), p. 12

Cooper, J. L. (1980). *The police and the ghetto.* Port Washington, NY: Kennikat Press.

Crank, J. P. (1998). *Understanding police culture.* Cincinnati: Anderson Publishing.

Christopher Commission. (1992, July). *Report of the Independent Commission on the Los Angeles Police Department.* City of Los Angeles.

Davis, K. A. (2000, May 4). Board chosen to explore police-minority relations: Almond picks URI scholar to lead panel. *Providence Journal*, p. A1.

Davis, M. (2000, January 30). Friendly fire victims haunt fellow police. *Providence Journal*, p. A1.

Duggan, P. (1995, February 14). Praise and tears for officer slain in the line of duty: DC leaders laud dedication of policeman shot by colleague. *Washington Post*, p. E1.

Dulaney, M. (1996). *Black police in America.* Bloomington: Indiana University Press.

Fogelson, R. M. (1977). *Big-city police.* Cambridge, MA and London, England: Harvard University Press.

Fyfe, J. J., ed. (1982). *Readings on police use of deadly force.* Washington, DC: Police Foundation.

Fyfe, J. J. (1995). "Training to Reduce Police-Civilian Violence." In *And justice for all: Understanding and controlling police abuse of force.* William Geller and Hans Toch, (Eds.), Washington, DC: Police Executive Research Forum.

Goldberg, J. (1999, June 20). The color of suspicion. *New York Times Magazine*, 51–57, 64–65, 85–86.

Kappeler, V. E., Slader, R. D., & Alpert, Geoffrey P. (1998). *Forces of deviance*, 2d ed. Prospect Heights, IL: Waveland Press.

Kelling, G. L. (1997/1999). Efforts to reduce police brutality should not interfere with effective crime control. In T. L. Roleff (Ed.), *Police brutality* (pp. 48–51). San Diego: Greenhaven Press.

The Knapp Commission report on police corruption. (1973). New York: George Braziller.

Lane, R. (1967). *Policing the city: Boston 1822–1905*. Cambridge: Harvard University Press.

Lithty, T. (1999, September 2). City plays both sides in killing by officer. *Chicago Tribune*, p. 1.

Lithty, T., & Wilson, T. (1999, July 13). Cop chief moves to fire 4. *Chicago Tribune*, p. 1.

Marriott, M. (1995, September 3). Race lies & audiotape. *New York Times*, p. D4.

McFadden, R. (1997, December 27). After man is slain by officer, anger and calls for patience. *New York Times*, p. B1.

McGriff, M. (1999, May 28). Officer on patrol awaiting disciplinary hearing. *Philadelphia Tribune*, p. 3A.

McNamara, J.D. (1982, May 2). Dangerous nostalgia for the cop on the beat. *San Jose Mercury News*.

Mingis, K. (2000, January 28). Off-duty Providence police officer shot, killed by 2 other officers. *Providence Journal*, p. 1A.

Monkkonen, E. H. (1981). *Police in urban America 1860–1920*. Cambridge: Cambridge University Press.

Moore, M. H., & Kelling, G. L. (1983). To serve and protect: Learning from police history: *The public interest*, 70, 49–65.

Murr, A., (2000, June 12). "A murder in the family," *Newsweek*, p. 64.

Niederhoffer, A. (1969). *Behind the shield: The police in urban society*. Garden City, NY: Doubleday.

Nyden, P., Figert, A., Shibley, M., and Burrows, D. (1997). *Building community: Social science in action*. Thousand Oaks, CA: Pine Forge.

Nossiter, A. (1994, December 19). Officer linked to killing shocking a jaded city. *New York Times*, p. A14.

Olmsted, F. L. (1860). *A journey in the back country*. New York: Mason Brothers.

Peterson, I. (1999, April 21). Whitman says troopers used racial profiling. *New York Times*, p. 1A.

Prial, F. (1987, February 27). Judge acquits Sullivan in shotgun slaying of Bumpurs. *New York Times*, p. B1.

Quinnipiac College Polling Institute Poll. (1999, June). Hampden, CT: Quinnipiac College.

Reuss-Ianni, E. (1982). *Two cultures of policing*. Englewood Cliffs, NJ: Transaction.

Rockoff, J. (2000, April 19). Grand jury clears officers in Young's shooting death. *Providence Journal*, p. 1A.

Rockoff, J. (2000, February 3). How it all happened: A diner fight escalates, an officer is killed. *Providence Journal*, p. 1A.

Rockoff, J. (2000, January 29). Officer involved in peer's death had shot and wounded before. *Providence Journal*, p. 1A.

Sabar, A. (2000, February 12) The death of Sergeant Cornel Young, Jr.; The protest continues: Young's father joins call for outside probe. *Providence Journal*, p. 1A.

Serrano, R.A. (1991, July 10). Chief refuses to step down, defends police. *Los Angeles Times*, p. A1.

Sontag, D., & Barry, D. (1997, September 17). Using settlements to gauge police abuse: The price of brutality. *New York Times*, p. A1.

Sparrow, M., Moore, M. H., & Kennedy, D. M. (1990). *Beyond 911: A new era for policing*. New York: Basic Books.

Stoddard, E. R. (1968). The informal "code" of police deviancy: A group approach to "blue-coat crime." *The Journal of Criminal Law, Criminology and Police Science, 59*(2), 201–213.

Tobar, H., & Connell, R. (1991, July 10). Gates defends police at fiery council meeting; Violence: Commission gets briefing on charter provisions that could be used to discipline the chief. *Los Angeles Times*, p. A1.

Troutt, D. D. (1999). Screws, koon, and routine aberrations: The use of fictional narratives in federal police brutality prosecutions. *New York University Law Review, 74*, 18–122.

Six dead after church bombing: Blast kills four children; riots follow; two youths slain; state reinforces Birmingham police. (1963, September 16). *United Press International*.

Van Slyke, T., & Gordo, D. (1999, September). Controversial Web site vents Cops' fears, anger. *Chicago Reporter*, pp. 3,4.

Wade, R. (1964). *Slavery in the cities: The south, 1820–1860*. New York: Oxford University Press.

Walker, S. (1984). "Broken windows" and fractured history: The use and misuse of history in recent patrol analysis. *Justice Quarterly, 1*, 57–90.

Wilson, J. Q., & Kelling, G. L. (1982, March). The police and neighborhood safety: Broken windows. *Atlantic Monthly, 249*(3), 29–38.

Zambroski, J., Shafer, S. S., & Tangonan, S. (2000, March 3). Louisville police chief fired. *The Courier Journal*, p. 1.

Cases

Scott v. U.S. 436 U.S. 128 (1978)
Tennessee v. Garner 471 U.S. 1 (1985)
Illinois v. Wardlow 528 U.S. 119 (2000)

Women Officers on the Move

Susan E. Martin

For more than half a century after the acceptance of the first sworn female officer in 1910, women in policing were selected according to separate criteria from men, employed as "policewomen," and limited to working with "women, children, and typewriters" (Milton, 1972). It was only in 1972, with the passage of the 1972 Amendments to the Civil Rights Act of 1964, that women officers obtained the right to an equal opportunity in a law enforcement career. Since that date, many departments, often under court order, have eliminated discriminatory personnel policies. Despite these recent changes, however, women officers still face a variety of barriers to full occupational integration. This article examines: (1) the changes that have occurred in the status of women in policing in the past two decades; (2) the nature of the resistance of male officers to women in policing and the problems the women officers face as a result; and (3) current research and policy issues related to women in policing.

Evidence of Change in Police Personnel Practices

Since 1972 many of the discriminatory practices that restricted the selection and deployment of women in policing have been eliminated and the number of female officers has grown. How adequate is the pace of change? Price (1982) asserts that the sexual integration of policing has not kept pace with changes in other male-dominated occupations, using the example of the

Prepared especially for *Critical Issues in Policing* by Susan E. Martin.

increase of women law students from 8 percent in 1970 to 32 percent in 1980. Similarly, Reskin and Roos (1990), examining changes in occupational sex segregation between 1970 and 1988, categorized police work along with many blue-collar and craft jobs as those where women made disproportionately little headway. Fyfe, on the other hand, asserts that the changes in policing have been so dramatic that "the traditional view of policing as a nearly exclusive white male occupation is quickly becoming outmoded . . . (in) virtually every population category and geographic region" (1987:10). Moreover, 98 percent of the municipal departments serving populations greater than 50,000 had women officers assigned to field operations (patrol) units (Martin 1990).

Growth in the Number of Women Officers

The available evidence presents a mixed picture; there has been slow but steady growth in numbers of women officers and supervisors nationwide and an expansion of their assignments into all aspects of policing. Nevertheless, women continue to be significantly underrepresented in police work according to data collected annually by the FBI since 1970. In 1971, prior to the change in the civil rights law, women comprised only 1.4 percent of the sworn personnel in municipal departments and 2.7 percent of the officers in suburban agencies. By 1975 they constituted 2.2 percent of the municipal personnel, with the largest increases occurring in departments with populations between 250,000 and 1,000,000 (U.S. F.B.I. 1976). As shown in table 1, the proportion of women among all sworn officers in municipal agencies was 3.8 in 1980, 6.2 in 1985, 8.3 in 1990, 9.3 in 1994, and 11.2 in 2001. Figures for suburban county agencies are 8.1, 9.7, 11.3, 11.4, and 12.9, respectively. Thus, during approximately the past two decades, the proportion of women officers has grown steadily (except in rural counties), with the greatest increases occurring in the larger cities. The representation of women in suburban agencies also grew, so that proportions were similar in city and suburban departments. However, women's representation in cities with a population of less than 100,000 lags behind more densely populated areas. Similarly, women constituted only 4.2 percent of sworn state police personnel in 1987, 4.6 percent in 1990 (3.9 percent of whom were white), and 12.5 percent (9.1 percent of whom were white) in 2000 (U.S. Department of Justice 1992, 2000).

Data on the race, rank, and assignment of officers by sex until the latter part of the twentieth century has been "shockingly limited" (Walker 1985). Studies by the Bureau of Justice Statistics reported the race/ethnicity and sex of sworn local police for the years 1993 and 2000. As shown in table 2, in 1993 white women comprised 5.7 percent of sworn police personnel, black women 2.2 percent, and women of other ethnic groups less than one percent. By 2000, there had been a modest increase in these percentages, with the greatest for white women. Looking at the ratio of women to men from each of the racial/ethnic groups, however, the table indicates that black women made up 19 percent of black sworn personnel in 1993 (which increased to 23 percent in 2000). In 1993, women comprised only 11 percent of Hispanic and 7 percent of other ethnic sworn personnel. In 2003, these percentages were 12 and 11 percent respectively, thus reflecting a greater increase in women who were of other racial/ethnic backgrounds.

Data on the number of officers above the entry-level officer rank indicate that women's representation among supervisory personnel increased from less than 1 percent in 1978 to 3.3 percent of all supervisors in municipal agencies by the end of 1986 (including 2.3 percent white and 1 percent nonwhite women). Their representation decreases as one moves up the ranks; 3.7 percent of the sergeants, 2.5 percent of the lieutenants, and 1.4 percent of supervisory personnel of a higher rank are women (Martin 1990). According to a survey of the departments in the nation's 50 largest cities, women comprised 7.1 percent of supervisors, including 4.8 percent white women and 1.8 percent black women (Walker and Martin 1994). The fact that the proportion of women supervisors lags behind that of all personnel is not surprising since supervisors are selected from entry-level officers who are eligible for promotion after several years of service.

In sum, the statistics indicate both good news and bad news. On the one hand, women have made steady numerical and proportional gains in law enforcement agencies in all parts of the country. On the other hand, they still comprise only a "token" (Kanter 1977) proportion of all sworn police personnel and, like women in law and management,[1] are concentrated at the bottom of the police hierarchy but are virtually invisible in high-level administrative posts. Although women were promoted to sergeant at a rate

Table I   Percentage of Women Employed as Sworn Officers

	Year				
	1980[1]	1985[2]	1990[3]	1994[4]	2001[5]
Total Cities	3.8	6.2	8.3	9.3	11.2
Cities with pop. > 250,000	4.6	8.6	12.6	14.2	16.3
Cities with pop. 100,000–249,999	4.2	6.6	8.2	9.2	10.9
Cities with pop. 50,000–99,999	3.1	4.5	6.2	6.9	8.6
Cities with pop. 25,000–49,999	3.0	4.0	5.1	6.0	7.7
Cities with pop. 10,000–24,999	2.9	3.8	4.3	5.2	6.8
Cities with pop. < 10,000	3.2	4.7	5.5	6.4	7.8
Suburban Counties	8.1	9.7	11.3	11.4	12.9
Rural Counties	9.9	5.7	6.3	7.0	8.1

[1] Source: U.S. Federal Bureau of Investigation, 1981.
[2] Source: U.S. Federal Bureau of Investigation, 1986.
[3] Source: U.S. Federal Bureau of Investigation, 1991.
[4] Source: U.S. Federal Bureau of Investigation, 1995.
[5] Source: U.S. Federal Bureau of Investigation, 2002.

Table 2   Race, Ethnicity, and Sex of Full-Time Sworn Personnel in Local Police Departments, 1993 and 2000[1]

Race/Ethnicity	1993[2]			2000[3]		
	Total	Male	Female	Total	Male	Female
White	80.9%	75.2%	5.7%	77.4%	70.9%	6.5%
Black	11.3	9.1	2.2	11.7	9.0	2.7
Hispanic	6.2	5.5	.7	8.3	7.2	1.1
Other	1.5	1.4	.1	2.7	2.4	.3
Total	100.0%	91.2%	8.7%	100.0%	89.5%	10.6%

[1] Percents may not add to total because of rounding.
[2] Source: B. A. Reaves, 1996.
[3] Source: Bureau of Justice Statistics, 2003.

slightly higher than might be expected based on their representation among those eligible, the pace of their movement into supervisory ranks suggests that women are not likely to assume departmental policy-making positions for many years.

Changing Eligibility and Selection Criteria

The increase in female representation in policing is clearly related to the development of a substantial body of law requiring nondiscrimination on the basis of sex in terms and conditions of employment. More than thirty years ago police departments were brought under this legal edifice through the Equal Employment Opportunity Act of 1972 (amending Title VII of the Civil Rights Act of 1964), the Crime Control Act of 1973, the State and Local Government Fiscal Assistance Act of 1976, numerous state equal rights and fair employment practices laws and have been evolving case law in interpreting these laws.

Much litigation has been related to height and weight standards that eliminated most women and many Hispanics from eligibility for policing. Departments' failure to substantiate their claims that height is predictive of or correlated with superior job performance and the finding that there is no correlation between height and performance (White and Bloch, 1975) led courts to rule that the physical standards must be proved to be job relevant and necessary to safe and efficient job performance. In most cases such proof has been lacking. Consequently, differential height and weight eligibility requirements for male and female police applicants have been virtually eliminated since 1972. By 1979 only 23 percent of the departments surveyed by Sulton and Townsey (1981) retained any height and weight requirements for admission; by 1986 Fyfe (1987) found only 3.5 percent of the responding departments had minimum height standards (mean = 63.7 inches) and 3.7 percent had minimum weight standards (mean = 135.3 pounds).

Selection criteria also have changed. Most police departments use several criteria for selecting eligible candidates. These include a written examination, an oral interview, a psychological examination, a physical agility test, and a background check. Formerly, most female candidates were eliminated by the physical agility test and oral interview. The extent to which otherwise quali- fied women are screened out by the oral interview is unknown. The potential for bias is great unless interviewers are carefully screened, trained, and pro- vided with structured interview formats. Increasingly, however, departments have moved toward structuring and standardizing the interview process as lawsuits have prohibited arbitrary practices. By 1981 Sulton and Townsey observed that oral interviews no longer appeared to disproportionately elimi- nate women candidates in large urban departments.

Physical agility tests have been a source of much litigation, due to differ- ences between men and women in strength and agility, and the job related- ness of many of these tests has been questioned. The proportion of departments that use physical performance tests to assess fitness increased from 58 percent of responding agencies in 1982 to 76 percent in 1986 (Fyfe 1987:7). In 2000, 44 percent of local police departments used physical agility tests to select new officers (Bureau of Justice Statistics, 2003); most agencies changed the tests to conform with the law, which prohibits such tests from eliminating a disproportionate number of women (unless such tests can be shown to be reasonably job related and have a valid purpose). In *Harless v. Duck* [1619 F.2d 611(1980)], for example, the court found that the physical agility test under question was invalid under Title VII, stating:

> Defendant did not meet their burden of proving that the test was valid and job-related. First, the job analysis does not specifically define the amount of physical strength required or the extent of physical exertion required. Second, the same type of tests never have been validated. Third, there is no justification in the record for the type of exercises chosen or the passing marks for each exercise.

Based on a survey of 246 municipal departments serving populations over 50,000, Martin (1990) found that 20 percent of the applicants were women; virtually the same proportion of those accepted (20.6 percent) and completing training (19.2) were women. Thus it appears that there is not systematic bias in the selection process; however, the wide variation among departments, in the proportion of applicants that were female and in the proportion of those women that were accepted, suggests that the recruitment and selection prac- tices may favor women in some agencies and disadvantage them elsewhere. Furthermore, one of the factors that significantly reduced the rate at which women applied for police positions and at which those female applicants were accepted was the presence of a pretraining physical agility test.

Evaluations of Women's Performance

Many of the barriers to equal opportunity for women in policing were based on the belief that women could not adequately perform in the basic police role as patrol officers. In the early 1970s, as legal pressures to assign women to patrol mounted, nine evaluation studies of women on patrol were conducted in departments widely divergent in size and geographical location.[2]

In all but the second phase of the Philadelphia evaluation, the evaluators concluded that women officers were equally effective as comparison males in performing patrol duties. At the same time, the studies found some gender differences in performance that have implications for policing and found that male officers and supervisors tended to hold negative attitudes toward women officers. They noted that women were less aggressive, made fewer arrests, issued fewer traffic tickets, and were less likely to be involved in serious conduct unbecoming to an officer. The studies also found that the public was equally satisfied with male and female officers but that male supervisors rated the women as less effective than comparison men in handling violent situations. These nine studies undermined arguments that women are unable to perform patrol work adequately and that sex is a bona fide occupational qualification under Title VII. Consequently, they also contributed to the increased hiring of women officers.

A review of these evaluations (Morash and Greene, 1986) pointed out that despite findings generally favorable to women, gender biases were inherent in their evaluation designs. Most notable was the emphasis on traits stereotypically associated with "maleness" despite the lack of empirical evidence that the qualities evaluated were related to critical tasks performed by police. The study also indicated that there was a skewed sample of policing situations, two-thirds of which related to direct or potential violence, even though such incidents are far from frequent. In addition, the reports tended to assume that gender differences were the result of psychological or biological differences rather than the differences in the social experiences of the women officers in a workplace characterized by male officers' negative reactions to them. Although most studies observed differences in the treatment of the male and female officers and negative attitudes expressed by male officers and supervisors, they did not examine the intensity of these negative experiences nor consider their impact on women's performance.

Where the studies found differences in men's and women's behavior they did not consider the possibility that the women's style in resolving conflicts and disputes might have had a beneficial rather than a negative effect. For example, the women's lower arrest rates might mean that women were not taking enough initiative. Alternatively, it might indicate that women handled the situations better than male officers, if the latter caused incidents to escalate into confrontations that resulted in unnecessary arrests. A third explanation is that when a more experienced male patrolled with a female rookie, he tended to take charge of the situation and take credit for arrests more frequently than with male rookies. Thus, it is necessary to look beyond the numbers to an interpretation of their meaning.

BARRIERS TO THE INTEGRATION OF WOMEN INTO POLICING

The barriers to women in policing emanate from the structural characteristics of the occupation and the work organization, and the ways that cultural mandates and behavioral norms related to gender shape interpersonal interaction in specific occupational contexts.

Cultural and Structural Barriers to Gender Integration

In a study of men and women employed in corporations, Kanter (1977) suggests that occupational behavior is shaped by three key structural features of the organization and the individuals' position in it: the opportunity structure, the power structure, and relative numbers. These variables constrain and shape possibilities for action and press people to adapt to their situations.

Kanter observed that men and women behave differently in work organizations because men have more real power and greater opportunities for mobility. Both men and women, when placed in powerless and low-mobility situations, respond by lowering aspirations and developing different patterns of occupational behavior from those with greater power and opportunities. Blocked mobility leads to limited motivation which, in turn, sets in motion a downward cycle of deprivation and discouragement. Conversely, those with power and opportunities use these resources to gain allies and supporters and prove themselves, triggering an upward cycle of success. Although both cycles appear to be related to individual motivation, in fact they arise in response to organizational factors.

In addition, Kanter noted that number affects occupational behavior because minority individuals or "tokens" are treated differently than others in three ways. First, because tokens are highly visible, they face performance pressures. Second, because tokens polarize differences between themselves and dominants, they face heightened in-group boundaries and social isolation. Third, because dominants distort and stereotype tokens' characteristics, tokens are forced into stereotypic roles.

In addition to tokenism, sexism affects women workers. Even when female tokens have job skills and work commitment they are harassed by male coworkers and excluded from informal social networks, while male tokens not only do not face similar discrimination (Kadushin, 1976; Schreiber, 1979; Williams, 1989) but are the beneficiaries of advancement up the "glass escalator" (Williams, 1992). Reskin (1988) identified three additional practices that men adopt to prevent occupational equality when women workers intrude into the men's occupational world: they type jobs and tasks according to sex and give the less desirable and lower-paying activities to women; they treat women in a paternalistic manner; and they sexualize the workplace.

Paternalism involves men "helping" or "protecting" women by excusing them from difficult or undesirable tasks in exchange for submissive or dependent behavior. This "help," however, serves to control the women and deny them organizational rewards, stigmatizes them as inferior, and creates resentment by violating the men's sense of fairness (Jurik, 1985; Swerdlow, 1989; Padavic and Reskin, 1990).

The emphasis on women's gender includes sexual harassment, which results in women experiencing psychological stress that contributes to higher turnover rates (MacKinnon, 1978; Gutek and Morash, 1982) as well as dilemmas in responding to coworkers (Martin, 1978; Swerdlow, 1989).

Occupational behavior also is guided by socially prescribed norms guiding the ways people "do" or enact gender within the context of larger social structures. Gender is not a fixed attribute of individuals but emerges or is enacted in interactions (West and Zimmerman, 1987; Martin and Jurik, 1996). Thus the way men display appropriate "masculine" and women show "feminine" behavior emerges through "doing" gender in everyday social interaction, including those in the workplace. Consequently, gender is a pervasive feature of all aspects of organizational life including the images, interactions, workers' identities, and policies that result in gendered divisions of labor and power relations in work organizations (Acker, 1990). For example, the extent to which definition of police work has become associated with the male gender is indicated by the merging of the word for the work and the gender of the worker (i.e., "policeman"). Because the norms and expectations of "appropriate" behavior for police (as well as for persons in other occupations historically dominated by men) are associated with enacting "masculine" behavior, women entering these occupations encounter dilemmas on the job. On the one hand, as police, they are expected to display "masculine" behavior and interact with fellow workers as peers and equals; on the other hand, as women, their male coworkers expect and pressure them to display "feminine" behavior (including deference to men) which is deemed inappropriate for an officer (Goffman, 1956). Thus, policewomen have to decide when and how to "act like a cop" and still "act like a lady" on the job.

Police Work, the Police Culture, and Men's Opposition to Women Officers. In addition to the barriers women face in a variety of nontraditional occupations, certain aspects of police work lead to unique problems for women officers. Police officers have enormous discretionary decision-making authority. Across the wide variety of policing tasks there is always the potential for violence and the authority to use coercive means to enforce the officer's definition of the situation. The police role as the representative of the coercive potential of the state and as a legitimate user of force in everyday life helps explain certain attitudes and behavioral characteristics of the police and their work culture. The presence of danger and the potential for violence lead to a generalized suspiciousness, isolation from the community, and a cohesive, informal occupational group with its own stratification system and norms. These, in turn, heighten the barriers to informal acceptance of anyone who is perceived as an "outsider" and, therefore, cannot be counted on to conform to group norms.

The men's opposition to women officers has been amply documented (Bloch and Anderson, 1974; Sherman, 1975; California Highway Patrol, 1976; Martin, 1980; Charles, 1981; Hunt, 1990). Most of the men's objections to women officers focus on their physical differences from men and are phrased in terms of concern for physical safety and women's alleged inability to deal with physical violence. Nevertheless, a variety of other concerns underlie their opposition. Women threaten to disrupt the division of labor, the work norms, the work group's solidarity, the insecure occupational status and public image, and the sexist ideology that undergirds the men's definition of the work as "men's work" and their identity as masculine men.

The use of women on patrol implies either that the men's unique asset, their physical superiority, is irrelevant (as it is on most assignments) or that the man working with a woman officer will be at a disadvantage he would not face in a physical confrontation working with a male partner. Moreover, the possibility that women officers reduce the likelihood of a physical confrontation or act appropriately by protecting their male partner is no comfort because it undermines the gender stereotypes that permeate the male officers' perceptual world. Women are not "supposed" to fight or to control other male citizens. At the same time, for a male officer, being "defended" by a woman is regarded as an affront to his manhood.

Women also threaten work-group solidarity. They raise the specter of possible sexual intimacy between partners, fostering competition among the men and thus creating a competing set of loyalties. They also threaten the public image of police work and the mask of emotional detachment worn by male officers by exposing the fact that the day-to-day reality of policing does not revolve around crime fighting, but involves emotional labor and requires interpersonal skills. In addition, they inhibit men's use of crude language, their illicit on-the-job sexual activities, and the fringe benefit of enhanced masculinity that these confer.

Men's opposition to women in policing also reflects a "deeper concern about who has a right to manage law and order" (Heidensohn, 1992:215). In fact, according to Heidensohn, the view that "men 'own' order and have sole rights to preserve it" is the real but unstated issue underlying their assertions that women are unsuitable officers and will destroy men's solidarity. Instead, their resistance to women on patrol is better understood as emanating from a struggle over the ownership of social control. In sum, the men's opposition to women in their ranks stems from their threat to their definitions of the work, occupational culture, social status, and self-image as men's men which provides a psychological fringe benefit of the job.

Structural Barriers: Equality versus Equity.   Women enter policing at a disadvantage. Few went through an extensive anticipatory socialization process in which they vicariously rehearsed police roles. Compared with the men, fewer women have been in the military, had firearms training, or played team sports that involve physical contact and imbue the spirit of the team player.

At the training academy inequality may be fostered in several ways. An emphasis on meeting physical fitness standards that do not have to be maintained beyond the academy magnifies the importance of the physical differences between the sexes. Informal coddling of women by some physical education instructors who are protective or unable to deal with some women's manipulative efforts also negatively affects all the women. It allows some to move to the next stage of recruit training not fully prepared and fosters the expectation of those women that they can get along by being "different" rather than learning the lessons of group loyalty. It also undermines the confidence of male officers in women officers in general, and divides the women. At the same time, police training often fails to develop the interpersonal skills necessary to do the job well. These skills are usually more highly developed in women than in men, and their omission from the curriculum deprives the women of a job-relevant training opportunity in which they are likely to excel. Consequently, the new woman officer enters male turf on male terms with little recognition of the problems she will face, or acknowledgment of the interpersonal strengths she brings to the job.

The early months on the street are very important, since it is then that the reputation that follows an officer through a career is formed. Opportunities for learning and gaining self-confidence have a multiplier effect because once established, habits and reputations are difficult to change. Self-confidence grows with mastery of policing skills and positive feedback on performance. An officer who does not have, or does not take, opportunities to develop street patrol skills because of limited assignments, under-instruction, or over-protection is likely to act hesitantly, be viewed as a threat to others' safety, and be deprived of subsequent opportunities to handle situations.

Female rookies face several disadvantages on the street. They tend to have been sheltered from street life, and to be smaller and not as physically strong as the male rookies. They must overcome openly hostile attitudes of some of their trainers, supervisors, and partners; a dual standard of evaluation; and the performance pressures that "tokens" encounter.

Unless the timidity of some female rookies and the protectiveness of many of the men are consciously reversed, many women do not get opportunities to learn to act with decisiveness and confidence. Consequently, a self-fulfilling prophecy becomes a reality as they seek to manipulate others' expectations of them rather than altering their own behavior.

Cultural Mandate and Interactional Barriers. Women officers also face dilemmas in interacting with fellow officers and with citizens. As police officers, they are expected to interact with other police according to the norms governing relations among equals; as women they are expected to adhere to asymmetric norms governing male-female relationships where women are subordinates of men. Thus, in addition to dilemmas as "tokens," women officers must cope with norms that put them at a disadvantage in interactions with male officers.

Men's language keeps women officers "in their place" by constantly referring to them as "ladies" or "girls" (terms that suggest that they should be protected), or by calling those that do not conform to sex role stereotypes "lesbians," "broads," "bitches," or "whores."

Cursing also creates dilemmas. Many men are uncomfortable swearing in front of women officers but resent the inhibition on their expressiveness. Similarly, when women curse, men become offended and withdraw the deference they give to "ladies." If the women avoid cursing, however, their words are taken less seriously.

Frequent sexual jokes and gossip remind the women that they are desired sexual objects, visible outsiders, and feared competitors. In turn, this joking makes many of the women, concerned about even the appearance of impropriety, avoid interactions that might be viewed as having a sexual connotation. They maintain their moral reputation but sacrifice the opportunity to build close interpersonal relationships necessary for sponsorship and protection.

Gender stereotyping enables men to cast women into the roles that reflect in their linguistic categories, limit women's behavioral options, and have a negative impact on their work. Women either get pressed into enacting the "seductress," "maiden," "mother," or "pet" roles, or get labeled "lesbians" or "bitches" (Kanter, 1977). The former are deprofessionalized, protected from occupational demands, excluded from opportunities to develop occupational skills, and criticized for failing to fulfill their duties as officers. The latter are permitted to remain in the men's informal world, but their dangerous qualities are neutralized by defeminization and pejorative categorization.

Informal social exclusion and sexual harassment also remind the women that they are not "just officers." They are visible but excluded from career-promoting networks, vulnerable to harassment but held responsible for the outcomes of such interactions. They experience a more hostile interpersonal work environment than male officers as well as a unique group of work-related stresses. While the primary sources of stress for officers appear to be common to women and men (i.e., organizational and task-related concerns), both Wexler and Logan (1983) and Morash and Haarr (1995) have observed that women also endure an additional category of stressors. These include a lack of acceptance as officers; denial of information, sponsorships, and protection; and both sexual harassment and language harassment (i.e., deliberate exposure to profanity and sexual jokes).

Relating to Citizens. All police officers face recurrent uncertainties in relating to citizens who may seek to disrupt normal interaction by disavowing the officers' identity, and by ascribing to them irrelevant statuses based on age, sex, or race (Goffman, 1961). While citizens usually defer to the police officer who usually has higher social status than persons he or she encounters (Sykes and Clark, 1975), some seek to base the interaction on the officer's "irrelevant" status characteristics, thereby reversing the flow. Although all officers occasionally face such deference reversals, these situations continually threaten women officers' interactions and force the women to find ways to turn them to their advantage, minimize their occurrence, and limit their effects on the officer's control of the situation.

In police-citizen encounters, four possible combinations of gender and social category may arise: male officers with male or female citizens, and female officers with male or female citizens. Each combination has different expectations and management problems as police relate to citizens by doing gender while they seek to control the situation or otherwise enact the police role.

In interactions with male citizens, male officers have status superiority by virtue of their office and expect citizens to defer and comply. On the basis of shared manhood, however, they are status equals. This shared manhood can sometimes be effectively used as a resource for doing gender since it is to the citizen's advantage, saying, in effect, "act like a man (i.e., control yourself) and I won't have to exert my authority as an officer to overpower you." It also benefits the officer by minimizing the necessity of using force and allows him to act as a "good guy," giving a little to gain compliance. When suspects or offenders try to define the situation in terms of shared manhood, however, officers may view the interaction as denying the deference due to their office. When a male officer relies too heavily on the authority of the badge or rejects a male citizen's effort to be treated "as a man," the result is a "duel of manhood" which has a high probability of a physical or verbal confrontation that might well have been avoided.

Male officers' double-status superiority over female citizens generally leads to few problems arising in such interactions, except those related to sexuality. Male officers may use the authority of their office to gain control or gain compliance by asserting, "act like a lady and I'll treat you like one." If invoking the rules of chivalry works, the officer gains control while enhancing his sense of manly generosity. If it fails, he can still treat the woman as a wayward "girl" on whom he will not waste his time, or he may use force.

Interactions between female officers and male citizens are problematic because police expect to take control of situations and be shown deference by citizens; men may defer to the office but resist being controlled by or deferential to a woman. For that reason expectations regarding how a man relates to a woman and to a police officer generally are different and sometimes often are in direct conflict. Women officers usually are given deference, either out of respect for the uniform or because compliance does not challenge a man's manhood if he chivalrously complies, whereas fighting a woman may cause a man to lose status, particularly when there are witnesses. However, the man's deference is revocable, particularly if the officer acts "unladylike" in carrying out her occupational role obligations. Since they often are at a physical disadvantage, female officers may have to rely on the deference of males as a control strategy. Although most women usually try to minimize rather than activate their gender status, they recognize that men seek to redefine situations so as to affirm men's status superiority but that they must retain control.

When women officers encounter sexist or sexual comments they usually ignore them or reply "you wouldn't say that to a male officer, would you?" They may also use a variety of verbal and nonverbal cues involving use of the voice, appearance, facial expression, and body postures which also convey the message that despite their small stature, as police they are to be taken seriously. Learning to transmit these messages, however, requires altering long-standing habits such as smiling, and learning literally to "stand up to people."

In dealing with women citizens, female officers get both greater cooperation and more "hassles" than male officers. While their common gender status implies a reduction of social distance, it revokes the special consideration that female citizens expect from (male) police, and for this reason, may arouse the female citizen's anger at not being able to flirt or cry her way out of a situation. Women also are more willing to fight female officers than male officers. Conversely, women officers often are viewed as more sympathetic and so are able to gain the cooperation of female citizens, particularly victims, who refuse to talk to male officers.

Effective officers of both genders appeal both to "gender-appropriate behavior" on the part of citizens, and to their respect for the officer's authority to gain cooperation. They use a citizen's expectations and values to their advantage, draw on mutually shared statuses to diminish social distance, and only rely on the authority of their office when necessary. Ineffective officers, on the other hand, either too rigidly rely on their formal authority or cannot transcend the limitations on their behavior posed by adherence to traditional norms for doing gender. For female officers this means failure to use the authority of their office and overreliance on deference to them as women; for male officers this means overemphasis on aggressive "macho" behavior that may result in an avoidable confrontation.

In sum, a woman officer faces barriers and handicaps that are built into both the formal and informal work structures. These culturally mandated patterns governing male/female interaction force her to "think like a man, work like a dog, and act like a lady" (Martin, 1980:219).

ISSUES FOR THIS DECADE AND BEYOND

Have numerical increases and the passage of time required to achieve seniority and promotions reduced the barriers and limitations women officers face? What new problems challenge the women who move into supervisory positions, and the departments that hire women in greater numbers? These issues for future research will be addressed in the final section of this article.

Numbers: The Effects of Moving Beyond Token Status

Kanter (1977) observed that the proportion of minority individuals in work groups affects the manner in which minority members are treated. Her theory of tokenism suggests that members of a small minority suffer adverse conditions due solely to the small size of the subgroup. She distinguished four group types on the basis of proportional size of the minority: uniform groups with only one category of sex, race, or ethnicity; skewed groups in which minorities or "tokens" comprise up to 15 percent of the members; tilted groups typified by minority representation between 16 and 35 percent; and balanced groups. She asserts that minority members in tilted groups face barriers and constraints to acceptance that are less intense than in skewed groups because minorities can form coalitions affecting group culture.

An alternative minority proportion/inequality perspective, originating in race relations literature (Blalock, 1967; Marden and Meyer, 1973; Giles, 1977) asserts that minority individuals are less likely to be accepted by dominants when there are enough of them to threaten the economic and political security of the majority; thus, there is greater discrimination as the minority grows larger and more powerful.

In a test of these competing perspectives examining several work groups in a single organization where group membership ranged from highly skewed male to highly skewed female, South, et al. (1982) found some support for both perspectives. In measuring women's isolation from the work group they found no support for the hypothesis that token women have less contact with male workers and supervisors. However, consistent with the minority proportion hypothesis, female representation was negatively associated with the amount of encouragement for promotion women got from male supervisors. The proportion of women in a group was not significantly related to the quality of relations among women. The authors concluded that "token women are not found to face more severe organizational pressure than nontokens" (South, et al., 1982:587) and that an increase in the number of minority workers without alteration in the relations between dominants and subordinates is not likely to improve the position of minorities substantially, and may even worsen relations.

Other studies also cast doubt on the assertion that an increase in number alone will relieve the problems of tokenism for women. In a study of the effects of proportions on women managers in two companies with 6 and 19 percent female managers respectively, Harlan and Weiss (1981) found that there was no simple linear relationship between the amount of gender bias or stereotyping and the percentage of women in management. The women in the 19 percent company faced more overt bias and harassment, and women in both companies felt that they had to work harder and face more challenges to their authority than male managers. Deaux and Ullman (1983) found the attitudes of males in the steel industry toward women were more negative in the company with more female employees than in the one with fewer. In a study of the automobile industry, Gruber and Bjorn (1982) found men's sexual harassment of women became more frequent and severe as the proportion of women increased. Thus, it is unclear whether the increase in the number of women in policing has reduced the occupational dilemmas posed by tokenism. While some of the performance pressures due to visibility may have diminished, the organizational structures embedded in a broader social system of gender inequality remain in place, and as women move up the organizational hierarchy, they again face the problems of "tokens" as well as challenges to their authority from men who may tolerate working with women but resist working for them.

Assignments, Promotions and Women as Supervisors

For more than half a century women officers' assignments were limited to those viewed as compatible with their gender. Although women now are assigned to patrol just as men are, it appears that women officers continue to be disproportionately concentrated in support positions rather than line activities (Martin, 1990). Based on case studies of assignment patterns in three large agencies, it appears that, even with the same amount of time in policing, women have had more nonpatrol assignments than men and that a higher proportion of women than men hold staff support positions while men go into line units, such as special operations and traffic. These differences appear to arise from "pushes" away from patrol into "inside" assignments (Hunt, 1990) due to a hostile environment resulting from men's paternalism and harassment and from "pulls" toward assignments that offer more favorable hours and working conditions and that may reflect women's skills and interests. Similar questions arise with respect to racial patterns of assignments and how the combination of race and gender affect the occupational opportunities of minority women. The emerging literature on the intersection of race and gender suggests that because cultural images of white and black women differ, black women often are treated according to separate norms, are less often put on a pedestal or treated as "ladies," and afforded protection by white men (Martin, 1994). White women, particularly those who are physically attractive, appear to be more likely than black women to get inside assignments and protection on street patrol (Martin, 1994) and less likely to get recognition for superior performance (Belknap and Shelley, 1992).

Although it appears that women are gaining their "fair share" of promotions to sergeant in the large urban departments, questions arise with respect to opportunities for attaining higher rank, particularly top management positions that are based on political decisions rather than standardized examinations. Whether women in policing will be limited by a glass ceiling that women managers have encountered in other occupations remains an open question.

How have superiors and subordinates reacted to women supervisors? Limited interview data suggest that a woman sergeant's position is not an easy one. Like all new sergeants, they face problems adopting an effective supervisory style and "thinking like management." In addition, women sergeants face renewed difficulties as tokens, tend to lack mentors to help them, come in for more testing of their authority than new male sergeants, and face many of the problems observed from studies of women managers in other occupations.

Harriman (1985) asserts that although there were few differences in the attitudes, motivation, and behavior of effective women and men managers, the women's careers progressed more slowly than those of their male cohorts. A review of studies of leadership found no differences in behavior between the sexes after controlling for situational and other demographic variables (Nieva and Gutek, 1981); other studies have noted a tendency to identify effective leadership traits with masculine traits (Schein, 1975) and to regard women as less effective or successful leaders (Harriman, 1985; Statham, 1986).

Research on the relationship between gender and the use of power have found that successful managers of both sexes get and use power strategies effectively. However, the strategies and styles most associated with competence (i.e., direct rather than manipulative; concrete resource mobilization rather than personal) are also associated with masculinity. All styles may be effective if used by a man, but masculine styles were found not to be effective when used by a woman. Thus women supervisors face a dilemma: they can manipulate and be unrecognized or be direct and risk ineffectiveness and hostility.

All performance evaluations are subjective. Not only may rating systems involve categories or activities that are gender stereotyped, but the choice of words in a written evaluation—as well as what is omitted—may exert subtle influence. Although women were found to be no less competent than men in a number of studies, there were differences in the way their performance was perceived and evaluated which resulted in an overall pro-male bias in performance evaluations (Harriman, 1985). For example, women were rated less desirable candidates for university department chairmanships (Fidell, 1970), and identical work was rated higher by both males and females when it was attributed to a man rather than to a woman (Mischel, 1974). The effects of subtle differences in written evaluations was identified by Thomas (1987) in a study of promotion evaluations in the Navy. Women candidates whose numerical evaluation scores were as high as the men's were much less likely to have written comments commending for a position of commanding officer. Not only did supervisors' silence work against them, but the written comments focused on gender stereotyped feminine traits (e.g., well groomed, supportive, sensitive) that are valued less highly than the masculine terms (aggressive, logical, mature) in which males were described.

In a study of men and women managers and their secretaries, Statham (1986) found not only that men and women managers tended to have different management styles,[3] but that each was critical of the other's style. Men saw women managers as too hovering and unwilling to delegate; the women viewed the autonomy that men gave subordinates as "neglect." These findings have implications for women's success because most women managers are supervised and evaluated primarily by men who regard their style as inadequate. For women police officials the problem is compounded by having mostly male subordinates who may share with male supervisors resistance to a "feminine" management style. The anticipation of such opposition was suggested by a survey of women eligible for promotion (Wexler and Quinn,

1985) that found that nearly half the women stated that their greatest concern in being a sergeant was related to the negative reception they expected within the department.

Turnover

Much of the literature on personnel turnover suggests that women in private industry have slightly higher turnover rates than men and that they leave jobs primarily due to family reasons, whereas men resign to accept other jobs. Others question these conclusions and suggest that women's turnover is related to their overrepresentation in jobs that are poorly paid, unsatisfying, and require a low skill level (Kanter, 1977) as well as to high levels of sexual harassment and discrimination (O'Farrell and Harlan, 1982; Jurik, 1985). Jacobs (1989) also found both an unexpectedly high proportion of women entering male-dominated jobs and a high turnover rate as well. This led him to conclude that the barriers to women's entry are lower than expected, but that employment in male-dominated occupations is less a permanent achievement for women than a temporary pass through a "revolving door."

The research on gender differences in turnover rates in policing is inconsistent. Women's turnover rate was found to be significantly higher than that of the men in the California Highway Patrol, the Royal Canadian Mounted Police (Linden and Minch, 1984), and one California sheriff's department troubled by a generally high turnover rate (Fry, 1983). Although women made up 6 percent of the sheriff's department's personnel, they accounted for 17 percent of those leaving the department in the three years prior to Fry's study. Their high turnover rate appeared to be related to their immediate assignment, however, since 71 percent of the women who resigned were assigned to the custody division (i.e., the jail) and 38 percent accepted employment with other law enforcement agencies. Another study (Sulton and Townsey, 1981) found that male and female turnover rates in municipal departments are similar. Martin (1990) found some support for both similarities and differences. Based on data from 303 municipal departments, women had a higher turnover rate during 1986 (6.3 percent) than men (4.6). The gender gap was even higher in state police agencies (8.9 percent for women versus 2.9 for men). At the same time, analysis of other factors affecting turnover indicated that in departments where women's turnover was high, men's separation rates also were high. The association between male and female turnover rates suggests that the same factors affect each group: internal policies that weed out officers who do not "fit" and alternative employment opportunities. Further research is needed on both turnover rates and reasons that officers leave a department.

Pregnancy Policy: The Emerging Legal Issue

While the decade of the 1970s marked great strides in assuring legal equality for women, it also brought before the court the "harder" issue: how to deal equitably with biological differences between the sexes. Because only women can get pregnant, there is no way within our legal framework to treat men and women equally and equitably at the same time.

Underlying our legal framework are a set of assumptions and power relations that limit legal reasoning and affect decision making. One assumption is that men and women naturally and biologically occupy different roles in life. This has led to the view that being a worker and mother are incompatible and has resulted in maternity leave and other employment policies that put hardships on women.

In the 1970s in several cases the Supreme Court ruled that employers did not violate Title VII of the Civil Rights Act by denying sick-leave disability insurance or health insurance coverage to female employees to cover disabilities resulting from normal pregnancy. The court found no sex discrimination in California's disability insurance plan that excluded pregnancy from coverage but covered sex-linked disabilities such as prostate operations (*Geduldig v. Aiello*, 1976). Likewise, in *General Electric v. Gilbert* (1976), the majority held that sex discrimination occurs only when men and women are treated differently with respect to a shared situation or characteristic. Since men cannot become pregnant, it was not discrimination against women to deny them health benefits for pregnancy. The employer simply removed one condition from the list of covered conditions.

In response, Congress passed the Pregnancy Disability Act in 1978, broadening the definition of sex discrimination to encompass pregnancy, childbirth, and related medical conditions. It prohibited an employer from: (1) requiring a woman to take leave set arbitrarily at a certain time during pregnancy; (2) failing to grant full reinstatement rights; (3) failing to pay disability or sick leave for pregnancy in the same manner as it pays for other employee disability or sick benefits; and (4) protecting a woman employee from "reproductive hazards" without scientific evidence that a hazard actually exists.

While clarifying Congressional intent, the law left the equal treatment/ special treatment question unresolved, as have two apparently contradictory Supreme Court decisions *(Wimberly v. Labor and Industrial Relations Commission of Missouri* and *California Federal Savings and Loan v. Guerra)*. These rulings leave it up to each state to decide whether to give pregnant women more favorable treatment than other workers that are physically unable to work. Federal law only requires states to treat women as well or badly as their disabled co-workers; states are permitted—but not obligated—to require employers to give additional benefits without being discriminatory.

Because police work poses the risk of unpredictable physical violence or injury that many departments regard as a "reproductive hazard," pregnancy raises a number of policy questions for departments which often are not covered by bargaining agreements and municipal personnel policies. Although many departments have "light duty" policies that permit officers who are temporarily disabled to work in noncontact positions, there appear to be no uniform policies or common practices with respect to: (1) the point at which the pregnant woman becomes "disabled" and, thereby, "unfit" for patrol or other duties; (2) the person(s) who make the determination of whether the woman should be reassigned or forced to take extended leave; and (3) the assignments that are suitable for an officer on light duty. As the number of officers who are pregnant at the same time increases, a department's deployment problems grow, increasing the need for consistent and clearly articulated policies that assure both adequate protection of the community and of the rights of pregnant officers.

In conclusion, the status of women in policing today is uncertain. Clearly the most blatant barriers that kept women out of police work for more than half a century have fallen, and women are entering policing in increasing numbers. Gaining admission to the occupation, however, is only a first step. Women officers still face discriminatory treatment that limits their options and opportunities for advancement. Nevertheless, as more women enter the occupation, move slowly into positions of authority, and serve as role models and sponsors for other women, there is reason for guarded optimism about the future of women in law enforcement, as well as a large number of questions waiting to be addressed.

Notes

[1] In 1985 only 2 percent of the top corporate executives of Fortune 500 companies were women (Powell, 1988:75) and 6 percent of law firm partners were women according to an ABA study (Goldberg, 1991).

[2] These studies assessed the Pennsylvania State Police (1973), Metropolitan Police of Washington, DC (Bloch and Anderson, 1974), the California Highway Patrol (California Highway Patrol, 1976), Denver (Bartlett and Rosenblum, 1977), Newton, Massachusetts (Kizziah and Morris, 1977), New York City (Sichel et al., 1978), and Philadelphia (Bartell Associates, 1978, Phases I and II) police departments.

[3] The women managers were described as "task-engrossed and person-oriented"; the men were "image-engrossed and autonomy-invested."

References

Acker, Joan. 1990. "Hierarchies, Jobs and Bodies: A Theory of Gendered Organizations." *Gender & Society* 4:139–58.

Bartell Associates. 1978. "The Study of Police Women Competency in the Performance of Sector Police Work in the City of Philadelphia." State College, PA: Bartell Associates.

Bartlett, H. W. and A. Rosenblum. 1977. *Policewoman Effectiveness.* Denver: Civil Service Commission and Denver Police Department.

Belknap, J. and J. K. Shelley. 1992. "The New Lone Ranger: Policewomen on Patrol." *American Journal of Police* 12: 47–75.

Blalock, H. 1967. *Toward a Theory of Minority-Group Relations.* New York: Wiley.

Bloch, P. and D. Anderson. 1974. *Policewomen on Patrol: Final Report.* Washington: Urban Institute.

Bureau of Justice Statistics. 2003. *Local Police Departments, 2000.* Washington, DC: U.S. Department of Justice.

California Highway Patrol. 1976. Women Traffic Officer Project, Sacramento.

Charles, M. T. 1981. "Performance and Socialization of Female Recruits in the Michigan State Police Training Academy." *Journal of Police Science and Administration* 9:209–23.

Deaux, K. and R. Ullman. 1983. *Women of Steel.* New York: Praeger.

Fidell, L. S. 1970. "Empirical Verification of Sex Discrimination in Hiring Practices in Psychology." *Journal of Psychology* 25:1094–98.

Fry, L. 1983. "A Preliminary Examination of the Factors Related to Turnover of Women in Law Enforcement." *Journal of Police Science and Administration* 11:149–55.

Fyfe, J. 1987. *Police Personnel Practices, 1986.* (Baseline Data Report Volume 18, Number 6). Washington, DC: International City Management Association.

Geduldig v. Aiello 417 U.S. 125 (1976).

General Electric v. Gilbert 429 U.S. 125 (1976).

Giles, M. 1977. "Percent Black and Racial Hostility: An Old Assumption Reexamined." *Social Science Quarterly* 58:412–17.

Goffman, E. 1956. "The Nature of Deference and Demeanor." *American Anthropologist* 56:473–502.

_____. 1961. *Encounters.* Indianapolis: Bobbs-Merrill.

Goldberg, S. B. 1991. "Token Women—The ABA Confronts its Glass Ceiling." *ABA Journal* 77:58–63.

Gruber, J. and L. Bjorn. 1982. "Blue-collar Blues: the Sexual Harassment of Women Autoworkers." *Work and Occupations* 9:271–98.

Gutek, B. and B. Morash. 1982. "Sex Ratios, Sex-Role Supervisors, and Sexual Harassment of Women at Work." *Journal of Social Issues* 38:55–74.

Harlan, A. and C. Weiss. 1981. *Moving Up: Women in Managerial Careers.* Wellesley, MA: Wellesley College, Center for Research on Women.

Harriman, A. 1985. *Women/Men/Management.* New York: Praeger.

Heidensohn, F. 1992. *Women in Control? The Role of Women in Law Enforcement.* New York: Oxford University Press.

Hunt, J. 1990. "The Logic of Sexism among Police." *Women and Criminal Justice* 1:3–30.

International City Management Association. 1972. "Personnel Practices in Municipal Police Departments." Urban Data Services.

Jacobs, J. 1989. *Revolving Doors: Sex Segregation and Women's Careers.* Stanford: Stanford University Press.

Jurik, N. 1985. "An Officer and a Lady: Organizational Barriers to Women Working as Correctional Officers in Men's Prisons." *Social Problems* 32:375–88.

Kadushin, A. 1976. "Men in a Woman's Profession." *Social Work* 21:440–47.

Kanter, R. 1977. *Men and Women of the Corporation.* New York: Basic Books.

Kelly, C. 1973. *Uniform Crime Report—1972.* Washington, DC: Government Printing Office.

Kizziah, C. and M. Morris. 1977. *Evaluation of Women in Policing Program: Newton, Massachusetts.* Oakland: Approach Associates.

Linden, R. and C. Minch. 1984. "Women in Policing: A Review." Unpublished manuscript. Ottawa, Canada: Ministry of the Solicitor General of Canada.

MacKinnon, C. 1978. *Sexual Harassment of Working Women.* New Haven: Yale University Press.

Marden, C. and G. Meyer. 1973. *Minorities in American Society.* New York: D. Van Nostrand.

Martin, S. E. 1978. "Sexual Politics in the Workplace: The Interactional World of Policewomen." *Symbolic Interaction* 1: 44–60.

_____. 1980. *"Breaking and Entering": Policewomen on Patrol.* Berkeley: University of California Press.

_____. 1990. *On the Move: The Status of Women in Policing.* Washington, DC: Police Foundation.

_____. 1994. "'Outsider within' the Station House: The Impact of Race and Gender on Black Women Police." *Social Problems, 41,* 383–400.

Martin, S. E. and N. C. Jurik. 1996. *Doing Justice, Doing Gender: Women in Law and Criminal Justice Occupations.* Thousand Oaks, CA: Sage.

Milton, C. 1972. *Women in Policing.* Washington, DC: Police Foundation.

Mischel, H. 1974. "Sex Bias in the Evaluation of Professional Achievements." *Journal of Educational Psychology* 66: 157–66.

Morash, M. and J. Greene. 1986. "Evaluating Women on Patrol: A Critique of Contemporary Wisdom." *Evaluation Review* 10: 230–55.

Morash, M. and R. Haarr. 1995. "Gender, Workplace Problems, and Stress in Policing." *Justice Quarterly* 12:113–40.

Nieva V. and B. Gutek. 1981. *Women and Work: A Psychological Perspective.* New York: Praeger.

O'Farrell, B. and S. L. Harlan. 1982. "Craftworkers and Clerks: The Effects of Male Coworker Hostility on Women's Satisfaction with Nontraditional Jobs." *Social Problems* 29: 252–65.

Padavic, I. and B. Reskin. 1990. "Men's Behavior and Women Interest in Blue-Collar Jobs." *Social Problems* 37: 613–28.

Pennsylvania State Police. 1973. "Pennsylvania State Police Female Trooper Study." Harrisburg: Pennsylvania State Police Headquarters.

Powell, G. 1988. *Men and Women in Management.* Beverly Hills: Sage.

Price, B. 1982. "Sexual Integration in American Law Enforcement." *The Future of Policing,* 205–13.

Reaves, B. A. 1996. *Local Police Departments, 1993.* (NCJ-148822) Washington, DC: Bureau of Justice Statistics.

Reskin, B. 1988. "Bringing the Men Back In: Sex Differentiation and the Devaluation of Women's Work." *Gender and Society* 2: 58–81.

Reskin, B. and R. Roos. 1990. *Job Queues, Gender Queues.* Philadelphia: Temple University Press.

Schein, V. 1975. "The Relationship between Sex Role Stereotypes and Requisite Management Characteristics among Female Managers." *Journal of Applied Psychology* 60: 340–44.

Schreiber, C. 1979. *Men and Women in Transitional Occupations.* Cambridge: MIT Press.

Sherman, L. J. 1975. "Evaluation of Policewomen on Patrol in a Suburban Police Department." *Journal of Police Science and Administration* 3:434–38.

Sichel, J. L., L. N. Friedman, J. C. Quint, and M. E. Smith. 1978. *Women on Patrol:* A Pilot Study of Police Performance in New York City. Washington, DC: National Institute of Law Enforcement and Criminal Justice.

Statham, A. 1986. "The Gender Model Revisited: Differences in the Management Styles of Men and Women." Unpublished manuscript. University of Wisconsin–Parkside.

Sulton, C. and R. Townsey. 1981. *A Progress Report on Women in Policing.* Washington, DC: Police Foundation.

Swerdlow, M. 1989. "Men's Accommodation to Women Entering a Nontraditional Occupation: A Case of Rapid Transit Operatives." *Gender and Society* 3: 373–87.

Sykes, R. and J. Clark. 1975. "A Theory of Deference Exchange in Police-Civilian Encounters." *American Journal of Sociology* 81: 584–600.

Thomas, R J. 1987. "Appraising the Performance of Women: Gender and the Naval Office." In B. Gutek and L. Larwood (eds.) *Women's Career Development*. Beverly Hills: Sage.

U.S. Department of Justice, Bureau of Justice Statistics. 1992. *State and Local* Police Departments, 1990. Bulletin NCJ-133284. Washington, DC: U.S. Department of Justice.

U.S. Federal Bureau of Investigation. 1976. *Uniform Crime Reports—1975.* Washington, D.C.: Government Printing Office.

_____. 1981. *Uniform Crime Reports—1980.* Washington, DC: Government Printing Office.

_____. 1985. *Uniform Crime Reports—1984.* Washington, DC: Government Printing Office.

_____. 1986. *Uniform Crime Reports—1985.* Washington, DC: Government Printing Office.

_____. 1991. *Uniform Crime Reports—1990.* Washington, DC: Government Printing Office.

_____. 1995. *Uniform Crime Reports—1994.* Washington, DC: Government Printing Office.

_____. 2002. *Crime in the United States, 2001.* Washington, DC: Government Printing Office.

Walker, S. 1985. "Racial Minority and Female Employment in Policing: the Implications of 'Glacial' Change." *Crime and Delinquency* 31: 555–72.

Walker, S. And S. E Martin. 1994. "Through the Looking Glass Ceiling: Patterns in Hiring and Promotion by Race, Ethnicity and Gender in American Policing, 1982–1992." Paper presented at the Annual Meeting of the American Society of Criminology. Miami, FL, November.

West, C. and D. H. Zimmerman. 1987. "Doing Gender." *Gender & Society* 1:125–151.

Wexler, J. G. and D. D. Logan. 1983. "Sources of Stress among Women Police Officers." *Journal of Police Science and Administration* 11: 46–53.

Wexler, J. G. and V. Quinn. 1985. "Considerations in the Training and Development of Women Sergeants." *Journal of Police Science and Administration* 13: 98–105.

White, T. W. and R B. Bloch. 1975. *Police Officer Height and Selected Aspects of Performance.* Washington, DC: Police Foundation.

Williams, C. 1989. *Gender Differences at Work: Women and Men in Nontraditional Occupations.* Berkeley: University of California Press.

_____. 1992. "The Glass Escalator: Hidden Advantages for Men in the 'Female' Professions." *Social Problems* 39:253–66.

SECTION VI
Community-Based Policing

The role of the community in the organization, maintenance, and control of law enforcement has come full circle since the police were first created as "organized watchers." In those early days of the police, it was the community or neighborhood that was the important focus of policing. Over the years, with the invention of two-way radios, automobiles, and computers, police work became impersonal and removed from the community level. However, since the 1990s, there has been an emphasis on reintegrating policing with the community and the neighborhood. In this section, we have included four articles that reflect the significance of community-based or community-oriented policing.

The first article in this section, entitled "Broken Windows" by James Q. Wilson and George L. Kelling, is a classic article reviewing the impact of reinstituting foot patrols in Newark, New Jersey. It was concluded that reinstituting foot patrols had not reduced crime rates but that residents in foot patrolled neighborhoods felt more secure than residents of other neighborhoods. Drawing upon an historical analysis, Wilson and Kelling suggest a return to a focus on order-maintenance policing as opposed to the current preoccupation with crime control. However, these authors have been criticized for what Samuel Walker calls the misuse of history in recent police patrol analysis. Walker's criticisms are outlined in the next article, "'Broken Windows' and Fractured History: The Use and Misuse of History in Recent Police Patrol Analysis." Walker argues that Wilson and Kelling's policy proposals may be worth pursuing, but that they are grounded in a romanticized version of the history of policing and therefore need to be more fully developed.

In the next selection, "Community Policing," Gary Cordner discusses the four dimensions of community policing: philosophical, strategic, tactical, and organizational. He notes that all the research on this topic focuses on the tactical dimension. Cordner suggests that since the evaluations thus far have been positive, research should now focus on the three other elements of community policing.

In the final selection for this section of the book, John Reitzel, Nicole Piquero, and Alex Piquero assess the problem-oriented policing movement. They describe its origins and how it differs from other styles of policing. They also include examples of how to evaluate programs that involve a problem-solving orientation. One of the most interesting aspects of this article is the juxtaposition of community-oriented policing and zero-tolerance policing.

Broken Windows

James Q. Wilson & George L. Kelling

In the mid-1970s, the state of New Jersey announced a "Safe and Clean Neighborhoods Program," designed to improve the quality of community life in twenty-eight cities. As part of that program, the state provided money to help cities take police officers out of their patrol cars and assign them to walking beats. The governor and other state officials were enthusiastic about using foot patrol as a way of cutting crime, but many police chiefs were skeptical. Foot patrol, in their eyes, had been pretty much discredited. It reduced the mobility of the police, who thus had difficulty responding to citizen calls for service, and it weakened headquarters control over patrol officers.

Many police officers also disliked foot patrol, but for different reasons: it was hard work, it kept them outside on cold, rainy nights, and it reduced their chances for making a "good pinch." In some departments, assigning officers to foot patrol had been used as a form of punishment. And academic experts on policing doubted that foot patrol would have any impact on crime rates; it was, in the opinion of most, little more than a sop to public opinion. But since the state was paying for it, the local authorities were willing to go along.

Five years after the program started, the Police Foundation, in Washington, DC, published an evaluation of the foot-patrol project. Based on its analysis of a carefully controlled experiment carried out chiefly in Newark, the foundation concluded, to the surprise of hardly anyone, that foot patrol had not reduced crime rates. But residents of the foot-patrolled neighborhoods seemed to feel more secure than persons in other areas, tended to believe that crime had been reduced, and seemed to take fewer steps to protect themselves

From *The Atlantic Monthly*, March 1982, pp. 29–38. Reprinted with permission of James Q. Wilson and George L. Kelling.

from crime (staying at home with the doors locked, for example). Moreover, citizens in the foot-patrol areas had a more favorable opinion of the police than did those living elsewhere. And officers walking beats had higher morale, greater job satisfaction, and a more favorable attitude toward citizens in their neighborhoods than did officers assigned to patrol cars.

These findings may be taken as evidence that the skeptics were right—foot patrol has no effect on crime; it merely fools the citizens into thinking that they are safer. But in our view, and in the view of the authors of the Police Foundation study (of whom Kelling was one), the citizens of Newark were not fooled at all. They knew what the foot-patrol officers were doing, they knew it was different from what motorized officers do, and they knew that having officers walk beats did in fact make their neighborhoods safer.

But how can a neighborhood be "safer" when the crime rate has not gone down—in fact, may have gone up? Finding the answer requires first that we understand what most often frightens people in public places. Many citizens, of course, are primarily frightened by crime, especially crime involving a sudden, violent attack by a stranger. This risk is very real, in Newark as in many large cities. But we tend to overlook or forget another source of fear—the fear of being bothered by disorderly people. Not violent people, nor, necessarily, criminals, but disreputable or obstreperous or unpredictable people: panhandlers, drunks, addicts, rowdy teenagers, prostitutes, loiterers, the mentally disturbed.

What foot-patrol officers did was to elevate, to the extent they could, the level of public order in these neighborhoods. Though the neighborhoods were predominantly black and the foot patrolmen were mostly white, this "order-maintenance" function of the police was performed to the general satisfaction of both parties.

One of us (Kelling) spent many hours walking with Newark foot- patrol officers to see how they defined "order" and what they did to maintain it. One beat was typical: a busy but dilapidated area in the heart of Newark, with many abandoned buildings, marginal shops (several of which prominently displayed knives and straight-edged razors in their windows), one large department store, and, most important, a train station and several major bus stops. Though the area was run-down, its streets were filled with people, because it was a major transportation center. The good order of this area was important not only to those who lived and worked there but also to many others, who had to move through it on their way home, to supermarkets, or to factories.

The people on the street were primarily black; the officer who walked the street was white. The people were made up of "regulars" and "strangers." Regulars included both "decent folk" and some drunks and derelicts who were always there but who "knew their place." Strangers were, well, strangers, and viewed suspiciously, sometimes apprehensively. The officer—call him Kelly—knew who the regulars were, and they knew him. As he saw his job, he was to keep an eye on strangers, and make certain that the disreputable regulars observed some informal but widely understood rules. Drunks and addicts could sit on the stoops, but could not lie down. People could drink on side streets, but not at the main intersection. Bottles had to be in paper bags. Talking to, bothering, or begging from people waiting at the bus stop was strictly forbidden. If a dispute erupted between a businessman and a customer, the businessman was assumed to be right, especially if the customer was a stranger. If a stranger loitered, Kelly would ask him if he had any means of support and what his business was; if he gave unsatisfactory answers, he was sent on his way. Persons who broke the informal rules, especially those who bothered people waiting at bus stops, were arrested for vagrancy. Noisy teenagers were told to keep quiet.

These rules were defined and enforced in collaboration with the "regulars" on the street. Another neighborhood might have different rules, but these, everybody understood, were the rules for *this* neighborhood. If someone violated them, the regulars not only turned to Kelly for help but also ridiculed the violator. Sometimes what Kelly did could be described as "enforcing the law," but just as often it involved taking informal or extralegal steps to help protect what the neighborhood had decided was the appropriate level of public order. Some of the things he did probably would not withstand a legal challenge.

A determined skeptic might acknowledge that a skilled foot-patrol officer can maintain order but still insist that this sort of "order" has little to do with the real sources of community fear—that is, with violent crime. To a degree, that is true. But two things must be borne in mind. First, outside observers should not assume that they know how much of the anxiety now endemic in many big-city neighborhoods stems from a fear of "real" crime and how much from a sense that the street is disorderly, a source of distasteful, worrisome encounters. The people of Newark, to judge from their behavior and their remarks to interviewers, apparently assign a high value to public order, and feel relieved and reassured when the police help them maintain that order.

Second, at the community level, disorder and crime are usually inextricably linked, in a kind of developmental sequence. Social psychologists and police officers tend to agree that if a window in a building is broken *and is left unrepaired*, all the rest of the windows will soon be broken. This is as true in nice neighborhoods as in run-down ones. Window-breaking does not necessarily occur on a large scale because some areas are inhabited by determined window-breakers whereas others are populated by window-lovers; rather, one unrepaired broken window is a signal that no one cares, and so breaking more windows costs nothing. (It has always been fun.)

Philip Zimbardo, a Stanford psychologist, reported in 1969 on some experiments testing the broken-window theory. He arranged to have an automobile without license plates parked with its hood up on a street in the Bronx and a comparable automobile on a street in Palo Alto, California. The car in the Bronx was attacked by "vandals" within ten minutes of its "abandonment." The first to arrive were a family—father, mother, and young son— who removed the radiator and battery. Within twenty-four hours, virtually everything of value had been removed. Then random destruction began—

windows were smashed, parts torn off, upholstery ripped. Children began to use the car as a playground. Most of the adult "vandals" were well-dressed, apparently clean-cut whites. The car in Palo Alto sat untouched for more than a week. Then Zimbardo smashed part of it with a sledgehammer. Soon, passersby were joining in. Within a few hours, the car had been turned upside down and utterly destroyed. Again, the "vandals" appeared to be primarily respectable whites.

Untended property becomes fair game for people out for fun or plunder, and even for people who ordinarily would not dream of doing such things and who probably consider themselves law-abiding. Because of the nature of community life in the Bronx—its anonymity, the frequency with which cars are abandoned and things are stolen or broken, the past experience of "no one caring"—vandalism begins much more quickly than it does in staid Palo Alto, where people have come to believe that private possessions are cared for, and that mischievous behavior is costly. But vandalism can occur anywhere once communal barriers—the sense of mutual regard and the obligations of civility—are lowered by actions that seem to signal that "no one cares."

We suggest that "untended" behavior also leads to the breakdown of community controls. A stable neighborhood of families who care for their homes, mind each other's children, and confidently frown on unwanted intruders can change, in a few years or even a few months, to an inhospitable and frightening jungle. A piece of property is abandoned, weeds grow up, a window is smashed. Adults stop scolding rowdy children; the children, emboldened, become more rowdy. Families move out, unattached adults move in. Teenagers gather in front of the corner store. The merchant asks them to move; they refuse. Fights occur. Litter accumulates. People start drinking in front of the grocery; in time, an inebriate slumps to the sidewalk and is allowed to sleep it off. Pedestrians are approached by panhandlers.

At this point it is not inevitable that serious crime will flourish or violent attacks on strangers will occur. But many residents will think that crime, especially violent crime, is on the rise, and they will modify their behavior accordingly. They will use the streets less often, and when on the streets will stay apart from their fellows, moving with averted eyes, silent lips, and hurried steps. "Don't get involved." For some residents, this growing atomization will matter little, because the neighborhood is not their "home" but "the place where they live." Their interests are elsewhere; they are cosmopolitans. But it will matter greatly to other people, whose lives derive meaning and satisfaction from local attachments rather than worldly involvement; for them, the neighborhood will cease to exist except for a few reliable friends whom they arrange to meet.

Such an area is vulnerable to criminal invasion. Though it is not inevitable, it is more likely that here, rather than in places where people are confident they can regulate public behavior by informal controls, drugs will change hands, prostitutes will solicit, and cars will be stripped. That the drunks will be robbed by boys who do it as a lark, and the prostitutes' customers will be robbed by men who do it purposefully and perhaps violently. That muggings will occur.

Among those who often find it difficult to move away from this are the elderly. Surveys of citizens suggest that the elderly are much less likely to be the victims of crime than younger persons, and some have inferred from this that the well-known fear of crime voiced by the elderly is an exaggeration: perhaps we ought not to design special programs to protect older persons; perhaps we should even try to talk them out of their mistaken fears. This argument misses the point. The prospect of a confrontation with an obstreperous teenager or a drunken panhandler can be as fear-inducing for defenseless persons as the prospect of meeting an actual robber; indeed, to a defenseless person, the two kinds of confrontation are often indistinguishable. Moreover, the lower rate at which the elderly are victimized is a measure of the steps they have already taken—chiefly, staying behind locked doors—to minimize the risks they face. Young men are more frequently attacked than older women, not because they are easier or more lucrative targets but because they are on the streets more.

Nor is the connection between disorderliness and fear made only by the elderly. Susan Estrich, of the Harvard Law School, has recently gathered together a number of surveys on the sources of public fear. One, done in Portland, Oregon, indicated that three fourths of the adults interviewed cross to the other side of a street when they see a gang of teenagers; another survey, in Baltimore, discovered that nearly half would cross the street to avoid even a single strange youth. When an interviewer asked people in a housing project where the most dangerous spot was, they mentioned a place where young persons gathered to drink and play music, despite the fact that not a single crime had occurred there. In Boston public housing projects, the greatest fear was expressed by persons living in the buildings where disorderliness and incivility, not crime, were the greatest. Knowing this helps one understand the significance of such otherwise harmless displays as subway graffiti. As Nathan Glazer has written, the proliferation of graffiti, even when not obscene, confronts the subway rider with the "inescapable knowledge that the environment he must endure for an hour or more a day is uncontrolled and uncontrollable, and that anyone can invade it to do whatever damage and mischief the mind suggests."

In response to fear, people avoid one another, weakening controls. Sometimes they call the police. Patrol cars arrive, an occasional arrest occurs, but crime continues and disorder is not abated. Citizens complain to the police chief, but he explains that his department is low on personnel and that the courts do not punish petty or first-time offenders. To the residents, the police who arrive in squad cars are either ineffective or uncaring; to the police, the residents are animals who deserve each other. The citizens may soon stop calling the police, because "they can't do anything."

The process we call urban decay has occurred for centuries in every city. But what is happening today is different in at least two important respects.

First, in the period before, say, World War II, city dwellers—because of money costs, transportation difficulties, familial and church connections—could rarely move away from neighborhood problems. When movement did occur, it tended to be along public-transit routes. Now mobility has become exceptionally easy for all but the poorest or those who are blocked by racial prejudice. Earlier crime waves had a kind of built-in self-correcting mechanism: the determination of a neighborhood or community to reassert control over its turf. Areas in Chicago, New York, and Boston would experience crime and gang wars, and then normalcy would return, as the families for whom no alternative residences were possible reclaimed their authority over the streets.

Second, the police in this earlier period assisted in that reassertion of authority by acting, sometimes violently, on behalf of the community. Young toughs were roughed up, people were arrested "on suspicion" or for vagrancy, and prostitutes and petty thieves were routed. "Rights" were something enjoyed by decent folk, and perhaps also by the serious professional criminal, who avoided violence and could afford a lawyer.

This pattern of policing was not an aberration or the result of occasional excess. From the earliest days of the nation, the police function was seen primarily as that of a night watchman: to maintain order against the chief threats to order—fire, wild animals, and disreputable behavior. Solving crimes was viewed not as a police responsibility but as a private one. In the March, 1969, *Atlantic*, one of us (Wilson) wrote a brief account of how the police role had slowly changed from maintaining order to fighting crimes. The change began with the creation of private detectives (often ex-criminals), who worked on a contingency-fee basis for individuals who had suffered losses. In time, the detectives were absorbed into municipal police agencies and paid a regular salary; simultaneously, the responsibility for prosecuting thieves was shifted from the aggrieved private citizen to the professional prosecutor. This process was not complete in most places until the twentieth century.

In the 1960s, when urban riots were a major problem, social scientists began to explore carefully the order-maintenance function of the police, and to suggest ways of improving it—not to make streets safer (its original function) but to reduce the incidence of mass violence. Order maintenance became, to a degree, conterminous with "community relations." But, as the crime wave that began in the early 1960s continued without abatement throughout the decade and into the 1970s, attention shifted to the role of the police as crime-fighters. Studies of police behavior ceased, by and large, to be accounts of the order-maintenance function and became, instead, efforts to propose and test ways whereby the police could solve more crimes, make more arrests, and gather better evidence. If these things could be done, social scientists assumed, citizens would be less fearful.

A great deal was accomplished during this transition, as both police chiefs and outside experts emphasized the crime-fighting function in their plans, in the allocation of resources, and in deployment of personnel. The police may well have become better crime-fighters as a result. And doubtless they remained aware of their responsibility for order. But the link between order-maintenance and crime-prevention, so obvious to earlier generations, was forgotten.

That link is similar to the process whereby one broken window becomes many. The citizen who fears the ill-smelling drunk, the rowdy teenager, or the importuning beggar is not merely expressing his distaste for unseemly behavior; he is also giving voice to a bit of folk wisdom that happens to be a correct generalization—namely, that serious street crime flourishes in areas in which disorderly behavior goes unchecked. The unchecked panhandler is, in effect, the first broken window. Muggers and robbers, whether opportunistic or professional, believe they reduce their chances of being caught or even identified if they operate on streets where potential victims are already intimidated by prevailing conditions. If the neighborhood cannot keep a bothersome panhandler from annoying passersby, the thief may reason, it is even less likely to call the police to identify a potential mugger or to interfere if the mugging actually takes place.

Some police administrators concede that this process occurs, but argue that motorized-patrol officers can deal with it as effectively as foot-patrol officers. We are not so sure. In theory, an officer in a squad car can observe as much as an officer on foot; in theory, the former can talk to as many people as the latter. But the reality of police-citizen encounters is powerfully altered by the automobile. An officer on foot cannot separate himself from the street people; if he is approached, only his uniform and his personality can help him manage whatever is about to happen. And he can never be certain what that will be—a request for directions, a plea for help, an angry denunciation, a teasing remark, a confused babble, a threatening gesture.

In a car, an officer is more likely to deal with street people by rolling down the window and looking at them. The door and window exclude the approaching citizen; they are a barrier. Some officers take advantage of this barrier, perhaps unconsciously, by acting differently if in the car than they would on foot. We have seen this countless times. The police car pulls up to a corner where teenagers are gathered. The window is rolled down. The officer stares at the youths. They stare back. The officer says to one, "C'mere." He saunters over, conveying to his friends by his elaborately casual style the idea that he is not intimidated by authority. "What's your name?" "Chuck." "Chuck who?" "Chuck Jones." "What'ya doing, Chuck?" "Nothin'." "Got a P.O. [parole officer]?" "Nah." "Sure?" "Yeah." "Stay out of trouble, Chuckie." Meanwhile, the other boys laugh and exchange comments among themselves, probably at the officer's expense. The officer stares harder. He cannot be certain what is being said, nor can he join in and, by displaying his own skill at street banter, prove that he cannot be "put down." In the process, the officer has learned almost nothing, and the boys have decided the officer is an alien force who can safely be disregarded, even mocked.

Our experience is that most citizens like to talk to a police officer. Such exchanges give them a sense of importance, provide them with the basis for gossip, and allow them to explain to the authorities what is worrying them (whereby they gain a modest but significant sense of having "done something" about the problem). You approach a person on foot more easily, and talk to him more readily, than you do a person in a car. Moreover, you can more easily retain some anonymity if you draw an officer aside for a private chat. Suppose you want to pass on a tip about who is stealing handbags, or who offered to sell you a stolen TV. In the inner city, the culprit, in all likelihood, lives nearby. To walk up to a marked patrol car and lean in the window is to convey a visible signal that you are a "fink."

The essence of the police role in maintaining order is to reinforce the informal control mechanisms of the community itself. The police cannot, without committing extraordinary resources, provide a substitute for that informal control. On the other hand, to reinforce those natural forces the police must accommodate them. And therein lies the problem.

Should police activity on the street be shaped, in important ways, by the standards of the neighborhood rather than by the rules of the state? Over the past two decades, the shift of police from order-maintenance to law-enforcement has brought them increasingly under the influence of legal restrictions, provoked by media complaints and enforced by court decisions and departmental orders. As a consequence, the order-maintenance functions of the police are now governed by rules developed to control police relations with suspected criminals. This is, we think, an entirely new development. For centuries, the role of the police as watchmen was judged primarily not in terms of its compliance with appropriate procedures but rather in terms of its attaining a desired objective. The objective was order, an inherently ambiguous term but a condition that people in a given community recognized when they saw it. The means were the same as those the community itself would employ, if its members were sufficiently determined, courageous, and authoritative. Detecting and apprehending criminals, by contrast, was a means to an end, not an end in itself; a judicial determination of guilt or innocence was the hoped-for result of the law-enforcement mode. From the first, the police were expected to follow rules defining that process, though states differed in how stringent the rules should be. The criminal-apprehension process was always understood to involve individual rights, the violation of which was unacceptable because it meant that the violating officer would be acting as a judge and jury—and that was not his job. Guilt or innocence was to be determined by universal standards under special procedures.

Ordinarily, no judge or jury ever sees the persons caught up in a dispute over the appropriate level of neighborhood order. That is true not only because most cases are handled informally on the street but also because no universal standards are available to settle arguments over disorder, and thus a judge may not be any wiser or more effective than a police officer. Until quite recently in many states, and even today in some places, the police make arrests on such charges as "suspicious person" or "vagrancy" or "public drunkenness"— charges with scarcely any legal meaning. These charges exist not because society wants judges to punish vagrants or drunks but because it wants an officer to have the legal tools to remove undesirable persons from a neighborhood when informal efforts to preserve order in the streets have failed.

Once we begin to think of all aspects of police work as involving the application of universal rules under special procedures, we inevitably ask what constitutes an "undesirable person" and why we should "criminalize" vagrancy or drunkenness. A strong and commendable desire to see that people are treated fairly makes us worry about allowing the police to rout persons who are undesirable by some vague or parochial standard. A growing and not-so-commendable utilitarianism leads us to doubt that any behavior that does not "hurt" another person should be made illegal. And thus many of us who watch over the police are reluctant to allow them to perform, in the only way they can, a function that every neighborhood desperately wants them to perform.

This wish to "decriminalize" disreputable behavior that "harms no one"—and thus remove the ultimate sanction the police can employ to maintain neighborhood order—is, we think, a mistake. Arresting a single drunk or a single vagrant who has harmed no identifiable person seems unjust, and in a sense it is. But failing to do anything about a score of drunks or a hundred vagrants may destroy an entire community. A particular rule that seems to make sense in the individual case makes no sense when it is made a universal rule and applied to all cases. It makes no sense because it fails to take into account the connection between one broken window left untended and a thousand broken windows. Of course, agencies other than the police could attend to the problems posed by drunks or the mentally ill, but in most communities—especially where the "deinstitutionalization" movement has been strong—they do not.

The concern about equity is more serious. We might agree that certain behavior makes one person more undesirable than another, but how do we ensure that age or skin color or national origin or harmless mannerisms will not also become the basis for distinguishing the undesirable from the desirable? How do we ensure, in short, that the police do not become the agents of neighborhood bigotry?

We can offer no wholly satisfactory answer to this important question. We are not confident that there *is* a satisfactory answer, except to hope that by their selection, training, and supervision, the police will be inculcated with a clear sense of the outer limit of their discretionary authority. That limit, roughly, is this—the police exist to help regulate behavior, not to maintain the racial or ethnic purity of a neighborhood.

Consider the case of the Robert Taylor Homes in Chicago, one of the largest public-housing projects in the country. It is home for nearly 20,000 people, all black, and extends over ninety-two acres along South State Street. It was named after a distinguished black who had been, during the 1940s, chairman of the Chicago Housing Authority. Not long after it opened, in 1962, relations between project residents and the police deteriorated badly. The citizens felt that the police were insensitive or brutal; the police, in turn, complained of unprovoked attacks on them. Some Chicago officers tell of times when they were afraid to enter the Homes. Crime rates soared.

Today, the atmosphere has changed. Police–citizen relations have improved—apparently, both sides learned something from the earlier experience. Recently, a boy stole a purse and ran off. Several young persons who saw the theft voluntarily passed along to the police information on the identity and residence of the thief, and they did this publicly, with friends and neighbors looking on. But problems persist, chief among them the presence of youth gangs that terrorize residents and recruit members in the project. The people expect the police to "do something" about this, and the police are determined to do just that.

But do what? Though the police can obviously make arrests whenever a gang member breaks the law, a gang can form, recruit, and congregate without breaking the law. And only a tiny fraction of gang-related crimes can be solved by an arrest; thus, if an arrest is the only recourse for the police, the residents' fears will go unassuaged. The police will soon feel helpless, and the residents will again believe that the police "do nothing." What the police in fact do is to chase known gang members out of the project. In the words of one officer, "We kick ass." Project residents both know and approve of this. The tacit police-citizen alliance in the project is reinforced by the police view that the cops and the gangs are the two rival sources of power in the area, and that the gangs are not going to win.

None of this is easily reconciled with any conception of due process or fair treatment. Since both residents and gang members are black, race is not a factor. But it could be. Suppose a white project confronted a black gang, or vice versa. We would be apprehensive about the police taking sides. But the substantive problem remains the same: how can the police strengthen the informal social-control mechanisms of natural communities in order to minimize fear in public places? Law enforcement, per se, is no answer. A gang can weaken or destroy a community by standing about in a menacing fashion and speaking rudely to passersby without breaking the law.

We have difficulty thinking about such matters, not simply because the ethical and legal issues are so complex but because we have become accustomed to thinking of the law in essentially individualistic terms. The law defines *my* rights, punishes *his* behavior, and is applied by *that* officer because of *this* harm. We assume, in thinking this way, that what is good for the individual will be good for the community, and what doesn't matter when it happens to one person won't matter if it happens to many. Ordinarily, those are plausible assumptions. But in cases where behavior that is tolerable to one person is intolerable to many others, the reactions of the others—fear, withdrawal, flight—may ultimately make matters worse for everyone, including the individual who first professed his indifference.

It may be their greater sensitivity to communal as opposed to individual needs that helps explain why the residents of small communities are more satisfied with their police than are the residents of similar neighborhoods in big cities. Elinor Ostrom and her co-workers at Indiana University compared the perception of police services in two poor, all-black Illinois towns—Phoenix and East Chicago Heights—with those of three comparable all-black neighborhoods in Chicago. The level of criminal victimization and the quality of police-community relations appeared to be about the same in the towns and the Chicago neighborhoods. But the citizens living in their own villages were much more likely than those living in the Chicago neighborhoods to say that they do not stay at home for fear of crime, to agree that the local police have "the right to take any action necessary" to deal with problems, and to agree that the police "look out for the needs of the average citizen." It is possible that the residents and the police of the small towns saw themselves as engaged in a collaborative effort to maintain a certain standard of communal life, whereas those of the big city felt themselves to be simply requesting and supplying particular services on an individual basis.

If this is true, how should a wise police chief deploy his meager forces? The first answer is that nobody knows for certain, and the most prudent course of action could be to try further variations on the Newark experiment, to see more precisely what works in what kinds of neighborhoods. The second answer is also a hedge—many aspects of order-maintenance in neighborhoods can probably best be handled in ways that involve the police minimally, if at all. A busy, bustling shopping center and a quiet, well-tended suburb may need almost no visible police presence. In both cases, the ratio of respectable to disreputable people is ordinarily so high as to make informal social control effective.

Even in areas that are in jeopardy from disorderly elements, citizen action without substantial police involvement may be sufficient. Meetings between teenagers who like to hang out on a particular corner and adults who want to use that corner might well lead to an amicable agreement on a set of rules about how many people can be allowed to congregate, where, and when.

Where no understanding is possible—or if possible, not observed—citizen patrols may be a sufficient response. There are two traditions of communal involvement in maintaining order. One, that of the "community watchmen," is as old as the first settlement of the New World. Until well into the nineteenth century, volunteer watchmen, not policemen, patrolled their communities to keep order. They did so, by and large, without taking the law into their own hands—without, that is, punishing persons or using force. Their presence deterred disorder or alerted the community to disorder that could not be deterred. There are hundreds of such efforts today in communities all across the nation. Perhaps the best known is that of the Guardian Angels, a group of unarmed young persons in distinctive berets and T-shirts, who first came to public attention when they began patrolling the New York City subways but who claim now to have chapters in more than thirty American cities. Unfortunately, we have little information about the effect of these groups on crime. It is possible, however, that whatever their effect on crime, citizens find their presence reassuring, and that they thus contribute to maintaining a sense of order and civility.

The second tradition is that of the "vigilante." Rarely a feature of the settled communities of the East, it was primarily to be found in those frontier towns that grew up in advance of the reach of government. More than 350 vigilante groups are known to have existed; their distinctive feature was that their members did take the law into their own hands, by acting as judge, jury, and often executioner as well as policeman. Today, the vigilante movement is conspicuous by its rarity, despite the great fear expressed by citizens that the older cities are becoming "urban frontiers." But some community watchmen groups have skirted the line, and others may cross it in the future. An ambiguous case, reported in *The Wall Street Journal*, involved a citizens' patrol in the Silver Lake area of Belleville, New Jersey. A leader told the reporter, "We look for outsiders." If a few teenagers from outside the neighborhood enter it, "we ask them their business," he said. "If they say they're going down the street to see Mrs. Jones, fine, we let them pass. But then we follow them down the block to make sure they're really going to see Mrs. Jones."

Though citizens can do a great deal, the police are plainly the key to order-maintenance. For one thing, many communities, such as the Robert Taylor Homes, cannot do the job by themselves. For another, no citizen in a neighborhood, even an organized one, is likely to feel the sense of responsibility that wearing a badge confers. Psychologists have done many studies on why people fail to go to the aid of persons being attacked or seeking help, and they have learned that the cause is not "apathy" or "selfishness" but the absence of some plausible grounds for feeling that one must personally accept responsibility. Ironically, avoiding responsibility is easier when a lot of people are standing about. On streets and in public places, where order is so important, many people are likely to be "around," a fact that reduces the chance of any one person acting as the agent of the community. The police officer's uniform singles him out as a person who must accept responsibility if asked. In addition, officers, more easily than their fellow citizens, can be expected to distinguish between what is necessary to protect the safety of the street and what merely protects its ethnic purity.

But the police forces of America are losing, not gaining, members. Some cities have suffered substantial cuts in the number of officers available for duty. These cuts are not likely to be reversed in the near future. Therefore, each department must assign its existing officers with great care. Some neighborhoods are so demoralized and crime-ridden as to make foot patrol useless; the best the police can do with limited resources is respond to the enormous number of calls for service. Other neighborhoods are so stable and serene as to make foot patrol unnecessary. The key is to identify neighborhoods at the tipping point—where the public order is deteriorating but not unreclaimable, where the streets are used frequently but by apprehensive people, where a window is likely to be broken at any time, and must quickly be fixed if all are not to be shattered.

Most police departments do not have ways of systematically identifying such areas and assigning officers to them. Officers are assigned on the basis of crime rates (meaning that marginally threatened areas are often stripped so that police can investigate crimes in areas where the situation is hopeless) or on the basis of calls for service (despite the fact that most citizens do not call the police when they are merely frightened or annoyed). To allocate patrol wisely, the department must look at the neighborhoods and decide, from first-hand evidence, where an additional officer will make the greatest difference in promoting a sense of safety.

One way to stretch limited police resources is being tried in some public-housing projects. Tenant organizations hire off-duty police officers for patrol work in their buildings. The costs are not high (at least not per resident), the officer likes the additional income, and the residents feel safer. Such arrangements are probably more successful than hiring private watchmen, and the Newark experiment helps us understand why. A private security guard may deter crime or misconduct by his presence, and he may go to the aid of persons needing help, but he may well not intervene—that is, control or drive away—someone challenging community standards. Being a sworn officer—a "real cop"—seems to give one the confidence, the sense of duty, and the aura of authority necessary to perform this difficult task.

Patrol officers might be encouraged to go to and from duty stations on public transportation and, while on the bus or subway car, enforce rules about smoking, drinking, disorderly conduct, and the like. The enforcement need involve nothing more than ejecting the offender (the offense, after all, is not one with which a booking officer or a judge wishes to be bothered). Perhaps the random but relentless maintenance of standards on buses would lead to conditions on buses that approximate the level of civility we now take for granted on airplanes.

But the more important requirement is to think that to maintain order in precarious situations is a vital job. The police know this is one of their functions, and they also believe, correctly, that it cannot be done to the exclusion of criminal investigation and responding to calls. We may have encouraged them to suppose, however, on the basis of our oft-repeated concerns about serious, violent crime, that they will be judged exclusively on their capacity as crime-fighters. To the extent that this is the case, police administrators will continue to concentrate police personnel in the highest-crime areas (though not necessarily in the areas most vulnerable to criminal invasion), emphasize their training in the law and criminal apprehension (and not their training in managing street life), and join too quickly in campaigns to decriminalize "harmless" behavior (though public drunkenness, street prostitution, and pornographic displays can destroy a community more quickly than any team of professional burglars).

Above all, we must return to our long-abandoned view that the police ought to protect communities as well as individuals. Our crime statistics and victimization surveys measure individual losses, but they do not measure communal losses. Just as physicians now recognize the importance of fostering health rather than simply treating illness, so the police—and the rest of us—ought to recognize the importance of maintaining, intact, communities without broken windows.

"Broken Windows" and Fractured History
The Use and Misuse of History in Recent Police Patrol Analysis

Samuel Walker

A fresh burst of creativity marks current thinking about police patrol in the United States. This revival follows a period of doubt and disorientation in the late 1970s when recent research shattered traditional assumptions about patrol strategy. The most notable proposal for a reorientation of police patrol is set forth in "Broken Windows" by James Q. Wilson and George L. Kelling. Drawing partly on recent patrol experiments and partly on a re-thinking of police history, Wilson and Kelling propose a return to what they see as an older "watchman" style of policing (Wilson and Kelling 1982).

This selection examines the use of history by Wilson and Kelling in their proposal for reorienting police patrol. Because the historical analysis is central to their argument, its viability may well depend upon how well they have interpreted police history. Kelling develops his view of police history even more explicitly in a subsequent article co-authored with Mark H. Moore (Moore and Kelling 1983).

We shall argue here that Wilson, Kelling, and Moore have misinterpreted police history in several important respects. Their proposal calls for a restora-

Reprinted with permission of Academy of Criminal Justice Sciences, from *Justice Quarterly*, 1 (1984): 57–90.

tion—a return to a former tradition of police patrol. Joe McNamara, Chief of the San Jose police, has already responded to the "broken windows" thesis by arguing that the good old days weren't all that good (McNamara 1982). This selection elaborates upon that point and argues that the tradition of policing cited by Wilson, Kelling and Moore never existed. This does not necessarily mean that the broken windows thesis is completely invalid. But if there is merit in the style of police patrol Wilson and Kelling propose, that style will have to be created anew. There is no viable older tradition to restore. Obviously, this is a far more difficult and challenging proposition than they have suggested.

POLICING AND BROKEN WINDOWS

Broken windows are a metaphor for the deterioration of neighborhoods. A broken window that goes unrepaired is a statement that no one cares enough about the quality of life in the neighborhood to bother fixing the little things that are wrong. While a broken window might be a small thing in and of itself, left unrepaired it becomes an invitation to further neglect. The result is a progressive deterioration of the entire neighborhood. Wilson and Kelling cite research in social psychology where abandoned cars were rapidly vandalized when some sign of prior vandalism invited further destructive acts (Zimbardo 1969).

Policing in America has failed, Wilson, Kelling and Moore argue, because it has neglected "the little things," the law enforcement equivalents of broken windows. This neglect is the product of the development of an efficiency-oriented crime control-focused style of policing over the past fifty years. Eric Monkkonen argues that the shift toward crime control began even earlier and was substantially complete by 1920 (Monkkonen 1981).

Two developments in the 1930s launched a radical reorientation of police patrol. The first was the greatly increased use of the patrol car, which took the patrol officer off the street and isolated him from the public. The second was the development of the Uniform Crime Reports system that then became the basic measure of police "success."

By themselves, these two developments might not have exerted such a profound effect on policing. The crucial difference was the influence of O. W. Wilson who forged a coherent theory of police management in the late 1930s. Wilsonian theory emphasized the suppression of crime as the primary mission of policing. Fulfillment of this mission depended upon maximizing the efficiency of patrol coverage. The automobile allowed a patrol officer to cover his beat more often during one tour of duty, and to do so in a more unpredictable fashion than foot patrol.

Wilson became the leading proponent of one-officer cars, claiming that two single officer patrol cars were twice as efficient as one two-officer car. He recommended that patrol beats should be organized according to a workload formula that distributed the work evenly among patrol officers. Finally, he concluded that rapid response time would increase apprehensions and generally enhance public satisfaction with police service (Walker 1977; Fogelson 1977).

Wilson tirelessly propounded his gospel of efficiency from the late 1930s onward. His text *Police Administration* became "the bible" of police management and instructed an entire generation of police executives (Wilson and McLaren 1977). Police departments converted almost entirely from foot to automobile patrol, invested enormous sums of money in sophisticated communications equipment, and encouraged members of the public to avail themselves of their service.

Lost in this process were the personal aspects of routine policing. The car isolated officers from the people in the neighborhoods, which became nothing more than a series of "beat assignments" to the officers. The most professionalized departments, in fact, took extra measures to de-personalize policing. Frequent rotation of beat assignments was adopted as a strategy to combat corruption.

The crime control orientation meanwhile caused the police to concentrate on more serious crimes—primarily, the seven felonies that comprised the Crime Index. Significantly, the police actively adopted the UCR system as the measure of their performance. It was not something imposed on them (Manning 1977). The police lost interest in lesser violations of the law and routine because they just did not count. These nuisances included drunks, loud and intimidating groups of teenagers, public drug dealing, and the like.[1]

According to Wilson, Kelling, and Moore, these nuisances are the "broken windows," the little things that convey the message that no one cares about the quality of life in this neighborhood. Wilson, Kelling, and Moore base much of their argument on the recent Newark Foot Patrol Experiment (The Police Foundation 1981). The presence of officers on foot patrol did not reduce crime, but did make people feel safer. Officers were able to establish and enforce informal rules of behavior for the neighborhood. It was all right to be intoxicated in public but not to pass out in the gutter, for example. Wilson and Kelling also cite with apparent approval the technique used by some Chicago police officers to maintain order in public housing projects: if groups of teenagers were troublesome, the officers would simply chase them away. "We kick ass," one officer explained (Wilson and Kelling 1982:35).

The "Broken Windows" article argues that policing should be neighborhood-oriented. More officers should be deployed on foot, and those officers should concentrate less on catching criminals and more on enforcing informal neighborhood norms of behavior. To a certain extent it advocates a form of team policing, although with some important differences.

Team policing experiments in the 1970s did not emphasize foot patrol, gave insufficient attention to street-level patrol tactics, and maintained the traditional crime control focus. Indeed, the incompatibility of some elements of team policing with the prevailing organizational structure and management philosophy was one of the factors in the failure of early team policing experiments (Sherman 1973; U.S. Department of Justice 1977; Schwartz and Clarren 1977).

"Broken Windows" offers an alternative model precisely because it focuses on what officers would actually do. It characterizes the recommended style of policing as a return to an earlier (pre-1930s) style of "watchman" or "constabulary" policing. At this point we turn our attention to the historical analysis that underpins this argument.

THE HISTORICAL FRAMEWORK

The historical framework presented by Wilson, Kelling and Moore consists of three components: the near-term, which embraces the last fifteen years; the middle-term, which includes the last fifty years; and the long-term, which involves all of police history before the last fifty years.

Their reading of near-term history is excellent. One of the most important developments of the past fifteen years has unquestionably been the enormous expansion of our knowledge about all aspects of policing. We can now discuss in an informed fashion issues that were *terra incognita* to the staff of the President's Crime Commission (Walker 1983). The most important findings constitute a systematic demolition of the assumptions underlying O. W. Wilson's approach to police management. We have learned that adding more police or intensifying patrol coverage will not reduce crime and that neither faster response time nor additional detectives will improve clearance rates. Few authorities on policing today could endorse the basic Wilsonian idea that improved management in the deployment of patrol officers or detectives is likely to reduce the crime rate.

Wilson's, Kelling's, and Moore's reading of the last fifty years of police history is mixed. They recognize the most significant developments in the period but misinterpret them in important respects. There are substantial implications of this misinterpretation for their proposed style of policing.

The development of American policing from the 1930s through the 1960s was a far more complex process than historians have lead us to believe. Wilson, Kelling, and Moore can be excused in large part because they have simply drawn upon the available historical scholarship. We will focus here on two aspects of police history since the 1930s that have not received sufficient attention. The first involves the impact of the patrol car and the second concerns the crime control orientation of policing.

THE TECHNOLOGICAL REVOLUTION

It is indeed true that American police departments largely converted from foot to automobile patrol between the 1930s and the present. We should, of course, be cognizant of the enormous variations that exist even today. Some departments are almost wholly motorized while others, primarily Eastern cities, still make heavy use of foot patrol (Police Executive Research Forum 1981).

And it is also true that car patrols remove officers from the sidewalks, isolate them from casual contacts with ordinary citizens, and damage police-community relations. This analysis is part of the conventional wisdom about policing.

The impact of technology was paradoxical, however. The mid-century revolution in American policing involved not just the patrol car, but the car in conjunction with the telephone and the two-way radio. These served to bring police officers into far more intimate contact with people than ever before. While the patrol car isolated police officers in some respects, the telephone simultaneously increased the degree of contact in other respects. Let us examine this paradox in detail.

In the days of foot patrol, officers had extensive casual contacts with people. But they occurred primarily on the streets or in other public places. The police did not often obtain entry to private residences. The reason for this is obvious: there was no mechanism whereby the ordinary citizen could effectively summon the police. The telephone radically altered that situation with profound ramifications for both policing and public expectations about the quality of life. Stinchcombe (1963) has discussed the impact of privacy considerations on routine police work.

The telephone made it possible for the ordinary citizen to summon the police, and the combination of the two-way radio and the patrol car allowed the police to respond quickly. As we know, the more professional departments acquired a fetish for responding as quickly as possible to all calls. The development of the 911 telephone number was simply the logical conclusion of this effort to advertise and encourage people to use police service. People have in fact availed themselves of this service. The number of calls for service has escalated to the point where serious attention has been given to the idea of restricting or otherwise managing those requests in the last few years (Gay 1977).

Technology radically alters the nature of police-citizen contacts. Most of those contacts now occur in private residences. Albert Reiss reports that 70% of all police-citizen contacts occur in private places, 12% in semi-public, and 18% in open public places (Reiss 1971:16). The police not only gain access to private places, but observe the most intimate aspects of peoples' lives, and are asked to handle their most personal problems.

Research has confirmed that the bulk of police work involves domestic disputes and other problems arising from alcohol, drugs, mental illness, and poverty. Officers refer to all this as "bullshit" or "social work" because it is unrelated to what they believe to be their crime control mission.

Police-citizen contacts became increasingly skewed. The police lost contact with "ordinary" people and gained a great deal of contact with "problem" people, who included not just criminal offenders but those with multiple social problems. David Bayley and Harold Mendelsohn once observed that police officers had more direct knowledge about minorities than did the members of any other occupation. This knowledge was a direct product of the heavy demands upon police service placed by low-income and racial minorities (Bayley and Mendelsohn 1969:156).

Our understanding of the full impact of the telephone on policing remains problematic. Not all experts on policing accept the argument advanced here. Some argue that the police were indeed intimately involved in people's lives prior to the advent of the telephone.[2] Unfortunately, there is no empirical evidence that would permit the resolution of this question. Prior to the late 1950s, there were no observational studies of police patrol activities and thus we have no reliable evidence on what American police officers did on patrol in the pre-telephone era.[3]

THE REVOLUTION IN PUBLIC EXPECTATIONS

One consequence of the technological revolution in policing has been a parallel revolution in public expectations about the quality of life. The availability of police service created and fed a demand for those services. The establishment of the modern police in the early nineteenth century was an initial phase of this process, which created the expectation that a certain level of public order would, or at least should, prevail (Silver 1967).

The technological revolution of the mid-twentieth century generated a quantum leap in those expectations. Because there was now a mechanism for getting someone (the police) to "do something" about minor disorders and nuisances, people came to expect that they should not have to put up with such minor irritations. Thus, the general level of expectations about the quality of life—the amount of noise, the presence of "strange" or "undesirable" people—has undergone an enormous change. Three generations of Americans have learned or at least have come to believe that they should not have to put up with certain problems.

The police are both the source and the victims of this revolution. They have stimulated higher levels of public expectations by their very presence and their policy of more readily available services. At the same time they are the prisoners of their own creation, swamped with an enormous service call workload. The recent effort to restrict or somehow manage this workload faces the problem of a public that expects rapid police response for any and every problem as a matter of right.

Documenting changes in public expectations concerning the police is difficult given the absence of reliable data about public attitudes or police practices prior to the late 1950s and early 1960s. Several indicators do provide evidence of short-term changes in public expectations. The development of three-digit (911) emergency phone numbers for the police increased the number of service calls. In Omaha, Nebraska, for example, the number of patrol car dispatches increased by 36% between 1969 and 1971, presumably as a result of a new 911 phone number (Walker 1983:110). These figures represent the dispatch of a patrol car, not the number of incoming calls. Omaha police officials estimate that about 35% of all calls do not result in a dispatch.

Additional evidence is found in data on the number of civilian complaints about police misconduct. In New York City, for example, the number of complaints filed with the Civilian Complaint Review Board (CCRB) increased from about 200 per year in 1960–62 to just over 2000 per year in 1967–68 and more than 3000 annually in 1971–74. It would be difficult to believe that the conduct of New York City police officers deteriorated by a factor of 10 or 15 during this period. Rather, the increase is probably the result of a lower threshold of tolerance for police misconduct on the part of citizens and the increased availability of an apparent remedy for perceived misconduct.

During the period under discussion, the procedures of the New York CCRB were reorganized several times. Each reorganization facilitated complaint filing and at the same time heightened public awareness of the availability of this particular remedy (Kahn 1975:113). The data on civilian complaints supports the argument made herein concerning police services generally: the availability of a service or remedy stimulates demand for that service, thereby altering basic expectations.

The Mythology of Crime Control

The conventional wisdom states that police organize their efforts around the goal of crime control. Wilson, Kelling and Moore restate this conventional wisdom, but the matter is a bit more complex.

There is an important distinction between the self-image of the police and the day-to-day reality of routine policing (Goldstein 1977). The emphasis on crime control is and has been largely a matter of what the police say they are doing. Peter Manning argues persuasively that the police consciously created and manipulated this self-image as a way of establishing greater professional and political autonomy (Manning 1977).

As we have seen, however, the day-to-day reality of policing contradicted this self-image. The sharp contrast between the crime-fighting imagery of the police and the peacekeeping reality of police activities was one of the first and most important findings of the flood of police research that began in the 1960s. When Wilson, Kelling, and Moore suggest that the police are completely crime control-oriented they seriously misrepresent the nature of contemporary policing.

The discrepancy between crime control imagery and operational reality also becomes evident when we look more closely at how police departments utilize their resources. The most recent Survey of Police Operational and Administrative Practices reveals enormous variations among departments (Police Executive Research Forum 1981). Many still distribute their patrol officers equally among three shifts, ignoring even the most rudimentary workload formulas, which were first developed by O. W. Wilson over forty years ago (Wilson and McLaren 1977: Appendix J). Departments typically do not revise the boundaries of their patrol districts on a regular basis. Districts remain unchanged for ten or twenty years, or longer. Meanwhile, the composition of the urban environment changes radically, as older areas are depopulated, new residential areas created, and so on.

THE QUESTION OF LEGITIMACY

The most important long-term development in American policing, according to Wilson, Kelling and Moore, has been the loss of political legitimacy. There can be little doubt that legitimacy, by which we mean acceptance of police authority by the public, is a major problem today.

The interpretation of police history offered by Wilson, Kelling, and Moore, which purports to explain how that legitimacy was lost, is seriously flawed. The evidence completely contradicts the thrust of their argument.

The police in the nineteenth century were not merely the "adjuncts" of the machine, as Robert Fogelson (1977) suggests, but were central cogs in it. Wilson, Kelling, and Moore maintain that this role offered certain benefits for the police, which reformers and historians alike have overlooked.

As cogs in the machine, the police served the immediate needs of the different neighborhoods. Political control was highly decentralized and local city councilmen or ward bosses exercised effective control over the police. Thus, the police carried out a wide range of services. Historians have rediscovered the social welfare role of the police, providing food and lodging for vagrants (Walker 1977; Monkkonen 1981). The police also performed political errands and were the means by which certain groups and individuals were able to corrupt the political process. These errands included open electioneering, rounding up the loyal voters, and harassing the opponents. Police also enforced the narrow prejudices of their constituents, harassing "undesirables" or discouraging any kind of "unwelcome" behavior.

Wilson, Kelling, and Moore concede that there was a lack of concern for due process, but argue there was an important trade-off. By virtue of serving the immediate needs and narrow prejudices of the neighborhoods, the police gained an important degree of political legitimacy. They were perceived as faithful servants and enjoyed the resulting benefits. All of this was destroyed by the reforms of the twentieth century. The patrol car removed officers from the streets, while the new "professional" style dictated an impersonal type of policing. Legal concerns with due process denied officers the ability to use the tactics of rough justice by which they had enforced neighborhood community norms.

This historical analysis is central to the reorientation of policing presented in the "Broken Windows" article. Wilson, Kelling, and Moore propose that the lost political legitimacy could be re-established by what they view as the older "watchman" style of policing. Unfortunately, this historical analysis is pure fantasy.

Historians are unanimous in their conclusion that the police were at the center of urban political conflict in the nineteenth century. In many instances policing was the paramount issue and in some cases the only issue. Historians disagree only on their interpretation of the exact nature of this political conflict. The many experiments with different forms of administrative control over the police (the last of which survives only in Missouri) were but one part of this long and bitter struggle for political control (Walker 1977; Fogelson 1977).

To say that there was political conflict over the police means that the police lacked political legitimacy. Their authority was not accepted by the citizenry. Wilson, Kelling, and Moore are seriously in error when they suggest that the police enjoyed substantial legitimacy in the pre-technology era.

The lack of legitimacy is further illustrated by the nature of the conflicts surrounding the police. Non-enforcement of the various laws designed to control drinking was the issue that most often roused the so-called "reformers" to action. Alcohol consumption was a political issue with many dimensions. In some respects it was an expression of ethnic conflict, pitting sobersided Anglo-Saxons against the heavy-drinking Irish and Germans. Drinking was also a class issue. Temperance and, later, prohibition advocates tended either to come from the middle class or at least define themselves in terms of the values of hard work, sobriety, thrift and upward mobility (Gusfield 1963). When nineteenth-century Americans fought over the police and the enforcement of the drinking laws, that battle expressed the deepest social conflicts in American society.

In one of the finest pieces of historical scholarship on the American police, Wilbur Miller explores the question of legitimacy from an entirely different angle (Miller 1977). The great difference between the London and New York City police was precisely the extent to which officers in New York were denied the grant of legitimacy enjoyed by their counterparts in London. Miller further argues that the problem of legitimacy was individualized in New York City. Each officer faced challenges to his personal authority and had to assert his authority on a situational level.

Miller does not argue that challenges to police legitimacy were patterned according to class, ethnicity or race. Thus, an Irish-American cop was just as likely to be challenged by a fellow countryman as he was by someone of a different ethnic background. To be sure, the poor, political radicals, blacks, and other people deemed "undesirable" were victimized more often by the police than were other groups, but it does not follow that the police enjoyed unquestioned authority in the eyes of those people who were members of the same class and ethnic groups as police officers.

THE MYTH OF THE WATCHMAN

With their argument that the nineteenth century police enjoyed political legitimacy, Wilson, Kelling, and Moore have resurrected in slightly different garb the old myth of the friendly cop on the beat. They offer this older "watchman" style of policing as a viable model for contemporary policing.

Quite apart from the broader question of political legitimacy, their argument turns on the issue of on-the-street police behavior.

Historians have not yet reconstructed a full picture of police behavior in the nineteenth century. At best, historians can make inferences about this behavior from surviving records. None of the historical accounts published to date presents a picture of policing that could be regarded as a viable model for the present.

What do we know about routine policing in the days before the patrol car? There is general agreement that officers did not necessarily do much work at all. Given the primitive state of communications technology, patrol officers were almost completely on their own and able to avoid effective supervision (Rubinstein 1974). Evidence suggests that evasion of duty was commonplace. We also know that corruption was the norm. Mark Haller (1976) suggests that corruption was possibly the primary objective of all of municipal government, not just the police department.

Wilbur Miller (1977), meanwhile, places the matter of police brutality in a new and convincing light. His argument that brutality was a response to the refusal of citizens to grant the police legitimacy speaks directly to the point raised by Wilson, Kelling, and Moore.

Recently some historians have attempted to draw a more systematic picture of police law enforcement activities. The most convincing picture is drawn by Lawrence Friedman and Robert Percival (1981) in their study of the Oakland police between 1870 and 1910. They characterize police arrest patterns as a giant trawling operation. The typical arrestee was a white, working class adult male who was drunk and was arrested for intoxication, disturbing the peace, or some related offense. But there was nothing systematic about police operations. The people swept up into their net were simply unlucky—there was no reason why they should have been arrested rather than others whose behavior was essentially the same. Nor was it apparent, in Friedman's and Percival's view, that the police singled out any particular categories of people for especially systematic harassment.

The argument offered by Wilson, Kelling, and Moore turns in part on the question of purpose: what the police saw themselves doing. Historians have established that police officers had a few purposes. The first was to get and hold the job. The second was to exploit the possibilities for graft that the job offered. A third was to do as little actual patrol work as possible. A fourth involved surviving on the street, which meant establishing and maintaining authority in the face of hostility and overt challenges to that authority. Finally, officers apparently felt obliged to go through the motions of "real" police work by arresting occasional miscreants.

We do not find in this picture any conscious purpose of fighting crime or serving neighborhood needs. That is precisely the point made by Progressive era reformers when they indicted the police for inefficiency. Wilson, Kelling, and Moore have no grounds for offering this as a viable model for contemporary policing. Chief McNamara is right: the good old days were not that good.

The watchman style of policing described by Wilson, Kelling, and Moore can also be challenged from a completely different perspective. The idea that the police served the needs of local neighborhoods and thereby enjoyed political legitimacy is based on a highly romanticized view of nineteenth-century neighborhood life. Urban neighborhoods were not stable and homogeneous little villages nestled in the city. They were heterogeneous, and the rate of geographic mobility was even higher than contemporary rates. Albert Reiss (1971:209–210) in *Police and the Public* critiques recent "community control" proposals on these very grounds: they are based on the erroneous impression that neighborhoods are stable, homogeneous, and relatively well-defined.

SUMMARY AND CONCLUSIONS

In "Broken Windows," James Q. Wilson and George Kelling offer a provocative proposal for reorienting police patrol. Their argument is based primarily on an historical analysis of American policing. They propose a return to a watchman style of policing, which they claim existed before the advent of crime control oriented policing in the 1930s. This historical analysis is further developed in a subsequent article by Kelling and Moore (1983).

In this article we have examined the historical analysis used by these three authors. We find it flawed on several fundamental points.

First, the depersonalization of American policing from the 1930s onward has been greatly exaggerated. While the patrol car did isolate the police in some respects, the telephone brought about a more intimate form of contact between police and citizen by allowing the police officer to enter private residences and involving them in private disputes and problems.

Second, the crime control orientation of the police has been greatly exaggerated. Crime control is largely a matter of police rhetoric and self-image. Day-to-day policing is, on the other hand, primarily a matter of peacekeeping.

Third, there is no historical evidence to support the contention that the police formerly enjoyed substantial political legitimacy. To the contrary, all the evidence suggests that the legitimacy of the police was one of the major political controversies throughout the nineteenth century and well into the twentieth.

Fourth, the watchman style of policing referred to by Wilson, Kelling, and Moore is just as inefficient and corrupt as the reformers accuse it of being. It does not involve any conscious purpose to serve neighborhood needs and hardly serves as a model for revitalized contemporary policing.

Where does this leave us? We should not throw the proverbial baby out with the bath water. The fact that Wilson and Kelling construct their "Broken Windows" thesis on a false and heavily romanticized view of the past does not by itself invalidate their concept of a revitalized police patrol. They correctly interpret the lessons of recent police research. Suppression of crime is a will-of-the-wisp that the police should no longer pursue. Enhancement of public feelings of safety, however, does appear to be within the grasp of the police. A new form of policing based on the apparent lessons of the Newark Foot Patrol Experiment, the failures of team policing experiments, and the irrelevance of most official police-community relations programs seems to be a goal that is both worth pursuing and feasible.

Our main point here is simply that such a revitalized form of policing would represent something entirely new in the history of the American police. There is no older tradition worthy of restoration. A revitalized, community-oriented policing would have to be developed slowly and painfully.

There should be no mistake about the difficulty of such a task. Among other things, recent research on the police clearly demonstrates the enormous difficulty in changing police officer behavior and/or the structure and process of police organization. Yet at the same time, the history reviewed here does suggest that fundamental long-term changes in policing are indeed possible. Change is a constant; shaping that change in a positive way is the challenge.

Notes

[1] James Fyfe argues that prosecutorial and judicial indifference to minor "quality of life" offenses is also responsible for neighborhood deterioration and that the police should not be singled out as the major culprits. By implication, he suggests that reorienting the police role would be futile without simultaneously reorienting the priorities of prosecutors and judges. Personal correspondence, James Fyfe to Walker.

[2] Lawrence W. Sherman accepts this view and dissents from the argument advanced in this article. Personal correspondence, Lawrence W. Sherman to Walker.

[3] The debate is conducted largely on the basis of circumstantial evidence. Sherman, for example, believes that literary evidence is a reliable guide to past police practices and cites *A Tree Grows in Brooklyn* as one useful example. Personal correspondence, Sherman to Walker.

References

Bayley, D. and Mendelsohn, H. (1969) *Minorities and the Police*. New York: The Free Press.

Fogelson, R. (1977) *Big City Police*. Cambridge: Harvard University Press.

Friedman, L. M. and Percival, R. V. (1981) *The Roots of Justice*. Chapel Hill: University of North Carolina Press.

Gay, W. (1977) *Improving Patrol Productivity*, Vol. I, Routine Patrol. Washington, DC: Government Printing Office.

Goldstein, H. (1977) *Policing a Free Society*. Cambridge: Ballinger.

Gusfield, J. (1963) *Symbolic Crusade: Status Politics and the American Temperance Movement*. Urbana: University of Illinois Press.

Haller, M. (1976) "Historical Roots of Police Behavior: Chicago, 1890–1925." *Law and Society Review* 10 (Winter): 303–24.

Kahn, R. (1975) "Urban Reform and Police Accountability in New York City, 1950–1974." In *Urban Problems and Public Policy*, edited by R. L. Lineberry and L. H. Masotti. Lexington: Lexington Books.

McNamara, J. D. (1982) "Dangerous Nostalgia for the Cop on the Beat." *San Jose Mercury-News*, May 2.

Manning, P. K. (1977) *Police Work*. Cambridge: MIT Press.

Miller, W. (1977) *Cops and Bobbies*. Chicago: University of Chicago Press.

Monkkonen, E. (1981) *Police in Urban America, 1860–1920*. Cambridge: Cambridge University Press.

Moore, M. H. and Kelling, G. L. (1983) "To Serve and Protect: Learning from Police History." *The Public Interest* 70:49–65.

Police Executive Research Forum (1981) *Survey of Police Operational and Administrative Practices—1981*. Washington, DC: Police Executive Research Forum.

Police Foundation (1981) *The Newark Foot Patrol Experiment*. Washington, DC: The Police Foundation.

Reiss, A. (1971) *The Police and the Public*. New Haven: Yale University Press.

Rubinstein, J. (1974) *City Police*. New York: Ballantine Books.

Schwartz, A. I. and Clarren, S. N. (1977) *The Cincinnati Team Policing Experiment*. Washington, DC: The Police Foundation.

Sherman, L. W. (1973) *Team Policing: Seven Case Studies*. Washington, DC: The Police Foundation.

Silver, A. (1967) "The Demand for Order in Civil Society." In *The Police: Six Sociological Essays*, ed. by David J. Bordua. New York: John Wiley.

Stinchcombe, A. (1963) "Institutions of Privacy in the Determination of Police Administrative Practice." *American Journal of Sociology* 69 (September): 150–60.

U.S. Department of Justice (1977) *Neighborhood Team Policing*. Washington, DC: Government Printing Office.

Walker, S. (1983) *The Police in America: An Introduction*. New York: McGraw-Hill.

_____. (1977) *A Critical History of Police Reform: The Emergence of Professionalization*. Lexington: Lexington Books.

Wilson, J. Q. and Kelling, G. L. (1982) "Broken Windows: Police and Neighborhood Safety." *Atlantic Monthly* 249 (March): 29–38.

Wilson, O. W. and McLaren, R. C. (1977) *Police Administration* (4th. ed.). New York: McGraw-Hill.

Zimbardo, P. G. (1969) "The Human Choice: Individuation, Reason, and Order versus Deindividuation, Impulse, and Chaos." In *Nebraska Symposium on Motivation*, edited by W. J. Arnold and D. Levine. Lincoln: University of Nebraska Press.

Community Policing
Elements and Effects

Gary W. Cordner

In less than two decades, community policing has evolved from a few small foot patrol studies to the preeminent reform agenda of modern policing. With roots in such earlier developments as police-community relations, team policing, crime prevention, and the rediscovery of foot patrol, community policing has become, in the 1990s, the dominant strategy of policing—so much so that the 100,000 new police officers funded by the 1994 Crime Bill must be engaged, by law, in community policing.

Despite all this activity, four complicating factors have made it extremely difficult to determine the effectiveness of community policing:

- *Programmatic complexity*—There exists no single definition of community policing nor any universal set of program elements. Police agencies around the country (and around the world) have implemented a wide array of organizational and operational innovations under the label "community policing." Because community policing is not one consistent "thing," it is difficult to say whether "it" works.

- *Multiple effects*—The number of intended and unintended effects that might accrue to community policing is considerable. Community policing might affect crime, fear of crime, disorder, community relations, and/or police officer attitudes, to mention just a few plausible impacts. The reality of these multiple effects, as opposed to a single

This article is a substantial revision (revised especially for *Critical Issues in Policing*) of an earlier article in *Police Forum* (July 1995).

bottom-line criterion, severely reduces the likelihood of a simple yes or no answer to the question "Does community policing work?"

- *Variation in program scope*—The scope of community policing projects has varied from single-officer assignments to department-wide efforts. Some of the most positive results have come from projects that involved only a few specialist officers, small special units, or narrowly defined target areas. The generalizability of these positive results to full-scale department-wide implementation is problematic.

- *Research design limitations*—Despite heroic efforts by police officials and researchers, most community policing studies have had serious research design limitations. These include lack of control groups, failure to randomize treatments, and a tendency to measure only short-term effects. Consequently, the findings of many community policing studies do not have as much credibility as we might hope.

These complicating factors are offered not as excuses but rather to sensitize us to the very real difficulty of producing reliable knowledge about the effects of community policing. Additionally, they identify priority issues that need to be addressed in order to substantially improve what we know about the effectiveness of community policing.

What is Community Policing?

Community policing remains many things to many people. A common refrain among proponents is "Community policing is a philosophy, not a program." An equally common refrain among police officers is "Just tell me exactly what you want me to do differently." Some critics, echoing concerns similar to those expressed by police officers, argue that if community policing is nothing more than a philosophy, it is merely an empty shell (Goldstein, 1987).

It would be easy to list dozens of common characteristics of community policing, starting with foot patrol and mountain bikes and ending with the police as organizers of, and advocates for, the poor and dispossessed. Instead, it may be more helpful to identify four major dimensions of community policing and some of the most common elements within each. These four dimensions of community policing are:

- The Philosophical Dimension
- The Strategic Dimension
- The Tactical Dimension
- The Organizational Dimension

The Philosophical Dimension

Many of its most thoughtful and forceful advocates emphasize that community policing is a new philosophy of policing, perhaps constituting even a paradigm shift away from professional-model policing. The philosophical dimension includes the central ideas and beliefs underlying community policing. Three of the most important of these are citizen input, broad function, and personalized service.

Citizen Input.   Community policing takes the view that, in a free society, citizens should have open access to police organizations and input to police policies and decisions. Access and input through elected officials is considered necessary but not sufficient. Individual neighborhoods and communities should have the opportunity to influence how they are policed and legitimate interest groups in the community should be able to discuss their views and concerns directly with police officials. Police departments, like other agencies of government, should be responsive and accountable.

Mechanisms for achieving greater citizen input are varied. Some police agencies use systematic and periodic community surveys to elicit citizen input (Bureau of Justice Assistance, 1994a). Others rely on open forums, town meetings, radio and television call-in programs, and similar methods open to all residents. Some police officials meet regularly with citizen advisory boards, ministry alliances, minority group representatives, business leaders, and other formal groups. These techniques have been used by police chief executives, district commanders, and ordinary patrol officers; they can be focused as widely as the entire jurisdiction or as narrowly as a beat or a single neighborhood.

The techniques used to achieve citizen input should be less important than the end result. Community policing emphasizes that police departments should seek and carefully consider citizen input when making policies and decisions that affect the community. Any other alternative would be unthinkable in an agency that is part of a government "of the people, for the people, and by the people."

Broad Police Function.   Community policing embraces a broad view of the police function rather than a narrow focus on crime fighting or law enforcement (Kelling and Moore, 1988). Historical evidence is often cited to show that the police function was originally quite broad and varied and that it only narrowed in recent decades, perhaps due to the influence of the professional model and popular media representations of police work. Social science data is also frequently cited to show that police officers actually spend relatively little of their time dealing with serious offenders or investigating violent crimes.

This broader view of the police function recognizes the kinds of nonenforcement tasks that police already perform and seeks to give them greater status and legitimacy. These include order maintenance, social service, and general assistance duties. They may also include greater responsibilities in protecting and enhancing "the lives of those who are most vulnerable—juveniles, the elderly, minorities, the poor, the disabled, the homeless" (Trojanowicz and Bucqueroux, 1990: xiv). In the bigger picture, the police mission is seen to include resolving conflict, helping victims, preventing accidents, solving problems, and reducing fear as well as reducing crime through apprehension and enforcement.

Personal Service.   Community policing supports tailored policing based on local norms and values and individual needs. An argument is made that the criminal law is a very blunt instrument and that police officers inevitably exercise wide discretion when making decisions. Presently, individual officers make arrests and other decisions based on a combination of legal, bureaucratic, and idiosyncratic criteria, while the police department maintains the myth of full or at least uniform enforcement (Goldstein, 1977). Under community policing, officers are asked to consider the "will of the community" when deciding which laws to enforce under what circumstances, and police executives are asked to tolerate and even encourage such differential and personalized policing.

Such differential or tailored policing primarily affects police handling of minor criminal offenses, local ordinance violations, public disorder, and service issues. Some kinds of behavior proscribed by state and local law, and some levels of noise and disorder, may be seen as less bothersome in some neighborhoods than in others. Similarly, some police methods, including such aggressive tactics as roadblocks as well as more prevention-oriented programs such as landlord training, may coincide with norms and values in some neighborhoods but not others.

Even the strongest advocates of community policing recognize that a balance must be reached between differential neighborhood-level policing and uniform jurisdiction-wide policing. Striking a healthy and satisfactory balance between competing interests has always been one of the central concerns of policing and police administration. Community policing simply argues that neighborhood-level norms and values should be added to the mix of legal, professional, and organizational considerations that influences decision-making about policies, programs, and resources at the executive level as well as enforcement-level decisions on the street.

This characteristic of community policing is also aimed at overcoming one of the most common complaints that the public has about government employees in general, including police officers—that they do not seem to care and that they are more interested in "going by the book" than in providing quality, personalized service. Many citizens seem to resent being subjected to "stranger policing" and would rather deal with officers who know them, and whom they know. Of course, not every police-citizen encounter can be amicable and friendly. But officers who generally deal with citizens in a friendly, open, and personal manner may be more likely to generate trust and confidence than officers who operate in a narrow, aloof, and/or bureaucratic manner.

The Strategic Dimension

The strategic dimension of community policing includes the key operational concepts that translate philosophy into action. These strategic concepts are the links between the broad ideas and beliefs that underlie community policing and the specific programs and practices by which it is implemented. They assure that agency policies, priorities, and resource allocation are consistent with a community-oriented philosophy. Three strategic elements of community policing are re-oriented operations, geographic focus, and prevention emphasis.

Re-oriented Operations. Community policing recommends less reliance on the patrol car and more emphasis on face-to-face interactions. One objective is to replace ineffective or isolating operational practices (e.g., motorized patrol and rapid response to low priority calls) with more effective and more interactive practices. A related objective is to find ways of performing necessary traditional functions (e.g., handling emergency calls and conducting follow-up investigations) more efficiently, in order to save time and resources that can then be devoted to more community-oriented activities.

Many police departments today have increased their use of foot patrol, directed patrol, door-to-door policing, and other alternatives to traditional motorized patrol (Cordner and Trojanowicz, 1992). Generally, these alternatives seek more targeted tactical effectiveness, more attention to minor offenses and "incivilities," a greater "felt presence" of police, and/or more police-citizen contact. Other police departments have simply reduced their commitment to any form of continuous patrolling, preferring instead to have their patrol officers engage in problem solving, crime prevention, and similar activities when not handling calls and emergencies.

Many police agencies have also adopted differential responses to calls for service (McEwen, Connors, and Cohen, 1986). Rather than attempting to immediately dispatch a sworn officer in response to each and every notification of a crime, disturbance, or other situation, these departments vary their responses depending upon the circumstances. Some crime reports may be taken over the telephone, some service requests may be referred to other government agencies, and some sworn officer responses may be delayed. A particularly interesting alternative is to ask complainants to go in person to a nearby police mini-station or storefront office, where an officer, a civilian employee, or even a volunteer takes a report or provides other in-person assistance. Use of differential responses helps departments cope with the sometimes overwhelming burden of 911 calls and frees up patrol officer time for other activities, such as patrolling, problem solving, and crime prevention.

Traditional criminal investigation has also been reexamined in recent years (Eck, 1992). Some departments have de-specialized the activity, reducing the size of the detective unit and making patrol officers more responsible for follow-up investigations. Many have also eliminated the practice of conducting an extensive follow-up investigation of every reported crime, focusing instead on the more serious offenses and on more "solvable" cases. Investigative attention has also been expanded to include a focus on offenders as well as on offenses, especially in the form of repeat offender units that target high-frequency serious offenders. A few departments have taken the additional step of trying to get detectives to expand their case-by-case orientation to include problem solving and crime prevention. In this approach, a burglary detective would be as concerned with reducing burglaries through problem solving and crime prevention as s/he was with solving particular burglary cases.

Not all contemporary alternatives to motorized patrol, rapid response, and criminal investigation are closely allied with community policing. Those specific operational alternatives, and those uses of the freed-up time of patrol officers and detectives, that are consistent with the philosophical and strategic foundations of community policing can be distinguished from those that conform to other philosophies and strategies of policing (Moore and Trojanowicz, 1988).

Geographic Focus. Community policing strategy emphasizes the geographic basis of assignment and responsibility by shifting the fundamental unit of patrol accountability from time of day to place. That is, rather than holding patrol officers, supervisors, and shift commanders responsible for wide areas but only during their eight or ten hour shifts, community policing seeks to establish 24-hour responsibility for smaller areas.

Of course, no single officer works 24 hours a day, seven days a week, week in and week out. Community policing usually deals with this limitation in one or a combination of three ways: (1) community police officers assigned to neighborhoods may be specialists, with most call-handling relegated to a more traditional patrol unit; (2) each individual patrol officer may be held responsible for long-term problem solving in an assigned neighborhood, even though s/he handles calls in a much larger area and, of necessity, many of the calls in the assigned area are handled by other officers; or (3) small teams of officers share both call-handling and problem solving responsibility in a beat-sized area.

A key ingredient of this geographic focus, however it is implemented, is permanency of assignment. Community policing recommends that patrol officers be assigned to the same areas for extended periods of time, to increase their familiarity with the community and the community's familiarity with them. Ideally, this familiarity will build trust, confidence, and cooperation on both sides of the police-citizen interaction. Also, officers will simply become more knowledgeable about the community and its residents, aiding early intervention and timely problem identification and avoiding conflict based on misperception or misunderstanding.

It is important to recognize that most police departments have long used geography as the basis for daily patrol assignment. Many of these departments, however, assign patrol officers to different beats from one day to the next, creating little continuity or permanency. Moreover, even in police agencies with fairly steady beat assignments, patrol officers are only held accountable for handling their calls and maintaining order (keeping things quiet) *during their shift*. The citizen's question, "Who in the police department is responsible for *my area*, my neighborhood?" can then only truthfully be answered "the chief" or, in large departments, "the precinct commander." Neither patrol officers nor the two or three levels of management above them can be held accountable for dealing with long-term problems in specific locations anywhere in the entire community. Thus, a crucial component of community policing strategy is to create some degree of geographic accountability at all levels in the police organization, but particularly at the level of the patrol officer who delivers basic police services and is in a position to identify and solve neighborhood problems.

Prevention Emphasis. Community policing strategy also emphasizes a more proactive and preventive orientation, in contrast to the reactive focus that has characterized much of policing under the professional model. This proactive, preventive orientation takes several forms. One is simply to encourage better use of police officers' time. In many police departments, patrol officers' time not committed to handling calls is either spent simply waiting for the next call or randomly driving around. Under community policing, this substantial resource of free patrol time is devoted to directed enforcement activities, specific crime prevention efforts, problem solving, community engagement, citizen interaction, or similar kinds of activities.

Another aspect of the preventive focus overlaps with the substantive orientation of community policing and problem-oriented operations. Officers are encouraged to look beyond the individual incidents that they encounter as calls for service and reported crimes in order to discover underlying problems and conditions (Eck and Spelman, 1987). If they can discover such underlying conditions and do something to improve them, officers can prevent the future recurrence of incidents and calls. While immediate response to in-progress emergencies and after-the-fact investigation of crimes will always remain important functions of policing, community policing seeks to elevate before-the-fact prevention and problem-solving to comparable status.

Closely related to this line of thinking, but deserving of specific mention, is the desire to enhance the status of crime prevention within police organizations. Most police departments devote the vast majority of their personnel to patrol and investigations, primarily for the purposes of rapid response and follow-up investigation *after* something has happened. Granted, some prevention of crime through the visibility, omnipresence, and deterrence created by patrolling, rapid response, and investigating is expected, but the weight of research over the past two decades has greatly diminished these expectations (Kelling, Pate, Dieckman, and Brown, 1974; Greenwood and Petersilia, 1975; Spelman and Brown, 1982). Despite these lowered expectations, however, police departments still typically devote only a few officers specifically to crime prevention programming, and do little to encourage patrol officers to engage in any kinds of crime prevention activity beyond routine riding around.

Moreover, within both informal and formal police cultures, crime solving and criminal apprehension are usually more highly valued than crime prevention. An individual officer is more likely to be commended for arresting a bank robber than for initiating actions that prevent such robberies. Detectives usually enjoy higher status than uniformed officers (especially in the eyes of the public), whereas, within many police agencies, crime prevention officers are seen as public relations functionaries, kiddie cops, or worse. To many police officers, crime prevention work is simply not real police work.

The preeminence of reactive crime fighting within police and popular cultures is understandable, given the dramatic nature of emergencies, crimes, and investigations. Much of police work is about responding to trouble and fixing it, about the contest between good and evil. Responding to emergencies and fighting crime have heroic elements that naturally appeal to both police officers and citizens. Given the choice, though, almost all citizens would prefer not being victimized in the first place to being dramatically rescued, to having the police successfully track down their assailant, or to having the police recover their stolen property. Most citizens would agree that "an ounce of prevention is worth a pound of cure." This is not to suggest that police should turn their backs on reactive handling of crimes and emergencies, but only that before-the-fact prevention should be given greater consideration.

A final element of community policing's preventive focus takes more of a social welfare orientation, particularly toward juveniles. An argument is made that police officers, by serving as mentors and role models, and by providing educational, recreational, and even counseling services, can affect peoples' behavior in positive ways that ultimately lead to reductions in crime and disorder. In essence, police are asked to support and augment the efforts of families, churches, schools, and other social service agencies. This kind of police activity is seen as particularly necessary by some in order to offset the deficiencies and correct the failures of these other social institutions in modern America.

The Tactical Dimension

The tactical dimension of community policing ultimately translates ideas, philosophies, and strategies into concrete programs, practices, and behaviors. Even those who insist that "community policing is a philosophy, not a program" must concede that unless community policing eventually leads to some action, some new or different behavior, it is all rhetoric and no reality (Greene and Mastrofski, 1988). Indeed, many commentators have taken the view that community policing is little more than a new police marketing strategy that has left the core elements of the police role untouched (see, e.g., Klockars, 1988; Manning, 1988; Weatheritt, 1988). Three of the most important tactical elements of community policing are positive interaction, partnerships, and problem solving.

Positive Interaction. Policing inevitably involves some negative contacts between officers and citizens—arrests, tickets, stops for suspicion, orders to desist in disruptive behavior, inability to make things much better for victims, etc. Community policing recognizes this fact and recommends that officers offset it as much as they can by engaging in positive interactions whenever possible. Positive interactions have further benefits as well, of course: they generally build familiarity, trust, and confidence on both sides; they remind officers that most citizens respect and support them; they make the officer more knowledgeable about people and conditions in the beat; they provide specific information for criminal investigations and problem solving; and they break up the monotony of motorized patrol.

Many opportunities for positive interaction arise in the course of call handling. Too many officers rush to clear their calls, however, often in response to workload concerns and pressure from their superiors, their peers, and dispatchers. As a result, they typically do a mediocre job of handling the immediate incident and make little or no attempt to identify underlying conditions, secure additional information, or create satisfied customers. The prime directive seems to be to do as little as possible in order to clear the call quickly and get back in the car and on the radio, ready to go and do little or nothing at the next call. Getting there rapidly and then clearing promptly take precedence over actually delivering much service or accomplishing anything. Community policing suggests, instead, that officers should look at calls as opportunities for positive interaction, quality service, and problem identification.

Even more opportunities for positive interaction can be seized during routine patrol, if officers are willing to exit their vehicles and take some initiative. Officers can go in and out of stores, in and out of schools, talk to people on the street, knock on doors, etc. They can take the initiative to talk not only with shopkeepers and their customers but also with teenagers, apartment dwellers, tavern patrons, and anybody else they run across in public spaces or who are approachable in private places. Police should insert themselves wherever people are and should talk to those people, not just watch them.

Partnerships. Participation of the community in its own protection is one of the central elements of community policing (Bureau of Justice Assistance, 1994c). This participation can run the gamut from watching neighbors' homes to reporting drug dealers to patrolling the streets. It can involve participation in problem identification and problem solving efforts, in crime prevention programs, in neighborhood revitalization, and in youth-oriented educational and recreational programs. Citizens may act individually or in groups, they may collaborate with the police, and they may even join the police department by donating their time as police department volunteers, reserves, or auxiliaries.

Under community policing, police agencies are expected not only to cooperate with citizens and communities but to actively solicit input and participation (Bureau of Justice Assistance, 1994b). The exact nature of this participation can and should vary from community to community and from situation to situation, in keeping with the problem-oriented approach. As a general rule, though, police should avoid claiming that they alone can handle crime, drug, or disorder problems, and they should encourage individual citizens and community groups to shoulder some responsibility for dealing with such problems.

Police have sometimes found it necessary to engage in community organizing as a means of accomplishing any degree of citizen participation in problem solving or crime prevention. In disorganized and transient neighborhoods, residents are often so distressed, fearful, and suspicious of each other (or just so unfamiliar with their neighbors) that police have literally had to set about creating a sense of community where none previously existed. As difficult as this kind of community organizing can be, and as far from the conventional police role as this may seem, these are often the very communities that most need both enhanced police protection and a greater degree of citizen involvement in crime prevention, order maintenance, and general watchfulness over public spaces.

One vexing aspect of community organizing and community engagement results from the pluralistic nature of our society. Differing and often conflicting interests are found in many communities, and they are sometimes represented by competing interest groups. Thus, the elders in a community may want the police to crack down on juveniles, while the youths themselves complain of few opportunities for recreation or entertainment. Tenants may seek police help in organizing a rent strike, while landlords want police assistance in screening or managing the same tenants. Finding common interests around which to rally entire communities, or just identifying common interests on which to base police practices, can be very challenging and, at times, impossible.

It is important to recognize that this inherent feature of pluralistic communities does not arise because of community policing. Police have long been caught in the middle between the interests of adults and juveniles, landlords and tenants, and similar groups. Sometimes the law has provided a convenient reference point for handling such conflicts, but just as often police have had to mediate, arbitrate, or just take the side of the party with the best case. Moreover, when the law has offered a solution, it has frequently been a temporary or unpopular one, and one that still resulted in the police taking sides, protestations of "we're just enforcing the law" notwithstanding.

Fortunately, nearly all citizens want to be safe from violence, want their property protected, and want some level of orderliness in their neighborhoods. Officers can usually find enough consensus in communities upon which to base cooperative efforts aimed at improving safety and public order. Sometimes, apparently deep conflicts between individuals or groups recede when attention is focused on how best to solve specific neighborhood problems. It would be naive to expect overwhelming community consensus in every situation, but it is equally mistaken to think that conflict is so endemic that widespread community support and participation cannot be achieved in many circumstances.

Problem Solving.   Supporters of community policing are convinced that the very nature of police work must be altered from its present incident-by-incident, case-by-case orientation to one that is more problem-oriented (Goldstein, 1990). Certainly, incidents must still be handled and cases must still be investigated. Whenever possible, however, attention should be directed toward underlying problems and conditions. Following the medical analogy, policing should address causes as well as symptoms, and should adopt the epidemiological public health approach as much as the individual doctor's clinical approach.

This problem solving approach should be characterized by several important features: (1) it should be the standard operating method of policing, not an occasional special project; (2) it should be practiced by personnel throughout the ranks, not just by specialists or managers; (3) it should be empirical, in the sense that decisions are made on the basis of information that is gathered systematically; (4) it should involve, whenever possible, collaboration between police and other agencies and institutions; and (5) it should incorporate, whenever possible, community input and participation, so that it is the community's problems that are addressed (not just the police department's) and so that the community shares in the responsibility for its own protection.

The problem solving process consists of four steps: (1) careful identification of the problem; (2) careful analysis of the problem; (3) a search for alternative solutions to the problem; and (4) implementation and assessment of a response to the problem. Community input can be incorporated within any or all of the steps in the process. Identification, analysis, and assessment should rely on information from multiple sources. A variety of alternative solutions should be considered, including, but not limited to, traditional enforcement methods. Typically, the most effective solutions are those that combine several different responses, including some that draw on more than just the police department's authority and resources.

A crucial characteristic of the problem-oriented approach is that it seeks tailored solutions to specific community problems. Arrests and law enforcement are *not* abandoned—rather, an effort is made in each situation to determine which alternative responses best fit the problem. Use of the criminal law is always considered, as are civil law enforcement, mediation, community mobilization, referral, collaboration, alteration of the physical environment, public education, and a host of other possibilities. The common sense notion of choosing the tool that best fits the problem, instead of simply grabbing the most convenient or familiar tool in the tool box, lies close to the heart of the problem solving method.

The Organizational Dimension

It is important to recognize an organizational dimension that surrounds community policing and greatly affects its implementation. In order to support and facilitate community policing, police departments often consider a variety of changes in organization, administration, management, and supervision. The elements of the organizational dimension are not really part of community policing *per se*, but they are frequently crucial to its successful implementation. Three important organizational elements of COP are structure, management, and information.

Structure. Advocates of community policing often look at various ways of restructuring police agencies in order to facilitate and support implementation of the philosophical, strategic, and tactical elements described above. Any organization's structure should correspond with its mission and the nature of the work performed by its members. Some aspects of traditional police organization structure seem more suited to routine, bureaucratic work than to the discretion and creativity required for COP.

The types of restructuring often associated with community policing include:

- *Decentralization*—Authority and responsibility can sometimes be delegated more widely so that commanders, supervisors, and officers can act more independently and be more responsive.

- *Flattening*—The number of layers of hierarchy in the police organization can sometimes be reduced in order to improve communications and reduce waste, rigidity and bureaucracy.

- *De-specialization*—The number of specialized units and personnel can sometimes be reduced, with more resources devoted to the direct delivery of police services (including COP) to the general public.

- *Teams*—Efficiency and effectiveness can sometimes be improved by getting employees working together as teams to perform work, solve problems, or look for ways of improving quality.

- *Civilianization*—Positions currently held by sworn personnel can sometimes be reclassified or redesigned for non-sworn personnel, allowing both cost savings and better utilization of sworn personnel.

Management. Community policing is often associated with styles of leadership, management, and supervision that give more emphasis to organizational culture and values and less emphasis to written rules and formal discipline. The general argument is that when employees are guided by a set of officially sanctioned values they will usually make good decisions and take appropriate actions. Although many formal rules will still probably be necessary, managers will need to resort to them much less often in order to maintain control over subordinates.

Management practices consistent with this emphasis on organizational culture and values include:

- *Mission*—Agencies should develop concise statements of their mission and values and use them consistently in making decisions, guiding employees, and training new recruits.

- *Strategic Planning*—Agencies should engage in continuous strategic planning aimed at ensuring that resources and energy are focused on mission accomplishment and adherence to core values; otherwise, organizations tend to get off track, confused about their mission and about what really matters.

- *Coaching*—Supervisors should coach and guide their subordinates more, instead of restricting their roles to review of paperwork and enforcement of rules and regulations.
- *Mentoring*—Young employees need mentoring from managers, supervisors, and/or peers—not just to learn how to do the job right but also to learn what constitutes the right job; in other words, to learn about ethics and values and what it means to be a good police officer.
- *Empowerment*—Under COP, employees are encouraged to be risk-takers who demonstrate imagination and creativity in their work—this kind of empowerment can only succeed, however, when employees are thoroughly familiar with the organization's core values and firmly committed to them.
- *Selective Discipline*—In their disciplinary processes, agencies should make distinctions between intentional and unintentional errors made by employees and between employee actions that violate core values versus those that merely violate technical rules.

Information. Doing community policing and managing it effectively require certain types of information that have not traditionally been available in all police departments. In the never-ending quality vs. quantity debate, for example, community policing tends to emphasize quality. This emphasis on quality shows up in many areas: avoidance of traditional bean-counting (arrests, tickets) to measure success, more concern for how well calls are handled than merely for how quickly they are handled, etc. Also, the geographic focus of community policing increases the need for detailed information based on neighborhoods as the unit of analysis. The emphasis on problem solving highlights the need for information systems that aid in identifying and analyzing community-level problems. And so on.

Several aspects of police administration under community policing that have implications for information are:

- *Performance Appraisal*—Individual officers can be evaluated on the quality of their community policing and problem solving activities, and perhaps on results achieved, instead of on traditional performance indicators (tickets, arrests, calls handled, etc.).
- *Program Evaluation*—Police programs and strategies can be evaluated more on the basis of their effectiveness (outcomes, results, quality) than just on their efficiency (effort, outputs, quantity).
- *Departmental Assessment*—The police agency's overall performance can be measured and assessed on the basis of a wide variety of indicators (including customer satisfaction, fear levels, problem solving, etc.)

instead of a narrow band of traditional indicators (reported crime, response time, etc.).

- *Information Systems*—An agency's information systems need to collect and produce information on the whole range of the police function, not just on enforcement and call-handling activities, in order to support more quality-oriented appraisal, evaluation, and assessment efforts.

- *Crime Analysis*—Individual officers need more timely and complete crime analysis information pertaining to their specific geographic areas of responsibility to facilitate problem identification, analysis, fear reduction, etc.

- *Geographic Information Systems* (GIS)—Sophisticated and user-friendly computerized mapping software available today makes it possible for officers and citizens to obtain customized maps that graphically identify "hot spots" and help them picture the geographic locations and distribution of crime and related problems.

WHAT DO WE KNOW?

Despite the programmatic and evaluation complexities discussed earlier, we do have a substantial amount of information from empirical studies of community policing. Table 1 summarizes the "preponderance of the evidence" on the effects of community policing based on a review of over 60 such studies (recent reviews have also been completed by Normandeau, 1993; Bennett, 1994; Leighton, 1994; and Skogan, 1994).

The first thing to note in table 1 is that almost three-fourths of the 28 cells are blank, indicating that the effects are unknown (completely or substantially untested). Nearly all of the evaluations conducted to-date have focused on the tactical dimension of community policing, leaving us with little or no information on the effects of philosophical, strategic, and organizational changes. This gap in community policing research is undoubtedly caused by a combination of two factors: (1) most community policing efforts, at least until recently, have been limited programmatic and street-level initiatives rather than large-scale strategic or organizational-change initiatives; and (2) evaluation of narrowly-focused programmatic initiatives is much easier and more feasible than evaluation of philosophical and organization-wide change.

The most useful way to summarize the evidence on the effects of community policing is to scan the tactical row of table 1.

Crime

The evidence is mixed. Only a few studies have used experimental designs and victimization surveys to test the effects of community policing on crime; many others have relied on simple before-after comparisons of reported crime or single-item victimization questions drawn from commu-

Table I   Preponderance of the Evidence on Community Policing

Effects/ Dimensions	Crime	Fear	Disorder	Calls for Service	Community Relations	Police Officer Attitudes	Police Officer Behavior
Philosophical: Citizen Input Broad Police Function Personal Service							
Strategic: Re-oriented Operations Geographic Focus Preventive Emphasis							
Tactical: Positive Interaction Partnerships Problem Solving	MIX	MIX	POS	MIX	POS	POS	MIX
Organizational: Structure Management Information					POS		

POS = positive effects (beneficial effects)
NEG = negative effects
MIX = mixed effects
Blank = unknown (completely or substantially untested)

nity surveys. Overall, a slight majority of the studies have detected crime decreases, giving reason for optimism, but evaluation design limitations prevent us from drawing any authoritative conclusions.

Fear of Crime

Again the evidence is mixed, but it leans more heavily in the positive direction. A number of studies have employed community surveys to make before-after comparisons of fear and related perceptions, some with experimental designs. Fear has typically been measured using a variety of survey items, lending the studies more credibility. The now widely-accepted view that community policing helps reduce levels of fear of crime and increases perceptions of safety seems reasonably well-founded, although some efforts have failed to accomplish fear reductions.

Disorder

The impact of community policing on disorder, minor crime, incivilities, and signs of crime has not been subjected to careful testing as frequently as its impact on crime and fear. The available evidence suggests, though, that community policing, and especially foot patrol and problem solving, helps reduce levels of disorder, lending partial support to the "broken windows" thesis (Wilson and Kelling, 1982).

Calls for Service

Community policing might reduce calls for service in several ways: problem solving might address underlying issues that generate calls; collaboration might increase call referrals to other government agencies; foot patrols and mini-stations might receive citizen requests directly, thus heading off calls to central dispatch; and workload management might find alternative responses for some types of calls. Although the ability of the last approach (workload management) to reduce the volume of calls dispatched to sworn units for immediate response has clearly been demonstrated (McEwen et al., 1986), the rest of the evidence on the effects of community policing on calls for service is mixed. Several studies have found positive effects but several others have not.

Community Relations

The vast majority of the studies that have looked at the impact of community policing on citizens' attitudes toward the police have uncovered positive effects. Clearly, citizens generally appreciate mini-stations in their neighborhoods, foot patrols, problem-solving efforts, and other forms of community policing. These very consistent findings are all the more remarkable because baseline measures of citizen satisfaction with, and support for, their police are frequently quite positive to begin with, thus offering relatively little room for improvement.

Police Officer Attitudes

A clear majority of the studies that have investigated the effects of community policing on officers' job satisfaction, perceptions of the community, and other related attitudes have discovered beneficial effects. Officers involved in community policing, especially if they are volunteers or members of special units, typically thrive on their new duties and responsibilities. Also, there is some evidence that organizing and managing officers differently (the so-called "inside-out" approach) can have positive effects on their morale and related attitudes (Wycoff and Skogan, 1993).

What is somewhat less certain, however, is (1) whether the positive effects of community policing on officers will survive the long term and (2) whether these benefits are as universal when *all* officers are required to engage in community policing. Whenever community policing is practiced only by specialists, as has generally been the case until recently in most departments, one condition that *is* nearly universal is conflict between the specialists and other members of the agency, frequently reflected in derogatory remarks about "the grin and wave squad."

Police Officer Behavior

Significant anecdotal evidence suggests that foot patrol, problem solving, permanent assignment, mini-stations, and other features of community policing lead to changes in some police officers' behavior, but these behavioral effects have only been lightly documented thus far (Mastrofski, Worden, and Snipes, 1995). Evidence also suggests that many officers resist changing their behavior, out of opposition to the philosophical underpinnings of community policing, doubts that community policing really works, or just plain habit.

CONCLUSION

A great deal of energy has been invested since 1980 in determining the nature of community policing and its effects. These efforts have paid off to the extent that the scope and variation of community policing is much better understood today and some of its effects have been fairly well documented. Since community policing has evolved significantly during this period, however, some of its elements have been more carefully evaluated than others. In addition, programmatic complexity, multiple effects, variations in scope, and research design limitations have hampered many of the community policing evaluations conducted thus far. Nevertheless, the tactical elements of community policing do seem to produce several beneficial outcomes for citizens and officers, and have the potential to impact crime and disorder. Whether the more philosophical, strategic, and organizational elements of community policing will become firmly rooted, and whether they will ultimately have beneficial effects, is yet to be seen.

References

Bennett, Trevor. 1994. "Community Policing on the Ground: Developments in Britain." In Dennis P. Rosenbaum, ed., *The Challenge of Community Policing: Testing the Promises*. Thousand Oaks, CA: Sage, pp. 224–46.

Bureau of Justice Assistance. 1994a. *A Police Guide to Surveying Citizens and Their Environment*. Washington, DC: Bureau of Justice Assistance.

———. 1994b. *Neighborhood-Oriented Policing in Rural Communities: A Program Planning Guide*. Washington, DC: Bureau of Justice Assistance.

———. 1994c. *Understanding Community Policing: A Framework for Action*. Washington, DC: Bureau of Justice Assistance.

Cordner, Gary W. and Robert C. Trojanowicz. 1992. "Patrol." In Gary W. Cordner and Donna C. Hale, eds., *What Works in Policing? Operations and Administration Examined*. Cincinnati, OH: Anderson, pp. 3–18.

Eck, John E. 1992. "Criminal Investigation." In Gary W. Cordner and Donna C. Hale, eds., *What Works in Policing? Operations and Administration Examined*. Cincinnati, OH: Anderson, pp. 19–34.

Eck, John E. and William Spelman. 1987. *Problem Solving: Problem-Oriented Policing in Newport News*. Washington, DC: Police Executive Research Forum.

Goldstein, Herman. 1977. *Policing A Free Society*. Cambridge, MA: Ballinger.

Goldstein, Herman. 1987. "Toward Community-Oriented Policing: Potential, Basic Requirements, and Threshold Questions," *Crime & Delinquency* 25: 236–58.

———. 1990. *Problem-Oriented Policing*. New York: McGraw-Hill.

Greene, Jack R. and Stephen D. Mastrofski, eds. 1988. *Community Policing: Rhetoric or Reality?* New York: Praeger.

Greenwood, Peter W. and Joan Petersilia. 1975. *The Criminal Investigation Process, Volume I: Summary and Implications.* Santa Monica: Rand Corporation.

Kelling, George L., Tony Pate, Duane Dieckman, and Charles E. Brown. 1974. *The Kansas City Preventive Patrol Experiment: A Summary Report.* Washington, DC: Police Foundation.

Kelling, George L. and Mark H. Moore. 1988. "The Evolving Strategy of Policing." *Perspectives on Policing* No. 4. Washington, DC: National Institute of Justice.

Klockars, Carl B. 1988. "The Rhetoric of Community Policing." In Jack R. Greene and Stephen D. Mastrofski, eds., *Community Policing: Rhetoric or Reality?* New York: Praeger, pp. 239–58.

Leighton, Barry N. 1994. "Community Policing in Canada: An Overview of Experience and Evaluations." In Dennis P. Rosenbaum, ed., *The Challenge of Community Policing: Testing the Promises.* Thousand Oaks, CA: Sage, pp. 209–23.

Manning, Peter K. 1988. "Community Policing as a Drama of Control." In Jack R. Greene and Stephen D. Mastrofski, eds., *Community Policing: Rhetoric or Reality?* New York: Praeger, pp. 27–46.

Mastrofski, Stephen D., Robert E. Worden, and Jeffrey B. Snipes. 1995. "Law Enforcement in a Time of Community Policing." *Criminology* 33, 4: 539–63.

McEwen, J. Thomas, Edward F. Connors III, and Marcia I. Cohen. 1986. *Evaluation of the Differential Police Responses Field Test.* Washington, DC: National Institute of Justice.

Moore, Mark H. and Robert C. Trojanowicz. 1988. "Corporate Strategies for Policing." *Perspectives on Policing* No. 6. Washington, DC: National Institute of Justice.

Normandeau, Andre. 1993. "Community Policing in Canada: A Review of Some Recent Studies," *American Journal of Police* 12,1: 57–73.

Skogan, Wesley G. 1994. "The Impact of Community Policing on Neighborhood Residents: A Cross-Site Analysis." In Dennis P. Rosenbaum, ed., *The Challenge of Community Policing: Testing the Promises.* Thousand Oaks, CA: Sage, pp. 167–81.

Spelman, William and Dale K. Brown. 1982. *Calling the Police: Citizen Reporting of Serious Crime.* Washington, DC: Police Executive Research Forum.

Trojanowicz, Robert and Bonnie Bucqueroux. 1990. *Community Policing: A Contemporary Perspective.* Cincinnati, OH: Anderson.

Weatheritt, Mollie. 1988. "Community Policing: Rhetoric or Reality?" In Jack R. Greene and Stephen D. Mastrofski, eds., *Community Policing: Rhetoric or Reality?* New York: Praeger, pp. 153–76.

Wilson, James Q. and George L. Kelling. 1982. "Police and Neighborhood Safety: Broken Windows," *The Atlantic Monthly* (March): 29–38.

Wycoff, Mary Ann and Wesley K. Skogan. 1993. *Community Policing in Madison: Quality From the Inside Out.* Washington, DC: National Institute of Justice.

Problem-Oriented Policing

John D. Reitzel, Nicole Leeper Piquero, & Alex R. Piquero

INTRODUCTION

To understand the current state of policing and its future direction, it is useful to briefly review its path to the present day. Historically, the policing enterprise has gone through numerous shifts in styles of law enforcement (Monkkonen, 1992; Reiss, 1992; Sherman, 1998). For example, some of the earliest forms of policing focused primarily on maintaining the public order while a dramatic shift after the Second World War altered the focus to a traditional or professional model of law enforcement, which lasted throughout much of the twentieth century. Amidst widespread disrepute with the "professional model" of law enforcement, the riots of the 1960s and the failed police-community relation efforts, particularly in minority, inner-city communities, the policing enterprise began to experiment with different forms of policing practices such as team policing, and in recent years, community and problem-oriented policing as well as community-problem solving policing.

In this article, we focus on the problem-oriented policing movement. In the second section, we describe its origins, how it differs from other styles of law enforcement, and what it looks like in practice. In the third section, we provide examples of several initial evaluations of problem-oriented policing programs. Section four presents three current examples of problem-oriented policing in action, one applied in a public housing setting and the other

Prepared especially for *Critical Issues in Policing* by John D. Reitzel, Nicole Leeper Piquero, and Alex R. Piquero.

applied to thwart violent crime. The fifth section outlines several implementation issues associated with successful executions of problem-oriented policing, and the sixth section concludes by outlining the probable future practices of problem-oriented policing and its juxtaposition against zero-tolerance policing.

WHAT IS PROBLEM-ORIENTED POLICING?

Problem-oriented policing originated largely as a function of the research undertaken during the traditional era of law enforcement. Specific concerns were raised regarding police effectiveness, police-community relations, police discretion, and police management and organization. The main concern levied against traditional methods of law enforcement was its reactive nature; that is, under the traditional law enforcement approach, police were reactive or incident-driven. Police aimed to respond to calls for service in a quick fashion and to resolve or dispense of individual incidents in a timely manner. Unlike the reactivity that is the hallmark of traditional law enforcement, the problem-oriented policing philosophy contends that reacting to calls for service is only the first step in police work. Herman Goldstein (1979), a pioneer in the problem-oriented policing movement, argued that police should go further and attempt to find a permanent resolution to the problem that was responsible for the initial call. At its core, the theory underlying problem-oriented policing is straightforward: identify the underlying condition(s) that are generating the repeated calls for service and develop problem-solving approaches that solve the underlying problem (Scott, 2000). To make this explanation more concrete, consider the following dental medicine example.

Suppose that at the beginning of last month you had a toothache. You reasoned that it is just one of those things that happens to you as you get older. You stop by the pharmacy to pick up some over-the-counter medicine to put on the tooth. When you get home, you apply the medicine before bed and when you wake up the next morning you notice that the pain has gone away. You feel, at least initially, that you have taken care of the problem. Now suppose that later that day you get the same toothache. You realize that this may be something more than a minor irritation and call your dentist for an appointment. During an examination, your dentist finds that you have a small cavity and she proceeds to fill it. For the next few weeks, you feel no pain in the tooth and once again assume that you have solved the problem. But just this past week, you again notice a pain in the tooth when you chew on it. Thinking that this is not normal, you call your dentist to get the tooth checked out again. This time, your dentist spots something that she did not see before: a root infection. After you settle down from the agony of having to endure a root canal, the dentist informs you that the problem has been taken care of. This is the essence of problem-oriented policing. Rather than responding to repeated calls-for-service (i.e., toothaches), the dentist has figured out what the underlying problem was (i.e., root infection), and has implemented a strategy that was designed to resolve the problem (i.e., a root canal).

At its core then, problem-oriented policing attempts to deal with the underlying problem(s) that may be responsible for the repeated calls-for-service. Such strategies operate under two assumptions. First, problem solving can be applied by officers throughout the police agency as a normal part of their police work. Second, routine problem-solving efforts can be effective in reducing and solving problems, thus curtailing repeated calls-for-service.

The problem-solving process follows a four-step procedure, referred to as SARA, that is interactive and reciprocal (Scott, 2000). In other words, it is constantly in operation and constantly re-produces itself over time. (See Figure A for an example of the SARA process). In the first stage, *Scanning*, the officer scans the area and identifies a problem. In the second stage, *Analysis*, the officer collects information from various sources in the community as well as from his/her own department and other law enforcement agencies. This is the heart of the problem-oriented process because officers are asked to break down the underlying problem into its component events (i.e., actors, incidents, responses). In the third stage, *Response*, the information obtained in the second stage is used to develop and implement potential solutions to the identified problem(s). In the fourth stage, *Assessment*, the officer evaluates the effectiveness of the response (i.e., did the problem get reduced and/or go away?). Depending on the outcome of the *Assessment* stage, the officer may return to the *Analysis* or *Response* stages to revise the response, collect more data, and/or redesign different problem-solving solutions. This is what makes the problem-solving process interactive and reciprocal. Thus, to the extent that officers address the underlying conditions, fewer incidents and repeat calls-for-service will ensue, and those that do occur, may be less serious. At the very least, information about the problem can help police to design more effective ways of responding to each incident (Eck and Spelman, 1987).

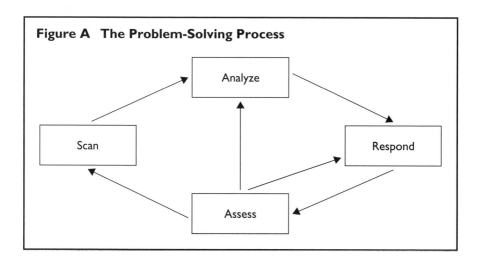

Figure A The Problem-Solving Process

Analyze

Scan

Respond

Assess

As could be reasoned, the problem-solving process takes as given the fact that the same problem-solving solution may not be transferable across different communities, cities, locations, and businesses. That is, problem-solving solutions need to be tailored to the specific makeup of actors and incidents in particular communities. At the same time, knowledge of effective problem-solving tactics in one locale may serve as a useful baseline for problem-solving tactics in other locales. We return to this point later in the article.

EARLY PROBLEM-SOLVING EVALUATIONS

In the 1980s, the problem-solving movement began to take shape and several police agencies began to adopt such an approach as their policing philosophy. At the same time, the National Institute of Justice, the research arm of the Department of Justice, funded evaluation studies of problem-oriented policing in an effort to gauge the effectiveness of problem-oriented policing. The Institute required that the problem-solving system follow five basic principles (Eck and Spelman, 1987):

1. Officers of all ranks and from all units should be able to use the system as part of their daily routine.

2. The system must encourage the use of a broad range of information, including but not limited to conventional police data.

3. The system should encourage a broad range of solutions, including but not limited to the criminal justice process.

4. The system should require no additional resources and no special units.

5. Any large police agency must be able to apply it.

To examine the effectiveness of problem-oriented policing, the Newport News, Virginia, Police Department was chosen to implement the system. By 1986, a number of problems had been identified. The type of problems varied by location (city vs. neighborhood) and by the type of event (criminal vs. disorder). The department chose two specific problems to concentrate their problem-solving efforts: burglaries from an apartment complex and thefts from vehicles.

Burglaries in Briarfield Apartments

Detective Tony Duke of the Crime Analysis Unit was assigned to study the apartment burglary problem. One of the first things that Detective Duke initiated was a survey of one-third of the households. The results of this survey confirmed that the residents believed burglary to be a serious problem, but others were equally concerned about the physical deterioration of the complex. Inspection of the apartment complex revealed that indeed it was in disrepair. After the survey results were studied, the patrol officer responsible for the area around the apartment complex enlisted the assistance of city agencies and the apartment manager to clean up the complex. Trash and abandoned appliances were removed, abandoned cars were towed, and potholes were filled and streets were swept (Eck and Spelman, 1987). Despite the success of the problem-oriented policing strategy, an evaluation of crime in and around the apartment complex showed a 35 percent reduction in burglaries, the police chief and officials from other city agencies proposed that the apartment complex should be razed. Tenants were provided with temporary housing while a new 220-unit apartment complex, a middle school, and a small shopping center were built in its place.

Vehicle Thefts in Newport News Shipyards

Thefts from vehicles parked near the Newport News shipyards accounted for almost 10 percent of all index crimes reported in Newport News. One officer who was given the task of solving this problem discovered that most of the thefts occurred in a few parking areas. After a number of interviews, the officer was able to identify a small number of suspects for the thefts and provided this information to patrol officers patrolling the area. In addition, the officer interviewed convicted offenders about the factors that made certain automobiles attractive and others unattractive. That information was given to the shipyard workers and a private security force to develop and implement a theft prevention strategy. As a result of these tactics, thefts were reduced by 55 percent since the proactive policing and arrests of repeat offenders began.

The two Newport News case studies provided evidence to many that officers can engage in a practice where they obtain information that underlies designated problems, and then execute concerted responses to help alleviate those problems. The preliminary work in Newport News set forward continued application of problem-solving efforts across many police agencies.

RECENT PROBLEM-SOLVING EFFORTS

Since the Newport News problem-oriented policing study, the strategy has been extended to varying problems in many different cities and across vastly different police agencies. Here, we discuss four recent efforts aimed at applying problem-oriented policing towards particular locations (public housing in Jersey City, NJ, and Philadelphia, PA) and at particular types of crime (violent crime in Jersey City, NJ, and violent crime, particularly homicide in Richmond, CA).

Problems in Public Housing in Jersey City and Philadelphia

Green-Mazerolle & Terrill (1997) and Green-Mazerolle, Ready, Terrill & Waring (2000) examined problem-oriented policing and public housing problems in Jersey City, New Jersey. In the first study, the researchers created problem-solving teams in six developments, each operating under the assumption that the problems affecting each of the developments varied across sites because of their unique physical, spatial, and cultural characteristics. The teams sought to identify high priority problems within and across each of the six developments that included drugs, graffiti, loitering, among others. Although each of the public housing sites had similar problems, the geographic distribution of the problems varied across the sites. For example, some sites had problems with drugs in lobbies while others had them in stairwells and still others had them in parking lots.

The key finding from the Green-Mazerolle and Terrill study is two-fold. First, officers can identify problems in public housing developments and thereby identify potential solutions to those problems. Second, the problem-solving process has to be applied uniquely across sites due to their varying characteristics. In addition, a number of key findings emerged from the Mazerolle et al. (2000) study. First, there was a negative correlation between the number of problem-oriented policing activities during each two-week study period and the number of crime calls for service. In other words, when the problem-oriented policing strategies were implemented, crime calls went down. This held even after controlling for the intervention period. Thus, the reduction finding was not significantly related to a general decline in crime rates in Jersey City as those areas under study saw much sharper decreases than the rest of the city. Second, and perhaps most importantly, the two sites where problem-oriented policing activities were implemented had much stronger results (i.e. much better predictive power) than the other sites that relied primarily on public housing or social service activities. Consequently, as they note, it seems that police presence as an authority role in problem solving is an important factor in successful problem-oriented policing strategies.

Problem solving in public housing has also been implemented in Philadelphia. Greene and his colleagues (1999) implemented and evaluated a problem-solving effort throughout the 11th Street Corridor in five public housing developments in North Philadelphia. Prior to problem solving, the Philadelphia Public Housing Police Department initiated an effort in which the officers assigned to the developments would undergo training in problem-solving and community-policing efforts. Then, the officers would be re-assigned to permanent foot patrol duty throughout the developments. After this was established, five problem-solving teams were created to provide a forum in which the police, residents, other public housing services, and other interested parties were able to discuss public safety concerns, as well as to design and implement local interventions.

The outcome evaluation revealed that the five developments suffered from many similar problems related to drug activity, youth programming, poor lighting, and recreational facilities. Interestingly, the outcome data revealed that the officers engaged in a higher amount of self-initiated radio-activity that is consistent with the proactive philosophy underlying problem-oriented policing. In addition, the residents of the developments noticed this increased level of police activity and reported that the police were instrumental in reducing community problems over the length of the program including drug selling, graffiti, and garbage and litter.

Violence in Jersey City

Shifting toward a problem-oriented study of violent crime places in Jersey City, Braga and his colleagues (1999) examined changes in crime within and across twenty-four high-activity, violent crime places that were matched into twelve pairs with one member of each pair allocated to treatment (i.e., problem-solving) conditions in a randomized block field experiment and the other member not allocated to treatment (i.e., the control group). Braga et al. (1999) describe the extent of violent crime across all of these places as ranging from assault and robbery to drug market violence to street fighting. The dynamics of the places range from transient populations to shoppers to indoor drug markets to middle-class neighborhoods. The physical characteristics of the places vary and include: a shopping mall, a drug house, a tavern, liquor stores, intersections, and college campuses.

After developing an understanding of the problems facing these locations, the officers developed situational interventions as responses to the particular problems. For many, the officers identified both physical and social disorder issues within the places. Although specific tactics and priorities varied across these places, the officers generally attempted to control them by cleaning up the environment through aggressive order maintenance and making physical improvements such as securing vacant lots and removing trash from the street (Braga et al., 1999). (Figure B describes the problem-solving strategies at the treatment places). Outcome data on crime and disorder revealed that the problem-oriented tactics of the officers was successful in reducing crime and disorder at violent places with little evidence of displacement.

Homicides in Richmond, California

In May of 2003, White and colleagues completed a study that examined the effects of problem-oriented policing strategies in reducing homicides (and violence) in the city of Richmond, California. Labeled the Comprehensive Homicide Initiative, and funded by the Bureau of Justice Assistance of the U.S. Department of Justice, the Richmond Police Department (RPD) began instituting a wide variety of problem-oriented policing and some community-oriented policing strategies in the fall of 1995 to combat what had previously been a sharp increase in homicide and violence rates. Though too numerous to list all the individual implementations, the strategies generally fell under headings: (1) Gun, Drug, & Gang-Related Violence (2) Domestic Violence (3) Targeting At-risk Youth and (4) Enhancing Investigative Capabilities. In order to gauge the effectiveness of the problem-oriented policing implementations, the researchers used an interrupted time-series analysis that measured the val-

Figure B   Problem-Oriented Policing Strategies at Treatment Places (From Most to Least Number of Places)

Responses
Aggressive Order Maintenance
Drug Enforcement
Required Store Owners to Clean Store Fronts
Public Works Removes Trash on Street
Robbery Investigations
Increased Lighting of Area
Housing Code Enforcement
Erected Fences Around Vacant Lot
Cleaned Vacant Lot
Boarded and Fenced Abandoned Buildings
Hung Signs Explaining Rules (e.g., No Drinking)
Surveillance of Place Using Videotapes
Evicted Troublesome Tenants
Improved Building Security by Adding Locks
Dispensed Crime Prevention Literature
Code Investigation of Tavern
Parking Enforcement
Razed Abandoned Building
Added Trash Receptacles
Changed Style of Trash Cans to Discourage Loitering
Opened and Cleaned Vacant Lot for Youth Recreation
Removed Graffiti from Building
Directed Patrol after School Hours
Removed Trash and Drug Paraphernalia from Alley
Remove Drug Selling Crew's Stashed Guns
Fixed Holes in Fence
Helped Homeless Find Shelter and Substance Abuse Treatment
Removed Piles of Lumber to Discourage Loitering

Source: Braga et al., 1999, Table 2, page 554.

ues of monthly levels of homicides (i.e., the dependent variable) and, for comparative purposes, gauged Richmond's results against all cities in California with over 75,000 residents (N = 75) during the same time period. This allowed them to compare whether the initiatives enacted were, in fact, responsible for the reduction in most "types" of homicides and violence, and it allowed them to tap into some other manifest and latent factors operating in Richmond. Their findings, although somewhat mixed, were noteworthy nonetheless. For instance, homicide rates for almost every type of homicide (e.g. homicides occurring outdoors, drive-by, homicides where the victim had prior convictions, etc.) dropped substantially except for homicides amongst gang members, which increased slightly. Additionally, similar to most homicide rates, the violent crime rate diminished as well. When compared to the other cities, the researchers claimed that while the findings were similar to only 10 of the 75 cities, those ten had also implemented problem-oriented and/or community-oriented policing. The other cities, excluding 19 cities that had so few homicides as to exclude them from the observation, significantly differed from Richmond. In short, White and colleagues' study is one of only a handful that directly examines the effects of problem-oriented policing strategies on violent crime and/or homicides. However, until we have more conclusive evidence about whether problem-oriented policing works or not, the findings here represent, at best, only tenuous support for problem-oriented policing.

INNOVATION AS A KEY TO SUCCESS

Every year since 1993, the Police Executive Research Forum (PERF) has given individual officers and/or entire police departments the Herbert Goldstein Award for Excellence in Problem-Oriented Policing in recognition of the best problem-oriented policing initiatives (Rojek, 2003). Accordingly, to aid in achieving a more definitive understanding of the types of problem-oriented policing models that are working or that are being recognized as innovative, Rojek (2003) conducted a study of the 53 Goldstein honored proposals awarded since its inception. His study reveals some important findings. Most noteworthy is that the winning proposals share two primary characteristics (in addition to keeping with the principles laid out by Goldstein). They are: (1) they are the most innovative in addressing persistent problems faced by police and (2) they show the most success in "reducing crime, disorder, and public-safety problems" (497).

Relating to the first characteristic, innovation, not only did each of the winning proposals address problems using innovative strategies, but also they did so at three different levels within the Goldstein paradigm (i.e., organizational, programmatic, and technique). For example, while many proposals shared similar techniques, of which Rojek grouped under broader categories for analytical purposes, such as crime prevention through environmental design, community mobilization, targeted enforcement efforts, his findings show that there were over 250 different innovative strategies applied across the 53 initiatives. Moreover, many of the strategies that were implemented may have already existed in some form within individual departments (e.g., targeted enforcement); however, some departments' combined multiple policing strategies in new ways or applied those utilized in other areas to a problem-oriented framework. As such, the innovation displayed by each of the departments seem to hold promise in increasing the technical knowledge base that may aid in improving problem-oriented policing strategies and, related to the second important finding, improve our knowledge about what policing strategies work best in reducing crime and other related problems (Rojek, 2003).

Two other points asserted by Rojek, though not necessarily related to one another, are worthy of mentioning here. First, his analysis of the initiatives runs somewhat counter to Eck's (1993) enforcement conception of problem-oriented policing. He states that problem-oriented policing "does not preclude the use of traditional law enforcement techniques," but rather, the "spirit" of the Goldstein model asserts that traditional enforcement strategies would be included with other types of problem-solving techniques (Rojek, 2003:507). Last, while the findings reveal potential for both reducing crime and disorder and, more generally for problem-oriented policing strategies, more time is needed to see if strategies that are shown to work can be sustained over time, and if not, why some do not work or are not sustained (Rojek, 2003).

IMPLEMENTATION ISSUES WITH PROBLEM-ORIENTED POLICING

Problem-oriented policing is a new organizational strategy that seeks to redefine the mission of policing, the principal operating methods, and the key administrative arrangements of police departments (Moore, 1992). Since problem-oriented policing involves a substantial change from traditional methods of law enforcement, some scholars have identified implementation problems that range from limited resources to accountability concerns to difficulty in changing the culture of policing. This last problem, changing the culture of policing, may in fact be the biggest obstacle of all since the traditional law enforcement mentality is deeply entrenched among current administrative arrangements (Moore, 1992). At the same time, there are approaches for changing the culture such that problem-oriented policing can become a viable police strategy. First, the organization must embrace openness as a value, thereby requiring that police become more exposed to the communities they police. Second, the values of the organization must be articulated in a manner so that all members of the police force know what is expected of them as they perform their duties. Third, and perhaps most important, the traditional, reactive method of policing must change from a centralized, reactive organization to one that is decentralized and marked by geographic organization. These changes are likely to alter the face of policing to one less preoccupied with making large numbers of arrests to one more focused on maintaining peace. The guiding principle of problem-oriented policing is to focus on identification and problem-solving techniques, which can lead to a better understanding of the problems that underlie the incidents to which the police are summoned.

With these concerns in hand, a fully problem-oriented police agency will be marked by at least seven characteristics (Eck and Spelman, 1987):

1. Problem solving will be the standard method of policing, not just an occasionally useful tactic.

2. Problem-solving efforts will focus on problems of the public, not police administration.

3. When problems are taken on, police will establish precise, measurable objectives.

4. Police managers will constantly look for ways to get all members of the department involved in solving problems.

5. Officers should consistently undertake thorough analysis using data from many sources, both internal and external to the police agency.

6. Officers will engage in an uninhibited search for solutions to all problems they take on.

7. All members of the department will be involved in problem solving.

Although implementing and sustaining these seven characteristics is likely to take time, police executives and the citizens they service should plan on a long- rather than short-term outlook at how the police define and execute their role. This process should continue, in tandem with the community, until the entire department adopts the problem-solving approach. Importantly, the problem-solving approach should be applied locally and situationally thereby recognizing that conditions, problems, and solutions are context specific such that they may not be translatable to other jurisdictions.

Conclusion

There is a good bit of evidence suggesting that police problem-solving efforts are effective at reducing crime and disorder at problem places (Goldstein, 1990; Sherman and Weisburd, 1995) and that such tactics do not necessarily move problems to surrounding areas (Braga et al., 1999). Thus, focused police efforts that attempt to modify the places, routine activities and situations that promote crime, violence, and disorder may present an effective option for police agencies in altering such negative social ills.

Although extant research on problem-solving tactics appears to support its continued application, the survivability of problem-oriented policing is unknown largely due to other popular, yet politically volatile, police strategies such as zero-tolerance policing. Problem-oriented policing and zero-tolerance policing are two ends of the policing continuum. For example, zero-tolerance policing, with its focus on attacking order maintenance and quality of life issues, is not concerned with (1) problem identification or analysis, (2) identification of underlying conditions and causes, nor (3) consideration of the wide range of possible alternatives to solving the problem. According to Cordner (1998), zero-tolerance policing places an overemphasis on formal control mechanisms, and as such it overrelies on the law enforcement and criminal justice system resources in order to quell social problems. All the while, zero-tolerance policing prefers a relative quick fix to crime and social ill problems with little concern for the long-term effects.

But do the data support the application of zero-tolerance over problem-oriented policing? Although little research has been directed at this issue, police and policy makers have credited zero-tolerance policing with the significant decrease in crime in New York City during the 1990s. Specifically, champions of zero-tolerance policing credit the 37 percent reduction in the Part I Crime Rate between 1990 and 1995 to the get-tough approach of the New York City Police Department and its significant increase in personnel; yet, at the same time, the San Diego Police Department experienced a similar decline with a problem-oriented policing approach and with a much smaller increase in sworn personnel. Thus, given that problem-oriented policing appears to be as successful as zero-tolerance in reducing crime, it may in fact be the preferred strategy for two reasons: (1) it costs less than zero-tolerance tactics, and (2) it requires fewer officers than traditional, enforcement-oriented policing (Cordner, 1998).

So, with this in mind, what does the future of problem-oriented policing look like? A close inspection of police agencies participating in the New England Consortium on Policing provides some evidence. Officers in these agencies are experimenting with computers in patrol cars that assist officers doing problem solving. For example, these problem-oriented policing modules contain information on the problem-solving stages and allow the officer to look up different types of available problem-solving strategies and their effectiveness. The computer program also allows them to input their situation-specific information into the database so other police officers can share in their knowledge. This approach is likely to continue as the use of computers becomes fully integrated into the policing operation and is likely to advance the types of problem-solving exercises and evaluations in the future. Whether this tactic aids in police efforts and leads to effective crime control policies remains an open, empirical question.

In sum, although problem-oriented policing still retains an element of reactiveness (i.e., a continued response to calls-for-service), at the same time it represents a significant shift in police emphasis and practice in that it attempts to identify and remove the problem underlying repeated incidents. In so doing, problem-oriented policing emphasizes a cooperation between the police, the community, and other local agencies. Importantly, problem-oriented policing also recognizes that citizens are concerned with issues much more than crime, like social and physical disorder, that permeate and infiltrate their overall quality of life (Skogan, 1990). By focusing on such concerns, police officers who practice problem-oriented policing can use their local knowledge and experience to improve the communities they serve (Eck and Spelman, 1987).

References

Braga, A. A., D. L. Weisburd, E. J. Waring, L. G. Mazerolle, W. Spellman, and G. Gajewski. 1999. Problem-oriented policing in violent crime places: A randomized controlled experiment. *Criminology* 37:541–580.

Cordner, G. 1998. Problem-oriented policing vs. zero tolerance. In T.O. Shelley and A.C. Grant (Eds.), *Problem-Oriented Policing: Crime Specific Problems, Critical Issues, and Making POP Work* (pp. 303–314). Washington, DC: Police Executive Research Forum.

Eck, J., and W. Spelman. 1987. Problem-solving: Problem-oriented policing in Newport News. *Research in Brief.* Washington, DC: National Institute of Justice.

Eck, J. 1993. Alternative futures for policing. In D. Weisburd and C. Uchida (Eds.), *Police Innovation and Control of the Police.* New York: Springer-Verlag.

Goldstein, H. 1979. Improving policing: A problem-oriented approach. *Crime and Delinquency* 25: 236–258.

Goldstein, H. 1990. *Problem-Oriented Policing.* Philadelphia: Temple University Press.

Green-Mazerolle, L., and W. Terrill. 1997. Problem-oriented policing in public housing: Identifying the distribution of problem places. *Policing* 20: 235–255.

Green-Mazerolle, L., J. Ready, W. Terrill, and E. Waring. 2000. Problem-oriented policing in public housing: The Jersey City evaluation. *Justice Quarterly* 17, 1: 129–155.

Greene, J. R., A. R. Piquero, P. Collins, and R. Kane. 1999. Doing research in public housing: Implementation issues from Philadelphia's 11th Street Corridor Community Policing Program. *Justice Research and Policy* 1: 67–95.

Monkkonen, E. H. 1992. History of urban police. In M. Tonry and N. Morris (Eds.), *Modern Policing: Crime and Justice, An Annual Review of Research.* Chicago: University of Chicago Press.

Moore, M. H. 1992. Problem-solving and community policing. In M. Tonry and N. Morris (Eds.), *Modern Policing: Crime and Justice, An Annual Review of Research.* Chicago: University of Chicago Press.

Reiss, Jr., A. J. 1992. Police organization in the twentieth century. In M. Tonry and N. Morris (Eds.), *Modern Policing: Crime and Justice, An Annual Review of Research.* Chicago: University of Chicago Press.

Rojek, J. 2003. A decade of excellence in problem-oriented policing: Characteristics of the Goldstein award winners. *Police Quarterly* 6, 4: 492–515.

Scott, M. 2000. *Problem-Oriented Policing: Reflections on the First 20 Years.* U.S. Department of Justice, COPS Office.

Sherman, L.W. 1998. American policing. In M. Tonry (Ed.), *The Handbook of Crime and Punishment.* New York: Oxford University Press.

Sherman, L., and D. L. Weisburd. 1995. General deterrent effects of police patrol in crime hot spots: A randomized controlled trial. *Justice Quarterly* 12: 625–648.

Skogan, W. 1990. *Disorder and Decline.* New York: The Free Press.

White, M. D., J. J. Fyfe, S. P. Campbell, and J. S. Goldkamp. 2003. The police role in preventing homicide: Considering the impact of problem-oriented policing on the prevalence of murder. *Journal of Research in Crime and Delinquency* 40, 2: 194–255.

SECTION VII
Use of Force

The authority to use force in the line of duty is one of the most controversial aspects of police work. While it is a necessary tool for officers in controlling crime and apprehending criminals, it also is the greatest source of police abuse of authority and citizen complaints. Police officers have the right to use force in certain specific situations, but questions are raised as to when it should be employed and how much force is necessary. The abuse of this authority is one of the most difficult problems facing police administrators today.

The beating of Rodney King in Los Angeles in 1991 provided an excellent example of the problems and consequences involved in the use of force. Regardless of the legal and policy-related responses to these events, the citizens of South Central Los Angeles made their opinions clear. This beating and the violent response to the not-guilty verdicts were tragic incidents, but unfortunately there is no reason to believe that these types of events will not be repeated.

In the first article for this section of the book, "The Split-Second Syndrome and other Determinants of Police Violence," Dr. James J. Fyfe distinguishes between police violence that is clearly extra-legal and violence that is simply the unnecessary result of police incompetence. He suggests that much of the problem with the excessive use of force is the result of officers being placed in situations that force the officer to make life and death decisions while under extreme time constraints or what he terms "the split-second syndrome." Dr. Fyfe concludes by proposing two principles that can be used to avoid the split-second syndrome: tactical knowledge and concealment.

In the second selection, "What We Know about Police Use of Force," Kenneth Adams reviews the available research on police use of force. Drawing upon a number of studies, he classifies the findings into three categories:

what we know with substantial confidence about police use of force, what we know with modest confidence, and what we do not know about police use of force. Although use of force is one of the most serious issues facing law enforcement today, it is applied by the police very infrequently and usually as we would want it to be used: at the lower end of the force continuum, without much injury to the officer or suspect, while the officer is trying to make an arrest and the suspect is resisting. However, it is the very few misuses of force that cause the serious problems that both citizens and police administrators have come to abhor.

The next article in this section is "Police Use of Deadly Force: How Courts and Policy-Makers Have Misapplied *Tennessee v. Garner*" by Michael Smith. Professor Smith, an attorney and PhD, analyzes this critical Supreme Court opinion and explains the various lower court interpretations. He examines the current standards adopted by police agencies and argues that a defense of life standard has practical advantages over less restrictive policies.

The final article in this section, "Police Operational Management: Rethinking the Legal Shell Game" by William C. Smith, addresses the legal and financial accountability of police agencies for injuries inflicted through the activities of their officers. There has been an accelerating trend in civil cases filed against police departments and more and more of them are successful. William Smith discusses how police agencies currently respond to the increasing threat and suggests a more effective model, involving the analysis of foreseeable risks and a constructive and practical approach to address those risks proactively.

The Split-Second Syndrome and Other Determinants of Police Violence

James J. Fyfe

Discussions of police violence are often blurred by the failure to distinguish between violence that is clearly extralegal and abusive and violence that is simply the unnecessary result of police incompetence. This distinction is important because the causes of these two types of violence, and the motivations of the officers involved, vary greatly. Extralegal violence involves the willful and wrongful use of force by officers who knowingly exceed the bounds of their office. Unnecessary violence occurs when well-meaning officers prove incapable of dealing with the situations they encounter without needless or too hasty resort to force.[1]

EXTRALEGAL POLICE VIOLENCE

It is tempting but probably simplistic, to conclude that extralegal police violence results exclusively from the aberrations or prejudices of individual officers or their commanders. If this kind of violence were totally—or even primarily—attributable to officers who regard their badges as licenses to vent

Anne Campbell and John Gibbs, eds. *Violent Transactions*. Basil Blackwell, 1986. Reprinted with permission of the publisher.

hostile and anti-social drives, we should be well advised to try to eliminate it by selecting and monitoring officers with greater care.

Certainly, these personnel processes are important, but it is probably useless to rely almost exclusively on them as the strategy for reducing extralegal police violence. First, our skill at predicting human behavior is not highly developed. Except in obviously extreme cases,[2] it is nearly impossible for personnel administrators to determine which police candidates for officers will eventually engage in extralegal violence. Second, as investigators of police corruption have suggested (City of New York, 1972), it is likely that characteristics of police work and police organizations, rather than characteristics of police officers, are the major determinants of police misconduct.[3]

Klockars (1980) makes such an argument in his formulation of a police "Dirty Harry Problem." He argues that some police perceive the procedural limitations under which they work as arbitrary barriers to achievement of one of their most important goals: the protection of good folk through the apprehension and conviction of criminals. Such officers operate on a presumption of suspects' guilt, and become frustrated when legal processes result in acquittals of people who have, in fact, committed the crimes of which they have been accused. Subsequently, to serve what they (and much of the public) see as justice, these officers resort to "dirty means"—fabrication of evidence, intimidation and even torture—to circumvent such perceived barriers to justice as judicial exclusion of illegally obtained evidence, and to make sure that their suspects ultimately receive in court what the officers regard as their just due. Even though the actions of such officers may reflect a widely held view that there should be little distinction between factual guilt and legal guilt (Packer, 1968), they involve, Klockars asserts, wrongful moral choices by the officers themselves. The best way, according to Klockars, of preventing such wrongful choices is to punish the individual officers and the police agencies who make and tolerate them.

As Klockars acknowledges, however, his approach to this kind of violence is not entirely satisfactory. To penalize individual officers who have been trained and socialized by their employers to believe that policing cannot be done by the book and that abuse and misconduct are the most effective means of accomplishing police goals is probably unfair and would almost certainly be ineffective. Extralegal police violence is probably more closely attributable to politically expedient, but morally wrong, definitions of appropriate police conduct at the highest levels of police agencies than to the deviance of street-level officers. Thus, a better way to reduce such violence is to alter the organizational expectations and norms to which the officers who commit abuses conform.

For that reason, Klockars is much more persuasive in his suggestion that police *agencies* bear penalties for extralegal violence than in his qualified advocacy of individual punishment. Certainly, officers who apply wrongful definitions to their work may *deserve* to be punished. But such wrongful definitions are likely to survive them and to dictate the behavior of other officers unless their superiors—and the citizens whose taxes ultimately pay for disciplinary measures against the police—learn that the costs of encouraging or tolerating the use of dirty means to achieve good ends are intolerable.

Thus, as the United States Supreme Court indicated in *Monell vs. New York City Department of Social Services,*[4] one way to correct high-level tolerance or encouragement of public officials' misconduct is to make citizens liable for their employees' misdeeds. Implicit in this approach is the theory that concerned citizens will then demand that officials behave in a manner that is more consistent with both law and their financial interests. But, because the citizenry usually does not comport with this neat theory, this approach is not totally satisfactory either.

Citizens are often apathetic rather than concerned about the operations of their officials, including the police. Many of them simply expect officials to be there when needed, and become concerned only when officials have failed to meet this responsibility, or when they have personally experienced or witnessed what they regard as a grave injustice at the hands of officials. Further, many of the most concerned citizens regard with great distaste and little empathy the people against whom the police employ extralegal violence. The citizens who have the time to devote to civic affairs belong to the middle and upper classes, who rarely are the victims of police abuse; but it is they who sit on the juries that determine whether police have exceeded the bounds of their authority and, if so, whether the citizens—themselves included—should compensate the victims.

There is probably no better way to reform the wrongful behavior of police officers than to hit in the pocket the citizens to whom they are accountable. But this tactic often fails because those same citizens determine whether and how hard their pockets should be hit, and because they often do not regard as peers the victims of police abuse. Consequently, reality demands that more operationally practicable means of reducing extralegal police violence be found.

One such method is simple but rare: the engagement of leaders willing to disabuse the citizenry of their unrealistic expectations of the police. In a democracy, rates of crime, levels of disorder and the safety of "good people" are more closely associated with social conditions than with the number of police or the willingness of the police to employ dirty means to achieve the good ends of order and public safety. Few elected officials or police chiefs, however, are willing to run the risk of appearing to be soft on crime by announcing to apathetic citizens that crime and disorder are *their* problems rather than police problems and that, unless they are willing to give up many of their freedoms, no level of police presence or toughness is likely to improve matters.[5]

Were more mayors and police chiefs willing and courageous enough to do so, the pressures upon them and their personnel to achieve ends that lie beyond their means would dissipate, as would the temptation to bend the rules in attempts to achieve the impossible.[6] Until we grow a new breed of elected executives and police chiefs who are somehow able to change unrealistic public expectations of the police, however, we will not remove the major source of extralegal police violence, but must expect it to continue, however dissipated by other, less direct, approaches.

INCOMPETENCE AND UNNECESSARY POLICE VIOLENCE

While extralegal police violence is egregious, it probably occurs far less frequently—and probably less frequently injures sympathetic and factually innocent victims—than does police violence emanating from simple incompetence. Such violence occurs when police lack the eloquence to persuade temporarily disturbed persons to give up their weapons, but shoot them instead. It occurs when, instead of pausing to consider and apply less drastic and dramatic alternatives, officers blindly confront armed criminals in the midst of groups of innocent people. It occurs when officers called to quell noisy but nonviolent disputes act in a way that provokes disputants to violence to which the police must respond in kind. In short, it occurs when well-meaning police officers lack—or fail to apply—the expertise required to resolve as bloodlessly as possible the problems their work requires them to confront.

Much unnecessary violence occurs because many of us, including many police, have not adequately analyzed the role of the police or the problems they confront. Thus, we have not devised adequate solutions to these problems, and have instead settled for a standard of performance from the police that is far below what we should tolerate from other groups.

THE ROLE OF THE POLICE

A common conceptualization is that the police, along with the courts and correctional agencies, are a component of the criminal-justice system. This observation is true but, for two major reasons, it may lead to shallow analysis of the police and their problems. First, the courts (excluding civil courts) and correctional agencies devote their efforts exclusively to crime-related matters, but police officers do not. The clients of court personnel are those who have been charged with or victimized by crime; without exception, they are alleged criminals and their presumed victims. The people with whom the officials of correctional agencies interact most directly are those who are awaiting trial on criminal charges, or those who have been convicted of crime; without exception they are alleged or convicted criminals. But, in addition to bringing the alleged perpetrators and victims of crime to the attention of the courts, police regularly interact with people in circumstances in which criminal behavior is doubtful or clearly absent. The clientele of the police includes participants in minor disputes and traffic accidents, those who are lost and in need of travel directions, those who suffer sudden illness or injury, and many others whose problems have nothing whatever to do with crime, criminal law or criminal justice.

In addition, in many cases in which it is clear that some violation of criminal law has occurred, police possess greater discretion to devise informal and unrecorded dispositions of offenders than is true of any other criminal-justice officials. The police officer who sends a disorderly group of teenagers on their way on the grounds that it is more just—or more convenient—than arresting them may do so in the knowledge that no official record of his encounter with them will appear anywhere. What he does and says in such a case disappears into the ozone and, unlike a court or correctional-agency decision to release, cannot be objectively reconstructed by reference to any transcript or detailed official document.

In large measure, the police officer decides which of the people with whom he interacts shall come to the attention of the courts. He exercises a degree of discretion that is usually unrestricted by the prior decisions of any public official.[7] He cannot sentence offenders or impose harsh correctional conditions upon them, but he often has the power to choose between letting them go free and initiating a process likely to result in the imposition of penalties by other officials. He also has great power to impose upon his clientele penalties that do not require court agreement with his actions. Should he decide to arrest rather than to release, nothing a prosecutor, judge, defense attorney or correctional-agency official can do is likely to erase that arrest from the police record. Even when he recognizes that conviction is unlikely, the police officer knows that arrest will result in substantial inconvenience and cost.

But, as has been made clear in several attempts to define the police role, the police cannot be comprehensively discussed or understood in terms of their responsibilities to apprehend criminals or to enforce laws. Their job, Wilson (1968) suggests, includes the duty to see that popular conceptions of order are maintained. The police serve to prevent "behavior that either disturbs or threatens to disturb the public peace or that involves face-to-face conflict among two or more persons" (p. 16).

Goldstein (1977) concurs in part, arguing that law enforcement does not describe the role of the police, but instead defines only one of many methods that they may apply to achieve this goal. Bittner (1970) points out another method employed by police to maintain order: the use or threatened use of legitimate force (that is, as approved by both the government and most of the people served by the police) to coerce individuals to behave in accordance with society's expectations.

Still, the functions of the police are so complex that they are not adequately captured by even the broad "order-maintenance" descriptor. Just as many police tasks have little to do with crime or law, many have little to do with threats to public order, and many involve no coercion or threat or use of force. The police are on duty 24 hours a day, seven days a week, Sundays and holidays included, in order to tackle a variety of problems and crises. These range from tree-bound cats, through lost children and persons locked out of their homes, to people who have been horribly mangled in automobile accidents. In none of these cases is the quality of police response less critical for those concerned—the mother of a lost child, or the man whose femoral artery has been severed in a car crash—than in cases where the police are required to exercise their law-enforcement and order-maintenance responsibilities.

The breadth of police work is what makes Goldstein's definition of the role of the police the most comprehensive and satisfactory. He observes that

> The police function, if viewed in its broadest context, consists of making a diagnostic decision of sorts as to which alternative might be most appropriate in a given case. In this respect the total rule of the police differs little from their role in administering first aid to sick and injured persons. (1977, p. 41)

Goldstein is correct. Police officers, like doctors, lawyers, psychologists and marriage counselors, are human-service workers. Like these others, police are paid to diagnose problems that befuddle the rest of us, to treat those within their competence, and to refer to more specialized agencies and officials those problems that they themselves cannot solve. Just as we call upon the doctor to investigate and treat internal complaints not responsive to our own treatment efforts, so we call upon the police to investigate and treat complaints deriving from certain external conditions that we cannot otherwise ameliorate—noisy neighbors, assault or robbery, the injury of a loved one by a hit-and-run driver.

Police officers, however, treat their clients and professional problems under conditions that do not affect most other human-service workers, and that greatly increase the potential for violence. Police-client interactions are uniquely *urgent, involuntary* and *public.* Unless we and the police fully appreciate the causal relations between these three conditions and violence, we inadequately diagnose police problems. The result is that we witness and experience violence that need not have occurred.

Urgency of Police-Citizen Encounters

Police are generally unable to select the times at which they will perform their services. They are expected to respond to and resolve our problems *now,* while we routinely agree to wait until two weeks from Thursday to obtain help for our medical and legal dilemmas. In Bittner's terms, the police task consists of resolving problems *"that-ought-not-to-be-happening-now-and-about-which-somebody-had-better-do-something-now"* (1974, p. 30). As a consequence, police usually encounter their clients in circumstances analogous to those faced by hospital emergency-room personnel: they deal with people immediately after their problems have come to light, and must treat not only the substance of these problems, but also the shock that accompanies their clients' discoveries that suddenly all is not well.

Involuntariness of Police-Citizen Encounters

The constraint of time usually denies police officers the luxury of picking and choosing their clientele from among those deemed in need of police attention, and places great limits on their ability to refer clients and problems to more highly qualified specialists. When we do get to see our family doctor, he may diagnose but decline to treat a problem that he views as most amenable to resolution by a more specialized colleague. But a police officer summoned to a late-night domestic dispute cannot withdraw with a referral to a better trained and more competent officer who does not come on duty until the morning. Regardless of his ineptness, and because his clientele includes the neighbors who cannot sleep because of the noise, he is duty-bound to establish at least temporary peace before he leaves, even if he has to coerce some of his clients to accept his prescriptions.

Therein lies another unique characteristic of police work: many of those who come to police attention do not seek it, but become unwilling clients through the intervention of third parties or of officers themselves. When this happens, just as officers cannot usually decline clients who come to their attention, so their clients cannot withdraw from treatment no matter how distasteful they find it. Given the choice, very few of the clients arrested or brought to book by the police would consent to this form of treatment.

Public Setting of Police-Citizen Encounters

Unlike even emergency-room personnel, police officers are unable to choose the places in which they perform their services. The work of police patrol officers occurs not in private offices, but in public settings or other locations in which the problems of their clientele have come to light. As a result, police officers suffer the disadvantage of performing in places in which clients' behavior is not constrained by the formality and decorum of a professional setting and the realization that one is on another's territory. The clientele of the police are governed only by the behavioral rules of the street.

Another consequence of the public setting of police work is that officers must be attentive not only to the immediate problems of the clients they have been summoned to treat, but also to third-party reactions to their efforts. If they are to avoid criticism and even interference from bystanders, police officers summoned to restrain emotionally disturbed or drug-crazed persons on the street must do so in a way that is demonstrably proper and humane.

The police officers' concern with the *appearance* of propriety and humaneness is not shared by mental-health professionals who work in residential facilities, or who administer shock therapy to patients in the privacy of their clinics. Nor is it shared by others who must render their services in public places. Ambulance personnel, for example, often perform their work in public, but it rarely involves resolution of disputes or other competing interests, so they need not concern themselves with their audiences' perceptions of their fairness. In addition the work of ambulance personnel usually involves more distastefully gory and less intriguing and public problems than those of the police, so that bystanders watch the proceedings less closely. It is much easier, less nauseating, and more interesting to watch the police subdue a street drunk than it is to watch a team of emergency medical technicians treat a man whose leg has been severed in an automobile accident. Finally, the techniques used by ambulance personnel are far more arcane than are those of the police: few bystanders have any experience or expertise in stanching the flow of blood or treating shock, but nearly everybody has attempted to resolve a dispute, calm an unreasonable or unruly person, and seen the ways in which television police subdue suspects. Consequently, few bystanders feel competent to judge or protest the work of ambulance personnel, but many view themselves as qualified to assess the work of the police. As can be seen from cases where riots have been precipitated by bystanders' dissatisfaction with police actions, some are even willing to demonstrate their disagreement violently and immediately.

Police officers must also be acutely aware that the presence of an audience of bystanders may affect their clients' behavior. In some cases, the embarrassment of having one's problems aired in public may cause—or increase—irrational behavior on the part of the client. In others—the crowd encouraging the young man poised to jump from a high roof comes to mind—bystanders may become direct actors in police encounters. In still others, as Muir observes, police respond to street disputes that are "played out on two levels—in the relationship between the two antagonists, and in the relationship of the crowd to the disputants. Police officers have to perceive both levels" (1977, p. 102). Muir describes a situation in which police arrived at a crowded recreation center and found a bat-wielding young man confronting an aide. This case, which superficially appeared to be an attack by an inner-city youth upon an older authority figure, could be satisfactorily resolved only if the police took time to learn the antagonists' motivations and the importance of the crowd. Here, the young man suspected that the aide had raped his 13-year-old sister, so that

> From the point of view of the brother of the victim of the alleged rape, he was retaliating not only from a desire for retribution but to deter future marauders. . . . The brother was establishing face in the neighborhood, a reputation for dogged revenge; in thrashing his sister's rapist, he was making a harsh example for all the crowd to see. . . . He was publishing his message for those persons that really counted, those who might think they could push his family around. In the brutish neighborhood he and his family inhabited, the brother was making himself "a man of respect." . . .
>
> In the relationship between the crowd and the brother, the crowd's definition of honorable conduct became crucial. Depending on its expectations of him, his attack on the aide would have different meanings. . . . Anyone who had the talent to influence the crowd's philosophy in this matter could make a great deal of difference to what the brother felt he had to do to establish face. (pp. 102–3)

To summarize, then, a proper analysis of the police role requires acknowledgement of many unique characteristics of the work of street-level officers. Policing is a form of human-service work that requires officers to diagnose the problems they confront, and to decide which of several means of solving them—invoking the law, threatening to invoke the law, employing force or, as in Muir's example, attempting to persuade—is most likely to be successful. The broader discretion available to police officers than to other criminal-justice officials, however, is limited by several constraints unique to policing. There is an urgency about police work that does not affect court or correctional-agency officials or most others whose work involves diagnosis and treatment of human ills. The police cannot select the times or places at which they treat their clientele. They often must do so at odd hours and in very public places. Consequently, if they are to avoid criticism or adverse response by third parties, they must be greatly concerned not only with *doing* the right thing, but also with *appearing* to do the right thing. This compounds the difficulties of police work, because the people they treat are often adversaries rather than individuals who have come to the police for help. The people at the core of police problems often do not agree with police diagnoses of those problems or even that any problem exists. They do not see the police as individuals who have come to help them. Once the police have come, however, neither they nor the police may withdraw until the problem at hand is at least temporarily remedied.

The urgent, involuntary, and public relationship between police officer and client creates a high potential for violence. To avert it, police must often apply considerable diagnostic skills, and must learn to manipulate these causal variables in ways that diminish the likelihood that violence will result. If urgency and time constraints sometimes lead to violence, it follows that police should slow the pace of their encounters with citizens so that cooled tempers and the restoration of reason may eventually lead to nonviolent outcomes. If involuntariness sometimes leads to violence, it follows that police should attempt to diminish their clients' feelings that something is being done *to* them, by trying to win their confidence and devising problem solutions that at least appear to be collaborative rather than exclusively coercive. If the public settings of police-citizen encounters sometimes lead to violence, it follows that police should inject as much privacy as possible into these encounters.

There is evidence that attempts by police to manipulate time and involuntariness, and to make more private highly volatile encounters between police and citizens, do reduce violence. Recent police efforts to diagnose and plan for hostage situations and situations involving armed and barricaded persons have led to a high rate of bloodless resolution of these situations. The time-manipulative techniques employed in these situations include avoidance and delay of armed confrontation unless it is clear that lives are in imminent danger. Involuntariness is manipulated by trained negotiators who attempt to determine the motives and win the confidence of their subjects, and to convince them that surrender is in their own best interests. Privacy is introduced into these situations by carefully controlling media access to hostage-takers and *vice versa*, and by clearing the public from the immediate areas. These privacy techniques serve the multiple purposes of protecting uninvolved citizens, eliminating the audiences to whom hostage-takers may wish to play, reducing hostage-takers' loss of face at the time of surrender, and eliminating the possibility that the attention of bystanders or the media will encourage hostage-takers or barricaded persons to further rash actions (see, for instance, Schlossberg and Freeman, 1974).

Despite the apparent success of such defusing techniques, many of us—and many police leaders—often encourage officers to think of themselves as rough and ready men and women of action whose prime function it is to show up quickly at emergencies and to make their diagnoses on the spot. Unless we more strongly encourage officers to develop the requisite diagnostic skills to deal with certain types of situations when they occur, we are likely to witness many more hasty and inaccurate diagnoses and many unnecessarily violent attempts to treat police problems.

POLICE DIAGNOSTIC EXPERTISE

As too many experiences have demonstrated, police often do not attempt diagnosis until they are in the midst of treating critical problems. The 1965 Watts riot began when, despite the violent reaction of a large and growing crowd drawn by the protests of the suspect's mother, two police officers persisted in their attempts to arrest a drunken driver whom they had already identified and could presumably retake later under quieter circumstances. The 1971 Attica prison riot resulted in the deaths of 39 inmates and hostages when New York State police officers, who usually work alone or in small groups in rural areas, were armed with shotguns and armor-piercing rifles and directed to storm and retake the tear-gas-filled, heavily-walled yard of a maximum-security prison inhabited largely by inner-city convicts. A block in Philadelphia burned down in 1985 when, in an attempt to evict a radical group, a police helicopter dropped onto the roof of an adjoining wooden house an incendiary device that had apparently never before been used by police in any field situation.

Looking back, it is easy to say that these decisions should not have been made. It would probably have been wiser for the police in Watts to have retreated, and to have returned to make their arrest in quieter and less public circumstances. In Attica and Philadelphia, continued negotiation or less drastic tactics probably would have better served the fundamental police responsibility to protect life than did the hastily devised tactics that were employed.

THE SPLIT-SECOND SYNDROME

It is difficult to define the factors that led well-meaning officials to make the bad decisions just reviewed, but it appears that they are reflections of what might be called a "split-second syndrome" that affects police decision-making in crises. This syndrome serves both to inhibit the development of greater police diagnostic expertise and to provide after-the-fact justification for unnecessary police violence. It also serves as a guide to many of the equally unfortunate low-visibility decisions made by individual police officers every day.

The split-second syndrome is based on several assumptions. First, it assumes that, since no two police problems are precisely alike, there are no principles that may be applied to the diagnosis of specific situations. Thus, no more can be asked of officers than that they respond as quickly as possible to problems, devising the best solutions they can on the spur of the moment. This, of course, places an extraordinary burden upon officers, who must make life-or-death decisions under the most stressful and time-constrained conditions.

Second, because of these stresses and time constraints, a high percentage of inappropriate decisions should be expected, but any subsequent criticism of officers' decisions—especially by those outside the police, who can have no real appreciation of the burdens upon officers—is an unwarranted attempt to be wise after the event. Thus, if we are to maintain a police service whose members are decisive in the crises to which we summon them, we had best learn to live with the consequences of the decisions we ask them to make. If we do not, we risk damaging police morale and generating a police service whose members are reluctant to intervene on our behalf.

Finally, the split-second syndrome holds that assessments of the justifiability of police conduct are most appropriately made on the exclusive basis of the perceived exigencies of the moment when a decision had to be taken. So long as a citizen has, intentionally or otherwise, provoked the police at that instant, he, rather than the police, should be viewed as the cause of any resulting injuries or damage, no matter how excessive the police reaction and no matter how directly police decisions molded the situation that caused those injuries or damages.

Thus, should police receive a report of an armed robbery in a crowded supermarket, they should be granted great leeway in their manner of response, because no two armed-robbery calls are precisely alike. If, in the course of responding, they decide that, to prevent the robber from escaping, the best course of action is to confront him immediately in the midst of a crowd of shoppers, they should not be told they should have acted otherwise. When they do challenge the alleged robber and he suddenly reacts to their calls from behind by turning on them with a shiny object in his hand, the only issue to be decided by those who subsequently review police actions is whether, at that instant, the suspect's actions were sufficiently provocative to justify their shooting him. That is so regardless of how the prior actions of the police may have contributed to their peril; regardless of how predictable it was that the suspect would be alarmed and would turn toward the police when they shouted to him; regardless of how many innocent bystanders were hit by bullets; and regardless of whether the reported armed robber was in fact an unhappy customer who, with pen in hand to complete a check for his purchase, had been engaged in a loud argument with a clerk during which he had said that the store's prices were "robbery."

The underpinning of the split-second syndrome, in short, is the assumption that the sole basis on which any use of force by the police needs to be justified is the officers' perceptions of the circumstances prevailing at the instant when they decide to apply force. The officers involved in the incident described above did, of course, possess much information that would lead them to believe that the subject of their call was a robber. When he turned on them, they were entitled, in the heat of the moment, to believe that their lives were in imminent danger. When they made the split-second decision to pull the trigger, they were also entitled to believe that no less drastic action would adequately protect their lives, so they were fully justified in shooting. Under the split-second syndrome, this shooting was a legitimate use of force under provocation.

But such an analysis lends approval to unnecessary violence, and to failure of the police to meet their highest obligation: the protection of life. Split-second analysis of police action focuses attention on diagnoses and decisions made by the police during one frame of an incident that began when the police became aware that they were likely to confront a violent person or situation. It ignores what went before. As the successful application of hostage techniques illustrates, it also ignores the fact that there are general principles that may be applied by officers to a variety of highly predictable, potentially violent situations.

It requires no great diagnostic ability to determine that the officers involved made a significant contribution to the bloody finale of the incident described above. Officers who respond to reports of robberies by charging through the front door and confronting suspects from exposed positions are almost certain to find themselves in great danger, real or perceived, and to face split-second decisions involving their lives, the lives of suspects and the lives of bystanders. Thus, instead of asking whether an officer ultimately had to shoot or fight his way out of perilous circumstances, we are better advised to ask whether it was not possible for him to have approached the situation in a way that reduced the risk of bloodshed and increased the chances of a successful and nonviolent conclusion.

AVOIDING SPLIT-SECOND DECISIONS

Even though most potentially violent situations encountered by the police are not as clear-cut as the one described in the previous section, opportunities usually do exist for officers to attempt to prevent the potential for violence from being realized. Police are usually assigned to the same geographic areas for long periods, but in my experience they are rarely encouraged to leave their patrol cars when there is little happening and to survey the places in which they might someday be asked to confront potentially violent situations. Were they to do so, they would be able to formulate tentative advance plans for dealing with reported supermarket robberies, warehouse burglaries and the like. Most often, police are directed by radio to scenes of potential violence (Reiss, 1971) and so are usually not on the spot at the time. Thus, even in the few minutes it takes them to get there, they have some opportunity to avoid split-second decisions by analyzing available information and planning their responses in advance of arrival. If they do not, and if they fail to structure their confrontations in a manner that is most likely to avert bloodshed, almost any violence that results is unnecessary, and should be condemned rather than rewarded with headlines, honors and medals.

Two principles, tactical knowledge and concealment, may be useful diagnostic tools in deciding how to deal with potentially violent people and situations.[8] Tactical knowledge includes prior knowledge of the setting and actors involved. Most often, police officers summoned to potentially violent situations have far less tactical knowledge than is desirable. While they usually know only what they have been told over the radio, any potential adversaries know precisely what is happening, where it is happening and who is involved. Since this places officers at a great disadvantage, it is important that they employ techniques for enhancing their tactical knowledge before committing themselves beyond the point of no return. If they fail to do this, they may easily fall prey to the more knowledgeable violent subjects of their calls, or may misinterpret the actions of innocent persons—such as the outraged shopper with a pen—in a way that may create violence where none exists. Like the military, they must be expected to learn as much as possible about the settings in which they may have to intervene.

Concealment includes disguising one's intent or identity, as well as employing actual physical cover or shelter. Officers—especially those in uniform—are usually at a disadvantage where this factor is concerned. When they respond to scenes of potential violence (for instance, armed robberies in progress), they are readily identifiable, while the subjects of their calls (the robbers) usually are not. Consequently, officers should employ all possible means of concealing themselves or their presence until the moment of least hazard. Doing so generally involves confronting from positions of concealment subjects who are temporarily without concealment. In the example of the reported supermarket robbery, this might mean that responding officers should avoid losing concealment by actually entering the supermarket, and should instead surreptitiously take up positions of concealment outside it (for instance, behind parked cars) and wait for their suspect to come to them. The military knows that the safest way to confront potential adversaries is to wait for the appropriate moment to ambush them from positions of concealment, but police are often encouraged to charge up hills.

The use of concealment not only minimizes the risk of officers, bystanders and suspects, but may also prevent tragic mistakes. I can recount several occasions in which officers responding to such calls have neglected to seek concealment, have encountered armed individuals from positions of total exposure, have—with some justification—perceived imminent danger to themselves, and have shot persons later found to be plain-clothes police officers or crime victims who had armed themselves to pursue the actual perpetrators. Many of these tragedies might have been avoided if the officers involved had instead confronted these individuals from positions of physical cover. From such positions, officers make themselves near impossible targets, and are able to give their perceived adversaries opportunities to identify themselves or to drop their weapons without placing themselves in jeopardy.

Application of these principles requires that officers diagnose the most critical problems they face—those that may require the use of extreme force—*before* they occur, and that they attempt to apply to their resolution techniques of tactical knowledge and concealment. We demand that from the military and from the fire service, both of which spend considerable time diagnosing and planning for exigencies that we are someday likely to ask them to resolve. We do not tolerate it when their actions in emergency situations demonstrate that they have been taken by surprise and forced to react on the basis of instinct rather than of careful advance diagnosis and planning. But, when police resort to forcible means to resolve readily foreseeable problems that could have been peacefully resolved with advance diagnosis and planning, we not only tolerate but also often reward their behavior. The police officer who shoots and kills an armed robber is often rewarded for his efforts with a medal. Should he instead kill a shopper with a pen, he is likely to be viewed as the unfortunate victim of a shared tragedy who, under the circumstances, had no choice but to take the action he did.

We should pay less attention to the outcomes of potentially violent situations than to questions of whether officers respond to them in ways likely to reduce the potential for violence. If we do not, we fail to legitimize genuinely unavoidable provoked force, and we reward and encourage an operating-style that eschews advance diagnosis, planning and training, and relies on officers' ability to make the most critical decisions under the worst possible conditions. That operating-style can only lead to frequent bad decisions by officers, who in the heat of the moment cannot reasonably be expected to devise solutions of equal quality to those that could be reached through careful advance planning. These results are grossly unfair to the public and to street-level police officers.

Thus, to reduce unnecessary police violence, we must define the police as diagnosticians, and we must demand that they learn that role thoroughly long before they actually confront someone who they have reason to believe is armed and dangerous. As we have done where hostage situations are concerned, we must define as successful those encounters where the police have done everything reasonably possible to avoid violence, and we must cease rewarding easily avoided split-second violence.

Notes

[1] As Bittner suggests, it is also necessary to distinguish between all types of violence and "the exercise of provoked force required to meet illegitimate acts" (1970, p. 36). There is little

doubt that the police must be granted considerable license to employ such force, and, in our condemnation of what Bittner calls "provocative violence" by officials, we should be careful to avoid retracting the legitimacy of police authority to employ necessary provoked force. The police simply cannot function without this authority. We should take care too to distinguish between legitimate provoked force and incompetence-related violence. The former is that *required* to put down threats against officers or other challenges to official authority. The latter is unnecessary, and occurs only because officers lack the expertise to employ readily available and less drastic means of putting down such threats and challenges.

[2] As a result of bureaucratic procedures or administrative apathy, guns and law-enforcement powers have sometimes been granted to, or not withdrawn from, officer candidates or in-service officers whom personnel investigations have shown to possess gross psychological instability or character flaws. I have reviewed police personnel folders that disclose that officers accused of misconduct had been hired by officials who knew that they had previously been excluded or dismissed from police service in other agencies because of congenital brain defects, extensive criminal records, long histories of drug abuse, assaults on supervisors and coworkers, or giving false sworn statements at previous official investigations of allegations that they had committed extralegal violence.

[3] Friedrich reports that the data he analyzed did "not support the notion that police use of force depends very much on the individual characteristics of the police" (1980, p. 89). Sherman's extensive survey (1980) of studies of police behavior found virtually no empirical support for assertions that individual officer characteristics are measurably related to any type of performance in office.

[4] The major import of the judgment in this case is that public agencies are liable when plaintiffs can demonstrate in court that they have suffered constitutional deprivations at the hands of public officials, and that the unconstitutional acts of these officials were directly caused by agency custom and practice. Thus, if an individual were able to demonstrate that he had been unconstitutionally beaten and arrested by a police officer, and that the police department involved had a history of encouraging or tolerating such misconduct, he would presumably be entitled to money damages from both the officer and the government agency that employed him.

[5] In addition, elected officials, who serve as intermediaries between citizens and police, may often be tempted to react defensively to judgments against police, regardless of whether such defensiveness is in the citizens' best interests. Consequently, citizens' ire may be redirected at what may be portrayed by elected officials as the arbitrariness of the courts, rather than at the police misconduct that gave rise to judgments against the taxpayers. For an elected mayor to acknowledge that his police department has operated unconstitutionally is not easy. It requires him to admit that the person he appointed as police chief (or who was otherwise determined to have been best qualified for that position) has performed his duties in a manner that violates the fundamental law of the land.

[6] See Manning (1977), who argues that the police have assumed—or been given—the "impossible mandate" of responsibility for crime control and order maintenance, and that most police are unwilling to admit that they cannot accomplish it.

[7] This is not to suggest that police currently operate with no *a priori* restrictions. As Goldstein (1977) points out, police operations are greatly influenced by legislators, and by the decisions made by prosecutors and judges in prior *similar* matters. My point is that police make decisions about specific individuals and situations before they have come to the attention of other officials.

[8] These principles were first articulated in a training-program I developed in 1976 while on the staff of the New York City Police Academy.

References

Bittner, E. 1974. Florence Nightingale in Pursuit of Willie Sutton: A Theory of the Police. In H. Jacob (ed.), *The Potential for Reform of Criminal Justice*, Beverly Hills: Sage.

Bittner, E. 1970. *The Functions of the Police in Modern Society*. Rockville, Md: National Institute of Mental Health.

City of New York Commission to Investigate Allegations of Police Corruption and the City's Anti-corruption Procedures. 1973. *Commission Report*. New York: George Braziller.

Friedrich, R. J. 1980. Police Use of Force: Individuals, Situations and Organizations. *Annals of the American Academy of Social and Political Sciences*, 452, 82.

Goldstein, H. 1977. *Policing a Free Society*. Cambridge: Ballinger.

Klockars, C. 1980. The Dirty Harry Problem. *Annals of the American Academy of Political and Social Science*, 452, 33.

Manning, P. 1977. *Police work*, Cambridge: MIT Press.

Monell vs. New York City Department of Social Services. 1978. 436 US 658.

Muir, W. K. 1977. *Police: Streetcorner Politicians*. Chicago: University of Chicago Press.

New York State Commission on Attica. 1972. *Attica*. New York: Bantam Books.

Packer, H. L. 1968. *The Limits of the Criminal Sanction*. Stanford: Stanford University Press.

Reiss, A. J., Jr. 1971. *The Police and the Public*. New Haven: Yale University Press.

Schlossberg, H. and Freeman, L. 1974: *Psychologist with a Gun*. New York: Coward, McCann and Geohagan.

Sherman, L. W. 1980. Causes of Police Behavior: The Current State of Quantitative RESEARCH. *Journal of Research in Crime and Delinquency,* 17, 69.

Wilson, J. Q. 1968. *Varieties of Police Behavior: The Management of Law and Order*. Cambridge: Harvard University Press.

What We Know about Police Use of Force

Kenneth Adams

Ambrose Bierce, a social critic known for his sarcasm and wit, once described the police as "an armed force for protection and participation."[1] In this pithy statement, Bierce identifies three critical elements of the police role. First, by describing the police as "armed," their ability to coerce recalcitrant persons to comply with the law is emphasized. Because police carry weapons, it follows that the force they use may have lethal consequences. The capacity to use coercive, deadly force is so central to understanding police functions, one could say that it characterizes a key element of the police role.

Second, the primary purpose of police is protection, and so force can be used only to promote the safety of the community. Police have a responsibility for safeguarding the domestic well-being of the public, and this obligation even extends in qualified ways to protecting those who violate the law, who are antagonistic or violent toward the police, or who are intent on hurting themselves. In dealing with such individuals, police may use force in reasonable and prudent ways to protect themselves and others. However, the amount of force used should be proportional to the threat and limited to the least amount required to accomplish legitimate police action.

Third, the concept of participation emphasizes that police and community are closely interrelated. Police are drawn from the community, and as police they continue to operate as members of the community they serve. The commu-

Use of Force by Police: Overview of National and Local Data. National Institute of Justice Research Report, 1999, NCJ 176330.

nity, in turn, enters into a solemn and consequential relationship with the police, ceding to them the power to deprive persons of "life, liberty, and the pursuit of happiness" at a moment's notice and depending on them for public safety. Without police, the safety of the community is jeopardized. Without community support, police are dispossessed of their legitimacy and robbed of their effectiveness.

This three-element definition of police makes it easy to understand why abuse of force by police is of such great concern. First, there is the humanitarian concern that police are capable of inflicting serious, even lethal, harm on the public. Second, there is the philosophical dilemma that in "protecting" the whole of society, some of its constituent parts, meaning its citizens, may be injured. Third, there is the political irony that police, who stand apart from society in terms of authority, law, and responsibility, also are part of society and act on its behalf. Thus, rogue actions by a few police, if condoned by the public, may become perceived as actions of the citizenry.

Recent developments in policing have elevated concerns about police use of force beyond ordinarily high levels. In particular, community policing, which is becoming widespread as a result of financial incentives by the federal government, and "aggressive" policing, which is becoming widely adopted as a solution to serious crime problems, have come to the fore as perspectives of choice by policing experts. Community policing emphasizes the role of the community as "coproducers" of law and order in conjunction with the police. Communities naturally vary in attributes, and they vary in how they are defined for the purposes of community policing. Consequently, some communities look to add restrictions on police use of force, while others are satisfied with the status quo, and still others seek to ease current restrictions. Regardless of the community's orientation on this issue, community policing means increased levels of accountability and responsiveness in key areas, such as use of force. Increased accountability hinges on new information, and new information stimulates debate.

The other emerging perspective is "aggressive" policing, which often falls under the rubric of broken windows theory, and, as a strategic matter, is concerned with intensifying enforcement against quality-of-life and order maintenance offenses. The influence of aggressive policing can be seen in the proliferation of "zero tolerance" enforcement strategies across the nation. The concern is that the threat posed by petty offenders may be exaggerated to the point that use of force becomes more commonplace and abuses of force more frequent.

The Violent Crime Control and Law Enforcement Act of 1994 mirrored congressional concern about excessive force by authorizing the Civil Rights Division of the U.S. Department of Justice (DOJ) to initiate civil actions against police agencies when, among other conduct, their use of force reaches a level constituting a pattern or practice depriving individuals of their rights. DOJ exercised that authority when, for example, it determined that an urban police department engaged in such conduct and negotiated a consent decree that put in place a broad set of reforms, including an agreement by the department to document its use of force and to implement an early warning system to detect possible abuses.[2]

Use-of-force concerns also are reflected in the attention the media give to possible instances of police abuse. An accumulation of alleged abuse-of-force incidents, widely reported in the media, encourages overgeneralization by giving the impression that police brutality is rampant and that police departments across the nation are out of control. For example, Human Rights Watch states, "Allegations of police abuse are rife in cities throughout the country and take many forms."[3]

Before considering the details of recent research efforts on police use of force, it is useful to summarize the state of our knowledge.[4] We know some details about police use of force with a high degree of certainty. These items represent "facts" that should frame our understanding of the issues. Other details about police use of force we know in sketchy ways, or the research is contradictory. These items should be subject to additional research using more refined methods of inquiry. Finally, there are some aspects of police use of force about which we know very little or next to nothing. These items represent critical directions for new inquiry.

As is often the case with important policy questions, the information that we are most confident of is of limited value. In many cases, it does not tell us what we really need to know, because it does not focus squarely on the important issues or is subject to competing interpretations. Conversely, the information that is most critical for policy decisions often is not available or is very difficult to obtain. Such is the case with police use of force. The issues that most concern the public and policy makers lack the kinds of reliable and solid information that advance debate from the realm of ideological posturing to objective analysis. Nonetheless, it is important to take stock of our knowledge so that it is clear which issues can be set aside and which should be the target of efforts at obtaining new knowledge.

What, then, is the state of knowledge regarding police use of force? We begin with issues about which we have considerable information and a high degree of confidence in our knowledge. Discussed next are issues where knowledge is modest and considerably more research is merited. Finally, we conclude with issues that are critical to debates over police use of force and about which little knowledge exists.

WHAT WE KNOW WITH SUBSTANTIAL CONFIDENCE ABOUT POLICE USE OF FORCE

Police use force infrequently.

Whether measured by use-of-force reports, citizen complaints, victim surveys, or observational methods, the data consistently indicate that only a small percentage of police-public interactions involve the use of force. As Bayley and Garofalo observed, police-citizen encounters that involve use of force and injury are "quite rare."[5]

Because there is no standard methodology for measuring use of force, estimates can vary considerably on strictly computational grounds. Different definitions of force and different definitions, of police-public interactions will yield different rates[6] (see "Working definitions"). In particular, broad definitions of use of force, such as those that include grabbing or handcuffing a suspect, will produce higher rates than more conservative definitions. The Bureau of Justice Statistics' (BJS) 1996 pretest of its Police Public Contact Survey resulted in preliminary estimates that nearly 45 million people had face-to-face contact with police over a 12-month period and that approximately 1 percent, or about 500,000 of these persons, were subjected to use of force or threat of force[7] (see chapter 2 in *Use of Force by Police*). When handcuffing is included in the BJS definition of force, the number of persons increases to 1.2 million.

Working Definitions

Police use of force is characterized in a variety of ways. Sometimes, these characterizations are functionally interchangeable so that one can be substituted for another without doing injustice to the factual interpretation of a statement. At other times, however, differences in terminology can be very consequential to a statement's meaning. For example, "deadly force" refers to situations in which force is likely to have lethal consequences for the victim. This type of force is clearly defined and should not be confused with other types of force that police use.

In contrast, "police brutality" is a phrase used to describe instances of serious physical or psychological harm to civilians, with an emphasis on cruelty or savageness. The term does not have a standardized meaning; some commentators prefer to use a less emotionally charged term.

In this report, the term "excessive force" is used to describe situations in which more force is used than is allowable when judged in terms of administrative or professional guidelines or legal standards. Criteria for judging excessive force are fairly well established. The term may also include within its meaning the concept of illegal force.

Reference also is made to "excessive use of force," a similar, but distinctly different, term. Excessive use of force refers to high rates of force, which suggest that police are using force too freely when viewed in the aggregate. The term deals with relative comparisons among police agencies, and there are no established criteria for judgment.

"Illegal" use of force refers to situations in which use of force by police violated a law or statute, generally as determined by a judge or magistrate. The criteria for judging illegal use of force are fairly well established.

"Improper," "abusive," "illegitimate," and "unnecessary" use of force are terms that describe situations in which an officer's authority to use force has been mishandled in some general way, the suggestion being that administrative procedure, societal expectations, ordinary concepts of lawfulness, and the principle of last resort have been violated, respectively. Criteria for judging these violations are not well established.

To varying degrees, all of the above terms can be described as transgressions of police authority to use force.

Expanding and contracting definitions of "police-public" interactions also work to affect use-of-force rates but in an opposite way from definitions of force. Broad definitions of police-public "interactions," such as calls for service, which capture variegated requests for assistance, lead to low rates of use of force. Conversely, narrow definitions of police-public interactions, such as arrests, which concentrate squarely on suspects, lead to higher rates of use of force.

The International Association of Chiefs of Police (IACP) is in the process of compiling statistics on use-of-force data being submitted by cooperating agencies. These data indicate that force is used in less than one-half of 1 percent of dispatched calls for service. From this point of view, one might well consider police use of force a rare event. This figure is roughly consistent with the preliminary estimate reported by BJS, although the IACP figure is subject to the reporting biases that may exist in police agency data. Furthermore, IACP data are not yet representative of the national picture because of selection bias; the estimate is based on a small percentage of police departments that voluntarily report information on use of force.

Garner and Maxwell found that physical force (excluding handcuffing) is used in fewer than one of five adult custody arrests (see chapter 4 in *Use of Force by Police*). While this figure hardly qualifies as a rare event, it can be considered low, especially in light of the broad definition of force that was used.

In characterizing police use of force as infrequent or rare, the intention is neither to minimize the problem nor to suggest that the issue can be dismissed as unworthy of serious attention. Society's ends are best achieved peaceably, and we should strive to minimize the use of force by police as much as possible. However, it is important to put police use of force in context in order to understand the potential magnitude of use-of-force problems. Although estimates may not completely reassure everyone that police are doing everything they can to minimize the use of force, the data do not support the notion that we have a national epidemic of police violence.

Another purpose for emphasizing the infrequent nature of police use of force is to highlight the methodological challenges of trying to count or study infrequent events. In this regard, methodological approaches can vary considerably in terms of cost efficiency, reliability, and precision of information obtained. In BJS's 1996 pilot household survey of 6,421 persons, 14 respondents, or roughly 1 in 450, said that they were subjected to use of force or threat of force by police over a year's time. The household survey approach has the benefit of providing national-level estimates based on data that are free of police agency reporting biases. However, as noted by BJS, the preliminary estimates derived from such a small number of respondents are subject to a wide margin of error. This issue is particularly important if one is interested in tracking changes over time, because a very small change in reporting can have a very large impact on estimates. In the survey's continuing development, the next pilot test will use a sample about 10 times the size of the 1996 pilot test as well as involve a redesigned questionnaire.

Police use of force typically occurs at the lower end of the force spectrum, involving grabbing, pushing, or shoving.

Relatively minor types of force dominate statistics on police use of force. Garner and Maxwell (see chapter 4 in *Use of Force by Police*) observed that police use weaponless tactics in roughly 80 percent of use-of-force incidents and that half the time the tactic involved grabbing the suspect. Alpert and Dunham (see chapter 5) found that in Miami 64 percent of use-of-force incidents involved grabbing or holding the suspect. In the BJS pilot national survey, it was estimated, preliminarily, that about 500,000 people were "hit, held, pushed, choked, threatened with a flashlight, restrained by a police dog, threatened with or actually sprayed with chemical or pepper spray, threatened with a gun, or experienced some other form of force."[8] Three-fifths of these situations, however, involved only holding. Finally, Pate and Fridell's survey of law enforcement agencies regarding use of force and civilian complaints also confirms that minor types of force occur more frequently than serious types.[9]

As a corollary finding, when injuries occur as a result of use of force, they are likely to be relatively minor. Alpert and Dunham (see chapter 5 in *Use of Force by Police*) observed that the most common injury to a suspect was a bruise or abrasion (48 percent), followed by laceration (24 percent). The kinds of police actions that most captivate the public's concerns, such as fatal shootings, severe beatings with fists or batons that lead to hospitalization, and choke holds that cause unconsciousness or even death, are not typical of situations in which police use force. These findings reassure us that most police exercise restraint in the use of force, even if one has concerns over the number of times that police resort to serious violence.

From a police administrator's point of view, these findings are predictable. Officers are trained to use force progressively along a continuum, and policy requires that officers use the least amount of force necessary to accomplish their goals.

Another affiliated finding is that police rarely use weapons. According to Garner and Maxwell (see chapter 4 in *Use of Force by Police*), 2.1 percent of adult custody arrests involved use of weapons by police. Chemical agents were the weapons most frequently used (1.2 percent of arrests), while firearms were the weapons least often used (0.2 percent of arrests). Most police departments collect statistics on all firearm discharges by officers. These data consistently show that the majority of discharges are accidental or are directed at animals. Only on infrequent occasions do police use their firearms against the public. One implication of these findings is that increased training in how to use standard police weapons will be of little value in dealing with day-to-day situations that involve use of force. Training, if it is to be effective in reducing the use of force, needs to focus on how to gain compliance without resorting to physical coercion.

Use of force typically occurs when police are trying to make an arrest and the suspect is resisting.

Research indicates that police are most likely to use force when pursuing a suspect and attempting to exercise their arrest powers. Furthermore, resistance by the public increases the likelihood that police will use force. These findings appear intuitively sound given the mandate that police have regarding use of force. Police may use force when it is necessary to enforce the law or to protect themselves or others from harm. The findings also seem logical in view of police training curriculums and departmental regulations. Alpert and Dunham (see chapter 5 in *Use of Force by Police*) find that police almost always follow the prescribed sequence of control procedures they are taught, except when suspect resistance is high, in which case they tend to skip the intermediate procedure.

The conclusion that police are most likely to use force when dealing with criminal suspects, especially those who are resisting arrest, is based on four types of data: arrest statistics, surveys of police officers, observations of police behavior, and reports by the public about their encounters with police.

Arrest statistics show that resisting-arrest charges often are involved in situations in which officers use force. The interpretation of this finding is ambiguous, however, because officers may bring such charges in an attempt to justify their actions against a suspect. Some commentators even would argue that resisting-arrest charges are a good indication that police officers acted inappropriately or illegally. Because we are relying on official reports by officers who are involved in use-of-force incidents, and because they have self-interest in presenting the situation in the most favorable light possible, we cannot rely on arrest records alone in determining what happened.

Fortunately, other research is available to help clarify the situation. The pilot national household survey by BJS included a series of questions about the respondent's behavior during contact with police.[10] The preliminary analysis revealed that of the 14 respondents in the sample who reported that police used or threatened force against them, 10 suggested that they might have provoked the officer to use force. The provocative behaviors reported by suspects include threatening the officer, assaulting the officer, arguing with the officer, interfering with the arrest of someone else, blocking or interfering with an officer's movement, trying to escape, resisting being handcuffed, and resisting being placed in a police vehicle.

Research by Alpert and Dunham (see chapter 5 in *Use of Force by Police*) confirms that. criminal suspects are not always cooperative when it comes to arrest. In almost all (97 percent) cases in which police officers used force in a Florida jurisdiction, the suspect offered some degree of resistance. In 36 percent of use-of-force incidents, the suspect actively resisted arrest, and in one-quarter of the incidents the suspect assaulted the officer. The researchers observed that the most common type of suspect force was hitting or striking a police officer (44 percent).

Garner and colleagues, after using statistical controls for more than 50 characteristics of the arrest situation, the suspect, and the police officer, found that forceful action by suspects was the strongest and most consistent predictor of use of force by police.[11] Furthermore, they found that while 22 percent of arrests involved use of force by police, 14 percent of arrests involved use of force by suspects. Police officers in Phoenix completed a use-of-force survey after each arrest to generate these data.

Finally, Bayley and Garofalo tallied 36 instances of force used by police or suspects out of 467 police-public encounters observed firsthand by researchers.[12] They found that in 31 incidents police used force against suspects and in 11 incidents suspects used force against police.

One implication of the research is that the decision to use some level of force probably has legal justification in most cases. Force is likely to be used when suspects resist arrest and attempt to flee, Also, in a significant number of instances, suspects use force against the police. These findings leave open the issue of *excessive* force, since issues of proportionality are not clearly addressed. However, the findings do suggest that many debates over excessive force will fall into gray areas where it is difficult to decide whether an officer acted properly, because there is credible evidence that the use of force was necessary.

What We Know with Modest Confidence about Police Use of Force

Use of force appears to be unrelated to an officer's personal characteristics, such as age, gender, and ethnicity.

A small number of studies suggest that use of force by police is not associated with personal characteristics, such as age, gender, and ethnicity. Bayley and Garofalo concluded that use of force is not related to age, although it may be related to experience.[13] Worden, in an analysis of observational data on 24 police departments in 3 metropolitan areas, concluded that the personal characteristics of police officers do not have a substantively significant effect on use of force.[14]

Likewise, Garner and colleagues. reported that the race of suspect and officer is not predictive of use of force.[15] However, they found that incidents involving male police officers and male suspects are more likely to involve force. Alpert and Dunham (see chapter 5 in *Use of Force by Police*) found that officer characteristics are of little utility in distinguishing between force and nonforce incidents.

Hence, gender and ethnicity appear unrelated to use of force. Given the limited research in this area, these conclusions should be accepted with caution and additional verification of these findings is needed.

It is widely accepted in criminology that violence, along with a wide variety of other risk-taking and norm-violating behaviors, is a young man's game. Thus, we should expect that young, male police officers should use force more than their female colleagues or older officers. The fact that this is not clearly the case seems surprising.

A lack of relationship between age and gender, on the one hand, and use of force, on the other, may be a function of police hiring and deployment practices. Retirement plans keep the age of police officers lower than that of most other occupations, and seniority, which is derivative of work experience, often brings more choice in work assignments, including duties that limit one's contact with criminal suspects on the street. Both these tendencies serve to constrain variation in the age of police officers who are exposed to potentially violent situations. This may attenuate the relationship between age and use of force. However, it is equally plausible that young male officers are assigned to high-crime areas where frequent use of force is necessary to gain compliance. Finally, it is possible that exposure to the police culture works to encourage the use of force, thus counterbalancing the decline in aggressivity that comes with age as demonstrated in criminological studies. More research is needed to disentangle these relationships.

The finding that an officer's race is unrelated to the propensity to use force runs counter to the argument that racial animosity lies at the heart of police abuse. Indeed, Alpert and Dunham's research (see chapter 5 in *Use of Force by Police*) indicates that officers are more likely to use force against suspects of their own race. The lack of relationship between race and use of force, as well as between gender and use of force, is probably disheartening to those who argue that integration of police agencies along racial and gender lines will do much to reduce the incidence of police violence. Again, more research is needed to understand the situation of minority and female police officers with regard to their use of force.

Use of force is more likely to occur when police are dealing with persons under the influence of alcohol or drugs or with mentally ill individuals. More research is needed.

Police come across a wide variety of situations in their work. They encounter problems that range from relatively minor to serious to potentially deadly. They also interact with people exhibiting various mental states, including persons who are hysterical, highly agitated, angry, disoriented, upset, worried, irritated, or calm.

Two situations that often give police officers cause for concern are when suspects appear to be under the influence of alcohol or drugs and when civilians appear to suffer from serious mental or emotional impairments. The concern stems from the fact that in such situations a person's rational faculties appear impaired. In dealing with problem situations, officers most often talk their way, rather than force their way, into solutions. For this reason, when a civilian is in a highly irrational state of mind, the chances of the police officer having to use force presumably increase and the possibility of injury to both officer and civilian increases as well.

Research carried out for the President's Commission on Law Enforcement and Administration of Justice observed that alcohol use by either a suspect or an officer increased the chances that force will be used.[16] Garner and colleagues found that alcohol impairment by suspects was a consistent predictor of police use of force, while drug impairment predicted increased use of force for some but not all measures of use of force.[17] In contrast, Alpert and Dunham (see chapter 5 in *Use of Force by Police*) observed that alcohol or drug impairment of suspects was unrelated to police use of force or subsequent injury. That finding is interesting because, although impaired civilians did not demonstrate an increased propensity to resist an officer's actions, when they did resist they were more inclined to do so by actively resisting or assaulting the officer.

Part of the disparity in findings between the President's Commission's research and more recent studies may be attributed to the fact that police officers today are better trained in how to deal with impaired civilians. Most police officers now receive training in a variety of violence reduction techniques, and this development is partly attributable to concerns over the President's Commission's findings and over the frequency with which police now are called to respond to large-scale violence, such as riots.

Questions about how police deal with civilians who appear to have impaired mental states are important from administrative and practical points of view. Police officers are expected to exercise restraint in dealing with impaired civilians, while at the same time they need to be cautious about protecting their safety as well as the safety of other civilians. This puts them in a precarious situation, one in which mistakes of judgment or tactics can have grave consequences.

From a practical standpoint, police regularly encounter civilians with impaired mental states, which makes the problem more than academic. Alpert and Dunham (see chapter 5 in *Use of Force by Police*) found that in 42 percent of use-of-force situations, suspects appeared to be under the influence of alcohol or drugs. Overall, the research on whether police use force more frequently in relation to civilians with impaired mental states is inconsistent. Further investigation, with an emphasis on implications for training, could reduce the risk of force and injury for both police officers and civilians.

A small proportion of officers are disproportionately involved in use-of-force incidents. More research is needed.

We often are told that a small number of people are responsible for most of the productive or counterproductive work in an organization. For example, we hear about the 80/20 rule in organizational management. That is, 20 percent of the workers account for 80 percent of the work. Policing has its counterpart explanation for deviant or illegal behavior. It is called the rotten apple or rogue officer theory, and it is often used to explain police corruption. Recently, a variation of this theory has become the principal explanation for use-of-force problems in police departments. In this context, we speak of "violence prone" police officers and we point to these individuals as the reason why a department has problems with the use of force.[18]

People with extraordinary work performance, either good or bad, are noticeable when compared with their colleagues, and their salience leads us to think that their work is highly consequential to the good fortunes or misfortunes of an organization. The utility of this perspective for police managers attempting to deal with illegitimate use of force lies in the presumed concentration of problem behaviors in the workforce. If only a handful of police officers accounts for most of the abuses, then effective solutions targeted at those individuals should deal with the problem. The nature of the solution, be it employee selection, training, oversight, or discipline, is less important than its degree of effectiveness and its ability to be directed at the problem group of employees.

The Christopher Commission, which investigated the Los Angeles Police Department subsequent to the Rodney King incident, highlighted the "violence prone" officer theory.[19] The Commission, using the department's database, identified 44 officers with 6 or more civilian allegations of excessive force or improper tactics in the period 1986 through 1990. For the 44, the per-officer average for force-related complaints was 7.6 compared with 0.6 for all officers identified as having been involved in a use-of-force incident for the period January 1987 through March 1991. The 44 officers were involved in an average of 13 use-of-force incidents compared with 4.2 for all officers reported to be using force.

Put another way, less than one-half of 1 percent of the department's sworn officers accounted for more than 15 percent of allegations of excessive force or improper tactics. The degree of disproportion (30:1) is striking and suggests that focusing efforts on a handful of officers can eliminate roughly 1 out of 7 excessive force incidents. This finding has led many police departments to implement early warning systems designed to identify high-risk officers before they become major problems. Most of these systems use administrative records, such as disciplinary records and citizen complaints, to monitor officer performance for possible problems.

The concept of an early warning system for risk management of problem police officers is not new. In the early 1980s, a report on police practices by the United States Commission on Civil Rights found that "[e]arly warning' information systems may assist the department in identifying violence-prone officers."[20] Consequently, it was recommended that "[a] system should be devised in each department to assist officials in early identification of violence-prone officers."[21]

Until recently, these systems received limited acceptance, owing in part to concerns over possible abuses. The abuses include use of inaccurate information, improper labeling of officers, misuse of confidential records regarding discipline and other personnel matters, and social ostracism by peers and community for officers identified as problematic. There also were concerns about limited resources and about increased legal liability for the organization and individual officers.

As Toch observes, the violence-prone officer paradigm often is based on a variety of loosely articulated theories of violent behavior.[22] The theories include concepts such as racial prejudice, poor self-control, and ego involvement. Furthermore, these theories often overlook the possibility that greater-than-average use of force may be a product of situational or organizational characteristics.

For example, an officer's work assignment may involve a high-crime area that contains a high proportion of rebellious offenders. Also, divisive, dehumanizing views of the world, such as "us-them" and "good guy-bad guy," that facilitate violent behavior may be supported by the organizational culture. Further, administrative views of work roles and products, communicated formally or informally, that emphasize crime control through aggressive police behavior may encourage confrontational tactics that increase the chances of violent behavior by either civilian or police officer. Unless the reasons for violence propensity are accurately identified, the effectiveness of interventions targeted at violent police officers is a hit-or-miss proposition.

Of the 44 officers identified by the Christopher Commission in 1991, 14 subsequently left the department as of October 1997. Of the 30 remaining officers, two had a use-of-force complaint that was sustained after review between 1991 and 1997.[23] This low number may be due to a variety of reasons, such as difficulties in sustaining citizen complaints, reassignment of work duties, negative publicity leading to a change in behavior, or greater circumspection when engaging in misconduct. However, the finding also may reflect regression to the mean. This is a statistical phenomenon postulating that extreme scores gravitate toward the mean or average score, thereby becoming less extreme over time.

For example, groups of police officers who receive many citizen complaints, or who are disproportionately involved in the use of force, or who frequently are given poor performance ratings, will tend to become "better" over time, in the sense of statistically looking more like the "average" officers, even if nothing is done about these problems. Statistical regression represents a serious threat to the validity of early warning systems based on the assumption that extreme patterns of behavior persist over extended periods of time.

What We Do Not Know About Police Use of Force

The incidence of wrongful use of force by police is unknown. Research is critically needed to determine reliably, validly, and precisely how often transgressions of use-of-force powers occur.

We do not know how often police use force in ways that can be adjudged as wrongful. For example, we do not know the incidence of excessive force, even though this is a very serious violation of public trust. We could pull together data on excessive force using police disciplinary records and court documents, for example, but the picture would be sketchy, piecemeal, and potentially deceiving. When it comes to less grave or less precise transgressions, such as "improper," "abusive," "illegitimate," and "unnecessary" use of force, the state of knowledge is even more precarious.

In discussing this issue, we will concentrate on excessive force, because these transgressions are of utmost concern to the public and because well-established professional and legal criteria are available to help us evaluate police behavior. Notwithstanding a generally agreed-upon terminology, we should recognize that developing a count of excessive force that is beyond all dispute is an unworkable task. This is so because difficult judgments are involved in deciding whether use of force fits the criteria for these categories in a given situation, and reasonable people will disagree in such judgments. We clearly need more accurate, reliable, and valid measures of excessive force if we are to advance our understanding of these problems.

Academics and practitioners both tend to presuppose that the incidence of excessive force by police is very low. They argue that, despite their short-comings, agency statistics provide a useful picture of the use-of-force problem. These statistics show that most officers do not engage in force on a regular basis, that few people are injured by police use of force, that only a small number of people complain about police misconduct involving use of force, and that only a handful of these complaints are sustained.

The argument has appeal. We believe that the vast majority of police officers are professionals who respect the law and the public. If use of force is uncommon, civilian complaints are infrequent, and civilian injuries are few, then excessive force by police must be rare. That conclusion may indeed be correct, but to the extent that it hinges on official police statistics, it is open to serious challenge.

Current indicators of excessive force are all critically flawed. The most widely available indicators are civilian complaints of excessive force and civil lawsuits alleging illegal use of force. Civilian complaints of excessive force are infrequent, and the number of substantiated complaints is very low. These figures are consistent with the argument that excessive force is sporadic. However, complaint mechanisms are subject to selection and reporting biases, and the operation of complaint systems, which typically is managed by police, wields considerable influence on whether people will come forward to complain.

Civil lawsuits against police are exceedingly rare relative to the number of times that police use force. Because the legal process is highly selective in terms of which claims get litigated, lawsuits are a very unreliable measure of illegal use of force. With both civilian complaints and lawsuits, small changes in administrative practices can have a large impact on the magnitude of the problem measured in these ways.

The difficulties in measuring excessive and illegal force with complaint and lawsuit records have led academics and practitioners to redirect their attention to all use-of-force incidents. The focus then becomes one of minimizing all instances of police use of force, without undue concern as to whether force was excessive. From this perspective, other records, such as use-of-force reports, arrest records, injury reports, and medical records, become relevant to measuring the incidence of the problem.

From a theoretical perspective, understanding all use-of-force incidents helps us to put wrongful use of force in perspective. However, because political, legal, and ethical issues are very serious when we are dealing with excessive force, pressures to know the incidence and prevalence of these events with precision will always be present.

As a corollary of our current inability to measure excessive force, we cannot discern with precision changes in the incidence of these events over time and across places. This means that we can neither determine whether excessive force problems are getting better or worse nor determine the circumstances under which those problems are more or less severe.

The impact of differences in police organizations, including administrative policies, hiring, training, discipline, and use of technology, on excessive and illegal force is unknown. Research is critically needed in this area.

A major gap in our knowledge about excessive force by police concerns characteristics of police agencies that facilitate or impede this conduct. Although many of the conditions that arguably lead to excessive or illegal force by police seem obvious, or appear to be a matter of common sense, we still greatly need systematic research in this area. We need to know, for example, which organizational characteristics are most consequential, which characteristics take on added significance in various environments, and which characteristics are redundant or derivative of other characteristics.

Many formal aspects of the organization—such as hiring criteria, recruit training, in-service programs, supervision of field officers, disciplinary mechanisms, operations of internal affairs, specialized units dealing with ethics and integrity, labor unions, and civilian oversight mechanisms—plausibly are related to levels of officer misconduct. It makes sense that poorly educated, badly trained, loosely supervised, and inadequately disciplined officers are likely to be problematic, and that when such officers are in the majority, the organization is on the road toward disaster. Yet, we lack research that systematically addresses these questions.

Less formal aspects of police organizations—officer morale, administrative leadership, peer culture and influence, police-community relations, relations with other government agencies, and neighborhood environments—also plausibly have a part in levels of officer misconduct. Alienated officers who do not have a clear vision of their role and responsibilities and who are working in disorganized agencies and interacting with the public under stressful circumstances probably are more likely to abuse their authority, including their authority to use force. Research that systematically addresses these questions is lacking.

Methodological investigation of relations between organizational elements and use-of-force transgressions will help explain police misconduct at a theoretical level. More importantly, research on these questions will allow us to deal effectively with police misbehavior. Faced with serious misconduct problems in a police agency, we need to focus scarce resources on those aspects of police organizations that are most clearly related to ensuring proper conduct of officers with regard to use of force. Generalized efforts to reform police organizations that are expected to reduce misconduct problems tend to be inefficiently focused and thus appear clumsy, inadequate, and misinformed.

Research must focus on establishing the relative cost-effectiveness of various strategies to reduce or eliminate police misconduct. Furthermore, only strategies that are solidly grounded in theory, practice, and empirical research will provide reliable solutions with predictable costs and benefits.

Influences of situational characteristics on police use of force and the transactional nature of these events are largely unknown. More research is necessary.

Research on police-citizen encounters reveals that use of force by police is situational and transactional. That is, police respond to circumstances as they first encounter them and as they unfold over time. For example, Bayley and Garofalo observed that the situations most likely to involve police use of force are interpersonal disturbance and violent personal crime.[24] Beyond this, however, we do not know much about the types of events that enhance the likelihood that police will use force.

Similarly, we have noted that when suspects attempt to flee or physically resist arrest police are more likely to use force. We also noted that in many cases both police and suspects use force against each other. However, these findings do not address the transactional nature of police-public encounters in that they do not describe the step-by-step unfolding of events and interactions. Knowing that police use force if suspects physically resist arrest, it matters if police use force without provocation and the suspect responds by resisting or vice versa.

A variety of situational elements plausibly are related to police use of force. If police are called to a scene where there is fighting, they may have to or believe they have to use force to subdue the suspects. If they are called to a domestic dispute where emotions are running high, they may have to or believe they have to use force to gain control of the situation. If they are called to intercede with a civilian who is recklessly brandishing a weapon, they may have to or believe they have to use force to protect themselves and others. Use of force in such circumstances maybe justifiable, but to the extent that it is predictable, we can prepare officers for these encounters and devise alternative strategies that minimize or eliminate the use of force.

Some situational factors may increase the chances that force of questionable legitimacy will be used. For example, officers sometimes use force on the slightest provocation following a high-speed car chase, when adrenaline levels are high. They may use force more frequently when they are alone, because they feel more vulnerable or believe that they can get away with it. They may use force more frequently as a way of emphasizing their authority when suspects are disrespectful or when there is a hostile audience to the encounter. At this point, however, knowledge about the types of police-citizen encounters in which police are likely to use force is rudimentary.

Police-public encounters are transactional in the sense that all the actors in a situation contribute in some way to its development and outcome. Understanding the transactional nature of police use of force is important because it emphasizes the role of police actions in increasing the chances that force will be used.

From this perspective, it is possible to minimize the use of force by modifying the behavior and tactics of police officers. By understanding the sequences of events that lead police to use force, we can gain a greater degree of control over those situations and possibly redirect the outcome. But we have only a basic understanding of the transactional nature of use-of-force situations, despite the fact that sequences of actions and interactions are highly germane to determining whether use of force was excessive or illegal.

Notes

[1] Bierce, Ambrose, *The Devil's Dictionary*, New York: Dover, 1958: 101.

[2] "Justice Department Consent Decree Pushes Police to Overhaul Operations," *Pittsburgh Post-Gazette*, March 1, 1998, C-1.

[3] Based on an investigation in 14 cities, Human Rights Watch described the brutality situation as follows: "[p]olice officers engage in unjustified shootings, severe beatings, fatal chokings, and unnecessarily rough physical treatment in cities throughout the United States, while their police superiors, city officials and the Justice Department fail to act decisively to restrain or penalize such acts or even to record the full magnitude of the problem." Human Rights Watch, *Shielded from Justice: Police Brutality and Accountability in the United States*, New York: Human Rights Watch, 1998: 1, 27.

[4] A previous summary of research on police use of force can be found in McEwen, Tom, *National Data Collection on Police Use of Force*, Washington, DC: U.S. Department of Justice, Bureau of Justice Statistics and National Institute of Justice, April 1996, NCJ 160113.

[5] Bayley, David H., and James Garofalo, "The Management of Violence by Police Patrol Officers," *Criminology*, 27(1)(February 1989): 1–27; and Bayley, David H., and James Garofalo, "Patrol Officer Effectiveness in Managing Conflict During Police-Citizen Encounters," in *Report to the Governor, Vol. III*, Albany: New York State Commission on Criminal Justice and the Use of Force, 1987: 131–88.

[6] Adams, Kenneth, "Measuring the Prevalence of Police Abuse of Force," in *And Justice For All: A National Agenda for Understanding and Controlling Police Abuse of Force*, ed. William A. Geller and Hans Toch, Washington, DC: Police Executive Research Forum, 1995: 61–97.

[7] Greenfeld, Lawrence A., Patrick A. Langan, and Steven K. Smith, *Police Use of Force: Collection of National Data*, Washington, DC: U.S. Department of Justice, Bureau of Justice Statistics and National Institute of Justice, November 1997, NCJ 165040.

[8] Ibid.

[9] Pate, Antony M., and Lorie A. Fridell, with Edwin E. Hamilton, *Police Use of Force: Official Reports, Citizen Complaints, and Legal Consequences*, Vols. I and II, Washington, DC: The Police Foundation, 1993.

[10] Greenfeld, Lawrence A., Patrick A. Langan, and Steven K. Smith, *Police Use of Force: Collection of National Data*.

[11] Garner, Joel, John Buchanan, Tom Schade, and John Hepburn, *Understanding Use of Force By and Against the Police*, Research in Brief, Washington, DC: U.S. Department of Justice, National Institute of Justice, November 1996, NCJ 158614.

[12] Bayley, David H., and James Garofalo, "The Management of Violence by Police Patrol Officers"; and Bayley, David H., and James Garofalo, "Patrol Officer Effectiveness in Managing Conflict During Police-Citizen Encounters."

[13] Ibid.

[14] Worden, Robert, "The 'Causes' of Police Brutality," in *And Justice For All: A National Agenda for Understanding and Controlling Police Abuse of Force*, 31–60.

[15] Garner, Joel, John Buchanan, Tom Schade, and John Hepburn, *Understanding Use of Force By and Against the Police.*

[16] Reiss, Albert J., Jr., *Studies on Crime and Law Enforcement in a Major Metropolitan Area*, President's Commission on Law Enforcement and Administration of Justice, Field Survey No. 3, Washington, DC: U.S. Government Printing Office, 1967.

[17] Garner, Joel, John Buchanan, Tom Schade, and John Hepburn, *Understanding Use of Force By and Against the Police.*

[18] Toch, Hans, "The 'Violence-Prone' Police Officer," in *And Justice For All: A National Agenda for Understanding and Controlling Police Abuse of Force*, 99–112.

[19] Independent Commission on the Los Angeles Police Department, *Report of the Independent Commission on the Los Angeles Police Department*, Los Angeles, CA: Independent Commission on the Los Angeles Police Department, 1991.

[20] United States Commission on Civil Rights, *Who's Guarding the Guardians? A Report on Police Practices*, Washington, DC: United States Commission on Civil Rights, 1981: 159.

[21] Ibid.

[22] Toch, Hans, "The 'Violence-Prone' Police Officer," 112.

[23] Office of the Inspector General, Los Angeles Police Commission, "Status Update: Management of LAPD High-Risk Officers," Los Angeles: Los Angeles Police Commission, 1997.

[24] Bayley, David, H., and James Garofalo, "Patrol Officer Effectiveness in Managing Conflict During Police-Citizen Encounters."

Police Use of Deadly Force
How Courts and Policy-Makers Have Misapplied *Tennessee v. Garner*

Michael R. Smith

I. Introduction

In 1985, the United States Supreme Court decided *Tennessee v Garner*.[1] In *Garner*, the Court held that a police officer may not use deadly force to apprehend a fleeing felon who does not pose a "significant threat of death or serious physical injury to the officer or others."[2] Thus, the actions of Memphis police officer Elton Hymon in shooting an unarmed, fleeing burglary suspect in the back of the head were unconstitutional, despite a Tennessee statute that permitted the use of deadly force under the circumstances.[3]

Although the Court's holding in the case was easy to discern,[4] Justice White, who wrote the opinion for a six justice majority, went on to give the following illustration of how the holding might be applied:

> Thus, if the suspect threatens the officer with a weapon or there is probable cause to believe that he has committed a crime involving the infliction or threatened infliction of serious physical harm, deadly force may be used if necessary to prevent escape, and if, where feasible, some warning has been given.[5]

Reprinted with permission of The University of Kansas School of Law, from *Kansas Journal of Law & Public Policy*, 7(2) (Spring 1998): 100–121.

Of course, this illustration is mere dicta, and in the strictest sense, it has no precedential value.[6] Nevertheless, lower courts, legislators, and law enforcement policy makers have seized upon Justice White's *obiter dictum* and have given it a life of its own. In fact, this language has become law in many states and official policy within many police agencies. Thus, at least some courts have read *Garner* to permit the use of deadly force by police officers to apprehend suspects fleeing from the commission of violent crimes, even if those persons do not appear to pose an immediate threat to police officers or to the public at large.[7]

The purposes of this article are to examine how the *Garner* decision has been translated into law and policy and to offer an argument for its reinterpretation. Section II of the article discusses the current state of police deadly force policy practice. It also presents an analysis conducted by the author of all reported lower court decisions that have applied *Garner* since the Supreme Court decided the case in 1985.[8] Following this analysis, Section III of the article presents a series of arguments for the adoption by legislatures and police agencies of strict defense of life policies[9] governing the use of deadly force by police.

II. Current Legal and Policy Practice Regarding Deadly Force

A. Deadly Force Statutes and Policies

Prior to the *Garner* decision, some states, including Tennessee, followed the ancient common law rule that allowed law enforcement officers to use deadly force to apprehend fleeing felony suspects, regardless of their potential threat.[10] *Garner*, of course, modified that rule. As a result of *Garner*, some state legislatures and law enforcement agencies were forced to change their rules governing the use of deadly force.[11] Today, it is possible to distinguish four deadly force policy types.

1. Defense of Life. The most stringent policy governing deadly force permits law enforcement officers to use deadly force only when they or other persons are threatened with death or serious injury. Idaho[12] and New Mexico[13] are examples of states that have codified this rule. The Commission on Accreditation for Law Enforcement Agencies (CALEA) requires that agencies seeking national accreditation have a policy that permits the use of deadly force only when necessary to defend human life or in the defense of any person in immediate danger of serious physical injury.[14]

The requirement for immediacy that appears in the CALEA standard does not appear in the deadly force statutes of Idaho or New Mexico. The CALEA standard makes clear that deadly force is not to be used unless the threat posed by the criminal suspect is imminent. With defense of life statutes and policies such as those maintained by Idaho and New Mexico, it is unclear how temporally proximate the suspect's threatening actions must be to the use of deadly force by a police officer. For example, do the Idaho and New Mexico statutes permit a police officer to use deadly force in order to prevent the escape of an unarmed, serial murderer? Is the future threat of such a person immediate enough to justify the use of deadly force under those statutes? To date, no court has directly addressed the issue of how imminent a threat must be in order to justify the use of deadly force under defense of life policies like those found in Idaho and New Mexico.

Clearly under the CALEA standard, deadly force would not be justified. Although the threat posed by the serial killer is real, it is not immediate in a temporal sense. As Geller and Scott point out in their excellent book *Deadly Force: What We Know*,[15] even trained psychologists using the very best diagnostic tools are unable to predict an offender's future dangerousness with any reasonable degree of accuracy. Given this fact, the CALEA immediacy requirement makes sense, even for persons known by the police to have violent criminal histories. If a criminal suspect is not presently posing a threat of death or serious injury to another, then a police officer operating under the standard advocated by CALEA would not be justified in using deadly force to apprehend that person.

2. Crimes Involving the Use or Threatened Use of Deadly Force. In addition to defense of life situations, the Model Penal Code[16] permits the use of deadly force if the arrest is for a felony[17] and the police officer believes that the underlying crime involved the use or threatened use of deadly force.[18] Justice White's dicta in *Garner* is substantially similar to the deadly force provision in the Model Penal Code. In fact, he cites the Model Penal Code provision several times in the *Garner* opinion.[19] While the Model Penal Code focuses on the type of force used or threatened by the suspect, Justice White's illustration focuses on the degree of harm caused or threatened by the suspect. If a suspect threatens or uses deadly force, then the suspect has necessarily threatened or caused serious physical injury and an officer would be justified in using deadly force to prevent the suspect's escape under either the Model Penal Code or the *Garner* illustration.[20]

3. Crimes Involving the Use or Threatened Use of Any Force. A variation on the Model Penal Code approach are policies that remove the deadly force or serious physical harm element from the suspect's conduct as a predicate to the use of deadly force. For example, Alaska allows its peace officers to use deadly force to apprehend any person that an officer reasonably believes "has committed or attempted to commit a felony which involved the use of force against a person."[21] Similarly, one provision of Oregon's deadly force statute permits the use of deadly force by police to apprehend any person that an officer reasonably believes committed "a felony involving the use or threatened imminent use of physical force against a person."[22]

Under a literal reading of statutes such as these, some degree of physical force in the commission of a felony is all that is required for a police officer to use deadly force to apprehend the perpetrator. Thus, rapes, robberies, or abductions not involving the use of a weapon or the infliction of serious injury would seemingly qualify as crimes for which a police officer could use deadly force to prevent the suspect from escaping. Even an aggravated purse snatching may be sufficient under these policies to provoke a deadly response by police. By eliminating the deadly force or serious physical harm element, policies such as these substantially broaden the circumstances under which police are allowed to use deadly force. Whether this approach is constitutional or represents wise law enforcement policy is discussed further in Section III.

4. Forcible Felony Rule. The final deadly force policy type allows police officers to use lethal force to apprehend persons suspected of committing certain specified felonies. Policies or statutes embodying this rule usually provide a list of violent felonies for which the use of deadly force is appropriate to effect an arrest or to prevent the perpetrator's escape. New York's deadly force statute, for example, lists the crimes of kidnapping, arson, escape in the first degree, burglary in the first degree, or an attempt to commit any of these offenses.[23] In addition to its provision on crimes involving physical force discussed above, the Oregon deadly force statute also contains a subsection that is identical to New York's with regard to violent felonies.[24]

Interestingly, both the New York and Oregon statutes list burglary in the first degree as a crime for which a police officer may be justified in using deadly force. Of course, burglary was the crime that *Garner* was suspected of having committed when he was shot and killed by the Memphis police, and the Supreme Court disapproved of the use of deadly force under the facts of that case.[25] However, first degree burglary in New York[26] and in Oregon[27] is an aggravated form of burglary where the suspect is armed with a deadly weapon or causes physical injury to someone. Thus, these statutes assume some injury caused by, or potential threat from, the suspect before deadly force would be appropriate. Again, whether the physical harm or threat thereof contemplated by these statutes is sufficient to justify the use of deadly force by police is discussed below.

5. Policy Overlap. Although it is analytically useful to think of these four policy types as distinct, in practice they tend to coexist within a single policy framework. Consequently, it is common for a single deadly force policy or statute to contain provisions representing several of the four policy types discussed above. Again, the Oregon statute is a good example of this. Section 161.239(1)[28] contains separate subsections that represent (1) a defense of life policy,[29] (2) a forcible felony policy,[30] and (3) a policy allowing deadly force in response to a crime involving physical force.[31]

Jurisdictions that have more lenient deadly force policies typically have separate provisions that cover defense of life situations. Thus, if a particular state or law enforcement agency permits its officers to use deadly force as a response to any felony involving the threat of physical force, then that state or agency will also permit its officers to use deadly force in defense of human life. On the other hand, jurisdictions that have adopted highly restrictive deadly force policies usually allow deadly force to be used only in defense of life situations.

B. Judicial Interpretation of *Tennessee v. Garner*

This section presents the findings from an analysis of all reported court decisions that have applied *Tennessee v. Garner* to cases involving the intentional use of deadly force by law enforcement officers.[32] The sample of cases discussed below was obtained by Shephardizing *Garner* and then reviewing each of the resulting lower court cases in which *Garner* was cited.[33] This resulted in a sample of 577 state and federal cases that mentioned *Garner* between the day it was decided, March 27, 1985, and the day on which the sample was drawn, August 7, 1997.

Of course, many of those cases did not involve a deadly force incident and cited *Garner* for some purpose other than its constitutional rule governing deadly force. Cases such as those were discarded and did not become part of the final analysis. Moreover, cases that involved disputed factual issues where the court denied a motion for summary judgment also were excluded.[34] The purpose of the analysis was to examine only those cases in which a court decided as a matter of law, that the use of deadly force was appropriate or inappropriate or where a court upheld a jury verdict based upon the jury's finding that the officer had acted properly or improperly in using deadly force. Of the 577 cases that cited *Garner*, only seventy-two fit the criteria outlined above. These seventy-two cases represent judgments on the part of judges or juries that the officers involved were or were not justified in using deadly force under the standards articulated by the Supreme Court in *Tennessee v. Garner*.

Table 1 below breaks down the seventy-two cases into the number of cases per suspect action category. The left-hand column indicates what the suspect was doing when shot by police, while the right-hand column shows the number of reported cases for each action category. These categories exhaust all of the suspects' actions in the seventy-two case sample. Table 1 clearly shows that appellate courts most often reported decisions involving

Table 1   Suspect's actions when deadly force used by police

Action	Number of Cases
Direct threats with a deadly weapon	52
Fleeing from crime involving use/threatened use of deadly force	8
Fleeing from nonviolent crime	5
Nonviolent crime-in-progress	2
No apparent criminal activity involved	2
Direct threats of nondeadly force	1
Armed with weapon, but not threatening anyone	1
Fleeing from crime involving use of nondeadly force	1

incidents where a suspect directly threatened someone with deadly force. All other categories contain few cases relative to this category.

Table 2 indicates the number of cases from each category where the court or jury approved or disapproved of the officer's use of deadly force. In none of the fifty-two cases involving direct threats of deadly force by a suspect did a court or jury disapprove of the officer's proportional response. On the other hand, Table 2 also illustrates that as the threat posed by a suspect becomes less imminent, courts and juries are more willing to disapprove of the use of deadly force by police under the *Garner* standard.

Table 2   Appropriateness of police use of deadly force

Suspect's Actions When Deadly Force Used by Police	Deadly Force Appropriate	Deadly Force Inappropriate
Direct threats with deadly weapon	52	0
Fleeing from crime involving use/threat of deadly force	8	1
Fleeing from nonviolent crime	2	4
Nonviolent crime in-progress	0	1
No apparent criminal activity involved	0	3
Direct threats of nondeadly force	0	2
Armed with weapon, but not threatening police	0	1
Fleeing from crime involving use of nondeadly force	0	2

1. Flight Cases Where the Use of Deadly Force Held Appropriate.   Setting aside the fifty-two cases where suspects were directly threatening someone with a deadly weapon when shot by police, Table 2 indicates that courts in ten other cases applied the Fourth Amendment standard from *Garner* and found the use of deadly force by police to be appropriate where the suspect was fleeing from the commission of a crime. These cases are summarized in Table 3.[35]

These cases demonstrate how in some instances, lower courts have extended the holding of *Garner* to permit the use of deadly force even where the suspect does not pose an immediate threat of death or serious injury to others.

Daniels v. Terrell[46] and *Ryder v. City of Topeka*[47] are illustrative. In *Daniels*, a Missouri state trooper attempted to pull over the driver of a car for running a red light. The automobile abruptly stopped and one or both of the occupants opened fire on the trooper's vehicle. The suspects then sped away with the trooper in pursuit. Periodically during the course of the chase, the suspects would fire at the trooper with a revolver and a rifle. Eventually, the suspect vehicle stopped in a housing project and the passenger ran away on foot. The driver, however, jumped from the car and ran directly at the trooper who was still in his vehicle slowing down as he reached the scene. The trooper shot at the now unarmed suspect through the window of his patrol car, and

Table 3   Use of deadly force held appropriate

Case	Court	Suspect Behavior When Shot	Disposition	Court's Rationale
Daniels v. Terrell[36]	E.D. Mo	Unarmed suspect fleeing on foot after shooting at state trooper	Judgment for defendant officer	Deadly force justified to apprehend suspect who just committed crime involving use of deadly force
Ridgeway v. City of Woolwich Twp. Police Dept.[37]	D. N.J.	Robbery suspect fleeing on foot after using his vehicle to ram police car	Summary judgment for defendant officer	Suspect posed an immediate threat of death or serious injury to others
Smith v. Freland[38]	6th Circuit	Suspect fleeing in vehicle from officer after high speed chase where suspect rammed officer's car	Summary judgment for defendant officer affirmed	Suspect posed an immediate threat of death or serious injury to others
Ford v. Childers[39]	7th Circuit	Bank robbery suspect fleeing bank on foot	Directed verdict in favor of defendant officers affirmed	Deadly force justified to apprehend a person who was armed and dangerous
Hill v. Jenkins[40]	N.D. Ill.	Armed suspect fleeing on foot from robbery	Summary judgment granted to defendant officer	Deadly force justified to apprehend an armed person whom just committed a robbery
Cole v. Bone[41]	8th Circuit	Suspect driving tractor trailer at a high rate of speed refused to stop for police	Court reversed denial of summary judgment in favor of defendant officers	Suspect posed an immediate threat of death or serious injury to others
Ryder v. City of Topeka[42]	10th Circuit	Suspect fleeing on foot from the scene of a robbery	Jury verdict in favor of defendant officer affirmed	Evidence sufficient for jury to conclude that suspect posed a threat of serious injury to the officer or others or that deadly force was necessary to prevent escape
Garcia v. Wyckoff[43]	D. Colo.	Auto theft and burglary suspect escaped police custody and fled on foot	Summary judgment granted in favor of defendant officer	Court distinguished *Garner* on the grounds that (1) suspect was only injured by police bullet, (2) was in lawful custody when he escaped and (3) continued to flee even after repeated warnings
Montoute v. Carr[44]	11th Circuit	Suspect running away from police armed with a sawed-off shotgun	Denial of officer's motion for summary judgment reversed	Suspect posed an immediate threat of death or serious injury to others
Hendrix v. Matlock[45]	5th Circuit	Armed suspect fleeing from a marijuana field	Jury verdict in favor of defendant officers upheld	"Shocks the conscience" standard for excessive force liability was appropriately applied

then exited his vehicle, and fired more shots at the suspect driver as he ran from the scene. These shots caused the driver to fall and allowed the trooper to place him under arrest.[48]

Under these circumstances, the district court had no trouble ruling that the trooper was justified in using deadly force to apprehend the plaintiff driver. Following a bench trial of the driver's Section 1983 suit against the trooper, Judge Gunn wrote that "the credible evidence also supports the conclusion that, at a minimum, plaintiff was seeking to escape and was fired upon only after a warning had been given."[49] Thus, even assuming that the plaintiff was merely seeking to escape when he was shot and was no longer a direct threat to the trooper, the court ruled that the trooper's use of deadly force was appropriate under *Garner*. In entering judgment for the defendant trooper, Judge Gunn quoted[50] Justice White's dicta from *Garner* which suggests that deadly force is an appropriate response to apprehend those who use or threaten to use deadly force in the commission of a crime.[51]

For some, *Daniels* represents a measured extension of *Garner*'s holding based upon explicit language found in the *Garner* opinion itself. On a visceral level, it is quite easy to condone the trooper's actions. Furthermore, if *Garner* requires an imminent threat of death or serious injury as a prerequisite for the use of deadly force to apprehend a fleeing felon, then it is arguable that the plaintiff in *Daniels* did pose an immediate threat to the officer or others even if he was unarmed at the moment deadly force was used to apprehend him. After all, he had repeatedly tried to murder a police officer just moments before he was shot. The court in *Daniels*, however, did not use this rationale to justify its ruling in favor of the trooper. For Judge Gunn, it was sufficient that the plaintiff was fleeing from the commission of a violent crime. Whether this rationale should support the use of deadly force by police is the subject of Section III.A. below.

In contrast to *Daniels*, the facts of *Ryder v. City of Topeka*[52] are more problematic. In that case, Topeka detectives staked out a pizza restaurant that was suspected of being the target for an armed robbery. After foiling one robbery and arresting several suspects,[53] the detectives received information that another robbery was to take place later that same evening. Remaining in their concealed positions at the rear of the restaurant, the officers watched another group of suspects enter a short time later. As the suspects exited the rear entrance, the officers announced their presence and with guns drawn, ordered the suspects to halt. One of the suspects fled and was chased by a Topeka detective. The officer fired a warning shot but the suspect continued to flee. As the suspect began to run around a building into a darkened residential area, the detective shot the suspect in the back. It was only after she fell paralyzed to the ground that the officer noticed that she was a young girl.[54]

After a jury trial, the district court entered judgment in favor of the defendant officer upon the jury's finding that the officer had not violated the plaintiff's constitutional rights. Among other issues, the plaintiff appealed the trial court's denial of her motion for J.N.O.V. [judgment notwithstanding the verdict]. Again relying on Justice White's dicta from *Garner*, the court of appeals identified two situations that would justify an officer's belief that a suspect posed a threat of serious harm: (1) if the suspect threatens the officer or another with death or serious injury or (2) if the suspect flees from the commission of an inherently violent crime.[55]

Reviewing the facts known to the detectives on the night of the offense, the court concluded that the defendant officer was "presented with no demonstrable evidence that would justify the belief that Ryder, or other members of her group, used, or would have used, force to facilitate the commission of the crime."[56] Moreover, the court noted that the evidence available to the detectives suggested that this robbery was actually a fraudulent theft facilitated by an employee of the pizza restaurant and not an armed robbery at all.[57] Nevertheless, the court later held that the jury was justified in concluding that at the moment the defendant officer fired his weapon, he had probable cause to believe that the plaintiff posed a serious threat to himself or others. The court reached this conclusion based upon the nature of the location where the plaintiff was shot, a darkened alley, and evidence presented at trial which suggested that the second group of robbery suspects might be armed with a gun or a knife.[58]

The logical inconsistencies in the court's opinion are striking. On one hand, the court plainly states that the defendant officer had no reason to believe that the plaintiff would have used force to facilitate the commission of the crime. Nor was any evidence presented which suggested that the plaintiff threatened the officer in any way. Yet despite the complete lack of evidence that the plaintiff was dangerous, the court concluded that the jury was justified in finding that the defendant was in fear for his safety or the safety of others. In the final analysis, the court of appeals upheld a jury verdict that permitted the use of deadly force against an unarmed, teenage girl who ran away from the police after committing what the court itself described as a fraudulent theft. Of course, what allowed the court to justify its decision was the illustration written by Justice White in *Garner*.

2. Cases Where the Use of Deadly Force Was Held Inappropriate. The cases that appear in Table 4 each involve situations where the suspect did not pose an imminent threat to public safety but where the officers involved, nevertheless, used deadly force to apprehend the suspect or prevent the commission of a crime. In each case, a court ruled that the use of deadly force under the circumstances was inappropriate under the *Garner* standard. Several of these cases are worthy of further discussion.

If *Ryder v. City of Topeka* is an example of how far a court is willing to stretch the concept of reasonableness under the Fourth Amendment, *Soba v. McGoey*[73] represents the opposite extreme. In that case, the plaintiff robbed a tavern in Brooklyn, New York. He was armed with a sawed-off shotgun. He left the restaurant and walked down the street holding the shotgun in plain view. At a nearby intersection, he was confronted by New York City Police

Table 4 Use of deadly force held inappropriate

Case	Court	Suspect Behavior When Shot	Disposition	Court's Rationale
Moody v. Ferguson[59]	D. S.C.	Fleeing vehicle from scene of traffic stop	Judgment for plaintiff	Suspect posed no threat to safety of others
Soba v. McGoey[60]	S.D. N.Y.	Walking away from armed robbery holding a sawed-off shotgun	Jury verdict in favor of plaintiff affirmed	Evidence sufficient for jury to conclude that suspect did not pose an immediate threat to defendant officers
Gutierrez-Rodriguez v. Cartagena[61]	1st Circuit	Driving away from plainclothes officers	Jury verdict in favor of plaintiff affirmed	Shooting of unarmed plaintiff who had committed no crime amounted to reckless disregard of plaintiff's constitutional rights
Acosta v. City of San Francisco[62]	9th Circuit	Fleeing in an automobile from the commission of a purse snatching	Court reversed J.N.O.V. granted to defendant officer	Evidence was sufficient for jury to conclude that suspect did not pose an immediate threat of death or serious injury to officer
Guzman Rosa v. Alba[63]	D. Puerto Rico	Breaking open a backyard fence to gain access to a storage shed	Judgment for plaintiff	Unarmed suspect did not pose a threat to the officer or others
Davis v. Little[64]	D. Conn.	Escaped felon fleeing on foot from officers	Judgment for plaintiff	Unarmed suspect did not pose an immediate threat of death or serious injury to officers or others
Grandstaff v. City of Borger[65]	5th Circuit	Innocent person shot by police who mistook him for wanted fugitive	Jury verdict in favor of plaintiff survivors affirmed	Officers were grossly negligent in failing to identify the person that they shot
Sherrod v. Berry[66]	7th Circuit	Driver of vehicle shot as he reached into jacket pocket while being questioned by police	Jury verdict in favor of plaintiff survivors affirmed	Evidence was sufficient for jury to conclude that officer was not in immediate fear of his life or safety
Pruitt v. City of Montgomery[67]	11th Circuit	Suspected burglar fleeing on foot from behind auto parts store	Summary judgment in favor of plaintiff affirmed	Unarmed fleeing burglary suspect posed no threat of injury to officer or others
Gilmere v. City of Atlanta[68]	11th Circuit	Drunken suspect attempting to flee police abuse	Bench verdict in favor of plaintiff affirmed	Officers were not justified in using deadly force against a suspect whom they had beaten and who lunged at officer in an attempt to flee
McCummings v. New York Transit Authority[69]	N.Y. Ct. of App.	Suspect fleeing from the commission of a strong-arm robbery	Jury verdict in favor of plaintiff affirmed	Evidence was sufficient for jury to conclude that the defendant officer did not know that the suspect had committed a violent crime when he shot the suspect in the back

continued

Table 4   Use of deadly force held inappropriate *(continued)*

Case	Court	Suspect Behavior When Shot	Disposition	Court's Rationale
Young v. City of Centreville[70]	Ill. App. Ct.	Burglary suspect fleeing on foot	Jury verdict in favor of plaintiff affirmed	Jury could have concluded that officers were not justified in using deadly force against a fleeing, unarmed suspect who posed no threat to the officers or others
Wallace v. Estate of Davies[71]	Ind. Ct. App.	Suicidal man holding a shotgun	Jury verdict in favor of plaintiff affirmed	Evidence was sufficient for jury to conclude that the man did not pose an immediate risk to the officers or others
Zuchel v. City of Denver[72]	10th Circuit	Walking toward officers with a pair of fingernail clippers in his hand	Jury verdict in favor of plaintiff affirmed	Evidence was sufficient for jury to conclude that suspect did not pose an immediate threat of death or serious injury to others

Officer McGoey who was responding to the scene of the robbery. Seeing the shotgun in the plaintiff's hands, Officer McGoey opened fire. Just then two more officers arrived, jumped out of their police car and also began firing. The plaintiff received six different gunshot wounds but miraculously survived.[74] Although the testimony about the plaintiff's exact position relative to the officers was in conflict, the jury apparently believed that he was not, at the moment that he was shot, pointing the shotgun at the two officers who arrived in the police car. The jury rejected these two officers' claims of self-defense and returned a verdict in favor of the plaintiff on his civil rights claims.[75]

In reviewing the officers' motion for J.N.O.V, the district court ruled that sufficient evidence existed for the jury to conclude that Officer McGoey fired in self-defense, but that the two other officers did not.[76] In denying the officers' J.N.O.V. motion, the court never discussed whether the shooting of the plaintiff would have been justified under the theory that he was fleeing from the commission of a crime involving the threat of deadly force. Thus, Justice White's dicta from *Garner* played no role in the district court's analysis. The court limited its analysis to whether the plaintiff posed an immediate threat of death or serious injury to the arriving officers and thus whether the jury was justified in rejecting their claims of self-defense.

Even under a strict interpretation of *Garner*, however, the court's ruling is questionable. *Garner* held that a police officer may not use deadly force to apprehend a fleeing felon who does not pose an immediate risk of death or serious injury to the officer or others.[77] Implicit in this ruling is the logical corollary that an officer *may* use deadly force to apprehend a fleeing felon who *does* pose an immediate and serious risk to the safety of others.

In *Soba*, the plaintiff had just committed an armed robbery and was fleeing the scene with a sawed-off shotgun in his hands. At the moment that he was shot his get away was obstructed by several uniformed police officers. Even if he was not pointing the shotgun directly at the officers, it presumably would have taken him only a split second to lower the weapon or to turn and fire it at the officers. To hold police officers liable for using excessive force when coming face-to-face with a suspect fleeing the scene of a robbery while armed with an extremely lethal weapon is not only grossly unfair to the officers involved, but is likely to cause hesitancy on the part of the next police officer facing a similar situation. Hesitancy in the face of a demonstrable threat like that posed by the plaintiff in *Soba* is likely to get police officers or innocent citizens killed.[78]

Contrast the facts of *Soba* with the facts of *Davis v. Little*.[79] In *Davis*, a Waterbury, Connecticut, police officer stopped the plaintiff for allegedly running a stop sign. A routine check of the plaintiff's driver license revealed that he was an escaped felon from the North Carolina correctional system. The officer placed Davis under arrest and put him in the back of his patrol car. At some point, several minutes later, Davis jumped out of the car and began to flee.[80] At that point, two other officers who had been sent to assist spotted Davis, jumped from their car with their guns drawn, and ordered him to halt. Again, the testimony about what occurred next was in conflict,[81] but Davis apparently eluded these officers and again attempted to run away. He did not get far, however, when one of the officers shot him eight times and ended his attempt to escape.

The plaintiff's Section 1983 claims of excessive force under the Fourth Amendment were tried before a United States magistrate sitting as a district court judge. The magistrate found in favor of the plaintiff and against the officer who shot him. In so ruling, the court restated the holding from *Garner* as permitting deadly force only if "(1) it is necessary to prevent escape *and* (2) the police officer has probable cause to believe the suspect poses a significant threat of death or serious injury to h/er or to a third person, *and* (3) where feasible the officer warns the suspect that s/he might use deadly force."[82]

The court held that the officer had no articulable basis for believing that Davis was armed or posed a serious threat to the officer or to others. The court stated that even if Davis assaulted the officers as they claimed, he did so without intending to inflict serious injury to them. Thus, under the *Garner* standard, the officer who shot Davis was not justified in using deadly force to apprehend him.[83]

The court's ruling in *Davis* is sound. Unlike in *Soba* where the suspect had just committed a robbery and was armed with a deadly weapon when confronted by the police, the plaintiff in *Davis* was unarmed and as the court noted, gave no indication that he was a serious threat to the safety of others. The plaintiff's assaultive conduct, if any, was not aggravated in nature and was apparently designed to allow him to escape. Neither *Garner*, nor the Fourth Amendment, permit the police to use simple assault as a justification for deadly force, even if the assault was committed by a known felon. In contrast to the cases in Table 3, the majority of cases from Table 4 depict courts that are unwilling under *Garner* to allow police officers to use deadly force against suspects who are not directly threatening the lives of others. This more reasoned approach stays faithful to the true holding of *Garner* without turning Justice White's dicta into law. The following section of this article provides an in-depth examination of why this approach is preferable from a constitutional, as well as pragmatic, standpoint.

III. Toward a New Constitutional Threshold for the Use of Deadly Force

A. The Constitution vs. The Reasonable Officer

In *Graham v. Connor*,[84] the Supreme Court held that the Fourth Amendment reasonableness standard is the appropriate test to apply when police subject citizens to seizures. Prior to *Graham*, many lower courts had applied a Fourteenth Amendment due process test to determine whether a seizure was lawful.[85] However, in *Graham*, which involved the application of non-deadly force by police, the Court stated that "all claims that law enforcement officers have used excessive force—deadly or not—in the course of an arrest, investigatory stop, or other 'seizure' of a free citizen should be analyzed under the Fourth Amendment . . . rather than under a 'substantive due process' approach."[86] Thus, the Court held that an officer's actions in using force should be judged according to whether the officer acted reasonably under the circumstances.[87] Factors to be considered in judging reasonableness are (1) the severity of the crime at issue, (2) the immediacy of the threat posed by the suspect, (3) whether the suspect is actively resisting arrest or (4) whether the suspect is attempting to flee.[88]

Although *Graham* involved the use of non-deadly force, virtually all lower courts have applied its same reasonableness standard to cases where police used deadly force.[89] In doing so, however, courts have often failed to conduct a searching inquiry into the reasonableness of the officer's actions in a particular case. This is especially troublesome in cases where the justification for the use of deadly force is the suspect's flight from the commission of a crime.

For example, in none of the cases discussed in Table 3, where the use of deadly force was found to be appropriate, did lower courts apply the factors suggested by the Supreme Court in *Graham* relevant to deciding whether an officer acted reasonably in using deadly force. Instead, most of these courts merely relied on the Supreme Court's dicta from *Garner* suggesting that deadly force may be used to apprehend fleeing suspects who commit crimes of violence. By short-circuiting the reasonableness inquiry, courts have abdicated their responsibility to decide the very Fourth Amendment reasonableness question that the *Graham* test was designed to answer.

In cases where an officer uses deadly force to apprehend a suspect fleeing from the scene of a violent crime, the question of whether the officer acted reasonably requires a judicial determination of what the Fourth Amendment permits in such cases. It is premature to ask whether a reasonable officer would have used deadly force under the circumstances without first deciding whether the constitution allows police to use deadly force in those circumstances at all. Simply because a reasonable officer would have used deadly force under existing law does not mean that the constitution should permit him to do so. After all, before the Supreme Court decided *Garner*, it was perfectly reasonable for a Tennessee police officer to use deadly force to apprehend any fleeing felon. Before courts decide whether an officer acted reasonably in resorting to deadly force, the courts must properly define the boundaries of when deadly force may be used. This is a relatively easy task when human lives are directly threatened because it is surely reasonable under the Fourth Amendment to use deadly force to neutralize an imminent threat to innocent lives.

However, if the suspect is no longer armed or does not otherwise pose an immediate threat to the safety of the officer or others as in the cases from Tables 3 and 4, then courts must decide the constitutional question of whether deadly force is appropriate in that instance. Despite the overly expansive reading that lower courts have given to *Garner*, the Supreme Court has not decided that question and lower courts have abdicated their responsibility to do so by inappropriately relying on the *Garner* dicta without conducting a careful constitutional analysis of the issue. As a result, lower courts have failed to appropriately balance the extent of the government intrusion against the need for that intrusion in cases where suspects are fleeing from the commission of crimes involving some degree of force.[90]

B. The Constitutionality of Using Deadly Force to Apprehend Fleeing Suspects Who Pose No Immediate Threat to Public Safety

Garner has clearly answered the question of whether police may use deadly force to apprehend fleeing felons who are not armed and who have committed non-violent offenses.[91] Despite Justice White's suggestion in *Garner* that police may use deadly force to apprehend those who commit crimes involving the use or threatened use of serious physical harm,[92] the use of deadly force under those circumstances is unconstitutional if those persons no longer pose an imminent threat of death or serious injury to others.

As the Supreme Court noted in *Garner*,[93] the proper Fourth Amendment analysis of this issue requires that courts "balance the nature and quality of the intrusion on the individual's Fourth Amendment interests against the importance of the governmental interests alleged to justify the intrusion."[94] When conducting this analysis in *Garner*, the Court initially noted that the intrusiveness of the seizure in deadly force cases is the most extreme of any state action.[95] The right to life is the most fundamental of all rights and is at risk each time that a police officer pulls the trigger. Also weighing in on the intrusiveness side is society's interests in a judicial determination of guilt arrived at through the proper application of due process and procedural safeguards. The effective use of deadly force frustrates these interests by ensuring that a criminal suspect will never be tried.[96] On the other hand, the government has a decidedly important interest in arresting those who break the criminal law. Without accountability for criminal actions, anarchy will eventually follow.

Where then should the line be drawn? At what point does the use of deadly force become unreasonable and therefore unconstitutional? In the 1970s and early 1980s, a number of studies were conducted that may help answer these questions. In his 1973 study of fifty Los Angeles County police departments, Uelman found that departments with the least restrictive shooting policies reported more than twice the deadly force rate than did departments with the most restrictive policies.[97] Furthermore, he attributed the differences largely to the shooting of fleeing felons in the non-restrictive departments. In 1983, Sherman re-analyzed some data that had been collected a decade earlier by the Kansas City Police Department.[98] He found that controlling for changes in reported crimes and arrests, the Kansas City police shot fewer people and a larger proportion of them posed serious threats to public safety after the police chief instituted a more restrictive shooting policy. Significantly, the percentage of shootings at fleeing suspects decreased from 46% to 22% after the policy change.[99] In his landmark research of shootings by New York City police, Fyfe found significant reductions in the number of shootings by NYPD officers after a defense of life policy was instituted in that department.[100] Non-defense of life shootings decreased by more than 80%. More recently, an internal study conducted by the Dallas Police Department measured a 39% decrease in police shootings following the 1988 adoption of a defense of life deadly force policy.[101] Consequently, these and other studies suggest that more restrictive deadly force policies can have a substantial impact in reducing the number of police shootings and in particular, shootings of fleeing felons.[102] But do restrictive shooting policies decrease police or public safety, and do they result in more criminals escaping justice to commit further crimes?

Fyfe found that the restrictive shooting policy adopted by the NYPD not only reduced police shootings of civilians but also reduced the number of police officers shot.[103] At the same time, the policy had no adverse impact on either crime or arrest rates. Following restrictive policy changes prompted by the *Garner* decision, the Memphis police actually made more felony arrests per officer than before adopting the more restrictive shooting policy.[104] Finally, a 1971 report by Chief Gain of the Oakland Police Department found that only two officers believed that a new department ban on shooting burglary suspects resulted in more burglars escaping.[105] Thus, it appears that not even police officers themselves believe that more restrictive deadly force policies are likely to allow criminals to escape apprehension.

After their exhaustive review of the published and much of the unpublished literature on the impact of restrictive police shooting policies, Geller and Scott concluded that the "[a]doption of restrictive policies usually has been followed by marked decreases in shootings by police, increases in the proportion of the shootings that are responses to serious criminal activity, greater or unchanged officer safety, and no adverse impact on crime levels or arrest aggressiveness."[106] Thus, the available social science data supports the conclusion that increased restriction on the use of deadly force by police represents good public policy.

In addition to the impressive body of research that points to the obvious advantages of restrictive shooting policies, the Supreme Court has indicated that actual policy practice is important in deciding the constitutional question of when deadly force should or should not be used. In *Garner*, for example, the Court cited a number of studies that examined the types of shooting policies utilized by American police departments.[107] These studies indicated that by 1985 when *Garner* was decided, most large police departments had already prohibited the use of deadly force to apprehend all fleeing felons.[108]

Currently, CALEA requires that agencies seeking national accreditation have written policies that prohibit the use of deadly force except to defend human life against an imminent threat of death or serious injury.[109] Under this standard, a law enforcement agency cannot receive national accreditation if it permits its officers to use deadly force to apprehend a fleeing suspect, even one who committed a violent offense, unless the suspect also poses an immediate risk to officers or public safety. Furthermore, although no current studies are available that give the percentage of departments that have adopted such restrictive policies, approximately 380 agencies have achieved national accreditation and the number is growing yearly. These agencies have met rigorous guidelines established by the Commission and are considered among the most professional in the United States.[110]

As law enforcement agencies strive toward increased professionalism and respect for human rights, they invariably must review their policies on deadly force. Those among them that seek national recognition and accreditation restrict their officers' use of deadly force to situations where human life is in immediate jeopardy. The standard set forth in policies such as these has become the new benchmark for reasonableness. Without an immediate threat, an officer's use of deadly force is per se unreasonable. Under this standard, cases such as *Ford v. Childers* and *Hill v. Jenkins* listed in Table 3 above probably would have been decided differently.

C. A New and Improved Reasonableness Test for Defense of Life Situations

The current reasonableness standard found in *Graham* merely asks whether a reasonable officer under the circumstances would have felt the need to use force. Given the argument set forth above that the threat of death must be immediate, a better approach would be for the Supreme Court to adopt a two-part reasonableness test in deadly force situations.

The first part of this test would ask whether a reasonable officer would have believed that lives were in immediate danger. In *Zuchel v. City and County of Denver, Colorado*,[111] a Denver police officer shot and killed a man who minutes before had been involved in an argument with several youths over a bicycle. Although the eyewitness testimony was partially inconsistent, it appeared that the decedent turned toward the police officer with something in his hand that later turned out to be a pair of fingernail clippers.[112] The court of appeals held that the evidence was sufficient for a jury to conclude that the officer's use of deadly force was unconstitutional because he did not have a reasonable belief that he or another person was in immediate danger.[113]

Zuchel demonstrates that the belief on the part of a police officer that lives are in immediate danger must be reasonable under the circumstances. If the officer is frightened easily or seems too ready to use deadly force without sufficient justification, then the officer may be liable for using excessive force.

Secondly, a reasonableness test for the use of deadly force should require that the officer employ that force with the amount of skill and judgment that a reasonable officer would use under the circumstances. An officer who reasonably believes that a person's life is in danger may not be justified in using deadly force if, for example, his bullets have a high probability of striking innocent persons. An officer who fires a shotgun into a crowded room in order to incapacitate an armed and threatening suspect would not be acting reasonably. The harm created by the officer's conduct in that hypothetical would outweigh its benefits.[114]

Thus, in cases where an officer alleges that he or she used deadly force to defend against an imminent threat to human life, the jury should be given a two-part reasonableness test: (1) Would a reasonable officer under the circumstances have believed that his or her own or someone else's life was in immediate danger, and (2) did the officer employ deadly force with the skill and judgment of a reasonable officer under the circumstances? This test maintains the Fourth Amendment emphasis on reasonableness found in *Graham*, while at the same time recognizing that instruments of deadly force have a much greater capacity for causing collateral damage than instruments of non-deadly force. Thus, part two of the alternative standard suggested above requires reasonable skill on the part of officers when using such instruments.

IV. THE PRACTICAL BENEFITS OF STRICT DEFENSE OF LIFE POLICIES[115]

A. The Risk of Civil Liability Is Reduced

Table 2 from above illustrates that no court or jury in a reported case found fault with an officer's use of deadly force to defend himself or another person from an imminent threat with a deadly weapon. All of the remaining cases where courts imposed liability on an officer involved the use of deadly force in response to some event that itself was not life-threatening.

Although this group of reported cases does not represent a random sample of all liability claims filed against police officers arising from the use of deadly force, there is no reason to believe that a larger sample would yield different results. It is highly unlikely that a jury would hold a law enforcement officer civilly liable for appropriately using deadly force to defend someone's life.[116] On the other hand, a jury is much more likely to find fault with an officer's use of deadly force in situations where the officer used deadly force as a means of apprehending a fleeing criminal suspect.[117] In today's climate of sue first and ask questions later, law enforcement agencies and local governments could cut their exposure to large civil judgments simply by encouraging officers through official policy to use deadly force only as a last resort to save their own or someone else's life.

B. Police-Community Relations May Improve

The use of force by police, and particularly the use of deadly force, has always been a major source of friction between police and citizens. This is especially true in inner-city, minority communities where police-community relations are frequently strained to begin with. For example, the 1989 shooting of a black motorcyclist by a Miami police officer sparked two days of rioting that resulted in one death and the destruction of twenty-two businesses.[118] In 1992, the shooting of a drug dealer by New York City police caused a Hispanic neighborhood to erupt in widespread violence.[119] More recently, the beating death of Malice Green by Detroit police officers resulted in widespread community outrage and the convictions of two police officers for murder.[120]

Even under ideal conditions, the use of deadly force by police may be problematic for police-community relations. Adopting defense of life policies before a crisis occurs may go a long way toward defusing community outrage over a questionable police shooting. Strict policies on the use of deadly force signal to communities that police agencies take their responsibilities for using deadly force seriously. Communities that know that their police are permitted to shoot only in defense of human life have a clear and intuitive benchmark by which to hold officers accountable.

C. "Better" Police Shootings

As the evidence from the research on deadly force indicates, restrictive shooting policies decrease the number of police shootings without comprising the safety of officers or citizens.[121] By limiting the use of deadly force only to those situations where a person's life is in immediate danger, restrictive shooting policies can help control the shooting of fleeing criminal suspects—an entire category of police shootings in some jurisdictions.

Furthermore, strict defense of life policies can help reduce the number of "bad" or mistaken shootings by police. According to many deadly force policies, police may shoot at fleeing suspects if they have probable cause to believe that those persons have committed crimes of violence.[122] It is not difficult to imagine a scenario where a police officer receives information from a citizen that a certain person has just committed a violent crime. Upon seeing that person running from the scene of the crime, the officer would probably be justified in using deadly force to apprehend the person, even though the officer did not witness the crime himself. Although the officer may have probable cause to arrest under those circumstances,[123] he should not be permitted to shoot the person in the back. After all, the citizen-witness may be mistaken or, worse still, be using the police for his own improper motives. Arrests can be remedied if the information upon which the arrest was made later proves inaccurate or deliberately contrived. However, allowing police to shoot based upon the low evidentiary showing of probable cause invites mistakes of a deadly sort.

Strict defense of life policies would help eliminate these types of shootings by requiring officers to reasonably perceive an immediate threat to human life before resorting to deadly force. Under this standard, the sight of an apparently unarmed person running away would not provoke a deadly response on the part of police even if they possessed information that the fleeing person allegedly committed a violent crime.

V. Conclusion

Following the Supreme Court's decision in *Tennessee v. Garner*,[124] lower courts have, in some cases, approved the use of deadly force by police officers to apprehend fleeing criminal suspects believed to have committed violent crimes. The law enforcement policies and court decisions that permit the use of deadly force under these circumstances generally rely on dicta from the *Garner* decision which suggests that deadly force may be appropriate to prevent the escape of someone who has committed or threatened to commit a crime involving serious physical harm.[125]

Some courts, however, have read *Garner* more narrowly and have disapproved of the police use of deadly force in those instances where a suspect does not pose an immediate risk of death or serious injury to the officer or others. This is the better constitutional rule. *Graham v Connor*[126] requires that the use of force by police be reasonable under the Fourth Amendment. Several research studies into the use of deadly force by police have found that restrictive shooting policies result in fewer police shootings without comprising the safety of officers or citizens and without adverse impact on crime levels. In recent years, law enforcement agencies that seek national accreditation are required to adopt strict defense of life policies that permit the use of deadly force only when someone's life is in immediate jeopardy. From a policy perspective, this is the new standard of reasonableness among professional law enforcement agencies and should be the new constitutional standard as well.

Law enforcement policies that permit the use of deadly force only in the defense of human life have several practical advantages over less restrictive policies. First, defense of life policies reduce the risk of civil liability. In no reported case has a judge or jury imposed liability on an officer who used deadly force under the reasonable belief that human life was in imminent danger. However, a significant number of officers have been held liable for using deadly force as a means of apprehending fleeing criminal suspects who did not pose an immediate threat of death or serious injury to others. Moreover, restrictive shooting policies are advantageous from a police-community relations perspective. Such policies can help reduce the tension between police and citizens over the use of deadly force, particularly in inner-city, minority communities that have historically suffered from police abuse. Finally, defense of life policies will help reduce the number of shootings that may occur when officers use deadly force to apprehend fleeing suspects based upon information derived from citizens who are mistaken or who have malicious intentions.

The use of deadly force by police is a necessary component of the government's responsibility to ensure the safety and welfare of the citizenry. However, by using deadly force, police officers short-circuit the adjudication process and impose the death penalty without benefit of trial. A constitutional rule and administrative policies that prohibit the use of deadly force, except to defend a person's life from imminent danger, will help ensure that deadly force is truly used as a last resort.

Notes

[1] 471 U.S. 1 (1985).

[2] *Id.* at 1.

[3] *See* Tenn. Code Ann. § 40-7-108 (1982).

[4] The second sentence of Justice White's opinion reads, "we conclude that such [deadly] force may not be used unless it is necessary to prevent the escape and the officer has probable cause to believe that the suspect poses a significant threat of death or serious physical injury to the officer or others." *Garner*, 471 U.S. at 3.

[5] *Id.* at 11–12.

[6] *Black's Law Dictionary* 408 (5th ed. 1979) (defining dicta as "[e]xpressions in court's opinion which go beyond the facts before court and therefore are . . . not binding in subsequent cases."

[7] *See Ford v. Childers*, 855 F.2d 1271 (7th Cir. 1988); *Daniels v. Terrell*, 783 F. Supp. 1211 (E.D. Mo. 1992); *Hill v. Jenkins*, 620 F. Supp. 272 (N.D. Ill. 1985).

[8] *Garner* was decided on March 27, 1985. The analysis of lower court cases that applied or interpreted *Garner* included all cases from that date through August 7, 1997.

[9] The phrase "strict defense of life policy" is used throughout this article. It refers to those statutes and administrative policies that permit the use of deadly force by police only to defend persons from an immediate threat of death or serious physical injury.

[10] The Supreme Court noted in *Garner* that even before 1985 when the case was decided, many states and police agencies had adopted deadly force policies that were more restrictive than the common law fleeing felon rule. *See Tennessee v. Garner*, 471 U.S. 1, 18–19 (1985). In his 1982 study for the International Association of Chiefs of Police, Kenneth Matulia found that only 7.5% of surveyed agencies had policies that permitted the use of deadly force to apprehend any suspected felon. *See* Kenneth J. Matulia, *A Balance of Forces* 161 (1982).

[11] In 1992, Walker and Fridell surveyed police departments in the 100 most populous cities in the United States about their policy response to the *Garner* decision. They found that 30.2% of the surveyed agencies changed their deadly force policies as a result of *Garner*. See Samuel Walker & Lori Fridell, *Forces of Change in Police Policy: The Impact of Tennessee v. Garner*, 11 *Am. J. of Police*, at 97, 101 (1992).

[12] See Idaho Code § 18-4011(2) (1997) (providing that a law enforcement officer may use deadly force to overcome resistance to some legal process if the officer has "probable cause to believe that the resistance poses a threat of death or serious physical injury to the officer or to other persons." Subsection (3) allows the use of deadly force to prevent the escape of a person suspected of committing a felony but only if that person also "poses a threat of death or serious physical injury to the officer or other persons.").

[13] See N.M. Stat. Ann. § 30-2-6(B) (Michie 1997) (states that homicide by a law enforcement officer is justified if the officer "has probable cause to believe he or another is threatened with serious harm or deadly force." Furthermore, the statute requires the officer "[w]henever feasible, . . . [to] give warning prior to using deadly force.")

[14] See Commission on Accreditation for Law Enforcement Agencies, Inc., *Standards for Law Enforcement Agencies* 1.3.2 (3d ed. 1994).

[15] William A. Geller & Michael Scott, *Deadly Force: What We Know* 255 (1992).

[16] Model Penal Code § 3.07(2)(B) (Proposed Official Draft 1962).

[17] *See id.* at § (2)(b)(i)

[18] *See id.* at § (2)(b)(iv)(1)

[19] *See Garner*, 471 U.S. at 6 n.7, 18 n.21.

[20] Examples of states that have adopted either the Model Penal Code's formulation of deadly force or Justice White's illustration from *Garner* are Connecticut and Hawaii. *See* Conn. Gen. Stat. §53a-22(c)(2) (1997) (providing a peace officer may use deadly force to "effect an arrest or prevent the escape from custody of a person whom he reasonably believes has committed or attempted to commit a felony which involved the infliction or threatened infliction of serious physical injury. . . ."); *See* Haw. Rev. Stat. § 703-307(3)(d) (1996) (providing a law enforcement officer is justified in using deadly force if the "actor believes that the crimes for which the arrest is made involved conduct including the use or threatened use of deadly force. . . .").

[21] Alaska Stat. § 11.81.370(a)(1) (Michie 1996).

[22] Or. Rev. Stat. § 161.239(l)(a) (1996).

[23] See N.Y. Penal Law § 35.30(1)(a)(ii) (Consol. 1996).

[24] *See* Or. Rev. Stat. § 161.239(1)(b) (1996) (kidnapping, arson, escape in the first degree, burglary in the first degree, or any attempt to commit such a crime)

[25] *See Garner*, 471 U.S. at 3.

[26] *See* N.Y. Penal Laws § 140.30 (Consol. 1996).

[27] *See* OR. Rev. Stat. § 164.225 (1996).

[28] *Id.* § 161.239(1).

[29] *See id.* § 161.239(1)(c).

[30] *See id.* § 161.239(1)(b).

[31] *See id.* § 161.239(1)(a).

[32] Cases where a judge or jury found that the shooting was accidental were not included in the analysis. Accidental shootings are not seizures under the Fourth Amendment and so the standards enunciated in *Garner* are not applicable to such cases. *See Pleasant v. Zmieski*, 895 F.2d 272 (6th Cir. 1990); *Glasco v. Ballard*, 768 F. Supp. 176 (E.D. Va. 1991).

[33] Because Shephard's printed volumes lag several months behind, the author also conducted an electronic search using Westlaw for the most recent cases that mentioned *Tennessee v. Garner*.

[34] *See Anderson v. Liberty Lobby, Inc.*, 477 U.S. 242, 248 (1986) ("summary judgment will not lie . . . if the evidence is such that a reasonable jury could return a verdict for the nonmoving party.").

[35] All of the cases that appear in Tables 3 and 4 involve either state tort claims, claims brought against officers under 42 U.S.C. § 1983 (1994), or both.

[36] 783 F. Supp. 1211 (E.D. Mo. 1992).

[37] 924 F. Supp. 653 (D.N.J. 1996).

[38] 954 F.2d 343 (6th Cir. 1992).

[39] 855 F.2d 1271 (7th Cir. 1988).

[40] 620 F. Supp. 272 (N.D. Ill. 1985).

[41] 993 F.2d 1328 (8th Cir. 1993).

[42] 814 F.2d 1412 (10th Cir. 1987).

[43] 615 F. Supp. 217 (D. Colo. 1985).

[44] 114 F.3d 181 (11th Cir. 1997).

[45] 782 F.2d 1273 (5th Cir. 1986).

[46] 783 F. Supp. 1211 (E.D. Mo. 1992).

[47] 814 F.2d 1412 (10th Cir. 1987).

[48] *See Daniels*, 783 F. Supp. at 1212.

[49] *Id.* at 1213.

[50] *See id.*

[51] *See Tennessee v. Garner*, 471 U.S. 1, 11-12 (1985).

[52] 814 F.2d 1412 (10th Cir. 1987).

[53] The court describes these juvenile suspects as "girls." One of them was armed with a knife at the time that she was arrested leaving the rear entrance of the restaurant. *See id.* at 1415.

[54] *See id.* at 1415-16.

[55] *See id.* at 1418-20.

[56] *Id.* at 1420.

[57] *See id.*

[58] *See id.* at 1421-22.

[59] 732 F. Supp. 176 (D.S.L. 1989).

[60] 748 F. Supp. 227 (S.D.N.Y 1990).

[61] 882 F.2d 553 (1st Cir. 1989).

[62] 83 F. 3d 1143 (9th Cir. 1996).

[63] 671 F. Supp. 882 (D.P.R. 1987).

[64] 670 F. Supp. 1115 (D. Conn. 1987).

[65] 767 F.2d 161 (5th Cir. 1985).

[66] 827 F.2d 195 (7th Cir. 1987).

[67] 771 F.2d 1475 (11th Cir. 1985).

[68] 774 F.2d 1495 (11th Cir. 1985).

[69] 613 N.E.2d 559 (N.Y. 1993).

[70] 523 N.E.2d 621 (Ill. App. Ct. 1988).

[71] 676 N.E.2d 422 (Ind. Ct. App. 1997).

[72] 997 F.2d 730 (10th Cir. 1993).

[73] 748 F. Supp. 227 (S.D.N.Y. 1990).

[74] *See id.* at 228.

[75] *See id.* at 230.

[76] *See id.*

[77] *Tennessee v. Garner*, 471 U.S. 1 (1985).

[78] Under similar facts, the court of appeals in *Montoute v. Carr*, 114 F.3d 181 (11th Cir. 1997) reversed the trial court's denial of the officer's motion for summary judgment. In that case, the plaintiff had just fired a sawed-off shotgun into the air while surrounded by a crowd of people. He was fleeing the scene holding the shotgun when confronted by the officers. He repeatedly ignored commands to drop the shotgun and continued to flee. One officer shot him in the buttocks as he ran away. In holding that the officer's use of deadly force was appropriate as a matter of law, the court of appeals stated "we accept [that] . . . Montoute never actually pointed the sawed-off shotgun at anyone. But there was nothing to prevent him from doing either, or both, in a split second. . . . An officer is not required to wait until an armed and dangerous felon has drawn a bead on the officer or others before using deadly force." *Id.* at 185.

[79] 670 F. Supp. 1115 (D. Conn. 1987).

[80] The testimony about what actually transpired in the officer's patrol car differed. The officer testified that Davis, an ex-professional boxer, punched him several times in the head before fleeing on foot. Davis denied hitting the officer. *See id.* at 1116-17.

[81] The officers claimed that Davis pushed and struck them while Davis claimed that he used some "fancy footwork" to cause them to lose their balance. *Id.* at 1117.

[82] *Id.* at 1120 (citations omitted) (emphasis in original).

[83] *See id.*

[84] 490 U.S. 386 (1989).

[85] This test derived from the Second Circuit case *Johnson v. Glick*, 481 F.2d 1028 (2d Cir. 1973). This case set forth four factors to be used in determining whether the use of force was excessive and therefore violative of substantive due process: (1) the need for the use of force, (2) the relationship between the need for force and the amount of force used, (3) the extent of injuries caused by the force, and (4) whether the force was applied in good faith or whether it was applied maliciously or sadistically for the purpose of causing harm. *See id.* at 1033.

[86] *Graham*, 490 U.S. at 395.

[87] *See id.* at 396. The Court noted that the reasonableness test is fact-specific and that an officer's conduct should be judged from the perspective of a reasonable officer on the scene, "rather than with the 20/20 vision of hindsight." *Id.*

[88] *See id.*

[89] *See, e.g., Salim v. Proulx*, 93 F.3d 86 (2d Cir. 1996); *Reynolds v. County of San Diego*, 84 F.3d 1162 (9th Cir. 1996); *Sevier v. City of Lawrence*, 60 F.3d 695 (10th Cir. 1995); *Maravilla v. United States*, 60 F.3d 1230 (7th Cir. 1995); *Daniels v. Terrell*, 783 F. Supp. 1211 (E.D. Mo. 1992).

[90] *See, e.g., Graham v. Connor*, 490 U.S. 386, 396 (1989); *Tennessee v. Garner*, 471 U.S. 1, 8-9 (1985); United States v. Place, 462 U.S. 696, 703 (1983).

[91] The answer is clearly no. *See Garner*, 490 U.S. at 11.

[92] *See id.*, at 11-12.

[93] *Id.* at 8.

[94] *United States v. Place*, 462 U.S. 676, 703 (1983).

[95] *See Garner*, 471 U.S. at 9.

[96] *See id.* at 9-10.

[97] *See* Gerald Uelman, Varieties of Police Policy: A Study of Police Policy Regarding the Use of Deadly Force in Los Angeles, 6 *Loyola-L.A. L. Rev.* 1 (1973).

[98] *See* Lawrence W. Sherman, Reducing Police Gun Use: Critical Events, Administrative Policy and Organizational Change, in *Control in the Police Organization* 98–125 (Maurice Punch ed., 1983).

[99] *See id.* at 118.

[100] *See* James J. Fyfe, Administrative Interventions on Police Shooting Discretion: An Empirical Examination, in *Classics in Policing* 191 (Steven G. Brandl & David E. Barlow eds., 1996).

[101] *See* Dallas Police Department, *Review of Dallas Police Department's Use of Force* 2 (1990).

[102] *See* Geller & Scott, *supra* note 15, at 257–67, for an excellent review of the literature surrounding the impact of restrictive deadly force policies on police shootings.

[103] *See* Fyfe, *supra* note 100, at 197.

[104] *See* New Memphis Police Department Shooting Policy Saves Lives, Reduces Friction with Community, *Crime Control Digest*, Mar. 30, 1992, at 7.

[105] *See* Charles Gain, *Discharge of Firearms Policy: Effecting Justice Through Administrative Regulation* 15 (December 23, 1971) (unpublished memorandum).

[106] Geller & Scott, *supra* note 15, at 267.

[107] *See Tennessee v. Garner*, 471 U.S. 1, 18-19 (1985).

[108] *See id.*

[109] *See* Commission on Accreditation for Law Enforcement Agencies, Inc., *supra* note 14.

[110] *See* Interview with Gerald Williams, Director of the Law Enforcement Management Institute of Texas and former director of the Commission on Accreditation for Law Enforcement Agencies, in Huntsville, TX (April 18, 1997).

[111] 997 F.2d 730 (10th Cir. 1993).

[112] *See id.* at 735-36.

[113] *See id.* at 736.

[114] In a related analysis, the necessity or choice-of-evils defense is only available to criminal defendants if the harm sought to be avoided by their conduct is greater than the harm caused. *See generally* Wayner LaFave & Austin W. Scott, Jr., *Criminal Law* § 5.4 (2d ed. 1986).

[115] The term "strict defense of life policy" refers to those policies that permit the use of deadly force only to defend against an immediate threat of death or serious injury to a human being.

[116] *See Soba v McGoey*, 748 F. Supp. 227 (S.D. N.Y. 1990). However, it is possible that a court or jury would disagree with an officer's perception concerning the immediacy of a threat.

[117] *See supra* Table 4.

[118] *See* Police Are Biased, Panel Tells Miami, *N.Y. Times*, July 29, 1989, at 6.

[119] *See* J. Dao, Angered by Police Killing, a Neighborhood Erupts, *N.Y. Times*, July 7, 1992, at A1.

[120] *See* Victor E. Kappeler et al, *Forces of Deviance: Understanding the Dark Side of Policing* 283 (1994).

[121] *See supra* notes 97–106.

[122] *See supra* sections II.A.(2)-(4).

[123] In *Illinois v. Gates*, 462 U.S. 213 (1983) the Supreme Court held that probable cause is a commonsense determination, based upon all available facts, that a fair probability exists that contraband or evidence of a crime will be found in a particular place. Although *Gates* involved a search based upon information from an informant, courts have generally applied the same standard of probability when deciding whether probable cause existed to arrest a person. *See* Wayne R. LaFave & Jerold H. Israel, *Criminal Procedure* § 3.3 (2d ed. 1992). Furthermore, when police receive information about a crime from an average citizen (rather than a police informant), the Court has not required supporting information regarding the citizen's credibility. *See Jaben v. United States*, 381 U.S. 214 (1965). In fact, police routinely make arrests based upon the word of one citizen versus another.

[124] 471 U.S. 1 (1985).

[125] *See id.* at 11-12.

[126] 490 U.S. 386 (1989).

Police Operational Management
Rethinking the Legal Shell Game

William C. Smith

INTRODUCTION

The legal and financial accountability of police agencies for injuries inflicted through the activities of their officers occupies a large part of the contemporary discussion of police practices and management. Much of that discussion, however, has become focused on an after-the-fact discussion of police misconduct, typically using a legal analytical postmortem framework based upon case-law precedent. This method is based upon analysis of police liability, not upon an analysis of police management or decision making. Its primary focus is the legal dissection of prior police actions as opposed to providing analytical insight to potentially controllable aspects of critical police functions. In the context of assisting police executives in the avoidance of past mistakes, analysis of solely the legal aspects of prior police actions loses sight of the fact that neither are police officers judges nor are they equipped to operationally implement the court decisions upon which so many departments have made themselves dependent. While this is not to say that case law is unimportant to a police agency's management of operational risks, it is proposed that a more effective approach for police administrators to manage their operations should be based, not upon legal analysis of liability, but, instead, upon assessment of operational exposure, complemented by a review

Prepared especially for *Critical Issues in Policing* by William C. Smith.

of applicable case law, where necessary. It is proposed that the approach most effectively suited to addressing police operational management is one based upon global principles of risk management rather than one based upon a necessarily parochial analysis of legal liability alone.

THE CONVENTIONAL WISDOM

Historically, perhaps due to lack of in-depth academic study or simply because of a relatively recent boom in police civil litigation, there has come to exist a belief, if not a mantra, which states that because the courts are the primary mechanism by which the police are held accountable for their actions, those same courts must also be the source of guidance for police operations. As Kappeler has so aptly noted:

> It is often thought that the future of police liability depends solely on the judicial branch of government. Police executives often feel that they can only sit back and wait for the next pronouncement of the judiciary to shape department policy and operations. . . . While it is certainly important for the police to understand the law of civil liability and its judicial interpretation, it is equally important for police executives to realize that they shape the contours of liability law as it affects critical police operations.[1]

Strict reliance on judicial pronouncements of liability as guidance for a department's operational decision-making strategy is an inherently flawed proposition for a number of reasons. First, the decision reached by a court in the adjudication of any single case will be fact specific. Notwithstanding that law enforcement actions similar to those before a court may occur in the future, the interpretation of necessarily different facts by a different trial judge may result in a substantially different finding regarding liability.[2] Second, the perceptions and views of judges, as well as those of the attorneys representing the parties, may hinge more on the procedural or settlement aspects of a case than on its substantive aspects; the result being that the case's ultimate outcome may provide binding effect on the department but offer no operational guidance to those most affected by it.[3] Obviously, where settlement occurs, there will be no precedential value of the case, but the fact remains that a mutually acceptable financial settlement reached in a particularly egregious set of circumstances may actually prolong police avoidance of addressing questionable police actions.[4] Third, even the periodic announcement of so-called "bright line" rules or guidance by a court is so often mired in legal rhetoric or logic as to be virtually meaningless from a practical standpoint.[5] Fourth, many lawyers who provide "operational" legal guidance to law enforcement agencies, tend to focus solely on the specifics of case holdings in providing advice to their clients, whereas legally educated extrapolation from the holding, or even dicta, in the case might potentially prove more useful to the practical management of police risks.[6] Fifth, although law enforcement executives understand and respect the impact and effect of judicial rulings, they may often find that the legal nuances of court decisions represent nothing more than the rigid application of a legal rule to what was a dynamic police operational scenario fraught with significant decision-making issues.[7] Finally, the inconsistencies between courts addressing similar police factual situations leaves many law enforcement executives uncertain of which "rule" ultimately is in effect for purposes of operational management.[8]

Because of the seemingly increased scrutiny police agencies face in their daily operations, it is crucial that operational guidance have a foundation that addresses the demonstrated needs of the police agency as opposed to merely addressing the hypothetical legal constructs upon which a finding of liability might ultimately be based.

POLICE OPERATIONAL ACCOUNTABILITY: A BRIEF OVERVIEW

In our media conscious society, police agencies face scrutiny of their operations on a daily basis. Much of what has been termed "media sensationalism" has come about due to a variety of factors including victim outrage and high dollar civil judgments as well as a public fascination with the spectacle of enforcement itself. As an example, in 2003, the City of Los Angeles Police Department decided to significantly curtail its pursuit operations, through the introduction of a more restrictive pursuit policy. The decision was met with an outpouring of disappointment from many Angelenos who had paid for pager services to alert them whenever a police agency became engaged in a vehicular pursuit.[9] Although not alone in their fascination with police operations, those citizens of Los Angeles have become symbolic of an evolving public mind-set that views police operations as a phenomenon not only to be closely observed but, as well, to be potentially called into question in less-than-favorable outcomes. The upshot of the foregoing is that the police find themselves increasingly subject to a watchful, and frequently critical, public eye. This modern public eye, through available media and personal technology, has the benefit of an extended time frame to analyze, digest, and criticize police split-second decisions that become preserved for repeated and in-depth analysis in a sort of electronic amber. The downside to this increased exposure is that, where police administrators come to rely solely upon after-the-fact analysis of potential liability of their actions, the benefit of "front-end" operational control is lost.

Enhanced public scrutiny, coupled with an increasingly litigious society, has brought to the forefront police-targeted lawsuits based upon allegations of police wrongdoing or carelessness. In such a crucible of discontent, the police often find themselves attempting to mount a viable legal defense against citizen allegations or seeking reasonable settlement thereof. Simultaneously, however, the police must also conduct and implement an effective analysis in an attempt to preclude future recurrences of questionable actions. That forward-looking analysis can only fall short, however, where it is structured solely upon the legal rationale that provides the department with its fact-specific defense. In effect, a police agency's reliance solely upon a liability-driven model for management of operational risks is akin to playing a shell game with high, but unknown, stakes for both police and public.

Criminal versus Civil Accountability

The manner in which the police are held accountable for their actions may also impact the fashion in which a department develops its operational control strategy. In a very basic sense, police accountability may either be criminal or civil. And the question of the form of the accountability will likely hinge on a balancing of issues of public policy and trust against other legal principles underlying compensation for private injuries. Stated more basically, whether the accountability is criminal or civil, or both, may impact police accountability for injuries and how the department elects to manage its operations.

Although an infrequent occurrence, the police may be held criminally accountable for the injuries inflicted through their operations. In the realm of assigning responsibility, the decision to bring criminal charges against a department or its officers is an extremely rare one, with most prosecutors opting instead to allow private victims to pursue their own remedies, absent some flagrant abuse of the public trust. The decision to prosecute criminally is a significantly different one than a private citizen's decision to pursue civil remedies.[10]

In exercising the prosecution function, a public prosecutor elects to vindicate a violation of a public right. Although not unheard of in state court proceedings, decisions to pursue departments or officers criminally are far more likely to be brought about through federal criminal channels, such as happened in the Rodney King case in Los Angeles in the early 1990s where two officers were charged with federal criminal civil rights violations under Title 18 of the United States Code.[11] The far more common approach, indemnification for victim injuries, comes about through the filing of civil suits against offending officers or their employers.

Although the purposes of criminal and civil proceedings against the police are not synonymous, both serve to impose accountability upon a wrongdoer for either publicly or privately impermissible conduct, and both serve as a control mechanism external to those imposed by the police themselves.[12] Although criminal prosecution concerns itself with remedying the wrongdoer's violation of a public interest generally, its ultimate impact may also benefit individuals.

The criminal prosecution's emphasis on societal wrong or violation of the interests of the public as a whole, as opposed to violation of a specific victim's private interests, is one that directly addresses the police role itself. As public guardians, the police are tasked with the protection of public order and preservation of the public trust. The commission of a criminal act by the police represents a direct departure from their publicly granted authority and, as such, constitutes a fundamental breach of the rights of all citizens. Because the police criminal act is so antithetical to the role of the law enforcement profession, the accountability imposed by a criminal prosecution is both direct and unambiguous. Where a crime has been committed by the police, issues of departmental policy and training are seldom directly implicated, as may be the case in a civil action, nor is the question of an offending officer's knowledge of the law an issue; for all citizens are presumed to "know the law."[13] Succinctly, at least in theory, the commission of a crime by a police officer, with its associated discussions of foreseeability, causation in fact, qualified immunity, and myriad other legal issues, is a far more clear-cut proposition in terms of culpability than is the commission of a tort.

Likewise, in the realm of criminal prosecution, a police officer's culpability is not contingent upon that officer's perceived "reasonableness" as a police officer. For these as well as many other reasons, the impact of the criminal prosecution of a police officer on the department is relatively straightforward and unambiguous. The is due, in significant part, to the relative clarity of "the rules" and the assumption that the police are familiar with them. The well-defined contours of the criminal law serve as a daily infrastructure for guidance to police officers and departments; an infrastructure in which the components are somewhat clearly labeled and logically connected to each other.

The vast majority of cases seeking to hold the police accountable, however, are not criminal cases, but instead those in which an individual private citizen victim seeks redress for injuries attributable to the police. These actions, typically seeking compensation for personal injury, as opposed to societal punishment for police misconduct, are commonly referred to as tort actions. It is in the realm of tort accountability that the lack of clear-cut guidance for the police has created a legal shell game.

State Law Torts: A Basic Component

Legally speaking, a tort is "a legal wrong committed upon the person or property [of another] independent of contract" and may involve either:

1. a direct invasion of a legal right of the individual;
2. the violation of some public duty which results in special damage to the individual; or
3. the violation of a private obligation which results in damage to the individual. (*Black's Law Dictionary*, 6th Ed., West Publishing Co.)

Torts are of different varieties. Under state tort law, the negligence tort and the intentional tort are particularly applicable to police actions.

Negligence can be generically defined as a "unintentional failure to conform one's conduct to a standard which the law says is reasonable." The difference between a tort in negligence and an intentional tort is that in an intentional tort ". . . the actor is expressly or impliedly judged to have possessed intent or purpose to injure" (*Black's Law Dictionary*, 6th Edition). Difficulty may arise in determining whether a person allegedly committing a tort had the intention to cause injury. For example, *Black's Law Dictionary* states that "intentionally" means that one does something "purposely, and not accidentally" or "desires to cause consequences of his act or . . . believes consequences are substantially certain to result." This definition, of necessity, involves something of a subjective analysis of the reasonableness of the actions of the person causing the injury.

Because accountability in tort must take into consideration the "reasonableness" of conduct under a particular set of circumstances, the law has developed numerous fictions to address standards of expected behavior in societal interactions. One of the best known of these is the so-called "reasonable man" standard. The "standard" essentially requires an evaluation of "what" a hypothetically reasonable person would have done when confronted with similar facts to those facing the person accused of negligent conduct.

Although engaged in activities that are by and large not permitted for the average citizen, police officers have no special body of law that delineates the parameters of their civil wrongs but, instead, are subject to the same "reasonableness" analysis as any other allegedly "negligent" citizen. Although police officers do "benefit" from having their allegedly negligent actions examined from the perspective of a "reasonable" police officer, the examination is typically conducted by non-police.[14]

State negligence torts involving public officials, such as the police, will likely fall subject to state legislative creations commonly known as "tort claims acts." Tort claims legislation came about as a partial abolition of the ancient doctrine of "sovereign immunity" and was, in large part, a reaction to the complete immunity of government for tortious acts for which private actors could be held accountable. The purpose of the legislation has been to encourage settlement of negligence claims against the state and its political subdivisions. Or, where that is not feasible, to allow suits to proceed, but subject to limitations on the amount of monetary damages the claimant may recover against the entity or against the public employees who can be individually sued. Because most tort claims legislation not only "caps" the amount of recovery allowed against the government agency and allows numerous "exemptions from liability" for government agencies, governmental entities are shielded from any full potential damage award for their negligence. The availability of those statutory exemptions, while an attractive proposition to state and local law enforcement agencies has, however, in the minds of many police agencies, produced a detachment from financial, and even professional, accountability for the actions of their officers. The typical representation of such a mind-set is the attitude that once a negligence claim is filed, all concerns "belong to" an insurer. This mind-set, taken in conjunction with reliance upon a case-based approach to operational management, augurs a narrow vision of police operational management responsibilities with potentially dangerous and self-perpetuating effects.

Constitutional Torts and Section 1983

Another major source of civil accountability for law enforcement agencies is that commonly referred to as the "constitutional tort." This type tort is substantially different in nature than the garden variety state law tort and involves the violation of a federally protected statutory or constitutional right. The basis for this type tort in cases initiated against the police is overwhelmingly Section 1983 of Title 42 of the United States Code.

Typically the right that is alleged to have been violated in the section 1983 action will be one set out in the Bill of Rights to the United States Constitution or will constitute a "due process" violation under the Fourteenth Amendment, which makes the first ten amendments applicable to the states.

Divergent Concerns: State Torts versus Constitutional Torts

There are numerous and significant differences between state torts and constitutional torts, and those differences greatly impact police operational accountability.

In the realm of Section 1983 actions, the concerns addressed through tort claims exemptions and defenses for negligent acts are, in large part, silent. Although Section 1983 cases may be, and are, brought in state court settings, the prospects for governmental protection, as envisioned under the tort claims acts, are absent. Neither the limited recovery provisions or the vast number of typical "exemptions from liability" found in that legislation are applicable when the cause of action arises under Section 1983, as the basis for the 1983 claim will not be one founded upon the simple negligence of the police.

While this lack of state tort claims act protections and the absence of caps on damage awards might seem to make the federal statute a more attractive vehicle for plaintiffs to sue governmental entities, the trade-off in difficulties of proof and nonavailability of state tort imputed theories of recovery, such as *respondeat superior*, may serve to quell what otherwise might be the overwhelming weapon of choice in a plaintiff's arsenal.

Although the financial losses that may come about from a plaintiff's successful prosecution of a state tort or Section 1983 claim can be significant, the fact remains that the blockbuster judgments that so often serve as the fodder and scare tactics of some police legal training courses, are, in reality, relatively rare. Experienced officers and administrators, while cognizant of the possibility of such judgments, realistically are aware that they are less than likely under most circumstances.[15] The presence of this knowledge has worked an interesting, and arguably dysfunctional, approach in some departments with respect to their efforts to control operational risks.

The Case-Based Approach: Cliffs and Ambulances

The accountability that injured parties seek to impose upon municipalities and their police officers poses potentially severe short-term and long-term financial consequences, not only in terms of settlements and judgments but, as well, in terms of increased insurance premiums and overall risk management costs. These substantial costs notwithstanding, the approach of many police departments in attempting to alleviate the recurrence of liability triggering conduct has been based upon the aforementioned "case-based" approach, in which specific police behavior leading to a determination of liability is examined and a strategy is developed to avoid those specific behaviors in the future. Although avoiding certain behaviors, which has led to some level of legal culpability, based upon a court's holding, is a laudable goal, the approach is all too often one of "too little too late." Further, focus solely on culpable activities without analysis of the environment in which the activities arose, and the decision-making process that produced them, ignores the dynamic and interactive aspect of police operations.[16]

A fundamental limitation of the case-based approach to liability management is that it is exactly that: it is an approach to "liability" management. At the risk of belaboring an obvious definition, "liability" can be understood as "[t]he quality or state of being legally obligated or accountable; legal responsibility to another or to society enforceable by civil remedy or criminal punishment" (*Black's Law Dictionary*, 7th Edition, West Group 1999). It is thus a determination of responsibility, arrived at after the fact, through judicial decree or through acknowledgment, such as by a settlement of the parties. Of necessity, executive management based upon a determination of liability is an after-the-fact approach. To put this observation in everyday vernacular, liability is what happens when risk management fails, and accordingly, any lesson learned through a determination of liability has no prospective application for the factual situation from which it arose. To borrow the words of a police chief, long ago used to describe the impact of a finding of liability on a department: "It doesn't do any good to park an ambulance at the bottom of the cliff." Yet, many departments remain aloof from the concept that effective management of police operational risks requires action to avoid ever reaching the edge of that cliff.

Two fundamental aspects of the American legal system complicate a department's reliance on the case-based approach: "holding" and "precedent." Both underlie the legal effect of a court's ruling, whether civil or criminal, and the extent to which the court's ruling will prospectively affect others who are not party to the immediate case.

The "holding" in a case is a particular court's "determination of a matter of law pivotal to its decision." (Black's supra) and "precedent" can be defined as "[a] decided case that furnishes a basis for determining later cases involving similar facts or issues." (Black's supra) In other words, a court's holding in a particular case may come to have precedential value in other situations involving similar facts and issues. In this basic sense, both holding and precedent are useful concepts for addressing a law enforcement agency's prospective liability exposures. The difficulty arises, however, in that many departments have come to view case holdings and their precedential value in the purely legal way that lawyers do in the management of litigation or in the conduct of legal research. That is, the available reported cases are analyzed, after the fact, to see whether a defense may be available for actions that potentially form the basis for a determination of liability. This after-the-fact legal approach does little to address the operational behaviors that gave rise to the claim. Adherence solely to a case-based approach effectively puts a police agency in a "triage" mode next to the ambulance at the bottom of the cliff, awaiting the victim's prognosis and the almost certain ensuing medical bill. In terms of a department's responsibility to its constituent community and the public at large, this approach can be likened to a shell game.

Because the outcome of each lawsuit filed against a police department will hinge on the facts of the particular case and, to some extent, on the court and the predisposition of the assigned judge, the case-based approach is fraught with speculation and financial hazard. The financial hazards are not solely those attendant to settlement or judgment costs, but include, as well, the attorneys' fees and costs incurred in the pre-trial portion of the case, which can represent the lion's share of the litigation costs. As it is well-established that the majority of lawsuits filed against police agencies are settled, the upshot is that significant attorneys' fees, expert witness fees, and litigation costs will likely be incurred. Those costs are in addition to the agency and officer time that will be consumed by the process. The foregoing begs the question of whether there is a more efficient and predictable means of addressing potential liability and, as such, encouraging effective operational management and accountability. The answer is clearly "yes."

Reevaluating Police Accountability: Risk and Exposure Analysis

The duty of the police, so often stated, is to "protect and serve" the public. Inherent in this maxim is a requirement of social responsibility, finding its roots in such hoary treatises as Rousseau's *Social Contract*. The importance of that duty comes squarely into play when one attempts to define the nature of the protection to be provided and the nature of the duty owed to members of the public. At a basic level, every police officer understands that the role of the police officer is as a public servant, accountable to the citizenry. A disconnect from this role can occur, however, when the activities of the police in furtherance of their duty either unnecessarily endanger the public, lose sight of the duty, or become removed from their accountability. The disconnect can occur in any number of ways, ranging from cases of condoned departmental corruption at one extreme of the spectrum to merely ineffective departmental management at the other end. Irrespective of the causation, the reality remains that breaches of police duty pose potential liability exposure for the department. How, then, given the myriad and evolving theories of recovery trotted out by attorneys on behalf of injured plaintiffs, can a case-based approach to liability management address those exposures? The answer is that it cannot.

Where departments rely solely upon the pronouncements of courts to provide operational guidance, the translation of judicial holding to practical guidance comes to resemble an abstract mosaic. The "reasonableness" standard, long the judicial hallmark to which department administrators seek to hold their officers accountable, is a less than clear standard because of the importance that some police administrators attach to "what the court said," as opposed to "what the court meant." In the latter context, the meaning of a court's ruling must be viewed in the practical environment of police operational exposure, not in the theoretical vacuum of a legal advisor's explanation of a case's holding. Effective police management cannot rely upon a piecemeal analytical approach relying solely on court rulings for operational guidance. An effective approach must, instead, incorporate factual analysis of known departmental operational exposures as an aid to line-level decision making. Where necessary, legal analysis must be factored into the analysis. In sum, it is proposed that the dog should wag the tail.

At the risk of using overused terminology, the case-based approach is reactive, not proactive, and invites mismanagement through both police executive inaction and through an abdication of responsibility for departmental operational control to insurers, legal advisors, and defense counsel.

Taking proactive steps to prepare before becoming involved in a potentially hazardous task is neither novel nor earthshaking, but instead a commonsense proposition. Most of us would agree that the better we prepare ourselves for a known potential hazard, the better we will be able to deal with it should it occur. In its most basic form, this is the definition of the concept known as risk management, a fundamentally different approach to operational management than that offered in the case-based approach.

The goals of effective risk management are two-fold. The first is to *identify* the likelihood of real and potential hazards, prior to their occurrence. The second is to put into place reasonable and cost effective *protective measures* that will help prevent the hazards from becoming actual or from inflicting devastating injury should the hazards be unavoidable. Ideally, risk management for law enforcement agencies should be what is called a "front-end" proposition. That is, preparations should put into place well in advance of a foreseeable dangerous or high risk event. To this extent, a risk management approach to operational accountability does not await a court's determination of responsibility, but instead seeks to identify exposures, or risk-inviting activities, that may potentially result in injuries, which may become the subject of litigation. In this respect, case law is important in the development of risk management strategies, but does not dictate them.

The risk management process consists of four basic steps:

1. *Identifying the hazards or potential hazards that face an organization.* These hazards and potential hazards are commonly referred to as "exposures." Exposures can vary widely from such concerns as an inadequate training budget to outdated equipment. The first task in the risk management process is the identification of the exposures for the agency. There are many

reasons that an agency's command staff may be unwilling or reluctant to address the possibility that their policies or practices may be deficient or otherwise open to attack. Nonetheless, unless the administration is content to await judicial guidance, a proactive review of the department's operational posture should be undertaken. At a minimum, the review should involve the department's "critical functions."

From a national perspective, a handful of functions appear to present the greatest operational exposure for law enforcement agencies. The purpose of the critical functions assessment is to identify those functions that, if improperly performed by the agency's officers, create the greatest exposure for the agency and the public. A critical function may be one that does not occur frequently but has great potential for injury, such as an officer's use of deadly force with a firearm, or it may be one that does occur with relative frequency and that has high potential for serious injury, such as a vehicular pursuit.

In evaluating departmental operational exposure, the agency should review with its past claims and lawsuits, the current and historical litigation status of the agency, to include settlement decisions and conduct an assessment of actual line officer practices and officer opinions. A number of sophisticated loss forecasting tools are also available that, properly used, will allow for a better grasp of the potential frequency and severity of claims. The critical functions assessment should help focus on current, past, and potential problem operational areas within the department and not just on those for which the department has been sued.

2. *Determining the means of reducing (i.e. eliminating or curtailing) the identified exposures.* Once the agency has conducted its assessment, means to address significant exposures must be identified. The means must be realistically within the capability of the organization. There is no single method of exposure reduction that will be appropriate under all circumstances for all functions. Likewise, exposure reduction measures should not be directed just to functions that have resulted in litigation or claims, as this approach would amount to nothing more than a case-based approach. Instead, exposure identification must involve honest and intelligent projection of potentially problematic areas, based upon feedback from line officers and supervisors and observed trends. Examples of exposure reduction might include such activities as increasing the amount of training provided in certain "critical function" areas (such as the use of force), reviewing the organization's progressive discipline policy, or revising the organization's policies.

3. *Implementing appropriate measures for reduction of exposure.* This is the logical consequence of step 2 and may include the use of such risk management processes as policy development, training, increased supervision, post-incident reporting requirements, and enhanced public relations efforts. Implementation of the measures that have been identified as "workable" involves more, however, than a broad statement to the affected agency members that

implementation will occur. Successful implementation will require "buy-in" by the officers who will be affected by it. This implementation should take place in a carefully orchestrated process that is capable of converting conceptual risk reduction measures into usable tools for the agency.

4. *Monitoring the effectiveness of the selected exposure reduction measures and implementing changes as appropriate.* This step requires a recognition that the risk management process is not a one-time undertaking but a constantly evolving program that should be continually updated. This step will also entail the use of case law to fine-tune the risk management process as necessary. The initial identification of feasible measures is merely the first step in a continuing dynamic process. Measures initially selected for implementation may become outdated because of changes in technology, the law, line level or supervisory trends, or the agency's mission itself. When those changes occur, the agency must be willing and prepared to reevaluate and adjust the risk management strategy. It is the ability to detect these changes, rather than wait for them to become the subject of litigation, which is crucial to the successful risk management program.

Conclusion

The accountability that injured parties seek to impose upon municipalities and their police officers poses potentially severe long-term financial and operational consequences for those affected. Yet, many police administrators are apparently willing to accept that the rulings of courts in and of themselves provide a viable basis for managing their agency's operations and instilling accountability. Because of the after-the-fact nature of this case-based approach, departments may not actively seek out potentially problematic functions within their control until litigation occurs. Such an approach ignores the responsibility of the police to the public and relies on judicial pronouncements that do not directly address the decisions that police officers are required to make in the operational arena. Although case law analysis is beneficial and necessary for a department's operational efforts, it cannot be substituted for an administrator's understanding of the department's operational posture and shortcomings. Far more beneficial in the management of departmental operations is an approach that relies on the analysis of foreseeable risks generated by the department's activities and a constructive and practical approach to address the risks, supplemented by case law as appropriate. This risk management model is preferable because it requires a proactive analysis of the department's operations and requires an administrator to address affirmatively and meaningfully any identified deficiencies.

The proportional percentage of law enforcement claims to a municipality's overall loss exposure has historically been exceptionally high. Rather than relying upon a judicial determination of liability, with its corresponding financial impact, the better approach is to identify critical functional areas of the department's mission and to take an active role in managing them. Because of the findings that a critical functions assessment may bring to light, the administrator must have the courage to address the observed deficiencies rather than hope that a suit will not be filed. Rather than rely upon a case-based approach, effective accountability and management for police operations requires that a proactive risk management process be implemented by which administrators identify the risks of their operations and then act upon those identified risks to reduce the agency's possible liability exposure as well as to increase public safety and public trust.

Notes

[1] Kappeler, Victor, "Shifting Conceptions of Police Civil Liability and Law Enforcement" in *Critical Issues in Police Civil Liability*, 3rd Edition, Prospect Heights, IL: Waveland Press (2001), p. 189.

[2] While the concept of "precedent" may dictate the law inferior courts are required to follow, the trial court's determination of established facts may preclude application of the apparently applicable precedent.

[3] The decision to settle cases is a source of contention with many officers who may view their actions in a particular case as justified and in accordance with departmental policy and guidance only to find that an insurer or counsel determines settlement of the case is most financially expedient.

[4] In the context of section 1983 litigation, the uncorrected actions may ultimately lead to municipal exposure for a widespread custom or practice that can be said fairly to represent the "policy" of the municipality. See, e.g. *Monell v. New York City Department of Social Services*, 436 U.S. 658 (1978), and its progeny.

[5] As an example, see the US Supreme Court decision in *County of Sacramento v. Lewis* (523 US 833; 1998) in which the court provided long anticipated clarification of the standard to be applied in pursuit cases involving Fourteenth Amendment substantive due process claims. Although the decision announced a "shocking to the conscience" standard for such claims, most observers remain uncertain of the operational impact or application of the case.

[6] While strict compliance with a higher court's holding is a *sine qua non* for judges who are bound by applicable appellate precedent under principles of stare decisis, the "hypothetical" indicia provided by a court's dicta may ultimately prove more useful to a police department's efforts at managing risks. As an example, see the US Supreme Court's now "famous" footnote 10 in *Canton v. Harris*. It should bear noting, as well, that many courts, themselves, may incorrectly interpret the holding of a higher court, thereby perpetuating inaccurate guidance to departments where the guidance is solely case-based. (See, Michael R. Smith, "Police Use of Deadly Force: How Courts and Policy-makers Have Misapplied *Tennessee v. Garner*," *Kansas Journal of Law and Public Policy*, Spring, 1998, and in this volume, article 26).

[7] As an example, courts addressing deadly force seizure cases involving fleeing suspects are wont to rely upon mechanical application of *Garner*'s two pronged "revised fleeing felon rule" to the exclusion of the more extensive "objective reasonableness" analysis seemingly required after *Graham v. Connor* (see Smith, supra, footnote 6). From time to time, even the courts are reluctant to apply heretofore accepted rigid rules of construction such as the Fourth Amendment exclusionary rule.

[8] Cases addressing substantive due process violations in police pursuits are particularly pertinent. Even after *County of Sacramento v. Lewis* (supra footnote 5), courts continue to grapple with the concept of what conduct is "conscience-shocking." See, e.g *Feist v. Simonson*, 222 F.3d 455, 464 (8th Cir.2000), overruled by *Burch v. Helseth*, F.3d 867, 871 (8th Cir. 2001).

[9] In March 2003, the problem of media coverage of police pursuits had become so pervasive in the opinion of law enforcement officials that both Los Angeles City and County officials

requested the local press to curtail coverage of police pursuits in the interest of protection of public safety. See "The Reporters Committee for Freedom of the Press" Web statement at http://www.rcfp.org/news/2003/0310lachas.html

[10] For an overview of the problems in holding police departments accountable, especially in the context of the Los Angeles Police Department's "Rampart Scandal," see, Michael Rowan, "Leaving No Stone Unturned: Using RICO as a Remedy for Police Misconduct," 31 *Fla. St. U. L. Rev.* 231 (Fall 2003).

[11] See, generally, *Koon v. United States* (No. 94-1664), 518 U.S. 81 (1996).

[12] See Alpert and Smith: "Developing Police Policy: An Evaluation of the Control Principle," *American Journal of Police*, Volume 13, No. 2, 1 (1994).

[13] This maxim is sometimes alternatively stated as "ignorance of the law is no excuse." The quotation originated with Thomas Jefferson who, in 1787 wrote to Andrew Limozin, commenting on our system of justice, that "Ignorance of the law is no excuse, in any country. If it were, the laws would lose their effect, because it can be always pretended. . . ." (See http://etext.lib.virginia.edu/jefferson/quotations/jeff1275.htm).

[14] In non-bench trials, the fact-finder is the jury, which, through the process of "voir dire," and other jury selection techniques, is generally devoid of members who either are, or ever have been, law enforcement officers; the result being that the factual aspects of the police actions to be litigated will be evaluated by a group unfamiliar with police operational practices or procedures, except as they may be "instructed" by expert witnesses retained by the litigants themselves.

[15] See Vaughn, Cooper and del Carmen, "Assessing Legal Liabilities in Law Enforcement: Police Chiefs' Views," *Crime and Delinquency*, Volume 47, No. 1, 3 (2001).

[16] See Alpert and Smith, "How Reasonable is the Reasonable Man: Police and Excessive Force," *Journal of Criminal Law and Criminology*, Volume 85 No. 2, 481 (1994).

Police work incorporates a number of job characteristics that present police officers with an unusual and unique set of personal hazards. Of course there is the real danger of being killed or assaulted while carrying out one's duties as an officer. In addition, there is an unusual degree of stress involved in police work, which has been associated with the ever-present threat of danger to oneself or to others and with the potential or actual use of (deadly) force. This unusual degree of stress has been linked to the frequent occurrence of divorce, alcoholism, and suicide among police officers. Over the past decade, law enforcement administrators have increasingly become concerned about the personal hazards of police work and have focused on the identification and treatment of these problems.

The first selection, "Gender and Police Stress: The Convergent and Divergent Impact of Work Environment, Work-Family Conflict, and Stress Coping Mechanisms of Female and Male Police Officers" by Ni He, Jihong Zhao, and Carol Archbold, explores the impact of work environment on the physical and psychological stresses of police officers. They find that work-family conflict and destructive coping mechanisms are the main factors leading to physical and psychological problems. One very practical implication of their research is for police administrators to devise management programs to minimize stress as much as feasible and help officers devise effective coping strategies to deal with the stressors inherent to police work.

The final article, "Toward an Understanding of the Physical Hazards of Police Work" by Steven Brandl and Meghan Stroshine, examines the hazards of policing by separating injuries that occur as a result of accidents from those that result from felonious acts. They find that assaults on officers are relatively rare events, as are serious injuries and death. Most of the incidents resulting in injury are the result of accidents, leading to their contention that policies must deal with accidental and felonious hazards to be effective in creating a safer work environment for officers.

Gender and Police Stress
The Convergent and Divergent Impact of Work Environment, Work-Family Conflict, and Stress Coping Mechanisms of Female and Male Police Officers

Ni He, Jihong Zhao, & Carol A. Archbold

INTRODUCTION

Police work is often considered to be a highly stressful occupation. Not only are police officers frequently exposed to the most violent, antisocial, and mistrustful elements of society, they are also expected to exercise discretion under critical circumstances (Crank and Caldero, 1991; Violanti and Aron, 1994). Researchers have long argued that police officers' job performance can be affected deleteriously, when officers experience chronic stress (McGreedy, 1974; Goodman, 1990). However, most of the early research fails to examine the differences of the impact of stress among both male and female police officers. Early police stress studies focus primarily on male police officers.

Observations and subsequent policy implications derived from police stress research based solely on male police officers may not be applicable to

Reprinted with permission of Emerald Journals, from *Policing: An International Journal of Police Strategies & Management*, 25(4) (2002): 687–708.

female police officers. Research on stress and gender in occupations outside of the scope of policing indicates that there are significant differences in the perceptions and coping skills of male and female workers (Barnett et al., 1987). Though limited, there is also research that suggests that female police officers experience stress derived from sources that are different from male police officers, and that female officers cope with stress differently than male officers (Pendergrass and Ostrove, 1984; Brown and Campbell, 1990). There have been few studies that examine stress coping mechanisms of both male and female officers through direct comparison.

The concern of the impact of stress and female police officers should be given more attention now that female police officers have become a steadily growing demographic in many police agencies. The representation of female police officers in U.S. police agencies grew from 4.6 percent in 1980 to 14.3 percent in 1999 (National Center for Women and Policing, 2000; Martin, 1993). The increase in the presence of female police officers, coupled with research findings that suggest that stress can have a negative impact on job performance, provides justification for additional research on gender and police stress.

In spite of the plethora of literature on the general relationship between police work and job-related stress, there is a paucity of empirical evidence pertaining to the study of gender differences in coping with police stress. Most of the earlier studies on police stress did not have sample sizes large enough to allow for meaningful comparisons between male and female police officers (Burke, 1993). The current study uses survey data from a large metropolitan police department located in the New England area to explore the impact of work environment, work-family conflict, and coping mechanisms on physical and psychological stresses of both male and female police officers. Among those who responded to the survey, there were 943 male officers and 157 female officers. This relatively large sample size allows us to perform an in-depth analysis of gender-specific police stress using clinical measurements.

The purpose of the current study is to investigate whether levels of clinically developed measures of psychological and physical stress are similar between male and female police officers, and the impact of work environment, work-family conflict, and stress coping mechanisms on the stress of both male and female police officers. In our analysis, we use three indexes to measure the levels of physical and psychological stress in the workplace considering both male and female officers. Four categories of explanatory variables including work environment, work-family conflict, coping mechanisms, and demographic variables are also employed to predict levels of stress among male and female police officers.

Literature Review

Researchers who study stress across a wide variety of professions often utilize gender as a key factor in their studies. Stress studies using clinically developed survey instruments consistently show that females report significantly higher levels of psychological and physical stress than their male counterparts (for a review of the literature, see Derogatis and Savitz, 1999). Moreover, these studies have revealed that male and female employees possess different conceptualizations and adaptations to stress. First, male and female workers often have different views on what is stressful—the source of stress (Stotland, 1991). Second, male and female workers usually adopt different coping strategies when they are under stress (Barnett et al., 1987, p. 350). It is argued that females are more likely to use "emotional-focused" coping strategies compared to males who are more proficient with "problem-focused" coping strategies (Billings and Moos, 1981; Stone and Neale, 1984). It is possible that the gender differences found in the perceptions and coping mechanisms used to deal with stress among male and female workers in non-police-related occupations might also be found among male and female police officers.

Gender and Stress in Police Work

Research shows that gender is a key explanatory factor in predicting the sources and coping strategies of stress among police officers (Pendergrass and Ostrove, 1984; Brown and Campbell, 1990). For example, previous literature reveals that female police officers are likely to encounter higher levels of harassment, overt hostility, and other negative social interactions on the job compared to their male counterparts (Deaux and Ullman, 1983; Balkin, 1988; Martin, 1990). A common explanation for this maltreatment of female officers is that police organizational culture, in general, is adversarial toward them. Moreover, the negative side of police work may bear its mark more on female police officers than their male counterparts. Wexler and Logan (1983, p. 48) revealed that, "The sources of stress mentioned were negative attitudes of male officers, training, exposure to tragedy and trouble, group blame, and rumors." Therefore, both the internal organizational culture and external work environment are much less favorable to female officers.

The studies that were previously discussed suggest that stress may have different effects on male and female police officers. However, there has been little research focused specifically on psychological and physical stress between male and female police officers, using the same measurement. Most of the previous studies on police stress and gender focus on male or female officers separately due to limitations of the collected data (e.g. Wexler and Logan, 1983).

Sources Associated with Occupational Stress Among Police Officers

In this section, we highlight five major convergent and divergent sources of police stress identified in the literature. It is evident that police work is often cited as one of the most stressful occupations (Eisenburg, 1975; Selye, 1978; Alkus and Padesky, 1983; Loo, 1984; Kroes, 1985; Violanti, 1985;

Reese, 1986; Dantzer, 1987; Goodman, 1990; Burke, 1993). The sources associated with stress in police work are well documented by scholars and practitioners (Symonds, 1970; Cruse and Rubin, 1973; Kroes et al., 1974; Reiser, 1974; 1976). Major sources of police stress that are frequently highlighted in the literature include:

- stress from the work environment;
- availability of peer support and trust;
- social and family influence;
- bureaucratic characteristics of police organizations; and
- accessibility of coping mechanisms.

The first major source of stress identified in police work is associated with the unique work environment of police officers. The danger associated with police work is usually highlighted in surveys of law enforcement officers where police officers are asked to rank-order a list of possible stressors. Not surprisingly, the death of a partner or having to take a life in the line of duty are typically among the top stressors identified by officers (Coman and Evans, 1991; Violanti and Aron, 1993). Other elements of stress often mentioned in the literature include making violent arrests and gruesome crime scenes (Violanti and Aron, 1993). Overall, violent and unpredictable incidents involved in police work are commonly considered to be the leading sources of both psychological and physical stress among law enforcement officers.

Next, a substantial body of literature addresses the important role of peer support and trust of coworkers and supervisors in buffering the effects of stress related to police work (House and Wells, 1978; LaRocco et al., 1980; House, 1981; Dignam et al., 1986; Ganster et al., 1986; Quick et al., 1992; Morris et al., 1999). Researchers have argued that peer support is especially salient to police officers because the nature of their work requires them to place their lives in the hands of fellow police officers in dangerous situations and because work-related stress may only be completely comprehensible to fellow police officers (Ellison and Genz, 1983; Graf, 1986). Further, research indicates that police officers who perceive themselves as having a strong work-related peer support system also perceived their jobs as being less stressful (LaRocco et al., 1980; Graf, 1986). With respect to gender, peer support from fellow officers is regarded as especially important to female and minority officers who are "breaking and entering" into an occupation that has traditionally been dominated by white male officers (Walker, 1985; Martin, 1990).

Bureaucratic characteristics of police organizations are identified as a third major source of stress among police officers (Violanti and Aron, 1993). Studies have identified the unique characteristics of police agencies as a significant factor predicting stress among police officers (Spielberger et al., 1981; Maslach, 1982; Martelli et al., 1989; Brown and Campbell, 1990). Organizational stressors include the events precipitated by police administration that are troublesome to members of the organization. Given the bureaucratic nature of police organizations (such as impersonal rules, and a distinct chain of command) individual input at the workplace is often reduced to a minimal level (Coman and Evans, 1991). Furthermore, Golembiewski and Kim (1991) make the argument that the quasi-military nature of police organizations tends to breed alienation among police officers. This is especially problematic as police officers are required to exercise considerable discretion while being tightly controlled by a plethora of administrative rules surrounding their work.

The fourth major source of stress in police work involves work/family relationships. Research on work/family interface have long recognized that the personal lives of police officers are affected by the unique nature of police work, which, in turn, makes officers perceive their job as more psychologically and physically stressful (Hughes et al., 1992; Galinsky et al., 1993; 1996). Several studies have identified work-family conflict as an important predictor of psychological burnout among police officers (Jackson and Maslach, 1982; Burke, 1989; 1993). This is particularly true for female officers because the demands of their domestic role as wife and mother are greater than those of male police officers (Martin, 1980, p. 200). For example, research findings suggest that marriage is distinctly beneficial for most husbands but much less for most wives (Bernard, 1972), and married women experience more strain than do married men (Gove and Tudor, 1973). However, very few studies have empirically examined this issue within the context of gender and police work.

The final source of police stress concerns the availability and choice of coping mechanisms adopted by male and female police officers in order to reduce their stress. Although coping literature is replete with varied definitions of the concept of coping, most researchers agree that only the conscious use of a cognitive or behavioral strategy that is intended to reduce perceived stress or improve a person's resources to deal with stress reflects the coping process (Evans et al., 1993; Anshel, 2000).

A review of the literature on stress reveals that individuals in a variety of professions usually take two approaches to reduce psychological and physical stress (Burke, 1993). The first approach focuses on positive coping strategies that usually involve gaining family and social support in an attempt to reduce stress. A few examples of positive coping strategies include support group meetings, sharing stressful experiences with others (including family members), and religious-based support groups. The second approach used to cope with stress includes negative coping strategies. Generally, negative coping strategies involve self-destructive methods to reduce stress, including increased cigarette smoking and avoidance of friends and family members. Violanti et al. (1985) also observed that certain stress-related job "demands" of policing are also associated with alcohol use. They argued that psychological and physical stress is directly or indirectly related to alcohol use. Similarly, Haar and Morash (1999) found that male and female officers use different coping methods, attempting to reduce their stress at the workplace.

Not surprisingly, positive coping mechanisms are considered to be the more appropriate approach to reduce psychological and physical stress. Several studies indicate that improper or maladaptive coping contributes to the intensity of perceived stress instead of reducing stress levels (Lazarus, 1990; Aldwin, 1994). In addition, failure to cope effectively with stress can lead to long-term and chronic stress (Loo, 1984). Police officers who use maladaptive coping skills (e.g. excessive alcohol intake, smoking, overeating, or drug use) are more likely to experience chronic, long-term stress (Hurrel, 1986). Consequently, ongoing and long-term police stress can result in burnout, reduced motivation and, ultimately, withdrawal from police work (Maslach, 1976; Violanti and Aron, 1993).

After reviewing the body of literature on police stress and gender, it is clear that we do not clearly know how some of the main sources of stress related to police work impact both male and female officers. Using a comparison of both male and female officers, the current study explores the impact of work environment, coping mechanisms, and work-family conflict on psychological and physical stress of male and female police officers.

METHODOLOGY

The current study utilizes data that was originally used in Gershon's (1999) study titled "Police stress and domestic violence in police families in Baltimore, Maryland, 1997–1999." We acquired this data set from Inter-university Consortium for Political and Social Research's (ICPSR #2976) Web site.

The sampling strategy that was used in data collection for Gershon's study involved three steps:

1. obtain the total number of sworn employees in each precinct for all shifts;

2. attend one or two roll calls for each shift in all nine of the Baltimore precincts and main headquarters to obtain a convenience sample of volunteers; and

3. distribute self-administered questionnaires to police officers who volunteered to participate in the study.

The reported response rate was 68 percent in the original study (see Gershon, 1999 for more details). The five-page instrument distributed to Baltimore police officers included questions regarding symptoms of psychological and physical stress and likely stressors, perceptions of current stress levels, coping mechanisms to deal with stress, and health outcomes related to stress.

Dependent Variable

The instrument developed to measure police stress in Gershon's (1999) survey was adopted with minor modifications from the brief symptom inventory (BSI), a brief form of the Symptom Check List 90 (Derogatis and Melisaratos, 1983). The original BSI instrument comprised 53 items, which measure nine dimensions of psychological and physical symptoms of stress. Each of the items is rated on a five-point scale of distress ranging from not at all (0) to extremely troublesome (4). The BSI was developed in 1975 and is designed to assess the psychological symptom patterns of community residents and psychiatric and medical patients (Derogatis and Savitz, 1999). Its psychometric validity has been tested and sustained in numerous empirical studies reported in the USA (for a review see Derogatis and Savitz, 1999).

Gershon's (1999) survey includes three of the nine dimensions of stress symptoms and uses a four-point scale of distress ranging from never (1) to always (4). The first dimension is somatization, a scale that reflects the psychological distress arising from perception of bodily dysfunction. Complaints typically focus on cardiovascular, gastrointestinal, respiratory, and other systems with strong autonomic mediation. Aches, pains, and discomfort localized in the gross musculature are also frequent manifestations of stress. The second dimension is anxiety, a scale in which general indicators such as restlessness, nervousness, and panic attacks are represented. The third dimension is depression, a scale that reflects a broad range of the elements constituting the clinical depressive syndrome. Symptoms of dysphoric effect and mood are represented, as are signs of withdrawal of interest in activities, lack of motivation, and loss of vital energy (for a detailed discussion of dimensions see Derogatis et al., 1973). Survey items contained in each scale are presented in Appendix 1.

Independent Variables

The current study also includes six independent variables in three major contexts including:

1. work environment;
2. work-family conflict; and
3. stress coping mechanisms.

Three variables are used to represent the characteristics unique to the police work environment. First, negative exposures related to police work are used to measure the dangerous or negative aspects of work events that police officers often experience (e.g. making violent arrests, shooting someone, attending police funerals, etc.). Second, camaraderie is a measure of peer support and trust within police officers' immediate work groups (e.g. cooperation between units, and trust between police partners). And third, unfairness measures police officers' perceptions of treatment as an officer both within the context of bureaucratic nature of police organization and by the media.

Work-family conflict and its impact on psychological and physical stress of individual police officers are measured by spillover. Unhappiness in someone's personal life and workplace burnout are thought to have significant influence on stress levels. This would include those situations where police officers are too physically and emotionally exhausted to deal with their spouses or significant others, and they begin to treat family the way that they treat suspects at work. This study examines how the "spillover" of conflict associated with family and work impacts stress of both male and female police officers.

This study also uses two measures of coping mechanisms including constructive and destructive coping mechanisms. Constructive coping is a measure of direct, positive, and active responses to work-related stress (e.g. talk to spouse, relative, and friends about the problem; make a plan of action and follow it; pray for guidance and strength; etc.). Destructive coping measures the negative and avoidance techniques used to deal with work-related stress (e.g. stay away from everyone; yell or shout at spouses/significant others or family members; smash or break things; increased smoking, drinking, and/or gambling; or pretend that nothing is wrong).

Five demographic variables are used as control measures in this analysis:

1. ethnicity;
2. marital status;
3. education status;
4. rank; and
5. years of service.

Previous studies suggest that the rank of officers and years of police service are important occupational characteristics associated with exposure to stressors and experience of their consequences (Robinson, 1981; Gudjonsson and Adlam, 1985; Fielding, 1987; Brown and Campbell, 1990). Other studies found inconsistent and weak relationships of stress and individual demographic characteristics (e.g. Maslach, 1982; Burke and Richardsen, 1993; Burke, 1993). We include these five control variables to ensure that the potentially intervening effects of respondent demographic background or work experience are not accounting for any observed relationships between work environment, work-family conflict, coping mechanisms, and the reporting of stress symptoms among officers. See Appendix 2 for the correlation matrix of all the variables included in this study.

FINDINGS

Table 1 reports the major demographic characteristics of the survey respondents. The survey sample includes 943 male officers (86 percent) and 157 female officers (14 percent). There are 696 officers who identified themselves as white (66 percent), and 355 officers who identified themselves as African American (34 percent). Few respondents are in the other racial categories. For the simplicity of comparison, percentages for the variable ethnicity are calculated based on white and African American officers only. About 60 percent of officers in this survey are married. The majority of the respondents (70 percent) do not have a college degree. A total of 18 percent of the survey respondents stated their ranks as sergeant or higher. The average length of police service is about 12 years.

Table 1   Descriptive statistics of demographic variables

Variables	Mean (SD)	n	%
Gender			
Female = 0		157	14.3
Male = 1		943	85.7
Ethnicity			
White = 0		696	66.2
African American = 1		355	33.8
Marriage			
Not married = 0		441	40.1
Married = 1		658	59.9
Education attainment			
BA and + = 0		326	29.8
Less than BA = 1		768	70.2
Rank			
Supervisor = 0		202	18.4
Officer = 1		898	81.6
Years of service	11.52 (9.28)		

Our first research question examines the levels of clinically developed measures of stress between male and female officers in the Baltimore City Police Department. Table 2 presents the results of a comparison between male and female police officers on all of the dependent and independent variables using *t*-tests. The findings indicate that female officers have statistically significant higher levels of stress in two of the three indexes measuring psychological and physical stress. The means of depression and somatization among female officers (1.58, 1.54) are both higher than those of their male counterparts (1.47, 1.36), respectively. However, no statistically significant difference was found between male and female officers on anxiety.

Among the three sets of independent variables, statistically significant differences were found between male and female officers in all three measures of work environment. Male officers were found to have experienced more work-related negative exposures (1.34) and tended to report higher levels of camaraderie (3.62) than do their female counterparts (1.22, 3.44), respectively. Male officers reported a higher level of unfairness in the department (3.04) than their female counterparts (2.81). There were no statistically significant differences detected between male and female officers in the means of spillover. And finally, we found statistically significant gender differences in coping mechanisms employed by police officers. Female officers seemed to use more constructive coping (2.66) than male officers (2.35). Although statistically significant, the differences in the destructive coping measures were rather marginal when male (1.56) and female officers (1.50) are compared.

Table 2   Testing the differences between male and female police officers in Baltimore PD

	Baltimore PD Scale mean (SD)	Male officers Scale mean (SD)	Female officers Scale mean (SD)	t-test
Dependent variable				
Somatization	1.39 (0.38)	1.36 (0.36)	1.54 (0.45)	4.58*
Anxiety	1.27 (0.36)	1.27 (0.36)	1.26 (0.37)	−0.16
Depression	1.47 (0.39)	1.45 (0.38)	1.58 (0.45)	3.56*
Work environment				
Negative exposures	1.33 (0.65)	1.34 (0.65)	1.22 (0.61)	−2.21*
Camaraderie	3.60 (0.80)	3.62 (0.80)	3.44 (0.84)	−2.70*
Unfairness	3.00 (0.66)	3.04 (0.66)	2.81 (0.62)	−3.98*
Work-family conflict				
Spillover	2.38 (0.78)	2.40 (0.78)	2.30 (0.77)	−1.43
Coping				
Constructive coping	2.39 (0.60)	2.35 (0.60)	2.66 (0.57)	5.98*
Destructive coping	1.55 (0.33)	1.56 (0.33)	1.50 (0.32)	−2.17*

Note: * $p < 0.05$

Tables 3 and 4 show the results of separate multivariate analyses used to answer our second research question (whether the sources of stress and coping strategies are indeed similar between the two gender groups). Both the unstandardized and standardized (beta) coefficients are reported to document the relative contribution of each individual variable to the equations for the three dimensions of stress.[1] In both the male and female police officer samples, the R^2 statistics for all of the regression models are statistically significant, ranging from 0.24 on the anxiety dimension (female sample) to 0.34 on the depression dimension (male sample).

In the male police officer sample, the results of regression analysis indicate that the majority of the independent variables have statistically significant impact on all three stress indexes. More specifically, we found that four variables are particularly important in predicting the levels of both psychological and physical stress among male officers. These four variables include:

1. negative exposures to police work;
2. camaraderie (work environment);
3. spillover effect (work-family conflict); and
4. destructive coping (coping strategy).

Moreover, all of the signs of the four statistically significant variables are pointed in the hypothesized directions (see Table 3). We also discovered that married male officers have less psychological stress compared to unmarried male officers. And it appears that the years of service in the police force is a statistically significant contributor to depression, as reported by male officers.

Table 3   Regression analyses, male officers sample

| | Physical stress | | Psychological stress | | | |
| | Somatization | | Anxiety | | Depression | |
	b	β	b	β	b	β
Work environment						
Negative exposures	0.086	0.157*	0.088	0.163*	0.067	0.115*
Camaraderie	−0.076	−0.174*	−0.043	−0.099*	−0.074	−0.159*
Unfairness	−0.007	−0.013	−0.008	−0.016	0.035	0.062
Work-family conflict						
Spillover	0.102	0.227*	0.090	0.204*	0.102	0.214*
Coping						
Constructive coping	0.010	0.016	0.015	0.025	−0.006	−0.009
Destructive coping	0.259	0.238*	0.330	0.308*	0.339	0.294*
Demographic						
Ethnicity	−0.059	−0.075	−0.041	−0.054	−0.034	−0.041
Marriage	−0.033	−0.045	−0.064	−0.089*	−0.060	−0.078*
Education	0.011	0.014	0.012	0.016	−0.000	−0.000
Rank	0.021	0.024	0.014	0.017	−0.002	−0.002
Years of service	0.001	0.031	−0.000	−0.021	0.003	0.075*
Adjusted R^2 =	0.288*		0.276*		0.340*	

Note: * p < 0.05

In comparison, our regression analysis using the female officer sample revealed some more interesting findings (see Table 4). First, none of the work environment measures yielded statistically significant impact on female police officer stress. It seemed that female officers' stress was not influenced by the three variables measuring work environment.[2] In addition, it is also interesting to note that none of the demographic variables were statistically significant predictors of female officers' psychological and physical stress.

Second, similar to those findings from the male officer sample, spillover (work-family conflict) and destructive coping (coping strategy) were statistically significant contributors to female officer stress. However, unlike those found in the male officer sample, constructive coping is now a statistically significant "buffer" to depression for female officers. It is important to point out that although fewer variables are significant in predicting stress levels of female officers, the explanatory power of the two variables (i.e. spillover and destructive coping) are high judging by their respective beta weights. The

Table 4   Regression analyses, female officers sample

	Physical stress Somatization		Psychological stress			
			Anxiety		Depression	
	b	β	b	β	b	β
Work environment						
Negative exposures	0.083	0.102	0.047	0.070	0.093	0.116
Camaraderie	−0.051	−0.093	−0.037	−0.082	−0.057	−0.107
Unfairness	−0.023	−0.031	0.044	0.071	0.030	0.041
Work-family conflict						
Spillover	0.104	0.174*	0.112	0.226*	0.117	0.199*
Coping						
Constructive coping	0.067	0.080	−0.057	−0.082	−0.127	−0.154*
Destructive coping	0.510	0.345*	0.365	0.299*	0.516	0.355*
Demographic						
Ethnicity	0.051	0.054	−0.009	−0.011	0.039	0.042
Marriage	0.059	0.063	0.072	0.090	0.103	0.111
Education	−0.008	−0.008	−0.020	−0.024	−0.082	−0.083
Rank	0.102	0.073	0.031	0.027	0.103	0.075
Years of service	0.012	0.156	0.003	0.047	0.007	0.093
Adjusted R^2	0.297*		0.241*		0.333*	

Note: * $p < 0.05$

variance explained measures (R^2) obtained from the three regression analyses using the female sample ($R^2 = 0.30$, 0.24, and 0.33 respectively) are similar to those obtained using the male officer sample ($R^2 = 0.29$, 0.28, and 0.34 respectively).

DISCUSSION AND CONCLUSIONS

In regard to our first research question, the findings of this study indicate that female officers do have statistically significant higher levels of somatization and depression compared to their male counterparts, respectively. These findings are generally consistent with relevant previous research findings in the area of psychology and mental health (e.g. Derogatis and Savitz, 1999). Nevertheless, we find no evidence to suggest that male and female police officers differ statistically in the clinically developed measure of anxiety.[3]

To answer our second research question, a multivariate analysis examines the sources of stress and coping strategies used by male and female officers. We found both convergent and divergent effects of work environment, work-family conflict, and coping strategies on the physical and psychological stress of police officers. In both male and female officer samples, there appears to be convergent impact of spillover and destructive coping on all three measures of stress (somatization, anxiety, and depression). Judging from the signs and values of the standardized regression coefficients (beta), the impact of spillover and destructive coping are consistently the largest, which suggests that both are among the most important job stressors in police work.

There are unmistakable signs of divergent effects of some work environment, coping, and demographic variables on stress that appear to be gender specific. For example, in the analysis using the female officer sample, neither the work environment variables nor the demographic variables are statistically significant predictors of any measures of stress. Yet, unlike the corresponding finding from male officer sample, constructive coping has been found to reduce depression among female officers.

To further our understanding of the intricate nature of police work environment, we compared the percentage of male and female police officers that agreed to specific individual items (see Appendix 3 for analysis of item responses). The results of comparison between the two groups revealed that constructive coping was found to be a statistically significant stress-reducing factor for one type of female police officer stress—depression. About half of all the female officers in the sample indicated that they have frequently or always used the following coping strategies:

- rely on your faith in God to see you through this rough time (female—61.9 percent; male—35.3 percent);
- pray for guidance and strength (female—59.1 percent; male—28.5 percent);
- talk with your spouse, relative or friend about the problem (female—52.3 percent; male—37.1 percent); and
- make a plan of action and follow it (female—48.0 percent; male—44.2 percent).

Apparently, there are differences between male and female officers in using constructive coping strategies. Male police officers appear to rely far less on spiritual guidance and on consulting spouse, other family members, and friends when dealing with stress. We suggest that this observation has significant policy implications.

Policy Implications

The results of this study provide the basis for several policy implications related to police stress and gender. First, our findings suggest that police administrators should pay attention to the convergent factors that lead to police officer stress. Stressors such as work-family conflict and negative coping are common among both male and female officers. To ameliorate the stress associated with work-family conflict, police management should play a leading role in creating greater flexibility in accommodating police officers' professional, personal, and family needs. In more practical terms, efforts need to be made to actively solicit input from both police officers and their family members. For example, police stress training sessions targeting work-family conflict should consider the possibility of involving both police officers and their spouses/significant others.

Second, with regard to improving police officers' coping skills, police stress management programs should be tailored to fit the specific needs of a police department. A sensible approach would involve the following three major components:

1. assessment of police officers' physical and psychological stress, which includes identifying both internal and external stressors;

2. monitoring police officers' adaptive and maladaptive coping skills; and

3. effective use of appropriate intervention strategies such as peer counseling.

In particular, peer counseling could be a realistic and effective way to deal with police officer stress (Klyver, 1983). Some male police officers are notoriously shy in seeking professional help for fear of being viewed as weak by fellow officers (Graf, 1986).

Finally, police stress management programs could also benefit from learning the divergent impact of work environment and coping mechanisms on police stress that is gender specific. Our study indicates that work environment has had greater impact on stress of male police officers. While negative exposures to work-related incidents remain a significant stressor to male officers, camaraderie among colleagues could counteract its negative impact on the well-being of male police officers. Although we did not find a statistically significant impact of work environment on female officers' stress in this study, the signs of the indicators of work environment were similar in both gender groups. Additionally, it is encouraging that constructive coping has been found to have a significant impact on reducing depression for female police officers. The constructive coping techniques used by female officers that result in decreased depression could be promoted among male police officers in pursuit of similarly positive impact on their stress. In sum, employee stress is an important issue that no police agency can afford to overlook. Stress management in policing is essential because police work is such a highly stressful profession. In addition, police officers unable to deal effectively with stress might fail to provide efficient quality police services to citizens.

We would like to point out three caveats in regard to the findings of our study. First, we acknowledge that the findings derived from our analysis were based on a large police department located on the East Coast. Therefore, the results might be more informative to large police agencies, compared to medium-sized or smaller police agencies. Second, we would caution the possible risk of model specification errors. Third, although we are able to test our hypotheses based on larger sub-samples of male ($n = 943$) and female officers ($n = 157$) than many of the previous police stress and gender studies, we would prefer even greater numbers from broader jurisdictions in future studies on this topic.

We invite other police scholars and practitioners to join in the study of police stress management with an eye on further exploring possible group (e.g. gender, race) differences. Longitudinal and cross-sectional studies are needed to both increase our understanding of the sources of police stress and to develop more effective responses to manage police officer stress. We hope that our study of the convergent and divergent impact of work environment, work-family conflict, and coping mechanisms on female and male officer stress is a step forward in police stress research.

Notes

[1] Multicollinearity is a potential serious problem associated with the use of ordinary least square (OLS) regression analysis. Accordingly, the variance inflation factor (VIF) often is used to detect whether collinearity exists among independent variables. Some researchers use a VIF score of 4 or greater as an indication of noteworthy multicollinearity (Fisher and Mason, 1980; Judge et al., 1988). The collinearity statistics run on theses data showed that none of the VIF values exceeded 2. It is safe to say that multicollinearity was not a problem in our analysis.

[2] Our reviewers correctly pointed out that since we are using a convenience sample originated from a single site the generalizability of our findings might be limited.

[3] To our best knowledge, there is no prior study in policing using similar clinical measures of stress as used in our current study. This renders a difficult exercise for us to compare our findings to the existing literature in the field of policing.

References

Aldwin, C. (1994), *Stress, Coping and Development*, Guiford, New York, NY.

Alkus, S. and Padesky, C. (1983), "Special problems of police officers: stress related issues and interventions," *Counseling Psychologist*, Vol. 11, pp. 55–64.

Anshel, M. H. (2000), "A conceptual model and implications for coping with stressful events in police work," *Criminal Justice and Behavior*, Vol. 27, pp. 375–400.

Balkin, J. (1988), "Why policemen don't like policewomen," *Journal of Police Science and Administration*, Vol. 16, pp. 29–38.

Barnett, R. C., Niener, L. and Baruch, G. K. (1987), *Gender and Stress*, The Free Press, New York, NY.

Bernard, J. (1972), *The Future of Marriage*, Bantam Books, New York, NY.

Billings, A. G. and Moos, R. H. (1981), "The role of coping responses and social resources in attenuating the stress of life events," *Journal of Behavioral Medicine*, Vol. 4, pp. 139–57.

Brown, J. A. and Campbell, E. A. (1990), "Sources of occupational stress in the police," *Work and Stress*, Vol. 4, pp. 305–18.

Burke, R. J. (1989), "Career stages, satisfaction and well-being among police officers," *Psychological Reports*, Vol. 65, pp. 3–12.

Burke, R. J. (1993), "Work-family stress, conflict, coping and burnout in police officers," *Stress Medicine*, Vol. 9, pp. 171–80.

Burke, R. J. and Richardsen, A. M. (1993), "Psychological burnout in organizations," in Golembiewski, R.T. (Ed.), *Handbook of Organizational Behavior*, Dekker, New York, NY, pp. 263–98.

Coman, G. and Evans, B. (1991), "Stressors facing Australian police in the 1990s," *Police Studies*, Vol. 14, pp. 153–65.

Crank, J. P. and Caldero, M. (1991), "The production of occupational stress in medium-sized police agencies: a survey of line officers in eight municipal departments," *Journal of Criminal Justice*, Vol. 19, pp. 339–49.

Cruse, D. and Rubin, J. (1973), *Determinants of Police Behavior: A Summary*, Criminal Justice Monograph, U.S. Department of Justice, No. 2700-00215, U.S. Government Printing Office, Washington, DC.

Dantzer, M. L. (1987), "Police-related stress: a critique for future research," *Journal of Police and Criminal Psychology*, Vol. 3, pp. 43–8.

Deaux, K. and Ullman, J. C. (1983), *Women of Steel*, Praeger, New York, NY.

Derogatis, L. and Melisaratos, N. (1983), "The brief symptom inventory: an introductory report," *Psychological Medicine*, Vol. 13, pp. 595–605.

Derogatis, L. and Savitz, K. (1999), "The SCL-90-R: brief symptom inventory and matching clinical rating scales," in Maruish, M. (Ed.), *The Use of Psychological Testing for Treatment, Planning and Outcomes Assessment*, Lawrence Erlbaum Associates Inc., Mahwah, NJ.

Derogatis, L., Lipman, R. and Covi, L. (1973), "SCL-90: an outpatient psychiatric rating scale-preliminary report," *Psychopharmacology Bulletin*, Vol. 9, pp. 13–28.

Dignam, J. T., Barrera, M. and West, S. C. (1986), "Occupational stress, social support, and burnout among correctional officers," *American Journal of Community Psychology*, Vol. 14, pp. 177–93.

Eisenburg, T. (1975), "Job stress and the police officer: identifying stress reduction techniques," in Kroes, W. H. and Hurrell, J. J. Jr. (Eds.), *Job Stress and the Police Officer: Identifying Stress Reduction Techniques*, HEW Publication No. NIOSH 760187, U.S. Government Printing Office, Washington, DC.

Ellison, K. W. and Genz, J. L. (1983), *Stress and Police Officer*, Charles Thomas Publishers, Springfield, IL.

Evans, B. J., Coman, G. J., Stanley, R. O. and Burrows, G. D. (1993), "Police officers' coping strategies: an Australian police survey," *Stress Medicine*, Vol. 9, pp. 237–46.

Fielding, N. G. (1987), *Joining Forces: Police Training Socialization and Occupational Competence*, Routledge, London.

Fisher, J. E. and Mason, R. L. (1980), "The analysis of multicollinear data in criminology," in Fox, J. A. (Ed.), *Methods in Quantitative Criminology, Academic Press*, New York, NY, pp 99–125.

Galinsky, E., Bond, J. T. and Friedman, D. E. (1993), *The Changing Workforce: Highlights of the National Study, II*, Families and Work Institute, New York, NY.

Galinsky, E., Bond, J. T. and Friedman, D. E. (1996), "The role of employers in addressing the needs of employed parents," *Journal of Social Issues*, Vol. 52, pp. 111–36.

Ganster, D. C., Fusilier, M. R. and Mayes, B. T. (1986), "Role of social support in the experience of stress at work," *Journal of Applied Psychology*, Vol. 7, pp. 102–11.

Gershon, R. (1999), "Police stress and domestic violence in police families in Baltimore, Maryland, 1997–1999," computer file, ICPSR version, Johns Hopkins University (producer), Baltimore, MD, Inter-University Consortium for Political and Social Research (distributor), Ann Arbor, MI.

Golembiewski, R. and Kim, B. (1991), "Burnout in police work: stressors, strain, and the phase model," *Police Studies*, Vol. 14, pp. 74–80.

Goodman, A. M. (1990), "A model for police officer burnout," *Journal of Business and Psychology*, Vol. 5, pp. 85–99.

Gove, W. R. and Tudor, J. F. (1973), "Adult sex roles and mental illness," *American Journal of Sociology*, Vol. 78, pp. 812–35.

Graf, F. A. (1986), "The relationship between social support and occupational stress among police officers," *Journal of Police Science and Administration*, Vol. 14, pp. 178–86.

Gudjonsson, G. H. and Adlam, K. (1985), "Occupational stressors among British police officers," *Police Journal*, Vol. 58, pp. 73–85.

Haar, R. N. and Morash, M. (1999), "Gender, race and strategies of coping with occupational stress in policing," *Justice Quarterly*, Vol. 16, pp. 303–36.

House, J. S. (1981), *Work Stress and Social Support*, Addison-Wesley, Reading, MA.

House, J. S. and Wells, J. A. (1978), "Occupational stress, social support, and health," in McLean, A., Black, G. and Colligan, M. (Eds.), *Reducing Occupational Stress: Proceedings of a Conference*, National Institute of Safety and Health, Washington, DC, publication No. 78–140, pp. 8–29.

Hughes, D., Galinsky, E. and Morris, A. (1992), "The effects of job characteristics on marital quality: specifying linking mechanisms," *Journal of Marriage and Family*, Vol. 54, pp. 31–42.

Hurrel, J. J. (1986), "Some organizational stressors in police work and means for their amelioration," in Reese, J. T. and Goldstein, H. A. (Eds.), *Psychological Services for Law Enforcement*. National Symposium on Police Psychological Services, FBI Academy, Quantico, VA.

Jackson, S. E. and Maslach, C. (1982), "After-effects of job-related stress: families as victims," *Journal of Occupational Behavior*, Vol. 3, pp. 63–77.

Judge, G. G., Hill, R. C., Griffiths, W. E., Lutkepohl, H. and Lee, T. C. (1988), *Introduction to the Theory and Practice of Econometrics*, 2nd ed., Wiley, New York, NY.

Klyver, N. (1983), "Peer counseling for police personnel: a dynamic program in the Los Angeles Police Department," *Police Chief*, Vol. 50, pp. 66–8.

Kroes, W. H. (1985), *Society's Victim: the Police Officer*, Charles Thomas, Springfield, IL.

Kroes, W. H., Margolis, B. L. and Hurrell, J. J. (1974), Job stress in policemen," *Journal of Police Sciences and Administration*, Vol. 2, pp. 145–55.

LaRocco, J., House, J. and French, J. (1980), "Social support, occupational stress, and health," *Journal of Health and Social Behavior*, Vol. 21, pp. 202–18.

Lazarus, R. S. (1990), "Theory-based stress measurement," *Psychological Inquiry*, Vol. 1, pp. 3–13.

Loo, R. (1984), "Occupational stress in the law enforcement profession," *Canadian Mental Health*, pp. 10–13.

McGreedy, K. (1974), "Selection practices and the police role," *Police Chief*, Vol. 41, pp. 41–3.

Martelli, T. A., Waters, L. K. and Martelli, J. (1989), "The police stress survey: reliability and relation to job satisfaction and organizational commitment," *Psychological Reports*, Vol. 64, pp. 267–73.

Martin, S. E. (1980), *Breaking and Entering: Policewomen on Patrol*, University of California Press, Berkeley, CA.

Martin, S. E. (1990), *On the Move: The Status of Women in Policing*, The Police Foundation, Washington, DC.

Martin, S. E. (1993), "Female officers on the move: a status report on women in policing," in Dunham, R. and Alpert, G. (Eds.), *Critical Issues in Policing: Contemporary Readings*, 2nd ed., Waveland Press Inc., Prospect Heights, IL, pp. 327–47.

Maslach, C. (1976), "Burnout," *Human Behavior*, Vol. 23, pp. 16–22.

Maslach, C. (1982), *Burnout: The Cost of Caring*, Prentice Hall, Englewood Cliffs, NJ.

Morris, A., Marybeth, S. and DuMont, K. (1999), "Contextual factors affecting the organizational commitment of diverse police officers: a levels of analysis perspective," *American Journal of Community Psychology*, Vol. 27, pp. 75–105.

National Center for Women and Policing (2000), *Equal Denied: The Status of Women in Policing: 1999*, National Center for Women and Policing, Los Angeles, CA.

Pendergrass, V. and Ostrove, N. (1984), "Survey of stress in women in policing," *Journal of Police Science and Administration*, Vol. 12, pp. 303–9.

Quick, J. C., Murphy, L. R., Hurrell, J. J. and Orman, D. (1992), "The value of work, the risk of distress, and the power of prevention," in Quick, J. C., Murphy, L. R. and Hurrell, J. J. Jr. (Eds.), *Stress and Well being at Work: Assessments and Interventions for Occupational Mental Health*, American Psychological Association, Washington, DC, pp. 3–14.

Reese, J. T. (1986), "Policing the violent society: the American experience," *Stress Medicine*, Vol. 2, pp. 233–40.

Reiser, M. (1974), "Some organizational stresses on policemen," *Journal of Police Science and Administration*, Vol. 2, pp. 156–9.

Reiser, M. (1976), "Stress, distress, and adaptation in police work," *The Police Chief*, January, pp. 24–7.

Robinson, P. (1981), "Stress in the police service," *Police Review*, Vol. 20, pp. 2254–9.

Selye, I. (1978), "The stress of police work," *Police Stress*, pp. 1:1–3.

Spielberger, C. D., Westberry, L. G., Grier, K. S. and Greenfield, G. (1981), *The Police Stress Survey: Sources of Stress in Law Enforcement*, Human Resources Institute, Tampa, FL.

Stone, A. A. and Neale, J. M. (1984), "New measure of daily coping: development and preliminary results," *Journal of Personality and Social Psychology*, Vol. 46, pp. 892–906.

Stotland, E. (1991), "The effects of police work and professional relationships on health," *Journal of Criminal Justice*, Vol. 19, pp. 371–9.

Symonds, M. (1970), "Emotional hazards of police work," *American Journal of Psychoanalysis*, Vol. 30, pp. 155–60.

Violanti, J. M. (1985), "The police stress process," *Journal of Police Science and Administration*, Vol. 13, pp. 106–10.

Violanti, J. M. and Aron, F. (1993), "Sources of police stressors, job attitudes and psychological distress," *Psychological Reports*, Vol. 72, pp. 899–904.

Violanti, J. M. and Aron, F. (1994), "Ranking police stressors," *Psychological Reports*, Vol. 75, pp. 824–6.

Violanti, J. M., Marshall, J. R. and Howe, B. (1985), "Stress, coping, and alcohol use: the police connection," *Journal of Police Science and Administration*, Vol. 2, pp. 106–10.

Walker, S. (1985), "Racial minority and female employment in policing: the implications of glacial change," *Crime and Delinquency*, Vol. 31, pp. 555–72.

Wexler, J. G. and Logan, D. D. (1983), "Sources of stress among women police officers," *Journal of Police Science and Administration*, Vol. 13, pp. 98–105.

APPENDIX 1. COMPOSITE INDEX CONSTRUCTION

Dependent Variables
    Response categories are rated from 1 (never) to 4 (always).

Somatization (alpha = 0.76):
    Questions. In the past six months, how often did you have:
- Pains or pounding in your heart and chest.
- Faintness or dizziness.
- Headaches or pressure in your head.
- Nausea, upset stomach, stomach pains.
- Trouble getting your breath.
- A lump in your throat.

Anxiety (alpha = 0.85):
    Questions. In the past six months, how often did you have:
- Suddenly scared for no reason.
- Feeling that something bad was going to happen to you at work.
- Spells of terror or panic.
- Feeling so restless you could not sit still.

Depression (alpha = 0.67):
    Questions. In the past six months, how often did you have:
- Loss of sexual interest or pleasure.
- Feelings of low energy or slowed down.
- Feelings of being trapped or caught.
- Blame yourself for things.
- Feeling blue.
- Feeling no interest in things.
- Feeling hopeless about the future.
- Thoughts of ending your life.
- Crying easily.

Independent Variables

Negative exposures (alpha = 0.79):
    Questions. If you have ever experienced any of the following, please indicate how much it emotionally affected you. Please check N/A if you have not experienced it.
- Making a violent arrest.
- Shooting someone.

- Being the subject of an IID investigation.
- Responding to a call related to a chemical spill.
- Responding to a bloody crime scene.
- Personally knowing the victim.
- Being involved in a hostage situation.
- Attending a police funeral.
- Experiencing a needle stick injury or other exposure to blood and body fluids.

Response categories are: 0 (N/A), 1 (not at all), 2 (a little) and 3 (very much).

Camaraderie (alpha = 0.53):

Questions: Please check the box that best describes how much you agree with the following statements:

- There is good and effective cooperation between units.
- I can trust my work partner.

Original response categories are from 1 (strongly agree) to 5 (strongly disagree). Categories have been reversed coded in current study.

Unfairness (alpha = 0.60):

Questions. Please check the box that best describes how much you agree with the following statements:

- Compared to my peers (same rank), I find that I am likely to be more criticized for my mistakes.
- I feel that I am less likely to get chosen for certain assignment because of "who I am" (e.g. race, gender, sexual orientation, physical characteristics).
- Within the department, gender-related jokes are often made in my presence.
- When I am assertive or question the way things are done, I am considered militant.
- Media reports of alleged police wrong-doing are biased against us.
- The department tends to be more lenient in enforcing rules and regulations for female officers.

Original response categories are from 1 (strongly agree) to 5 (strongly disagree). Categories have been reversed coded in current study.

Spillover (alpha = 0.65):

Questions. Please check the box that best describes how much you agree with the following statements:

- I often get home too physically and emotionally exhausted to deal with my spouse/ significant other.
- I catch myself treating my family the way I treat suspects.

- At home, I can never shake off the feeling of being a police officer.
- I expect to have the final say on how things are done in my household.

Original response categories are from 1 (strongly agree) to 5 (strongly disagree). Categories have been reversed coded in current study.

Constructive coping (alpha = 0.66):
Questions. When dealing with stressful events at work, how often do you:

- Talk with your spouse, relative or friend about the problem.
- Pray for guidance and strength.
- Make a plan of action and follow it.
- Exercise regularly to reduce tension.
- Rely on your faith in God to see you through this rough time.

Response categories are from 1 (never) to 4 (always).

Destructive coping (alpha = 0.57):
Questions. When dealing with stressful events at work, how often do you:

- Stay away from everyone; you want to be alone.
- Smoke more to help you relax.
- Yell or shout at your spouse/significant other, a family member, or a professional.
- Let your feelings out by smashing things.
- Hang out more with your fellow officers at a bar.
- Gamble.
- Increase your sexual activity.
- Try to act as if nothing is bothering you.

Response categories are from 1 (never) to 4 (always).

Appendix 2. Correlation Matrix

Table A1

	1	2	3	4	5	6	7	8	9	10	11	12	13	14
1. Somatization	1.000													
2. Anxiety	0.612*	1.000												
3. Depression	0.663*	0.674*	1.000											
4. Negative exposure	0.277*	0.267*	0.287*	1.000										
5. Camaraderie	-0.267*	-0.205*	-0.289*	-0.119*	1.000									
6. Unfairness	0.217*	0.250*	0.295*	0.258*	-0.263*	1.000								
7. Spillover	0.383*	0.402*	0.422*	0.206*	-0.153*	0.350*	1.000							
8. Constructive coping	-0.074*	-0.113*	-0.146*	-0.041	0.078*	-0.153*	-0.237*	1.000						
9. Destructive coping	0.435*	0.490*	0.485*	0.253*	-0.159*	0.287*	0.474*	-0.124*	1.000					
10. Ethnicity	-0.057	-0.093*	-0.074*	-0.155*	0.012	-0.058	-0.072*	0.326*	-0.082*	1.000				
11. Marriage	-0.008	-0.030	-0.027	0.198*	-0.025	0.052	0.014	-0.022	-0.021	-0.157*	1.000			
12. Education	0.030	0.045	0.018	-0.077*	0.024	0.070*	0.089*	-0.035	0.070*	0.079*	0.002	1.000		
13. Rank	-0.064*	-0.041	-0.084*	-0.257*	0.102*	-0.026	-0.035	-0.003	-0.009	0.148*	-0.134*	0.223*	1.000	
14. Years of service	0.139*	0.085*	0.160*	0.473*	-0.185*	0.062*	0.017	-0.132*	0.071*	-0.219*	0.272*	-0.105*	-0.476*	1.000

Note: *$p < 0.05$

APPENDIX 3. ANALYSIS OF SELECTED ITEM RESPONSES

Constructive coping (percentage responded that they have frequently or always done the following things when dealing with stressful events at work):

- Rely on your faith in God to see you through this rough time (male—35.3 percent; female—61.9 percent).
- Pray for guidance and strength (male—28.5 percent; female—59.1 percent).
- Talk with your spouse, relative or friend about the problem (male—37.1 percent; female—52.3 percent).
- Make a plan of action and follow it (male—44.2 percent; female—48.0 percent).
- Exercise regularly to reduce tension (male—37.3 percent; female—27.9 percent).

Spillover (percentage strongly agree or agree with the followings items):

- I often get home too physically and emotionally exhausted to deal with my spouse/ significant other (male—42.4 percent; female—41.7 percent).
- I catch myself treating my family the way I treat suspects (male—74.2 percent; female—81.2 percent).
- At home, I can never shake off the feeling of being a police officer (male—63.3 percent; female—71.1 percent).
- I expect to have the final say on how things are done in my household (male—61.3 percent; female—59.3 percent).

Destructive coping (percentage responded that they have frequently or always done the following things when dealing with stressful events at work):

- Stay away from everyone; you want to be alone (male—10.5 percent; female—13.1 percent).
- Smoke more to help you relax (male—11.3 percent; female—13.0 percent).
- Yell or shout at your spouse/significant other, a family member, or a professional (male—5.6 percent; female—6.5 percent).
- Let your feelings out by smashing things (male—1.2 percent; female—1.9 percent).
- Hang out more with your fellow officers at a bar (male—5.5 percent; female—1.3 percent).
- Gamble (male—1.1 percent; female—1.2 percent).
- Increase your sexual activity (male—14.4 percent; female—8.5 percent).
- Try to act as if nothing is bothering you (male—28.2 percent; female—21.4 percent).

Negative exposures (percentage responded that the following items affect them emotionally very much):

- Attending a police funeral (male—53.5 percent; female—64.5 percent).
- Being the subject of an IID investigation (male—34.9 percent; female—27.3 percent).
- Experiencing a needle stick injury or other exposure to blood and body fluids (male—29.7 percent; female—29.7 percent).
- Making a violent arrest (male—19.4 percent; female—18.8 percent).
- Personally knowing the victim (male—15.7 percent; female—20.6 percent).
- Responding to a bloody crime scene (male—15.2 percent; female—18.1 percent).
- Shooting someone (male—8.9 percent).
- Being involved in a hostage situation (male—8.1 percent; female—6.5 percent).
- Responding to a call related to a chemical spill (male—4.6 percent; female—3.9 percent).

Camaraderie (percentage strongly agree or agree with the followings items):

- There is good and effective cooperation between units (male—27.8 percent; female—33.5 percent).
- I can trust my work partner (male—6.2 percent; female—11.9 percent).

Toward an Understanding of the Physical Hazards of Police Work

Steven G. Brandl & Meghan S. Stroshine

In the literature, there exist various claims and debates concerning the dangerousness of the police occupation and its dangerousness in relation to other occupations. Most of the extant studies on the topic have come to the conclusion that policing is dangerous (see Fridell & Pate, 1997, p. 603) or, at the very least, that certain tasks of the job are dangerous (Edwards, 1995; Garner & Clemmer, 1986; Hirschel, Dean, & Lumb, 1994; Kaminski & Sorensen, 1995; Konstantin, 1984; Lester, 1981; Stanford & Mowry, 1990). This conclusion is most often arrived at through the analysis of assault and homicide data. Defining dangerousness in this narrow manner, however, is quite unlike other occupations. In most other occupations, the hazards associated with the job are defined in terms of any injuries and illnesses that occur during the course of the job (e.g., Bureau of Labor Statistics, 2000), including those that result from violence (National Institute for Occupational Safety and Health, 1992, 1997; Peek-Asa, Howard, Vargas, & Kraus, 1997) and accidents (Centers for Disease Control, 1998, 2001).

Part of the reason researchers have defined the dangerousness of the police occupation in such a narrow manner is that police officers have a rather unique occupational reality; assaults and homicides are an issue in the police occupation but are not for most other occupations. Whereas it may be true that assaults and homicides pose a greater risk for police officers given

Police Quarterly 6(2) (June 2003): 172–191, copyright © 2003 by Sage Publications, Inc. Reprinted by permission of Sage Publications, Inc.

the nature of their job, the exclusion of injuries that are the result of accidents presents at least two problems. First, defining dangerousness strictly in terms of assaults and homicides likely distorts an accurate picture of the physical dangers of the job and may severely underestimate the hazards of police work. This is problematic both conceptually and practically. Conceptually, an understanding of the dangers faced by officers is central to understanding the nature of police work and all of its complexities (Skolnick, 1994). Dealing with danger—potential or actual—is a critical factor shaping how police perceive themselves, their role, and the citizens with whom they come into contact (Skolnick, 1994). If one wishes to draw accurate conclusions about the nature of police work and the dangerousness of the police occupation, one must not focus exclusively on injuries and deaths that result from felonious acts; the dangers posed by accidents must also be considered. Practically, the injuries and deaths of police officers have enormous costs. Regardless of how injuries or deaths are sustained (accidentally or feloniously), these incidents translate into lost wages, medical expenses, insurance claims, and decreases in productivity. Of course, these assaults as well as accidents may also have dramatic consequences for officers and their families. It is reasonable to expect that some of the injuries sustained by officers could be prevented, if research is used to develop proper training and policy (Bayley & Garofalo, 1989; Edwards, 1995; Edwards & Tewksbury, 1996; Feldstein, Valanis, Vollmer, Stevens, & Overton, 1993; Fyfe, 1979; Hirschel et al., 1994; Kaminski, Edwards, & Johnson, 1998; Kaminski & Sorensen, 1995; Sherman, 1980). Without examining accidental deaths and injuries, however, it is not possible for police managers to address adequately the totality of the risks faced by police officers.

A second problem that emerges from relying solely on assaults and homicides to define the dangers associated with the policing profession is that it becomes difficult to accurately compare the dangerousness of police work to other occupations. This is problematic because dangerousness is a relative phenomenon. Danger is most meaningful when one can compare the hazards of one occupation with the hazards of another.

In short, operationalizing danger strictly as assaults and homicides precludes an appreciation of both the absolute dangers of policing (by overlooking a potentially significant area of threat) as well as the relative dangers of policing (by preventing the comparison of the danger in police work to danger in other occupations). These issues are addressed in the current study by (a) expanding the conceptualization of dangerousness to include injuries that occur as a result of accidents; (b) comparing accidental injuries to those that result from felonious acts; and (c) comparing injury incidents of varying natures and causes across occupations, fire fighting in particular. By analyzing the nature and frequency of police injuries sustained either by accident or assault for police officers and comparing these to injuries sustained by firefighters, one may develop a more complete appreciation of the relative physical hazards of police work.

Literature Review
The Absolute Dangers of Police Work

As noted, most studies on the dangerousness of police work have examined assaults and homicides (e.g., Edwards, 1995; Fridell & Pate, 1997; Hirschel et al., 1994; Meyer, Magedanz, Dahlin, & Chapman, 1981; Uchida, Brooks, & Kopers, 1987). These studies have shown that assaults are most common in disturbance and arrest situations, that the injuries are usually relatively minor, and that they are most commonly inflicted via person weapons (e.g., hands and feet).

Alpert and Dunham (1999) analyzed injury incidents that occurred in situations in which the police used physical force in controlling subjects and in which subjects used force against the police. They found that the most common type of force used by subjects was striking or hitting the police officer (44%), followed by pushing or pulling the officer (27%) and grabbing or holding the officer (20%). The most common injuries sustained by officers were bruises or abrasions, followed by sprains or strains and lacerations. Of the injured officers, 2% were bitten by the suspect, 2% suffered broken bones, and 1% were injured by gunshots.

Kaminski and Sorensen (1995) took a different approach and identified factors that differentiated between assaults that involved a physical attack and resulted in officer injury and assaults that involved a physical attack but did not result in officer injury. Using data originally collected and analyzed by Uchida et al. (1987), the researchers found that officers were more likely to be injured as a result of an assault when more than one officer was involved, when the suspect/assailant used bodily force as opposed to a weapon, when the suspect was under arrest or was fighting with officers, and when the suspect was sober. The researchers also found that there was a curvilinear relationship between officer height and odds of being injured; the odds of injury decreased up until the officer was 70 inches tall, then the odds of injury increased. In addition, officers with more years of service were generally less likely to be injured when assaulted. Officer weight, age, gender, and education were not related to the odds of injury.

On an ongoing basis, the FBI regularly reports on the killings, assaults, and other deaths of police officers in their annual publication, *Law Enforcement Officers Killed and Assaulted* (Federal Bureau of Investigation, 1998). The FBI report shows that for the years 1989 through 1998, 682 officers were feloniously killed in the line of duty. Almost the same number of officers were killed accidentally ($n = 636$), most often in motor vehicle, motorcycle, or aircraft accidents. More than a half a million officers (623,887) were assaulted in this 10-year time frame. Relatively little attention is given to accidents in the report, even though accidents are a cause of a large proportion of all deaths. No information is provided about accidents that did not result in deaths. In short, because of the focus on assaults, homicides, and deaths in the previous research, little is known about the nature and frequency of accidental and nonfatal injuries to police officers.

One exception is a study conducted by Brandl (1996), which compared accidental injuries to ones that resulted from felonious acts. Brandl examined more than 2,000 incidents resulting in police officer injuries or deaths. He found that a relatively small proportion of injury incidents resulted from assaults (10%), about one-half of all incidents resulted from accidents (e.g., 54%) (e.g., automobile accidents, slips, and falls), and the remaining incidents resulted from uncooperative or resisting subjects (36%) (e.g., officer was injured during a foot pursuit of subject). In addition, Brandl found that the most serious injuries were most often due to accidents, most medical treatment was due to accidents. and most days off were the result of accidents. For example, Brandl found that 52 incidents resulted in broken bones during the study period. Of these, 6 were as a result of assaults, 21 were due to accidents, and 25 were the result of uncooperative suspects. Medical attention was sought by officers in 50% of accidents, 43% of incidents with uncooperative suspects, and 37% of assaults. Fourteen percent of assaults resulted in at least 1 day off of work due to the injury, 18% in uncooperative suspect incidents, and 20% in accidents. As Brandl's study attests, there is clearly value to examining accidental injuries and deaths in police work. Failure to do so results in an incomplete and inaccurate picture of the dangers of police work.

The Relative Dangers of Police Work

Few studies have empirically compared injuries sustained by police officers to injuries sustained by incumbents of other occupations. *The Census of Fatal Occupational Injuries* (Bureau of Labor Statistics, 2000) showed that policing ranked 8th of the 10 most dangerous industries,[1] but of course, this conclusion does not take into consideration nonfatal incidents. Violanti, Vena, and Marshall (1996) compared the cause of death among police and other municipal workers. This study showed that a larger proportion of police officers died as a result of suicide and homicide than other municipal workers, but a smaller proportion died as a result of accidents. No comparisons were provided with regard to nonfatal injuries. Peek-Asa et al. (1997) examined assaults across occupations and found that, not surprisingly, police departments reported the highest rates among the 9 industries that reported any assaults.[2] The police group was calculated to be 73.1 times more likely to be assaulted at work than the overall industry average. The researchers also found that most injuries that resulted from assaults, regardless of the occupation, were relatively minor, most being contusions, sprains, and strains. No comparisons were provided for deaths or accidents. Finally, Feuer and Rosenman (1986) examined the rate and causes of death among a sample of retired police officers and firefighters and found that the mortality of these two groups did not differ from that of the general population, with the exception of increased rates of skin cancer and heart disease among firefighters and increased heart disease among police officers. Although this study does make comparisons between the police and firefighters, no comparisons are provided with regard to accidents, assaults, or homicides. Indeed, given the current state of the research, we know little about the physical risks of policing—particularly the risks posed by accidents and other nonfatal incidents—compared to other occupations.

Study Objectives

In this study, we explore the absolute dangers associated with police work by broadening the definition of danger typically used by researchers in this area. Specifically, we examine injuries that occurred as a result of assaults, resisting subjects, and accidents. In doing so, we provide a more comprehensive picture of the dangers associated with police work than that currently found in the literature (cf. Brandl, 1996).

This study also explores the relative dangers of police work by comparing the injuries reported by police officers to those reported by firefighters in the same Midwestern municipality. Police officers and firefighters were compared for several reasons. First, both organizations share common characteristics: Both are responsible for providing emergency uniformed services to the public, both have the same source of funding (i.e., municipal tax revenue), both have similar compensation levels (i.e., parity), and both are occupations in which the nature of the work poses hazards above and beyond those typically found in the workplace. In particular, police officers deal with suspects who may or may not peacefully acquiesce to the instructions of police officers. Similarly, firefighters find themselves at risk during the course of fighting fires and assisting people in precarious situations. Clearly, other municipal employees do not have such responsibilities or corresponding risks. Second, police and fire departments have been previously compared to each other in the past (e.g., Feuer & Rosenman, 1986; Fyfe, 1995). Finally, in this study, police officers (police officers and detectives) and firefighters (firefighters and heavy equipment operators) about whom data were collected were employed by the same municipality, resulting in injury report forms and associated reporting procedures that enabled consistent comparisons. In short, it appears reasonable that if police officers are to be compared with other municipal employees, firefighters would be would be most appropriate. By analyzing the nature and frequency of police injuries sustained by either accident or assault with those sustained by firefighters, one is able to develop a more complete appreciation of the relative hazards of police work.

Method

Data

At the time of the study (1997), the police and fire departments served a population of approximately 600,000, of which approximately 40% were members of racial minority groups (30% of the population was African

American). The largest segment of the population was employed in the manufacturing sector. The median annual household income was approximately $41,000, with about 84% of families above the poverty level (of 2000). The overall crime rate in the city most often ranks in the lower half of the 25 most similarly sized municipalities in the country. In 1997, the police department employed more than 2,000 sworn officers (of which about 1,700 were patrol officers or detectives), and the fire department employed approximately 1,000 sworn members (of which about 700 were firefighters or heavy equipment operators).

Data Source

As mandated under worker's compensation laws and departmental policies, city employees were required to complete a standard Report of Accident form upon sustaining a work-related injury (via an accident or assault). The report was typically completed by the employee's supervisor at or near the time the incident occurred. The report contained data on the employee's demographic characteristics, employment information, the date and time of the incident, a description of injuries, whether medical attention was sought, and a narrative that explained the circumstances of the incident.

In a single report, several specific injuries may have been documented (e.g., officer fell and received abrasions to hands and knees). Therefore, although each report documented one incident for a particular individual, several injuries may have been sustained and recorded in the report. If more than one employee was injured (or killed) as a result of the same incident (e.g., motor-vehicle accident), a separate report documenting the particular injuries sustained would have been filed for each individual. As such, the unit of analysis in this study was the injury incident.

Data Collection

Injury incidents that occurred in 1997 were analyzed. For the police, a data coding form was completed on all reports that identified a police officer or detective as the injured party. For the fire department reports, a coding form was completed on all reports in which it was determined that a firefighter or heavy equipment operator was the injured party. These four positions represent line-level personnel in each of the respective departments. As a result of the coding process, a total of 1,054 police injury reports and 530 fire department injury reports were included and analyzed in the study.

Variables

The data for the study were obtained from the injury reports and were transcribed as recorded by the supervisor who completed the reports. Specifically, the variables of interest consisted of (a) nature of the injury incident, (b) nature of the most serious injury sustained, (c) total number of injuries sustained, (d) activity that resulted in the injury incident, (e) whether medical attention was sought as a result of the incident, and (f) whether time was lost from work as a result of the incident (for police only).[3]

The nature of the injury incident was defined as either as a result of an accident, a resisting subject, or an assault. The incident was considered a result of an assault on the employee if it appeared that the employee was directly injured by the intentional assaultive acts of the subject. Specifically, if the employee was hit, kicked, bit, shot, stabbed, or spat on, the injury was considered a result of an assault. An injury incident was considered a result of a resisting subject if it was indicated in the report that the subject was fleeing, resisting (arrest or treatment), or was otherwise uncooperative. In all other instances, the injury incident was considered a result of an accident.

The nature of the most serious injury sustained had the following values: laceration/abrasion, sprain/strain, contusion, other muscle pain, contact with bodily fluid,[4] other contact with infectious disease, broken bones/dislocated joints, other pain, human bite, dog bite, contact with hazardous material, smoke/fume inhalation, bee/wasp sting, torn ligaments/tendons, eye injury (other than black eye), gunshot wound, burns, electrical shock, exhaustion/heat stroke, or other injury. The process of determining what constituted the most serious injury when more than one injury was identified was not often clear-cut. Specific medical details on the injuries were usually not provided in the reports. In some cases, it was easier to identify the more serious injury (e.g., fractured ribs vs. sprained finger) than in others (puncture to foot vs. contusion to elbow). When intuitively such a determination was difficult to make, the first injury listed on the report was considered most serious.

As for the total number of injuries sustained, injuries were counted separately if it appeared that each injury would likely require separate treatment. As common examples, pain and contusion to foot was considered one injury, whereas contusion to foot and laceration to hand were considered two injuries.

The activity that led to the incident assumed several values: controlling/arresting subject, conducting investigation, apprehending fleeing subject (on foot), vehicle accident, processing prisoner (e.g., controlling prisoner in lockup), other vehicle-related (e.g., slammed hand in car door), during training, on departmental premises (e.g., slip and fall), other physical activity (e.g., changing tire, foot patrol), assisting citizen/victim (e.g., first aid), when using police/fire equipment (not at fire/crime scene), during fire rescue/discovery, doing forced entry, fighting fire/injured at scene (e.g., using equipment at a fire scene), during shooting incident, post-shooting incident (related to stress), other work-related stress (usually self-diagnosis on report), and other activity (e.g., slip and fall where activity engaged in is not specified).

Medical attention was considered to have been sought and received if a treating practitioner (e.g., a medical doctor) was identified in the report. Finally, the number of work days lost due to the incident/injury was coded as it appeared in the report.

RESULTS

The results of the analyses are presented in Tables 1 through 3. Table 1 reports the results of the analyses on police injury incidents, Table 2 shows the analyses on police incidents disaggregated by the nature of the incident, and Table 3 provides a comparison of police and fire personnel injury incidents.

It is seen in Table 1 that just greater than 10% ($n = 110$) of all police injury incidents were the result of an assault, approximately 39% ($n = 413$) were due to subjects who were resisting or otherwise uncooperative, and the remaining 50% ($n = 531$) were a result of accidents. With regard to the nature of the most serious injury sustained by police officers, five types of injuries were common and distinguishable in frequency from the others: laceration/ abrasion (19.4% of all injuries), sprain/strain (18.9%), contact with infectious disease (18.3%),[5] contusion (16.6%), and other muscle pain (15.6%). These five types of injuries account for 88.8% of all injuries to police officers and detectives. In addition, it is seen that there were no deaths, three gun shot wounds, and no knife wounds.

Table 1 also shows the activities that led to the injury incidents. The most common activities resulting in injury incidents for the police were as follows: controlling/arresting suspect (43.8%), conducting investigation (14.1%), apprehending fleeing suspect on foot (11.6%), and vehicle accident (8.7%). These four categories account for 78.2% of all incidents. By far, the most common activity resulting in injury to police personnel was controlling/ arresting suspects.

As depicted in Table 1, approximately one-half of all incidents ($n = 516$) were serious enough to warrant immediate medical attention; however, 87.7% ($n = 909$) did not result in any time lost from work. Finally, on average, police officers sustained 1.43 injuries per incident (1,507 separate injuries were documented in the 1,054 reports/incidents). Considering the total number of patrol officers and detectives in the department, there were 0.610 incidents reported per officer.

Table 2 shows the key variables disaggregated by the nature of the incident. In assaults against the police, the most common injuries were contusions (37.3%), human bites (19.1%), and contacts with infectious disease (17.3%). When incidents resulted from a resisting subject, lacerations/abrasions (27.1%) and sprains/strains (24.9%) were the most common injuries reported. In accidents, contact with infectious disease was the most prevalent injury (24.7%), followed by other muscle pain (18.1%). Perhaps surprisingly, Table 2 also shows that many of the most severe injuries were not the result of assaults. For example, of the 28 incidents that involved broken bones/dislocated joints, only 2 resulted from assaults. Similarly, none of the 5 torn ligaments/tendons resulted from assaults, and none of the 3 gunshot wounds resulted from assaults.

Table I   Characteristics of injury incidents for police officers

	n	%
Nature of injury incident	1,054	100.0
Accident	531	50.4
Resisting subject	413	39.2
Assaultive subject	110	10.4
Nature of most serious injury	1,054	100.2
Laceration/abrasion	205	19.4
Sprain/strain	199	18.9
Contact with infectious disease	193	18.3
Contact with bodily fluid	98	
Blood-to-blood contact	16	
Other contact with infectious disease	95	
Contusion	175	16.6
Other muscle pain	164	15.6
Broken bones/dislocated joints	28	2.7
Human bite	22	2.1
Other pain	10	0.9
Contact with hazardous material	8	0.8
Smoke/fume inhalation	7	0.7
Torn ligaments/tendons	5	0.5
Eye injury (other than black eye)	4	0.4
Gunshot wound	3	0.3
Burns	2	0.2
Knife wound	0	0.0
Death	0	0.0
Other	29	2.8
Activity resulting in injury	1,050	100.2
Controlling/arresting subject	460	43.8
Conducting investigation	148	14.1
Apprehending fleeing subject (on foot)	122	11.6
Vehicle accident	91	8.7
Processing prisoner	52	5.0
Other vehicle related	36	3.4
During training	31	3.0
On department premises	23	2.2
Other physical activity	22	2.1
Assisting citizen/victim	17	1.6
Using equipment (not at fire scene)	12	1.1
During fire rescue/discovery	6	0.6
Doing forced entry	3	0.3
Fighting fire/at fire scene	1	0.1
During shooting incident	1	0.1
Other	26	2.5
Medical attention sought	1,016	100.0
No	500	49.2
Yes	516	50.8
Time off work due to injury	1,037	100.0
No	909	87.7
Yes	128	13.3

Rate of injury incidents (per officer) = 0.610
Number of injuries per incident = 1.43

Note: Missing data excluded from the table; percentages may not sum to 100 due to rounding.

Table 2 Characteristics of injury incidents for police officers by nature of incident

	Assaultive subject		Resisting subject		Accident	
	n	%	n	%	n	%
Nature of most serious injury	110	100.0	413	99.8	531	100.2
Laceration abrasion	13	11.8	112	27.1	80	15.1
Sprain/strain	3	2.7	103	24.9	93	17.5
Contact with infectious disease	19	17.3	43	10.4	131	24.7
Contact with bodily fluid	19		40		39	
Blood-to-blood contact	16		0		0	
Other contact with infectious disease	0		3		92	
Contusion	41	37.3	66	16.0	68	12.8
Other muscle pain	10	9.1	58	14.0	96	18.1
Broken bones/dislocated joints	2	1.8	15	3.6	11	2.1
Human bite	21	19.1	1	0.2	0	0.0
Other pain	1	0.9	2	0.5	7	1.3
Contact with hazardous material	0	0.0	4	1.0	4	0.8
Smoke/fume inhalation	0	0.0	0	0.0	7	1.3
Tore ligaments/tendons	0	0.0	4	1.0	1	0.2
Eye injury (other than black eye)	0	0.0	1	0.2	3	0.6
Gunshot wound	0	0.0	0	0.0	3	0.6
Burns	0	0.0	1	0.2	1	0.2
Knife wound	0	0.0	0	0.0	0	0.0
Death	0	0.0	0	0.0	0	0.0
Other	0	0.0	3	0.7	26	4.9
Activity resulting in injury	110	99.9	413	100.1	528	100.0
Controlling/arresting subject	99	90.0	282	68.3	79	15.0
Conducting investigation	0	0.0	0	0.0	148	28.0
Apprehending fleeing subject	2	1.8	120	29.1	0	0.0
Vehicle accident	2	1.8	6	1.5	83	15.7
Processing prisoner	5	4.5	2	0.5	45	8.5
Other vehicle related	0	0.0	2	0.5	34	6.4
During training	0	0.0	0	0.0	31	5.9
On department premises	0	0.0	0	0.0	23	4.4
Other physical activity	0	0.0	0	0.0	22	4.2
Assisting citizen/victim	1	0.9	0	0.0	16	3.0
Using equipment (not at fire scene)	0	0.0	0	0.0	12	2.3
During fire rescue/discovery	0	0.0	0	0.0	12	1.1
Doing forced entry	0	0.0	0	0.0	3	.6
Fighting fire/at fire scene	0	0.0	0	0.0	1	.2
During shooting incident	1	0.9	0	0.0	0	0.0
Other	0	0.0	1	0.2	25	4.7
Medical attention sought	106	100.0	402	100.0	508	100.0
No	35	33.0	200	49.8	265	52.2
Yes	71	67.0	202	50.2	243	47.8
Time off work	107	100.0	407	100.0	523	100.0
No	99	92.5	359	88.2	451	86.2
Yes	8	7.5	48	11.8	72	13.8

Note: Missing data excluded from the table; percentages may not sum to 100 due to rounding.

Table 3 Characteristics of injury incidents for police officers and firefighters

	Police		Fire	
	n	%	n	%
Nature of injury incident	1,054	100.0	530	100.0
Accident	531	50.4	526	99.2
Resisting subject	413	39.2	0	0.0
Assaultive subject	110	10.4	4	0.8
Nature of most serious injury	1,054	100.2	530	100.1
Laceration/abrasion	205	19.4	46	8.7
Sprain/strain	199	18.9	151	28.5
Contact with infectious disease	193	18.3	44	8.3
Contact with bodily fluid	98		11	
Other contact with infectious disease	95		33	
Contusion	175	16.6	40	7.5
Other muscle pain	164	15.6	132	24.9
Broken bones/dislocated joints	28	2.7	11	2.1
Human bite	22	2.1	1	0.2
Other pain	10	0.9	5	0.9
Contact with hazardous material	8	0.8	7	1.3
Smoke/fume inhalation	7	0.7	22	4.2
Torn ligaments/tendons	5	0.5	1	0.2
Eye injury (other than black eye)	4	0.4	21	4.0
Gunshot wound	3	0.3	0	0.0
Burns	2	0.2	18	3.4
Knife wound	0	0.0	1	0.2
Death	0	0.0	0	0.0
Other	29	2.8	30	5.7
Activity resulting in injury	1,050	100.2	530	99.9
Controlling/arresting subject	460	43.8	0	0.0
Conducting investigation	148	14.1	0	0.0
Apprehending fleeing subject (on foot)	122	11.6	0	0.0
Vehicle accident	91	8.7	8	1.5
Processing prisoner	52	5.0	0	0.0
Other vehicle related	36	3.4	62	11.7
During training	31	3.0	27	5.1
On department premises	23	2.2	54	10.2
Other physical activity	22	2.1	17	3.2
Assisting citizen/victim	17	1.6	79	14.9
Using equipment (not at fire scene)	12	1.1	50	9.4
During fire rescue/discovery	6	0.6	7	1.3
Doing forced entry	3	0.3	9	1.7
Fighting fire at fire scene	1	0.1	199	37.5
During shooting incident	1	0.1	0	0.0
Other	26	2.5	18	3.4
Medical attention sought	1,016	100.0	524	100.0
No	500	49.2	264	50.4
Yes	.516	50.8	260	49.6
Rate of injury incidents (per officer or firefighter)	0.610		0.717	
Number of injuries per incident	1.43		1.09	

Note: Missing data excluded from the table; percentages may not sum to 100 due to rounding.

The activities resulting in injuries varied according to the nature of the injury incident. Controlling/arresting subject was the activity that most commonly led to assaults (90.0%). In incidents resulting from a resisting subject, controlling/arresting subjects (68.3%) and apprehending fleeing suspects (29.1%) were most common preceding activities. In accidents, conducting investigations (28%), followed by vehicle accidents (15.7%) and controlling/arresting subjects (15.0%), was most common.

Table 2 also shows that medical attention was most likely sought as a result of assaults (67.0%) and least likely in accidents (47.8%). However, the opposite pattern held for time lost from work: Accidents were most likely to result in time off work (13.8%), and assaults were least likely (7.5%).

Table 3 allows for a comparison of injuries reported by police and fire department personnel. Table 3 shows that more than 99% of fire department personnel injury incidents were the result of accidents; only 4 (of 530, or 0.8%) incidents were due to an intentional assaultive act on the part of a subject. Furthermore, for fire department personnel, two types of injuries were common and distinguishable from the others: sprain/strain (26.4%) and other muscle pain (25.0%).These two types of injuries account for 51.4% of all injuries to firefighters and HEOs. Contacts with bodily fluid (especially (blood-to-blood contacts), human bites, and dog bites were more likely to occur among police officers; whereas smoke/fume inhalation, eye injuries, and burns were more likely to occur among firefighters. Like the police department, the fire department did not experience any work-related deaths in 1997.

It is seen in Table 3 that the most common activities resulting in injury incidents for firefighters or heavy equipment operators were as follows: fighting fire/while at fire scene (37.5%), assisting citizen/victim (14.9%), other vehicle related (11.7%), and while on department premises (10.2%). These four categories accounted for 74.3% of all incidents. Of the injuries that occurred as a result of fighting fire/while at fire scene, the greatest proportion resulted from using equipment at the scene (75 of the 199 injury incidents, or 37.7%; results not tabled).

Table 3 also shows that similar to the police, fire department personnel sought medical attention as a result of the incident in 49.6% (260 of 524) of the incidents. Finally, on average, fire department personnel sustained 1.09 injuries per incident (578 injuries reported in 530 incidents). Considering the total number of personnel in the department, there were 0.717 incidents reported per employee.

CONCLUSION

On the basis of this descriptive study, several conclusions can be drawn. First, based on the analysis of injuries to police officers, it is seen that assaults on officers—the focus of much previous research—are relatively rare events, as are serious injuries and deaths. The overwhelming majority of incidents, regardless of the task engaged in, are not as a result of assaults and, of course, do not result in deaths. Rather, most injury incidents are a result of accidents. Particularly prevalent in accidents are contacts with infectious diseases (24.7%, $n = 131$). This is a dimension of danger that is rarely captured in the conceptualization of danger used by most police researchers. Yet these incidents—which include exposures to relatively minor diseases such as chicken pox or head lice to far more serious diseases such as hepatitis or HIV—are part and parcel of dealing with the public. The frequency of these incidents, however, highlights the continuing need for proper education and training for officers (see Edwards & Tewksbury, 1996). Contact with persons having HIV, for example, may be a less frightening experience for officers who have received training on the disease and the different means by which the virus may be transmitted. Officers may also take the precaution of wearing gloves at all times to reduce the likelihood of coming into contact with bodily fluids.

Second, felonious incidents differ from other types of incidents. Most of the most serious injuries sustained by police officers are not a result of assaults. As noted, the most serious injuries are most often due to accidents, most medical treatment is due to accidents, and most days off of work are as a result of accidents. These findings are consistent with those reported by Brandl (1996). Little question, if all or even some portion of assaults could be prevented through policies and training, which is the intent of much of the prior research in identifying high-risk or dangerous activities, there would still exist a large percentage of injury incidents to police officers. Simply put, consideration of the physical hazards of police work must include not only assaults and homicides but also accidents.

Third, with regard to a comparison of police and fire department personnel injuries, the frequency (i.e., rate) of incidents reported by police and fire department personnel is similar, but the nature of the injuries and the causes of the injuries are not. The differences in activities that lead to injuries for police and fire personnel reflect important differences in the nature of the occupations and the tasks that are expected to be performed. As such, it is, at a minimum, safe to conclude that the risks, dangers, and physical demands of police work and fire fighting are different. In particular, the police are much more likely to be injured during confrontations with antagonistic people. As such, a relatively large proportion of the actual risks of police work derive from, at least indirectly, the actions of people, with those actions resulting in injuries to police officers. In contrast, most of the risks of fire fighting are associated with using equipment (vehicles, hoses, ladders, axes, etc.), assisting citizens, and performing living activities (preparing meals, cleaning, maintenance, etc.). It is worthwhile to note that when fire department personnel are injured in interactions with citizens, it is most often a result of providing some sort of assistance to them (e.g., first aid). Accordingly, despite the common comparison between firefighters and police officers and the similarities of their occupations, policing and fire fighting are clearly different jobs in terms of their dangers and demands. In this regard, perhaps police work could be more accurately compared to the work of correctional officers or custodial personnel in mental institutions.

Fourth, in considering further the comparison of police and fire department personnel injuries, specifically the nature of the injuries sustained, how these injuries occur, and the significance of these injuries, it is important to realize that there is not only a physiological dimension to injuries but a psychological one as well. With regard to the physiological dimension, one could debate the significance of police officers' typical contusion/abrasion/laceration injuries versus firefighters' typical muscle sprains and strains—different medical opinions may lead to different conclusions. More meaningful, perhaps, is the likely difference in the psychological effects that stem from the typical injuries sustained by police officers and firefighters. Of particular relevance here are those injuries that occur as a result of an assault on the officer or an otherwise resisting, combative subject. One might expect that injuries that occur as a result of one person doing harm to another person are more psychologically significant than injuries that occur as a result of physical exertion. Although this expectation could not be tested given the nature of the data collected here, previous research does support this contention. Briefly, Violanti (1994) found that police officers ranked being physically attacked the third most significant stressor in their work, just behind killing someone in the line of duty and having a fellow officer killed. According to Cullen, Link, Travis, and Lemming (1983), heightened perceptions of danger among police officers contribute to increased work stress and, furthermore, to the manifestation of depression. McMurray (1990) reported that officers who were assaulted expressed increased levels of alienation and decreased levels of job satisfaction and work-related support. In short, even though injuries that result from assaults are relatively rare in police work (and even more so in fire fighting), the likely psychological effects of injuries that result from these interactions may likely have dramatic long-term negative consequences for officers' physical and emotional well-being and, as such, may be much more significant than injuries that occur in other ways.

This study provides direction for future research. First, as demonstrated in this study, in assessing the physical dangers of police work, one needs to include not only assaults and homicides but also injuries that result from accidents. Second, it is necessary to measure the psychological effects of physical injuries. Future research that seeks to document the hazards of police work would be well advised to broaden the conceptualization of risk/hazards to include psychological effects. Third, it would be worthwhile to examine the long-term physiological impact of injuries. Although injuries are usually minor, long-term cumulative effects may have reaching and lasting consequences. Fourth, it may be useful to compare injuries across police departments of different sizes with different workloads, policies, and structures. In addition, further cross-occupational comparisons may cast additional light on the relative dangers of police work. A final important direction for future research is to examine individual-level variation in injury incidents (Hansen, 1989). Kaminski and Sorensen (1995) took a first step in this direction when they examined individual-level variation in whether officers were injured as a result of an assault, but they did not address the larger questions, namely the following: Are some officers at more risk of accidents, assaults, or other injuries than others? Are some officers more at risk of ill psychological effects of injuries than other officers? Are there accident-, assault-, or injury-prone officers? What characteristics do they share? Studies designed to address these issues may contribute to our understanding of the dangers of police work.

Notes

[1] The other industries identified were agriculture, mining, construction, manufacturing, transportation, wholesale trade, retail trade, finance, and services. No further details are provided regarding the nature of the jobs within these occupations.

[2] The other industries identified were hotel management, bus driver, school bus driver, retail, hospitals, schools, correctional facilities, and private security.

[3] Given the work schedule of firefighters and heavy equipment operators (two 24-hour shifts a week) and the manner in which the fire department injury reports were completed, it was not possible to determine for fire department personnel whether work time was lost as a result of the injury incident.

[4] A "blood-to-blood" contact occurred when a subject's blood came into contact with the employee's blood, either by aggravating an existing wound or as a result of a new wound.

[5] Note that approximately one-half of contacts with infectious disease involved actual contact with bodily fluid. Sixteen of these incidents involved blood-to-blood contact.

References

Alpert, G. P., & Dunham, R. G. (1999). The force factor: Measuring and assessing police use of force and suspect resistance. In *Use of force by police: Overview of national and local data*. Washington, DC: National Institute of Justice.

Bayley, D. H., & Garofalo, J. (1989). The management of violence by police patrol officers. *Criminology, 27*, 1–23.

Brandl, S. G. (1996). In the line of duty: A descriptive analysis of police assaults and accidents. *Journal of Criminal Justice, 24*, 255–264.

Bureau of Labor Statistics. (2000). *Census of fatal occupational injuries*. Washington, DC: U.S. Department of Labor, Bureau of Labor Statistics.

Centers for Disease Control. (1998). Surveillance for nonfatal occupational injuries treated in hospital emergency departments—United States, 1996. *Morbidity and Mortality Weekly Report, 47*, 302–306.

Centers for Disease Control. (2001). Fatal occupational injuries—United States, 1980–1997. *Journal of the American Medical Association, 285*, 2440–2444.

Cullen, F. T., Link, B. G., Travis, L. R., & Lemming, T. (1983). Paradox in policing: A note on perceptions of danger. *Journal of Police Science and Administration, 11*, 457–462.

Edwards, T. D. (1995). Felonious killing of state police and highway patrol officers: A descriptive and comparative evaluation. *American Journal of Police, 14*, 89–105.

Edwards, T. D., & Tewksbury, R. (1996). HIV/AIDS: State police training practices and personnel policies. *American Journal of Police, 15*, 45–62.

Federal Bureau of Investigation. (1998). *Law enforcement officers killed and assaulted.* Washington, DC: Government Printing Office.

Feldstein, A., Valanis, B., Vollmer, W., Stevens, N., & Overton, C. (1993). The back injury prevention project pilot study. *Journal of Occupational Medicine, 35,* 114–120.

Feuer, E., & Rosenman, K. (1986). Mortality in police and firefighters in New Jersey. *American Journal of Industrial Medicine, 9,* 517–527.

Fridell, L. A., & Pate, A. M. (1997). Death on patrol: Killings of American law enforcement officers. In R. G. Dunham & G. P Alpert (Eds.), *Critical issues in policing.* Prospect Heights. IL: Waveland.

Fyfe, J. (1979). Administrative interventions on police shooting discretion: An empirical examination. *Journal of Criminal Justice, 7,* 309–324.

Fyfe, J. (1995). Good policing. In B. Forst (Ed.), *The socioeconomics of crime and justice.* New York: M. E. Sharpe.

Garner, J., & Clemmer, E. (1986). *Danger to police in domestic disturbances.* Washington, DC: U.S. Department of Justice.

Hansen, C. (1989). A causal model of the relationship among accidents, biodata, personality, and cognitive factors. *Journal of Applied Psychology, 74,* 81–90.

Hirschel, J. D., Dean, C. W., & Lumb, R. C. (1994). The relative contribution of domestic violence to assault and injury of police officers. *Justice Quarterly, 11,* 99–117.

Kaminski, R. J., Edwards, S. M., & Johnson, J. W. (1998). The deterrent effects of oleoresin capsicum on assaults against the police: Testing the velcro-effect hypothesis. *Police Quarterly 1,* 1–20.

Kaminski, R. J., & Sorensen, D. W. (1995). A multivariate analysis of individual, situational and environmental factors associated with police assault injuries. *American Journal of Police, 14,* 3–48.

Konstantin, D. (1984). Homicide of American law enforcement officers. *Justice Quarterly, 1,* 29–45.

Lester, D. (1981). Occupational injuries, illnesses, and fatalities in police officers. *Police Chief, 48*(10), 43, 63.

McMurray, H. L. (1990). Attitudes of assaulted police officers and their policy implications. *Journal of Police Science and Administration, 17,* 44–48.

Meyer, C. K., Magedanz, T., Dahlin, D., & Chapman, S. (1981). A comparative assessment of assault incidents: Robbery related ambush and general police assaults. *Journal of Police Science and Administration, 9,* 1–18.

National Institute for Occupational Safety and Health. (1992). *Homicide in U.S. workplaces: A strategy for prevention and research* (DHHS Publication No. 92-103). Morgantown, WV: U.S. Department of Health and Human Services, Public Health Services, Center for Disease Control, National Institute for Occupational Safety and Health.

National Institute for Occupational Safety and Health. (1997). *Current Intelligence Bulletin 57: Violence in the workplace risk factors and prevention strategies* (DHHS Publication No. 96-100). Morgantown, WV: U.S. Department of Health and Human Services, Public Health. Services, Center for Disease Control, National Institute for Occupational Safety and Health.

Peek-Asa, C., Howard, J., Vargas, L., Kraus, J. F. (1997). Incidence of non-fatal workplace assault injuries determined from employer's reports in California. *Journal of Occupational and Environmental Medicine, 39,* 44–50.

Sherman, L. W. (1980). Perspectives on police and violence. *Annals, 452,* 1–12.

Skolnick, J. H. (1994). *Justice without trial: Law enforcement in a democratic society.* New York: Macmillan.

Stanford, R. M., & Mowry, B. L. (1990). Domestic disturbance danger rate. *Journal of Police Science and Administration, 17*, 244–249.

Uchida, C. D., Brooks, L. W., & Kopers, C. S. (1987). Danger to police during domestic encounters: Assaults on Baltimore County police, 1984–86. *Criminal Justice Policy Review, 2*, 357–371.

Violanti, J. M. (1994). Ranking police stressors. *Psychological Report, 75*, 824–826.

Violanti, J. M., Vena, J. E., & Marshall, J. R. (1996). Suicides, homicides, and accidental death: A comparative risk assessment of police officers and municipal workers. *American Journal of Industrial Medicine, 30*, 99–104.

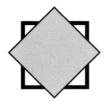

Index